AGRO BASED AND PROCESSED FOOD PRODUCTS

AGRO BASED AND PROCESSED FOOD PRODUCTS

Written By

EIRI BOARD OF CONSULTANTS & ENGINEERS

ENGINEERS INDIA RESEARCH INSTITUTE

4449, Nai Sarak, Main Road, Delhi - 110006 (India)

Ph:. 91-11- 23918117, 23916431, 23840361, 9312282370

Fax: 91-11- 2391 6431, 23918117

* E-Mail : eirisidi@bol.net.in

* Website: www.eiriindia.org

Sole Distributor :

Indian Institute of Consultants, 4/27, Roop Nagar, Delhi - 110007

PRINTED & PUBLISHED BY

ENGINEERS INDIA RESEARCH INSTITUTE

4449, Nai Sarak, Main Road, Delhi - 110006 (India)
Ph:. 91-11- 23918117, 23916431, 23840361, 9312282370
Fax: 91-11- 2391 6431, 23918117
* E-Mail : eirisidi@bol.net.in
* Website: www.eiriindia.org

DISTRIBUTED BY

SMALL INDUSTRY RESEARCH INSTITUTE (SIRI)
INDIAN INSTITUTE OF CONSULTANTS

ISBN : 81- 86732-89-6

Printed in New Delhi (INDIA)

Rs. 1100

Printed & Published by Sudhir Gupta for "Engineers India Research Institute"
4449 Nai Sarak, Main Road, New Delhi - 110 006
Printed at Swastik Offset, Shahadra, Delhi - 110032.

Preface

The book "**AGRO BASED AND PROCESSED FOOD PRODUCTS**" covers almost all the basic and advanced details to setup your own manufacturing industry. The main chapters are: Roller Flour Mills, Milled Products of Wheat, Flour Mix for Bakery Products, Traditional Wheat Products, Developments in Pasta and Special Food Products, Methods for Prolonging Shelf-life of Fresh Fruits and Vegetables, Technology of Fruit Juice and Pulp Concentrates, Technology of Aroma Recovery for Fruit Juices, Palm Oil, Coconut Processing, Protein Foods from Oilseeds, Livestock Feed Technology, Post-harvest Technology of Prawn, Manufacture and Quality of Tea, Coconut Products and Technological Innovations, Technology of Basmati Rice Processing, Spirulina: a Classical Health Food, Pulse Production Technology, Fermented Soya Products, Brewing and Distilling, Processing of Hot-serve Cereals, Special Dietary Foods and Ingredients, Food Additives, Use of Antimicrobials in Food Preservation, Role of Antioxidants in Food Preservation, Preservation of Fruits and Vegetables, Beverages, Sugars and Sweeteners, Milk and Milk Products, Meat and Meat Products, Sea Foods, Poultry, Eggs and Egg Products, Candied Foods, Fruits and Fruit Products, Vegetables and Vegetable Products, Processing of Foods using High Hydrostatic Pressure, Technology for Pellet based Snacks, Confectionery, Cocoa, Coffee and Tea, Plant Economics of Alcoholic Beverages and Vinegar from Coconut Water, Plant Economics of Aquaculture Prawn Farming, Plant Economics of Bakery Unit, Buns, Cake, Toffee, Plant Economics of Bread Plant, Plant Economics of Beer Industry (Export Oriented), Plant Economics of Confectionery Industry, Plant Economics of Corn Flakes, Plant Economics of Chewing Gum, Plant Economics of Cattle Feed, Plant Economics of Coconut Products & Bye Products Processing Unit, Plant Economics of Coir Pith, Plant Economics of Desiccated Coconut Powder from Coconut, Plant Economics of Dall Mill, Plant Economics of Dairy Products & Milk Packaging in Pouches, Plant Economics of Egg Powder, Plant Economics of Food Dehydration, Plant Economics of Fruit Juice Making & Packing in Plastic Containers, Plant Economics of Feed Mill for Mixed Feed (Poultry & Cattle), Plant Economics of Instant Noodles with Taste Maker Spice, Plant Economics of Indian Made Foreign Liquor, Plant Economics of Meat, Plant Economics of Macaroni, Plant Economics of Processed Food (Fruit Juice, Ketchup Jelly Canning of Fruits, Pickles etc.), Plant Economics of Palm Oil, Plant Economics of Protein and Protein based Products, Plant Economics of Poultry & Broiler (Hatchery) Farming, Plant Economics of Roller Flour Mill, Plant Economics of Modern Rice Mill, Plant Economics of Snack Food (Crax size), (Roll & Ball type), Plant Economics of Soybean Products, Plant Economics of Soya Milk & Soya Paneer, Plant Economics of Sugar Plant, Plant Economics of Tea Processing and Packaging, Plant Economics of Vermicelli, Plant Economics of Wheat Porridge (Dalia), Suppliers of Plant and Machinery, etc.

The book has been written for the benefit and to prove an asset for entrepreneurs who want to setup their own industry.

Director

ENGINEERS INDIA RESEARCH INSTITUTE

Nai Sarak, Main Road
Delhi - 110 006 (INDIA)
e-mail: eirisidi@bol.net.in

Contents cum Subject Index

1
ROLLER FLOUR MILLS

This business environment has instigated numerous new developments in milling engineering, aiming mainly at:

LOWER PRODUCTION COSTS THROUGH

- design of high capacity equipment to allow the construction of larger mill units
- reduced investment by saving building volume and costs,
- design of equipment requiring less maintenance to save labour and to reduce the duration of production stoppages.
- saving of energy by:
    - the application of air recycling systems for all screen room equipment, and
    - automatic air controls for the mill pneumatic system.

AUTOMATION TO GOVERN THE COMPLETE PROCESS TO

- Improve on management control,
- assure flour consistency by precise adjustment of equipment, quick production changeovers and repeatable milling results.
- optimisation of flour quality.
- provide quality and production records.
- eliminate unsocial working hours and overtime.
- assist and reduce personnel.

IMPROVED WORKING CONDITIONS FOR STAFF BY

- design of easy adjustable and safely operating equipment
- noise reduction.
- special regard to plant safety.

ULTIMATE PRODUCT CONTROL BY

- the application of on-line quality control systems to assure consistently high performance of milling products in bakeries and to eliminate consequential damages.

- best possible sanitation through appropriate equipment and plant design.

Now let us have a survey on some of them and start with the following:

1. SCREEN ROOM

Considering the growing consciousness in environmental respects, the farmers use less pesticides and fertiliser, resulting in poorer wheat qualities supplied to the mill. This calls for an improved screen room performance and well equipped wheat blending systems in order to obtain clean wheat grits of uniform properties - the basic condition for favourable mill performance.

The new Transflowtron wheat measures working on the principle of loss in weight feeding, do not only meter and accurately feed each wheat according to PC controlled blending recipes, but also supply data for stock and production control.

For proper wheat cleaning, large air volumes are required consuming much energy and filter area. The development of an air/dust separator (making use of centrifugal forces as well as the vector of dust velocity), allows reuse of the separation air. The consequent application of this principle for the Aspirator, Combinator and Dry stoner resulted in substantial savings on energy consumption upto 50% for a 22 t/h screen room. This has been made possible by a drop in fresh air requirement of over 90%. In addition, a reduction in building space could be obtained since less filters and fans are needed.

Another important machine in the cleaning section today is the Automatic Moisture Controller MYFA. This equipment allows one to keep the moisture content for conditioning at the optimum. With this machine, a lot of money can be saved in a very short period of time.

2. MILL

The merger of milling companies has led to a concentration in production plants and the construction of flour mills with much higher capacities like 400 to 600 tonnes per unit per day. This demands the development of the correspondingly sized equipment. The new square-type sifters have a nominal sifting area of upto 87 sqm, i.e., approx. 36% more than the largest type previously available. Its application reduces the number of equipment units, saves building volume and costs.

During previous years, the process technique of conventional milling has been optimised to such a degree that the extraction rate achieved as at present in new efficient plants is difficult to be improved upon. For this reason, it is no surprise that news of dehulling processes with promising results have attracted a lot of attention.

A great number of tests, which have been made by us in dehulling various wheat types to differing degrees and with varying conditioning procedures showed that

- the ash curves are the same or inferior to those of our conventional milling process and that especially the ash content of the first reduction flours is higher
- the extraction calculated on wheat prior to dehulling is the same or lower as compared with the results in modern mills without dehulling
- the baking quality of flours with the same colour or ash is the same

At the same time, the energy requirement and capital expenditure are substantially higher, i.e., within the range of 15%.

On the other hand, the new milling process with the double grinding of stocks without sifting introduced some three years ago has proven to be a great success. Already more than 250 mills have been built and commissioned all over the world using the new technique mainly for Ist/2nd break, A/B and D/E passages. Seven mills have been sold upto the day equipped with 8 roller mills only. The milling results are found to be the same as those with the conventional system. However, it may be noted that the

- power requirement (and air) of the pneumatic system is reduced by approx. 13% due to the elimination of the lifts for 2nd break, B and E passages
- the sifting area required is reduced by 8%
- the requirement in building volume is reduced by 15 to 20%
- lower capital expenditures.

3. QUALITY ASSURANCE

A baker remains a happy customer as long as the flour supplied to him has the same consistent quality and is preserved clear from any infestation. Legislation of food for human consumption enforces these demands and continuous on-line flour quality records can save the miller consequential damage claims.

The inframatic NIR Online Measurement System PerCon-Buhler is field proven and continuously records the protein and moisture contents as well as an ash/colour value. In addition, closed loop control systems are available for the control of the

- protein content by the addition of gluten with loss in weight feeders
- moisture content by the addition of water with computer controlled water feeders.

The treatment of flour with a sterilator kills moths and weevils, reduces the risk of infestation in flour silos and assures long shelf-life. The machine can be fitted into a pneumatic lift and owing to its design reduces the pressure of the blowlines considerably - compared to earlier models,

4. FLOUR SILO

In many flour mills around the world, flours and additives are mixed by means of batch-blending systems permitting the production of tailor-made flours and sophisticated production records. The disadvantages of such systems are their power and building requirements.

The latter especially allows the incorporation of such systems in some existing plants at high capital expenditures only. However, the developments in electronic continuous-flow scales such as Differential dosing scale (Loss-in-weight feeder) for capacities from 2 to 3000 kg/hr, and Transflowtron/ Transflowmeter, which are continuous flour flow controllers (measures of the loss-in-weight principle), feeding flow capacities from 1 to 40 t/hr. have provided new tools to the process engineers, permitting the construction of fully automatic, continuous blending plants.

A flour blending system with Transflowtron blending control has been developed. The different flours are weighed as well as the accurate quantities of additives - pre-selected by recipe - and blended in continuous streams. The batch mixer is not required and a self-cleaning homogeniser or mixing screw ensures the finished products to be homogeneous. This system allows the pre-commissioning of packing or bulk loading jobs. A computer control system manages production without personnel, provides production and quality records as well as stock and loading statistics.

The major difference between batch-blending and continuous-blending systems is, with a view to accuracy, the job-start stage. With the batch-blending, even the first batch includes all components as each single one is accurately weighed and the batch thereafter thoroughly mixed. Whereas with continuous blending there is an inaccuracy owing to start-up lags and spouting at the beginning of the job for approx. 250 kg. However, this problem can easily be solved by the use of a "start-up" hopper, into which the flour is fed at the beginning of the job and fed back to the stream afterwards. For this reason, the continuous blending system has its special advantages for large plants in which quantities of at least 4 tonne per each flour are blended.

2
Milled Products of Wheat

For the preparation of chapati and its variants such as roti, phulka, parotha, wheat ground in disc mill of metallic or stone discs has been found to be better suited than that ground in other types of mills such as pin mill, hammer mill, roller mill, etc. Among the types of wheat, medium hard wheat containing 9-10% gluten protein, 14-15% damaged starch, is more suitable for the preparation of chapati and roti. Phulka in addition to these requirements needs a flour in a much finer granulation. Resultant atta is not well suited for obtaining good chapati as it has lower damaged starch content. Poori is a deep-fat fried product and requires flour with lower bran content to enable the product to puff fully during frying

Refined flour, from roller flour mills, with low ash (0 4-0.5%) and medium protein content (9-10%), is preferred in the preparation of other traditional products like nan and South Indian parotha. A dough of good extensibility is a desirable characteristic for the preparation of parotha. This enables the stretching of the dough into a thin sheet needed for layering

The available information on the quality requirements indicates the urgent need to collect the exhaustive scientific data regarding quality requirement of milled products of wheat for the preparation of various indigenous products which would go a long way in making available the desired quality flour for different indigenous products.

INTRODUCTION

India ranks 3rd in the world production of wheat and is next only to China and USA. The present production in India is estimated at 56.5 million tonnes which is about five times higher than the production in 2½ decade ago. Unlike in many of the developed countries where wheat is used mostly in bakery products, in India, it is mainly used in the preparation of various traditional products like chapati, phulka, roti, parotha, nan, puri, upmav etc These products are mainly made in households/restaurants and eaten fresh.

Most of these traditional products are prepared from milled flour (maida) wheat products like (suji, resultant atta etc. are used in roller flour mills.

Whole wheat flour obtained by grinding wheat in a plate/stone mill is also used instead of resultant atta on which simulates whole wheat flour. (Tara et al). The composition of whole wheat flour (atta) and resultant atta given in Table 2.1, indicates that there is little difference in the components except that ash and damage starch contents are lower in the latter. Considerable variation also exists in mill atta separated in different mills.

Table 2.1. Characteristics of Resultant atta and Whole Wheat Flour

Characteristics (%)	*Resultant atta*	*Whole-wheat flour*
Ash	1.31	1.68
Protein	10.80	10.60
Dry gluten	9.90	9.90
Ether extractives	3.20	2.30
Crude fibre	2.09	2.24
Starch	52.20	54.50
Damaged starch	7.00	14.50
Water absorption capacity	62.80	73.50

a. Values are the average of 18 samples and are expressed on a 14% moisture basis.

b. Required to prepare chapati dough or optimum consistency.

There are quite a number of other indigenous products that are made either from maida or suji which are the main products of roller flour milling industry. Over 2 million tonnes of maida is used in Nan, South Indian Parotha and other flour confectionery products like - Sohan halwa, Sohan Papri, Jilebi, Bombay halva, etc. However, suji is used mainly for the preparation of upmav or 'Khara Bhath' in households/restaurants.

The quality of these products naturally depends on the quality of the raw materials used. Though there is a considerable information on the semi quality requirements of maida/ semolina for different bakery or paster products, very little information is available on the quality requirement for various indigenous products except for chapati (Auslies and Ram 1971) and for other traditional products. The information available is reviewed in this paper.

TRADITIONAL PRODUCTS - CHAPATI AND ITS VARIANTS

Chapati and its culinary variations like roti, phulka parotha etc., comes under the category of unfermented flat breads. The quality requirement of whole wheat flour for chapati as reported by Auslin and Ram (1971) is given in Table 2.2. The most important criteria of quality of flour for chapati are ash, protein/gluten and damaged starch contents. The flour having low or high ash content is reported to affect the texture of chapati (Haridas Rao,

1982). This is indicated by the fact that the mill atta which normally contains lower ash content or flour of lower extraction rates yields chapati with rubbery texture. The optimum ash content in flour is found to be 1.3-1.5%. The protein or gluten content in wheat or flour milled from it should be in the range of 9 to 10%. Hence, most of the Indian wheats grown in our country are suited for the chapati preparation. The damaged starch content in whole wheat flour not only affects the water absorption capacity, but also influences the texture, taste, flavour and keeping quality of chapati (Haridas Rao et al 1987). The reported optimum level is 14 to 15%. Low damaged starch containing flour makes chapati hard with bland flavour, while too highly damaged starch content on the other hand, gives sticky dough and undesirable dark coloured spots in chapati (Table 2.3). Only wheat milled in either platemill or stone mill gives wheat flour having desired damaged starch content. Therefore, chapati made from flour processed in plate mills has better quality as compared to that processed in roller flour mill and chapati made from mill atta has bland flavour, taste and hard texture (Table 2.4).

Table 2.2. Characteristics of Whole-wheat (aestivum) Flour Suitable for *chapati* Making

Characteristics	*Level*
Ash (%)	1.2 - 1.5
Protein (%)	9.0 - 10.5
Sedimentation value (ml)	25 - 35
Pelshenke value (ml)	120 - 150
Total sugars (%)	2.5 - 4.0
Diastatic activity (mg/10g flour)	250 - 375
Damaged starch (%)	14 - 15
Water absorption capacity (%)*	70 - 75

*Required to prepare dough of optimum consistency.

Table 2.3. Effect of Damaged Starch Content on the Quality of Dough and *Chapati*

Damaged starch (%)	*Water absorption (%)*	*Rolling characteristics*	*Appearance (20)*	*Pliability (cm)*	*Texture (25)*
10.6	71.0	Tough	10.5[a]	1.6[a]	12.4[a]
13.7	75.5	Easy	15.4[b]	1.8[b]	15.8[b]
15.5	77.5	Easy	16.2[b]	2.0[c]	16.1[b]
19.6	82.5	Easy but sticky	10.0[a]	2.3[d]	16.3[c]

The average values followed by different letters differ significantly at 5% level.
*Maximum score

Table 2.4. Quality Characteristics of chapati made from Resultant atta and Whole Wheat Flour

Characteristics	*Resultant atta*	*Whole wheat flour*
Color volume (%)	57.5	40.0
Aroma	Mild to bland	Pleasant wheaty
Texture	Slightly hard and leathery	Soft
Taste	Bland	Sweet

A fine ground flour is desirable for chapati making. The coarse flour with more than 70-80% overtailings on 10XX (132 u) sieve, yields chapati having poor appearance and rough texture (Haridas Rao, 1982). The normal practice of removing about 5% of coarse bran in the household from whole wheat flour do not affect the quality of chapati.

Efforts are now being made to improve the quality of mill atta with respect to chapati making. This could be achieved by increasing the damaged starch content by any one of the methods given below:

1. Applying higher roll pressure on reduction rolls
2. Giving higher speed differentials than normal (1:1.25) for the reduction rolls
3. Use of finely grooved rolls to reduce the size of middlings and semolinas.
4. Reducing the tempering time and conditioning moisture
5. Repeated grinding of the flour : In this method finer sieves are used, then coarser flour goes to next reduction passage. Hence, the product will be ground again in that passage thereby increasing the starch damage.

50 (410 μ)		50 (410 μ)		
9 N (150 μ)	→	11 N (118 μ)	→	The overtails will be more here which will be sent to the next passage.
10 N (132 μ)		12N (112 μ)		

The extent of starch damage depends on the type of wheat, the degree of tempering of wheat prior to milling, pressure and grinding surface of the rolls and fineness of the flour. So in the repeated grinding we can regrind some part of the finished products by increasing the pressure in the subsequent rolls. Thus, it is the milling process which is responsible for mechanical damage to the starch.

GRINDING IN HAMMER MILL FOLLOWED BY 2 REDUCTION PASSAGES

The other method is by conditioning the wheat to 145% moisture and grinding in hammer mill by keeping 1500 μ sieve. The ground material is taken to the plan-sifter and sieved through 300 μ sieve. The overtailings are passed through two reduction rolls and the materials sieved through 50 W (410 μ) sieves. The overtailings are removed as bran The extraction rate of such processed flour is 90-92% and has the composition as given in Table 2.5. The flour has higher ash as well as damaged starch content when compared to mill atta. The chapati made from such a flour has softer texture, better flavour and taste.

Table 2.5. The Composition of Differently Milled Atta

Characteristics	Resultant atta	Hammer milled atta
Moisture (%)	12.4	12.2
Ash*(%)	1.25	0.93
Damaged starch*	7.4	9.7
Farinograph water absorption* (%)	57.4	60.8
WB shea r value of chapati (X 0.1 lbs)	11	9

*Values are expressed on 14% moisture basis.

The recovery of mill atta in a flour mill ranges from ac low as 5.0% to ac high as 30% In different roller flour mills depending on the demand for such product. Generally, North Indian flour mills recover more of atta as compared to mills situated in Southern part. There is also considerable variation in the quality of atta separated from different mills. This needs to be standardised. There is no ISI specifications for mill atta, but it is available for whole wheat flour. The quality requirements of atta for chapati and its variant tandoori roti and parotha are similar.

PHULKA

Phulka is similar to chapati except that it is made thinner (0.5-1.0 mm) and puffed fully on live coal or gas flame. The main requirement of flour is its particle size distribution which should be very fine and over 80% should pass through 130 μ sieve.

Sheeting and puffing quality are important in case of phulka which are mainly influenced by the particle size, ash and gluten contents in the flour. The desired quality characteristics are given in Table 2.6. Similar to chapati, flour from medium hard wheat is desirable.

Sheeting characteristics are better when made from mill atta as it contains higher amount of endosperm particles of finer particle sizes. In case of whole wheat flour milled in plate mills, the grinding need to be done twice : first coarse grinding followed by fine grinding to obtain fine flour. Grinding in a single stage by keeping closer clearance results in excessive damaged starch resulting in sticky dough, hence affects sheeting.

There are mainly two types of phulka, one made only with flour and water and the other made using additional salt and fat. The latter is also known as Gujarathi type phulka. Both the types are served fresh after smearing fat on the surface. The quality requirements are the same for both types of phulka.

Table 2.6. Quality Characteristics of Flour for phulka.

Wet gluten (%)	30 - 32
Diastatic activity (mg maltose/10 g flour)	275 - 300
Ash (%)	125 - 140
Farinograph water absorption (%)	70 - 75
Dough development time (mm)	2.5 - 4.0
Stability (mm)	2.5 - 8.0
Mixing tolerance index (BU)	50 - 100
Damaged starch (%)	13 - 15.0
10 XX (throughs) (%)	50 - 55

*On 14% moisture grains.

The other chapati variants made from whole wheat flour/mill atta are parotha and tandoori roti, and the quality characteristics of flours required are similar.

POORI

It is the deep-fat-fried product and the type of raw material required is the same as used for chapati. However, some of the households prefer to use mill atta as the poori made from it will have better whitish colour and good puffing during frying. Some prefer to use blend of maida and whole wheat flour. Whole wheat flour milled in a plate mill is also used as such, but the product has dull brownish colour, though it has better texture and flavour.

Like chapati, medium hard wheat flour is desirable for poori, and the product made from whole wheat flour is better with respect to texture, taste and flavour. However, colour is brownish. Excess damaged starch in the flour results in a sticky dough and the product does not puff completely during frying due to sticky nature.

Hence, it is desirable to have flour with damaged starch ranging from 12 to 14% and ash from 1.0 to 1.2%. The gluten content should range from 9-10.0%.

Important traditional products based on refined flour (maida) are nan and South Indian type parotha.

NAN

Nan is a lactic fermented product unlike bread which is yeast fermented. The shape varies from circular to elliptical and is made thicker than chapati with thickness ranging from 0.75 to 1.0 cm. Soft texture is desired in nan - similar to bread. The crumb colour of nan should be white hence a flour with low ash content is desirable. Lower ash, would also help in obtaining soft textured product due to increased volume obtained during baking in a tandoori oven. Medium strong flour with protein content ranging from 9.5 to 10.5% is desired for the preparation of nan.

SOUTH INDIAN PAROTHA

South Indian Parotha is made from maida and the product has a number of laminations. Laminations are obtained by sheeting and stretching the dough to a thin transparent film and folding the sheet. Oil is applied during folding. The folded dough is again curled and it is again sheeted. The product is baked on a hot plate by applying oil during baking. The quality of flour should be such that one should be able to make a thin film by stretching without tearing. Hence, it should be a strong flour, having high resistance to extension as well as extensibility. The flour should have white colour, hence low ash containing flour is desired. Damaged starch is not important as the dough is not fermented. The quality of flour could be improved by adding cystine or proteolytic enzyme which increases the extensibility.

TRADITIONAL FLOUR-BASED CONFECTIONERY PRODUCTS

Several indigenous sweet preparations are made from whole wheat flour maida. Some of the popular products are Sohan halwa, Bombay halwa, Jilebi, Chirote etc. Though the preparations of these products are restricted to hotels, restaurants and sweetmeat stalls, the turnover is quite large (Venkatesh et al, 1982). There is no information on the quality requirements of flour for preparation of the above sweet products.

Sohan halwa is made using the blend of germinated wheat flour and maida. The water extract of the above is heated with continuous stirring while adding sugar and fat (Venkatesh et al 1984). The heated mass is poured on the mould and cooled for solidification. There is no information on the quality of wheat flour required for preparing the above product.

The other sweet product is sohan papri which is mainly based on maida. Maida with some part of Bengalgram flour are mixed and roasted in fat, then added to sugar syrup at 80°C and thoroughly kneaded. The kneaded mass is stretched to obtain thread like structure spread on a tray and cut into small pieces.

Jilebi is another sweet made from wheat flour. Wheat flour is mixed with small quantity of black gram flour and made into a slurry by adding water. The slurry is made acidic with citric acid or butter milk. The batter is passed through thick cloth or coconut shell with a hole, on to frying pan and deep-fat-fried.

Chiroti is made from the semolina and its particle size distribution plays an important role in determining the quality. The required particle size is that it should pass through 525 μ sieve and retain over 290 μ sieve. The semolina should be free from bran. Semolina is mixed with water, the dough formed is rolled laminated with fat repeatedly. This is again rolled in to circular shape and dough fat fried

CONCLUSION

It is very clear that though a number of indigenous traditional products are prepared in India, from wheat very little scientific information is available on the technology of preparation, quality requirements of ingredients, keeping quality etc. This information is very important in order to mechanise the preparation of these products.

The information regarding the quality requirement of milled wheat products which forms the main ingredient is all the more necessary to prepare products of improved quality and maintain the consistency in the quality. It is clear that there is no information on the above aspect except for chapati. Hence, there is an urgent need to study the quality requirements of flour for different indigenous products as major part of the wheat produced is consumed in the form of traditional products. The information will be useful for the milling industries to produce specific flours and make available to different end users. This would go a long way in improving the traditional food based industries in the country.

3
FLOUR MIX FOR BAKERY PRODUCTS

When one thinks of bakery products only the wheat flour based products comes to one's mind. Wheat is the major cereal crop of the world. It was cultivated and consumed by almost all civilisations throughout the world and it continues to be even now. It has a unique history interwoven with folklore. The bakery products also are as old as wheat itself. History records wheat cultivation where modern man was supposed to have first appeared in South-western Asia. It is rather a Herculian task to trace the history of wheat when man used wheat as his food fifteen thousand years before Christ. There are several archaeological evidences to show that wheat has been a part of man's civilisation since times immemorial.

Worldwide, wheat is consumed mainly as baked product such as bread and its variations, biscuits, cookies, pasta products, pizzas and as breakfast cereals and other extruded products such as noodles. This is particularly because it has specific properties to withstand rigorous machining and processing conditions due to the gluten forming proteins present in wheat. Wheat is also consumed by cooking in the form of semolina.

Many other cereals have found almost equal status to wheat. Other major cereals of the world are maize, rice, barley, oat, sorghum and rye. These cereals are consumed as staple food by specific populations.

In Asian and South East Asian countries, consumption of rice perhaps is more than wheat. The people of different countries have varying preferences for the type of rice and its use. Rice is boiled and consumed as cooked rice which is a common practice in Asia and South East Asia. It is also consumed in many other form either alone or as composite flour preparation, may be deep fried as snack food, or processed as flaked rice, puffed rice or rice semolina. Traditional food fermentations have been developed based on rice especially Indian products such as idli and dosa which are gaining popularity internationally. Rice crackers as a baked product are being marketed in some of the western countries.

Also known as corn, maize is popular in African and American continents. America is the biggest domestic user of corn. Maize is utilised in the form of grits, meal, flour, starch, protein, germ, etc.

Barley was used as a bread grain by ancient Greeks and Romans. In the present day it is still used as an enzyme supplement in bakery industry. In Europe, North America and Asia, Barley and/or its sprouts are incorporated in weaning foods as a source of malt.

Rye cultivation for human use has been relatively recent. It was cultivated in Germany and in Southern Europe during 4th Century BC. Rye generally occurred as a weed in wheat or barley crops. In bakery industry, it is generally incorporated in wheat and barley flour in rye bread formulations rich in dietary fibre.

Oat is generally used in bakery products as oat meal or bran. In recent times, there has been a tremendous growth in bakery products and breakfast cereal items containing oat bran as it has been endowed to possess hypocholesteremic properties. Oat meal is also used in cake manufacture.

Other minor millets such as sorghum, bajra and ragi are endemic to certain populations. However, in India the above minor millets have been used as flour for making preparations such as Rotis or is consumed as a gelatinised mass or as a porridge.

Pulses along with cereals have been part and parcel of man's diet. It is by far well known that pulses are an excellent source of vegetable protein and some important vitamins and minerals.

Owing to the presence of certain anti-nutritional factors in some of the pulses, they are consumed by human beings in various forms such as germinated grams, roasted, deep fried and puffed products. Traditionally the pulse flours are processed into either sweetmeats or savoury items which vary according to the ethnic tastes of the civilisation. They include blackgram, greengram, horsegram, Bengalgram, peas, etc. In recent times, legume based processed foods are popular such as weaning food based on malted greengram, extruded foods containing legumes and cereals, puffed and sprouted legumes, protein beverage and milk substitutes, high protein snack foods, textured vegetable proteins as meat analogues and protein isolates as alternate whipping agents to egg.

It is needless to emphasise on bread as an oriental fermented food product. However, in recent times, flours of other sources such as soyflour, rice flour and flours of other cereals are being incorporated.

The beneficial effects of traditional food fermentations are well known. Some of them have now been produced on industrial scale and mass marketed as processed foods. Many of them are based on mixed flours.

Leavened breads without wheat flour such as Idli has been highlighted earlier which is an ethnic product of the Indian subcontinent.

"Trahanas" an ancient fermented product of wheat is a native to Cyprus, Greece and Turkey. It is prepared from crushed wheat flour and sheep's fermented milk and stored in the form of biscuits. Similar products are seen in Egypt, Lebanon, Jordan, Iraq and North Africa.

"Mahewu" is a popular South African maize beverage prepared from an admixture of maize porridge with wheat flour. Wheat flour is added after cooling the maize porridge and the fermentation is allowed till it attains about 3.5 pH.

"Ogi" and "Soy-Ogi" are similar products from Nigeria which is used both as a food for adults and as a weaning food. Soy-ogi is a protein enriched product with more than 20% protein and 2.4 PER.

There are several home made and cottage scale products based on admixtures of flours. Snack foods such as "Murukku", "Sevai", "Papads" and several other sweetmeat preparations are locally sold as deep fried or shallow fried items.

However, due to non-availability of technologies, they have remained as home scale or cottage scale items. Regarding fabricated foods, only soy chunks, nuggets, noodles and other extruded products are just beginning to woo the fast changing populations in our country. In European and American markets, there are endless list of extruded and co-extruded products which are ready-to-eat and which are either boiled, cooked, fried and roasted products with admixtures of fat, milk, nuts and fruits.

Attempts are now on to identify the traditional food fermentations which involve drying or frying as a potential product type for bakery industry and development of technologies. Extrusion process has opened new vistas in snack food sector with its versatility and its ability in processing composite flours and can be considered as extension of the bakery products.

Expanded cakes or second generation snacks such as Fried Collettes can be prepared by incorporating high fibre and high protein making them nutritionally sound with reduced calories. Example of fried collettes is a mixture of corn meal and cheese powder. Spin-off of the expanded cakes are baked collettes such as Corn Curl which utilises other cereal grain flours, tuber flours, fibre and proteins. Fibre, cellulose, brans, pectin and protein isolates are used to prepare low, calorie high protein snack foods.

Third generation snack foods such as "Crunchy" could be either hard in texture where generally flour of one cereal grain is used or could be soft and frothy textured wherein starch from many cereal/tuber crops are incorporated.

Confectionery type "Carob bars" can be prepared by incorporating many other flours such as wheat flour, milk powder, dry fruit powder, potato flour, apple fibre, rice flour, cocoa powder or oat flour along with "Carob" flour base .

Though dry fruits and nuts are being used by a baker and a confectioner, the potential of incorporation of nut based flours is an interesting area not exploited commercially. Bakery technology offers an immediate scope for utilisation of flour mixes of various raw materials as it is cost effective compared to extrusion process and is also a widely accepted snack food.

Rye breads, wholemeal breads with bran incorporation can make them nutritional with higher dietary fibre content and with reduced calories. Flat breads such as "Italian flat bread" or "Crisp breads" can be prepared with mixtures of flour and brans as a source of dietary fibre. Incorporation of "Guar Gum", "Xanthun Gum" in bread formulations not only serve as a source of dietary fibre but are known to increase the shelf-life of breads by retaining higher moisture content. Spice powders such as garlic or onion not only impart specific flavours but can to an extent replace existing food additives used in bread manufacture.

Incorporation of some of the above flour mixes for manufacture of some existing biscuit and cookies either savoury or sweet variety are already popular in developed countries. Oat bran cookies, Ritz crackers, rice crackers, digestive biscuits are some of the examples among many varieties of biscuits and cookies available in the market. Even, in our own country, products such as "Rice land", "Digestive" are fibre rich sweet biscuits available in the market. Biscuits such as "Thin Arrowroot", "Ritz crackers" are also being marketed.

It is evident from the scientific literature available that it is a global trend for the development of flour mixes for bakery products. We may observe that flours such as Grain Amaranth, prune juice concentrate in breads, waxy rice in muffins, sunflower kernels, sorghum-peanut composite flour, wheat and corn flour for breads and tomato seed meal in breads are being looked into as flour mixes for bakery products.

In our own Research Development Centre, attempts towards product development by utilising flour mixes are in progress and the author believes that flour mixes in bakery industry would be one of the future thrust areas towards commercialising, health oriented, aesthetical and nutritionally sound bakery products suitable to the ethnic tastes of Indian palate.

4
TRADITIONAL WHEAT PRODUCTS

1. INTRODUCTION

For thousands of years, cereals have been the staple food for most people. The saving in energy and the increased productivity when cereals are consumed directly are so great that even the Sumerians 4000 years ago, recognised that 'a given acreage of land put down to wheat or barley filled more stomachs, more quickly and more cheaply than the same land given over to livestock". Although no record exists of where and when human use of whoat was originaled, there is little doubt that history of wheat usage as food is the history of human civilisation itself.

As we near the dawn of the 21st pacentury, it is evident that food is a global business, and eating patterns around the world seem to be moving in directions that will make them increasingly similar in the future. The globalisation of food consumption patterns is occurring along two tracks. First, basic food commodities such as wheat-based products available and eaten in countries around the world are becoming more alike. Simultaneously, more diverse food preferences are developing within countries, and a greater variety of foods are being purchased by individuals. International trade, telecommunications, travel and an increasingly international media are fostering the homogenisation of food consumption patterns and concerns across countries and the diversification of food preferences within countries. These food trends are occurring in the context of the more general globalisation of world economies and mass culture. In that context, the concept of "traditional products" has a vague and somewhat misleading connotation.

Wheat, a major source of nourishment for most nations, is consumed today in different ways, with each product produced having a range of variation in processing, appearance, taste, and shelf-life. Every wheat-based product has a country of origin and has been the part of tradition of a nation or culture at a point of time - from India's chapati to British shortbreads. For the purpose of this review, discussions will be focussed on wheat-based products which are not yet widely mass produced in large scale production lines and yet have a secure place in the diet of millions of people.

Wheat is cleaned, cooked in boiling water, dried, and roasted to produce roasted whole wheat kernel which is consumed as a snack. Or, it is moistened, partially tempered, and pearled to produce pearled wheat which is used in many ways. For example, it could be cooked with meat and mashed to a paste for the production of harees or haleem. The partially tempered wheat is broken and sized to produce Jereesh, which substitutes for rice in many countries. It might be used for the production of bulgur, or milled to produce semolina which is the essential ingredient for a whole range of pasta products, and couscous, the traditional North African dish. The most diverse consumption of wheat is in the form of flour. Wheat flour is used to produce a whole range of breads, rolls, noodles, cookies, pastries, and other sweet products. Finally, wheat bran and germ have many diverse applications as food and feed

II. TRADITIONAL WHEAT PRODUCTS

A. Couscous

Couscous is a name given to a processed semolina (Fig. 4.1) which is a major staple in North African countries. The term couscous is locally used for the popular stew dish prepared and served with steamed couscous. Semolina requirements for optimum quality couscous are not well known. It might be similar to those of pasta. However, further studies are needed to conform this relationship. The size of the semolina granules and their level of starch damage may play a role in the end product's quality from the standpoint of absorbing sauce and mouthfeel. The yellow colour, and homogeneity of particle size are the most desirable characteristics of couscous. Couscous should absorb high amounts of sauce and particles should keep their integrity, the factors which affect the eating quality of the final product.

Fig. 4.2 shows the diversity of traditional wheat-based products. For the past three decades, research and development efforts have been focussed on many of the traditional processes, and specifying objectively, the attributes of final products. Among wheat-based products, pan bread, followed by cookies, crackers, and to a lesser extent, pasta have been studied the most and the volumes of references are devoted to their wheat quality requirements, milling and production processes, and shelf-life. In contrast, other wheat based products, even though they constitute the staple diet of many nations, are least studied. In this article the processing techniques and the state of research on four traditionally-made products will be discussed briefly and suggestion on future course of action will be made.

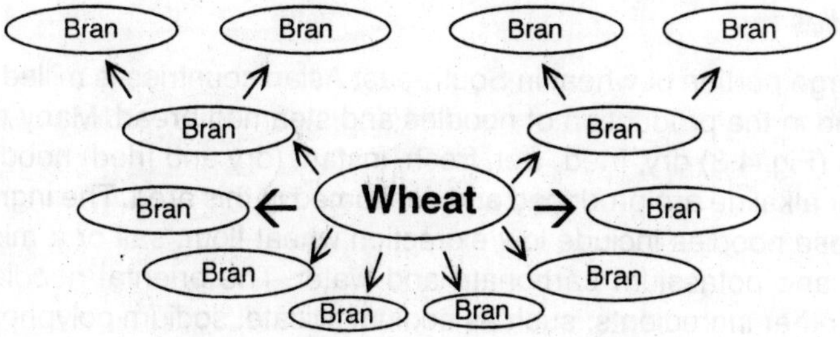

Fig. 4.1. Traditional wheat-based products

Semolina
↓
Blending with salted water
↓
Agglomeration
↓
Shaping
↓
Steaming
↓
Disagglomoration
↓
Drying
↓
Cooling
↓
Grading
↓

↓	↓	↓
Course Couscous	Medium Couscous	Fine Couscous

Fig. 4.2. Processing steps of couscous

5. Ravioli

The same press used for short goods is required. A die to form a dough sheet however has to be added. The dough sheet is passed onwards to the ravioli machine, where the ravioli is stamped out and the necessary meat is injected. The formed raviolis will be either filled into tins, deep-frozen or dried in a macaroni short goods dryer.

B. Noodles

A large portion of wheat in South-east Asian countries is milled to flour and used in the production of noodles and steamed bread. Many types of noodles (Fig. 4.3) dry, fried, wet, fresh, instant (dry and fried) noodles and salted or alkaline are produced and consumed in this area. The ingredients of Chinese noodles include low extraction wheat flour, salt or a mixture of sodium and potassium carbonate and water. The oriental noodle might contain other ingredients, such as sodium silicate, sodium polyphosphate, lecithin, fat, ground vegetable and various flours, starches and gums. The water absorption and mixing time are found to be the most and the least important variables in noodle making respectively. Flour protein significantly affected noodle quality. According to reports, high protein gives a dark and strong cooked noodle, with a relatively soft and mushy surface. Protein is the single most important factor other than flour colour, affecting the colour of fresh noodle sheets.

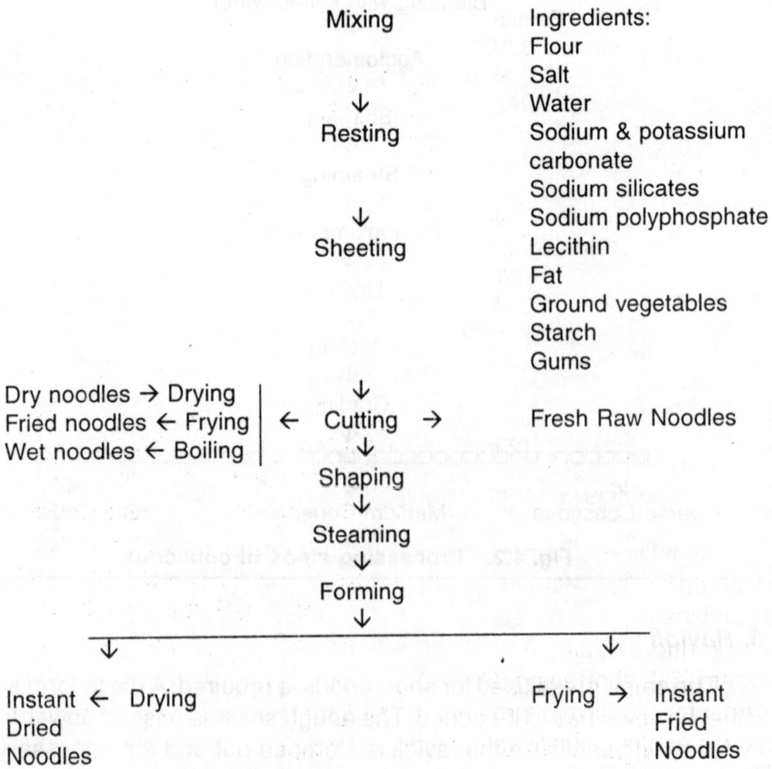

Fig. 4.3. Processing of oriental noodles

The alkaline salts that are commonly used in noodle preparation results in development of a unique flavour and quality, and are responsible for their yellow colour. Sodium carbonate in Chinese noodles has affected the properties of partially·cooked noodles and protein affected the firmness of this prdocut. Excellent quality product has been prepared from wheat flour of 10.0-11.5% protein, 1.4-1.7 sodium chloride and 0.7-1.2% sodium carbonate.

C. Steamed Bread

The formulae of steamed bread include flour, water, yeast and depending on the country and it might also include sugar and shortening (Fig. 4.4). Both, straight and sponge and dough procedures are used for this product. The internal quality factors of steamed bread include texture, grain, firmness and colour. The skin of steamed bread should be smooth and shiny. Height, width, volume and symmetry of this product are considered important.

Sponge mixing
↓
Fermentation
(60 mm 32°C, 85% RH)
↓
Dough mixing
↓
Sheeting
(12-16 times)
↓
Dividing and rounding
(120 g)
↓
Proofing
(45 mim, 38°C, 85% RH)
↓
Steaming
(12 mm)

Ingredients	
-Flour	100
-Yeast	0.7%
-Sugar	2.0%
-NFDM	2.0%
-Shortening	2.0%
-Water	42-48%

Fig. 4.4. Processing steps of steamed breads

The influence of ingredients and processing variables on the quality of steamed bread has been studied. It has been reported that water absorption, a combination of sugar and yeast and processing variable significantly affects the product's quality. An optimum formula has been found to contain flour, sugar (8%), shortening (2%), yeast (1.0%) and optimum water, with 3.5 hr fermentation, 58 mm. proofing, and 10 mm. steaming. With respect to flour protein content significant differences in bread volume has been reported. The research findings suggest that flour of low to medium protein content produce optimum quality product. In contrast to this finding, it has been reported that high protein, high strength flour are desirable. It has been concluded that protein content and strength are the most important factors determining steamed bread quality and 95% of the variability could be explained by six variables in which the protein and dough strength are the dominant factors.

D. Flat Breads

Breads of the world can be divided into three groups with respect to their specific volume (volume/weight):

a. those with high specific volume such as western pan bread;
b. those with medium specific volume such as French, rye and steamed bread; and
c. those with low specific volume such as flat breads of the world

Flat bread could be divided into two groups with respect to their cross section:

a. single-layered flat bread such as Middle Eastern tanoor bread, Indian chapati and European and American flat breads; and
b. double layered flat breads such as Arabic (pita) and Egyptian Baladi bread (Fig. 4.5)

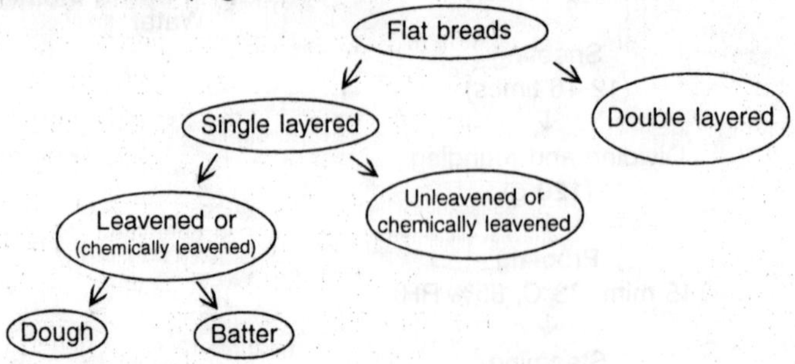

Fig. 4.5. Classification of Flat Breads

Numerous reports are devoted to pan bread and French bread in scientific and technical journals. However, the research on flat breads is limited. These products are mainly prepared from the four essential ingredients of leavened products. Many types of flat bread, such as Indian flat breads are prepared without leavening agent. Research on flour quality requirements for flat bread has shown that optimum products are produced from flour of moderate protein content and dough strength. It has been shown that flour from hard wheat results in a product of superior quality in some type of products to that of soft wheat. Level of starch damage being achieved during the milling of hard wheat is partially responsible and results in flour of high water absorption capacity and superior crust colour in the final product. Flat breads are usually produced from flour of high extraction rate (80% to whole meal). This common practice has many advantages. Firstly, it increases the water absorption of the flour, and secondly it improves the handling quality of the dough. These factors have a significant impact on the quality of final product.

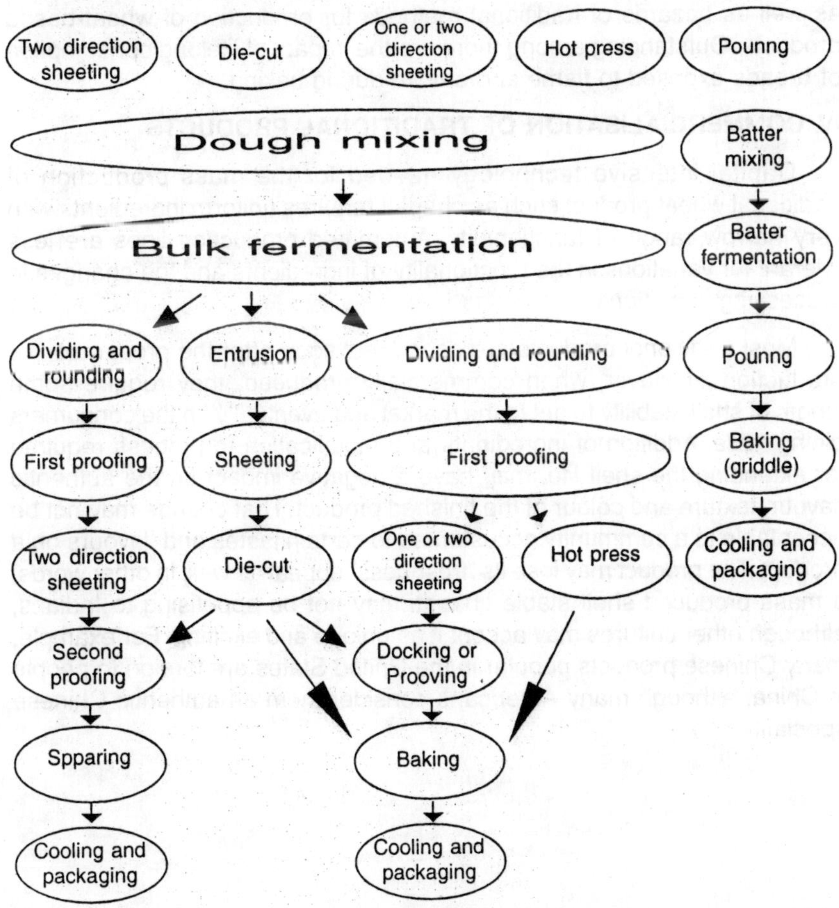

Fig. 4.6. Processing Steps of Flat Breads

III. FUTURE TRENDS

In the next few decades, as the Information Age Technology continues to penetrate the most remote corners of the world, consumption of food will go hand in hand with other cultural changes toward a universal availability of raw material and prepared foods. This would further help in commercialisation of traditional wheat products. Therefore, much research is needed on developing practical and reproducible methods for laboratory production of traditional wheat products. The wide variety of traditional products makes it mandatory to focus on better understanding of their physical, chemical and rheological properties and on the development of new products based on characteristics of the traditional wheat products.

More of research is also needed to identify the potential health benefits as well as hazards of traditional methods for production of wheat-based products. Outstanding among them are the impact of lifelong consumption of breads exposed to flame and smoke during baking.

IV. COMMERCIALISATION OF TRADITIONAL PRODUCTS

Capital intensive technology needed for the mass production of traditional wheat product such as chapati requires uniform ingredients with very narrow range of functionality. Automated production lines are less tolerant for variations in the functionality of ingredients and the changes in processing conditions.

Most traditional products are consumed soon after the preparation or production. However, when commercially produced, they require some length of shelf stability to get to the market and eventually on the consumers dining table. Addition of ingredients and modification to process required for extending the shelf life, may have a negative impact on the authentic flavour, texture and colour of the finished product. That change may not be acceptable to a community accustomed to certain tastes and flavours on a product. The product may lose its "freshness" appeal as well. In other words, a mass produced shelf stable chapati may not be appetising to Indians, although other cultures may accept it as unique and exciting. For example, many Chinese products popular in the United States are foreign to people in China, although many Americans consider them an authentic Chinese speciality.

5
DEVELOPMENTS IN PASTA AND SPECIAL FOOD PRODUCTS

Buhler Ltd., Uzwil, started manufacturing milling equipment in Switzerland in 1860 itself. Very soon many customers showed interest in macaroni machines and therefore, the management decided to design such machines as well. About 25 years ago snacks, breakfast cereals, baby food manufacturing machines were added, We are proud to state that our company has done a lot of pioneering work in these fields, and today macaroni products are among the most important commodities of the world and due to the long shelf-life and high proteln content of 12 to 14 % (rice about 7%) the demand is growing fast.

In this age of fast food, various kinds of snacks are very much liked and the consumption is growing very rapidly. Cereal, flour or semolina are the raw materials required to manufacture these products and the storage and preparation plants are essential for the same.

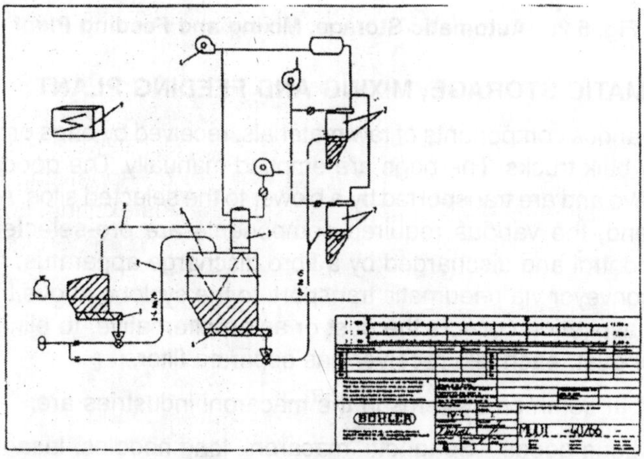

Fig. 5.1. Discontinuous Feeding and Mixing Plant

The automatisation of such plants can be chosen according to the available manpower and financial sources

1. DISCONTINUOUS FEEDING AND MIXING PLANT

The operation of this plant is as follows:

The necessary quantity of the various raw materials are weighed on a platform scale and fed manually into the feeding hopper. The below mounted screw conveyor forwards the blend into the mixer. The blend is uniformly mixed and discharged via the bottom slide and the screw conveyor forwards the goods into the air-lock and via the blower into the cyclone mounted above the doser of the extruder. The dust is collected by a jet-air filter.

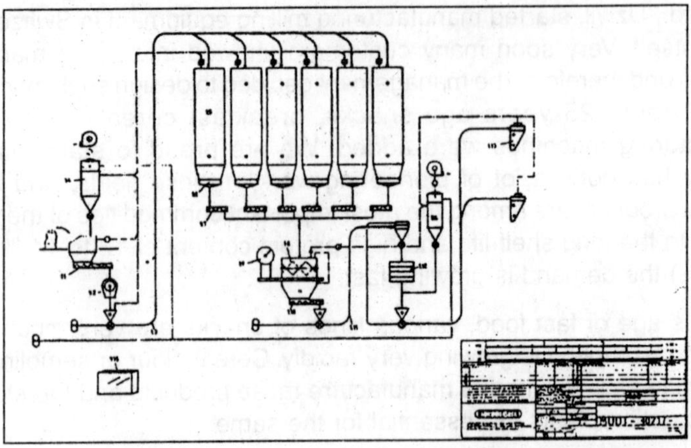

Fig. 5.2. Automatic Storage, Mixing and Feeding Plant

2. AUTOMATIC STORAGE, MIXING AND FEEDING PLANT

The various components of raw materials, received by bags or in certain cases, by bulk trucks. The bags are emptied manually. The goods pass a control sieve and are transported by a blower to the selected silos. According to the blend, the various required components are pre-selected by the weigher control and discharged by a fibro discharge apparatus, dosed by a screw conveyor via pneumatic transport, to the cyclone above the doser. A central aspiration collects the dust or as an alternative, to eliminate the mixture of dust, each silo receiver has separate filter.

The four common systems in the macaroni industries are:-

- Long goods - Spaghetti, macaroni, long noodles, lasagne
- Short goods - Elbows, sea-shells, soup shapes lasagne, vermicelli, noodles

- Nest goods
- Twisted goods

The most popular ones are the long and short goods. The nest and/or twisted goods are only popular in certain countries. I will therefore only explain the main ones.

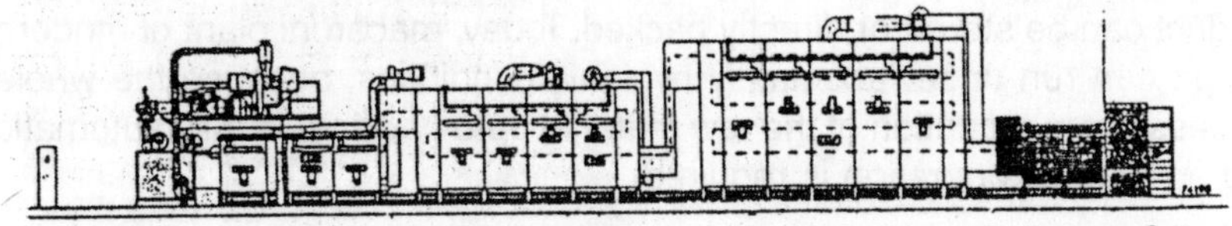

Fig. 5.3. Continuous Long Goods Line

3. CONTINUOUS LONG GOODS LINE

The required raw material is forwarded via a blower to the cyclone above the feeder. The feeder regularly doses the raw material and liquid and leads it into the mixer of the extruder and is homogenizely mixed. It further passes via a vacuum device into the main worm, where the dough is extruded under heavy pressure and go through a rectangular die of 2000 mm width. The spaghetti is simultaneously spread over two sticks.

The loaded sticks pass the dryers which have different climates and are controlled independently by automatic climate controls. Before conveying to the stripping off and cutting machine, the goods pass through a cooler and cooled to the ambient climate. At the end, the spaghetti is stripped off and cut to the required length. Then the empty sticks return below the dryers, automatically to the spreader, where new products can further be loaded. The drying time is between 5 and 10 hours depending on the system of the line. The cut spaghetti is packed manually or with an automatic packing machine.

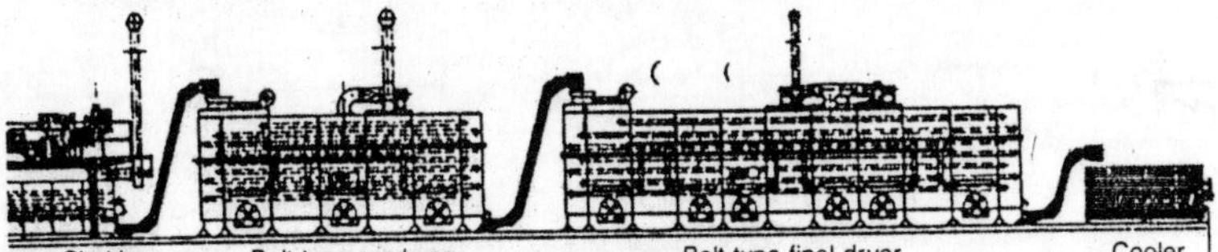

Fig. 5.4. Continuous Short Goods Line

4. CONTINUOUS SHORT GOODS LINE

The feeding of the mixer is the same as described for long goods. However, the extruded dough is pressed through a round die. The product (sea-shells, elbows, etc.) is cut directly at the die, and the length can be chosen in accordance to the requested shape. The wet product (about 30% water) passes through a shaking pre-dryer and final dryer. The dryers are equipped with several belts and a cooler is installed at the end.

The drying temperature is between about 70 and 100°C and the drying time, depending on the chosen system between 3 and 7 hours. The finished product can be stored or directly packed. Today, macaroni plant of modern design can run under absolutely hygienic conditions, because the whole process (from reception of the raw material upto packing) is fully automatic and no manual operation is required.

Before ending my explanation on the macaroni production, I would like to add some comments on the production of ravioli and stamped goods.

5. RAVIOLI

The same press used for short goods is required. A die to form a dough sheet however has to be added. The dough sheet is passed onwards to the ravioli machine, where the ravioli is stamped out and the necessary meat is injected. The formed raviolis will be either filled into tins, deep-frozen or dried in a macaroni short goods dryer.

6. STAMPED GOODS

The same press used for ravioli is required. The dough sheet passes a stamping machine and the goods are dried in the standard short goods dryer. The off-cuts of the sheet is re-processed in the mixing dough.

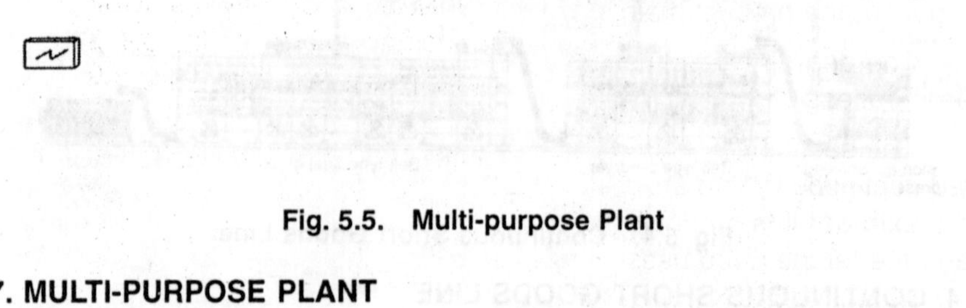

Fig. 5.5. Multi-purpose Plant

7. MULTI-PURPOSE PLANT

This plant is designed and built according to the space available and the following products can be produced:

- Standard short goods macaroni
- Instant short goods macaroni
- Direct expanded snacks
- Shaped snacks
- Various flakes
- Baby food
- Instant flour
- Bread crumbs
- Couscous
- Breakfast cereals
- Co-extrusion products

STANDARD SHORT GOODS

The manufacturing process of this product has already been explained.

INSTANT SHORT GOODS MACARONI

The difference between instant macaroni and standard macaroni lies in the cooking process. The standard macaroni is cooked for about 7-10 mins. To prepare instant macaroni either boiled water is poured over the dried product (taking about 3.5 to 4 mins) or cooked for about 1.5 to 2 mins (to enable such a process a steamer between the press and the dryers is needed) and the meal gets ready for eating.

DIRECT EXPANDED SNACKS

The raw materials used are maize, rice, wheat flour or semolina. The moisture content before extrusion is about 16-17%. The basic fact for the expansion of snacks is that the pressure is generated in the product cells by heating, which turns the locked-up moisture into the steam. If the cell walls are elastic and the steam cannot escape, the individual cell walls expand and further lead to an expansion of the volume of the total product.

When the steam finally escapes and dried and the temperature gets reduced, the product maintains its inflated volume.

The degree of expansion varies widely - depending on raw materials and processing. The process can be described as follows:

The semolina or flour dampened with the necessary water quantity is fed continuously into the main screw. As the material is moved forward in the extruder it is gradually compressed more; pressure increases rapidly and the temperature rises considerably owing to steam and heating.

As the compressed mass is released through the forming dies into the atmosphere, the water flushes off as steam, expanding the product into a light cellulose structure of a shape determined by the die orifice.

The strands are cut off by rotating knives to suitable lengths, dried with a hot air dryer and packed

SHAPED SNACKS

The production of shaped snacks is quite different from that of the direct expanded ones.

The advantages of these products are as follows:

a. There is practically no limit in shapes
b. Raw material with protein content can be processed as well
c. Pellets can be stored for a long time and fried just before distribution.

The diagram for such a line is as follows:

The raw material (wheat, rice corn or potato, flour or starch) is dosed into a mixing trough and the necessary quantity of water is added (the water content is about 30%).

The mixture is fed continuously to the main screw, where the gelatinisation takes place.

The gelatinised product can either be dried (and reground for the second process) or put into a second extruder where the wet product is directly formed to the final shapes.

This product passes through three continuous belt dryers, which are controlled by climate controls (automatically)

After a drying time of about 4-6 hours, the product is made ready for frying, flavouring and packing or the pellets can be stored, The flavour can be adopted to the requirements of customers.

It may be noted that the cheese taste maintains a leading position in Europe, but other flavours (onion, paprika, bacon, peanuts, etc.) are also much appreciated. Children prefer the fruit and sugar taste,

VARIOUS FLAKES

Normally flakes are made as fragments or as whole grains (the corn flakes even out of hominy grits). In the past, we received many applications for processing flakes of a mixture of various raw materials or raw material enriched with additional protein, vitamins or fibre. Such products can be manufactured on special flaking plants only. Therefore, we developed a new method. The various raw materials are mixed in our multipurpose extruder and the necessary moisture is added. The dough is gelatinised and small pellets are extruded at a moisture content of about 30%. The pre-dryer evaporate part of the water and the pellets are flaked in a roller mill. The partly dry flakes are either roasted to a crispy final product or dryed in a final dryer. At the end, the goods are packed. They are then made ready for shipment.

BABY FOOD

We developed a process that guarantees a nutritional baby food - made out of vegetables, containing protein.

One of the most important machines in this process is once again the multipurpose extruder which has already been discussed.

The raw materials used for processing are wheat, lentils, chickpeas, soya, etc. Wheat, chickpeas and lentil flour are mixed with water. After leaving the extruder, the product is directed into a steamer and the dryer, heated with hot water and the moisture is reduced to about 15%. The goods are ground to flour and the necessary milk powder, minerals, vitamins and flavours are admixed and the mixture is packed and made ready for the market. The taste of the baby food can be modified with various types of flavours. There is another process on the market, where the raw material made into a slurry and then dried on drum driers. We are able to supply such plant as well.

INSTANT FLOUR

The production is similar to that of the baby food. However, instead of a blend of various raw material a single type of material is used. After gelatinising, the goods are dried and ground to a flour and then packed.

This flour is mainly used for instant soup, etc.

BREAD CRUMBS

Bread crumbs are used more and more for pattering fish or meat or as a filler for sausages.

The raw material is pre-gelatinised, formed in a certain size of pellets dried, roasted, regrinded and packed.

COUSCOUS

A food consisting of agglomerates of semolina granules, can be produced from durum wheat as well as from soft wheat varieties. The product passes the following processing stages

- Blending of semolina and water
- Mixing agglomeration
- Detaching (reduced and shaped)
- Steaming (pre-cooked)

- Drying into uniformed moisture
- Grading and separation
- Size reduction according to the customers demand
- Storage and packing

BREAKFAST CEREALS

These products are produced in the same way as direct expanded snacks. Mainly the shape is changed and instead of spraying the goods with spices, the final product is sprayed with caramel, sugar, etc.

SOYMILK AND OTHER SOYA PRODUCTS - FROM THE TRADITIONAL PRODUCTION TO THE NEW MANUFACTURING PROCESSES

Soya is increasingly viewed as being the miracle destined to save humanity and its senseless and irresponsible demographic growth. Over the last few years, production of soya has risen to almost 100 million metric tonnes. If we assume that the total quantity of soya be applied for human nutrition, the annual crop can cover 30% of the protein needs of mankind. Of course, in making this assumption, we are not giving due consideration to the fact that there is a wide gap between purely statistical figures and the reality of implementing such scheme of nutrition. The first barrier for using soya for human consumption is a psychological one. From an economic point of view, soya's relevance is as a source of oil and protein, the oil normally being considered for human use and the protein for animals. Soya as a whole is not viewed as a foodstuff, i.e., by its own right like, say milk, meat or grain. There is however an exception to this mistrust, its value as a food has long been known to the Chinese,

TECHNOLOGY OF THE FUTURE

The introduction of soya in our future nutrition must not be limited to Tofu. We must therefore redefine our aim. Soya must be made available to food manufacturers in a form allowing it to be readily incorporated in the products as demanded by the market.

However this readily means:

- without impairing the texture or the taste of such products;
- without reducing their sanitary or bacteriological quality;
- without entailing excessive additional investments;
- without generating new waste or by-products requiring expensive disposal.

We believe full fat soya powder is the most promising for, it is natural, it contains all of the valuable constituents of soya, it is inexpensive to produce, and it does not generate any waste that cannot be re-used. The following products can be made of soya powder.

- Tofu
- Soymilk
- Ice cream
- Sausages, hamburger, etc.
- Bread
- Macaroni
- Yoghurts
- Drinks, etc.

Today soya is used more and more for human food, due to the high nutritional value and it can replace a certain amount of animal protein with vegetable protein to increase the health of the people.

I sincerely hope that these explanations give you additional information. Should you need more details or should you have a firm project, please do not hesitate to contact us. Should you plan a trip to Europe, please inform us, so that we can organise a visit to our headquarters in Uzwil/Switzerland, where our research and developing centres are also located. It would be a pleasure to assist you in this very interesting field and we are looking forward to meet you soon again.

6

METHODS FOR PROLONGING SHELF-LIFE OF FRESH FRUITS AND VEGETABLES

INTRODUCTION

The developing countries around the world have varied agro-climatic conditions and are uniquely placed to produce almost different types of fruits and vegetables. India produces around 611 million tonnes of fruits and vegetables worth Rs.7,000-8,000 crores from 720 million hectares of land. Post-harvest losses to the extent of 20-30% were found to occur due to improper post-harvest handling and marketing. The principal causes of post-harvest losses are mechanical injuries, shrivelling due to excessive moisture loss, microbial infections and sprouting and chilling injuries (Table-6.1). However, the nature and extent of damage depends on the commodity involved, agro-climatic conditions and marketing.

Post-harvest losses can be reduced to some extent by breeding of fruits and vegetables for longer shelf-life, improvement in pre-harvest factors and harvesting techniques, and proper methods of handling. Some of these aspects are discussed in this paper with emphasis on emerging technologies.

POST-HARVEST HANDLING METHODS

1. Selection of varieties: The selection of appropriate varieties mediated through modern breeding practice is one of the important aspects in the development of suitable post-harvest handling techniques. In the recent past, it is gaining increasing popularity giving molecular geniticist a key role to play. The intrinsic genetic characteristic derived/gained thereof are directed towards attainment of decrease resistance, textural qualities and alterations in the induction pattern of cell wall degrading enzymes like polygalacturonase and pectin methyl esterase.

2. Harvesting method: Improper harvesting practices usually result in mechanical injuries like bruising and cuts. Care in harvesting and handling is necessary to preserve quality of fruits and vegetables. These mechanical injuries cause abnormal post-harvest behaviour altering quality attributes like flavour, texture and colour. Therefore, it is essential to follow appropriate harvesting method besides keeping in view specific harvesting indices.

Table-6.1. Causes of Post-harvest Losses

Group	*Commodity*	*Principal causes of post-harvest losses and poor quality*
Root vegetables	Carrots Beets Onions Garlic Sweet potato	1. Mechanical injury 2. Improper caring 3. Sprouting and rooting 4. Water loss (shrivelling) 5. Decay
Leavy vegetables	Lettuce Spinach Cabbage	1. Water loss (witting) 2. Loss of green colour 3. Mechanical injuries 4. Decay
Flower vegetables	Broccoli Cauliflower	1. Mechanical injuries 2. Yellowing and other discolouration 3. Abscission 4. Decay
Immature fruits and vegetables Egg plant Okra	Cucumbers Squash Snap beans Pepper	1. Over maturity at harvest 2. Water loss 3. Bruising and other mechanical injuries 4. Chilling injury 5. Decay
Mature fruits, vegetables and all fruits	Tomato Melons Citrus Bananas Mangoes Apples	1. Bruising 2. Over ripeness and excessive softening at harvest 3. Water loss 4. Compositional changes 5. Decay

3. Methods of Storage

(a) Surface decontamination of fresh produce: Fungicides, bactericides and senescence inhibitors are applied to fruits and vegetables for the purpose of reducing decay either directly or indirectly during storage and marketing. Treatments currently utilised in the produce industry are specific to the fresh product to certain extent (Table-6.2). The two basic methods for applying chemicals to crops after harvest are by fumigation and by solution or suspension in water and wax formulations.

Table-6.2. Treatment Utilised to Control Post-harvest Decay of Fresh Produce

Crop	*Treatment*
Apple	Sodium 0. Phenylphenate
Pear	Thiabendazole, Benomyl
Banana	Thiabendazole, Benomyl
Citrus fruits	Sodium carbonate, +Borax Sodium O. Phenylphenate Thiabendazole, Benomyl, Biphenyl, 2-4 dichloro phenoxy acetic acid
Grape	Sulphur dioxide fumigation
Peach	Hot water
Cherry	Bonomyl
Pineapple	Sodium O. Phenylphenate, Salicylanitide
Papaya	Hot water
Mango	Hot water, Benomyl
Potato	Hypochlorite
Vegetables	Chloromines

Source: Vijav Sethi and Maini, SB. 1989

The common fumigants used for the fumigation of fresh produce are sulphur dioxide, nitrogen trichloride and biphenyl. Fumigation of grapes with SO_2 during storage and transit has been the standard practice for controlling decay of this crop. The usual practice is to fumigate grapes as soon as possible after harvest with 1% SO_2 (vol/vol) followed by a periodic fumigation with a 0.25% SO_2 at 7-10 day intervals during storage. Nitrogen trichloride has been used extensively to control decay or lemons during storage, but in recent years the practice has been declining because of the corrosion problems associated with its use. Citrus fruits destined for distant markets are treated with biphenyl to control decay during the transit and storage periods. This fungistat is impregnated into fruit wraps or into paper sheets placed at the bottom and top of the fruit container.

(b) Use of waxes and emulsions: The use of waxes and emulsions results in the fall in respiratory rate with a simultaneous restriction in the physiological loss in weight. The emulsion can act as a carrier of fungicidal and bactericidal compounds. Protein, lipids and carbohydrates are widely used in the edible emulsions out of which sucrose esters of fatty acids and casein in combination with alginic acid and acetylated monoglycerides are the important ones. Chitosan derived from the shells of crustaceans in combination with laurel oils like coconut oil was the latest innovative application.

(c) Hormonal and chemical control of ageing/ripening: A variety of hormones and growth substances, viz., gibberellic acid, kinetin and Vitamin

K are reported to be effective in retarding the senescence of fresh fruits and vegetables. However, from the economics point of view, they were not found viable.

Among chemical regulants the use of calcium chloride and ethylene scrubbers were common. Defence Food Research Laboratory, Mysore standardised a method to extend the shelf-life of assorted fresh fruits and vegetables (salad items) pre-packaged in perforated polyethylene pouches as 3 kg units.

Fruits like apple, orange, mosambi, guava, mango and pears and salad vegetables like carrot, radish, tomatoes, cucumbers, green chillies. onion and ginger may be treated in this way. However, citrus fruits and tuber vegetables were not subjected to dip treatments. The shelf-life of different fresh commodities was found to be extended by 3-5 days.

Pre-treatment and Packaging Method

Wash in bleaching powder solution (0.04%)

↓

Dip treatment in calcium chloride solution (2% for 10 mm)

↓

Air drying to remove surface moisture

↓

Selective application of antifungal paste at the stem end of fruits (0.5% sorbic acid in petroleum jelly)

↓

Loading of racks in multipurpose ventilated plastic crates (15 kg crate)

↓

Use of ethylene absorbing sachets (40 g/crate)

↓

Lidding and transport

The use of ethylene absorbents is an established practice wherever ethylene accumulation at physiologically active concentration occurs. Ethylene is a gaseous ripening hormone which when accumulated in the storage atmosphere can promote senescence of different fresh fruits and vegetables. There is a need to remove the accumulated ethylene using ethylene scrubbers. Such formulation can be used either in a blanket form or in the sachet form and is suitable for use cold rooms or under ambient conditions respectively.

(d) Controlled atmosphere storage: Controlled atmosphere storage generally refers to in an atmosphere in which CO_2 usually is lowered and that of CO_2 increased, with simultaneous maintenance of low temperature, which is highly effective in controlling the post-harvest decay of fruits like tomato. Controlled atmosphere has been known to significantly increase the efficacy of low temperature storage, but cannot be a substitute to refrigeration.

(e) Low temperature storage: The optimum low temperature storage conditions and the expected shelf-life of fruits and vegetables have been thoroughly investigated. The compatibility of storing together different fresh commodities at low temperature for certain period of time is determined by their tolerance for low temperature and volatile gas generation in storage.

(f) Modified atmosphere storage: Modified atmosphere (MA) storage does not differ in principle from controlled atmosphere (CA) storage, except that control of gas concentration is less.

The types of flexible plastic packaging materials used for the modified atmosphere packaging of fresh produce are low density polyethylene, cellophane, rubber hydrochloride (Pilo film) and polyvinyl chloride.

Many workers have tested MAP with a wide variety of fresh produce. CA/MA conditions reduce respiration rates as long as the levels of O_2 and CO_2 are within the limits tolerated by the commodity This, combined with the decreased ethylene production and reduced sensitivity to ethylene action results in delayed senescence as indicated by retention of chlorophyll, textural quality and other sensory attributes. Exposure of fresh fruits and vegetables to 02 levels below or CO2 levels above tolerance limits may increase anaerobic respiration and consequently accumulation of ethanol and acetaldehyde may form causing off flavours.

(g) Irradiation: Gamma irradiation at low dose levels improves the shelf-life of fruits like banana, mango and papaya, etc. by delaying the ripening and senescence and in addition causes distinfestation. When combined with physical process like hot water treatment, irradiation extends the market life by reducing post-harvest decay caused by fungal pathogens. Irradiation causes suppression of sprouting in tuber crops like potato and onion.

(h) Zero energy cool chambers: Indian Agricultural Research Institute has developed a zero energy cool chamber for retaining the freshness of the fruits and vegetables during storage for a short period. The Central Food Technological Research Institute, Mysore, has also developed an evaporative cooling storage chamber.

Another way of obtaining evaporative cooling effect is the continuous pumping of moist air over the fresh produce resulting in significant restriction of physiological loss in weight and overall deterioration of produce quality.

FUTURE PROSPECTS

The data base necessary to design commercially feasible preservation methods for fresh produce is available by and large. The need of the hour is a concerted effort to translate the methods into commercial practice. A nationwide refrigeration network is needed for transport and storage. Packaging costs and taxation pattern need consideration to make the system viable.

7
TECHNOLOGY OF FRUIT JUICE AND PULP CONCENTRATES

1. TRENDS IN FRUIT JUICE PROCESSING

Several important technological advances have appeared in the fruit juice processing industries during the past decades. Some of the more important ones concerning orange juice processing are presented here.

Fruit juices can be made directly from the fruit or made from juice concentrate by dilution with water. Orange juice is most popular, occupying about 60% of the total consumption. The next is apple juice which occupies about 20% of the total consumption. In the United States, the annual consumption of apple juice is about 19 million standard cases; grapefruit juice 8.6 million cases; and pineapple juice, 9.2 million cases. Other juices of significant quantities are tomato juice, cranberry juice citrus grapefruit juice and many others.

In 1987-88, 16 million gallons of frozen orange concentrates and 3 million gallons of frozen grape concentrates were made in the United States.

Fruit juice production is regulated in most countries. Juices from acidic fruits such as apricots, berries, kiwifruit and lemon are not suitable for direct consumption because of their high acid content. They are made into nectars, juice drinks or sweet musts.

Preparation of the fruits for processing involves washing, rinsing, trimming and sorting to remove undesirable ones. The stone seeds, stems or calyx are removed in the pulping process. Disintegration is accomplished mechanically in mills, thermally by heating or thermo break at 80°C or by freezing at -50°C. The yield can be increased by enzymic pectin degradation particularly for apple juice, berry juice and kiwifruit juice.

Separation of the juice is achieved using continuous or batch process such as vacuum filtration or extraction. Newer methods involve application of pectic and cellulase enzymes for soft tropical fruits. The production line involves fruit washing and sorting, fruit mashing- milling, enzyme treatment, filtration, thermal processing to inactivate enzymes and to destroy microorganisms, filling and sealing into containers and canning or refrigeration for the super market. The juice may also be preserved by filling or aseptic canning into cans, bottles or containers made of laminated pouches with polypropylene lining.

For non-pulpy juices, clarification with pectic enzymes is a very important step. Sometimes, it is necessary to use gelatin, alone or together with colloidal silicic acid to remove excessive tannins. Turbidity caused by small particles or proteins is removed by adsorption on bentonite or kieselguhr as filter aid. Another method to remove excessive tannins is the use of polyvinylpyrrolidone prior to filtration. Clarification of juice is achieved by filtration through porous pads or layers of cellulose, kieselguhr or cellulose acetate sheets of controlled porosity. Centrifugation is another method for removal of pulpy materials.

Oxygen-sensitive juices must be deaerated by an evacuation step or purging with nitrogen gas or carbon dioxide gas.

Citrus juices, such as lemon, orange and grape are heat-treated to inactivate the endogenous pectinesterase, which would otherwise provide pectic acid that can aggregate and flocculate in the presence of calcium ions.

The final step in fruit juice preservation involves pasteurisation, preservation by freezing, storage under an inert gas atmosphere or aseptic processing.

Pasteurisation kills the microorganisms and inactivates polyphenoloxidases and other undesirable enzymes. A high-temperature short-time heat treatment is the preferred process, using plate heat-exchangers or swept-film type heat exchangers at 82 to 90°C for 15 to 150 sec with subsequent rapid cooling. The product is stored in germ-free containers.

Preservation by freezing generally involved transforming the juice or concentrate into an ice slurry ast -2.5°C to -5.6°C, then packing and cooling to the retail-market storage temperature.

Storage under an inert atmosphere makes use of the fact that filtered, sterilised juices are microbiologically stable at temperature below 10°C and under an atmosphere of more than 14.6 g carbon dioxide/litre. To obtain such a concentration of carbon dioxide, the filled storage tank has to be at a pressure of 5.9 bar at 10°C and 4.7 bar at 5°C.

II. CITRUS JUICE PROCESSING

Florida is one of the more important citrus fruit production areas in the United States. It produces primarily 650 Brix frozen orange concentrate but also some grapefruit concentrate and lemon juice concentrate. By-products produced are cold pressed peel oil, citrus essences, d-limonene and citrus pellets.

Orange juice concentrate : Fruit is harvested at proper maturity to the plant in trucks with 20 tonne capacity and discharged by gravity into conveyor belts. Fruit is sampled during this operation to determine the Brix:Acid ratio and juice content which can be used for selective blending of loads to achieve specific quality parameters. Before storage into bins, a first grading is done to remove unsound fruit.

Fruit is pulled out from the bins in conveyor belts, washed and graded again before juice extraction. Most processors use pumps to convey the fruit in water to the surge bins in order to minimise bruising. Detergents and chlorinated water rinse can be used and often condensate from juice evaporation is used in the washing step. After washing and grading, fruit is sized and juice is extracted in FMC extractors and conveyed in a totally closed system to finishers to separate juice sacs from the juice.

The finished juice is centrifuged to reduce the pulp level and defects, collected in large evaporator feed tanks and concentrated in a TASTE unit which stands for "Thermally Accelerated Short Time Evaporator". This evaporator is a single pass unit and, because of the multi-stage, multi-effect design, it generally provides a good steam economy. The evaporator contains an essence recovery unit to recover aqueous and oil phase components. The essences are added back to the concentrate during the blending operation.

Concentrate from the evaporator comes out at about 30°C and is further chilled to 5°C to -18°C and stored in large bulk tanks of 250,000 gallon capacity. Some processors use polypropylene lined steel drums as containers. The concentrate from the storage tank is usually blended to provide a 650 Brix concentrate of uniform quality. Essences are added back to enhance product quality and flavour. Distribution of the product is done in bulk with concentrate being transported from the plants in insulated tank trucks to the port. At the port, the concentrate is stored in cold storage tanks and later loaded in the ships, which will ultimately take the product to various port located abroad. A flow chart is shown in Fig 7.1.

III. CITRUS BY-PRODUCTS RECOVERY

The recovery of citrus by-products is important to the industry. It brings in additional revenue and solves the disposal problem of fruit waste material. The major by-products recovered from oranges are cold pressed peel oil and citrus pellets which are used as cattle feed.

Fruit unloading
↓
Bin Storage
↓
Washing
↓
Grading
↓
Essential oil Emulsion ← Extraction → Peel & Rag
↓
Finishing
↓
Centrifuging
↓
Evaporation → Aqueous and oil phase essences
↓
Essences & oil ← Blending
↓
Tank Farm
↓
Shipment

Fig. 7.1. Concentrate Production

Recovery of cold pressed oil from orange occurs simultaneously during juice extraction. A flow chart for orange oil recovery is shown in Fig. 7.2. An oil emulsion in water is produced with small pieces of peel which are separated later in a screw type finisher. The oil emulsion recovered at the finisher goes to a desludge centrifuge which splits the feed stream into three separate parts, an oil rich phase usually containing 65-80% oil, an aqueous phase and a thick mass with solid particles called sludge. The aqueous phase is filtered and a portion of it is recycled back to the extractors. The oil rich emulsion is then sent to a polisher centrifuge to remove all remaining water. The clear oil is usually placed in drums and dewaxed.

The frozen pulp or juice sacs are recovered from the juice stream after the extractor. Small peel particles and immature seeds are removed with liquid cyclones which operate at relatively high pressures. After removal of excess juice, the clean pulp is stabilised, finished and packaged in fibreboard cartons or drums.

Cattle feed is produced from the peel, seeds and core material. As these materials are discharged from the extractor they are conveyed by screw conveyors to the feed mill. The combined material is reduced in size in a hammer mill and lime, in the dorm of calcium hydroxide, is added. The mixture goes to a reaction screw where lime assists in the release of water and then sends to a screw press. In this operation 60% of the feed is recovered as a liquid, which is concentrated to 300 Brix and added back to the peel and cores at the hammer mill.

Extractor
↓
Oil slurry
↓
Finisher
↓
Oil emulsion
↓
Desludging centrifuge
↓
Oil rich emulsion
↓
Polishing centrifuge
↓
Drum filling
↓
Cold storage

Fig. 7.2. Oil Recovery Flow Chart

The press cake is then conveyed to a direct fired kiln drier, where the moisture is reduced to a maximum of 10%. The press liquor is concentrated in a waste heat evaporator which uses the hot combustion gases and steam from the kiln drier. The dried cake is cooled in a rotary air cooler and pelletised to reduce bulk density.

IV. CONCENTRATION TECHNOLOGY

Concentration technology has undergone drastic changes since the early 1940s. The citrus juices were concentrated in low temperature falling film evaporators. These evaporators operated under high vacuum stripping off most of the volatile aromas. Later on, the TASTE (thermally accelerated short-time evaporator) was developed and adopted by the citrus industry. This evaporator used several stages or effects heating the juice to higher temperature for shorter times. It also had systems for recovering essences which were added back to the juice making the finished product more attractive.

In the late 1970's, the freeze concentration process was developed and used by the citrus industry in making concentrates. Concentration is accomplished by separating ice crystals from the liquid. The juice must be heat pasteurised prior to concentration to inactivate enzymes and lower microbiological counts. The process is more expensive and the equipment is mechanically complex. It is used for concentration of orange juice and instant coffee extracts. It is very important that a special FMC Premium juice extractor be used to minimise the quantity of peel oil and peel extractives getting into the juice.

Membrane concentration: In the late 1980s, the Fresh Note Process was developed by the Separa Systems, a joint venture of FMC Corporation and DuPont. It uses both ultrafiltration and reverse osmosis membranes to concentrate citrus juices to high Brix levels. The principle of operation of the process is that incoming orange juice stream is first separated into a clarified serum and a pulp stream by an ultrafiltration membrane module. The clarified serum is then passed through a reverse osmosis membrane module, where it is concentrated to 600 Brix. The pulp stream is sent to a pasteurizer where the enzymes and microorganisms are inactivated. The flavour and aromatic compounds are protected from heat since they pass freely through the ultramembrane and are concentrated in the reverse osmosis membranes without the use of any heat. In fact, the process is carried out in a chilled condition. This membrane concentration system is mechanically simpler than the freeze concentration system Product quality is equal to or better than that from freeze concentration. The Fresh Note system is almost a completely automated and simplified operation.

V. PRODUCTION AUTOMATION

New systems have been installed at several citrus processing plants around the world which have automated the fruit handling prior to the juice extraction system. Juice room automation has resulted in increased juice extraction, improved clean-up efficiency, increased yield and more consistent higher quality juices. Some of the juice room automation systems use computer logic with touch CRT screen graphics. In other locations, keyboards have been employed. Either way the systems allow the operator to monitor all operations of the juice room without leaving the control room. Automation of evaporators has been carried out successfully on a limited scale on some smaller evaporators. Some Florida citrus processors have operational automated evaporators in various stages of commercialisation.

VI. JUICE QUALITY ENHANCEMENT

Recently, a number of new technologies have been introduced into the citrus industry aimed at improving the quality of citrus juices. These include debittering systems, deacidification systems, decolourisation systems and bulk aseptic storage systems.

Several debittering systems have been developed in the past decade. Each of these systems uses a clarification stage to remove pulp and a debittering stage using a resin column to remove bitter substances such as limonin and nariginin from the juice. Some of these systems use centrifugation to clarify the juice prior to treatment with the resin while another system uses an ultrafiltration membrane system in conjunction with centrifuges to clarify the juice. The resins used are primarily adsorption type which adsorb the bitter molecules. The bitter constituents are later removed when the column is regenerated. Debittering systems are being used commercially to process naval orange and grapefruit Juice. Another system which uses the same principle as debittering is deacidification which uses ion-exchange resins to selectively remove acids. In some areas of the world it has been found to be beneficial to both debitter and deacidify Juices from citrus to improve the quality.

VII. VOLATILE COMPOUNDS IMPORTANT TO ORANGE FLAVOUR

Orange flavour has been widely studied in an effort to discern the components important to flavour and aroma of good quality juices. Several recent reviews have discussed the current status of fresh and processed orange juice flavours.

Table 7.1 lists volatile components of orange believed to contribute to Juice flavour. Comparison of the mean values and range of values for the components found in fresh versus processed juice reveals some differences between them. Hand-extracted fresh orange Juice contained considerably less limonene than did processed juices. Consequently, other components contributed largely by peel oil (myrcene, alpha-pinene, octanal, nonanal, decanal and linalool) were also present in considerably higher quantities in processed juices. Alpha-terpineol, which makes a negative contribution to juice flavour, was present In relatively high amounts at or above the taste threshold level in some processed juices. Ahmed et al., (1978) evaluated ten of the compounds listed in Table 1 for their importance to orange flavour and found acetaldehyde, citral, ethyl butanoate, limonene, linalool, octanol and alpha-pinene to make important contributions.

Table-7.1: Volatile Compounds important to Orange Flavour

	Amount in orange juice (ppm)			
	Fresh[a]		Processed[b]	
Component	*mean*	*range*	*mean*	*range*
Terpene hydrocarbons				
d-Limonene	35	22-67	154	80-290
Myrcene	0.7[c]	0.05-2	2.6[d]	-
Alpha-Pinene	0.031	0.025-0.041	1.0	0-5.0
Valencene	2.0	0.028-7.0	1.3	0-14.8
Aldehydes				
Acetaldehyde	9.5	5.3-15	6.3	0.72-12.2
trans-2-Pentenal	<0.01[d]		0.0075[e]	
Hexanal	0.06	0.03-0.1	0.14	0-0.33
Octanal	0.009	0.001-0.14	043	0.19-0.83
Nonanal	0.02[c]	<0.01-0.04	0.09[d]	-
Decanal	0.012	0.007-0.018	0.47	0-1.73
Citral	0.18[c]	0.05-0.3	0.48[d]	-
Sinensal	—	—	0.11[d]	-
Esters				
Ethyl acetate	0.20	0.06-0.4	0.14	0-0.32
Ethyl propionate	0.1f	—	—	
Methyl butanoate	0.029	0.009-0.06	0.013	0-0.07
Ethyl butanoate	0.62	0.09-1.2	0.30	0.01-0.89
Ethyl 2-methylbutanoate	0.05[c]	<0.01 -0.1	—	
Ethyl 3-hydroxyhexanoate	0.055[c]	0.14-1.0	0.13[f]	-
Alcohols				
Ethanol	923	285-1260	568	14-1150
trans-2-Hexen-1 -01	0.007	0.005-0.008	0.01	0-0.14
cis-3-Hexen-1-01	0.14	0.08-0.28	0.62	0-2.1
Linalool	0.15	0.10-0.33	1.4	0-6.1
Alpha-Terpineol	0.08	0.06-0.11	0.46	0-2.5

a From Lizotte and Shaw (1992) for hand-extracted Valencia orange juice, unless otherwise noted.

b Adapted from data of Nisperos-Carriedo and Shaw (1990) and Shaw et al. (1992) unless otherwise noted,

c Values adapted from Shaw (1991)

d Shaw (1986)

e Moshonas and Shaw (1973)

f Moshonas and Shaw (1987)

g Moshonas and Shaw (1986)

8
TECHNOLOGY OF AROMA RECOVERY FOR FRUIT JUICES

Flavours (aromas) are a very heterogeneous group of substances including far more than 100 individual compounds with, as a rule, very low odour thresholds. Major substances categories are differentiated such as, for example, alcohols, esters, aldehydes, terpenes and lactones. Fruits can be classified according to their aromatic substances. Fruits whose flavours are determined by one or a small number of known compounds have a so-called character of impact. Then, there are fruits with more or less undefined flavours comprising a large number of compounds. Storage of natural fruit juices without further treatment, e.g., cold sterile storage or pasteurisation, leads in time to a clear negative alteration in the flavour. Studies have shown that this is also the case with the cut-back method previously used for orange juice. The surest way to maintain the original quality of flavour and juice for longer periods is to concentrate the fruit juice, applying an integrated flavour recovery method, followed by separate storage of the flavour/fruit juice concentrate. The technology used is of the essence. One typical characteristic of flavour substances is that they are released from the product along with the water when it evaporates. To obtain the aromatic (flavour) substance from a fruit juice, the flavour must first enter a vapour phase. The evaporation volume required for complete evaporation of the various fruit flavour substances varies. This is followed by the actual aroma extraction process in a rectification column, where the aroma substances are separated as volatile substances from the water, which is less volatile, then condensed and chilled. About 1% of the original juice volume is extracted in the form of a water-clear flavour concentrate containing some alcohol. Separate preparation and storage of the aroma concentrate facilities storage for over a year if the applicable storage conditions such as low temperature, oxidation prevention and light exposure are maintained.

Fruit juice concentrates are semi-finished goods, the properties of which allow for worldwide marketing. Most fruits have been internationally standardised according to the RSK - Values (guide values and ranges of identification parameters including the revised method of analysis) providing clear requirements for product qualities. The long shelf life of fruit juice concentrates and the enormous volume reduction involved simplify handling and contribute to cost reductions for storage and transport. Rationalised, longer-term storage can also contribute to price stabilisation. 100% fruit juice is reduced to about 17% concentrate, which contains all of the valuable-contents of the fruit juice with the exception of the highly volatile flavour substances (above all sugar, minerals, acids, vitamins and others more). Centrifugal tubular and plate evaporators are available to make the concentrates. Conventional plate evaporators have plates with a pattern of crossed lines similar to the patterns on heat exchanger plates. They are inexpensive, but are also especially sensitive to solids and fibres in the product. The plate evaporator SIGMASTER is different in this respect: its impressed pattern consists of parallel tubes resulting in clear flow channels that prevent product deposits. Fruit juice concentrate evaporators are always built in several effects. The multiple-effect design increases the potential overall capacity of a system, reduces total energy consumption and allows for particularly gentle product processing, since the evaporation temperatures are reduced from one effect to the next. The considerable increase in specific vapour volume at falling temperatures must be taken into consideration when designing the various effects. The increasing concentration of the juice causes a concurrent increase in viscosity and a raising of the boiling point. Special problems involved in evaporating fruit juice to obtain concentrate are: deposits, increase in viscosity, thermal load (acceleration of Maillard reaction) and precipitations. Not all evaporator types are equally suitable for all fruit juices. The plate evaporator SIGMASTER is ideal for use with all fruits. Clear and clouded juices, juices containing fibres and purees can be evaporated to reduce them to commercial concentrations within a brief period without thermal damage. Hydroxymethylfurfural, furfural and dimethylhydroxyfuranone are among the indicators for thermal loads of all kinds. Remember that improper storage of concentrates is the cause of much greater increases in these indicator compounds than the evaporation process itself.

Process of fruit juice concentrate production, evaporator types, heat-transfer, heating surface calculations, problems in concentration of different fruit juices and trouble management, storage conditions, aroma recovery, aroma yields are given in Tables and Figures in this paper as follows:

Concentration of Fruit Juices

Fruits and Fruit juice concentrates: Comparison of Sugar concentration

Fruit	*Sugar concentration in °Brix* Natural Fruit Juice	Concentrate Intern. Std
Orange	12	65
Pineapple	14	60
Passion fruit	15	50
Apple	12	70
Cherry	14	65

General Advantages of Fruit Juice Concentrate Production

Cost Reduction	Less volume for transport and storage
Increased Stability	Microbiologically (a_w- value), chemically (separation juice and aroma)
Price Stabilisation	Over year reserve stocks
International Trade	International standard

General Scheme of Evaporator types

The Process of Fruit juice Concentration: Water Evaporation

100 % Natural Fruit Juice			
Orange 12° Bx 10000 kg Juice including sugar 1200 kg acids 50 kg minerals 30 kg proteins vitamins aroma 0.1 kg	1 %	**Aroma Concentrate** 100 Kg	flavours (appr. 100 g) more than 100 differ.
	20 %	**Fruit Juice Concentrate** 2000 kg 65° Bx	Sugar 1200 kg acids 50 kg minerals 30 kg proteins, vitamins, others
	79 %	**Distilled Water** 7900 kg	no aroma no minerals no sugar

The Different Types of Plate Evaporators

Centrifugal Evaporator

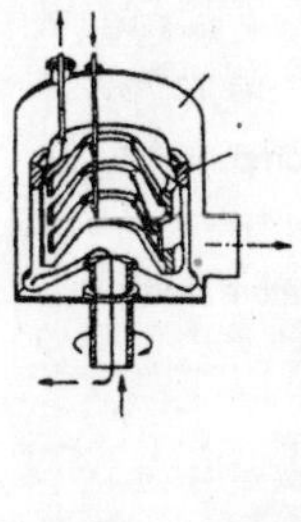

Tubular Evaporator

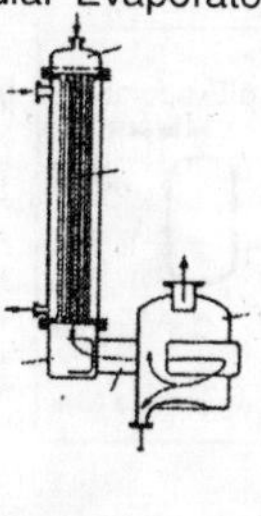

Plate Evaporator Type SIGMASTER

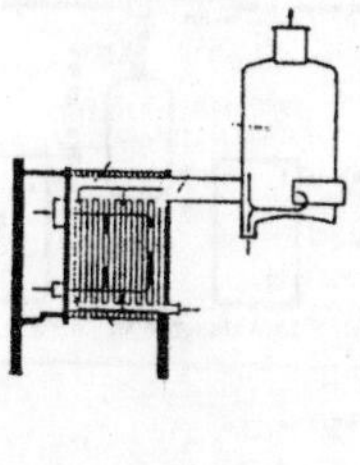

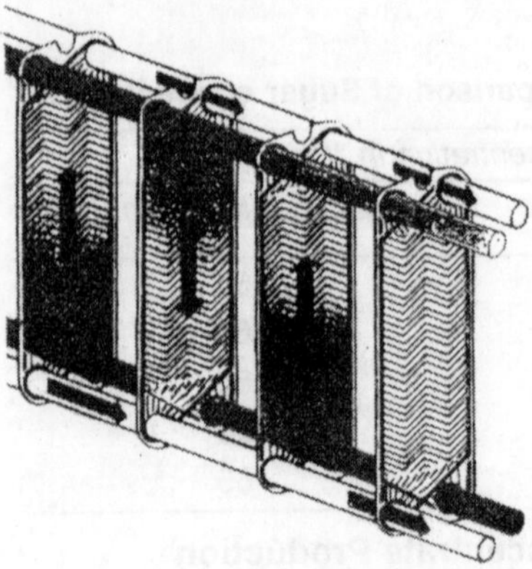

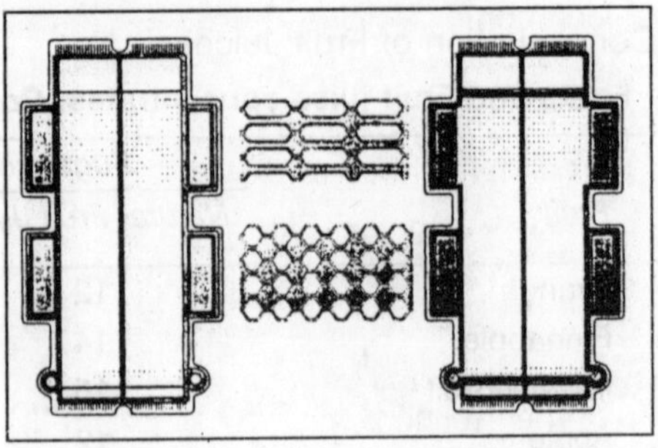

SIGMASTER - Evaporator Plate

Multiple Effect Evaporation

General Principle

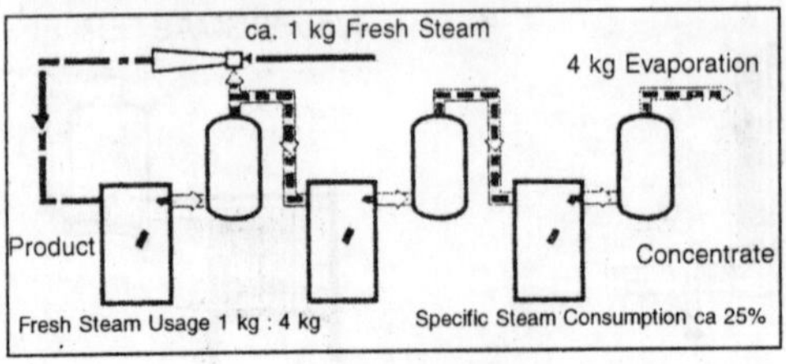

Advantages:

Lower Steam Consumption
Increased Capacity
Product Saving
Decreasing Temperature from Effect to Effect

Calculation of required heat transfer Q

$Q = m_E * r$

$m_E = m_F * (C_C - C_F) : C_C$

Q = heat transfer [k]
m_E = evaporation capacity [kg/h]
m_F = feed mass [kg]
C_F = feed concentration [° Bx]
C_C = final concentration [° Bx]
r = evaporation enthalpie [kj/kg]

Orange juice first effect

m_F = 10000 kg/h
c_F = 12 °Bx
c_C = 20 °Bx
r = 2309 kj/kg (80 °C, 474 mbar)

m_E = 10000 * (20 – 12)/20 = 4000 kg

Q = 4000 * 2309 = 9236000 kj

Calculation of required heating surface A

$Q = k * A \Delta T$

Q = heat transfer [kj]
k = heat transfer coefficient [W/K]
ΔT = temperature difference [k]

Surface to concentrate

Orange juice first effect:
ΔT = 10k
k = 2500 W/K (80 °C)

$A = Q/k * \Delta T$
A = 9236000/2500 * 10 = 370m²

Decreasing of Temperature = Increasing of Specific Steam Volume and Evaporation Energy

temp. [°C]	*p [mbar]*	*spec. steam vol. [m³/kg]*	*evap. enthaipie [kj/kg]*
100	1013	1.67	2257
90	701	2.36	2283
80	474	3.41	2308
70	313	5.05	2334
50	123	12.05	2383

Rising concentration causes higher boiling points and an enourmous increasing of viscosity

Concentration [°Brix]	*Boiling Point [°C, 150 mbar]*	*product viscosity 35°C [mpas]*
10	55.1	
60	57.6	28
70	59.6	90
80	63.4	1100

Thermal Stress: Acceleration of the Maillard - Reaction

Compounds of Interest	**Reaction Mechanisme**		**Indicating Compounds**
reducing sugars	maillard-reaction (complex) →		hydroxymethyfurfural
amino acids	factors:	temperature	furfural
polyphenols		oxygen	dimethylhydroxyfuranon
organic acids		concentration	optical density 420 nm

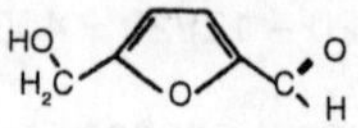

hydroxymethylfurfural

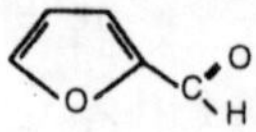

furfural

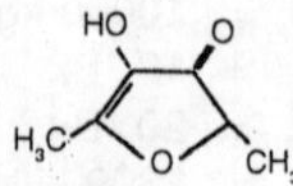

2.5-dimethyl - 4 - hydroxy -3- fruanor

Concentration of fruit juices by evaporation: Possible Troubles

Problem	*clear apple juice*	*berry & cherry juice*	*toma-toes*	*orange juice with fibres*	*Purees*	*Grapes*
layer formation	o	o	•	•	•	o
high viscosity	o	o	•	o	•	o
thermal stress						
cooking flavour	o	•	?	•	o	o
browning	o	•	?	•	o	o
vitamin degradation	o	•	?	•	o	o
precipitations	o	o	o	o	o	•

• = Problem o = No Problem

Evaporators and their Trouble - Management

		Evaporator Type		
Problem	*centrifugal*	*tubular*	*plate type A*	*Sigmastar*
layer formation	o	•	••	o
high viscosity	•	••	•	o
thermal stress	o	•	•	o
precipitations	o	•	••	o
Overall Height	4 m	10 m	4 m	4 m
investment Price	••	•	o	•

• = Problem •• = Critical o = No Problem

Orange Juice Processing

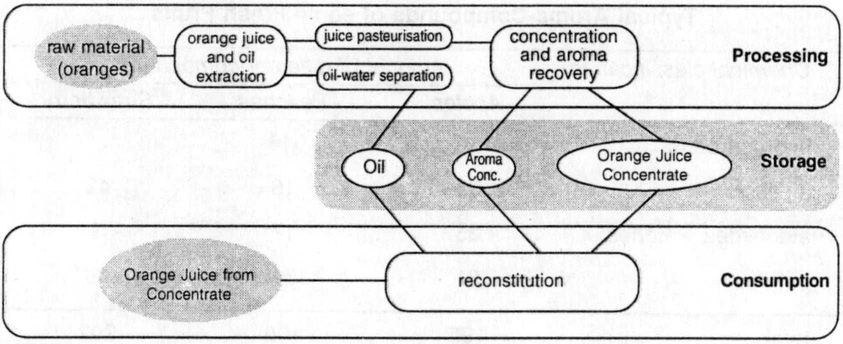

Aroma Yield in Aroma Recovery Plant

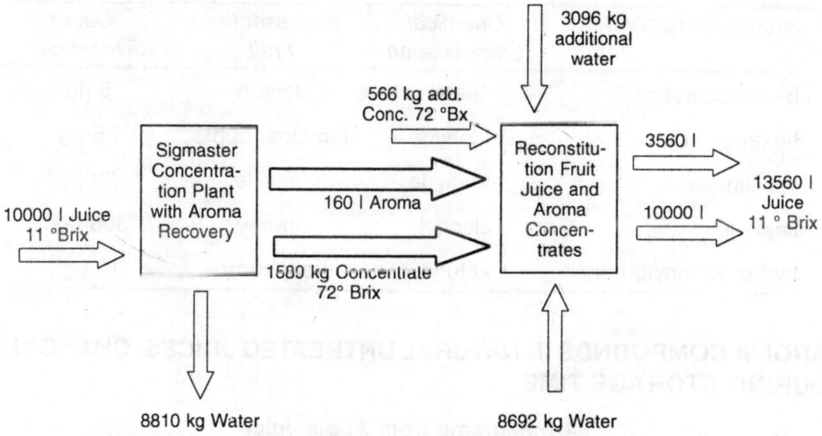

SUMMARY

Flavours in Juices	Low odour thresholds Large amount of individual components Alteration during Storage
Aroma Saving	Concentration of Fruit Juices with aroma recovery Separate storage of aroma concentrate and juice concentrate
Product Quality	Raw material Process equipment Storage conditions

Aroma Recovery from Fruit Juices

Typical Aroma-Compounds of some Fresh Fruits

Chemical classification	*Amount of different compounds*		
	Apples	*Peaches*	*Strawberry*
hydrocarbons	18	16	
alcohols	33	16	42
aldehydes, ketones	35	17	3
esters	91	34	06
total	195	106	202

Odour Thresholds of some Aroma Compounds

Aroma Compound	*Chemical Classification*	*Representive Fruit*	*Odour Threshold*
ß- cyclocitrol	ester	lemon	5 µg/l
hexanal	aldehyde	tomatoe, apple	4,5 µg/l
vanillin	aldehyde	vanille	20 µg/l
linalool	alcohol	orange	300 µg/l
hydroxyphenylbutanon	ketone	raspberry	10 µg/l

AROMA COMPOUNDS IN NATURAL UNTREATED JUICES: CHANGING DURING STORAGE TIME

Aromagrame from Apple Juice

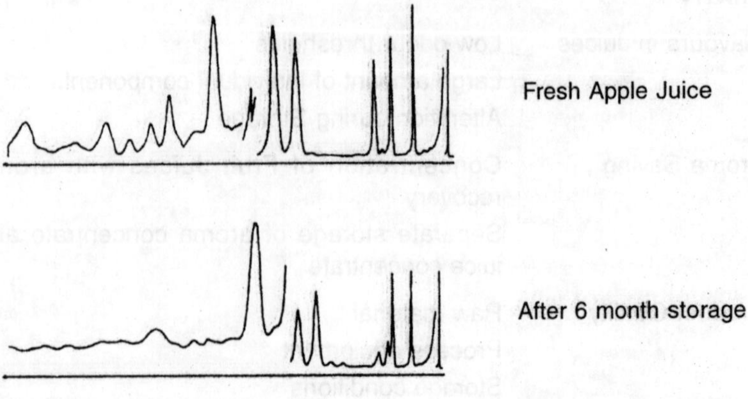

AROMA YIELD DEPENDING ON EVAPORATION RATE

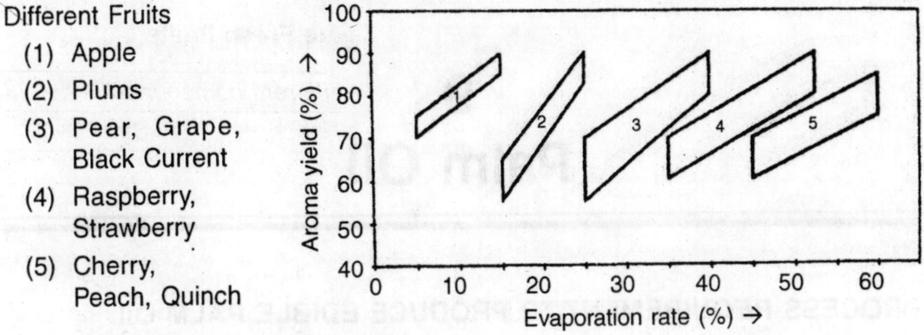

Concentration with Aroma Recovery

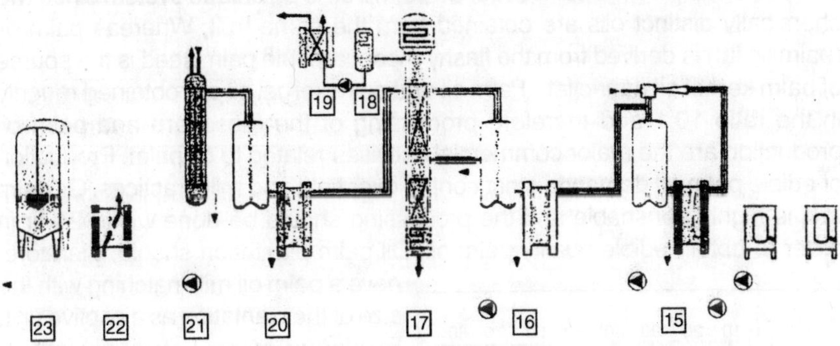

Aroma Recovery System

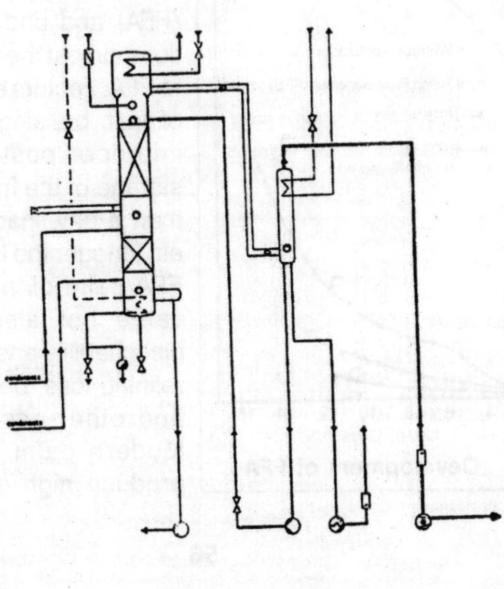

9
Palm Oil

PROCESS REQUIREMENT TO PRODUCE EDIBLE PALM OIL

Oil palm fruit is a sessile drupe with a fleshy mesocarp which encloses a stony endocarp called palm seed. Oil palm fruit is an unique system since two chemically distinct oils are obtained from the same fruit, Whereas palm oil (palmitic fat) is derived from the fleshy mesocarp, the palm seed is the source of palm kernel oil (lauric fat). Palm oil and palm kernel oil are obtained roughly in the ratio 10:1 and therefore processing of the mesocarp and palm oil production are the major commercial activities related to oil palm. Production of edible palm oil demands strict control over field and mill practices. Oil palm fruit is highly perishable and the processing should be done within 24 hr in order to obtain edible quality palm oil. Oil palm plantation should, therefore, have a palm oil mill matching with the size of the plantation as a captive unit. Presence of an extremely active lipase in the mesocarp releases excessive amounts of free fatty acids (FFA) and under favourable conditions almost the entire oil is converted to FFA. Factors such as over ripening of fruit, bruising of the fruits due to improper post-harvest handling, storage of the fruit bunches for more than a day, inadequate sterilisation, etc., trigger the lipase (Fig. 9.1). High FFA palm oil not only fetches low value but also results in poor bleachability and colour fixation, high refining loss, poor oxidation stability and other associated problems. Modern palm oil mills (POM) to produce high quality red palm oil

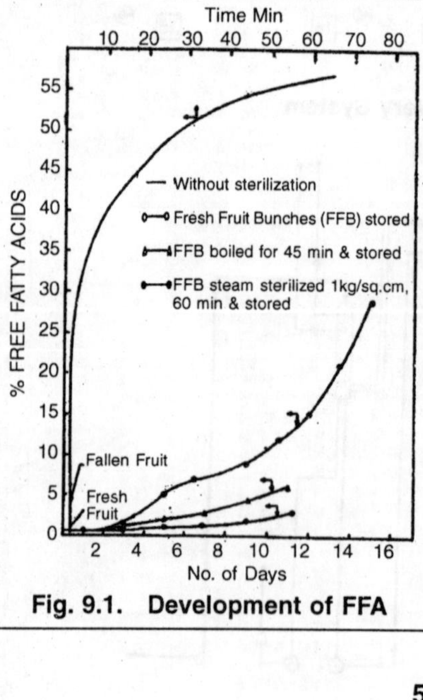

Fig. 9.1. Development of FFA

(RPO) are designed to match the size of the captive plantation. Considering the agricultural situation in India and the rural infrastructure, Regional Research Laboratory, Trivandrum (RRLT) has developed different models of POM based on the R&D efforts on the post- harvest science and technology on oil palm. As a result, minimum commercially viable capacity of 1 tonne Fresh Fruit Bunches (FF9) per hr has been arrived at taking into account, the capital investment, recurring expenditure, technological inputs for process efficiency and product quality, etc. (Sundaresan, et al.,1990). The basic design of the I tonne POM could be easily adopted for 2 tonnes with minor modifications.

This has been achieved by designing a screw press to facilitate continuous extraction. The basic design, therefore, has the flexibility to handle 200-400 hectares of plantations and can also take care of larger plantations (1000 hectares and above) at their immature stages. Various steps of the process to produce edible quality RPO are summarised (Fig. 9.2). (The description of the process applies to 1-2 t.FFB/hr POM designed and commissioned by RRL-T).

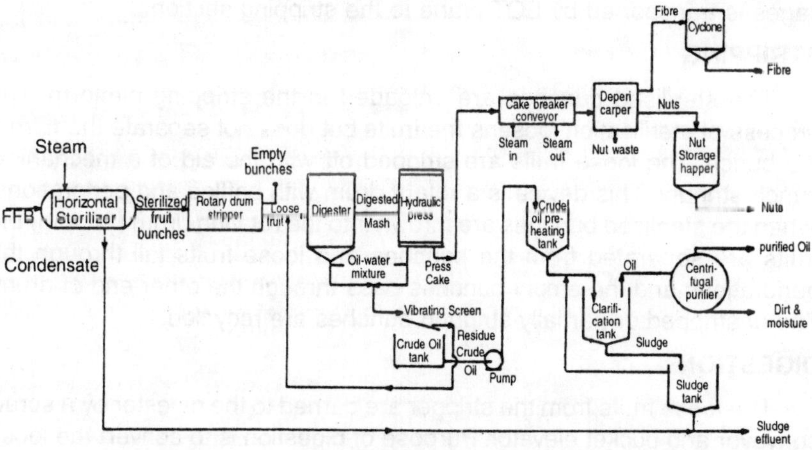

Fig. 9.2. Flow sheet of the Palm Oil Mill

HARVESTING AND HANDLING OF FRESH FRUIT BUNCHES

Oil palm fruit takes about six months for full maturation. Harvesting of FFB of right maturity is very important with respect to yield and quality of palm oil, since immature fruits yields less oil and over mature fruits have high free fatty acids (Arumughan, et al., 1989). Laboratory studies on oil palm fruit lipases and the factors influencing the enzyme action have shown that the lipases are bound to the fat globule membrane and does not have access to its substrate (triacylglycerols) in an intact fruit. Factors such as over maturity, bruising while harvesting and transport, and delay in processing leading to disruption of the membrane trigger the enzyme activity resulting in release of FFA to the extent of 60.0% depending on the severity of damage (Mohankumar, et al., 1990). Good field practices, therefore, are extremely important to produce high quality edible palm oil. After arrival of the FFB in sound condition, delay in processing particularly in the peak season would also enhance the FFA. Capacity of the POM should therefore be well matching with the plantation area to avoid this situation.

STERILISATION

This serves the dual objectives of inactivation of the lipases and loosening of the fruits from the bunch. It also softens the cell wall and coagulates proteins that facilitate oil extraction in the subsequent stages. A horizontal type steriliser is adopted to minimise bruising of fruits. The FFB are loaded in a perforated cage and placed in the steriliser. The steriliser is a long cylindrical vessel provided with steam inlet and outlet, pressure gauge, etc. Sterilisation of FFB for 60 mm at 45 psi has been found to be optimum to achieve the objectives mentioned above. The sterilised bunches with cages is transported by EOT crane to the stripping section.

STRIPPING

The sterilised bunches are unloaded in the stripping platform. The process of sterilisation loosens the fruits but does not separate them from the bunch. The loose fruits are stripped off with the aid of a mechanical bunch stripper. This device is a rotary drum with baffles and perforations. When the sterilised bunches are thrown into the rotating drum (20 rpm) the fruits are separated from the bunches and loose fruits fall through the perforations and the empty bunches pass through the other end of drum. The unstripped or partially stripped bunches are recycled.

DIGESTION

The loose fruits from the stripper are carried to the digestor by a screw conveyor and bucket elevator. Purpose of digestion is to convert the loose fruit into pulp and in the process the cell walls are broken facilitating release of oil with the help of thermal and mechanical energy. The digestor is a vertical jacketted cylindrical vessel fitted with a centrally mounted agitator having specially designed blades rotating at slow speed (25 rpm). The loose fruits are charged into the digestor from the top with the aid of an elevator. Live steam is injected into the jacket and into the vessel to maintain the temperature at 95°C. The digested mash with semi-solid consistency is discharged through a discharge chute at the bottom.

PRESSING

The digested mash consisting of oil, water, seed, fibre and other suspended matter is charged into a perforated cage and subjected to pressing. The hydraulic press is fitted with a plunger matching with the cage diameter. The pressing is done while the mash is hot (80-90°C) at 750 psi. The hot oil water mixture with suspended solids is expelled through the perforations leaving the solid press cake in the cage. Hydraulic pressing is a batch process, labour intensive and the oil recovery is slightly less as compared to screw press. Whereas hydraulic press is suitable for 1 tonne POM because of low capital and maintenance cost, screw press is advantageous for larger plants. A twin screw press has been designed and fabricated by RRL-T suitable for 2 tonne plant. Performance of the press has been evaluated and the oil recovery is 3.0 to 5.0% higher than that of hydraulic press. The screw press has been fabricated for the first time indigenously for palm oil extraction.

CLARIFICATION

The oil water mixture is filtered to remove the fibrous debris and is collected in the clarification tank. Clarifier is a vertical cylindrical vessel fitted with steam coil. The oil water- mixture is diluted with hot water (1:2) and heated to 95°C. The oil being lighter, rises to the top and is decanted continuously into a collection tank. The watery sludge at the bottom is discharged as waste.

PURIFICATION

The crude palm oil from the clarifier is passed through a high speed centrifuge at 80°C to remove the traces of solid impurities and water. 500 lit/hr bowl type centrifuge is employed.

VACUUM DRYING

Excess moisture in the oil leads to FFA release and quality deterioration on storage. Vacuum drying is adopted in the process to remove the excess moisture, The vacuum drier designed to bring down the initial moisture content of 0.4% to less than 0.2% with a throughput of 500 lit/hr.

OIL STORAGE

The raw palm oil is stored in tanks provided with steam coils (80 KL capacity).

NUT RECOVERY

Palm kernel oil is derived from the palm nut recovered from the press cake. After extraction of palm oil, the press fibre has a moisture content of 45-50%. Mechanical recovery of the seeds involves breaking and drying the press cake followed by separation of the nuts. The nut recovery unit has also been designed to match the one to two tonne FFB/ hr palm oil mill. The unit consists of a steam jacketted paddle-conveyor and cake breaking section, vertical column for fibre/nut separation, a cyclone for fibre collection and a nut polishing section. During the passage. the press cake is broken with the help of the rotating paddles and the press cake is also dried as it is heated by the steam jacket. The dried press cake is separated into fibre and nut in a vertical separating column using suction. The lighter fibre is drawn into a cyclone and the heavier nuts are allowed to fall into a horizontal rotating nut polishing drum. The fibre thus separated is used as boiler fuel. Final removal of residual fibre from the nuts is achieved in the polishing drum along with grading of the nuts based on size. The 1 to 2 tonne POM envisages only upto the nut recovery stage and the nuts as such are saleable products.

ESSENTIAL FEATURES OF THE INDIGENOUS PALM OIL MILL

Unlike in Malaysia, the oil palm cultivation in India is essentially in the hands of small holders, mostly in the range of 2.0 to 10.0 hectares. Furthermore, they are spread out in large areas without adequate transport facilities, Considering the process requirements for the production of edible palm oil, POM of smaller capacities (1.0 to 2.0 t FEB/hr) is more practical. However, larger POMs (10.0 to 20.0 t FFB/hr) can also coexist if the situation demands. There are several advantages in the Indian context for the smaller POMs. Better control over the field factors to produce high quality RPO, can be exercised. A group of farmers under the cooperative umbrella will be able to establish and maintain the POM. The capital investment per unit capacity is actually lower compared to the larger plants because of the totally indigenous design and fabrication. Lower gestation period (12 months) further adds to the economic viability of the smaller POMs. Process efficiency of the 2.0 FFB/hr POM with the screw press is at par with the larger plants. Because of the better control over the field and mill conditions high quality palm oil with 2.0 to 3.0% FFA can be produced in the smaller POMs. The technology was demonstrated first in 1989 at Palode by commissioning a demonstration unit. Subsequently a commercial POM of 2 tonnes FFB/ hr has also been commissioned in West Godavari District of Andhra Pradesh in 1992. The techno-economic viability of these POMs have been analysed based on the data collected from them. Chemical characteristics of edible and raw palm oil is given in Table 9.1.

INVESTMENT

Capital investment for establishing 1 and 2 t FFB/hr POM is presented in Table 9.2. These mills are designed to process the palm fruits from 200 and 400 hectares of plantation respectively with sufficient flexibility to handle 10 to 20% more during the peak harvesting season. The total investment of Rs. 85.0 lakh for 1 t and Rs. 136.0 lakh for 2 t mills include mechanical equipments, material handling systems, utilities, civil and other overheads. The capital cost per unit throughput of FFB works out to be much lower than that of larger mills primarily due to the total indigenous design and fabrication using the infrastructure available in the country.

Table-9.1: Chemical Characteristics of Edible Raw Palm Oil

Chemical parameters	
Colour (Lovibond unit, 1)	28R+10Y
Total Carotene (ppm)	700
Tocopherols (ppm)	800
Free Fatty Acids (%)	2.0
Moisture and impurities (%)	0.2
Iodine value	52
Saponification value	195
Unsaponifiable matter (%)	0.5
Peroxide value	Nil
Anisidine value (OD at 400 nm)	0.14
Diene value (E_{233} 1%)	0.17
Triene value (E_{265} 1%)	0.15
Iron (ppm)	4
Copper (ppm)	0.5
Melting Point (°C)	36.00

Arumughan, et al., 1989

ECONOMICS OF OIL PALM

The palm oil mill of 1 t. FFB/hr is the minimum commercially viable unit that functions as a captive unit and the raw material (FF9) is procured from the farmers. The paprocurement price for the FFB is normally fixed based on the oil recovery, quality of the FFB and palm oil obtained therefrom. The oil content of FFB may vary from 18.0 to 22.0% for the tenera palms depending on the quality of the hybrid. Normally 10.0 to 150% of the oil value is taken as the procurement price. At present, Rs. 2,000/- per tonne FFB is fixed as the procurement price in Andhra Pradesh which is equivalent to 11.0% of the oil value of the FFB assuming an oil content of 20.0%. The oil content of FFB has not been established under the field conditions prevailing in India, which needs detailed investigations. The price fixed for the FFB at present, therefore, is only based on the limited data available. The product output of the 1 t. mill is 600 tonnes of edible grade red palm oil and 300 tonnes of palm seed, Based on the sale price of Rs. 20,000/- per tonne of RPO and Rs. 3,000/- per tonne of palm seed, the cost of production of RPO is about Rs. 15,000/- of which Rs. 11,000/- accounts for the cost of FFB/ After the payback period (7 years) for the term loans and depreciation, the cost of production arrived at is about Rs.13,000/- per tonne of palm oil. Palm oil, therefore, is the cheapest edible oil vis-a-vis other edible oils produced in India. Considering the yield pattern of oil palm, it is more economical to establish the POM when the plantation is between 4 and 5 years, though the palms starts yielding from third year onwards.

Table-9.2: Cost of Equipments/Utilities/Services for 1 and 2 t. FFB/hr Palm Oil Mill

Sl. No.	*Description*	*Cost (Rs. in lakhs)* 1 t. FFB/hr	2 t. FFB/hr
A.	MECHANICAL EQUIPMENTS		
I.	Horizontal sterilisers	5.00	6.00
2	Rotary drum stripper	2.00	2.50
3.	Digestor	3.50	4.00
4.	Screw press	—	6.00
5.	Hydraulic press	300	—
6.	Clarifier	0.60	1.00
7.	Centrifuge	1.80	3.00
8.	Vacuum drier	1.50	2.00
9.	Vibrating screen	0.50	0.50
10.	Palm seed recovery unit	6.50	8.00
	Sub total	24.90	33.00
B.	MATERIAL HANDLING, AUTOMATION AND ACCESSORIES		
1.	EOT crane	2.00	3.00
2.	Pallet trucks	0.90	1.00
3.	Conveyors (screw, belt and bucket)	2.00	5.00
4.	Steel structure, platforms etc.	2.00	5.00
5.	Process pumps, pipes. etc.	1.00	2.50
6.	Storage tanks	2.50	6.00
7.	Intermediate tanks	0.50	0 50
8.	Industrial balance	0.50	0.50
9.	Miscellaneous	3.00	5.00
	Sub-total	14.40	28.50
C.	UTILITIES		
1.	Agro waste fired boiler	5.80	8.00
2.	Steamline	2.70	5.00
3.	Electrical	4.50	8.50
4.	Generator	—	3.00
5.	Water supply	1.50	4.00
6.	Spares and accessories	2.50	3.00
	Sub-total	17.00	31.50
D.	OTHER OVERHEADS		
1.	Erection and commissioning	2.50	5.00
2.	Engineering consultancy	3.50	7.00
3.	Technical know-how fee	3.00	3.00
4.	Contingency	4.30	6.00
	Sub-total	13.70	21.00
	GRAND TOTAL	85.00	136.00

As far as the return to the farmers is concerned, the estimated net annual income is Rs. 30,000/- per hectare based on the prevailing costs of inputs and outputs as described before. If the POM is established and operated under farmers' cooperatives, the net income could be more than Rs. 40,000/- per hectare to the farmers. Oil palm development and processing under the farmers' cooperatives is well matching with the concept of Small Farmers Agribusiness Consortium (SFABC) envisaged to promote agro processing and rural development by Government of India.

PRODUCT UTILISATION

Palm oil is the most versatile of all glyceride oils for its varied uses in food and industry. For food uses, the RPO is further subjected to refining, fractionation, etc., to meet the international requirements as most of the palm oil produced is exported. As far as India is concerned, the palm oil production envisaged is primarily to meet the domestic requirement. Palm oil and its products should, therefore, be tailored to suit the Indian situation. On account of the inherent properties, palm oil can be more profitably used as follows:

RED PALM OIL (RPO) AS NUTRITIONAL OIL

RPO is the most abundant natural source of alpha- and beta-carotenes (Table-9.3) One 'g' of RPO has retinol equivalent of around 300 U and there is no comparable natural source of "Pro vitamin A". It is, therefore, not surprising that the people in the West African countries where RPO is the staple cooking medium, do not suffer from vitamin A deficiency. However, among the Indian population, of the four major nutritional deficiencies that of vitamin A is the most predominant accounting for most of the preventable blindness among children. Popularisation of RPO as dietary fat would go a long way in combating vitamin A deficiency particularly among the deprived sections in the country. Nutritional and toxicological studies conducted at the National Institute of Nutrition, Hyderabad, already established the efficacy of RPO for vitamin A supplementation (Manorama and Rukmini, 1989; 1990; 1991). A multi-centered studies under the aegis of Nutrition Foundation of India covering about 6,000 preschool children are currently under way. In these studies 5 g of PRO is fed to the children as part of their noon meal. Anthropometric and clinical parameters related to vitamin status before and after feeding RPO for one year are recorded. Based on the outcome of this pilot study wider use of RPO could be recommended among the general population.

Apart from the classical role of beta-carotene, recent findings strongly suggest that alpha- and beta-carotenes protect tissues against carcinogenesis (Peto, et. al., 1981; Nenkes, et. al., 1986; Schwartz, et al., 1986). RPO also contains high levels of tocopherols and tocotrienols (800 ppm) which are now known to have anti-thrombotic and anti-cancer properties. Almost the entire quantity of carotenes and substantial portion of the tocopherols are lost when RPO is subjected to refining as practised now. With increasing availability in the coming years, RPO could be made more acceptable and much more efforts are required by the R&D institutions and non-government agencies. A detailed investigation to establish the relation between consumption of palm oil and cardiovascular diseases or nutritional benefits have been initiated at RRL with the financial support of Palm Oil Research Institute of Malaysia (PORIM). Nutritional properties of carotenoids and tocopherols have recently been reviewed.

Table-9.3: Composition (%) of Carotenolds in Palm Oil

Carotene	*Tenera*	*Pisifera*	*Dura*
Phytoene	1.27	1.68	2.49
Cis-beta-carotene	0.68	0.10	0.15
Phytofluene	0.06	0.90	1.24
Beta-carotene	56.02	54.39	56.02
Alpha-carotene	35.06	33.11	24.35
Cis-alpha-carotene	2.19	1.64	0.86
α-carotene	0.69	112	2.31
γ-carotene	0.33	0.48	1.16
δ-carotene	0.83	0.27	2.00
Neurosporene	0.29	0.63	0.77
Beta-Zeacarotene	0.74	0.97	0.56
Alpha-Zeacarotene	0.23	0.21	0.30
Lycopene	1.30	4.50	7.80
Total carotenes (ppm)	673.00	428.00	997.00

Choo, et al., 1990

REFINED BLEACHED AND DEODOURISED (RBD) PALM OIL

The deep red colour of RPO is due to the extremely high levels of carotenes and this is one of the reasons for the consumer resistance of this oil. The FFA level beyond the legally permitted limit may also come in the way of marketing RPO for direct edible use. The fruity flavour could be yet another impediment against acceptance of RPO by the general consumers. In the event of large scale production in the future, RPO may have to be refined to satisfy the requirements of a wider market. Conditions have been optimised to produce refined, bleached and deodourised palm oil (RBD palm oil) on commercial scale (5-10 tonnes/batch) and test marketed by RRL successfully. It is further envisaged to design a palm oil refinery matching with the capacity of the 2 t. POM. The RBD palm oil is semisolid in consistency at the ambient conditions of India, due to the presence of high melting glycerides. This product is comparable with 'Vanaspathi' or 'Ghee' in appearance and texture and is cheaper than the palmolein.

SPECIALITY FATS FROM PALM OIL

Other than the products mentioned above, palm oil could be further processed to obtain products for sophisticated uses in confectionery, bakery margarine, etc. The liquid palmolein is produced from palm oil under controlled crystallisation. About 30% of the palm oil is removed as high melting stearin. While the liquid palm olein is a popular cooking oil, the by-product, stearin can be further processed to confectionery and bakery fat. Various types of margarines are formulated to substitute costly table butter. Carotene - rich margarine can be formulated which could be a cheaper substitute for table butter. Moreover, RPO as part of the margarine may find better acceptability among the general consumers in India RPO can also be blended with the traditional cooking oil specific to the region at appropriate ratio and these RPO blends may find better marketability and acceptability in different geographic regions of the country.

10
COCONUT PROCESSING

INTRODUCTION

Coconut is one of the main sources of vegetable oils in the South-east Asian and the Pacific regions. Of the total production of coconuts in Asia, more than 50% is converted to copra for extraction of oil (Table-10.1). The balance is used to extract the coconut milk for culinary purposes or is converted to desiccated coconuts or coconut cream. The per cent coconut production diverted to extract coconut milk varies widely from country to country. In Sri Lanka, nearly 75% is consumed domestically, whereas the figures for Indonesia and Philippines are 40% and 10% respectively. The coconut milk is an oil-in-water emulsion containing 35% oil, if no water is added for extraction.

For extraction of the oil, the coconut kernels are dried to produce copra. The oil is extracted from copra in mechanically driven screw presses followed by the solvent hexane to extract the residual oil from the cake. The residue copra meal (poonac) is used as an animal feed. The copra meal after mechanical expulsion of oil retains about 10% of the oil.

The distribution pattern of coconut lands by acreage indicates it to be a small holder crop in most of the countries. This limits large scale processing of coconut. As a result, the conventional methods of processing continue to be used more widely in the coconut industry.

In the international markets the coconut oil is faced with inconsistent prices due to the adverse publicity regarding low PUFA content. Much research and publicity are needed to remove the fears already established on the effects of coconut oil in relation to heart diseases.

PRODUCTION OF COPRA

The coconut kernels are converted to copra by drying either in the sun as whole or split nuts or in direct heating dryers or in indirect hot air dryers. The quality of copra depends on the type of dryer used, the final moisture content and the presence or absence of smoke deposits. Traditionally coconut oil was expelled from the copra in large stone mortars by crushing using power from draft cattle. The oil is expelled today in power driven screw expellers.

Processing of coconuts for copra and expulsion of oil carry several inherent problems. The economics of reducing the moisture content from 36% in fresh kernels to 8% in copra limit application of costly indirect drying methods. The kernels are dried mostly in the sun followed by direct dryers using the components from the coconut palm, the shells, husks, leaves and fronds. A cleaner product is obtained when only coconut shells are used as fuel. Of the different types of kilns used in the region, those designed similar to "Ceylon Copra Kiln" burning only coconut shells under well controlled conditions, minimise the discolouration due to smoke constituents on the kernels and cause uniform drying. Direct, uncontrolled fires used in drying of copra results in deposition of carcinogenic Polycyclic Aromatic Hydrocarbons (PAH) on copra. The PAH get extracted in to coconut oil. The resulting copra and oil are of poor quality due to dark colour.

The fresh coconuts are highly susceptible to growth of the fungus Aspergillus flavus/ parasiticus and accumulation of aflatoxin. The smoke curing process is shown to inhibit the toxin accumulation. Drying of copra to moisture content below 10% avoids aflatoxin contamination. During storage the kernels need to be protected from insects and high humidity. Prolonged storage of copra makes expulsion of oil easy (due to partial degradation of tissues) but results in poor quality oil. The intermittent sundrying of the kernels at domestic level causes increased aflatoxin contaminations. This practice is observed very much in small coconut holdings where the farmers dry a few kg of kernels for oil extraction at the nearby 'mini oil expellers' for local consumption.

As a means to overcome the poor quality characteristics associated with the oil produced through copra, many attempts have been made to develop new processing technologies. Essentially, the new approach by-passes the production of copra and solvent extractions and aims at separating edible oil and edible proteins directly from the fresh kernels. Some processes yield additional by-products such as coconut syrup and coconut flour. Although these processes were capable of increasing the food value of coconuts as a source of edible oil and edible proteins they did not achieve industrial success. The reasons for the failure of the processes are many. The extraction processes were incapable of achieving high recovery of oil compared to extraction from copra The technologies applied were of a high cost level and limited their application in the third world countries. The production of coconuts was insufficient in certain countries to meet the scale of operations of the processes. The technologies failed to demonstrate economic viability and there was no ready market for the edible proteins isolated by the new processes. Thus, the industry has relied on production of oil through copra. The current trend is to develop the drying technology to obtain a cleaner product avoiding PAH as well as aflatoxin contaminations. Much research is carried out currently in developing efficient and appropriate dryers.

DESICCATED COCONUT

Desiccated coconut produced by indirect drying of the shredded coconuts enjoys an important position in the coconut industry as a foreign exchange earner in the region. The desiccated coconut is valued for its appearance, in addition to its flavour much sought in the confectionery industry. However, production of desiccated coconut has still not achieved the standards required in modern food processing. The emphasis in the desiccated coconut industry today is to maintain high quality and sanitary standards in the production lines. Modernisation of the processing techniques is an immediate need of the desiccated coconut industry to remain competitive in the Western markets.

COCONUT CREAM

The changes in family employment patterns has made it necessary to move away from the habit of extraction of coconut milk in the traditional way. As a result, there is an emerging market for a cream or a milk concentrate that could be diluted and used in place of coconut milk. This has resulted in development of small scale alternate technologies for production of coconut cream and coconut milk concentrates. Techniques have been developed in the TDRI, UK and at the CISIR, Sri Lanka. The method is already employed in Sri Lanka for production of coconut cream for local and export markets. This may lead at a later stage to development of large scale processing of coconut cream or milk.

COCONUT MILK

Processing of coconut milk for preservation in different forms is expanding today The milk is usually extracted from freshly grated coconuts or desiccated coconut. Technologies are employed to can milk in sweetened or unsweetened form. The milk can also be pasteurised and refrigerated in the same way as dairy milk. However, it is necessary to remove protein and add stabilisers if the milk is to be heat treated, to prevent denaturing of proteins. Spray- dried coconut milk is available in the region since 1979. Creamed coconut produced mainly from desiccated coconuts is gaining wide acceptability both in Asia and the West.

However, the new coconut products suffer marketing and acceptability problems due to lack of standards for canned products (the oil content in present market canned milk vary between 10 and 23%), use of non-standard names (milk is named either coconut milk or coconut cream), lack of precise information on the additives used, use of sub-standard raw materials, poor plant sanitary conditions, inaccurate information on coconut equivalent of the contents per can or bottle, and high variation in colour and texture of the products It is time that the industry takes measures to develop quality standards, labelling guidelines, nomenclature and grading of the new products based on moisture/total solids, free fatty acids, rancidity, flavour, colour and texture.

Although markets are expected for these new products in the West, it needs much propaganda by the coconut industry to benefit in view of adverse campaign against coconut oil and high competition in the Western markets from cream and milk based other materials having competitive textural and flavour properties.

BLENDED OILS

A better approach in overcoming the adverse publicity based on low polyunsaturated fatty acids content (PUFA) in the coconut oil may be to make use of the special nature of the coconut oils (having a high concentration of medium chain fatty acids) to use it as a base for easily digestible foods for the children and elderly and in designing blends with other edible oils to provide edible oil blends of high nutritional acceptability. Formulations of this nature are already available. (Table-10.1).

Table-10.1: Copra and Coconut Production In Asia (in '000 MT)

Country	*Coconut*	*Copra**	*% Copra*
Fiji	210	88	42
India	3,900	1,468	38
Indonesia	11,100	4,487	40
Malaysia	1,200	855	71
Papua New Guinea	767	579	75
Philippines	9,200	8,092	88
Samoa	200	75	38
Soloman Islands	230	130	57
Sri Lanka	2,300	608	26
Thailand	800	235	29
Vanuatu	260	155	60
Vietnam	360	268	74
Asia	30,527	17,040	

*coconut equivalent

BASIC INFORMATION

Compositional data on nutrients in coconut, coconut oil, cream, copra meal, coconut water and coconut milk published in different sources show much anomalies. It is essential to develop a computerised data base on analytical values before the industry embraces on development of new products.

The future developments in processing ot coconuts should be addressed for improvements in the small scale coconut cream or milk production and in formulation of blended edible oils of high nutritional quality for the Western markets. Continued production of desiccated coconut of good quality would sustain the market.

11
PROTEIN FOODS FROM OILSEEDS

The first topic described here is on the importance of the control of the enzymes contained in soybeans in the manufacturing of soybean protein foods. For instance, the grassy-beany flavours of soy milk are developed through lipoxygenase-lyase pathways, the objectionable after-tastes of soy milk are strengthened by the action of beta-glucosidases and the gel hardness of tofu is decreased by the lipid peroxides produced through the action of lipoxygenases.

The second topic is the improvement of soybeans through breeding or genetic engineering. Recently soybean seeds lacking lipoxygenases have been obtained through breeding for a practical use. The genetic engineering trials of soybeans have been carried out successfully on the improvements of the gelating properties, the emulsifying abilities and the nutritive values through the modification of a gene encoding soybean storage proteins.

The third topic is the manufacturing of soy sauce through a bioreactor, by which the manufacturing period decreased from 6 to 8 months to about 2 weeks.

INTRODUCTION

In the Orient, there are many kinds of indigenous soybean protein foods which have evolved over many centuries (Fukushima, 1981, 1985, 1989, 1991a, b). Recently, however, worldwide attention has been paid to soybean proteins and their products as an economical protein source. The present paper deals with the recent progress on the improvements of the flavours, nutritional qualities, and manufacturing techniques, for oilseed proteins and their products.

CONTROL OF ENZYMES CONTAINED IN SOYBEANS AND QUALITY IMPROVEMENTS OF THEIR PRODUCTS

1. Control of Lipoxygenase-Hydroperoxide Lyase Pathways and Improvements of Grassy-Beany Flavours

Most of grassy-beany off-flavours contained in soybean protein foods are formed during the processing treatments through the lipoxygenase-hydroperoxide lyase pathways for converting linoleic acid to cis-3-hexenal, as shown in Fig. 11.1. In order to prevent the generation of grassy-beany flavours, various trials have been carried out for the inactivation of lipoxygenases contained in soybeans such as heat treatments, acid or alkaline treatments and so on. Recently, however, breeding trials on eliminating endogenous lipoxygenases from soybeans have been carried out as the fundamental solution of this problem. Generally, soybean seeds contain 3 kinds of lipoxygenase isozymes, called L-1, L-2 and L-3. So far, the mutant soybean seeds lacking 2 or 3 of these isozymes have been obtained. Among these mutant seeds, only the homogenate of the L-1, L-3 double deficient mutant seed generated n-hexanol practically under the condition without adding free linoleic acid, as shown in Table-1, indicating that the lipoxygenase- 2 is responsible substantially for the production of grassy-beany flavours. Accordingly the use of L-1, L-2 deficient, L-2, L-3 deficient, or L-1, L-2, L-3 triple deficient mutant seed, for soybean protein foods, will be very promising for the improvement of their grassy-beany

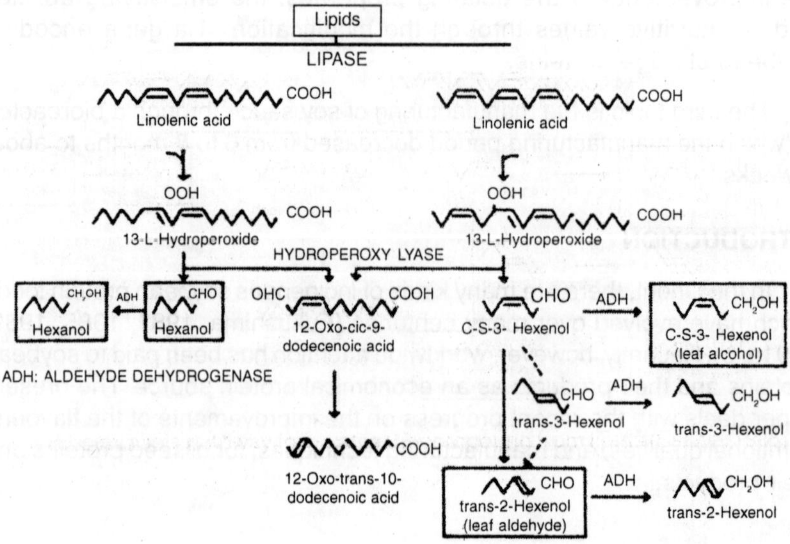

Fig. 11.1. Biosynthesis pathway for volatile C6-compound from lipids (Sekiya, 1985)

flavours. In fact, it was ascertained by the sensory evaluation that the generation of grassy-beany flavours did not occur substantially in the homogenate of these mutants.

Table-11.1: n-Hexanal Generation in Soybean Homogenates Lacking Lipoxygenase Isozymes In Absence and Presence of Linoleic Acid (Takamura, et al., 1991)

Soybean	*n-Hexanal generation (nmol/mg protein)*	
	Linoleic acid absent	*Linoleic acid present*
Wild type	1.34 ± 0.06*	2.03 ± 0.24
L-1,-2-3 deficient	0.14 ± 0.09	1.41 ± 0.05
L-2,-3 deficient	0.15 ± 0.01	3.56 ± 0.74
L-1,-3 deficient	1.86 ± 0.35	6.31 ± 0.66
L 1,-2 deficient	0.14 ± 0.03	0.37 ± 0.04

*Values are means ±SD (n=3)

2. CONTROL OF BETA-GLUCOSIDASES AND IMPROVEMENTS OF OBJECTIONAL AFTER-TASTES

(a) *Compounds Responsible for the Objectionable After-tastes and their Location in Soybeans*

The typical off-flavours of soybean products other than grassy-beany flavours are objectionable after-tastes which are referred to astringent, bitter and chalky flavours. These objectionable after-tastes are caused by soybean glycosides such as "saponins", "isoflavone glycosides" and their "aglycones".

Soybean saponins are divided into two groups: "group A saponins (Shiraiwa, et al., 1991a)" and 'group B saponins (Shiraiwa, et. al.., 1991c; Kudou, et al., 1992)", as shown in Figs. 11.2 and 11.3. The "group A saponin" consists of 6 different kinds of saponins: Aa, Ab, Ac, Ad, Ae and Af. These "group A saponins" are all acetyl-soyasaponins. On the other hand, 8 kinds of "group B saponins" were separated as Ba, Bb, Bb', Bc, Bd, Be, BdA and BeA. However, it was elucidated that BdA and BeA are major genuine soybean saponins and the others are all artifacts. BdA is changed to Ba and Bd, and BeA is changed to Bb and Be, by heating during the analytical processes. The "group B saponins" are not acetylated.

Another "glycoside group" responsible for the objectionable after-taste is isoflavones. Nine kinds of isoflavones are isolated from soybeans (Fig. 11.4). Among these, major soybean isoflavones are 6"-0-malonyl diadzin, 6"-0-malonylglycitin and 6"-0-malonylgenestin, but they are thermally unstable and converted into their corresponding acetyl isoflavone glycosides by heating at 80°C.

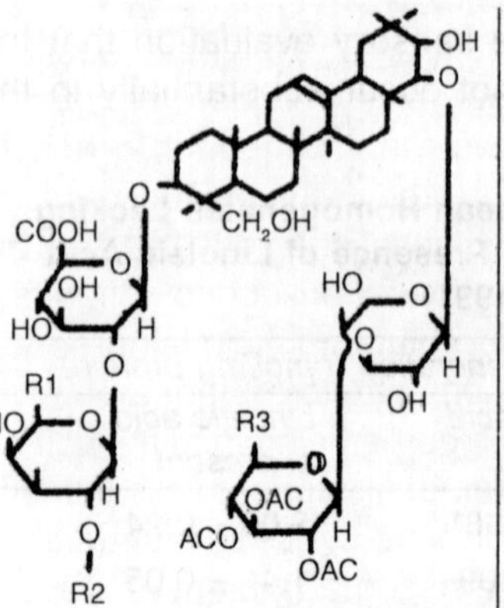

	R1	R2	R3
Aa	CH_2OH	β-D-glc	H
Ab	CH_2OH	β-D-glc	CH_2OAc
Ac	CH_2OH	α-L-rha	CH_2OAc
Ad	H	β-D-glc	CH_2OAc
Ae	CH_2OH	H	H
Af	CH_2OH	H	CH_2OAc

Fig. 11.2. Soybean 'group A saponins' and their structures

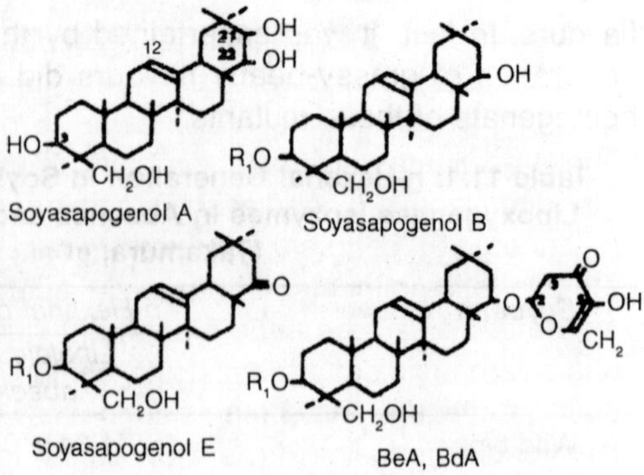

	Aglycone	R1
Ba	B	β-D-glc(1→2)-β-D-gal (1→2)-β-D-glcUA
Bb	B	α-L-rha(1→2)-β-D-gal (1→2)-β-D-glcUA
Bb	B	β-D-glc(1→2)-β-D-glcUA
Bc	B	α-L-rha(1→2)-α-L-ara (1→2)-β-D-glcUA
Bd	E	β-D-glc(1→2)-β-D-gal (1→2)-β-D-glcUA
Be	E	α-L-rha(1→2)-β-D-gal (1→2)-β-D-glcUA
BdA		β-D-glc(1→2)-β-D-gal (1→2)-β-D-glcUA
BeA		α-L-rha(1→2)-β-D-gal (1→2)-β-D-glcUA

Fig. 11.3. Soybean 'group B saponins' and their structures

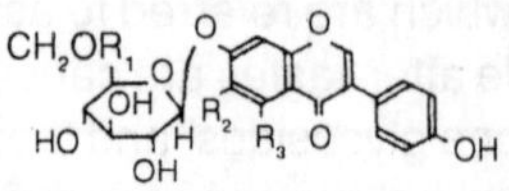

Compound	R_1	R_2	R_3
1. Daidzin	H	H	H
2. Glycitin	H	OCH_3	H
3. Genistin	H	H	OH
4. 6"-θ-Malonyldaidzin	$COCH_2COOH$	H	H
5. 6"-θ-Malonylglycitin	$COCH_2COOH$	OCH_3	H
6. 6"-θ-Malonylgenistin	$COCH_2COOH$	H	OH
7. 6"-θ-Acetyldaidxin	$COCH_3$	H	H
8. 6"-θ-Acetylglycitin	$COCH_3$	OCH_3	H
9. 6"-θ-Acetylgenistin	$COCH_3$	H	OH

Fig. 11.4. Soybean isoflavone glycosides arid their structures

The flavour characteristics and the thresholds of these saponins, iso-flavones and their aglycones, are shown in Figs. 11.5 and 11.6. The objectionable after-tastes of saponins are much more intense than those of their aglycones, whereas the objectionable after-tastes of isoflavones are weaker than those of their aglycones. In general, the objectionable after-tastes of glycosides are strengthen by malonylation or acetylation (Fig. 11.6). The objectionable after-tastes of the "group A saponins' are decreased by heating. This is due to the deacentylation of the 'group A saponins" through the heating, which are all acetyl-saponins.

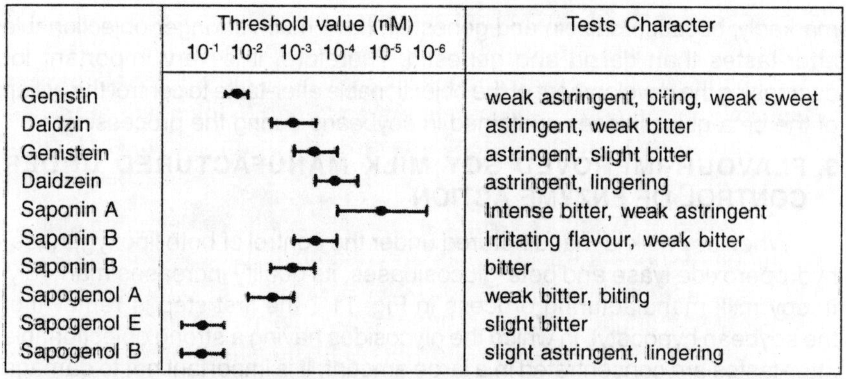

Fig. 11.5. Flavor characteristics of soybean glycosides and their aglycones.

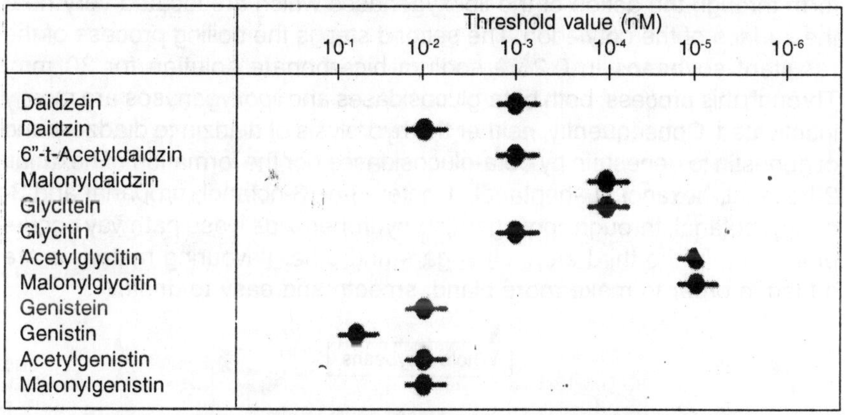

Fig. 11.6. Threshold values of soybean isoflavone glycosides.

It should be noted that the soybean glycosides described above are concentrated in soybean hypocotyl. Namely the "group A saponins", glycitin and glycitin derivatives, are present only at the hypocotyl, which possess very strong objectionable after-tastes. Further, 30 to 50% of the total glycosides of whole soybean exists in the hypocotyl which only forms 2 to 3% of the total weight of soybeans. Therefore, the flavour of soybean products can be improved markedly by using hypocotyl-removed soybeans as a material.

(b) Necessity of the Control for Beta-glucosidase Action

There are 3 kinds of beta-glucosidases in soybeans: beta-glucosidases A, 9 and C Among these, the beta-glucosidases B and C are major ones, of which optimum pH of the action are 5.5 and 5.2 respectively. Daizin and genestin, the major isoflavones of soybean cotyledon, are hydrolyzed by these beta-glucosidases to produce daizein and genestein during the processing. As a result, the objectionable after-tastes in soybean products increase markedly, because daizein and genestein have much stronger objectionable after-tastes than daizin and genestin. Therefore, it is very important for decreasing the development of the objectionable after-taste to control the action of the beta-glucosidases contained in soybeans during the processing.

3. FLAVOUR-IMPROVED SOY MILK MANUFACTURED UNDER CONTROL OF ENZYME ACTION

When soy milk is manufactured under the control of both lipoxygenase-hydroperoxide lyase and beta-glucosidases, its quality increases markedly. In soy milk manufacturing process in Fig. 11.7 the first step is removal of the soybean hypocotyl, in which the glycosides having a strong objectionable after-tastes are concentrated in a large amount, It is important not to damage the cotyledon during this step, because the grassy-beany flavours come forth through the action of the lipoxygenases which are located very near the surface of the cotyledon. The second step is the boiling process of the resultant soybeans in 0.25% sodium bicarbonate solution for 30 mm. Through this process, both beta-glucosidases and lipoxygenases are mostly inactivated. Consequently, neither the hydrolysis of diadzin to diadzein and of genestin to genestein by beta-glucosidases nor the formation of hexanal, 2-hexanal, hexanol, 1 -heptanol, 1-octen-3-ol, 3-octanol, propanal and 3-methyl butanal, through lipoxygenase-hydroperoxide lyase pathway occurs practically. In the third step, oil sugars and other flavouring materials are added in order to make more bland, smooth and easy to drink.

Whole Soybeans
↓
Dried
↓
Hull and hypocotyl removed
↓ → Hull and Hypocotyl
Soaked in alkaline hot water
↓
Ground in hot water
↓
Separated
Residue → ↓ ← Flavours, Oil, Sugar, etc.
Mixed and standardized
↓
Homogenised
↓
Sterilized
↓
Packed aseptically
↓
Soy Milk

Fig. 11.7. Manufacturing process of flavour-improved soy milk.

4. CONTROL OF LYPOXIGENASES AND IMPROVEMENTS OF GEL HARDNESS

Soybean proteins form gel by heating. In the Orient, there is an indigenous food called tofu, which is produced by utilising this gel-forming ability of soybean proteins. Soy milk containing about 5% of proteins forms gel as a whole by heating under the presence of coagulants such as $CaSO_4$, $MgSO_4$, glucono-delta-lactone, and so on. Such a gel of soy milk is called "Kinugoshi-tofu", as shown in Fig. 11.8.

The hardness of soy milk gel is important for the quality of Kinogoshi-tofu and it is influenced by the manufacturing conditions of soy milk. As shown in Fig. 11.9, the hardness of the soy milk gel decreased with the elevation of the grinding temperature in the range of 2 to 50°C. At the same, the free -SH groups of soy milk decreased, which will take part in the intermolecular -SH/-S S- interchange reactions. The intermolecular disulfide bonds are very important for the strength of the network structure of the gel.

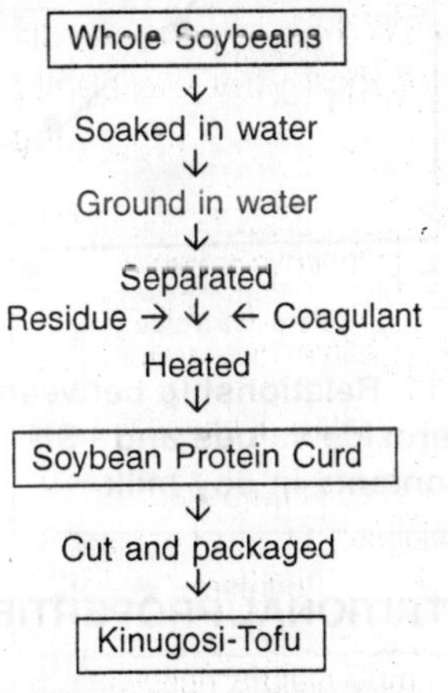

Fig. 11.8. Manufacturing process of kinogoshi-tofu.

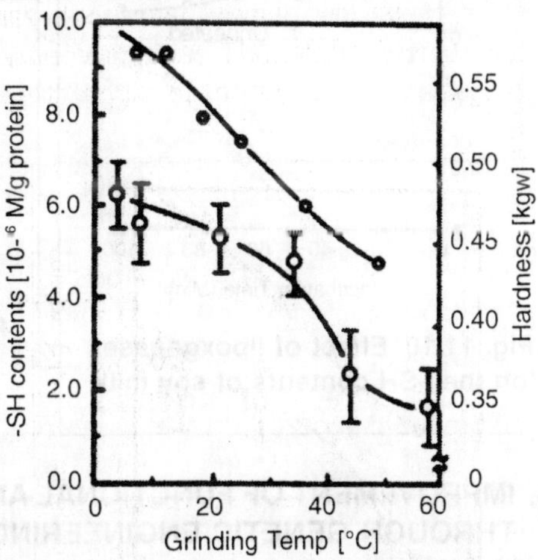

Fig. 11.9. Effect of grinding temperatures of soy milk on -SH contents and gel hardness

It is known that in wheat flour, the lipid hydroperoxides produced by lipoxygenases react with the free -SH groups of flour proteins. Therefore, there is the possibility that the decrease of the -SH groups with the elevation of temperature may be ascribed to the reaction between the -SH groups and lipid hydroperoxides in the soy milk, because the lipid hydroperoxides are considered to be produced much more with the elevation of the temperature through the action of the lipoxygenases present in soy milk. In order to ascertain this possibility, the experiment to add lipoxygenases was carried out to the heated soy milk, in which the lipoxygenases are inactivated. In the unheated soy milk, the -SH groups decreased markedly with time, whereas in the heated soymilk they did not decrease substantially, until the lipoxygenases are added (Fig. 11.10).

Further, the coefficient values between the peroxide values and -SH contents in the soy milk showed the very high negative value of -0.994 (Fig. 11.11), indicating that the -SH groups in soy milk are oxidised by the lipid hydroperoxides produced through the lipoxygenase action. From these results it should be mentioned that the hardness of tofu gel can be controlled through the control of the action of the lipoxygenases. In this connection, the hardest tofu gel is produced under an anaerobic condition.

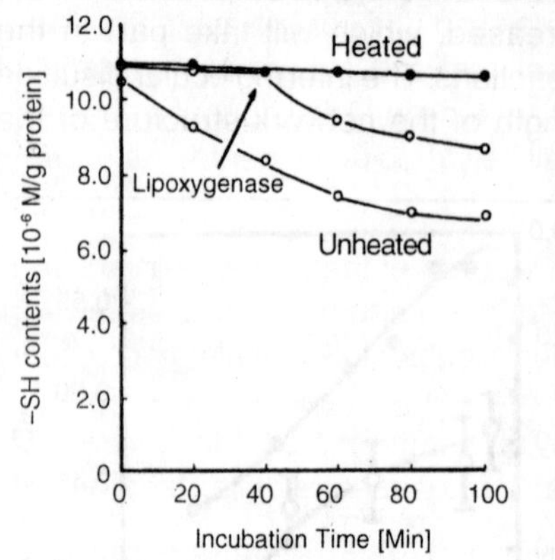

Fig. 11.10. Effect of lipoxgenases on the –SH contents of soy milk

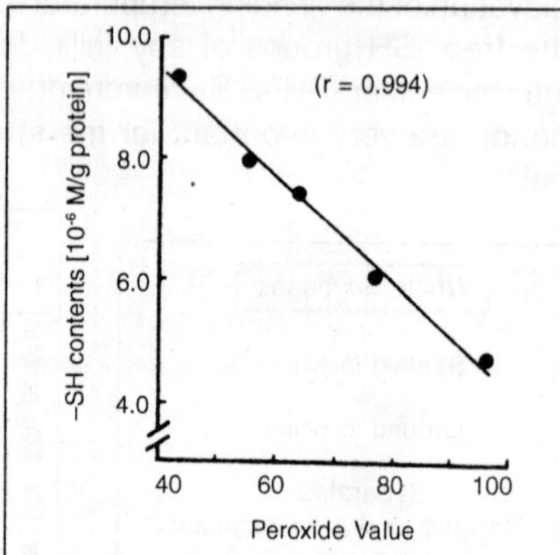

Fig. 11.11. Relationship between the peroxide values and –SH contents in soy milk

5. IMPROVEMENT OF FUNCTIONAL AND NUTRITIONAL PROPERTIES THROUGH GENETIC ENGINEERING

Generally speaking, three approaches will be considered to improve the qualities of oilseed proteins through genetic engineering. They are the control of gene expression, the introduction of foreign genes, and the modification of genes encoding storage proteins, Among these three approaches, the last one will be described here mainly, which is the modification through protein engineering techniques. There are four ways on the modification: (i) the exchange of domains, (ii) the deletion or the insertion of the sequences in the variable regions of storage protein genes, (iii) the insertion of synthetic DNA or foreign gene fragments to the variable genes, and (iv) the site-directed mutagenesis. The genes modified thus are introduced and expressed in transgenic plants.

(1) Exchange of Domains

A soybean 11S globulin molecule composes of 6 subunits, each of which has acidic (A) and basic (B) domains linked by disulfide bonding and is designated as A-S S-B (abbreviated as A-B). So far, 5 kinds of subunits, are identified as $A_{1a}B_{1b}$, $A_{1b}B_2$, A_2B_{1a}, A_3B_4 and $A_5A_4B_3$. Among these subunits, the functionalities and nutritional values are different. For instance, the numbers of methionine which is the limiting amino acid of soybean proteins are different in each subunit, as shown in Table-11.2. By exchanging the B_{1a} domain of A_2B_{1a} with the B_{1b} domain of $A_{1a}B_{1b}$, the gene encoding A_2B_{1b}, which contains 9 methionines in total was already obtained (Utsumi, 1990). This gene will be expressed in a transgenic soybean plant as a stable subunit which can be self-assembled, because both A_2 and B_{1b} are present in soybean seeds actually.

Table-11.2. Methionine Contents of Soybean 115 Globulin Subunits

Subunit	*Numbers of methionine residues*		
	A chain	*B chain*	*Total*
A_{1a} B_{1b}	3	3	6
$(A_{1a}$ $B_{1b})^*$	3	4	7
A_{1a} B_2	3	2	5
A_2 B_{1a}	5	2	7
A_3 B_4	2	2	4
A_5A_4 B_3	2	0	2

$^*B_{1b}$ is a mutant of B_{1b}

(2) Deletion of Variable Domains and Insertion of Synthetic DNA Sequences

The deletion or the insertions of gene fragments must be done in the variable regions of the storage protein genes, because the variable regions have little function in forming and maintaining the storage protein structure and may tolerate modification. Otherwise, the conformational problems of the expressed proteins will occur in a transgenic plant.

Wright suggested that existence of 5 variable regions of I, II. III, IV and V on the A_{1a} B_{1b} subunit, as shown in Fig. 11.12 wright, 1988). These regions exist in the hydrophilic region, which suggests that they are located on the surface of the protein.

From the research on the mechanisms of the functionalities of soybean proteins it is assumed that the increase of the hydrophobicity and the decrease of the conformational stability of the subunit structures will improve the emulsifying ability and further heighten the heat-induced gel forming speed and the gel hardness. Therefore, the removal of the hydrophilic variable domains and the insertions of hydrophobic continuous plural methionines into the variable domains will improve both the gel-forming and emulsifying abilities of the 11S golbulin molecules. Kim, et. al.., deleted the nucleotide sequences corresponding to each of the pavariable domains from the cDNA encoding the A_{1a} B_{1b} subunit and they inserted a synthetic DBA encoding 4 continuous methionines into cDNA region corresponding to each of the variable domains. In order to evaluate whether these modified A_{1a} B_{1b} proteins are able to form proper conformation and to exhibit expected functional properties before the modified genes are transferred to a soybean plant, Kim, et. al.., constructed a high-level expression system of A_{1a} B_{1b} subunit cDNA in Escherichia coli strain JM105. As a result, some of the modified proteins were accumulated as soluble proteins in the cells at a high level (mostly 10-20% of total bacterial protein content) and self-assembled into trimmers Table-11.3 shows the emulsifying activity of the modified proteins: $A_{1a}B_{1b}$–3, Δ I, Δ V8 (the deletions of the N-terminal 3 amino acids, of the variable domain I, of the 8 amino acids from the variable domain V), IV+4Met, and V+4Met (the insertions of 4 methionines to the variable domain IV and V). These modified proteins exhibited higher emulsifying activities than 11S globulin. Especially those of A V8 and V+4Met were more than 2 times higher than the native one, indicating that the hydrophobicity of C-terminal region may be closely related to the emulsifying properties of 11S globulin. On the gel forming abilities, AI, IV+4Met and V+4Met formed gels having significantly higher hardness by 100°C heating than that of the native 11S globulin gel, while A V8 formed a slightly softer gel Among these the modified proteins V±4Met seems to be an ideal soybean protein, of which nutritional values and functionalities are both improved. In order to improve the protein qualities in soybean seeds, the experiments of the expression of these modified genes in transgenic soybean plants are under progress at present.

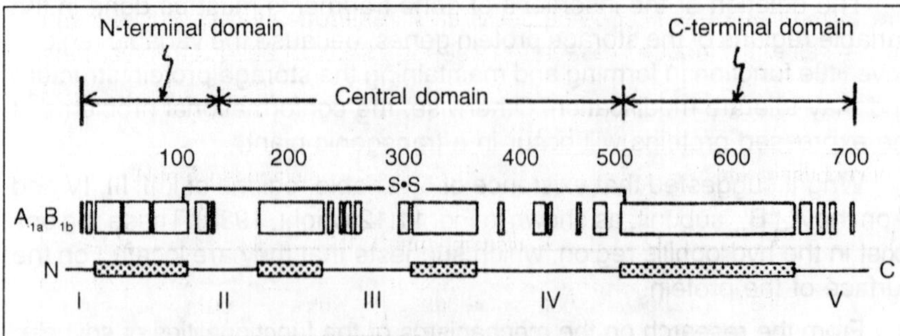

Fig. 11.12. Variable and reserved regions of $A_{1a}B_{1b}$, subunit of soybean 11S globulin. -S - S-, disulfide bond between N-terminal and C-terminal domains; Numerals, residue numbers counted from N-terminal residue; ——, variable region I, II, III, IV, and V: ▒▒▒, reserved region: ▭, amino acid sequence of A_{1a} B_{1b}.

Table-11.3. Emulsifying Activity of Modified A_{1a} B_{1b} Subunit

Modified A_{1a} B_{1b}, Subunit	*Emulsifying activity* (%)*
Soybean 11S globulin	100
A_{1a} B_{1b}-3	130
Δ I	132
Δ V8	215
IV + 4Met	134
V ÷ 4Met	211

* Emulsifying activity was expressed as relative value (%) compared with the soybean 11S globulin.

MANUFACTURING OF SOY SAUCE THROUGH BIOREACTOR

Soy sauce is one of the typical soybean protein foods which is made through fermentation processes It is a liquid product and takes 6 to 8 months for the fermentation in the conventional method. Recently, however, the manufacturing method of soy sauce using bioreactors with immobilised whole cells has been developed, by which the total manufacturing time is shorten for only two weeks.

The manufacturing process of soy sauce through bioreactors is quite different from the conventional method. The first step of the bioreaclor method is to make the filtrate from the digestion mixture. This filtrate is put into the feed tank A, followed by the successive pass of the reactors B and C to the buffer tank D, from which the resultant filtrate was fed to the bioreactors E and F separately in the ratio of ten to one to be mixed in the product tank C. The reason why the reactors E and F were set in parallel is for the control of the amount of 4-ethylguaiacol (4-EG) produced by C. versatilis. The paimmobilization of glutaminase, P. halophilus, Z. rouxii and C. versatilis, were carried out by chitopearl, alginatesilica gel, alginate gel and alginate gel, respectively. Lactic acid fermentation, alcohol fermentation and 4-EG production, continued for over 100 days at a satisfactory level without alteration of the residence time. A constantly increased level of glutamic acid was found in the effluent from the glutaminase column. The net fermentation period through these four bioreactor columns was only 2 days. This shortening of the fermentation is possibly due to the high density of immobilized cells in gel and free cells in the liquid. The quality of the Bioreactor soy sauce was considered to be similar to that of the conventional sauce, based on the results of the analysis of chemical components and sensory evaluation. Therefore, it seems that this bioreactor system is feasible for the production of soy sauce and soy sauce-like seasonings.

12
Livestock Feed Technology

TECHNOLOGICAL INNOVATION IN LIVESTOCK FEEDING SCIENCE

First is technological innovations being used in livestock feeding science. Animal scientists are always seeking improved efficiency and better use of available feed resources. By adapting modern technology, the availability of nutrients to the animals has been increased.

1. Protection of protein and fat is one of the technologies developed recently, to make available more nutrients to the animal. Balanced compound feed formulations based on this technology, making protein and fat by-pass the rumen microbial activity, are available in our country, though in limited quantity.
2. Work on methane inhibition at rumen level so as to make more metabolisable energy available to the system is in progress.
3. Manipulation of rumen fermentation in order to alter the rumen metabolism for increasing animal production, is another method.
4. For promoting growth and production, probiotics are also being utilised.
5. Innoculation of roughages with microbial inoculum is another innovation.
6. Modification of rumen microorganisms using D.N.A. recombinant technology is also being tried.
7. Biotechnological tools to overcome problems of mycotoxicosis.
8. Improving the nutritional value of feed stuffs by genetic engineering are also catching up the attention of research workers.

Out of these many ideas, feeding of probiotics for increasing animal productivity seems to be quite feasible and suitable under Indian conditions, Also by-pass protein/fat feeds will be helpful to the dairy farmers.

Animal feed industry in India is not in a position to accept in toto, the methods of feeding adapted by developed countries where a great percentage of grains produced are utilised for conversion into animal products. In our country there is an ongoing competition between men and animals for the available feed resources particularly grains. Therefore, we will have to devise methods of utilising the crop residues, cakes, brans and other by-products from agriculture not suitable for human consumption. Under the circumstances, prevailing in India, it is extremely important to find out suitable technologies to enrich and make better use of waste materials available from the agricultural sector using technological innovations in livestock feeding science.

MANUFACTURING TECHNOLOGY

The modern machinery consuming less energy giving more production with least wear and tear have always been our goal. Machines are also designed to reduce the down time, automation in the operations of the machine are also fast progressing. Introduction of extruders is the recent innovation in feed industry. Extruders are more commonly used in fish feed production where pellets of varying hardness are required. Microprocessor based batching system is also a new addition to the livestock feed industry.

When we think about the innovations in manufacturing technology in our country, we will have to reckon with certain prevalent operation conditions such as:

1. Irregularity in power supply;
2. Lower level capital investment;
3. Limitations of operating and maintenance personnel;
4. Absence of infrastructure for bulk transportation of raw materials and finished products;
5. Large quantity of high fibre/low density materials to be handled;
6. Impurities like metal pieces, twine, stones, etc., in the raw materials.

All these limitations prevent us from adapting technologies available in foreign countries as such. The methodology has to be suitably modified to suit the Indian conditions.

Efficiency of the grinders available in India is to be increased. Pellet mills of higher capacity adapted for pelleting high fibre feeds are also required. Pelleting technology has to be fine tuned and automated. More number of extruders and preconditioners are required for making special feeds. Machinery for making complete feeds with roughage are also essential.

In developed countries feed industry is utilising automatic inline electronic weighers, compact high capacity cleaning machines and grinding machines, automatic microprocessor controlled batch weighers, modern bin level indicators, system for mixing molasses higher than 10%, accurate and high quality flow meters, expanders for increasing digestability, efficient aspiration systems and roughage boilers, special grinders and pelletisers. As the level of automation is very high, the manpower used is very low and therefore, the system may not be very ideal for existing Indian conditions.

Absence of bulk handling in India is one major handicap for increasing the level of automation and sophistication of our plants. The cleaner feed mills are better feed mills and therefore, an efficient aspiration system is a must for our feed mills. It is true that some organisations in India have planned to put up mega plants producing 1,000 MT per day. Since the scope for high level automation is low and because of factors affecting the availability of raw materials and distribution of finished products, Indian feed mills will continue to serve the market in close vicinity and therefore, are likely to remain lower capacity plants.

To augment livestock production and to maintain increasing number of cross-bred animals of high genetic potential in good health, adoption of modern technology is essential for the ultimate benefit of the dairy farmer and the consumer of livestock products in our country.

Before I conclude I would like to say a few words about the organisation I represent. I am here in the capacity as the Chairman of The Compound Livestock Feed Manufacturers Association of India, popularly known as CLFMA. Our association is an All India Association of Feed Manufacturers having members from public, private and cooperative sectors, with registered office at Bombay. CLFMA is doing yeoman service in the popularisation of balanced compound feeds. Many of our members have well established research set up and are coming out with innovative products aimed at increasing livestock production.

CLFMA proposes to set up an International Institute of Feed Technology at Bangalore, in collaboration with National Dairy Development Board and International Institutes like Switzerland Institute of Feed Technology (SIFT), Buhler International Limited, Kansas State University and Barneveld College. This is an ambitious project for which we expect substantial financial and material help from our collaborators. The Institute will be able to train veterinarians arid Engineers in practical aspects of mill management and animal nutrition so as to make them capable of managing feed mills independently.

13
Post-Harvest Technology of Prawn

PRAWNS OF COMMERCIAL SIGNIFICANCE

Although about 100 species of prawns are reported from Indian waters, only the following species are known for their commercial importance. They are classified as Penaeid and Non-penaeid. Penaeid species include Parapenaeopsis stylifera, Metapenaeus affinis, M. dobsoni, Penaeus indicus, M. monoceros, Solonocera indica, Penaeus semisulcatus, Parapenaeopsis hardwickii, P. merguioensis, P. monodon, P. uncta, P. pencillatus and Parapenaeopsis sculptilis. The non-penaeid species include Acetes indicus Palaemon tenuipes, Hippolysmata ensirostris, Palaemon styliferus and Machrobrachium. Among these P. indicus, P. monodon, P. semisulcatus, P. merguensis, Parapenaeopsis sp and Macrobrachium sp are of high export value. Continuous demand for penaeid prawns in the export market have boosted prawn farming in India and the total annual production of cultured shrimps in India is estimated to be around 35500 t. P. indicus, P. monodon and P. merguensis are produced through farming for exports mainly in the southern states of India.

HARVESTING OF PRAWNS

Prawns are caught throughout the coastline of India and the magnitude of catches varies from region to region. They are caught from inland waters, inshore and offshore regions. Generally shrimp fishery is day fishery. Catches made by both country boats and trawlers from different locations are transported to processing centres after subjecting to preprocessing and/ or icing as the case may be.

A shrimp trawl contains an assortment of shrimp, fish, crabs and often mud or debris. Some shrimps are killed Immediately after entering the trawl particularly if large quantities of fish are also caught. Before icing shrimps are separated from trash and are usually beheaded. Beheading of prawns extend the keeping quality, retard spoilage and reduce contamination in prawn tails. In country boats the prawns, immediately after catch, are stored as such in the boat and nets and transported to land. In both the cases there is lapse of period, for about 4-12 hr by the time the prawns are transported and iced.

PREPROCESSING OF PRAWNS

The prawn freezing factories receive their supplies of raw materials from all over the coastal areas. Some factories have separate peeling centres in most of these places and the prawns collected from nearby fishing villages are peeled and deveined or beheaded and deveined as the case may be, cleaned with the water available in the vicinity and packed in ice at these centres before transporting to the factories. It often happens that the material thus transported takes more than 8-24 hr to reach the factories where they are finally processed Icing of the material at the peeling site helps in preventing bacterial spoilage during the long period of transport, since freshness of prawns are not maintained after 4 hr and spoilage sets in causing damage to the commodity owing to their high protein content at ambient temperatures. Method of icing plays a very important role in bringing about the cooling. Crushed ice and prawns are put in split bamboo baskets or plywood boxes, alternating each other, the proportion of ice varying widely depending upon season, availability, cost, etc. Common salt is also sprinkled along with ice in some places which causes quicker cooling. Lids made of the same material as the basket are stitched on and the whole basket is given an outer wrapping with gunny and two or four handles. These are transported in insulated/refrigerated trucks and refrigerated rail wagons.

One blemish which usually occurs in prawns when they are preserved in ice is the formation of black spots on shells followed by a general blackening of the shell and meat (melanosis). A dip treatment of the prawns in dilute solutions of sodium bisulphite or storage in ice incorporated with the above said chemical is practiced to control melanosis.

PROCESSING OF PRAWNS

Prawn products exported from India include frozen shrimp, individually quick frozen shrimp (IQF), canned shrimp, dried shrimp, shrimp powder, accelerated freeze-dried (AFD) shrimp, cooked sushi shrimp and prawn pickles. Frozen prawns are marketed as whole, headless shell-on, peeled and deveined (P&D), peeled and undeveined (PUD) cooked and peeled, peeled and cooked and peeled deveined and cooked.

Prawns received in the freezing or processing factories, as raw prawns and or iced prawns are deiced, washed, cooked and peeled or peeled and cooked as the case may be, glazed and freezed at -40°C in contact plate freezers/tunnel freezers, after which it is dipped in ice water to give a thin coating of ice, wrapped in polyethylene paper and packed in waxed duplex cartons and stored at -18 to -20°C till they are exported.

FACTORS THAT INFLUENCE THE QUALITY OF PRAWNS DURING PREPROCESSING

Prawns in their natural environment carry a commensal bacterial load, of 10/g of total heterotrophic bacteria. According to Thatcher and Clark (1968) when fish harbours more than 106 microorganisms per gm or cm^2 it is considered to have a very short potential shelf-life or may even to be at incipient spoilage. Spoilage is caused mainly as a result of bacterial activity over the flesh substrates in which most of the macromolecules are broken down into more readily usable metabolites. observed that Penaeus indicus freshly caught and unprocessed is spoiled mainly due to species of Vibrio, at ambient temperatures and by Pseudomonas at 2-4°C in a short period of 4-8 hr and 2 days respectively. The bacterial load and the composition of bacterial flora are governed by feeding of prawns; their living habits; quality of water - clean or polluted with sewage; geography of the area - inland, brackish, offshore or near shore; seasons -monsoon or post-monsoon; and temperature. Deep-sea species carry only marine bacteria whereas inshore species collected from littoral or sublittoral zones which are subject to pollution may in addition carry significant numbers of terrestrial types. Contamination of bacteria of public health significance takes place during catching and post-harvest handling of prawns as a result of contact with man who handles them, net, onboard deck surfaces, air, containers used for storage, water used for washing and flies and insects.

Unless desired to have whole individuals it is better to behead the prawns as soon as they are caught and stored as a lot. Unlike fishes the head portions of prawns which contain the digestive system undergo immediate spoilage within hours. If the head portion is not removed the spoiled head leaches out the spoilage flora along with the digested materials that contaminates not only the fleshy tail area but also other unspoiled prawns. Secondly prawn shells and appendages carry a lot of dirt and mud and could enhance the spoilage rate Hence, they are often peeled to reduce the spoilage rate, However, peeled meats are exposed to more contamination and needs appropriate precautionary measures such as a wash with brine. Beheading and peeling at primary centres at landing site reduce percentage of raw material wastage.

Quality of water used for the preparation of ice and the type of ice used, also determine the quality of prawns during storage and transportation. Flake ice makes better contact without bruising the body of prawns. Adequate icing is required to compensate melting of ice and to maintain the temperature well below 2°C. Otherwise there will be loss of quality.

Sanitary conditions and maintenance of hygiene in peeling centres at the primary centres and the processing factories also influence the magnitude of contamination by pathogenic bacteria.

BACTERIA OF PUBLIC HEALTH SIGNIFICANCE IN PRAWN

Contaminating bacteria of public health significance include Escherichia coli, Faecal streptococci. Staphylococcus aureus, Salmonella, Shigella, Vibrio cholerae, V. parahaemolyticus, Clostridium welchii and CL botulinum. E. coli and faecal streptococci are absent in offshore waters but their presence is reported in the nearshore waters. The water gets contaminated by direct contact with faecal matters. One gram of faeces contain 10-10 E. coli and 10-10 streptococci, Prawns caught from sewage contaminated water will have more number of these organisms. Flies and insects also act as a source for contaminating the product with these organisms. Since their presence is an indicative of faecal contamination there is every likelihood that the product might be contaminated with other pathogenic organisms. Staphylococcus contamination in the fishery product is being considered as an indication of unsatisfactory condition of worker's hygiene.

PRESENT QUALITY CONTROL PROGRAMME IN INDIA

Inspection of fishery products and certification of their exportworthiness is being carried out by Export Inspection Agency following Indian Standards Institution specifications laid down for cooked frozen prawns. In the In-plant Quality Control (IPQC) scheme already introduced by the Export Inspection Agency, trained inspection officers posted in each processing plant supervise the entire processing operations. Now Government of India has entrusted the entire responsibility of quality control to the processors themselves by introducing a system of modified n-plant quality control (MIPQC). This scheme envisages making available the required technical and financial assistance to the processors for setting up their own quality testing laboratories. The processors are to appoint their own quality control personnel and are authorised to self certify their products as fit for export. In the new scheme, the responsibility of the EIA gets limited to assisting the processors technically to maintain high standards of quality of their produce.

NEED FOR QUALITY UPGRADATION

Food borne illness is on an increase in the developed countries due to seafood as the eating habits of people have taken a new turn nowadays for reasons pertaining to health. Hence, the consumers in the developed and developing countries who import seafood demand strict quality standards. Consequently the future of any food processing industry therefore depends upon the capacity of the industry to meet these standards. Till recently more emphasis has been paid for end product inspection to ensure the quality of seafoods. But inspection of the finished product alone can be of no avail in improving its quality because quality has to be built up in it stage by stage. As the industry has developed with the processing technologies reinforced with the most modern machineries the concept of quality has changed its definition from consumer satisfaction and the end product assessment of quality to the new approach of Quality Assurance through a Quality System. Moreover introduction of a wide range of ingredients, new processing technologies, modern manufacturing machines and new packaging materials lead to safety challenges.

FAO/WHO food standards implemented by Codex Alimentarius Commission and ICMSF are the two most influential international agencies on food safety. Both these agencies have given a lot of importance to the promotion and implementation of Hazard Analysis of Critical Control Point (HACCP) concept in seafood industries. HACCP provides more specific and critical approach to the hazards in food industry than traditional inspection and quality assurance approach. Now the concept of HACCP is being advocated and accepted by all developed, developing and underdeveloped nations as a key system. The salient features are well recognized by many nations and are now in the process of application n their processing industries.

ISO 9000 is considered by some as the European alternative to HACCP. There are a few similarities between these two systems eventhough ISO 9000 has a much broader scope. ISO 9002 Is the quallty system appllcable to fish products which ensure quality at the production and installation and guarantee quality between producer and seller. Certification under ISO 9002 will be a stamp of approval by not only EC countries but by other countries also.

By incorporating the HACCP principles and appropriate modification of IPQC scheme the quality of prawn could be improved a lot and our foreign exchange earnings could be enhanced in the international market.

CONSTRAINTS IN SEAFOOD INDUSTRY AFFECTING QUALITY

The quality standards prescribed and exercised by Export Inspection Agency of India are in fact more rigid and stringent and at par with most of the exporting countries. However, admittedly there are setbacks in infrastructural developments and domestic quality system particularly in the areas from landings to the preprocessing and processing.

Under conditions obtaining in the fishing industry in India at present it is extremely difficult if not possible to exercise strict control on the quality of the harvested species due to various constraints like small size of the majority of the fishing boats, employment of small country boats which contribute two thirds of the country's marine fish catches and where even carrying of ice onboard is rather a difficult task and lack of proper understanding on hygienic handling practices among the illiterate fishermen. In addition, frequent power failure, potable water shortages, inadequate transport facilities, port and warehousing problems are also major constraints in applying HACCP concept in India.

CRITICAL POINTS REQUIRING QUALITY MANAGEMENT

Preprocessing and processing are the areas identified apt for application of HACCP concept adopting preventing methods and sensory evaluations with supporting documents. These areas are dealt together due to identical nature. The critical points that need quality management and monitoring during preprocessing and processing includes (a) receiving raw material for peeling, (b) washing, weighing, icing, (c) storing, (d) peeling, washing and preservation, (e) transporting to main processing plant, (f) receiving at the processing plant (g) icing and storing in the plant, (h) washing and packing, and (i) freezing.

CONCLUSION

Indian foreign exchange earnings could be considerably improved in the future through export of prawns which are often referred as "breathing dollar". India has nearly a million ha in the coastal area suitable for farming out of which 65000 ha are utilised for shrimp farming at present. Optimum exploitation of the untapped resources of the EEZ and effective utilisation of brackish water areas for prawns culture through semi-intensive and intensive prawn production in India is needed. Improved post-harvest technology, especially effective pre-processing and implementation of quality assurance system can alone safeguard our commodity against raw material wastage and food safety aspects.

Infrastructural facilities such as adequate warehousings and ports, uninterrupted and smooth shipment at all ports, uninterrupted power supply, potable water supply, road transport facilities, adequate landing centres, creating awareness on the public health significance in the local fishermen by Government agencies besides implementation of HACCP and ISO 9000 standards at all levels of procuring, pre-processing, processing, production and export may be worthwhile and beneficial not only for prawn industry, but also for the augmentation of foreign reserves for India.

14
Manufacture and Quality of Tea

The manufacture of tea is a specialised operation and involves modem methods of biochemical engineering. The freshly harvested shoots can be processed into several types of commercial tea each with its own flavour and taste. The bulk of the harvested tea in India is processed into black tea, followed by green tea; the latter type is manufactured chiefly for export. Other types of tea are produced only on experimental scale.

BLACK TEA

Four principal operations are involved in the processing of tea leaves (a) withering, (b) rolling, (c) fermenting, and (d) drying.

Withering—This operation removes moisture from the leaf which makes it less brittle, roll well and take a twist. It is generally done by spreading the leaves evenly on racks or shelves or in withering troughs protected from the weather. In north-east India, withering is effected by allowing natural breeze to pass over the leaves in houses having open sides. In south India, the leaves are generally withered in enclosed lofts with provision for blowing-in warm air. The leaf is withered for 16-18 hours during which period the moisture in the leaf is reduced by about 40% and the leaf acquires a kid-glove feel. Some chemical changes also occur during withering. A slight increase in caffeine and a relatively large increase in some of the amino acids are the earliest chemical manifestations. These changes and the degree of wither are partly responsible for the characteristics of the liquor and physical appearance and quality of the made tea.

Rolling — The withered leaf is passed on to rollers where it is twisted to cause sufficient damage to the individual cells and to initiate enzymic oxidation. Rolling is usually done for 30 minutes and the rolled mass is sifted and the finer portions of the leaf are allowed to ferment whereas the coarser portions are subjected to heavy rolling. Sometimes, a third rolling may be given. A continuous process to cause more extensive cell-damage, and thoroughly expose the catechins to the enzyme polyphenol oxidase has been developed.

Three major manufacturing methods commonly used are: i) orthodox, which employs non-cutting rollers, ii) crushing, tearing and curling *(CTC),* which employs rotorvanes and cutting-rollers, and iii) Laurie Tea Process (LTP), which uses hammer-mill-type cutter.

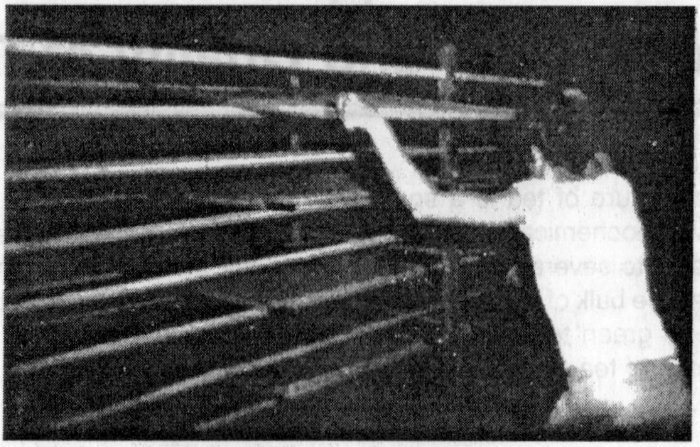

Withering of tea leaves in trays

A tea processing factory with orthodox machines

The orthodox process uses conventional crank rollers while the CTC machine consists of two engraved metal rollers operating like a mangle and gives an instantaneous nip to the leaf. Presently, many factories use the rotorvane, which acts like the common domestic mincing machine, to pre-condition the withered leaf prior to feeding to CTC machine. CTC maceration improves the aflavin and thearubigin content, and briskness, brightness and thickness of black teas, whereas the orthodox process produces more caffeine and volatile flavour compounds which make tea with superior flavour. CTC teas, being more economic, are popular in India.

A different method, Legg Cut manufacture, is used in certain tea estates in Dooars in West Bengal. The fresh leaf is directly processed and the liquor made from this tea compares well with those from withered teas but possesses a characteristic brassy or metallic taste. The green-leaf-processing can also be made continuous by using the rotorvanes in conjunction with the Legg Cut manufacture.

Fermenting— The main operation in the manufacture of black tea is enzymic oxidation, originally termed 'fermentation' which still continues. Fresh shoots contain about 25% solid matter, nearly half of it as insoluble substances like crude fibre, cellulose, protein and fats. The water-soluble portion contains, apart from caffeine, about 30 different polyphenolic substances, many amino acids, sugars and some organic acids. Within the leaf, but spatially separated from the polyphenolic bodies, are present enzymes called polyphenolic oxidases. Fermentation brings about a series of enzyme catalyzed reactions by bringing the polyphenolic bodies (mainly epigallocatechin and its gallate) in contact with the enzyme. The polyphenolic bodies undergo change to theaflavins and thearubigins. The concentration of yellow-coloured theaflavins and the red-and- brown thearubigins in the manufactured tea have remarkable influence on the colour, strength, brightness and briskness of liquor. Fermentation also imparts mellowness to the brew. The proportion of theaflavins and thearubigins can be brought to an optimum level by proper control of the conditions of fermentation. Various fractions of the rolled leaf are spread on clean cement floors or other suitable platforms to a thickness of 2.5-10.0 cm, depending upon the season and condition of the leaf, and allowed to ferment for 2-4 hrs depending upon the type of roller used under high humidity and low temperature (24.0- 26.5°) C. The colour of the leaf also changes from green to a bright coppery red. Too high a temperature results in over-fermentation and inferior product. Recently, a new method of fermentation using rotating drums has been introduced which yields uniformly good grade of tea.

Drying or firing— The fermented leaf is dried with hot air (82-93°)C for 30-40 mm to arrest further changes and to make the product fit for packing and keeping. The dried product contains 3-4 % moisture, and can withstand long storage and transit.

A tea processing factory with CTC machines

A chromatic stalk sorter

SORTING AND GRADING

Tea after firing is a mixture of particles of different sizes, ranging from dust to leaf about *5* cm long and 1.3 cm wide. It is sorted into uniform grades acceptable to the buyers and blenders. Sorting is done preferably on the day following firing by sifting in multisieved machines, the large residue remaining after each sifting being cut or broken. Sifting and cutting of the residue is alternately repeated as many times as necessary. Stalk is also removed during sorting. Specialised chromatic stalk sorters are also used in many tea factories. There are different grades of tea for both CTC and orthodox teas. The three main sizes for the CTC teas are brokens, fannings and dusts. Under each of these, the grades are sorted out. The broken grades include broken pekoe one and broken pekoe; the fannings comprise pekoe fannings one and pekoe fannings; and dusts contain pekoe dust, dust one and dust. There are four sizes for orthodox teas - whole-leaf, brokens, fannings, and dusts. The whole-leaf grades encompass tippy golden flowery orange pekoe, golden flowery orange pekoe, flowery orange pekoe one, flowery orange pekoe, and orange pekoe; the brokens include tippy golden broken orange pekoe, golden broken orange pekoe, flowery broken orange pekoe, broken orange pekoe one, broken orange pekoe, and broken pekoe; fannings contain broken orange pekoe fannings, golden orange fannings, orange fannings, and pekoe fannings; and dusts encompass pekoe dust, dust one, and dust.

Different grades of tea
(upper left — Tippy golden broken orange pekoe, upper right — Flowery broken orange pekoe, centre — Dust, lower left — Tippy golden flowery orange pekoe, and lower right — Golden orange fannings).

The broken grades (fannings and dusts) usually give a stronger tea than leaf-grades. About 450 gins of orange-pekoe gives about 100 cups of good tea, that of broken grade gives 150 cups, and fannings still more. Commercially broken grades (fannings and dusts) are particularly important for restaurants where quick service is demanded. Further, a greater quantity of broken tea can be packed in a given chest than the leaf-tea. An examination of a sample of good-quality black tea reveals many golden-yellow leaf particles in the bulk. These are unopened terminal buds of the plucked shoots. The number of these yellow particles or tips is an indication of the amount of fine leaves in the bulk and also of the quality of manufactured tea.

CUP CHARACTERS

All teas, except for the Darjeeling teas, teas from the Nilgiris, and those from high altitudes of south India, which possess aroma are sold for other cup characters, such as briskness, strength, body and brightness. In south India blacker teas are valued higher, whereas in north India teas are neither marked up nor discounted for their colour. The manufacturing process is, therefore, manipulated to produce specific requirements of these regions, although the basic process remains the same.

In the earlier years, tea in south India was manufactured mainly by the orthodox method which produced bright and brisk liquors with little strength. But, at present, the bulk of tea manufactured at mid elevations in south India is through the CTC processing technology which gives thick and brisk liquor. In the Nilgiris and at high elevations in Kerala, tea is still manufactured by the orthodox method; in the rest of the areas at mid elevations, up to 1,500m and above sea-level, roughly half the tea is manufactured by CTC and the rest by the orthodox process. In north India, several factories are fitted with dual processing system to meet demands.

The colour of CTC teas is due to many factors. The colour transition from green to reddish-green and brown/black during the manufacture depends on two major and many minor chemical reactions. The first set is the oxidation of colourless phenols into highly coloured products, theaflavins and thearubigins, and the second set is the degradation of chlorophylls to pheophytins and pheophorbides. The main constituents for aroma in Assam clones are linalools whereas geraniol is characteristic of China clones. The light leaf Assam jats generally produce blacker teas than the dark leaf jats. 'TV 18' and 'TV 19' produce black teas,. Clone 'TV 1' produces brownish tea. Fine plucking enhances blacker appearance of CTC teas. The monoterpenes, especially linalools, are present in more quantity in finely plucked shoots of five-days plucking round, which progressively decrease with increased plucking interval up to 11 days under north-east Indian conditions. Loss of terpenes in made tea results in a deleterious organoleptic quality which in turn is responsible for lower valuation of tea. Cambodia clones predominate in chlorophylls whereas carotenoids are predominant in China clones.

A wither of 75-80% is necessary for making CTC teas with an acceptable degree of blackness. The first CTC cut should be sharp so that stalks and fibres are not exposed, followed by sharp second and third cuts. The sharper the cut the blacker the tea. Firing at a higher temperature and in a shorter time makes blacker teas at the expense of quality of liquor.

GREEN TEA

Green tea is manufactured by eliminating the withering and fermentation steps. The leaves are directly heat-treated, rolled and dried. The heat treatment consists of either pan-firing (Chinese method) or steaming (Japanese method) to inactivate the enzymes. In the Japanese technology, the freshly plucked leaves are steamed for at least two minutes in cylindrical drums which inactivates the oxidizing enzymes, fixes the green colour, eliminates its raw smell and gives the leaf the elasticity required for rolling. In the Chinese method, the green leaf is kept in a cast-iron pan and turned with turning forks for about ten minutes to destroy the oxidising enzymes. In Russia, this is done in the steaming machine with a chain of trays encased in a closed chamber into which steam under pressure is passed.

Steaming is the common practice in Assam, whereas in Dehra Dun and Kangra valley the leaves are pan-fired. The heating should be completed within a few minutes to maintain the bright green colour of the leaves without scorching or reddening. The leaves are then rolled and immediately dried. In India, rolling is done in a conventional roller unlike the Japanese process in which the rolling is done in a drum. The pan-fired product is reported to be of better quality than the steam-cured product. The dried green tea is improved by polishing with soapstone or French chalk. Besides polishing, the Chinese type of green tea is usually coloured with indigo. The common grades of green tea are: Fine Young Hyson, Young Hyson, Hyson No.1, Twanky, Fannings or Soumee and Dust. The first grade forms nearly 90 per cent of the total, whereas the remainder is made up mostly of broken fragments. If carefully made, green tea should have more or less the same composition as fresh leaf. However, there is usually an appreciable decrease in soluble tannins (20% in fresh leaf, 14% in prepared leaf), though the total tannin content of green tea is higher than that of black tea made from the same leaf. The caffeine content also is higher. A larger quantity of green leaf is required for obtaining a given weight of finished green tea than of black tea.

Green tea manufactured in Japanese style in south India finds a market in Japan. Under south Indian conditions, green leaf acceptable to the Japanese market can be made only from China jat and some of the small-leaved hybrids. Green tea made from Assam jat yields a bitter type of liquor which is not relished.

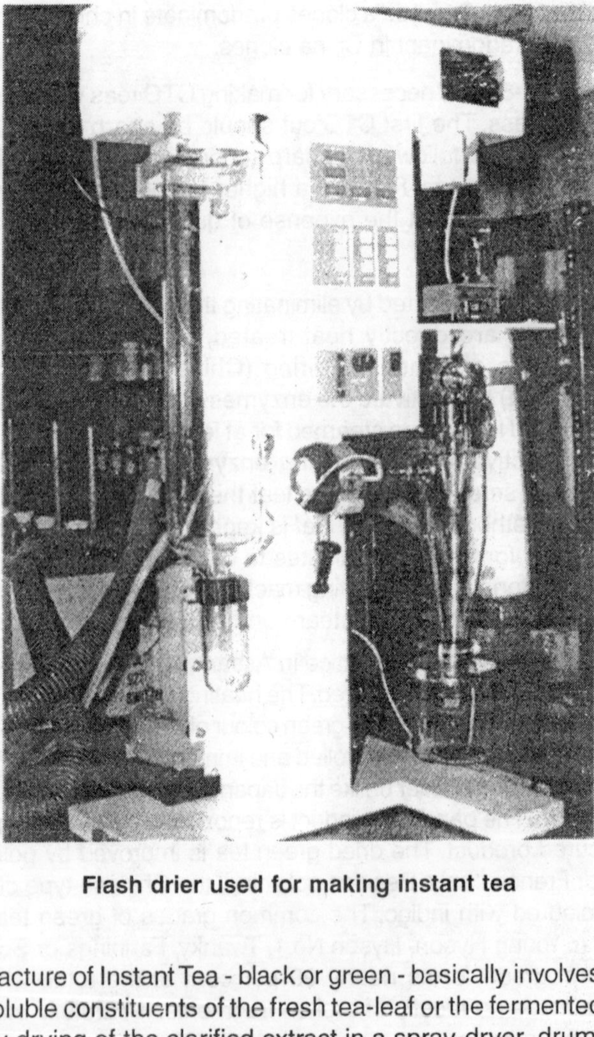

Flash drier used for making instant tea

Manufacture of Instant Tea - black or green - basically involves extraction of water-soluble constituents of the fresh tea-leaf or the fermented leaf mass followed by drying of the clarified extract in a spray-dryer, drum-dryer or a freeze-dryer.

OOLONGA TEA (WULONG TEA)

It is a semi-fermented product where the manufacturing process is similar to that employed for green tea, except that the leaf is slightly withered and a light fermentation allowed before it is dried.

A similar semi-fermented type is Jasmine tea, prepared by spreading jasmine flowers over the dried leaf, which absorbs their fragrance, and then sifting out the dried flowers.

Brew of fermented (left), partially fermented (centre) and unfermented tea (fight)

BRICK-TEA

Both black and green teas can be made into bricks. Black brick- tea is made chiefly from the waste left over after the manufacture of black tea, including siftings, dust and stalks. Green brick-tea is made of leaves only. The material is steamed over a boiler and when flaccid and soft, pressed in heavy moulds under hydraulic pressure, into bricks. A small quantity of dust treated with boiled glutinous rice-water is sometimes mixed with coarse choppings before moulding, to impart fineness. Before use the tea is whittled off the edge and ground. It is used in Tibet and Central Asia. Tablet-tea is made from the fine residual dust left from the screening of better grades.

LET-PET OR LEPPET TEA

It is peculiar to Myanmar (Burma), the Shan States and some of the hill regions between Myanmar and Assam. It is manufactured by boiling or steaming the green leaves and preserving them in pits or siloes.

A similar tea, La tea, chiefly prepared in Thailand consists of siloed teas which are used more as pickles or vegetables than as beverages.

In contrast to the well-known forms of tea, green, black and oolong, some researchers recognize six categories of tea - green, brown, black, white, blue and red, and believe that the earlier and most commonly used names are erroneous and lead to confusion. The classification is based on processing methods as enzymes play a crucial role in the conversion of one form of tea into another. With red teas, chemical reactions play a major part with internal constituents undergoing numerous changes. In case of green teas few chemical reactions take place and the internal substances are almost unchanged. In the other categories of tea, the effect lies between these two extremes. White teas undergo withering for a rather long period, while blue teas become blue over a comparatively short time. Black teas are allowed to ferment in wet vats for a short period whereas brown teas are piled up in dry vats for a long period.

TEA-TASTING

To satiate all tastes, there are teas with a variety of flavours. The geographical location of the plantations, daily or even hourly weather changes, genetics, agricultural practices and manufacturing techniques significantly affect the quality of tea. Tea manufactured on an estate in the morning may well be quite different from that produced in the afternoon or the evening. A tea-taster's palate evaluates these countless varieties of tea to ensure the right cup reaches the right consumer.

A taster's palate and olfactory sense are extremely sensitive and highly discriminatory. In assessing the characteristics of tea, the taster first examines the dry tea for colour, uniformity, twist, tip, bloom or sheen, size, fibre and aroma, and then passes on to the infused leaf. For preparing the infusion, porcelain cups of a standard size which holds 140 ml liquid is used. Infusion is prepared by taking 2.8 g of tea which amounts to a 2.0 per cent brew, by timing to 6 mm, and the liquor is poured off into a porcelain bowl. For valuation and auction, the liquor is tasted without milk. Milk and sugar are sometimes added to liquor to assess changes in quality due to interaction. It also helps to check colour and brightness.

The quality of liquor depends on the amount of unchanged catechins, primary products and polymers. The tea-tasters' report relate to appearance, colour, strength, pungency and flavour. Liquor should be bright and clear when first poured, with a distinct reddish tinge that gives a faint, pink meniscus. The 'cream' separating from cooling of a strong infusion consists mainly of theaflavins, thearubigins and caffeine. Briskness of liquor is a measure of stimulation on the palate. It depends on the complex formation between theaflavins and caffeine and declines in the later stages of fermentation due to the transformation of theaflavins into thearubigins. In non-flavoury plain teas, quality generally refers to a proper balance of characters. The colour and strength are dependent on the polyphenolic content of the shoots. The strength of liquor develops during fermentation and may be due to theaflavins, thearubigins and bis-flavanols.

Manufactured tea leaves and tea brew kept ready for visual examination and tea tasting (top); A tea taster sipping the brew to assess its characteristics (bottom)

BLENDING

The manufactured tea does not reach the consumer directly; but is blended. The object of blending is to produce a product with uniform character so that the consumer may get a similar product in every packet purchased by him. In blending, many desirable qualities in the brew, such as colour, strength, pungency and flavour, are incorporated. The appearance of the dry leaf is also considered to satisfy certain specialised markets. Profusion of tip is another specialized characteristic. Blackness and good twist are more desirable than a brown stalky appearance or a flaky consistency. The concerted opinion of a panel of tea- tasters provides a reliable evaluation of the teas' worth.

QUALITY

There are two factors which contribute to the quality of tea - (i) the genetic constituent of the individual plant, and (ii) environment in which the plant is reared which may either be natural or imposed.

Certain morphological characteristics of the leaf have been found to be associated with the quality of tea. The pubescent types produce better tea than the glabrous ones. It is well known that 'tip' in tea is due to hairy buds and leaves, and the tippy teas are quality-teas. *Pek-ho* in Chinese denotes the white hair or down on the younger leaves, and till the beginning of the century the finest grades of Indian tea were the pekoes. The quality of tea is also associated with the colour of mature leaf. For example, the light-leaved Assam types produce better quality tea than the dark-leaved types. The liquor colour, strength, overall quality and flavour of light-leaved selection are better than dark-leaved ones. The darkest green- and the palest green-leaved bushes produce poorer quality than the medium green ones. The quality of tea has also been attributed to the ratio of theaflavins, which contribute briskness, and thearubigins, which contribute the colour; the former is the precursor for the latter.

The flavour quality changes with variations in geographical and climatic conditions. In general, better teas are produced in subtropical regions and at higher altitudes. Teas produced at Darjeeling are of the finest quality and esteemed throughout the world and command higher prices than teas produced elsewhere. Dry -season teas are of superior quality to monsoonal teas. During the wet weather, the catechins are at their maximum on the plains with moderate enzymic activity leading to poor quality. The first flush and the second flush produced between March and June are most sought after and command a high value for export. There are also short-term fluctuations in the chemical constituents that are basic to the production of good-quality tea.

Of the imposed factors, the most important are fertilisers, shade, irrigation and the cultural manipulations of bushes. The finest teas are not produced in the periods of heaviest cropping, and in general nitrogen is the most effective nutrient for augmenting crop. The most variable factor affecting the quality of tea is the management. The first shoots emerging after pruning do not produce the finest teas. It is the 'second flush' teas of Assam which are noted for their quality. The polyphenol content diminishes with age of leaf, therefore, the standard plucking of two and a bud produces superior quality teas compared to inclusion of more leaves. Unshaded tea has an advantage in brightness of infused tea over shaded tea. Besides these environmental factors, the processing of tea, the duration of fermentation and the moisture content of the finished tea (normally about 3 per cent), also affects the quality of tea.

PURITY STANDARD

A chemical definition of tea has been laid down in the Prevention of Food Adulteration Act of India. The characteristics included in the definition and the limits prescribed are: total ash, 5-8%; water- soluble ash, not less than 40% of total ash; acid-insoluble ash, not more than 1 %; alkalinity of soluble ash - 1.0-2.2% as K2O; and, crude fibre not more than 17%. The Act also requires that the tea shall be free from added colouring-matter. Teas which do not measure up to this specification are considered to be adulterated and are not allowed to be sold either for domestic consumption or for export. This specification is, however, not a quality standard but only a purity standard which helps in detection of spent tea-leaf, tea-waste and other possible adulterants in tea.

PACKING

Various grades of manufactured tea are packed in plywood boxes lined with aluminium foil and parchment paper. The boxes hold about 40-55 kg leaf-tea and 50-65 kg broken grades. Fannings and dust are packed in smaller boxes holding 35-40 kg. During sorting, tea invariably absorbs additional moisture depending upon the humidity of the sorting room. It is important that tea should be sorted in a room with a 65% Relative Humidity, when it neither picks up nor loses moisture. The product may need a second firing before packing if the moisture exceeds 6-7% where the post fermentation or mellowing takes place. Tea packed with much less moisture does not 'mature' after packing, whereas tea containing much more moisture is liable to 'go off' on keeping.

KEEPING-QUALITY

A well-made tea packed in a standard plywood teachest can keep well for nine months or more, provided the temperature of storage is not high.

But tea is extremely hygroscopic and under unfavourable storage conditions can pick up a great deal of moisture. Tea with high moisture content 'goes off' quickly, becomes musty and, finally, mouldy. Cold storage and inert gas packing are used in Japan for preservation of quality in green tea, which usually has poor shelf-life.

WORLD FAMOUS *TRINITEA*

Tea is grown in several regions in India, the main areas being concentrated in the north-east India and in and around the Nilgiris or the Blue Mountains in the south. The three world famous Indian teas are Darjeeling, Assam and Nilgiri.

Highly prized by connoisseurs, Darjeeling tea is often known as the 'champagne of teas'. There is no other area in the world which can produce the 'muscatel' flavour. Since it has no equal. Darjeeling tea fetches the highest price in the auctions.

It is the result of a number of natural factors such as climate, elevation, type of the bushes, soil and even the air. Most of the bushes belong to the China jat, China hybrid and hybrid Assam. Darjeeling teas are characterised by the presence of an abundance of fine hairy growth on the underside of the leaf, on the bud and sometimes even on the stalk.

Darjeeling tea accounts for only 3 per cent of India's total tea production contributing about 12 million kg. The cropping season in Darjeeling begins in March which is the first flush. The second flush is gathered during May and June.. Both the first and second flush are really excellent teas. The teas produced during the monsoon season contain a lot of moisture and are of standard quality. October yields another batch of vintage teas known as the 'autumnals'. Dormancy sets in winter when plucking conies to a standstill.

Each garden has its own factory where the leaves are processed by the 'orthodox' method to keep the flavour intact. The tea has a brownish-black, well-twisted appearance and shows a lot of golden tip. The liquor produced is high and golden in colour with the delectable flavour and aroma which is characteristic of Darjeeling tea.

Assam teas are well known throughout the world for their full- bodied, and strong-pungent liquor. Cropping begins as early as March and extends almost to mid-December. The plucking of the first flush goes on for two to two-and-a-half months. June starts off the season for the eagerly awaited second flush teas.

The leaves are characterised by an excessive amount of silvery pubescence called tip on their undersides giving the tea its excellent quality.

The tippy Assams of both first and second flush give a characteristic flavour besides the inevitable strong liquor. These teas are manufactured by the orthodox process of manufacture which imparts to the leaves a clean, black, well-twisted appearance with an abundant show of golden tip. They produce top- quality liquors with body, strength and sparkle.

Teas produced during monsoon, from July to September are suited for CTC manufacture. The liquor from such teas have enhanced characteristics of strength, grip and colour. As the climate becomes cooler, the autumnals make an appearance which are very similar to the second flush in quality.

Nilgiri teas are relatively mild teas growing all the year round unlike the seasonal Assams and Darjeelings. They are well known for their bright and brisk liquor and their mellow, light and clean flavour. Their fine, true flavour is the choice of connoisseur blenders across the globe. From Nilgiris come the teas that are known for their quality and cup-character. The soil, climate and water, all combine to achieve the quality of Nilgiri teas.

15

COCONUT PRODUCTS AND TECHNOLOGICAL INNOVATIONS

With the establishment of the Coconut Development Board, technological research activities were accelerated by sponsoring research projects through existing research institutions in the country. The technological innovations in the processing of coconuts and its by-products are given below:

(1) COPRA

Copra is the trade name of the dried coconut kernel and is prepared from fully matured coconuts. Copra is prepared in the form of cups and balls. Cup copra is prepared either by sun drying or by using different types of driers. Cup copra is mainly used for oil extraction although superior quality cup copra finds use in the edible sector. The ball copra is made only for edible purpose and is superior in quality. It is prepared by storing fully matured nuts for 10 to 12 months under the shade or in stores/sheds. When the kernel gets detached from the shells, the copra in the form of ball is removed after cutting open the shells. The yield and quality of copra vary depending on the maturity of the nut, variety, season of harvest, age of the palm, period of storage and agro-climatic conditions. Annual production of copra in the country is around 5 lakh tonnes, of which more than 10 per cent is ball copra. Production of ball copra is mainly concentrated in Karnataka and Tamil Nadu, whereas the bulk of the milling copra originates from Kerala. Drying methods adopted for conversion of copra are: -

(A) SUN DRYING

This is the most common and cheap method of drying practised at the rural level. The dehusked nuts are split into halves and the water in the nut is allowed to drain off for about two hours. The halves are placed with the kernel exposed to the sun and allowed to dry for 2-3 days. At this stage, the moisture content of the kernel gets reduced to 20-28 per cent and the kernel can be easily detached from the shell. To obtain good quality copra, the moisture is to be reduced to about 6 per cent for which seven days of continuous drying is essential. Any delay exceeding four hours to commence drying process after breaking the nut would lead to mould formation/bacterial growth, resulting in the deterioration of the quality of copra. Mould formation is faster in rainy season. In Kerala the rainy season lasts for about four months. Most of the copra produced during this season is of poor quality which will ultimately affect the quality of oil. Hence during this season artificial methods such as copra kiln, indirect hot air driers, electric driers, etc. are used for drying.

(B) KILN DRYING

In this process the coconut kernel is dried by the hot gases generated by the burning of coconut shells. The coconut cups are spread over a platform made of bamboo or wood, and are subjected to the heat of slow fire produced by burning coconut shells for 4 to 5 days. The shed housing the kiln is generally made of brick and the roof is either tiled or thatched with coconut leaves. The hot smoke generated by burning the shells passes through the stakes of copra and hastens drying process. The charge is loaded in the evening and the fire remains for four to five hours under low fire. Kiln drying is combined with sun drying during the day time. Since the hot smoke with a temperature of 40- 45°C directly comes into contact with the kernel, the copra produced by this method is of inferior quality and brownish in colour, with slight reduction of oil content when extracted.

(C) INDIRECT HOT AIR DRIER

It is gaining wide popularity among the large scale coconut processors due to increased efficiency and better quality of copra. In this type of dryer the coconut kernel is not exposed to direct contact with the combustion gases or smoke of the fuel applied, resulting in superior quality of copra. The drying process takes place by the hot air generated inside the drier. There are two types of indirect hot air driers, natural drought and induced drought. In natural drought driers the hot air generated in the kiln is passed over copra by means of an efficient dampened ventilator.

In the Induced drought driers, hot air is generated in a separate system and blown into the drying chamber by means of a blower which passes into the bottom of the drying chamber and is evenly distributed by baffles below the platform. These driers though more expensive than the conventional driers are generally preferred during rainy season to avoid fungal attack and deterioration of quality. The extra cost is usually compensated by reduction in drying time, low fuel cost and improved quality.

(D) SOLAR DRYING

Various trials conducted on drying of copra using solar energy have proved that the drying of copra in solar dryers is more efficient than the traditional sun drying. In solar dryers about 6-8 hours of drying is adequate for the kernel to detach from the shells, and bring clown the moisture level to 6-7 per cent. Four days of drying is found to be sufficient as against 7-8 days in the case of sun-drying.

(E) IMPROVEMENT IN DRYING

The most significant advance in copra drying technique has been made, designing an economical and safe oil fuel hot air system incorporating a process of circulating hot air which not only heats the product but also carries off the moisture liberated in the process. Studies conducted in mechanical drying of coconuts have shown that good quality copra can be obtained by drying the nuts at an air temperature of 70°C for the first eight hours and then completing the drying at 60°C.

(2) COCONUT OIL

Copra is the richest source of vegetable oil. On dry weight basis, copra contains 65-70 per cent oil. From the consumption pattern, it is seen that coconut oil does not enjoy much demand for industrial applications, its demand for edible uses is mainly confined to Kerala and some districts of neighbouring states, where it is used as a medium of cooking.

There are mainly two processing routes for oil extraction. One is the dry processing through the copra route and other is the wet processing through the coconut milk route. The former is the usual method adopted in our country. Extraction of oil through the copra route is usually realised in 'chekkus', rotaries and expellers. The yield of oil is estimated to be 63-65 per cent in the case of expellers, 58-60 per cent in 'chekkus' and 62-63 per cent in rotaries. Steam cooking is desired as a pre-treatment for enhancing the aroma of coconut oil.

In the rural sector copra is now seldom crushed in the primitive chekkus'. The 'chekku is a fixed wooden or stone mortar which revolves a wooden pestle, leaning against the sides of the mortar. The pestle is attached to a long pole which is moved round by a pair of bullock or even by human labour. The copra is crushed with the mortar as a result of the friction caused by the revolving pestle. The chekkus are suitable for crushing small quantities of copra, say about 100 kg in eight hours. The power driven 'chekkus' or rotaries, are similar in principle to traditional 'chekkus', except that the pestle is stationery and the mortar revolves against it, and are generally used in slightly larger mills. The crushing capacity of a rotary mill varies from 300 to 400 kg of copra in eight hours. About one kg of gum arabica is used for every quintal of copra, to facilitate the extraction of oil and to bind the cake. Although the efficiency of extraction of rotaries is very near to that of the expellers, the operational cost and maintenance expenses are slightly more in relation to the output. The expellers are the most efficient equipment used in oil milling in the commercial sector. Today there are expellers of diverse types with varying capacities. Usually three crushings are required to extract the available oil content in copra; but in the expellers of recent times, this has been reduced to two. The extraction of oil in the expeller takes place within a steel cage or barrel by means of a hardened steel worm or screw, so arranged on a revolving shaft, so as to produce increasing pressure as the copra is pushed from one end of the cage to the other. The oil escapes through the openings built on the barrel and the cake through an adjustable pressure orifice at the end of the barrel. Hydraulic presses are also used for direct crushing of copra and their capacity varies from 1 to 50 tonnes per hour. But these presses are getting out of use as they are very expensive and cumbersome. Solvent extraction process is used to extract the residual oil present in the rotary and expeller crushed cakes. In this process the cake is broken into bits and treated with a suitable solvent in a counter current extraction process. The solvent containing the dissolved oil is drawn off from the extracted residue arid filtered. The oil is separated from the solvent by distillation.

In India there are about 1,439 oil milling establishments consisting of about 121 expeller units and 1,318 rotary units. Seventy six per cent of these units are located in Kerala. Also 50 per cent of the total production of oil in the country which is around 3.25 lakh tonnes originates from Kerala State. Most of the expellers and rotary units in the country are not effectively working due to various reasons, the major reason being shortage of working capital and inadequate management. The Board has formulated a scheme to revive the existing rotary/expeller units for fuller utilisation of the installed capacity and for improving the overall production of coconut oil in the country.

3. DESICCATED COCONUT

Desiccated Coconut (DC) is the grated or shredded form of coconut meat. It is mainly used in biscuits, confectionery, bakery and other food industries. The process involves shelling, paring (removal of testa), disintegrating, drying, sieving and packing. In India, though the first desiccated coconut unit was established in the year 1952, the industry is still in its infancy. There are at present about 42 units in the country which are located in the states of Karnataka, Tamil Nadu and Kerala. The present total annual production of DC is estimated at about 15,000 tonnes. All the DC units in the country are in the small scale sector with capacities ranging from 0.5 to 1 tonne per day. This industry provides employment to more than 1,500 people on a regular basis. Though the DC units are located in the southern states of India, the consumption of DC in southern states is very limited. It is mainly consumed in the states of Maharashtra, Gujarat, Punjab, Delhi, Uttar Pradesh and West Bengal. There is tremendous scope for boosting the demand of DC for household uses for which the quality of

DC has to be improved. Also organised market promotional activities have to be undertaken. Now grade specifications for DC have been formulated with the efforts of the Board and co-operation of the DC manufacturing units, Also the Board has evolved a scheme for financing DC units for setting up laboratories based on Ag-mark grade specifications. This is likely to boost the overall demand for DC in the country.

4. COIR AND COIR PRODUCTS

Coir with an estimated GDP of Rs. 250 crores is an important agrobased cottage industry of great significance in India. It is a highly labour intensive industry covering wide range of activities including collection of husk, retting, fibre-extraction, spinning and manufacture of coir and coir products. Coir industry in India supports around half a million people belonging to economically weaker sections of the rural population. About 80 per cent of the workers in the coir industry are women. Coir industry in India produces a number of products from coir fibre and coir yarn ranging from doormat at the door step to beautifully woven tapestry. Coir mats, mattings, rugs, coir rope, curled coir, rubberised coir products, etc. are the products made out of coir.

Coir fibre is the most durable natural fibre in the world. In the changing world scenario, changing from synthetic fibres to natural ones, the coir fibre has a rosy future. But mechanisation and improvement in quality of the products are required to make them competitive in the international market. Among the coconut products and by-products, coir and coir products earn valuable foreign exchange to the tune of around Rs. 100 crores by way of export. Hence there exists a vast scope for fuller exploitation of coconut husk for the manufacture of coir and coir products. As coir industry depends on coconut for its raw material, increase in coconut production will directly benefit the coir industry. This will pave the way in enhancing the export of coir and coir products and thereby the export earnings.

EMERGING TECHNOLOGIES IN THE PROCESSING SECTOR

(A) WET PROCESSING OF COCONUT

A new method of oil extraction from fresh coconuts was developed a few years ago. In this process the white coconut meat is ground into a slurry, from which coconut milk is separated by pressing the slurry. The residual powder is desiccated coconut of medium fat content. The milk is sieved and concentrated. After separation of coconut cream containing most of the fat, from the low fat skim milk, it can either be dried into a powder or packed aseptically. The cream is stirred vigorously to get the virgin coconut oil by a process called phase inversion. This oil is clear, nutritious and due to its low fat content it has long shelf life and can be used for cosmetic, pharmaceutical and domestic purposes. The premium products derived from the process make it economically viable for a minimum capacity of 50,000 nuts per day. A plant, processing one lakh nuts per day, can produce 7.5 tonnes of virgin coconut oil, 0.8 tonnes of brown coconut oil from testa, 9 tonnes of medium fat desiccated coconut, 11.5 tonnes of coconut water, 16.5 tonnes of skimmed milk, 21 tonnes of fibre and 11.5 tonnes of coconut shell.

(B) COCONUT CREAM

Coconut cream is the concentrated milk extracted from fresh matured coconut kernel. This is a 'ready to use' product which can be either used directly or diluted with water for various preparations like curries, sweets, desserts, puddings, ice- creams, soft drinks etc. It could also be used in the manufacture of bakery products and for flavouring food stuffs. Processed and packed coconut cream has a shelf life of six months or more and once the container is opened it should be stored in refrigerators for subsequent use. The Board has set up a pilot plant for the manufacture of coconut cream at Kalamassery Industrial Estate, Kerala, under a sponsored project with the Regional Research Laboratory, Trivandrum. The technology of the above process has been transferred to a Kerala based entrepreneur, who has commenced production on a small scale and the commercial production is expected to be launched shortly.

(C) COCONUT MILK BASED CONSUMER PRODUCTS

Fresh coconut milk has many applications In households and food industries. Spray dried coconut milk powder is a product marketed In Philippines, Malaysia, etc. in laminated foil bags. The Board has sponsored a project on spray drying of coconut milk with the Central Food Technological Research Institute, Mysore. The technology tor the same is expected to be ready shortly. The composition of the product is 62 per cent fat, 14 per cent protein and 2 per cent moisture. It is reported that one tonne of white endosperm or kernel yields about 400 kg of powder. To make concentrated coconut milk or cream It is suggested to mix or blend 100 gm of powder with 120 ml of water. Other products of commercial value made out of coconut milk are coconut syrup/jam and coconut honey. The processed coconut syrup preserved in lacquered tin cans can find various end uses in the confectionery and bakery industries. It gives a delicious instant drink which is milk white in colour when mixed with water and is also an excellent bread spread. Another value added product prepared from coconut milk is coconut honey which is an excellent substitute for real honey in many household and confectionery applications. The product is a golden coloured thick paste with a nutty flavour. Besides its use in preparation of household and confectionery food items, it is an excellent bread spread and a base for soft drink.

Another promising coconut milk based product is the skim milk powder. It is a white and deliquescent powder possessing a fresh, sweet coconut flavour. The average composition of the powder is 24 per cent protein, 6 per cent fat and 5 per cent moisture. It is a valuable commodity in the food and beverage industry. It could also be an excellent low-fat coconut flavoured beverage base. The concentrated syrup made out of the skim milk is also a very delicious product and could be used just like jam and also is a base for the preparation of instant coconut soft drinks.

(D) COCONUT SHELL BASED PRODUCTS

Coconut shell is a natural product made up of hardened cellulose. On dry weight basis coconut shell is of the following composition:

Coconut shell composition

Cellulose	:	33.01%
Lignin	:	36.51%
Pentosans	:	29.29%
Ash	:	00.61%

The very high lignin content in the shell composition renders it to be very durable, enabling it to resist quick degradation and easy decomposition even under wet conditions. Although the lignin content is higher and cellulose content lower, coconut shell is similar in chemical composition to hardwood. The moisture content of shells shows considerable variation according to conditions and maturity. All dried coconut shells under average conditions may be reckoned to contain 6-9% moisture and thus retain less moisture than most woods which contain 10-25% on air dry basis. The weight of shells averages to about 25 per cent of the husked nuts. The uses to which shells are put are partly ornamental, partly domestic and partly industrial. Of the enormous quantity of shells produced annually in India, the bulk is mainly used as fuel in copra making units, households, laundries, smitheries, bakeries, lime kilns, brickyards, iron foundries and other local industries requiring such fuel. The other commercial uses of shells in the country is for the manufacture of shell powder and shell charcoal. The shell charcoal which was a relatively minor product in the past has now emerged as a major commercial commodity owing to its intrinsic value as a raw material for the manufacture of activated carbon which has got wide industrial applications.

1. COCONUT SHELL CHARCOAL

The manufacture of charcoal is a relatively simple process. It consists essentially of burning shells in a limited supply of air so that they are only carbonised and not burnt to ash as in the fire pit of a copra kiln. The tricky part of this operation, however is to get conditions right so that the coconut shells are carbonized just to the correct degree. The kiln in which the shells are burnt varies from a simple open air pit in the ground to expensive steel and brick work patented kilns.

In operating kilns a fire of shells is initially started at the bottom of the pit. More shells are added to this till those too have caught fire. The process is then continued until the pit is completely charged, making sure that before each new addition the shell is burning well. When the charge of shells is flaring steadily, fire should be damped down, if necessary by sprinkling water. This is deemed an appropriate stage for exclusion of air from the kiln and is done best by covering the glowing mass with corrugated iron sheets and then lining them on top with green coconut, pronder damp turf and soil. Sufficient space is however allowed under the sheeting for the large volume of smoke and vapour to escape as slow carbonisation proceeds within. As a rule it is not possible to open the pit until the third day. When this is done the mass of charcoal may catch fire, in which case, it is necessary to cool it by spraying water on the charcoal.

Now there are modern methods for commercial production of shell charcoal. The Waste Heat Unit Technology developed by the Natural Resources Institute, U.K. is one such method. The WHU technology reduces the smoke emission for a few minutes per day, at start-up and produces clean carbonised charcoal. The gas evolved during carbonisation is burned in a furnace producing heat energy for application in the coconut processing industry. The shells therefore can replace either imported fuel oil or locally felled wood. Application of the WHU (Waste Heat Unit) technology consequently reduces deforestation. In addition it maximises the utilisation of shell feed stock for charcoal production. Another important advantage is that the utilisation of WHU gives the processor a greater degree of energy sufficiency. This technology has been successfully introduced In Sri Lanka. Now the Coconut Development Board is in the process of introducing the WHU technology in India. This would create a lot of impact on the coconut based economy. The waste heat recovered from the shell carbonisation process could be effectively utilised for steam generation and power generation which could reduce the production costs in the coconut processing sector. The preliminary trials have shown that the application of WHU technology for the production of good quality copra, desiccated coconut and coconut oil, is an attractive commercial proposition. Moreover the use of coconut shell instead of wood as fuel source would reduce the pressure on an increasingly scarce resource and in many cases save on the import of costly fossil fuel. In addition the maximisation of the use of coconut shell for charcoal production would also enhance foreign exchange earnings through the export of charcoal or activated carbon prepared from it. Widespread, adoption of the technology in India would consequently result in gains to both the processor and the national economy.

2. ACTIVATED CARBON

Activated carbon may be defined as those carbonaceous materials in which millions of tiny holes are created by carbonising and activating substances of any biological origin. These tiny holes form an internal structure of inter- connected capillary passages not much larger than the molecules it absorbs. Although activated carbon could be produced from a variety of raw materials and by different methods of processing, the raw materials are to be carefully selected so as to produce combination of certain desired properties required for specific use for maximum effectiveness in each of its many applications. The other carbon sources utilised for activation are coal, lignite and wood. The shell based activated carbon is considered to be superior to those obtained from other sources mainly because of small macropores structure which renders it more effective for the adsorption of gas/vapour and for the removal of colour and odour of compounds. For each carbon source, specialised methods of processing are adopted by the processors to derive the selective adsorption characteristics. While shell based activated carbon is preferable in many applications, the problem encountered with its processing is that it has to compete with coal and other carbonaceous materials which are comparatively cheaper. But with the Introduction of new technology for shell based activated carbon, the barriers would soon be removed by producing better quality of activated carbon at increased output. As per the present figures available, there are about 12 units in India producing about 15,000 MT of activated carbon of different grades utilising various carbon sources like wood, lignite, rice husk, paddy husk and shell. There are also a few more shell based units likely to be installed in the current year and the production is expected to Increase to around 24,000 MT by the end of 19.93. The estimated present demand as per the information available from the Indian Chemical Manufacturers Association is around 25,000 MT which is expected to increase to 40,000 MT by the end of the year 1995.

METHODS OF PROCESSING

The process of activation is carried out to increase the internal surface area of the starting carbon material in order to create more sites for adsorption. The most commonly used processes are based on:

(i) Steam activation

(ii) Chemical activation (Phosphoric acid or zinc chloride)

The majority of the activated carbon industries throughout the world use steam activation process to produce quality activated carbon. In this process activated carbon is produced In two stages. Firstly the base carbonaceous material is converted into charcoal and in the second stage the pore structure will be enlarged to enable the charcoal to have accessible internal surface area. The first stage called carbonisation process is carried out using any one of the following equipments:

- Metallic portable kilns
- Brick kilns
- Continuous kilns
- Horizontal retorts

The second stage called steam activation process could be carried out using rotary kilns specially designed for the purpose. Here the charcoal is reacted with steam between 900-1100°C under controlled atmosphere. The reaction between steam and charcoal takes place at the internal surfaces of the charcoal removing carbon from the pore walls and thereby enlarging them. Here the temperature factor is very important. Below 900°C the reaction is too slow and is very uneconomical. At more than 1000°C the reaction becomes diffusion controlled and therefore takes place on the outside surface of the charcoal thereby resulting in loss of charcoal. Further the internal surface remains inactivated. It is, therefore, very much necessary to have a good design of rotary kiln which could provide sufficient residence time and at the same time have all necessary process control devices to control the other parameters involved in the process. With this the plant would be able to produce good quality activated carbon at increased output.

3. DESTRUCTIVE DISTILLATION OF SHELLS

When the coconut shells are heated in the absence of air to a sufficiently high temperature the highly complex substances of which the shell is constituted, breaks down, the shells as a whole suffering disruption and decomposition as in the case of wood. The products of the destructive distillation appear in all the three states of matter viz, solid, liquid and gas. Apart from the maturity of the shells and their moisture content, the chief factors governing the formation of distillation products are temperature, pressure, speed of distillation and the presence or absence of extraneous substances. The primary products of destructive distillation of coconut shells are retort charcoal which remains in the carbonising apparatus, pyroligneous liquor and settled tar which distills over, and uncondensable gases. Based on laboratory studies and commercial trials, the yield of these products are as follows: charcoal 34%, pyroligneous acid 40%, tar 6% and fuel gas 20%. The pyroligneous liquor further contains acetic acid contaminated with other compounds. It is a dark reddish coloured aqueous liquid with dark colour. During redistillation of this liquor, several useful products like methanol, acetone, acetate of lime and acetic acid carn be recovered.

4. COCONUT SHELL POWDER

As a result of intensive research during the past decade, an entirely new use for commercial exploitation has been found for coconut shell. This is the manufacture of coconut shell powder from shells. Early research work has established its value in the plastic and allied industries and now it is extensively used as a compound filler for the manufacture of synthetic resin glues and as a filler and extender for phenolic moulding powders. This unique filler is also being used successfully in specialised surface finishes, liquid products (as an adsorbent), mastic adhesives, resin casting, mild abrasive products, polyester type laminates, bituminous products and potent insecticides (as a diluent). Coconut shell flour gives a smooth and lustrous finish to moulded articles and also improves their resistance to moisture and heat. The demand is for fine grade of 200 mesh size and above. The present methods being adopted for shell powdering in India are by using a combination of hammer mill and pulverizer. The broken coconut shells are further broken up into pieces of about one inch square by passing through a disintegrator (hammer mill). This broken material is then fed into a pulverizer where the shells are powdered. The suction in this system draws up the particles into a cyclone which are further drawn to the exhaust end of the ducting and collected in bag filters fitted with linen bags. The separated particles are further fed into vibrating screen where they are graded into 100 mesh, 200 mesh and 300 mesh size particles. Suitable technology for obtaining higher proportion of fine mesh size is yet to be developed in the country. Since coconut shells are very hard and abrasive in nature it takes a long time to reach the desired particle size. This results in higher costs on electricity, machinery wear and tear, operational cost, etc.

Coconut shell flour is preferred to many other similar materials like wood bark powder, peanut shell powder etc., to use as phenolic extender in various chemical industries because of its uniformity inparticle size and chemical composition. With the introduction of newer ideas, research and progressive stream lining, the scope for the coconut shell flour in plastics and other allied Industries is expected to go up tremendously.

5. MISCELLANEOUS USES OF SHELLS

As the shell is hard and takes on high polish, it can be carved, decorated with lacquer, inlaid with silver or other metals and generally used with great ornamental effect. Articles of very attractive appearance are being manufactured by expert craftsmen in different parts of South India. The hard dense structure of the coconut shell permits sanding and polishing of the outer surface to a high luster. The shell of the coconut is a hard fine grained substance which is carved into all kinds of lovely intricate objects.

(E) COCONUT WATER

Coconut water from the tender young fruit is a delicious and nutritious beverage which can be sipped straight from the fruit or as a cool exotic concoction. The water in the matured coconut, constituting about 28 per cent of the nut, is considered as a waste product, causing problems in factories producing copra, desiccated coconut, and other coconut kernel products. It Is a very active pollutant because of its high Biological Oxygen Demand (BOD). The pollution problem has however motivated research in finding ways to effectively utilise the coconut water. Coconut water has a substantial amount of sugar, around 3 per cent that makes it a suitable fermentation substrate, although the addition of more sugar is necessary for appreciable fermentation to take place. Chemical analysis of matured coconut water showed that it contained 5.4% total solids, 2% soluble sugars, 0.5% minerals, 0.1% proteins, 0. 1% fat and 60 mg% acidity with pH 5.2. The corresponding figures for tender coconut water of about 7 months maturity are 6.5%, 5.7% 0.6%, 0.1%, 120 mg% and 4.5%. The quality of the mature and tender coconut water could be differentiated by their chemical composition. The Regional Research Laboratory, Trivandrum, Kerala has developed a process for the upgradation and preservation of mature coconut water as a soil drink. The main unit operations involve collection, upgradation and pasteurisation, filtration and bottling. The process essentially consists of upgrading the flavour of ripe coconut water to the level of tender water by supplementation with additives including sugar and preserving it by a judicious combination of heat sterilisation and permitted preservatives. The bottled coconut water was found to have a shelf life of about 45 days. Consumer acceptability studies for the product was also conducted by the Board in all metropolitan cities. The product was found to have a fairly good response from consumers. Although much research work had been carried out on bottling of coconut water, the commercial launching of this product has not taken place in India mainly due to problems like collection of large quantities of water, short time lag involved between collection and processing delicate flavour and low keeping quality.

However coconut water could be commercially exploited for the production of coconut vinegar. The Coconut Development Board in collaboration with Central Food Technological Research Institute, Mysore has developed a modern technique for producing quality vinegar from matured coconut water using vinegar generators. The vinegar generator is designed to provide the maximum surface exposure for a volume of fermented coconut water in order to supply enough air for the acetic acid bacteria to efficiently and quickly oxidize the alcohol to acetic acid. The generator assembly actually comprises a feed trough, an acetifier and a receiving trough. In essence, it is a counter current gas absorber wherein the acetic bacteria causes the oxidation of alcohol to acetic acid. The feed is uniformly sprayed over the surface of an inert porous packing medium (corn cobs) at the surface of which the oxidation takes place. The stock which drains off from the packing by gravity into the base of the generator is run out and pumped back into the feed vat from where it is recycled until acetification is complete. When the vinegar has reached its maximum strength (4.5%), it is aged before bottling. In certain coconut growing countries like Philippines, coconut water is used to produce a sweet dessert called Nata-de-coco which is also popular as a component of fruit salads, ice-cream and fruit cocktails.

Coconut water has also been found to speed up the growth of microbacterium tuberculosis organisms. When needed in large quantities for biological research, the organisms are usually grown on the surface of a culture medium. But with added coconut water, even when diluted 10,000 times, the normally required period of 20 days for maximum growth is reduced to 12 days.

Other research work on coconut water utilisation is currently being explored.

(F) COIR PITH AND MISCELLANEOUS PRODUCTS

Coir pith a waste from coir industry is being produced at 4.5 lakh tonnes annually and gets accumulated in the industrial yards causing environmental pollution, fire hazards and disposal problems. A study was carried out by the Tamil Nadu Agricultural University by treating the coir pith with Pleurotus sp. (edible mushroom) and urea and keeping it in the open yard for 30 days. The decomposed coir pith was analysed for its bio-chemical composition. The results indicated a definite reduction in lignin and cellulose content with an increase in total nitrogen and the plant mineral nutrients. The C:N ratio was narrowed down from 112:1 to 12:1 indicating the feasibility of using the inoculated coir pith as manure in agricultural farms in place of farmyard manure and compost. The coir pith is now being used on a limited scale in the coconut garden as a mulch material due to its potential quality of high moisture retentivity. It has been observed that pith could be successfully utilised for the manufacture of many commercial products such as hard boards, insulators, expansion joint fillers, etc. The pith in combination with cement has been reported to be an excellent thermal insulating material. Its use in the preparation of moulds for the production of ash trays, electric fittings, etc. has also been reported. It is reported that a process has been developed in the Philippines for the conversion of coir pith by a continuous process into charcoal briquettes with simultaneous production of tar and liquid condensates and a gas containing H_2 and CO which could be used as a domestic fuel.

Flow diagram showing destructive distillation of coconut shell

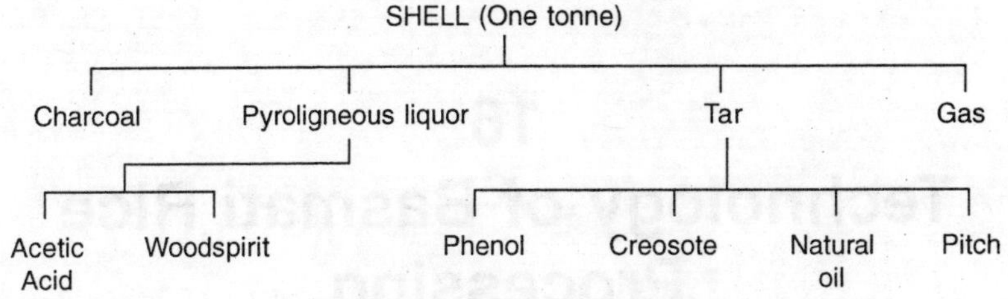

Flow diagram showing integrated processing of coconut

a. Integrated Processing Route 1

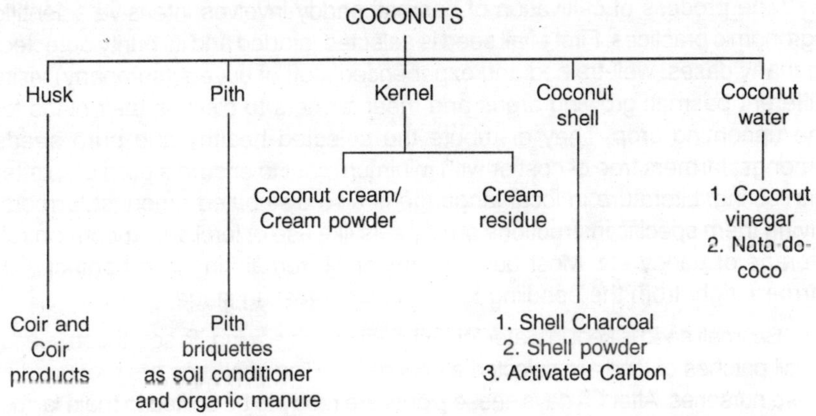

b. Integrated Processing Route II

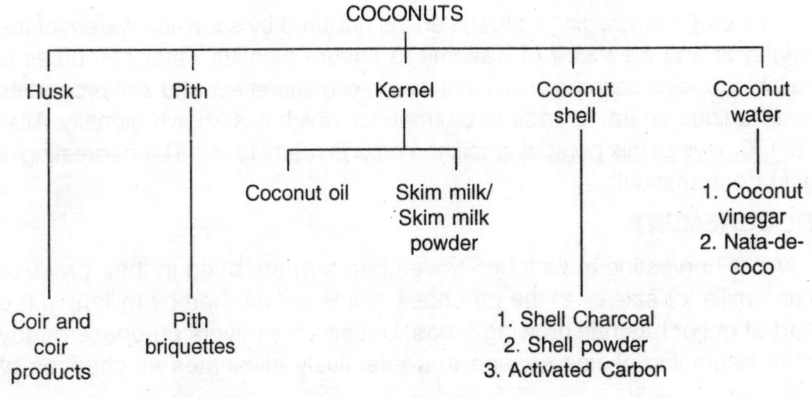

16
Technology of Basmati Rice Processing

CULTIVATION

The process of cultivation of basmati paddy involves intensive scientific agronomic practices. First of all seed is selected, graded and its purity detected. In many cases, well-trained and experienced staff of buyers (company) visits different basmati growing areas and meet farmers to discuss their plans for the upcoming crop. They distribute the selected healthy and pure seeds amongst farmers free of cost or with minimum cost to ensure a pure crop after harvesting. Literature in local language is also distributed amongst farmers, giving them specific instructions on aspects like use of fertilisers, pest-control, storage of paddy etc. Most buying companies remain in close contact with farmers right from the seedling to the final harvesting stage.

Basmati seed is kept in water for 24 hours before sowing. To sow these seeds, small patches of land are selected as nurseries. Rice seedlings are produced at these nurseries. After 25 days, these plants are ready to be shifted to main farms. During end-June or utmost by July-first half, when weather in basmati growing areas is too hot to bear, these sapplings are shifted from nurseries to water-flooded main fields. Transplanting is done manually one by one.

The crop from beginning to the end is nurtured by snow-fed waters of the Himalayas and the valley of Kashmir to ensure plentiful water resources is available to feed basmati crop. This water, climatic effect and soil properties impart unique characteristics to basmati for which it is known globally. After 120-130 days of this perspiring toil, the crop is ready to cut. The harvesting is again done manually.

PROCUREMENT

After harvesting in October-November, farmers bring in their produce to rice mills for sale or to the purchase points established by millers in the heart of major basmati growing areas. Usually, the buyers purchase paddy at the beginning of rice season that effectively eliminates all chances of mixing inferior varieties/grades. On the other hand, semi-processed rice available with brokers during rest of the year remains prone to mixing that is often hard to detect. Hence, paddy procurement plays a vital role in maintaining quality and purity of basmati rice.

Before a particular lot of paddy is purchased, it is subjected to various tests like tests for moisture content, kett-test, field admixture etc. Samples are then processed in mini mill to determine yield, kett-test and after-cooking characteristics in some cases. A lot is purchased only when it meets the stringent quality requirements of the buyer. Preference is, however, given to farmers who coordinate with particular buyer from seedling to harvesting stage. Quality of final product largely depends upon the quality paddy procured. Many buyers avoid indulging in such a laborious process and purchase semi-processed rice from brokers instead of paddy from farmers, compromising on the quality of the produce.

PROCESSING

Rice is a delicate grain; requires extra care in processing. Any rough handling during processing can cause the grains to break or develop cracks.

PHASE I

PADDY STORAGE

Paddy procured is stored under fumigation control to prevent any insects or microbial problems. Fumigation is done from time to time during storage. Stored paddy is transferred to processing plant for further processing when needed.

PRE-CLEANING

Paddy is thoroughly screened to remove any type of foreign material like stalks, dust etc. There are automatic pre-cleaners, which are scientifically designed to cater to the pre-cleaning problems.

Fig. 16.1. Different Types of Destoners

DRYING

On determining humidity limits of paddy through moisture testers, drying is carried out slowly and uniformly by blowing warm air to reduce the moisture to required levels. During drying, paddy is constantly stirred through automatic stirrers to keep the grains away from packing together and to allow more airflow through them. In traditional method, basmati paddy is allowed to slowly reduce its moisture by natural- sun-drying-method, to achieve optimum moisture content for husking. Paddy is spread over large fields during the day and left for drying in the sun. This gradual drying helps to avoid thermal cracks in rice grains, which would result in broken grains at later stages.

SECOND PRE-CLEANING

Dried paddy is again pre-cleaned to minimise any chances of the presence of foreign material. This basmati paddy is then used to produce raw or parboiled basmati rice.

PHASE II- PRODUCING BROWN BASMATI RICE

DE-HUSKING

Husk of the paddy is removed by De-Husking machinery, working with fully automatic rubber roll control system, which effectively removes outer husks of paddy, leaving bran layer of rice intact. Rice so produced is called Brown Basmati Rice.

Fig. 16.2. Huller and Husk Aspirator

Fig. 16.3 Paddy separator

PADDY SEPARATION

The De-Husked quantity still contains about 10-15% of paddy grains. This mixture is fed to Paddy Separators consisting of separating trays. The mixture is given special side way motion, separating brown rice from paddy. Paddy is returned to dehusking again and brown rice goes for further processing.

In brown rice production from minimal processing of paddy, only the outer husk is removed, leaving the germ and bran layer intact with the rice kernel, retaining most of the nutritional value. Bran is rich in protein, fat and crude fibre. This minimal processing therefore produces rice that is healthier to eat. The brown rice, after grading, is transported to warehouses.

WAREHOUSING

One of the main peculiarities of basmati rice is enhancement in its taste and aroma when it is seasoned for eight-to-nine months. This makes warehousing one of the very important steps in the whole production process. Stocks of brown basmati rice are stored in well-ventilated and spacious warehouses. These stocks are kept in most hygienic conditions under constant observation. During the period, stocks in warehouses are subjected to regular inspection and fumigation from time-to-time against disease and insect infestations. Good basmati rice should be aged for at least one year. The stored rice eliminates moisture from the grain and enhances its texture and flavour. Ageing also contributes to better cooking results, elongating 2-3 times its original size when cooked.

PHASE III- CONVERTING BROWN BASMATI TO WHITE AND PARBOILED BASMATI

For processing of White and Parboiled basmati rice in double polished forms, Brown Basmati rice is fed to fully automatic rice polishers.

RICE POLISHING

Rice polishing is conducted without addition of any chemicals to keep rice free from health hazards. For this purpose, Rice Polishers are designed in such a way that brown rice is polished by its own mutual friction among rice grains in polishing chambers to perform the polishing effect. Bran layer of brown rice is removed, producing pearly white kernels of basmati. Bran wastage produced here is removed by automatic vacuum systems, leaving behind double polished rice. Number of passes depends upon the degree of whiteness required.

Fig. 16.4 Different Types of Polishers and Whitners

PHASE IV- GIVING SILKY TOUCH

WATER POLISHING

Automatic water polishers are used to convert double polished rice into silky rice. This silky touch to rice is given with care and extra-vigilance to keep rice quality optimal.

Fig. 16.5 Water Polisher

Rice entering Water Polishers is moved through mist formed by mixing filtered air and distilled water coming from condensing chamber. This movement of rice through mist gives clean and glossy white appearance to the kernels.

PHASE V- GRADING BASMATI KERNELS

THICKNESS/LENGTH GRADING

Both- thickness and length of rice kernel are important in grading. Grading machines with multi-features have following capabilities—

1. Selecting uniform grains
2. Maintaining A.G.L. (Average Grain Length)
3. Removal of broken kernels
4. Rejection of short grains and shrivelled rice
5. Removal of any foreign material (if any)
6. Rejection oversized grains

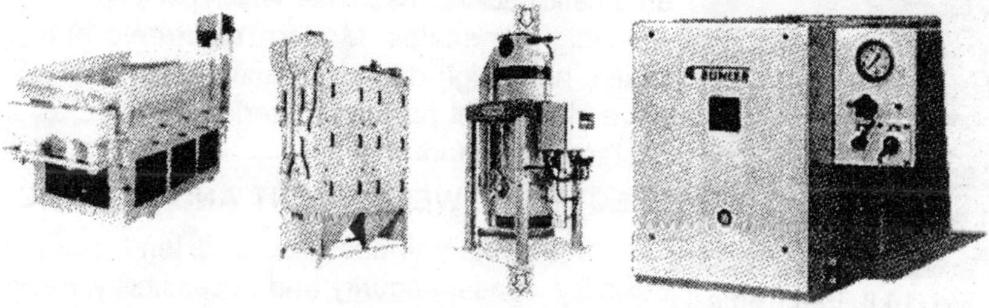

Fig. 16.6. Gravity Separator, Drum Grader, Dump Weigher, Automatic Flow Balancer

Grading machinery has been manufactured on gravity classification and centrifugal principles, incorporating many excellent features with eminent abilities to grade and clean rice kernels. Uniform grain length renders nice appearance to the finished product and adds to the presentation (before and after cooking).

PHASE VI- ADDING MAXIMUM VALUE TO BASMATI

COLOUR SORTING AND GRADING

The final step in rice processing is colour sorting. This is aimed at removing discoloured grains from processed rice to give the final product a uniform-colour look. Colour sorting is an intricate computer-controlled process where CCD (Charge, Coupled Device) technology is used for performing high- resolution-optical inspection of each and every kernel. It removes the high concentration of predominantly chalky and discolored kernels to give final product a uniform appearance.

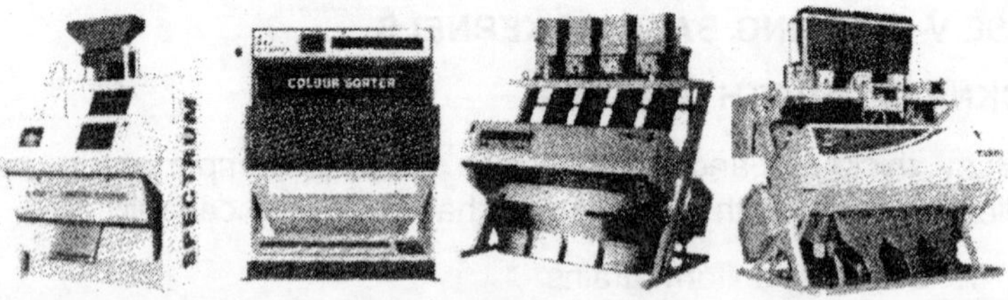

Fig. 16.7. Different Types of Colour Sorters

FINAL INSPECTION

Basmati rice sorted is finally inspected by Quality Control department and is sent to packing section.

Fig. 16.8. Electronic Weigher

PACKING

Processed basmati rice moves to specially designed packing bins where it is supplied to automatic packing machines, which pack rice on pre-set weighing scales. Modern electronic bagging scales have high degree of accuracy in weighing. Several kinds of packing material are used as per customer demand.

ELECTRONIC WEIGHTMENT AND BAGGING

Storage system is designed to extend maximum flexibility, space, security and accessibility. Packed rice is directly loaded to containers, which carries the premium rice to the end users.

General Flow Diagram of Basmati Rice Processing

Miller-Seed
↓
Farmer-Paddy
↓ ↓
Miller ← Broker-Semi Processed
↓
Storage-Paddy
↓
Pre Cleaning
↓
Drying
↓
Second Pre Cleaning
↓
De husking- Brown Basmati Rice
↓
Paddy Separation
↓
Warehousing
↓
Rice Polishing-Double Polished Rice
↓
Water Polishing- Silky Rice
↓
Colour Sorting and Grading
↓
Final Inspection by Quality Control
↓
Packaging
↓ ↓
Domestic Market Foreign Market

17
Spirulina: A Classical Health Food

INTRODUCTION

Spirulina is the genus of a filamentous blue-green algae. It is a very simple plant. It is unicellular, photosynthetic and mainly habitant of water. *Spirulina* comes under the division of Thallophyta. This means, it has no clear distinction into leaf, stem and root. It is microscopic in size and prokaryote in nature. That is, it lacks a nucleus. Broadly, *Spirulina* has also been classified under the umbrella of Single Cell Proteins (SOP).

In brief, SOP may be described as the dried cells of microorganisms like algae, certain bacteria, yeasts and moulds which are grown in large scale culture systems for use as protein sources for human or animal consumption. In addition, the products also contain other nutrients such as carbohydrates, fats, vitamins and minerals.

The concept of SOP production was developed in 1914- 1910 during the First world War, when the conventional foods were in short supply. During the First World War, yeast *(Saccharornyces cerevisiae)* was produced on mass scale in Germany from molasses which replaced upto 60% of imported protein. Similar type of incidence was also experienced during the Second World War (1939-1945) and then yeast *(Candida utilis)* was produced on large scale from manufacturing wastes. The organism *Candida utilis* was previously known as Torula yeast or *Torulopsis utilis.* After the war, many plants were set up for the mass production of *Candida utilis in* the USA and Europe.

Spirulina has been consumed as food by the human beings since ancient time. For example, in Central Mexico off Lake Texcoco, Spirulina maxima is harvested in huge amount for human consumption since centuries. Similarly, Spirulina platensis is harvested from Lake Chad of central Africa for the same purpose since long. Both Spirulina maxima and Spirulina platensis may be classified either in the genus Arthrospira or Spirulin. But the latter name has become more popular.

PRODUCTION

Spirulina can be produced by several methods, starting from cultivation in lakes, ponds or earth ditches to sophisticated bioreactors and fermentors. Outdoor cultivation may take place either in open or closed system. Open system shows wide variation in productivity which is dependent on the type of water, environmental temperature and sunlight radiation.

It is a herculean task to grow monoculture Spirulina species in open air system. Problem of propagation of mixed culture populations and frequent contamination by bacteria, fungi, protozoa, etc. hamper the production and deteriorate the quality of the end product. Ponds and ditches when used for mass production the surface of the water is either covered with polyethylene or other plastic material to reduce the risk of contamination. Seeding a large inoculum to dominate the culture is the another common practice to avoid the risk of infection. Slow agitation is essential to achieve the high productivity. It helps to prevent sedimentation, allows more homogeneous exposure of the cells to light, minimises nutrient requirement and temperature gradients. One of the important conditions of Spirulina production is that the water has to be alkaline in nature. The optimum pH of water ranges from 9 to 11.

In Mexico, from a lake of 900 hectares surface area about 1000 metric tons/year or 0.111 kg/m^2/year, Spirulina maxima was obtained. But on pilot scale experiments in China, it has been possible to produce 10 gm/m^2/day or more than 3 kg/m^2/year, Spirulina platensis from the ponds of about 100m^2. Currently, it is also known hat whey and dairy effluent may also be used as a substrate for the production of Spirulina maxima and Spirulina platensis with the addition of 4% sodium bicarbonate.

For the rapid growth of cells often CO_2 is injected in water. Sometimes, cheap organic material like molasses, manure and industrial wastes are also used. The water of lake Texcoco in Mexico has high concentration of carbonate and bicarbonate which are effectively consumed by *Spirulina maxima.* Nitrogen sources are usually urea, ammonia, nitrate and nitrites. The other important nutrients is phosphorus which may be added in its inorganic form in water.

In closed systems, *Spirulina* can be cultivated with photobioreactors (either by indoor or outdoor method) where a single species is inoculated for obtaining pure and clean cell mass. Closed system of production shows better control from the point of contamination which ultimately leads towards higher growth and comparatively good quality. However, this process increases the manufacturing cost. Photobioreactors which operate indoors are small because artificial light is required. Photobioreactors may be made up of either plastic or stainless steel material.

TABLE 17.1: Major Compositional Differences Among the Three Protein Rich Food-stuffs (on % Dry Wt. Basis).

	Soyabean	*Mushroom*	*Spirulina*
Protein	47.03	40.00	61.70
Fat	21.22	6.96	7.00
Minerals	5.00	12 17	9.00
Fibre	4.03	3.48	5.80
Carbohydrates	22.74	37.39	16.50

TABLE 17.2: Composition of Spirulina Maxima (on Dry Wt. Basis)

	S. maxima
Protein (g/100g)	48–61
Amino acids (g/l6gn)	–
Alanine	5.0–6.1
Arginine	4.5–9.3
Aspartic acid	6.0–15.2
Cystine	0.6–2.2
Glutamic acid	8.2–21.8
Glycine	3.2–4.0
Histidine	0.9–1.6
Isoleucine	3.7–4.5
Leucine	5.6–7.7
Lysine	3.0–4.5
Methionine	1.6–2.2
Phenylalanine	2.8–4.0
Proline	2.7–3.2
Serine	3.2–4.3
Threonine	3.2–4.5
Tryptophan	0.8–1.2
Tyrosine	3.9
Valine	4.2–6.0
Lipids (g/100g)	4–7
Carbohydrates (g/100g)	13–16
Minerals (g/100g)	4–9
Vitamins (mg/100g)	–
Thiamin	5.5
Riboflavin	4.0
Pyridoxine	0.3
Nicotinic acid	11.8
Pantothenic acid	1.1
Folic acid	0.05
Biotin	0.04
Cyanocobalamin	0.02
β-carotene	0.17
γ-Tocopherol	19.0

HARVESTING

Spirulina maxima and *Spirulina platensis* can be harvested by simple filtration process through screens or cloth. Thereafter, they are dewatered by centrifugation and for dried. The biomass is usually dehydrated by sun/ drum/spray drying.

Out of these three methods, drum drying technique is preferred most, because here both the net protein utilisation and digestibility of the product are increased. This may be due to the rupture of the cell walls during drying under controlled conditions. Cell walls of Spirulina are not easily digestible, therefore, any treatment to disrupt the cell wall will enhance both the digestibility and nutritive value. However, in the USA food grade Spirulina is generally produced by spray drying process. The product is held in the dryer at 60°C for a few seconds so that, the damage of heat sensitive nutrients and pigments can be avoided. Sometimes, the product is not dried and instead of this the product is used in the form of slurry. Lately, Spirulina is commercially produced for food use in Mexico, USA, Japan, Israel, Thailand, Taiwan, China, Germany and India.

NUTRITIVE VALUE

In Mexico and Africa Spirulinais consumed by the human beings since ages. On investigation, it is known that the nutritive value of Spirulina is very high. It is a very rich source of protein. This can be visualised from Table 17.1. For better understanding in the table, composition of the three protein rich food-stuffs has been highlighted. The protein content of Spirulina (61.70%) is higher than that of soyabean (47.03%) or mushroom (40.00%). The amino acids make up of the Spirulina are balanced except the sulphur containing amino acids methionine and cystine. It is a good source of vitamins, particularly the water soluble vitamins and essential fatty acids. In Spirulina the thiamin, riboflavin, nicotinic acid, pantothenic acid, folic acid and carotene contents are higher than many vegetable food-stuffs. However, the nutrients contents are highly dependent on the method of cultivation and processing conditions. For convenience of the reader, a detailed composition of Spirulina maxima has been highlighted in Table 17.2.

Recently, it is known that spray dried Spirulina platens/s powder is a fair source of iron (0.9 mg/100g) and the speciality of this product is, its absence from iron absorption inhibitors like oxalates and phytates. Mani et al., (2000), carried out studies on the effect of Spirulina supplementation on blood haemoglobin levels of anemic adult girls and concluded with the remarks that supplementation of *Spirulina had* fruitful effect on the blood haemoglobin levels which may be effectively used to combat against iron deficiency anaemia.

Spirulina can be supplemented in a variety of food formulations like cereal foods, breads, rolls, cookies, noodles, etc. It can also be used to decorate the salad. In Mexico, *S. maxima* has been chosen as a supplement for biscuit production, by a state company as a part of their national breakfast programme for the school students.

TABLE 17.3: Biological Value (BV) of Some Food-stuffs

Food-stuff	*BV*
Rice	68
Wheat	65
Maize	59
Bengal gram	68
Meat	74
Spirulina sp.	75
Fish	76
Spirulina sp. + methionine	82
Milk	84
Egg	94

Technology for the production of acceptable quality of milk beverage and yoghurt with the incorporation of Spirulina *has also been developed in China.*

The Biological Value (By) of Spirulina is substantially high. It is even higher than some common food-stuffs of our daily livelihood like rice, wheat, maize, Bengal gram, meat, etc. The BV of Spirulina is well comparable even with fish. Amino acid methionine if supplemented with Spirulina then the BV surpasses the fish BV and becomes comparable with milk. The BV of some food-stuffs are shown in Table 17.3.

In view of several merits of the Spirulina, currently it has been called as "all-in-one or 'super nutrient' for us. It contains some useful ingredients such as protein, vitamin B complex, iron, calcium, (ß-carotene, antioxidant, phycocyanin and G-linolenic acid. The usefulness of these ingredients are briefly specified in Table 17.4.

In addition to these beneficial effects, Spirulina also possesses some other medicinal values which can be seen at a glance from Table 17.5.

Number of pigments are also present in Spirulina. These include chlorophylls, carotenes, xanthines and phycocyanin. Out of these four pigments, phycocyanin is available exclusively from Spirulina. It produces a blue hue. Phycocyanin may be used as a colourant for sherbet, frozen confections, Ice-cream, soft drinks, sweets, etc. Now-a-days in Japan, blue chewing gum is made with the admixture of phycocyanin. Apart from this, phycocyanin helps to improve our body immunity.

TABLE 17.4: Usefulness of Some Ingredients in Spirulina

Ingredient	*Usefulness for our bodies*
Protein	For growth, to build up body muscles and tissues.
Vitamin B-Complex	To prevent beriberi, angular stomatitis, sore tongue, scaly skin, loss of appetite, pellagra, redness and burning sensation of eyes, etc.
Iron	To prevent anaemia and for the formation of haemoglobin.
Calcium	To build up strong bones and teeth, for proper contraction of heart and muscles.
β-Carotene	For the synthesis of Vitamin A and to keep eyes healthy.
Antioxidant	Retards the rate of becoming old.
Phycocyanin	Strengthens the body immunity system further.
G Linolenic Acid (GLA)	To control Cholesterol and keeps the skin tight and glossy

TABLE 17.5: Medicinal Values of Spirulina

* Effective for arthritis.
* Possibility of reduction of cancer (e.g. breast and uterus).
* Possibility of reduction of heart attack.
* Controls blood cholesterol level.
* Controls blood sugar.
* Prevents premature aging.
* Retards old age related problems.
* Free from side reactions.
* Cent percent vegetarian.

In US, Mexico, Chile and India Spirulina is available either in tablet or powder form whereas in Japan and Taiwan it is sold as powder or pellet form. In India, at present it is readily available from the pharmaceutical shops.

CONCLUSION

Although Spirulina has many merits and people have been consuming it as food for generations without any adverse effect but at the same time it has some demerits also. It has a dark green colour which is difficult to mask. Sometimes, it imparts an unfamiliar and bitter flavour. However, technology has been developed now to over come these problems and considering the pros and cons perhaps it will not be in appropriate if Spirulinais described as "a classical health food" or "the most powerful food on the earth".

18
PULSE-PRODUCTION TECHNOLOGY

The recent years have witnessed the growing imbalances in the production of foodgrains. The production achievements in wheat have exceeded the plan targets while the performance of most of the other cereals and millets has not been very satisfactory. Also, unfortunately the performance of pulses has always been below the expectation.

Realising the exceptional potential of pulses by virtue of several inherent advantageous characteristics, immense research efforts have been devoted to upgrade the pulse crops, since the last 2 decades. The All-India Co-ordinated Pulse Improvement Project (AICPIP), involving the ICAR institutes and agricultural universities, has made significant contributions through improved varieties and agrotechniques which offer considerable Potential for increasing the production of pulses.

A twin approach should be to (i) increase the productivity through package of practices and (ii) expand pulse cultivation through time and space as a result of identification of short-duration varieties of pulses for multiple cropping in place of low-yielding crops, and in *kharif* or *rabi* fallow areas wherever possible. The major contribution, however, can be stipulated by raising the productivity of pulses. With the existing technology in terms of improved varieties, fertilisers, Rhizobium cultures and Plant-protection measures, the productivity of pulse crops, like chickpea, pea, lentil and pigeonpea, can be increased substantially, provided these inputs are used judiciously and made available in time to the farmer. In the absence of major inputs, it will be difficult to decide targets of additional production which are likely to remain unfulfilled, keeping in view, the trends of the actual input utilization. The major production of pulses would, however, come from chickpea and pigeonpea. The pulse production can be stabilised if the available improved varieties of these 2 crops are brought under better standards of cultivation and proper crop management. Crop management would include both non-monetary and monetary inputs. Under the AICPIP, the relative role of various inputs has been worked out in detail for the important pulse crops. The data obtained for one such study conducted on chickpea is presented (Table 18.1).

Table 18.1: Effect of various production inputs on grain yield of chickpea (average of data from nine locations)

Treatment	*Grain yield (q/ha)*	*Per cent contribution*
Local practices	13.7	—
Improved package of practices (IPP)	19.0	—
IPP less fertilisers	15.5	18.4
IPP less Rhizobium inoculation	15.9	16.3
IPP less plant protection	16.2	14.7
IPP less weed control	14.0	26.3
IPP less irrigation	16.8	11.6
IPP+Local variety	15.9	—

Source: Chandra, S. 1982. Increasing pulse production in India. In: Constraints and Opportunities, Report. All-India Co-ordinated Pulse Improvement Project.

Another main thrust is expected in the form of introduction of short-duration pulses as a part of the multiple-cropping programme. By virtue of their early maturity or non-photo-insensitivity they can be grown successfully in non-conventional seasons and adopted in well-endowed lands without disturbing the cultivation of high-yielding cereals, cash crops or other economically important dominant components of the rotation.

Pulse-production technology may, however, be viewed as a means of helping farmers for upgrading the production of pulse crops. As the production of pulses increases resulting in increased income, the farmers would also try to spend more and more of their income for procuring the inputs. The potential of the improved technology for the 2 major pulse crops, chickpea and pigeonpea, grown in the main belts has already been demonstrated (Table 18.2).

Table 18.2: Comparative returns from chickpea and pigeonpea grown in the main belts under traditional and improved methods of cultivation

	Chickpea		*Pigeonpea*	
	Traditional method	*Improved method*	*Traditional method*	*Improved method*
Average yield (kg/ha)	900	1,600	800	1,600
Net profit (Rs/ha)	912	1,840	1.335	2,860
Output : input ratio	1.58	1.72	2.25	2.48

Source: Agronomy Report, 1982. All-India Co-ordinated Pulse Improvement Project.

CHOICE OF VARIETY

As a result of the co-ordinated and systematic efforts, a large number of improved varieties of different maturity durations suited to different agroclimatic zones and to various cropping systems have been developed along with appropriate production technologies over the years, through interdisciplinary research efforts. These improved varieties possess better yield potential and have performed convincingly well in farmers' fields under National Demonstrations and Lab-to-Land Programmes. For instance, under better management conditions, the improved varieties of chickpea have given 25-30 q/ha yield as compared with the national average of about 7.5 q/ha. As is evident from Figure 18.1, gaps exist in the production of chickpea between research farms and minikit trials, and the minikit trials and the national average. Similarly the yield of improved varieties of pigeonpea on research plots is 20-25 q/ha as compared to the national average yield of 7.2 q/ha. Improved varieties of other pulses, like greengram, blackgram, cowpea, lentil, etc., have also demonstrated better yield potential ranging from 1015 q/ha as compared with *3-5* q/ha of the local types. All this indicates that improved varieties capable of giving better productivity are available and calls for their immediate adoption for improving the overall production of pulses in the country.

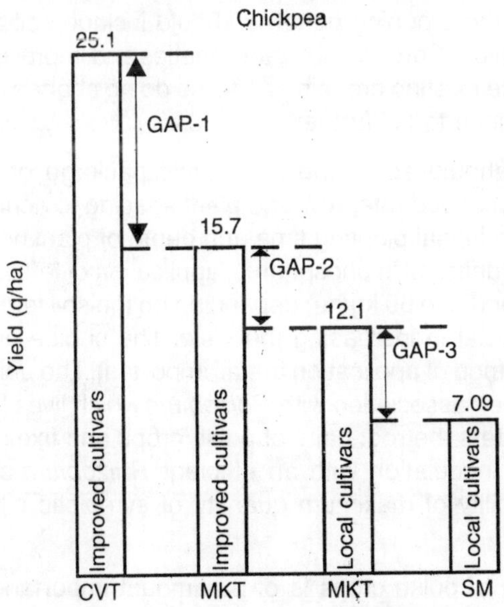

Fig. 18.1. Production gaps in chickpea—information compiled from the Co-ordinated Varietal Trials (CVT), Minikit Trials (MKT) and State Means (SM)) of 4 major chickpea-growing states of Haryana, Rajasthan, Madhya Pradesh and Uttar Pradesh.

However, for each variety, there is a limit beyond which no more manipulation *in* the package of practices can bring about further improvement in yield. Since the yield potentials have already been created, the most important consideration at present for significantly increasing pulse production should be to transfer the existent technology rather than generate higher yield potentials. The latter must remain an important objective, but effective production programmes should be planned at present based on the potentials already created. The plant breeders are continuing further improvement in the production potential of varieties through appropriate change in their genetic make up. With the basic objective of developing varieties better than the existing ones, the plant breeders all over the country have tailored a large array of improved varieties of different pulse crops. For improving production, maximum area must be brought under such improved varieties.

EFFICIENT AGRONOMIC MANAGEMENT

The long-term solution lies in improving the agronomic management of pulse crops in their traditional belts in Madhya Pradesh, Bihar, eastern Uttar Pradesh, Maharashtra and Andhra Pradesh. In these rainfed areas, where the pulse crops predominate, the physical factors which would contribute to the changes in the cropping patterns should include soil and moisture conservation, adoption of drought-tolerant varieties and improved techniques of dry farming. If the existing cropping patterns do no change, the supply of pulses would continue to fall further.

The farmers should adopt the agronomic package of practices as regards the optimum seed rate, row and plant spacing to achieve optimum plant population and ideal planting time and depth of planting. The soils of India are generally deficient in phosphorus; application of fertilisers specially phosphatic fertiliser (30 to 50 kg/ha) depending on the soil fertility, has been found to be beneficial in increasing the yield. The choice of fertiliser, its dose, time and method of application are all important. The unique property of pulse crops is their association with *Rhizobium* which lives freely in soils. The *Rhizobium* enters the root hairs of pulse crops and fixes atmospheric nitrogen. Artificial inoculation with an efficient *Rhizobium* culture would ensure the availability of maximum quantity of symbiotic nitrogen to the crop.

Timely sowing of pulse crops is of paramount importance to get the best out of the varieties, more so in rainfed areas. This factor is overlooked by the farmers as first preference is given to the main crops.

Kharif pulses should be sown immediately after the onset of monsoon. Delay in sowing results in very conspicuous reduction in yields because of decreased growth, increased seedling mortality and sometimes poor germination and attack of pests and diseases. Heavy rainfall adversely affects the sowing of *kharif* pulses. Sowing in the first fortnight of August is preferable to sowing in early or late September. Similarly, early rabi sowing in October is not desirable as compared to November sowing. Sometimes, even early November sowing g of chickpea is faced with the problem of low production owing to high humidity and excessive vegetative growth.

By and large *rabi* pulses, mainly chickpea, lentil and lathyrus, are grown under residual moisture conditions between mid-October and mid-November.

(a) Tillage operation. In high-rainfall areas, it is difficult to sow the crop in time during August, following the conventional method of tillage. Experimental results revealed that the yield of greengram sown by just opening drills between two rows of jute and rice stubble (after their harvest) may be as high as 8-10 q/ha, provided it is adequately protected against weed infestation and receives proper fertilisation. Pulse crops can be established successfully with minimum of tillage.

(b) Date of planting. Most *rabi* crops are sown under rainfed conditions. In such conditions the second fortnight of October appears to be the best and any delay in sowing reduces the grain yields (Table 18.3). However, there could be variation in the response depending upon the variety.

Table 18.3: Grain yield (kg/ha) of certain chickpea genotypes sown on 4 different dates under rainfed conditions

	Planting date			
Genotype	*October 20*	*October 30*	*November 10*	*November 20*
'BG 244'	1,817	1,531	1,331	1.320
'L 550'	1,586	1.620	1,343	1,105
'ICCC 22'	1,433	1,502	2.110	1,962

Source: Agronomy Report.

Wherever plenty of soil moisture is available the date of sowing could be profitably delayed up to mid-November. As such, the optimum date of sowing in chickpea keeps on changing from year to year for the same location, and from location to location during the same year. A consolidated effect of date of planting on the yield of chickpea at different centres is given in Table 18.4.

Normally, the end of October appears to be the suitable time for sowing of other *rabi* crops including lentil, pea and French-beans (rajmash) as seen in Tables 18.5 and 18.6.

Table 18.4: Effect of date of planting on yield (q/ha) of chickpea at different centres under irrigated conditions

Date of planting	*Ludhiana*	*Hisar*	*Delhi*	*Akola*	*Rajendra-nagar*	*Durga-pura*	*Kanpur*
	Average of data obtained from						
	6 years	*3 years*	*3 years*	*3 years*	*3 years*	*3 years*	*3 years*
October 10	14.2	34.3	20.1	183	10.8	—	18.3
October 25	13.8	32.6	21.7	17.4	12.5	14.7	21.3
November 10	10.9	27.5	19.7	14.2	12.3	15.2	24.7
November 24	7.9	21.6	14.4	10.7	11.5	12.7	23.2
December 9	—	—	—	—	—	—	16.8

Source: Agronomy Report, 1982. All-India Co-ordinated Pulse Improvement Project.

Table 18.5: Effect of genotype, planting date and row spacing on the grain yield kg/ha) in pea

Treatment	*Location*				
	Pantnagar	*Samba*	*Pandharpur*	*Varanasi*	*Mean*
Genotype					
HFP 4'	—	1.317	—	1,468	
KPSD 1'	714	828	1.156	1,557	1.064
'Pusa 10'	1,204	1,120	1,445	746	1.129
'Rachana'	1,114	1,185	1,010	1,224	1,441
LSD (P = 0.05)	63	NS	339	121	
Planting date					
October 10	1,117	—	—	—	57
October 25	1,363	2,425	1,766	—	1,851
November 10	1,222	1,031	1,352	—	1,202
LSD(P = 0.05)	81	237	133	—	
Row spacing (cm)					
20	1,177	1,049	—	1,269	1,165
30	1,237	1,176	—	1,228	1,234
LSD (P=0.05)	45			NS	
CV per cent	10.1	3.1		9.3	

Source: Agronomy Report, 1984-85. All-India Co-ordinated Pulse Improvement Project.
NS = Non-significant...

To sum up, for rabi pulses sowing under rainfed condition should be done around the last week of October. For irrigated conditions a delay of 5-20 days is desirable.

Table 18.6: Effect of genotype and planting date on grain yield (kg/ha) of rajmash at Pandharpur

Planting date	*Grain yield (kg/ha)*	*Genotype*	*Grain yield (kg/ha)*
October 15	1,192	PDR 14'	1,651
October 31	2,312	Waghya'	1,466
November 14	1,838	'V 2-63'	1,885
December 1	1,357		
LSD(P=0.05)	551	SE	141
		LSD (P=0.05)	NS

Source: Agronomy Report, 1984-85. All-India Co-ordinated Pulse Improvement Project.
NS = Non-significant.

The sowing of kharif pulses is generally done with the onset of rains. It has been found in many instances that achieving a good crop stand before the rains always results in higher yield. But this will require at least a pre-sowing irrigation, as has been clearly shown in pigeonpea, a major kharif crop (Table 18.7).

Table 18.7: Grain yield (q/ha) of pigeonpea as influenced by the date of planting

Planting date	*Varieties*			*Mean*
	TT6'	*T 21'*	*'290-21'*	
June 1, 1981	23.00	24.57	16.19	21.25
June 15, 1981	19.70	23.28	16.65	19.69
June30, 1981	15.58	17.86	15.37	16.27
Mean	19.75	21.90	16.07	
	Dates	Dates X Varieties		
SE	0.49	0.98		
CD (5%)	1.55	2.87		

Source: Deshmukh, R.B. and Bhapkar, D.G. 1982. Report, All-India Co-ordinated Pulse Improvement Project, Rahuri Centre.

For summer mungbean, which has come into prominence because of short- duration varieties, the end of March appears to be the best for sowing in northern India (Table 18.8). Any further delay not only reduces yield but creates problems for the sowing of the main kharif crops.

(c) Seed treatment. Germination of pulse crops is often affected due to a number of soil-borne fungi. An effective as well as a cheap technology is to treat the seeds before sowing with fungicides, like Captan, Bavistin, Brassicol or Thiram @ 2.5 g/kg of seed. Such treatments have proved very useful in bringing down the incidence of the soil-borne as well as seed-borne fungi in early stages of crop growth.

Table 18.8: Effect of genotype and planting date on grain yield (kg/ha) of summer mungbean

Planing date	*Yield of cultivar (kg/ha)*		
	'PS 16' (IARI)	*'K 851',(Uttar Pradesh)*	*'C 65'(Punjab)*
March 2l	790	940	760
March 3l	1,100	1,300	890
April 10	910	920	560
April 20	360	480	340

Source: Agronomy Report. 1982. All-India Co-ordinated Pulse Improvement Project.

SEED GERMINATION

There is no seed dormancy in pulse crops under field conditions and if enough moisture is available, the seedlings appear within 7-10 days after sowing. However, there is a certain percentage of hard seeds, especially in the *Vigna* group of crops. These seeds do not imbibe water and hence fail to germinate. The formation of hard seed coat is a function of environmental conditions prevailing at the time of crop maturity. The farmer can easily determine the percentage of hard seeds by simply soaking the seed sample in excess of water overnight. A seed lot containing a high percentage of hard seeds should not be used, or alternatively, its seed rate should be calculated accordingly.

Seed germination is also affected by the depth of sowing. Both hypogeal and epigeal mode of germination are found in pulses. *Rabi* pulses including chickpea, pea lentil and lathyrus follow hypogeal mode of germination wherein the cotyledons are left behind in the soil (Fig. 18.2). Sowing such seeds deep down neither delays nor retards germination. On the other hand the *kharif* pulses, excepting pigeonpea, show epigeal mode of germination wherein the cotyledons are first to emerge from the soil (Fig. 18.3). Naturally, such seeds if sown deep will fall to germinate. It is therefore, necessary that during *kharif,* when adequate moisture is available owing to the rains, the seeds should be sown superficially *and in* loose soil.

USE OF FERTILISERS

Since pulses have the capacity to fix nitrogen owing to their symbiotic relationship with the soil-inhabiting Rhizobium, supply of high doses of nitrogen by application of chemical fertilisers inactivates the inherent plant system. This results in substitution of the nitrogen supply source rather than supplementation. However, initial application of a small dose of nitrogen @ 15-20 kg/ha is beneficial. This helps the plant especially during the seedling stage.

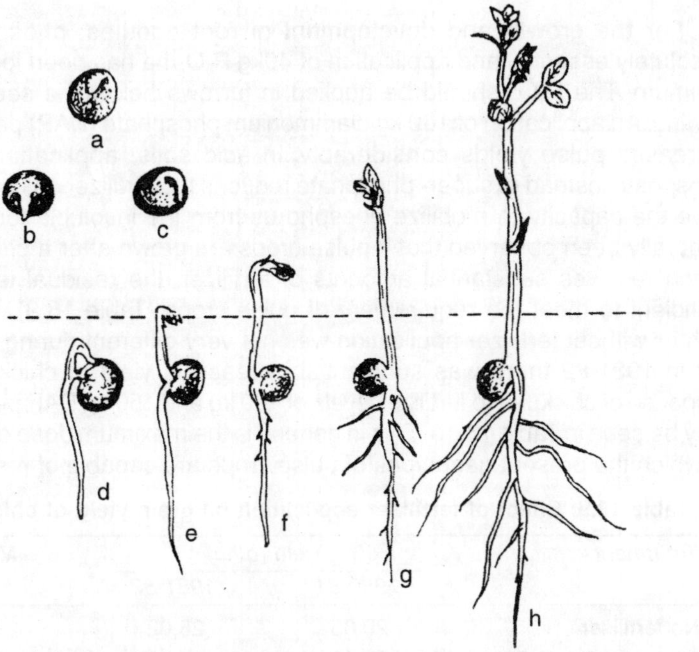

Fig. 18.2. Stages in hypogeal mode of germination in pea.

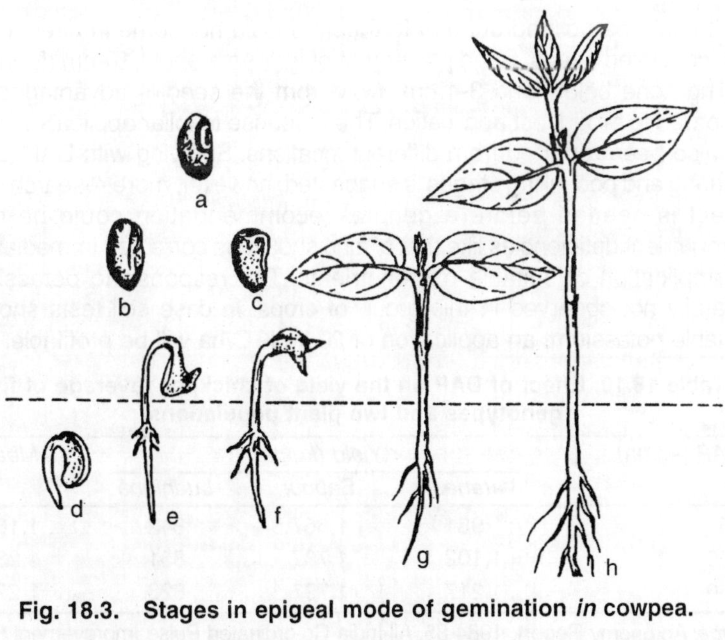

Fig. 18.3. Stages in epigeal mode of gemination *in* cowpea.

For the growth and development of root nodules, phosphorus is absolutely essential and application of 40kg P_2O_5/ha has been found to be optimum. The P_2O_5 should be applied in furrows below the seed before sowing. An application of 100 kg diammonium phosphate (DAP) per hectare increases pulse yields considerably. In acid soils, application of rock phosphate instead of super- phosphate reduces the fertilizer cost, as pulses have the capacity to mobilize phosphorus from the insoluble form. It has generally been observed that if pulse crops are grown after a cereal crop, which receives substantial amounts of fertilizer, the residual fertilizer is sufficient to meet the requirement of pulse crops (Table 18.9). The yield with or without fertilizer application was not very different during 1980-81, but in 1981-82 there was substantial increase in yield of chickpea. The response of chickpea to fertilizer levels of 100 kg and 150 kg DAP per hectare may be seen in Table 18.10. This in general is the maximum dose of fertilizer to which the present genotypes of pulse crops are capable of responding.

Table 18.9: Effect of fertiliser application on grain yield of chickpea

Treatment	*Yield (q/ha)*		*Mean*
	1980-81	*1981-82*	
No fertiliser	20.05	25.02	22.55
25kg N+50kg P_2O_5/ha	21.46	28.93	25.21

Source: Deshmukh, R.B. and Bhapkar, D.G. Report, 1982. All-India Co-ordinated Pulse Improvement Project. Rahuri Centre.

It might be pointed out that fertilisers should not come in direct contact with inoculated seeds. Band placement of fertilisers about 10-cm deep in the feeding zone below and 3-4 cm away from the seed is advantageous as compared to broadcast application. The response to foliar application of DAP has also been reported from different locations. Spraying with DAP (2%) at flowering and pod- filling stages is suggested, however, more research on this aspect is needed before a general recommendation could be made. Micronutrient deficiencies like that of zinc should be corrected immediately by the application of suitable micronutrients. The response to potassium is generally not observed in this group of crops. In case soil tests show low available potassium, an application of 20 kg K_2O/ha will be profitable.

Table 18.10: Effect of DAP on the yield of chickpea (average of five genotypes and two plant populations)

DAP (kg/ha)	*Yield (kg/ha)*			*Mean*
	Varanasi	*Sabour*	*Ludhiana*	
75	981	1,667	842	1.163
100	1,102	1,737	851	1,230
150	1,217	1,797	823	1 279

Source: Agronomy Report, 1984-85. All-India Co-ordinated Pulse Improvement Project.

RHIZOBIUM INOCULATION

Rhizobium inoculation of legume crops has long been considered an important factor for increasing yields. Experimental evidence suggests that anything up to 100% of the nitrogen requirement of pulse crops can be met with by providing efficient strains of *Rhizobium* coupled with sound agronomic practices. Not only do pulses meet their own requirement, but they also leave behind sufficient residual nitrogen for the succeeding crop. Studies reveal that generally 20-40 kg/ha of residual nitrogen may be left unused, although the amount varies with the crop, season and other factors. Owing to the important role of pulses in nitrogen economy of the cropping systems the Government of India is laying emphasis on increasing pulse production. Consequently, many microbiological laboratories have started producing *Rhizobium* culture and substantial funds are being provided to build up their laboratories.

Rhizobium, the bacterium found in the root nodules of leguminous plants, has the capacity to fix atmospheric nitrogen. By virtue of this, pulses have been used in different crop rotations. To activate the process of nodulation efficient *Rhizobium* cultures should be inoculated into the seeds. *Rhizobium* strains are variable in their performance. They are also specific to particular crops and even to a variety of a particular crop (Table 18.11). Efficient specific strains need to be isolated, tested and multiplied, and only suitable cultures should be supplied to farmers.

Table 18.11: Overall performances *of Rhizobium* strains and their interaction with different cultivars of chickpea at Hisar

Chickpea cultivar	*Rhizobium strain*	*Yield (q/ha)*		*Increase over control*	
		Control	*Inoculated*	*q/ha*	*Per cent*
'C 235'	F75'	21.20	28.40	7.20	34
	'F6'	21.20	27.60	6.40	30
	'Ca 11'	21.20	25.60	4.40	21
	'KG 31'	21.20	21.80	0.60	3
BG 209'	'Ca181'	26.00	28.90	2.90	11
	'F 75'	26.00	26.80	0.82	3
'Pant 114'	'KG 31'	21.40	32.00	10.60	50
	'F6'	21.40	28.70	7.30	34
	'Ca 181'	21.40	26,00	4.60	21
	F75'	21.40	25.90	4.50	21

Source : Microbiology Report, 1984. All-India Co-ordinated Pulse Improvement Project.

As *Rhizobium* use is a very low-cost input, it is necessary that the arrangements may be made for the mass-scale production of such bacterial cultures, and also for their proper storage and speedy distribution to farmers. The Gujarat State Co-operative Marketing Federation, Ahmedabad; Maharashtra Agro-Industries Corporation, Pune; National Agricultural Co-operative and Marketing Federation of India and the State Department of Agriculture in the different states are presently doing this type of work (for details *see* Annexures 18 and 19), however, the work needs to be streamlined and expanded. Many more units are being set up for the manufacture of *Rhizobium,* both in the private and public sectors.

The rhizobial cultures are available in packets of 250 g with a suitable carrier, such as peat, lignite, etc. The proper use of *Rhizobium* culture has been given in Annexure 16. About 10kg of seed, enough for one acre, is thoroughly mixed with the slurry of bacteria along with a carrier, dried under shade and sown as early as possible preferably the same evening or the next morning. Specific cultures are available for different pulses. In acidic or alkaline soils pelleting of the inoculated seed with $CaCO_3$ or $CaSO_4$ is very helpful.

If the seeds are dressed with fungicides, a double dose of bacterial culture may be used. Fungicides like Thiram, Captan, etc. @ 2.5-3.0 g/kg of seed are recommended to eliminate seed-borne inoculum and to ensure better germination. It should, however, be remembered that seed treatment with fungicides should precede and not follow the *Rhizobium* culture treatment. Mercurial preparations of fungicides like Ceresan should not be used if rhizobial inoculation is to be carried Out.

Experiments indicate that the seed inoculated before sowing with efficient strains of *Rhizobium* result in higher grain yields ranging from 3 to 50% over the uninoculated control (Table 18.11). In areas where pulses were not grown earlier, enormous yield increases were obtained due to *Rhizobium* treatment of seeds.

To successfully exploit the available technology, strict quality-control standards may be followed and proper extension services may be made available to the farmers. The Bureau of Indian Standards has specified the standards for *Rhizobium* inoculants, and it is imperative on the part of manufacturers to adopt these specifications so that farmers are provided with quality cultures.

The major limiting factors in rhizobial inoculation are the availability of the right type of culture to the farmers at the right time, and in adequate quantity. These factors are to be taken care of while popularizing rhizobial inoculation ,so that bad experience may not antagonize the farmer from using it. The efficacy of *Rhizobium* inoculation has been demonstrated on farmers' fields with extensive trials (Table 18.12) with a very high input : output ratio (Table 18.13).

Table 18.12: Response to *Rhizobium* inoculation at farmers' fields

Location	*Crop*	*Yield (q/ha)*		*Increase over control*	
		Control	*Inoculated*	*q/ha*	*Per cent*
Bangalore	Cowpea	9.00	9.50	0.50	6
	Blackgram	11.90	12.10	0.20	2
	Greengram	2.50	2.70	0.20	8
Navgaon	Chickpea	10.57	11.37	0.80	8
Ludhiana	Chickpea				
	location 1	3.80	3.92	0.12	3
	location 2	4.80	5.50	0.70	15
Berhampore	Chickpea				
	location 1	5.62	7.12	1.50	27
	location 2	5.82	5.88	0.06	1
Lam	Greergram	5.18	7.15	1.97	38
	Blackgram	9.45	10.30	0.85	9
Berhampore	Lentil				
	location 1	4.00	5.80	1.80	45
	location 2	5.67	6.69	1.02	18
	location 3	8.20	8.08	(–)0.12	
Berhampore	Pea				
	location 1	5.00	6.44	1.44	29
	location 2	5.49	6.00	0.51	9
Badnapur	Chickpea				
	location 1	7.00	8.42	1.40	20
	location 2	7.30	8.12	0.84	11
	location 3	6.45	7.69	1.24	19
	location 4	7.50	9.00	1.50	20
	location 5	7.50	8.57	1.07	14

Source: Microbiology Report, 1985. All-India Co-ordinated Pulse improvement Project.

Table 18.13: Input: output ratio in cultivation of pulses

Component	*Ratio*
Control: Rhizobium Inoculation (1)	1:1.5
Control: Phosphorus (P)	1:1.7
Control: I+P	1:1.8
Control: 1+ P +Weeding+ Plant Protection (package of practices)	1:2.4

LIMING

In the lateritic acid soil of the eastern hilly areas, liming is also very important for the production of pulses. In high-rainfall areas in the leached alluvial acidic soils, good response to liming in soybean has been reported (Chatterjee *et* at., 1972*). Research work on this aspect with reference to other pulses is very much limited.

USE OF MICRONUTRIENTS IN PROBLEMATIC SOILS

Molybdenum and iron are cofactors of the enzyme nitrogenase which mediates the fixation of atmospheric nitrogen. Sulphur and cobalt have clearly defined special roles. Boron deficiency prevents meristematic and vascular development of root nodules; perhaps, there is poorer translocation of the element to nodules than to other meristems in the plant. Molybdenum deficiency is most common in acid soils and can be corrected by liming. Low pH, low calcium, high aluminium and high manganese have also proved to be inhibitors of legume nodulation.

RESPONSE TO IRRIGATION

Experimental results clearly show that chickpea, lentil and pigeonpea, and other *rabi* pulses give increased yields if receding soil moisture is judiciously supplemented by irrigation (Tables 18.14-18.17).

Table 18.14: Effect of irrigation on grain yield of chickpea

Irrigation treatment	*Grain yield (q/ha)*
No irrigation	10.12
One irrigation at flowering stage	13.29
One irrigation at pod-development stage	14.37
Two irrigations one at flowering and one at pod-development stage	17.13

Source: Agronomy Report, 1982. All-India Co-ordinated Pulse Improvement Project

It must be kept in mind that though pulses in general will respond to one or two irrigations under moisture-stress conditions, the same irrigation can in fact reduce yields, if applied under situations when the moisture is not limiting. Thus, depending upon the residual moisture from monsoon, as well as winter rainfall, *rabi* pulses can give better yields with no irrigation to two or three irrigations, though the two situations are encountered during exceptional years. It is quite clear that pre-sowing irrigation appears to be essential, followed by one or two irrigations depending upon the state of soil moisture (Table 18.17).

*Chatterjee. B.N., Roy, B.. Maity, S. and Roquib. M.A. 1972. *Indian Journal of Agricultural Sciences* 42:130-4.

Table 18.15: Grain yield and economics of lentil under different irrigation levels at Pantnagar

Crop	*Number of irrigations*	*Gram yield (kg/ha)*	*Cost of cultivation (Rs/ha)*	*Gross return (Rs/ha)*	*Net return (Rs/ha)*
Lentil ('L 9-12')	Nil	1,632	1,326	3,264	1,938
	One	1,927	1,392	3,854	2,462
	Two	2,085	1,448	4,170	2,722

Source: Pandya. B.P. and Pandya, M.P. 1982. All-India Co-ordinated Pulse Improvement Project, Pantnagar Centre.

Table 18.16: Effect of irrigation on grain yield of pigeonpea

Irrigation treatment	*Grain yield of various cultivars (q/ha)*			*Mean*
	'TT6'	*'T21'*	*'N 290-21'*	
No irrigation	18.42	19.80	16.21	18.14
Two irrigations	20.48	24.01	15.93	20.14
	Irrigation	*Varieties*	*Irrigation X Varieties*	
SE	0.40	0.57	0.80	
CD (5%)	1.27	1.65	2.33	

Source: Deshmukh, R.B. and Bhapkar, D.G. 1982. All-India Co-ordinated Pulse Improvement Project. Rahuri Centre

Table 18.17: Effect of irrigation on grain yield (kg/ha) of some pulse crops

Location	*Crop*	*Irrigation levels*			
		No irrigation	*Pre-sowing irrigation (P)*	*P+one irrigation 40 days after sowing*	*P+2 irrigations 40+70 days after sowing*
Rahuri	Chickpea	657	1,114	1,713	2,077
	Field-pea	563	861	1.241	1,583
	Chickpea	513	639	999	1,158
Kanke	Lentil	611	667	1,014	806

Source: Agronomy Report, 1984-85. All-India Co-ordinated Pulse Improvement Project.

WEEDING AND INTERCULTURING

Weeds compete with the crops for the plant nutrients, space and light, and thus considerably reduce the yields by 40 to 100%. Pulse crops initially grow slowly, and so suffer because of the fast-growing weeds. The first *25* to 40 days are very critical for short-duration kharif pulses, and the first 45 to 60 days for medium- and late-maturing crops like pigeonpea. One or two interculturing and hand weedings during this stage are generally sufficient for weed control. Line sowing is also helpful for interculture operations through bullock-drawn implements and hand-hoes.

Chemical weed control is useful and economical also under certain situations. By using pre-emergence weedicides, the pressure on manual labour for timely and early weeding is reduced. The promising weedicides for pulses are Alachlor (1.0kg/ha), Prometryne *(0.5* kg/ha), Dosanex (1.0 kg/ha) and Nitrofen (1.0 kg/ ha); incorporation of Basalin (1.0 kg/ha) into the soil at pre-planting is also recommended (Table 31).

Table 18.18: Effect of weed-control measures on grain yield in chickpea

Treatment	*Grain yield (q/ha)*	*Per cent increase in yield*
Weedy check (control)	8.43	
Weed-free check (hand-weeding)	14.16	60.8
One mechanical hand-weeding	10.77	27.7
Two mechanical hand-weedings	12.48	48.0
Basalin @ 0.5 kg ai/ha	10.85	28.7
Basalin@ 1.0 kg ai/ha	11.31	34.1
Stomp @ 0.75 kg ai/ha	11.16	32.4
Ronstor @ 1.5 kg ai/ha	11.29	34.0

The results of the All-India Co-ordinated pulse Improvement Projection all the major pulse crops indicate that one or at the most two hand-weedings are more efficient in controlling the weeds than is the use of weedicides. It is, therefore, recommended that wherever labour is available, the practice of hand-weeding should be followed.

Intercropping with smothering pulse crops like greengram and blackgram, in alternate rows, or with one row of legume alternating with paired rows of the direct- seeded main crop, controls weeds effectively and has proved most remunerative. The best results have been obtained by sowing blackgram in between single and paired rows of the main crop; after first weeding and 20 days after sowing of the main crop.

PLANT-PROTECTION MEASURES

There are a number of diseases and insect pests which cause heavy losses resulting in poor production. Although, the most effective plant-protection measures would be in developing resistant varieties through genetic manipulation, it would be a long-term process. Until such varieties are available certain effective and economical plant-protection schedules that have been developed so far, for the avoidance of losses due to insect pests, like pod-borers in pigeonpea, chickpea, pea and lentil; galerucid beetles and jassids in greengram, blackgram, mothbean and cowpea; and powdery-mildew in pea, greengram, blackgram, etc. may be followed. No doubt, farmers are gradually adopting chemical control measures in high-return crops. But with comparatively small holdings and poor economy in pulse cultivation, farmers have to be motivated to adopt recommended plant-protection schedules to minimise the losses. Interestingly, the control of these major pests is rather easy, with the help of specific pesticides available in our country. Therefore, there is a need to adopt and popularise simple pest-control techniques, which will not only save the farmer a good deal of produce but will also help in stabilising the productivity of pulses. Attempts are also on to evolve effective biological control for certain pests of pulse crops, especially at the International Crops Research Institute for the Semi-arid Tropics (ICRISAT). However, commercial application is yet to commence.

Diseases. Some of the diseases of pulse crops have been widespread in different parts of the country for a long time, like wilt, blight diseases of chickpea and pigeonpea and also virus complex disease of chickpea, pigeonpea, greengram blackgram, cowpea and mothbean. Others, like sterility-mosaic virus of pigeonpea, *Ascochyta-blight* and *Botrytis* (grey-mould) in chickpea which hitherto were considered as minor diseases have assumed serious proportions. There is no effective and economical chemical control for these diseases. However, some of the varieties and agrotechnology developed by the scientists of the AICPIP of the ICAR and ICRISAT have indicated a high degree of resistance to these diseases, and thus losses can be minimised to a great extent. Another common disease is the powdery-mildew in pea, blackgram and greengram For this, sulphur dusting @25 kg/ha or sulphur spray in the form of Sulfex 0.3% has given encouraging results. Table 18.19 summarizes the effect of sulphur on the incidence of powdery-mildew in greengram.

Insect pests. Different pulse crops, like chickpea, pigeonpea, pea and others, suffer from very heavy incidence *of Heliothis (pod-borers)* which cause 30 to 90% damage. Interestingly, the control of this major pest is rather easy, with the use of pesticides, like BHC, DDT or Endosulfan, available in the country. In other *kharif* pulses, like greengram, blackgram, horsegram, mothbean and cowpea, leaf-eating insects and sucking insects, like galerucid beetles and jassids, cause heavy losses. Systemic insecticides, like Disulfoton or Phorate, effectively control the pest complex for a period of 4-6 weeks. In case, the infestation of any insect pest is noticed after this, the crops may be protected with a foliar spray of insecticides as mentioned above.

As a result of continuous research efforts at the IARI and other centres under the AICPIP effect of plant-protection measures on yields of different pulses have been worked out, the results of one such study are presented (Table 18.20).

Research work is in progress to develop chickpea varieties with high and stabilised yields by identification and incorporation of resistance to diseases like *Ascochyta-blight,* wilt and root-rot, and to insect pests like pod-borer. The following are the important donors or varieties of chickpea that may be sources of resistance to major diseases.

Disease	*Sources of resistance or tolerance*
Wilt	'P436-2', 'P231', 'P229', 'P391', 'P 692', 'P 858', 'P 1611','P 2089'. 'P 3183','P 3382', 'P 5901', 'P 8933'. 'P 11088'. 'P 4313-2-93, 'JG 74', 'JG 315', 'WR 315', 'H(WR) 355'
Root-rot	'H(WR) 355', 'K 295', 'P315' ('Kailash')
Ascochyta-blight	'G 12-34', '062-18', 'GG 588'. 'C 235', 'H 75-35', 'H 8 1-73', 'BG 257'. 'BG 261', 'ILC 72', 'ILC 2380', 'ILC 2957'
Wilt + Dry root-rot	'ICC 925'. 'ICC 12437'. 'ICC 12444', 'ICC 12450', 'ICC 12454'. 'ICC 12460'. 'ICC 12467', 'ICC 12472'
Wilt + Grey-mould	'ICC 11321', 'ICCL 80004'
Wilt + Blight	'ICC 3935'
Grey-mould + Blight	'ICC 1069'

The different sources of resistance available are being used in breeding programmes and in developing varieties possessing disease and pest resistance so as to minimise damage and impart yield stability.

For imparting stability to the production and minimise losses in pigeonpea due to diseases and pests, efforts have been made to identify sources of resistance and to incorporate these in agronomically suitable background. The following are the important donors or varieties of pigeonpea possessing resistance or tolerance to diseases.

Disease	*Sources of resistance or tolerance*
Wilt	'NP(WR) 15'. 'C 11'. 'Mukta', 'BDN 1'. 'ICPL 295'. 'ICPL 270', 'ICPL 337', 'ICPL 353','ICPL 338', 'DT 250', 'AWR 75115', 'ICPL 8863'. 'Bande Palore'
Sterility-mosaic virus	'Pant A3'. 'ICPL 343', 'ICPL 345', 'EMSMER 1', 'ICPL 341', 'ICPL 346', 'BSMR 2', 'Basant', 'Bahar'
Stem-blight	'Pant A 3', 'BDN l', 'ICPL 7065'. 'AS 3'

During the past few years, research emphasis in pigeonpea breeding has been on the development of new plant types. Efforts are being made to incorporate desirable characteristics such as reduced maturity, high harvest index, relatively determinate growth habit and significant response to increase in plant population. The dwarf and erect varieties of pigeonpea have the potential of being one of the components in intercropping systems. The dwarf varieties possess better harvest index and give better yields. In addition to the genetic dwarfism, agronomic dwarfism has been obtained in Bihar by sowing the crop in September-October instead of June-July, resulting in reduced vegetative growth and better yields.

Table 18.19: Effect of sulphur on the incidence of powdery-mildew in greengram

Treatment	*Per cent disease index*	*Yield (kg/ha)*	*Per cent increase in yield*
Control	21.76	288	—
Sulphur dust @ 25 kg/ha	5.38	359	24.65
Sulphur spray @ 0.3% Sulfex	4.92	409	42.01
SE	93.04	14	
CD(5%)	NS	38	

Source: Report, 1981. All- India Co-ordinated Pulse Improvement Project, Rahuri Centre. NS = Non-significant.

Table 18.20. Effect of plant-protection measures on yield of different pulses

Crop	*Variety*	*Yield (kg/ha)*			*% Avoidable*
		Untreated control (T)	*Treated with insecticide (C)*	*Increase in yield (kg/ha) (C-T)*	*loss* $\frac{C-T}{C} \times 100$
Greengram	'T2'	560	1,180	620	53
	'S9'	144	522	378	72
	'Pusa Baisakhi'	27	870	843	97
	'PS 7'	36	872	836	96
Pigeonpea	'S 8'	1,108	2,042	934	46
Blackgram	'S 1'	257	874	617	71
Chickpea	'T3'	1,225	1,716	491	29
Pea	'T163'	1.179	1,757	678	35

Source: Saxena, H.P. 1984. Control of pests to increase pulse production. In: *Pulse Production Constraints and Opportunities* (eds) H.C. Srivastava, S. Bhaskaran, K.K.G. Menon, S. Ramanujam and M.V. Rao, Oxford and IBH Publishing Co., New Delhi, pp. 269-72.

One of the major causes for poor yields in greengram is the occurrence of various diseases most importantly the yellow-mosaic viral disease. Development of disease- and pest—resistant varieties is an important aspect of green gram improvement programme. The donors or varieties of greengram identified/ developed for possessing resistance to certain diseases and pests are listed below.

Disease or Pests	*Sources of resistance or tolerance*
Cercospora leaf-spot	'11/99'
Macrophomina-blight	'PIMS 3', 'PIMS 4'
Yellow-mosaic virus	'11/99', 'ML 1', 'ML 5'. 'Hyb4-3', 'Hyb I2-4', 'ML 353', 'ML 371', 'MUG 125', 'PDM 62'
Pests	'ML267'. 'ML325'. 'IM529'

In blackgram varieties like 'T 9', 'T 27', 'Mash 40'. 'Khargaon 3', 'Pant U 19' and 'Pant U 30' have shown wide acceptability. These and other improved varieties need extensive popularisation.

As a result of breeding for disease resistance in blackgram the following donors or varieties have now been identified.

Disease or Pests	*Sources of resistance or tolerance*
Yellow-mosaic virus	'Mash 1-1', 'NP 16', 'NP 19', 'NP 21', 'K 86-10'. 'UG 133'
Powdery-mildew	'LU 188', 'Pant U19'. 'LBG 17'
Cercospora leaf-spot	'Pant U 19'
Pests	'LU 178'. 'LU 190'. 'LU 397'. 'UG 251', 'PU 19', 'PU 30'

Recently, the concept of new plant type has been introduced in developing better varieties of cowpea. The traditional varieties are highly photosensitive, late-maturing, trailing and/or of spreading nature. The improved plant type is visualised to have erect and compact growth habit, so that a higher plant population can be accommodated per unit area and better yields can be obtained. The attempts made at the TARI have been successful and 3 varieties, namely, 'V 16', 'V 37', and 'V 38', have been developed. Among the already existent cultivars 'C *152'*, 'FS 68', 'Pusa Phalguni', 'Pusa Dofasali', etc. are more promising and need large-scale adoption.

The varieties of lentil which have shown wide adaptability are 'L 9-12', 'Pant L 610', 'Pant L209', 'Pant L409' and 'T36'. However, wilt of lentil continues to be the major cause for poor yields, more so under rainfed conditions; 67 varieties were tested for wilt resistance at Dholi, and varieties 'GL *534', 'GL* 535' and LP 212' were found promising. Another disease which is important at certain locations is the lentil-rust. The 3 wilt-resistant varieties also show good resistance to rust, so their large-scale cultivation needs to be encouraged.

Pea varieties 'T 163', 'Hans' and 'EC 33866' have become popular. A recently developed variety 'Rachana' possesses resistance to powdery-mildew, and is likely to become popular in all the pea-growing areas of the country. However, diseases like powdery-mildew and to some extent rust and wilt continue to take a heavy toll. Varieties 'NDP 1', 'IP 928', 'JP 179', 'JP 885' and 'Batri Brown' have been found promising, showing resistance to rust. There is an urgent need to evolve more varieties resistant to powdery-mildew, which is a widespread disease.

19
Fermented Soya Products

Main fermented vegetable protein foods in Japan and China are soy sauce (shoyu in Japan, chiang-yu in China), fermented soy paste (miso in Japan, chiang in China), safu, and natto, which are all traditional foods. Chiang, which originated in China some 2,500 years ago, was introduced into Japan during the seventh century and transformed into the present Japanese shoyu and miso, which are now quite different from their Chinese counterparts. Their fermentations consist of koji fermentation by Aspergillus species and subsequent by brine, which contains lactic acid and alcoholic fermentations. The characteristic appetising aroma observed in Japanese style of soy sauce (shoyu) is derived through a special brine fermentation from the component of wheat which constitutes about one-half of the materials. During the recent 2 decades, the fermentation technology and engineering on shoyu and miso have made great progress in Japan. Sufu (Chinese soybean cheese) is a cheese-like product; originated in China in the fifth century. It is made through the fermentation by Mucor or a related mould from soybean protein curd called tofu, which is made by coagulating soy milk. This product is widely manufactured in China on a small scale, but it is not made and consumed in Japan. On the other hand, natto is the fermented soybean protein food common in Japan. It is a whole soybean product fermented by Bacillus species, and has originated in north-eastern Japan.

MISO

The Japanese fermented soya paste miso is now manufactured commercially in modernised factories on a large scale. There are many differences in the way fermented soybean pastes are consumed in Japan and in China. In China, chiang is used as the base for sauces served with meat, sea food, poultry, or vegetable dishes. In Japan, however, miso is mainly used as the base for soups. The average annual consumption of miso is 7.2 kg/ person in Japan.

The manufacturing methods for miso differ by the type of miso, but the basic process is all the same as shown in Fig. 19.1 for rice miso which is the most popular miso.

Miso can be classified into 3 major types (rice miso, barley miso, and soybean miso) on the basis of the raw materials. Rice miso is made from rice, soybean, and salt; barley miso is made from barley, soybean, and salt; and soybean miso is made from soybeans and salt. These types, are further classified by the taste into 3 groups, viz, sweet miso, semi-sweet miso, and salty miso. Each group is further divided by colour into white-yellow miso and red-brown miso. Among these miso, rice miso is the most popular one, forming 81% of the total miso consumption.

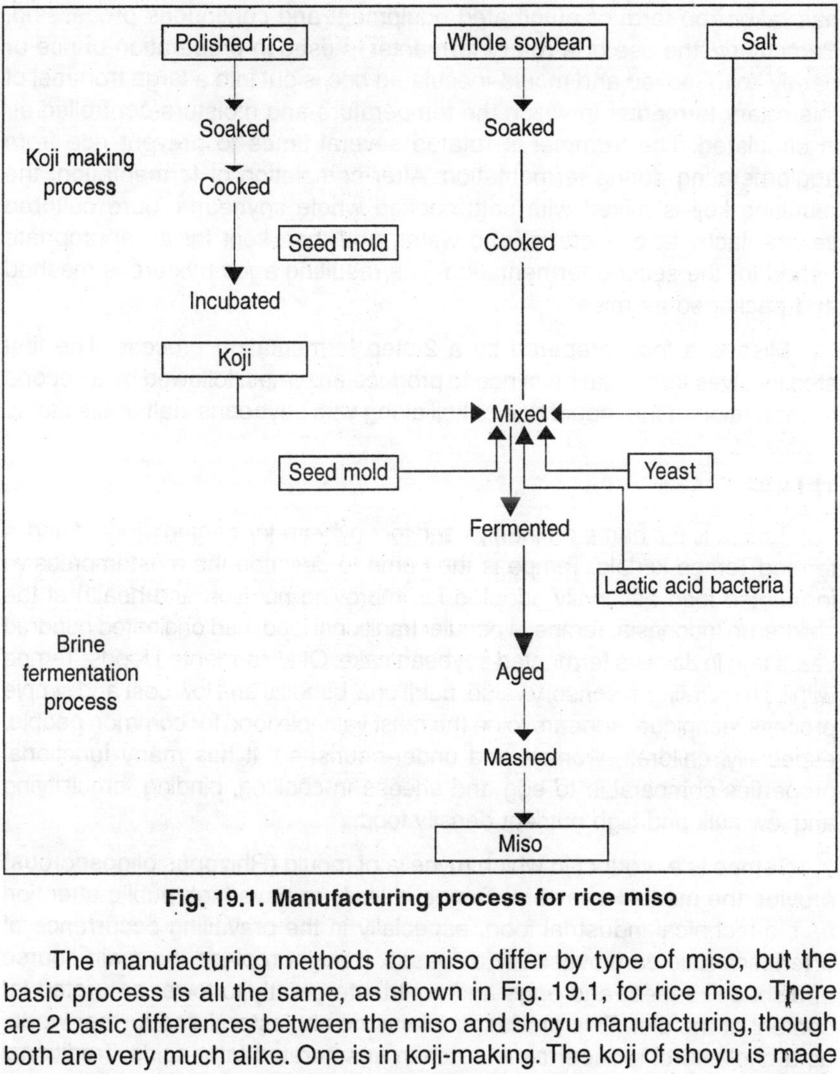

Fig. 19.1. Manufacturing process for rice miso

The manufacturing methods for miso differ by type of miso, but the basic process is all the same, as shown in Fig. 19.1, for rice miso. There are 2 basic differences between the miso and shoyu manufacturing, though both are very much alike. One is in koji-making. The koji of shoyu is made by using all the raw materials, that is, the mixture of soybean and wheat, whereas the koji of miso is made by using only carbohydrate materials, that is, rice or barley. The soybean is used in miso making without the inoculation of koji mould, except on soybean miso. The other difference is that miso is a solid paste, and therefore the making process has no filtration step, which has a very large influence on the cost in shoyu-making. The fungus and yeast used in miso manufacturing are very similar and sometimes the same as in shoyu manufacturing.

Recently, a revolution has occurred in the manufacture of miso, which has taken the form of automated equipment and continuous processing. Particularly, the use of a rotary fermenter is used in preparation of rice or barley koji. Cooked and mould-inoculated rice is put into a large trommel of this rotary fermenter in which the temperature and moisture-controlled air is circulated. The trommel is rotated several times to prevent rice from agglomerating during fermentation. After completion of fermentation, the resulting koji is mixed with salt, cooked whole soybeans, pure cultured yeasts, lactic acid bacteria, and water, and then kept for an appropriate period for the second fermentation. The resulting aged mixture is mashed and packaged as miso.

Miso is a food prepared by a 2-step fermentation process. The first step involves fermentation of rice to produce enzymes, followed by a second fermentation of the mould rice or koji along with soybeans, salt and suitable inoculum.

TEMPE

Tempe is the name ordinarily used for soybean-fermented product and is termed Tempe-kedale. Tempe is the name to describe the most impressive fermented food nationally adopted for improving nutrition and health of the children in Indonesia. Tempe, a popular traditional food, had originated hundred years ago in Java as fermented soybean cake. Of all fermented foods, Tempe with its high rating in sensory value, nutritional benefits and low cost and simple process technique, appears to be the most valuable food for common people, especially, children, women and under-nourished. It has many functional properties comparable to egg and cheese in cooking, binding, emulsifying and low bulk and high nutrient density food.

Tempe is a product in which mycelia of mould (Rhizopus oligosporous) provide the meat-like texture. Tempe is likely to have high public attention as bio-technical industrial food, especially in the prevailing occurrence of arteriosclerotic cardiovascular diseases. It might replace the main course of dishes like meat and eggs and contribute greatly to lower saturated fat content of the diet. This product contains no cholesterol and further works as a cholesterol reducer as it is rich in unsaturated fatty acids. Traditional method of its preparation with soybean is given in Fig. 19.2.

Soybean whole (1 kg)
↓
Clean and wash
↓
Boil (30 min)
↓
Wash and soak overnight (17 hr)
↓
Dehull (remove hulls on floatation in water)
↓
Steam for 45 mm. (until cooked but not too soft)
↓
Surface dry
↓
Mix well with 25 ml (1 1/2 tablespoon) of vinegar in a vessel (adjust pH 4.0-4.5)
↓
Inoculate (2 g tempe culture kg soybean)
↓
Pack evenly in perforated polythene pouches and seal
↓
Incubate in humid and warm place (40 hr), 320 to 36°C
↓
Fresh tempe → Chips; Toffees; Curry, Koftas
↓
Slice, steam blanch (15 mm.)
↓
Dehydrate (70°C) in oven/sun-dry
↓
Powder into desired grit size, pack in polythene pouches for future use
↓
Second generation tempe products (porridge, soups, cookies, halwas, chapati. etc.)
↓
Tempe can also be prepared with foodgrains other than soybean like maize, cowpea, groundnut etc.

Fig. 19.2. Tempe-Kedale (soybean) process

CHANGES IN SOYBEANS DURING TEMPO PREPARATION

Hessettine (1965) reported following changes in soybean during tempe preparation.

Proteins: Large amounts of proteins are broken down into simple amino acids. Total nitrogen remains about the same, but soluble nitrogen greatly increases. Ammonia is produced in last stages of fermentations.

Lipids: One-third of the neutral fat is hydrolysed to palmitic, stearic, oleic, linoleic, and linolenic acids. Rhizopus uses only linolenic acid. Total fat remains relatively constant.

Carbohydrates: Reducing sugars decrease. The pH changes little towards alkaline side. Hemicelluloses decrease.

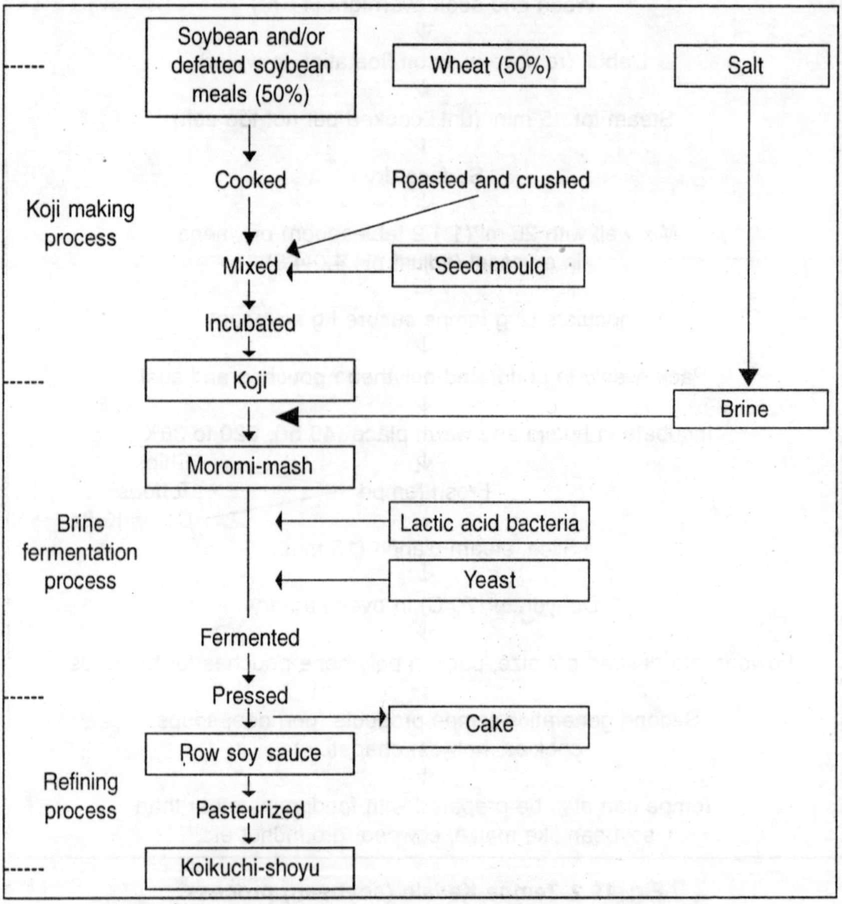

Fig. 19.3. Manufacturing process of Koikuchi-shoyu

Enzymes: Proteases and lipases are present in large amounts and amylases and pectonase in small amounts. Fermentation loss in dry weight is about 4%. Moisture content of produce is 55—65% and total water-soluble solids increase during fermentation.

In preparation of tempe, a mixed culture Rhizopus oligosporous and R. oryzae is used for bringing about fermentation. The resulting tempe contains tender cooked soybean bound together by a dense cottony mycelium of Rhizopus mould in a compact form like cake or in patties form. Tempe cake is cut into slices or cubes which are used in the preparation of curry, chips and toffees etc. Otherwise after dehydrating make it into powder form. It could be blended into various Indian preparations.

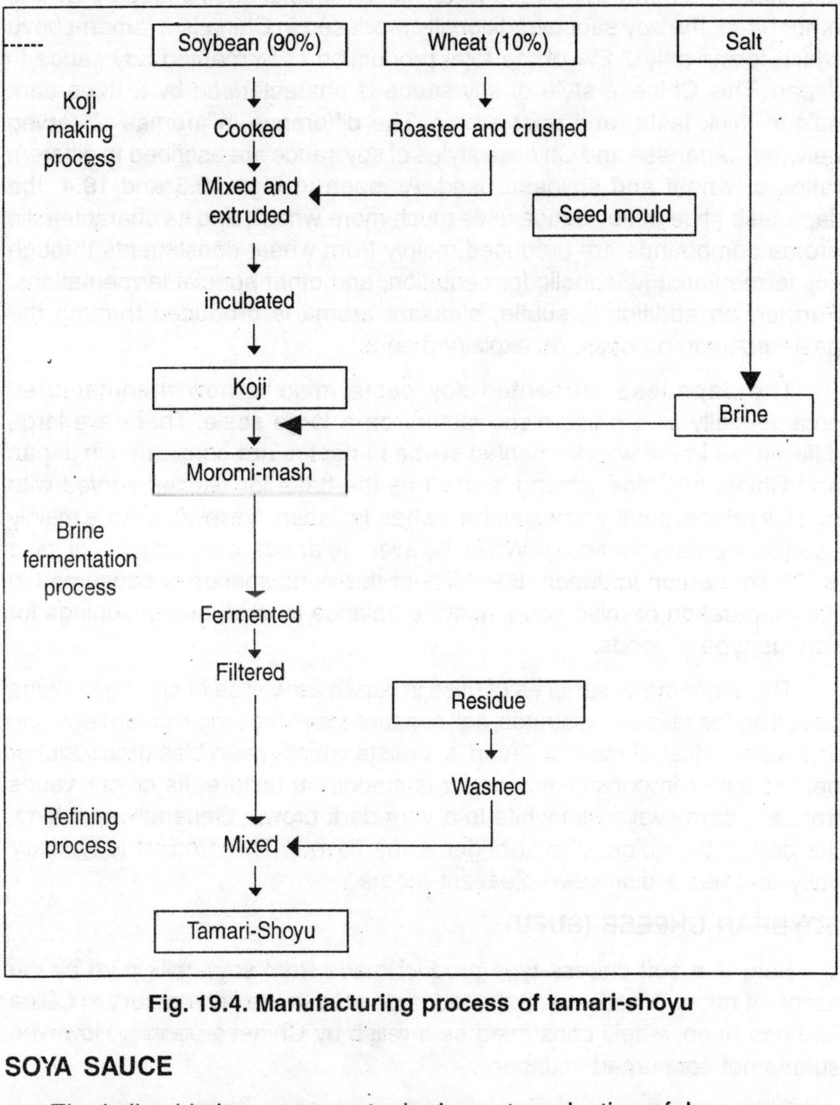

Fig. 19.4. Manufacturing process of tamari-shoyu

SOYA SAUCE

The koikuchi-shou represents the largest production of Japanese soy sauce. The forerunner of this type of soy sauce had been created in the 17th century and has been improved into the present product. It is an all-purpose seasoning, characterised by a strong aroma, myriad flavour, and is deep brownish red in colour. The second type of soy sauce is koikuchi-Shoyu, characterised by a lighter brown colour and milder flavour. It is used mainly for cooking when one wishes to preserve the original flavour and colour of the foodstuff itself. The other 3 types of soya sauces are produced and consumed only in isolated localities for special uses in Japan. On the other hand, the soy sauce traditionally produced in China is a tamari-shoyu which forms only 2.2% of the total production of fermented soy sauce in Japan. This Chinese style of soy sauce is characterised by a deep dark colour, thick taste, and poor aroma. The difference in aromas observed between Japanese and Chinese styles of soy sauce are ascribed to different ratios of wheat and soybean used. As seen in Figs 19.3 and 19.4, the Japanese style of soy sauce uses much more wheat, and its characteristic aroma compounds are produced mainly from wheat constituents through koji fermentation, alcoholic fermentation, and other special fermentations. Further, an additional, subtle, pleasant aroma is produced through the pasteurization process, as explained later.

The Japanese fermented soy paste miso is now manufactured commercially in a modernised factory on a large scale. There are large differences in the way fermented soybean pastes are consumed in Japan and China. In China, chiang is used as the base for sauces served with meat, seafood, poultry or vegetable dishes. In Japan, however, miso is mainly used as the base for soups. While the average annual consumption of miso is 7.2 kg/ person in Japan, 80—85% of this consumption is consumed in the preparation of miso soup, and the balance is used as seasonings for various type of foods.

There are many varieties of miso in Japan as well as of chiang in China based on the ratio of substrates, salt concentration, the length of fermentation and aging. Most of miso in Japan is a paste which resembles groundnut or peanut butter in consistency and it is smooth in texture. Its colour varies from a creamy yellowish white to a very dark brown. Generally speaking, the darker the colour, the stronger is the flavour. The product is typically salty and has a distinctive pleasant aroma.

SOYBEAN CHEESE (SUFU)

Sufu is a soft cheese-type product made from soya milk curd by the action of micro-organisms. Sufu had originated in the fifth century in China and has been widely consumed as a relish by Chinese people. However, sufu is not consumed in Japan.

Sufu-making process consists of 3 major steps, viz, preparation of soy milk curd, moulding process, and brining process. The first step, that is, soya milk curd-making is essentially the same process as used for making tofu. Tofu can be consumed directly and is widely eaten throughout the Far East. In the case of making sufu, however, tofu is made so hard that its water content may be less than 70%, while the water content of directly consumed ordinary tofu is about 90%.

The second process of sufu making is the moulding process. After the hard-made tofu is cut into 3 cm cubes, the cubes are heated for pasteurisation and for reducing water content of the cube surface, and then the mould is inoculated on it. The moulds belonging to the genus of Mucor or Actinomucor are usually used, and the moulds belonging to the genus of Rhizopus are also used sometimes. For instance, Actinomucor elegans, Mucor hiemalis, Mucor silvaticus, Mucor praini, Mucor subtilissimus, and Rhizophus chinensis, are used for the inoculation. The time of mould fermentation differs, depending on the varieties of moulds. It takes about 7 days at 12°C for Rhizopus chinensis, 3 days at 24°C for Mucor hiemalis and Mucor silvaticus, and 2 days at 25°C for Mucorpraini.

The last process of sufu-making is brining and aging. The freshly moulded cubes are placed in various types of brining solutions depending on the flavours desired. The usual brining solution consists of salted fermented rice mash, soya sauce moromi mash, fermented soya paste or 5% NaCl solution containing rice wine having ca. 10% ethyl alcohol. The time of aging ranges from 1—12 months, depending on the varieties of the brining solution. Finally, the product is bottled with the brine, sterilised, and marketed as sufu.

Sufu is a creamy cheese type product which has a mild flavour, and therefore it would be suitable for western people in using it the same way as cheese.

20
BREWING AND DISTILLING

INTRODUCTION

The fermentation of cereal grains to produce an intoxicating beverage must be at least as old as breadmaking, and may have been the second processing step invented for cereals, following closely on the development of the procedure of grinding grain and heating the meal with water to prepare gruels and porridges. It is tempting to speculate that a prehistoric human, having prepared a thin porridge of some grain, perhaps barley, satisfied his hunger with only a part of it, then let the remainder stand long enough for wild yeasts to ferment it. Later, satisfying his renewed hunger with the "spoiled" gruel, he would have been surprised, and presumably gratified, at the physiological effects of the alcohol which had accumulated. The incentive thus having been provided, experiments would have followed to refine the process by increasing the yield of active ingredients, improving the flavor, and changing the consistency from a semisolid to a liquid more or less free of sediment.

In its most primitive form, brewing is a simpler process than baking, which involves the preparation of a coherent piece of substantial size and the development of a method to cook it, even if the utensil is only a heated rock. Both require the availability of a vessel to hold liquid. The relationship of the timing of the invention of wine-making to the development of brewing must remain forever a matter of speculation, but it would seem these developments must have proceeded independently but along parallel lines.

So far as is known, the making of alcoholic beverages was not a part of any of the indigenous cultures of North or South America before the arrival of Europeans. Probably many of the early settlers in the New World were brewers in a small way, providing family and friends with beer of their own making, but the earliest known commercial brewery was established in 1544 near what is now Mexico City. A commercial brewery was built on the southern tip of Manhattan island before 1625 by Dutch immigrants. The

Molson brewery in Montreal was started in 1786 and has remained in continuous operation since then. Commercial brewing in the U.S. did not become widely important until the nineteenth century, when many Germans with brewing experience arrived in the country.

The brewing processes used today are fundamentally allied to those employed in ancient times, but the application of scientific methods has resulted in a closer control of the various steps. Now, each batch of product can be expected to resemble every other batch in flavor, color, and stability, so that failure to obtain a drinkable beer in a commercial brewery would be the occasion of much comment.

In this chapter, a brief general description of the brewing process will be given first, after which details of the various steps will be examined. The only part of distilling technology which will be discussed in detail will be the preparing and fermenting of wort.

PRODUCTION AND TRADE

In the last few years, beer production and consumption in the developed countries has, in general, showed slower rates of increase or reached a plateau, while growth in developing countries continues strong. China has shown the most dramatic growth in recent years.

The consumption of distilled beverages has shown little growth in the last few years.

THE BASICS OF BREWING

The main ingredient of beer is malt. Malt is usually prepared from barley which has been soaked in water, drained, and sprouted until the acrospire (plumule) has grown to an average length equal to three-fourths of the kernel length. The green or moist malt is then dried to halt growth. The drying step usually involves some toasting, which results in color and flavor changes, among other modifications. Malting allows the development of amylolytic enzymes which change starch to fermentable sugars, the substrates, acted upon by yeast to produce alcohol. Malt also contains proteins, protein breakdown products, and a host of other chemical entities which are sources of flavor and act as nutrients for yeast during fermentation. A full description of malt manufacture is given in the preceding chapter.

Malt is supplemented by corn and rice, which are not only cheaper carbohydrate sources but allow brewers to produce the paler, snappier, less filling beers preferred by many consumers. These adjuncts are heated to boiling in the presence of a small amount of malt to furnish amylolytic enzymes. Heating gelatinises the starch, permitting a more rapid attack by the enzymes, which then liquefy the gelatinised starch without converting it to sugar. Heating is usually applied in stages, the temperature being held for some time at specified levels to give different enzymes an optimum environment.

A conventional brewhouse contains as its minimum basic equipment a mash cooker and mash tub, a lauter tub or mash filter, and a wort kettle. The initial process in brewing is mashing, which is considered to include cleaning and grinding of the malt. Dried malt is willed to crush the husks so that the starches can hydrate more easily. The milled malt and water are put into a mash tub, where a series of controlled time-temperature changes enhance the action of enzymes on the proteins and starch, the latter being converted to fermentable sugars. The boiled adjunct (corn cones, broken rice, etc.) from the cooker is added during mashing, and thoroughly mixed in. The mash mixture, now called wort, passes to the lauter tub, which has a false bottom. Grain husks and other large particles collect on the false bottom and form a filter bed through which the carbohydrate-containing liquid, or wort, is strained.

Clear liquid wort is collected in the grant and then goes to the kettle where hops and (usually) corn sugar are added, then the mixture is boiled for about 2.5 hours. During boiling, some of the hydrolyzed protein is coagulated and any enzymes which remain, are inactivated. Virtually all the microorganisms are destroyed, so the wort is, in brewers' parlance, "sterilised." When boiling is completed, the wort is first strained in the hop strainer to remove hop leaves and stems, and then collected in the hot wort tank. After the wort temperature has been reduced to a suitable level in the cooler and cooler pan, yeast is mixed into it and the mixture pumped to the settlers where it remains for 10 to 12 hours. From the settlers, the wort is pumped to fermentation tanks where it remains, until fermentation is complete and the sugars have been converted to ethyl alcohol and carbon dioxide. Storage, addition of chillproofing materials, and carbonation follow.

A feature common to all schemes of beer production is the bringing together of yeast and brewer's wort under conditions which encourage the production of ethanol and carbon dioxide. In conventional batch processes, this primary fermentation step is continued until a desired amount of sugar has been converted to alcohol and the yeast has used up a certain amount of amino acids and other nutrients. The fermented wort is then matured in processes called conditioning, lagering, or ruh storage in order to develop desirable aromas and flavors and eliminate others. A considerable amount of time is required for the satisfactory accomplishment of this series of events. Typically, two to three weeks will elapse from, the beginning of primary fermentation until the completion of maturation, but some specialty beers may require months of processing. As a result, large amounts of liquid will be continuously present in an active brewery, and must be held under carefully controlled conditions if satisfactory results are to be obtained. This necessitates the availability of large and expensive equipment.

One factor which influences the size of fermentation vessels and the rate of beer production is the formation of large amounts of foam during fermentation. A fine white head appears near the sides of the vessel and above any attemperating coils about 8 to 16 hours after pitching. As fermentation proceeds, rocky or cauliflower-appearing heads ("krausen") appear and eventually reach a maximum state of development ("high kraeusen"). At the end of primary fermentation, in about 5 to 7 days, the head gradually collapses leaving a dark-colored, bitter tasting scum.

The scum must be separated from the beer by skimming or suction. Depending on the speed of fermentation and the type, shape, and size of the fermentation vessel, foam volume can reach as much as one-third of the total fermentation vessel capacity. There are known methods for minimizing foam formation and facilitating foam removal, but these add to the cost and complexity of beer production.

There are several different types of beer, with variations in flavor, color, carbonation, and alcoholic content resulting from differences in the kinds and proportions of ingredients and in the processing conditions. Most lager-type beers, such as Pilsener, Munich, Dortmund, and Vienna are produced by bottom fermentation, that is, with a yeast which sinks to the bottom of the tank during fermentation. Stout, porter, and ale are top- fermented beers. The term "lager beer' simply means that the beer has been aged after fermentation. Pilsener beer is a pale beer having a high hop level and a very stable head. Munich, or Munchener, beer is darker and sweeter than Pilsener and has a more pronounced malt flavor, due not only to use of a darker malt but also to a lower hop rate. Bock beer is a traditional spring time beer. It is darker in color and usually sweeter and fuller bodied than other types. Caramelized or roasted malt is used in its preparation.

Where the product is not identified in the following discussions, the process will be that used for brewing American lager beer. Most American lager beers do not closely resemble the European types, being, in general, lighter in color, milder in flavor, and higher in carbonation; they generally contain more hops. European beers demonstrate a wide range of characteristics, but can be quite dark, very high in malt flavor, and viscous. An extreme example is Guiness Stout.

Figure 20.1 includes a flow diagram of the brewing process.

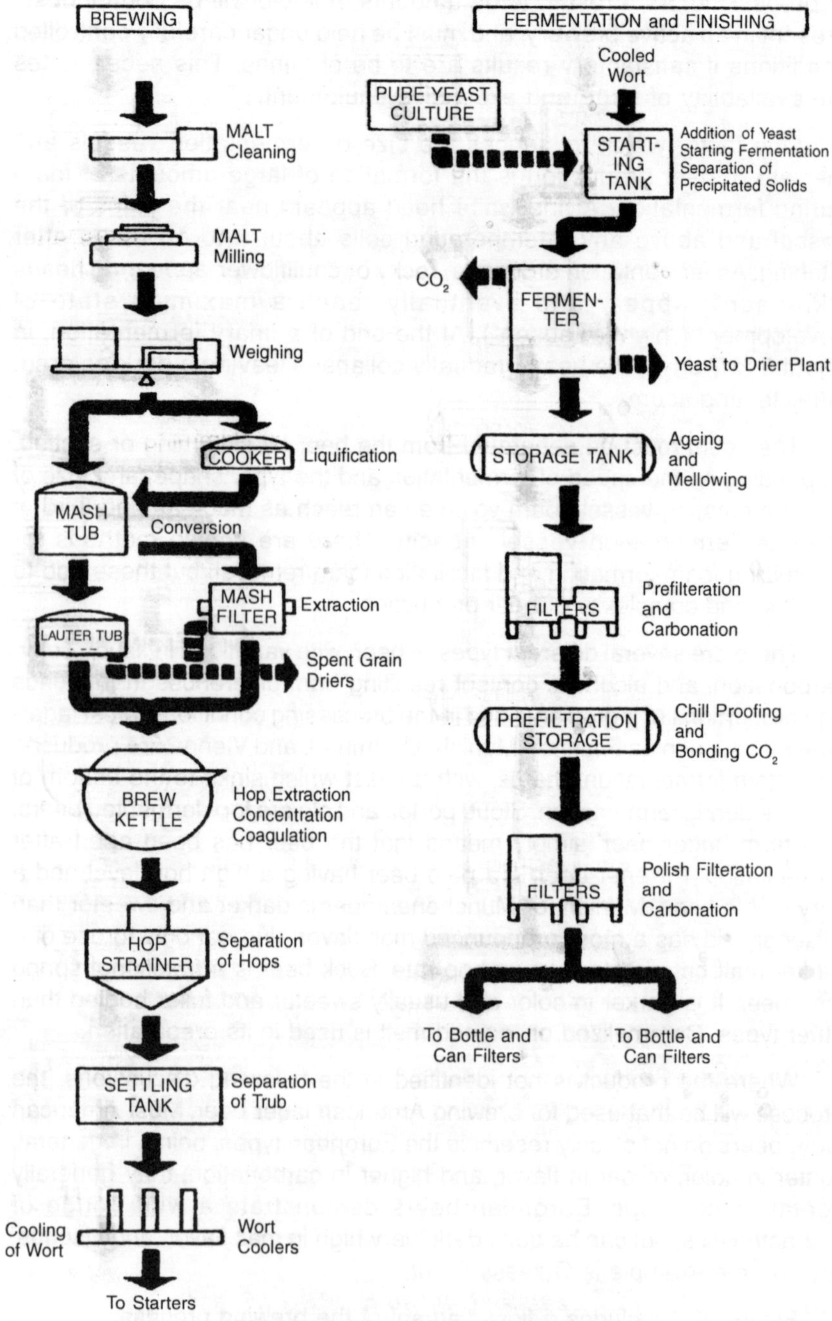

Fig. 20.1: The Brewing Process

RAW MATERIALS

Use of the proper ingredients is vital to the brewing industry, since it is impossible to brew a superior product from inferior starting materials. Table 20.1 shows the amounts of major raw materials used by U.S. breweries in a recent year. Some pertinent information regarding raw materials will be presented in the following paragraphs.

BARLEY

The traditional grain for beer brewing is barley, which has been made the subject of a preceding chapter. Over thousands of years, varieties suitable for malting and brewing have been selected and improved. As a result, present day barleys have certain characteristics favourable to the conventional brewing process which would be difficult to reproduce in other grains. Nonetheless, new methods of brewing as well as new and cheaper sources of enzymes and carbohydrates have opened the way for other grains to partially or completely replace barley malt. Tradition remains a powerful force in restraining switches to other beer ingredients.

Two factors probably have been the most important in promoting the use of barley as the primary grain for brewing: (1) it can be grown in a great variety of climatic conditions, and thus is found all over the world, and (2) its straw-like husks make it easier to process. The husks are not removed by threshing, and therefore protect the embryo during malting. They also assist in the clarification of wort by forming an efficient filter bed.

Table 20.1. MATERIALS USED AT BREWERIES[1]

Malt and malt products	4,813,247,201
Corn and corn products	1,040,831,950
Rice and rice products	1,129,018,834
Barley and barley products (unmalted)	637,530
Wheat and wheat products	104,024
Sorghum and sorghum products	217,630
Sugar and syrups	604,525,473
Hops	33,745,777
Hop extracts	9,092,356
Other	43,758,420
TOTAL	7,675,179,195

1. In pounds, during the calendar year 1989. Data from the Beer Institute.

The two main types of barley are the 2-rowed and the 6-rowed varieties. Two-rowed barleys, *Hordeum distichum,* are considered in Europe to be better for brewing. They are generally planted in the early spring. In the U.S., these barleys are cultivated primarily in the Pacific Northwest. Six-rowed barleys, *Hordeum hexastichum,* are known as winter barleys because they are usually sown in the fall and harvested in late spring or early summer. They are the most commercially important barleys grown in North America, and are extensively used for brewing. Barley grown in the Red River Valley is considered best for this purpose. Present practice is to select a pure line and strain of barley having known malting characteristics. The properties of barley varieties grown for animal feeds are usually substantially different from those of malting barleys. Seed for feed grain is selected primarily on the basis of its yield potential and disease resistance; physical and chemical characteristics of the harvested kernels being much less important than for malting barleys.

Manufacture of barley malt has been described briefly above, and in more detail in a preceding chapter. Malt used for brewing commonly has a diastatic power of 120 to 140 degrees Lintner and an a-amylase activity of 25 to 40 units. Distillers' malt is stronger, typically having a Linter value of 190' to 250' and an a-amylase strength of 50 to 70 units.

Specialty malts are available for making beers having unusual color, viscosity, and flavor. These are generally barley malts which have been subjected to modified kilning procedures. Higher than normal kilning temperatures lead to lark "caramel" malts which are valued for their coloring effect in bock beer and other dark brews. Caramel or roasted malts are available in different color grades. Crystal malt is kilned or roasted for 30 to 45 minutes at 140° to 167°F in the absence of air, then the cover is removed and the mass is heated at about 300°F for 1 to 2 hours in a normal draft.

ADJUNCTS

Barley malt is the traditional source of fermentable sugars for wort, and in some countries it still constitutes their only source by legal prescription. There are, however, other sources for sugars which are more economical and may have other advantages, such as blandness, lighter color, greater uniformity, or fewer processing problems. These include unmalted grains such as barley and rice which are added with the malt and saccharified by the malt enzymes, sugar, and syrups or dried syrups made by reacting grain or purified starch with bacterial or fungal enzymes, e.g., corn syrup. Sugar and syrups can be added to the cooled wort. Corn syrup of high dextrose equivalent is a common adjunct. Rice, corn, unmalted barley, sorghum grain, and some of the other adjuncts give a paler beer, and, frequently, a milder flavored beverage.

Adjuncts containing unmodified starch, such as broken rice or corn grits, must be cooked separately before they are added to the mash. The mix for precooking will consist of a relatively small amount of finely ground malt, the ground adjunct, and water. In the cereal cooker, this mixture is heated to about 158°F and held for about 30 min then boiled for 10 rnm. In brewing technology, it is common to express temperatures as degrees Reaumur (°R). In the Reaumur scale, zero is the freezing point of water (the same as zero on the Celsius scale), and each degree is equal to 1.25 degree Celsius/ Centigrade or 2.25°F. In this chapter, all temperatures will be stated in degrees Fahrenheit for convenience of the reader.

Rice is used in the form of grits, which are the broken grains obtained in the course of dehulling and polishing rice. Grits are considerably cheaper than unbroken kernels and the small size of the pieces is not a detriment as it is when rice is sold for home cooking. In fact, this characteristic is an advantage in brewing. The lipids content of rice grits should not exceed 0.5 to 0.7%, and the free fatty acid content should be low to avoid the development of rancid flavors in the beer.

Pre-boiling of corn can be avoided by using flakes obtained by passing degermed ground meal between heated cylinders so as to gelatinise the starch. Fat content of the corn meal should not exceed 1%, and the fat must not be rancid, as the free fatty acids would pass into the beer with disastrous effects on the flavor.

Corn syrups and corn syrup solids may be added to the kettle to increase the amount of fermentable sugars. Commercial preparations of hydrolysed corn starch contain variable amounts of dextrins, which are not usually considered objectionable since they give the beer a mellower flavor. Any "dextrose" used should have a neutral reaction in aqueous solution, and should not contain any iron or starch.

Although adequate alcohol and carbon dioxide content could be obtained from fermentations based entirely on purified sugars, some barley malt must be added to the wort, even if laws do not require it. It is needed not only to obtain the flavor which is expected in beer, but also for its enzyme activity, its contribution to the "body" and color of the beverage, and (in conventional breweries) for essential functions in the brewing process. Several patents have been issued covering the addition of nonmalt enzymes to adjuncts, which substantially eliminate the need for malt as an amylase and protease source. For example, one inventor claimed that malt:adjunct ratios as low as 40:60 can be used if 0.1 to 1.0% of proteolytic enzyme preparations (papain, bromelin, ficin, etc.) are added to the mash. A major advantage of such additions is that they eliminate the need for the carefully controlled temperature and time sequences customary in traditional brewing processes based on the functional participation of malt enzymes.

HOPS

Hops may have been first added to fermenting beer to contribute a different flavor or to mask unpleasant flavors, but they also had the important function of hindering the growth of unwanted microorganisms. Until the principle of using pure yeast cultures in combination with "sterilised" worts was adopted, their antiseptic properties may have been the most important contribution of hops to brewing. Brewers' hops are the dried fruit (cones) of the perennial plant *Humulus lupulus.* Male and female inflorescences are borne on separate plants and only the female ones are used in brewing. The flowers contain small lupulin glands which secrete the bitter resins and essential oils responsible for the value of hops in brewing. Hops are picked in late August or early September (in the Northern Hemisphere), and must be dried as rapidly as possible to prevent oxidation and polymerisation of the essential oils and bitter acids. Temperatures during drying should not exceed 122°F.

Hops grown in Czechoslovakia were traditionally considered to be the best in the world for beer making, but these have been gradually supplanted by hops from other locations. In the U.S., hops are grown mostly in Washington, Oregon, California, Idaho, and New York. American hops are characterized by a rather fruity flavor. The average chemical composition of kiln-dried hops is shown in Table 20.2.

Table 20.2. COMPOSITION OF KILN—DRIED HOPS[1]

Component	%
Moisture	12.5
Ash	7.5
Cellulose (gross)	13.3
Essential oils	0.4
Ether extract	18.3
Tannin	3.0
Nitrogenous matter	17.5
N-Free extract	27.5

1 DeClerck (1958)

From the standpoint of the brewer's art, the most important constituents of hops are their bitter resins and essential oils. The bitterness of hops is due almost entirely to the resinous materials previously mentioned. Hop oils contribute both flavor and aroma. Two resins are known: humulone (alpha-acid, alpha-resin) and lupulone (beta-acid, beta- resin). It has been shown by various investigators that humulone is a mixture of three closely related substances, called humulone, cohumulone, and adhumulone. Lupulone is also a mixture of at least three related compouds called lupulone, colupulone, and adlupulone. These resins, which are responsible not only for the bittering but also for the antiseptic qualities of hops, seem to be peculiar to this plant. When hops are stored, the resins are progressively oxidized and polymerized, thereby losing most of their desirable characteristics.

The composition of hop oil is very complex. About 70 to 80% of the oil consists of terpene-like hydrocarbons, but they are thought to contribute less to the aroma than the oxygenated compounds which are present. The terpenes consist chiefly of myrcene and humulene (alpha-carophyllene), with smaller amounts of other terpenes. These oils are subject to resinification and polymerisation when the hops are stored. A large proportion of the resin and oil content is lost during brewing.

Another important component of hops is tannin. This has been found to consist of a mixture of at least three different groups of substances, including flavanols and leucoanthocyanins. Hop tannin is converted to reddish-brown phlobaphene on oxidation, a behavior which is characteristic of catechol tannins. The tannin is precipitated along with barley albumin during boiling in the kettle.

Hops for brewing are selected chiefly on the bases of their external appearance and place of origin. Chemical analyses for moisture content and resins are useful.

It is common practice to ship whole hop blossoms in bales, but this has many disadvantages. The bales are difficult to handle and the hops are subject to rapid deterioration due to their exposure to oxygen, humid air, and light. Suppliers have developed extracts which contain all, or nearly all, the desirable components of hops and have many convenience features. Also, extracts reduce the loss of resins and oils during storage and allow much better standardization of the finished product.

These extracts can be added to the brewer's copper or to the fermented beer. Six gallons of refined hop extract will replace a 200-lb bale of dried hop blossoms. Hydrogenation or sodium borohydride reduction of the hop extract is said to reduce or eliminate the formation of odorous mercaptan-like compounds under the influence of light. Hydrogenation reduces the carbonyl group of the isohexenoyl side chains of isohumulones to a secondary alcohol group.

WATER

Water quality is of the utmost importance in brewing. It is literally impossible to produce a satisfactory beer with certain water supplies, unless

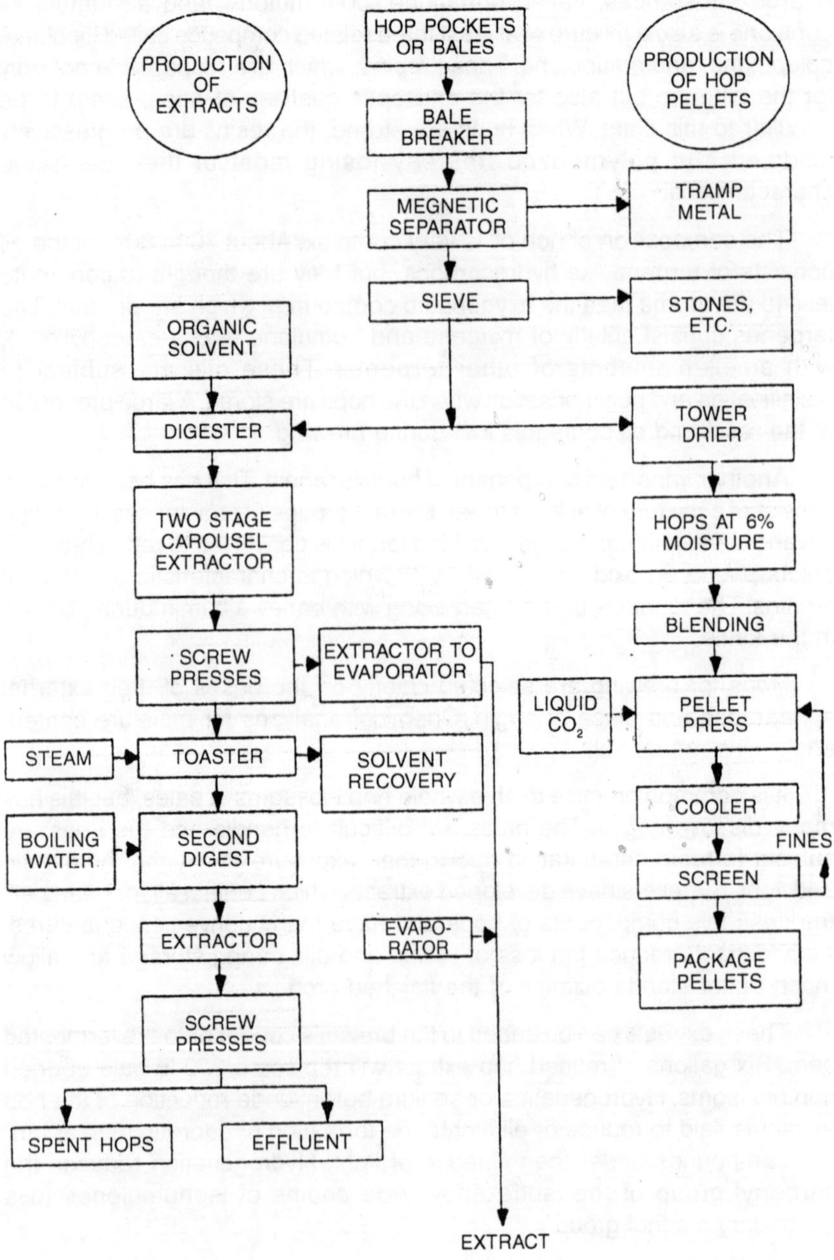

Fig. 20.2: Manufacturing hop pellets and hop extracts

corrective measures can be applied (and these may be too costly to be practical). Many of the famous breweries of old times were located near water sources having particularly good properties for the type of beer for which the breweries were noted. Pilsen beer was made from artesian water that was very soft—it had a very low mineral content. The Burton-on-Trent breweries used water with a high permanent hardness to make the Burton Bitter beers. Water with less calcium sulfate and more calcium bicarbonate was associated with sweeter darker beers from Munich, Dublin, and London. Dortmund beer is made from water containing both chlorides and bicarbonates. It is generally agreed that the mineral content of the water they used was an important factor in the success of these breweries. Of course, water treatment technology has advanced to the point where any potable water can be adapted for use in brewing any desired type of beer, although the cost of treatment may be prohibitive.

In most cases, the direct effect of the salts in normal potable water on the flavour of the beer brewed with it can be expected to be relatively slight because the amount of minerals contributed by the ingredient water is fairly small compared to the total mineral content of the finished beer. The type of inorganic compound may be very important, however, since different ions have different effects on the solubility of substances in malt, particularly the proteins, and on enzymatic and other reactions. Thus, the type of mineral constituent can exert a powerful indirect effect on the taste of the beer.

Pilsener beers require a very soft water, and dark beers a medium hard to hard carbonate water. For lightly hopped beers, a minimum residual carbonate hardness of 3 to 5 degrees is needed in order to avoid a relatively flat or bland taste in the finished beer. Water low in alkalinity and rather high in calcium sulfate hardness is needed so that mash pH will fall in the range of 4.6 to 5.7. This will give optimum enzyme activity. If the water is too soft, addition of calcium sulfate (gypsum) and sodium chloride may be required. Very soft water can be corrected with up to 0.15 gm of gypsum or calcium chloride per liter. The addition of hardening salts is called "burtonising." High wort pH leads to uneven saccharification during mashing, difficulties in separating wort from the spent grain (resulting in a low yield of extract), incomplete coagulation of proteins during boiling, sharper bitter flavour from the hops, and a biologically unstable beer susceptible to infection by lactic organisms.

The acidifying effect of calcium from the water supply or from added gypsum is due to the reaction of calcium ions with secondary phosphate ions derived from the malt, as indicated by the following equation. Although the triorthophosphate salt of calcium has a very low solubility, the reaction does not go to completion.

$$3\,Ca^{++} + 2\,HPO_4^{--} \rightarrow Ca_3(PO_4)_2 + 2H^+$$

Nitrites or nitrates, the latter being partially reduced to nitrite during fermentation, may interfere with yeast activity even if they are present at very low concentrations. Iron contributes an off-flavor and may discolor the beer by interfering with the clarification process. Iron in excess of one ppm has a deleterious effect on enzymes in the mashing step since it can combine with these proteins as well as with some other barley components.

Magnesium in excess of 30 mg/b imparts a reddish tint and an acrid flavour to beer. Chlorides are said to mellow and sweeten and soften beer, especially at levels of 20 to 60 mg/b. Higher concentrations are to be avoided, however. Copper in trace amounts has been blamed for accentuating the "gushing" phenomenon. Fluoride seems to stimulate yeast metabolism at concentrations of 1 to 5 mg/b, whereas inhibtion has been observed at levels higher than 10 mg/b. Silica may increase turbidity if more than 50 ppm are present, although this effect seems to have little practical importance. Bonnet (1955) and others have compiled lists of suggested limits for ions in brewing water.

Flavorants present in the raw water can be carried through the entire brewing process and appear in the finished beer. There are many types of these contaminants, but phenolic substances, and particularly chlorophenols, can be very troublesome, leading to medicinal or other unpleasant tastes and odors. Charcoal treatment to remove these compounds by adsorption is the most reliable means of correction.

The maltster must also consider the quality of water used in standardisation, or the final dilution made to attain precise alcohol limits just before the beer is packaged, The quality of this water is extremely important. One might even consider whether distilled water would not be preferable at this point. At any rate, the standardisation water must be free of compounds causing non-typical tastes and odors and of their precursors. It must contain no chlorine or other oxidants, and it must be deaerated immediately before use so that oxygen is not added to the blended beer. Deaerating systems have been described by Coors (1977). Briefly, these consist of hot systems in which 176°F water is sprayed into a vacuumised vessel and cold systems in which the chilled water is put through a packed tower to which vacuum is applied. The deaerated water is carbonated immediately, or it can be added to the beer which is then carbonated en route to the packaging equipment.

YEAST

American lager beer is generally fermented with a pure strain of *Saceharomyces uvarum* (formerly *S. carlsbergensis).* Strains of *S. cerevisiae* may be used for ales and porter. A bottom yeast is generally used for beer manufacture while top fermenting yeast is used for ale. The cells of top yeast gather in clumps and are carried to the top of the fermenting liquid while the cells of bottom yeast stay suspended in the bulk of the liquid or drift toward the bottom.

The effectiveness of a yeast strain in producing ethanol and carbon dioxide, and its ability to generate the minor constituents which affect beer flavor, are the characteristics considered by the brewmaster to be the most important. The property of flocculence is also of importance to the brewer. The flocculating ability of yeast is related to its capacity of forming aggregates of cells which either fall out of suspension in bottom fermentations or are carried to the surface in top fermentations. The more highly flocculating yeasts are removed from suspension relatively soon and thus do not have ready access to the fermentable materials in the bulk of the liquid. As a result, the degree of attenuation (i.e., the extent to which the sugars are converted to alcohol) tends to be reduced. Thus, highly flocculative yeasts give rise to sweeter, poorly attenuated beers while "powdery" yeasts lead to dry, well attenuated beers. On the other hand, the powdery yeasts are more difficult to remove from the beer and tend to be carried over into the storage tanks and even into the finished container, a highly undesirable situation.

Yeast is one of the main products of brewing. Probably not more than 20% of the yeast produced in batch fermentations is required for subsequent batches. The excess is disposed of through various commercial channels, e.g., to pharmaceutical companies and food flavoring manufacturers.

Most brewers prefer to isolate their stock culture from a pure brewery yeast culture and often derive it from a single-cell culture. A typical procedure relating to a pure mass culture of S. *uvarum,* was described by Strandskov (1965). Yeast reaching the fermenter was actively budding. Microbial infection was found in this procedure to be restricted to *Flavobacterium proteus,* which maintained a fairly constant relationship to yeast count in the fermenters of about 1.5% and did not adversely affect flavor.

ADDITIVES

There are many ingredients added to beers to assist in the processing and to modify characteristics in the finished beer. Agar, gelation, and sodium alginate have been added to beer prior to filtration in order to improve removal of colloidal substances which would cause clouding in the finished beverage. Other chillproofers or stabilisers, which are intended to reduce or eliminate the combination of high molecular weight proteins and tannins are enzymes such as papain, tannic acid, and adsorbents such as insoluble polyvinylpyrrolidone (PVPP). Most of these additives are expected to be removed in the filters along with the colloids with which they have combined, but some excess gums may be used as foam stabilisers to help build and maintain a head.

Fining agents are added at the onset of storage to speed up and improve sedimentation. Among the many fining agents which have been mentioned in the literature are bentonite, tannic acid, isinglass, carrageenan, and silicates. Many different substances have also been used or recommended as foam improvers, including ginseng (Owades 1989). Excess foam buildup during product blending and transfer can impede production, however, and this effect is minimized by adding silicone emulsions. All, or at least most, of the antifoam additives are removed prior to final packaging.

MASHING

Malt, which is received at the brewery as substantially whole kernels, must be reduced in size to facilitate extraction and enzyme action. Current techniques usually require grinding the malt into a wet or dry grist, retaining the husks in fairly large pieces while obtaining a maximum of finely ground barley flour. The husks will later serve as a very important component of the filter bed in the lautering process.

There are several variations of the method by which the ground malt is dispersed in water. In general, these variations have little effect on the finished product and are chosen to give maximum production efficiency.

The object of mashing the malt and adjuncts is to bring into solution the relatively small quantities of substances which are soluble without enzyme action, and to change insoluble substances into soluble ones through enzyme action. The enzymatic reactions have already been initiated during malting, but are speeded up and controlled by regulating the temperature during mashing. For example, the ratio of starch breakdown during malting to that during mashing is about 1 to 10. The chemical structure of the starch, proteins, gums, pectins, etc., is changed in such a way that the finished wort contains 10 to 14% total extract and no starch or dextrin giving a color with iodine. The pH should be 5.2 to 5.5, and must be regulated during mashing for optimum conversion of starch to sugars and to prevent turbidity caused by the complex nitrogenous substances which result from incomplete breakdown of proteins. Beers brewed from worts that are too alkaline show increased color and lack of stability.

CONTROL OF PH

Control of pH is achieved by adding lactic acid, mineral acids, or calcium sulfate to the mash. Calcium sulfate (gypsum) converts phosphates in the malt to acid phosphates. Malt contains about 1% phosphates calculated as PO_4. Twenty per cent of this is soluble phosphate, of which about half is present as alkaline phosphate and half as acid phosphate. The alkaline phosphate must be changed to acid phosphate in order to provide buffer action for regulating the pH. Calcium sulfate reacts with alkaline phosphates according to the equation:

$$3CaSO_4 + 4\ K_2HPO_4 = 2\ KH_2PO_4 + 3\ K_2SO_4 + Ca_3\ (PO_4)_2$$

Another function of the gypsum is to prevent conversion of acid phosphates to alkaline phosphates by the calcium carbonate present in the water, according to the equation:

$$4KH_2PO_4 + 3\ CaCO_3 = Ca_3\ (PO_4)_2 + 2\ K_2HPO_4 + 3\ H_2CO_3$$

The pH of the mash immediately after mixing with soft water is about 5.8 and the titratable acidity is about 0.05%. The acidity begins to increase at once due to liberation of acid phosphates, lactic acid, and other acids, such as amino acids, from the malt. The mash may be held at a temperature of about 95°F for 30 to 60 mm to promote acidification. If the mash is held too long at this temperature, however, butyric fermentation may occur. This holding period of 30 to 60 min is called the "lactic acid rest" and may be omitted if an added acidifying ingredient, such as lactic acid, is used.

TEMPERATURE CONTROL

After the lactic acid rest, the temperature is increased in stages by injecting steam and by adding adjunct mash from the cooker at appropriate times. "Rests" at specified temperature levels give time for specific enzyme reactions. In more modern practice, these temperature steps are consolidated.

The reason for periods during which there is no substantial increase in temperature is to give different enzymes a reaction period at their specific optimum temperature. Optimum degradation of proteins occurs between 113° to 140°F, while the greatest conversion of starches to fermentable sugars takes place between 140° to 149°F. The group of enzymes converting starch into dextrins and maltose is called "diastase." The separate enzymes known to be present in this group are ß-amylase and ßamylase. In early research, it was reported that a third enzyme, called amylophosphatase, which could split inorganic phosphates from starch without saccharification, was the agent responsible for the liquefaction of starch during mashing. The present view is that this liquefaction is due to the action of a-amylase. During mashing, liquefaction is pronounced at 122' to 176°F, with an optimum range of 158' to 167°F. Enzymes of fungal and bacterial origin, which are sometimes used to assist liquefaction of unmalted cereals, have high liquefying power and are destroyed at temperatures of about 190° to 200°F.

In order that starch can be liquefied in a reasonable length of time, it must be gelatinised. The temperature of gelatinisation varies with the type of starch and the size of the granules. For example, wheat starch gels at about 140°F, while rice starch gels at 176° to 185°F. Gelatinisation is accompanied by a sharp rise in viscosity, but viscosity decreases again as liquefaction occurs.

Starch is hydrolysed by both a- and ß-amylases, and these enzymes have different temperature optimums. The preferred conditions for ß-amylase are 122° to 145°F and pH 4.7 to 5.3, and the enzyme is destroyed at temperatures over 172°F. This enzyme is already quite developed in ungerminated barley but decreases during kilning because of the rather high temperature reached in that process. Beta-amylase splits maltose directly from the starch molecule, leaving behind a compound of the amylodextrin type. While sugar formation from up to 60% of the original starch proceeds rapidly, the iodine test (showing fairly large glucose polymers are still present) continues to be positive for a long time. With pure ß-amylase complete conversion may never be attained. During mashing, the length of time the mash remains at the temperatures most favorable for 13- amylase activity (140° to 149°F) determines the amount of maltose formed, and thus indirectly the alcohol content of the finished beer.

Alpha-amylase has optimum activity at 158°F and pH 5.7. It is more resistant to high temperatures but less resistant to low pH than ß-amylase, and it is practically inactive in ungerminated barley. Hydrolysis of starch by a-amylase leads chiefly to the formation of dextrins of the type giving a negative iodine reaction. Thus, a high mashing temperature (above the optimum for ßamylase) will yield wort having a high dextrin content and a low fermentable sugar content. The beer will then be relatively low in alcohol.

Beers low in alcohol content because of a high dextrin content in the wort are not as palatable as beers which have a higher alcohol content. In order to keep the -amount of fermentable sugar low the temperature of the mash must be raised quickly from 122° to 158°F so as to suppress ß-amylase activity, and this rapid rise prevents formation of the intermediate protein degradation products which are necessary as yeast nutrients and for adding body to the beer.

Starch degradation products other than maltose and dextrins are present in wort, evidently due to the action of amyloglucosidase in malt. Glucose polymer-affecting enzymes other than the diastase group seem to be present in malt. Maltase is present in detectable amounts, but is largely denatured by heat during the kilning of malt. Among the many different carbohydrates present are higher dextrins, maltotetraose, maltotriose, maltose, sucrose, glucose, isomaltose, panose, and fructose.

PROTEIN REACTIONS

Starch hydrolysis reactions are not the only important ingredient modifications occurring during mashing. Among the other essential reactions are the changes occurring in the proteins. American 6-row barleys contain 12 to 14% protein, of which roughly two-thirds is permanently insoluble under conditions existing during mashing. The remaining one-third, or about 3 to 5% of the dry matter of the malt, plays an important role in brewing. The proteins in brewing adjuncts such as grits, flakes, etc., are essentially inert insofar as mashing is concerned. The boiling in the cooker - seems to coagulate any adjunct proteins which might otherwise be soluble.

During mashing, part of the insoluble malt proteins are converted to solubles, but a small fraction of the dissolved proteins are coagulated during the subsequent boiling of the wort. The balance of the dissolved protein material is unaffected by boiling and is known as permanently soluble protein.

Several different proteolytic enzymes are present in malt, but their exact number and nature are not known, though some have been characterised. These proteinases have an optimum temperature range of 122° to 140°F and an optimum pH range of 4.3 to 5.7. They break down the soluble, complex proteins into simpler compounds of medium molecular weights. These substances have been categorised as albumoses, peptones, and polypeptides. They have a very favorable influence on the palatability and foam of beer. It is essential that all the proteins of high molecular weight be broken down, as proteins will cause turbidity and haziness if carried over Into the beer.

Further degradation of the medium weight nitrogenous products to peptides and amino acids is brought about by a group of enzymes known as peptidases. These low molecular weight products are important-as nutrients for the yeast If they, are present in excess, however, they may cause sluggishness or degeneration of yeast. They also tend to increase surface tension and decrease foam stability of the beer. High mashing temperatures favor the formation of peptones while lower temperatures favor the formation of peptides and amino acids.

EXAMPLES OF MASHING PROCEDURES

The two traditional types of mashing are called decoction and infusion. Infusion mashing, as employed in Britain for top fermentations, requires that conversion and extraction of wart be carried out in a single stage and at a single temperature in the mash tun. The mixed grist and water are allowed to stand in the mash tun and the temperature only gradually raised without boiling.

Decoction mashing is important, being used, for example, in central Europe for producing bottom fermentation beers. In this method, a part of the mash is withdrawn, boiled, and then returned to the mash tun to raise the temperature of the whole mash. There are also other systems adopted to meet specific needs. Proteolytic activities and saccharification are both favored by the decoction method British malts are generally highly modified to compensate for the enzymatically less favorable conditions of infusion mashing.

There have been many modifications of the traditional malting procedures. In a U.S. mashing process, there might be an albumin rest (protein rest), a sugar rest, a dextrinising rest, a conversion period, and a mashing-off stage. The conditions required and reactions occurring in each of these stages are summarised in the following paragraphs.

The *albumin rest or protein rest* consists of holding the mash for 30 to 60 minutes at 113°F. During this period, the proteinases are very active, forming low molecular weight nitrogen compounds such as amino acids, amides, and peptides from the proteins. Beta-amylase, which splits maltose units from the starch molecule, is only moderately active. Acidification and formation of buffering compounds take place.

During the *sugar rest*, the mash is held for 5 to 30 minutes at 133° to 144°F. This temperature range is near the optimum for ß-amylase, which is therefore very active. Alpha-amylase, which forms dextrins, is moderately active. Proteinases are very active, but at these temperatures produce more medium-molecular weight fragments such as polypeptides, rather than amino acids. For beers of restricted alcohol content, this temperature range should be passed over as quickly as possible. In some brewing schemes, the sugar rest is omitted entirely.

Conditions for the *dextrinising rest* are temperatures in the range 136° to 162°F and times of 15 to 45 minutes. The dextrin-forming alphaamylase is very active, while maltose production is much reduced. The proteinase which forms medium-molecular weight compounds is somewhat active, while the enzymes forming smaller molecules are only slightly active.

Conversion is performed at 162° to 167°F for 10 to 20 minutes, the times depending on the malt and previous mashing conditions. This is the optimum temperature range for quick and complete conversion of starch to dextrin by a-amylase. Some brewers prefer to carry out this step at 154 to 162°F. If the temperature exceeds 167°F, there is a risk that the amylases may be inactivated.

The *mashing-off* temperature is usually in the range of 167° to 176°F. Times will vary between 5 and 10 minutes. Under these conditions, most of the enzymes are inactivated, although a-amylase will retain some of its activity. The mashing-off temperature may be varied somewhat, depending on the alcohol content desired in the finished beer. For medium- to low-alcohol beers, a low mashing-off temperature may be chosen, because maltose formation during sparging (washing of drained mash bed to remove residual wort) is not objectionable.

A higher mashing-off temperature, 172° to 174°F, is used for beer of low to medium alcohol content to keep maltose formation within the desired limits. High mashing-off temperatures make the wort less viscous and facilitate the running off process (wort separation), but excessively high temperatures may lead to belated but incomplete action of previously uncoverted starch particles, causing turbid, slow-running worts as well as starch turbity in the cellar. With western malts it is advisable to keep the mashing-off temperature at 165° to 167°F.

PROCESSING THE WORT

FILTRATION

After the mashing process is completed, the water-soluble materials must be separated from the spent grain. This is accomplished by filtering the liquid through a bed of spent grain which is supported on a false bottom made of perforated plates. Filtration may take place in the mash tub itself, in a separate vessel known as a lauter tub, or in a filter press.

Filtration in the mash tub is inefficient, and is not common practice for that reason. Most frequently, filtration is carried out in the lauter tub. Mash is pumped into the tub and allowed to stand for about 0.5 hr, so that the spent grain can settle and form a bed on the false bottom. Taps leading from the bottom of the tub are then opened and the wort flows into the grant, a vessel in which the wort can be inspected and from which it can be transferred either to the kettle or back to the top of the lauter tub. Wort coming into the grant during the first 10 to 15 minutes of transfer is usually opalescent, and is pumped back into the lauter tub to be refiltered. As soon as the filtered wort is clear, it is transferred to the kettle. This fraction is known as the first wort.

Draining, or filtration, is continued until the fluid again appears opalescent and the rate of flow decreases, indicating that almost all of the liquid has run through. At this point the taps are closed. The filter bed contains a good deal of extract which must be recovered. This is done by spraying hot water onto the filter bed, raking it to mix it thoroughly with the water "mashing over"), allowing the grain to settle again, and drawing off the liquid as before. This process is called sparging. It is repeated until the last wort contains about 1% but not less than 0.75% extract. During sparging, the filtered liquid is pumped back as before until it comes through clear.

The sparging conditions must be controlled to ensure recovery of as much extract as possible without carrying over deleterious substances, such as silica and tannins, from the husks. In order to maintain optimum conditions, the sparging water is treated with additives to prevent alkalinity and the temperature of the sparge liquor is kept below 175°F. The temperature should not be lower than this, however, lest the the permeability of the filter bed decrease to a point such that the flow of liquid is impeded.

In some large breweries, filtration in the lauter tub is considered to be too slow for efficient operation, and a plate and frame mash filter is used instead. These filters are constructed similarly to the filter presses used in sugar refineries, but high pressure is not employed. The filter unit consists of hollow frames alterating with grooved plates covered with filter cloth. Wort passes through the filter cloth into the grooves and then through faucets into a collector similar to a grant. Sparging is carried out by passing the brewing water either from the pressure side or the inlet side of the filter press.

BOILING

After the wort is separated from the spent grain, it is boiled for about 1.5 to 2 hours Wort is boiled in order to sterilise and stabilise it, and to extract the constituents from hops which give beer its typical taste and aroma. According to Hough, the principal effects of wort boiling are: (1) arrest of enzyme activity, (2) sterilisation of the wort, (3) coagulation of proteins and tannins, (4) further precipitation of calcium phosphate and consequent fall in pH level, (5) distillation of volatile substances, (6) concentration of wort by evaporation of some of the water, (7) development of color and flavour by caramelisation of sugars, production of melanoidin, and oxidation of tannins, (8) extraction of resins from hops, (9) reduction of surface tension by hop oils and resins, (10) addition of essential oils and tannins from hops, and (11) modification of foam properties.

During boiling, most of the microorganisms are killed, some of the nitrogenous substances are coagulated, and some hop and malt components are volatilised. The slightly acid pH of the wort contributes to the destruction of microorganisms, and makes it unnecessary to raise the temperature much above the normal boiling point. Enzymes are also destroyed at this temperature, thus preventing further breakdown of starch and proteins. Dextrose is sometimes added to the kettle to bring the fermentable sugars to the proper level. The most striking phenomenon of the process is the so-called "hot break," which is the appearance of a precipitate that has formed from a reaction between the proteinaceous materials and the tannins from malt and hops.

Most of the colloidal proteins are subject to being coagulated by heat operating in conjunction with tannins extracted from malt husks and hops. Care must be taken to coagulate as much of the unstable protein as possible. One important factor is the pH, which should be near the isoelectric point of the proteins. This is generally considered to be about 5.2, and the pH should reach this value near the end of the boiling period (the pH drops by about 0.2 to 0.3 during boiling). Thus, the pH of the wort should be 5.4 or 5.5 at the start of the boil. Vigorous boiling also aids in the coagulation of proteins, since albumin particles, already denatured by heat, tend to accumulate on the surface of the wort around the bubbles of steam and air, and agglomerate more readily because of their proximity to each other. Excessively vigorous boiling in an open kettle may, however, have detrimental effects, such as the conversion of coagulated proteins into soluble forms through oxidation.

Hops are added chiefly to furnish two kinds of substances, essential oils and bitter resins. The resins are responsible for the typical bitter flavour of beer. They are insoluble in cold wort, but somewhat soluble in hot wort at its normal pH. As they are only sparingly soluble in water, their solubility in wort is attributed to their adsorption on colloidal particles which are later precipitated, and thus brought out of solution again. This loss is greater at lower pH levels, so that the pH of the wort should not be allowed to fall below 5.2. During boiling, the resins are partially hydrolysed, oxidised, and polymerised. The essential oils of hops are very volatile and evaporate during boiling. Therefore, if a good aroma is desired, more hops must be added near the end of the boiling period. Occasionally, hop oil is added to the finished beer.

Another change occurring during boiling is a darkening of the color, caused by a caramelisation of sugars, formation of melanoidins, and oxidation of tannin to phlobaphene. These changes, which are accompanied by the development of a malty flavor in the beer, are accentuated by a high pH and excessive aeration, while they may be prevented or greatly reduced by adding sulfur dioxide prior to boiling. The reducing power of wort is increased during boiling by the formation of so-called reductones, which are tautomeric compounds. Aeration of wort during boiling lowers its reducing power.

Boiling conditions have a considerable effect on the quality of the finished beer. Head retention and shelf-life are affected. Yeast behavior is dependent to some extent on the hop components and nitrogenous substances remaining in the wort after boiling. Beers from worts mashed at 145°F do not differ in their shelf-life whether boiled for 30 min or 2 hr, but, if they have been mashed at 155°, stability is greatly increased and head retention decreased, by boiling the wort for the longer time.

The spent hops and most of the hot break are removed by the hop strainer, in a piece of equipment called the Whirpool.

COOLING

The hot wort must be cooled before it is fermented, since the high temperatures would otherwise inactivate yeast. The wort is cooled to between 57° and 61°F when top-fermenting yeast is to be used and to between 43° to 46°F for bottom-fermenting yeast.

During cooling, two precautions must be observed: (1) care must be taken not to infect the wort with foreign microorganisms, the temperature range between 104° and 68°F being favourable to their growth, and (2) enough oxygen must be dissolved in the wort to shorten the lag time of fermentation. In addition, the protein coagulated in the hot break should be entirely eliminated during the cooling process, and the turbid material appearing during cooling (the "cold break') should be at least partly precipitated so that it will not be carried over into the finished beer.

Wort cooling was originally carried out in large open vessels called coolships. Heat was dissipated to the surrounding without mechanical assistance. This was a slow, inefficient process and very conducive to contamination of the wort by microorganisms from the atmosphere. Later, refrigeration was applied to smaller open vessels to increase the rate of cooling.

Modern brewery practice is to solve these problems by using closed coolers and pumping measured amounts of sterile air into the wort in the coolers. A common but older design is that of concentric pipes, the cooling liquid flowing through the central cylinder and the wort and air through the outer ones. Plate coolers are also very common. Aeration in closed systems can be accomplished by forcing sterile air through porous filter tubes, thus forming minute bubbles in the cooled or cooling wort. Too much air must be avoided, as an excess can result in oxidation of part of the coagulated protein, preventing efficient precipitation. The proteins precipitate partly by agglomeration of oppositely charged particles, such as the positively charged derived albumins and the negatively charged nucleoproteins. If these particles are approximately in balance, precipitation will be nearly complete. Oxidation may destroy the balance by changing the charge on some of the particles.

Wort enters the cooler at a temperature around 205° to 210°F, and is cooled to the fermentation starting temperature which, depending on the type of beer being made, can vary from 41° to 64°F. The rate of wort cooling has very little influence on the properties of the finished beer.

Cold break formation takes place below 140°F. The consistency and amount of this precipitate will depend upon the character of the malt, the type and amount of adjuncts, the mashing procedure, the runoff, the hopping rate, and the extent of wort boiling. "Pneumatic" removal of cold break can be carried out in large brewing units, usually with a pitching vessel, or cold break can be removed by centrifugation or by filtration through kieselguhr.

To minimise growth of bacteria, coolers are designed to chill wort rapidly to below their optimum growth range. In the later stage of fermentation, the danger of infection is much less, because the disappearance of sugars and development of alcohol due to yeast action provide a less favourable medium for most microorganisms. After fermentation, the temperature of the beer is kept low so that it remains essentially free of bacterial action. It is finally pasteurised, or in some cases, passed through filters which remove nearly all microorganisms.

COMPOSITION OF WORT

Obviously, the composition of wort will vary according to the ingredients used in its preparation as modified by processing conditions and equipment the ingredients have encountered. This means the composition will be different for each brewery, though the proximate analyses for the worts of standard beers prepared by different breweries may be quite similar. Ranges in the analytical values for worts intended for North American lager beers are shown in Table 20.3.

Table 20.3. COMMON WORT QUALITY PARAMETERS

Test and unit	*Range*
Extract, °Plato	10.8—12.5
Apparent extract after rapid fermentation, °P	1.9—3.1
pH	5.2—5.7
Color, degrees by standard method	1.8—2.5
Iodine reaction	*
Bitterness units	10—20
Turbidity, FTU	12—48
Total protein (N X 6.25), %	0.35—0.60
Free amino nitrogen, mg per L	140—260
Formol nitrogen, mg per L	190—250
Viscosity, cp	1.3—1.6

1 From Burger and LaBerge (1985). Analytical methodology as prescribed by the American Society of Brewing Chemists.

* Negative to trace of erythrodextrin

Different products, beers, ales, stouts, light beers, etc., will also require their own specific formulas and therefore the worts for them will vary. The composition of a "typical" UK wort, according to Hough (1985), is (quantities in grams per liter) fructose 2.1, glucose 9.1, sucrose 2.3, maltose 52.4, maltotriose 12.8, nonfermentable carbohydrates 23.9, total nitrogen as nitrogen 0.8, total amino acids as nitrogen 0.3, total amino acids as such 1.65, total phenolic constituents 0.25, iso-alpha-acids 0.035, and calcium ions 0.065. Combining some of these categories, we find that there are about 66 grams per liter of mono- and di-saccharides and about 37 grams per liter of higher saccharides, a total of about 10% by weight of the wort being carbohydrates. This is certainly a "rich medium," as Hough says.

Another source (Meilgaard 1977) gives the following composition of wort solids: carbohydrates 90 to 92%, nitrogen compounds (N X 6.25) 3 to 6%, salts and minerals 1.5 to 2%, free acids (as lactic acid) 0.5 to 1.0%, phenolic substances 0.1 to 0.2%, hop bitter substances and oils 0.05 to 0.1%, and lipids 0.03 to 0.06%. The same author gives a breakdown of the 3 to 6% of carbohydrates that are referred to as minor wort carbohydrates (reported as per cent of total carbohydrates): pentoses 0.031, galactose 1.1 to 1.6, disaccharides (i.e., maltulose, isomaltose, nigerose, and melibiose) 1.39 to 3.3, and trisaccharides (i.e., maltotriulose, panose, isopanose, and raffinose) 1.5 to 2.8. The pentoses are non-fermentable, some of the others are fermentable, at least by certain yeasts.

FERMENTATION

As previously mentioned, lager beer is produced with bottom fermenting yeast. In making this product, wort is cooled to between 43° and 50°F and pumped into a collecting tub or hot wort tank. It remains here for about four hours to give the turbidity (hot and cold breaks) time to settle out, and is then transferred to the pitching tub, leaving the sediment behind. Here it is pitched, that is, mixed with the required amount of yeast, usually 0.75 to 1 lb of yeast per barrel of wort. The foam formed during mixing is skimmed off. After about 24 to 48 hr, the "kraeusen" appear. These formations are collections of foam caused by evolution of gases which carry hop resins and nitrogenous materials to the surface. As soon as kraeusen appear, the wort is pumped to the fermentation tank, which can be either open or closed. Closed fermentors are usually employed so that the carbon dioxide produced by the yeast can be collected and injected back into the beer at a later stage in the processing.

The major and critical change occurring during fermentation is the conversion of fermentable sugars to alcohol and carbon dioxide. These reactions can summarized by the equation:

$$C_6H_{12}O_6 \rightarrow 2\ CO_2 + 2\ C_2H_5OH + 22 \text{ calories}$$

It can be seen from this equation that heat is generated in fermentation. Therefore, the temperature of the system will rise, but it should not be permitted to exceed 46° to 48° F. Temperature control can be accomplished by pumping cold liquid through coils (called attemperators) fitted in the tank.

Progress of the fermentation is followed by determining, with a saccharometer, the amount of sugar present. The readings begin to fall almost immediately after the wort is pitched with yeast, and fall more rapidly as fermentation progresses. The fermentation becomes very active 15 to 18 hr after pitching and reaches its maximum height in 70 to 80 hr after pitching. This high level is maintained for 48 to 72 hr, after which it decreases in intensity. Fermentation is usually complete in 7 to 9 days. Saccharometer readings will drop about 0.2 to 0.5% each day in the early stages, fall 1.0 to 1.5% per day in the middle stages, and then decrease about 0.1% in the final stages.

During the active period, the foam rises in height and becomes darker in color due to the accumulation of hop resins, proteins, dead yeast cells, etc. When the rate of fermentation begins to decrease, the head of foam starts to collapse because not enough gas is being generated to support it. Less heat is generated when fermentation slows down, and the rate of cooling can be moderated, but the temperature should not be allowed to rise above 59°F.

Fermentation is considered to be complete when the desired degree of sugar conversion (called attenuation) has taken place. If secondary fermentation during storage is to be performed, some sugar must remain; otherwise, fermentation will be continued to the stage of complete attenuation. When fermentation is determined to be complete, the beer is cooled slowly to 39°F and pumped off carefully, in a manner calculated to avoid disturbance of the sediment which has collected in the bottom of the tank. This sediment consists of three layers. The bottom layer is a sludge composed of materials which had been suspended in the wort. The middle layer is the yeast crop, which will be saved for pitching subsequent fermentations. The top layer is mostly hop resins.

The yeast collected in an average brewing operation is about 4 to 5 times the amount needed for pitching. It can be collected without prior separation and transferred through sanitised yeast lines to the yeast room where it is cleaned and washed. Stabilising procedures, mainly based on lowering of PH, are used to establish bacteriostatic conditions. Adding of antibiotics has also been suggested. If the yeast is to be kept longer than five days, it is compressed (dewatered) for storage, and then kept in a special "sterile" storage area. Yeast not required for brewery operations is filtered, dried,, and sold for use as stock feed and for human consumption.

In addition to the large amounts of carbon dioxide and ethanol which are produced in the fermenting vessels, much smaller quantities of many other compounds are generated. Some of these originate from side reactions of the yeast, while others are produced by infecting microorganisms. Volatile acids, which are initially low in the wort, rise sharply during the early stages of fermentation, but their rate of formation then drops rather quickly. A second and more gradual rise occurs during the latter part of the fermentation process. Beers which are entirely free from infection during processing are invariably low in volatile acids, containing only about 30 to 50 ppm.

Growth and multiplication of yeast cells are phenomena separate from fermentation, but in brewing these processes go hand in hand. To support them, nutrients are required, and these are supplied by the wort. The essential classes of substances which must be present for yeast nutrition are mineral salts, sources of carbon, nitrogen, and energy, and growth factors. The necessary mineral salts are ordinarily present in the wort, coming primarily from the malt but partially from the brewery water. A small portion (about 2%) of the metabolisable sugar in the wort is utilised by the yeast as a source of carbon and energy. Nitrogen requirements are satisfied by the amino acids and peptides present in the wort—more complex protein fragments and proteins themselves cannot be utilised by the yeast cells. *S. uvarum* can synthesize many of the growth factors which it requires, the specific capacity varying from strain to strain. Factors which must be present in the growth medium appear to be present in normal wort. They originate from malt, which is rich in the vitamin B complex and other growth factors.

Growth of yeast during beer fermentation can be divided into five well-defined phases: (1) a latent phase lasting a few hours during which no significant visible change occurs in the cells; (2) a lag phase, with slow growth, lasting only a short time and dependent to some extent on the amount of oxygen available to the cells; (3) a logarithmic phase of rapid increase in growth, continuing for about four hours at 64°F but only eight minutes under ideal conditions at 86°F; (4) a phase of declining growth during which the rate of reproduction falls slowly; and (5) a stationary phase during which the rate of multiplication is approximately equal to the rate at which the cells die and autolyse.

In addition attenuation, several other changes take place in the wort during fermentation. At the end of fermentation, the beer contains about 0.3% dissolved carbon dioxide and practically no dissolved oxygen. The pH falls, due to formation of carbon dioxide and organic acids, mostly lactic acid. The pH after bottom fermentation depends on the quantity of buffers present but is normally 4.2 to 4.4—occasionally 4.0 or even less. The nitrogen content falls by about a third, due mostly to the assimilation of amino acids and peptides by the yeast, but partly to the precipitation of complex proteins caused by low pH, the presence of alcohol, and denaturation at the surface of the carbon dioxide bubbles. Hop resins are largely eliminated by the fall in pH, adsorption on the yeast cells, and coagulation in the head. The bitter material in the head must be skimmed off carefully to avoid too sharp a taste in the finished beer. Finally, the color of the wort becomes paler during fermentation, partly because some of the pigmented substances are collected in the surface scum, partly because the reducing action of the yeast on oxidised tannin, and partly by the normal fall in color intensity accompanying the drop in pH.

The brewer wants the yeast to flocculate near the end of fermentation. The better the flocculation, the easier it is to remove the yeast and the fewer the number of cells which are carried over. Different strains of yeast vary markedly in their flocculation characteristics. These can also be affected by wort conditions. S. *uvarum* forms no yeast cap, and the cells settle readily—two of the reasons this species is highly preferred for brewing.

After fermentation is complete, as shown by the attainment of a specific gravity of 1.009 to 1.0 14, the beer is gradually cooled to the lagering temperature of about 27° to 30°F. During a further holding period of 2 to 3 days, additional suspended solids will settle out. Finally, the beer is pumped into the lager cellar.

Infection, or the introduction of undesirable microorganisms into the wort or beer, can have very serious consequences. Infection can result from several sources. The wort, the atmosphere, the pitching yeast, and the equipment are common avenues for the introduction of contaminating organisms. A number of different species may appear in the wort, but *Aerobacter aerogenes* is the most common. Bacteria appearing in the fermentation area are the classic brewery organisms, *Lactobacillus pastorianus, Pediococcus cerevisiae,* and *Flavobacterium proteus.* In the post-blending area, various lactobacilli species, and in the filling and bottling shop *Saccharomyces diastaticus* are frequent contaminants.

STORAGE

After the beer is pumped out of the fermentation tank, it is passed through a cooler. Here it will be quickly brought from its original temperature of about 39°F to 32°F. It is then sent through a diatomaceous earth filter. Diatomaceous earth is preferable filter mass at this point, as the latter has a tendency to become clogged. The brilliant filtered beer is pumped into pressure tanks in a storage cellar. Here it is stored at or near 32°F and is carbonated with carbon dioxide previously collected from the fermentation tanks. Rarely, the beer is not chilled but is stored at 39° to 43°F, in which case a secondary fermentation takes place. At 32°F no further fermentation occurs, but the beer undergoes important aging reactions. During this time yeast cells and other insoluble materials (mostly nitrogenous) settle out, and the flavor is improved as a result of complex chemical changes involving aldehydes, esters, and higher alcohols.

Storage periods may be as long as six months, or in the case of English draft beer, as short as I or 2 days. American lager beer is usually held for 3 to 12 weeks. Other types of beer are held in "ruh" storage for 5 to 7 days at 32°F. During storage, the brewer tries to achieve a balance between the beneficial changes taking place, such as esterification, and undesirable changes related to autolysis, oxidation, etc. The net result is generally a more pleasant aroma, a more mature and less yeasty flavor, and greater resistance to haze development during distribution and marketing.

In continuous aging processes, beer is transferred from one tank to another, with recarbonation at each transfer. The purpose of these operations is to flush out any dissolved air which is present and to permit long and intimate contact of the carbon dioxide with the beer, so that it is not only mechanically held in solution but also adsorbed by the colloidal particles which are present. The beer is kept under 5 to 6 psi counter pressure during storage and transfer. A period of about two weeks is considered sufficient for adequate carbonation under these circumstances.

Most American beers have slightly more carbonation than European products. About 2.8 volumes of carbon dioxide is a common level. Fermentation gas is often collected and liquefied for later use in carbonating the beer. The gas may be added through large porous stones in the lagering tanks, or it may be injected into the stream of beer as it flows to the packaging equipment.

Natural carbonation, or kraeusening, is accomplished by adding from 10 to 20% of vigorously fermenting wort to the fully fermented beer in the lager tank. The tanks are closed after this addition and gas is allowed to build up to a selected pressure.

Sometime during storage the beer is usually chillproofed. When beer is chilled to a low temperature, a colloidal haze appears, but it disappears again when the beer is warmed slightly. The nature of chill haze was a subject of controversy for many years, but it is now regarded as a mixture or complex of proteins and tannins. The protein component is an extremely diverse mixture of degraded globulin-like bodies, hordein, and glutelin derivatives. Chillproofing is a treatment designed to minimize the appearance of this turbidity. Chillproofing treatments include such additives as tannic acid (to precipitate the proteins), bentonites and other adsorbents, and proteolytic enzymes.

After its stay in the lagering tanks, the beer is considered finished. It may be diluted, or standardised, especially if high gravity brewing is being practiced. According to Coors (1977), it is not unusual for brewers to begin fermentation with 16 to 18 degrees Plato (degrees Plato are equivalent to grams of solids per 100 ml liquid) worts which must be diluted 30 to 40%

with water to make typical American products. The deaerated water can be carbonated, or the beer can be carbonated after the water is added. After the water is added, the mixture is placed into a secondary storage tank so the beer and water can "marry." Final quality checks can also be made during this time. It is also possible to blend in the water just prior to packaging, and allow the aging effect to take place in the container.

Beer possesses its final flavor and aroma after aging, but it may still be slightly hazy. To remove this defect, the beer is given a final filtration through a pulp mass composed mostly of cellulose fiber, or through a bed of diatomaceous earth or other filtering and adsorbing materials. A plate and frame filter is the usual type of equipment. The process is not a simple sieving procedure—most of the particles present at this time are of colloidal size and would not be removed by any ordinary type of filter. It appears that most of the particles are removed by adsorption on the filter mass. Thus, not only particles which can be optically detected as haze, but also other substances too finely divided to be detected will be removed. The final filtration removes some proteins, hop resins, coloring matter, higher alcohols, and esters.

After filtration, the beer is racked into casks or filled into bottles or cans. Filtration, racking, and bottling should be carried out in a manner to avoid loss of carbon dioxide, infection, and oxidation. To prevent loss of carbon dioxide, the beer is kept cold and racked or bottled against a counter pressure of carbon dioxide or air. Carbon dioxide is preferred, since a counter pressure of air may result in the dissolving of some oxygen in the beer, and this could lead to gradual oxidation. Danger of infection is minimised by sterilising the filters and other machinery, and by keeping them as clean as possible.

Beer to be packed in bottles or cans must either be heat pasteurised or filtered through membranes which will remove virtually all microbial contamination. Pasteurisation changes the flavor somewhat, so that draft beer tastes different from bottle beer. The availability of membranes suitable for filter sterilisation has made it possible to bottle draft-style (i.e., not heat-treated) beer. Beer should be given a rough filtration to remove coarse material, then treated with pectolytic and hemicellulytic enzymes before membrane filtration.

A TYPICAL FORMULA

Although ingredients used and their proportions vary according to the type of beer and the brewer's philosophy, the following formula for a batch of beer will provide the reader with a brief summary of the requirements. Process conditions are in outline form only. Consult other parts of this chapter for details of the processing steps and the equipment involved.

The mash cooker is filled with 3,500 lb of corn grits, 675 lb of malt, 70 barrels of water, 2.1 qt of lactic acid, and 3 lb of calcium sulfate. The mixture is brought to boiling.

The mash tub is filled with 10,000 lb of barley malt, 100 barrels of water, 1.6 qt of lactic acid, and 2 lb of calcium sulfate. The mixture is heated according to a mashing schedule, and at the end of the heating period the cooker mash from the preceding step is added.

The above mixture is first filtered through the spent grain bed without additions. For sparging, 3.2 qt of lactic acid and 5.0 lb of calcium sulfate are added to the sparge water. Then, 1.4 qt of lactic acid and 2.0 lb of calcium sulfate are added during the "mashover," that is, the raking of the grain bed to mix it with the sparging solution.

The clarified wort and spargings are filled into the kettle as they arrive from the grant. This step will require about four hours. The mixture is boiled for 2.5 hr with the addition of 16 lb of salt and 4.25 lb of potassium metabisulfite. Hops are added in two portions as follows: 50 lb at 30 mm and 50 lb at 20 mm before the end of the boiling period. This mixture is added to the kettle over a period of 20 mm, before the end.

Two hours before the end of boiling, 1,000 lb of dextrose and 5 to 6 barrels of water are mixed in a separate vessel. The temperature is not allowed to rise above 162°F at any time during mixing. This dextrose solution is added to the kettle over a period of 20 mm, starting one hour before the completion of boiling.

During storage the following additions are made for each 100 barrels of beer (a standard U.S. barrel of beer is 31 gallons): 160 grams of $K_2S_2O_5$, 600 grams of chillproof, and 5 lb of gum arabic.

DETERIORATION PROCESSES IN BEER

One of the most important factors affecting appearance, taste, foam stability and shelf-life of beer is oxidation of proteins. It has already been pointed out that the proteins of beer can be divided into groups according to their molecular weight, solubility, and other characteristics. Different investigators have expressed different opinions on how the proteins should be classified in order to better understand their effects on the quality of beer. One scheme which has proved to be useful over the years has been the characterization method of St. Johnston (1948), who classified the principal protein fractions of wort and beer as follows:

(1) Protein T — the chill-sensitive, globulin-tannin complex. Isoelectric point 6.4, completely soluble at 140°F with solubility diminishing below this temperature.

(2) Protein C — the coagulable albumin. Isoelectric point 6.0, readily coagulable by heat.

(3) Protein O — the oxyprotein or nucleoprotein. Isoelectric point 3.9.

(4) Fraction D — soluble fraction. Probably proteoses associated with dextrins

At the pH of beer, about 4.3, nucleoproteins wall carry a negative charge and albumins a positive charge, so that mutual precipitation is possible. The equilibrium between these protein fractions can easily be upset by oxidation. According to various workers, proteins having sulfhydryl groups can be oxidised to higher molecular weight compounds. In addition, albumins can be oxidised with an attendant change of the charge from positive to negative. The negatively charged oxidation products can then combine with unchanged positively charged proteins, thus increasing the apparent molecular weight and causing mutual precipitation.

The net result of oxidation is to shift the equilibrium between different fractions that has been so carefully set up during brewing. The distribution of protein fractions at various stages during brewing, and four months after bottling, is shown in Table 20.4. Upon examining the values shown here, it can be seen that the amount of protein in all fractions decreases during fermentation, accompanied by an increase in the ratio high/total and a decrease in the ratio low/total. This can be ascribed to the use by the yeast of nitrogenous substances, especially amino acids and other low molecular weight components. It will be noted that the total protein content remains essentially constant once fermentation has been completed, but that the distribution in different fractions changes markedly. The decrease in the high molecular fraction and in its ratio to the total during storage is a result of chillproofing. The chillproofing agents in common use today are essentially proteolytic enzymes, added for the specific purpose of hydrolyzing high molecular weight proteins which are associated with tannins in complex compounds. These combinations tend to precipitate at low temperatures, while the lower molecular weight compounds present after proteolysis do not form precipitable compounds.

The progressive post-bottling increase in high molecular weight compounds at the expense of the low molecular weight fraction is due to oxidation and the mechanisms described above. These changes are accelerated by pasteurisation, oxidation being favored by the high temperature and by the dissolving of air from the bottle head space during heating, resulting in more intimate contact of oxygen with the beer. As oxidation continues, it has a noticeable effect on the appearance and flavor of the beer. The brilliance of the liquid decreases progressively until a definite haze, known as oxidation haze, becomes visible. This haze is the result of the formation of high molecular weight protein complexes having colloidal dimensions. It is of a different nature from chill haze, as it does not disappear on warming. With the onset of oxidation haze, the beer acquires a definite "oxidation flavor" which is noticeable to the average consumer.

Table 20.4. PROTEIN DISTRIBUTION IN BEER AT VARIOUS STAGES

Protein fraction	*Kettle sample* %	*After fermen-tation* %	*After storage* %	*After pasteu-risation* %	*After four months* %
High molecular	0.154	0.145	0.072	0.086	0.125
Medium molecular	^ 133	0.096	0.081	0.086	0.105
Low molecular	u.207	0.111	0.196	0.180	0.118
Nonprotein	0.031	0.027	0.300	0.028	0.029
Total protein	0.524	0.379	0.379	0.379	0.380
High/total	29.3	38.31	18.9	22.7	33.0
Medium/total	25.3	25.3	21.4	22.7	27.6
Low/total	39.4	29.2	51.8	47.3	31.0
Non—protein/total	5.95	6.14	7.90	7.33	8.30

The distribution of protein fractions in beer at the time it is bottled can be used to estimate its probable shelf-life. Thus, if the proportion of high molecular weight components is greater than usual, the time required for visible haze to develop will be less than when this proportion is low at the start. One test which was used for many years to give an indication of the probable shelf-life of beer is the ITT (indicator time test) developed by Gray and Stone of Wallerstein Laboratories. This test measures the reducing power of beer, which increases as the proteins are oxidised. Results are, however, influenced by other factors besides the state of oxidation of the proteins. While the test is quite reliable in following the progress of oxidation in a single beer, its use to compare one beer with another sometimes leads to false conclusions. For example, the presence of hydrogen peroxide in beer has long been known to have a detrimental effect on its stability, and the presence of as little as 0.005% has been known to cause haziness. Hyrdogen peroxide is formed by the reaction of molecular oxygen and auto-oxidizable substances such as catechol, ascorbic acid, isoascorbic acid, and electron transfer systems, notably reduced flavin nucleotides. In the presence of peroxide, the ITT may show a zero or low value, even though haze and oxidation taste are present.

In view of the deleterious effects of oxidation flavor, many attempts have been made to prolong the shelf-life of beer by adding antioxidants.

For example, as early as 1939, recommendations were made to add ascorbic acid, and this substance has found rather wide application in the brewing industry. Others have pointed out that, in removing oxygen, ascorbic acid is changed to dehydroascorbic acid, which is a known oxidising agent for glutelins. Reductones prepared from sugars have been suggested to avoid this effect. The glucose oxidase-catalase system, which removes oxygen by enzymatic reaction with glucose, has also been recommended. A typical beer contains perhaps 0.001% glucose. This amount of reactant, though seemingly very small, is enough to bind several times the amount of oxygen normally present when the reaction is mediated by the glucose oxidasecatalase system.

Adding proteolytic enzymes to beer, as is done in chillproofing, will also lengthen the beer's shelf-life and delay the appearance of oxidation haze and decrease chill haze. These enzymes must be used with discretion, however, as too great a shift of the equilibrium toward low molecular fractions at the expense of the high and medium fractions will change the surface tension enough to cause foam instability and a poor head on the beer. All other things being equal, higher and more stable foams are obtained with lower surface tensions. As the molecular weight of the proteins decreases, the surface tension of the beer increases and the foam quality is adversely affected. Judicious use of proteolytic enzymes will result in an increase in the proportion of proteins in the optimum range without undue shifting of the equilibrium toward low molecular weight fractions.

Fig. 20.3. Small Brewery Pilot Plant

ANALYTICAL CONTROLS IN BREWING

Before the development of scientific analytical methods, brewing was entirely an art, and empirical methods for controlling quality were handed down from generation to generation, and from master brewer, to journeyman, to apprentice. While many phases of brewing are still largely an art, and a thorough practical knowledge of the factors to be considered at every stage is indispensable, the brewer now has at his command a host of scientific analytical methods to aid in controlling quality and to detect possible sources of trouble before they become serious. A pilot plant is included among the facilities of most modern breweries. Figure 20.3 shows a small brewery pilot plant.

Chemical and physical analyses are generally performed on the raw materials used, on the intermediate products obtained during brewing and storage, and on the finished product. A complete listing of all the tests used is beyond the scope of this chapter, and only a few of the most important analyses will be given to indicate the nature of examinations which may be carried out. Full directions for carrying out most of the analyses in general use are given in *Methods of Analysis of the American Society of Brewing Chemists*, hereafter referred to as ASBC Methods.

The data found in a typical analytical report on a sample of beer will include: type of container; clarity; sediment; clarity, chill test (-1 to 0°C); color, S.R.M.; apparent extract, degrees Plato; real extract, degrees Plato; alcohol, by weight, g/l00g; original extract, degrees Plato; apparent degree of attenuation, %; real degree of attenuation, %; reducing sugars, as anhydrous maltose, g/100g; iodine reaction; protein (N x 6.25); bitterness units; iron, mg/b; carbon dioxide, volumes (air corrected); sulfur dioxide, total mg/b; "air," ml per container; copper, mg/b; and foam. Some of these items are related. For example, a sample having a certain amount of alcohol by weight and a certain amount of apparent extract can have no variation in the alcohol by volume, the real extract, and the degree of attenuation. The alcohol by weight and the apparent extract readings are the most frequently used values in daily production and quality control of finished beer, according to Swistowicz (1977).

Table 20.5 lists the ranges of some of the components, as expected in North American lager beers. The ranges are taken from a table of Burger and LaBerge (1985), while the typical values are from Hsu (1988); analytical methods are those described in publications of the American Society of Brewing Chemists. In addition to the characteristics included in Table 20.5, brewers will usually monitor formol or amino nitrogen, dextrins, and sulfur dioxide.

Analyses applied to the ingredients used in beer, as well as to the packaging materials, etc., can be expected to vary somewhat from brewery to brewery, but a general outline of the quality control measures most commonly in effect will be given below.

Atypical evaluation of hop quality might include an examination of the cones for color, luster, size, and condition, tests for amount, color, and condition of lupulin, evaluation of aroma, determination of the amounts of leaves, stems, and seeds, and chemical tests for content of moisture, alpha resins, beta resins, gamma resins, soft resins, and total resins. A calculation of brewing value might be made by adding one-fourth of the beta resin content to the alpha resin content.

Brewing syrups and sugars would be initially examined for consistency or presence of lumps, color, odor, and taste. Clarity and color of 10% solutions would be judged. Specific gravity, as is extract, degrees Baume, moisture content, fermentable extract (as is and dry basis), dextrose equivalent, iodine reaction, pH value, protein content, ash content, diastatic power, and dextrose sucrose contents would be determined and reported.

Table 20.5. QUALITY CONTROL TESTS FOR AMERICAN LAGER BEER

Test and unit	*Range*	*Typical*
Original (wort) extract *Plato	10.7–12.1	11.5
Apparent extract, *Plato	1.9–3.0	2.08
Real extract, *Plato	4.0–4.8	3.90
Alcohol, % by volume	—	5.00
Alcohol, % by weight	3.4–4.0	3.92
Apparent degree of fermentation, %		81.9
Real degree of ferm., calculated %	62–68	66.1
Color, standard reference degrees	2.5–2.9	3.9
pH	3.9–4.4	4.26
Clarity, formazin turbidity units	35 max.	—
Foam stability, sigma value	110–150	—
Carbon dioxide, volumes	2.5–2.8	—
Air, ml per 12 fl. oz. (0.355 L)	1.0 max.	—
Iodine reaction	negative	—
Reducing sugars, %	—	0.97
Protein, %	—	0.37
Acid as lactic, %	—	0.21
Bitterness units, BU	—	11.9
Diacetyl, ppm	—	0.11
Calcium, mg per L	40–80	
Sodium, mg per L	40–220	
Copper, mg per L	0.15 max.	
Iron, mg per L	0.10 max.	

Cereal adjuncts would be examined for off-color, off-odor, foreign material, mold, weevils, and other possible gross defects. Chemical analyses normally applied include moisture content, oil content, extract (as is and dry basis), time of conversion, ash content, and protein content.

These and other analyses which are routinely applied in most modern breweries may appear to be long and unnecessarily detailed. While they may be so when considered individually, certain groups of tests serve to point out the most suble off-taste characteristics, such as sweetness, bitterness, and oxidation.

Other groups will point out deviations in characteristics such as foam stability and shelf-life. For example, the group of analyses associated with foam stability includes surface tension, surface activity, foam sigma, foam density, and protein and sugar distribution. Seldom are all of the tests conducted on an individual beer sample.

To reveal potential bitterness, the pertinent analyses are sulfur dioxide, iron, copper, tannins, carbon dioxide, air, and melanoidins. These substances are normally present in beer, but in very small amounts, well below the organoleptic threshold, i.e., the level at which a difference in flavor can be detected by taste panels or an expert taster. The approximate organoleptic threshold for each of these substances has been established, and it is used to evaluate the analytical results. For example, many expert tasters, perhaps not all, would agree that, if the amount of iron is 0.35 ppm or below, no off flavor can be detected, but a value of 0.70 ppm would almost certainly result in a distinct flavor. If 0.35 ppm is removed from beer testing at the high level, the flavor will again be normal.

When the threshold values have been established, it is easy to tell which substance or combination of substances is responsible for any off- flavor which may be detected, and the cause of the trouble can be corrected. Before accurate analytical methods were developed, correction of problems was necessarily based on trial and error techniques, and the length of time required to find the source of the deviation was largely a method of luck. Even more important than correction of an existing off-flavor is the ability to detect any "creeping trouble" before it actually results in a detectable change of flavor. For example, if the iron values for successive batches of beer showed a steady increase from 0.35 to 0.50 ppm, steps could be taken to find a reason for the increase and correct it before the organoleptic threshold was reached.

MODIFICATIONS IN PRODUCTS AND PROCESSES

VARIANT PRODUCTS

The variant products described here will be restricted to malt liquors, reduced-alcohol beers, and alcohol-free beers.

The simplest method for producing a "light" beer, reduced alcohol/ reduced calorie, is to dilute a regular beer with water. Some of the early varieties were allegedly made this way. Of course, this is not a new procedure. Many finished brews require some dilution with water to bring the alcohol content within legal limits and maintain product uniformity; also, substantial dilution is required if high gravity brewing is being practiced. It is obvious, however, that difficulties with taste, viscosity, appearance, stability, etc. will develop as the concentrations of all the constituents are substantially reduced. The product doesn't taste, look, or foam like 'real' beer. Fermentation of a diluted wort is another possibility; to the problems of taste are added the difficulties of obtaining a suitable fermentation with greatly altered concentrations of fermentables and other solubles. A possible solution would be to prepare a normal beer by customary techniques and then remove most or all of the alcohol by a method which causes few changes in the types and amounts of other ingredients. The product would be a reduced alcohol beer, though not necessarily a reduced calorie beer (depending on legal definitions of this term).

A great number of methods for reducing the alcohol content of fermented beverages can be found in the literature. Of course, it is no great problem to merely reduce the alcohol content, this can be done by well known methods such as distillation, freeze concentration, or membrane separation. Extraction with supercritical carbon dioxide can also be employed, and perhaps is the least harmful of the available methods, but it is also the most expensive to apply. Wiesenberger *et al.* (1989) say it is also not selective enough to permit a high degree of dealcoholization without removing other valuable constituents.

One method for making low-alcohol fermented beverages, which is apparently in use or has been used, is based on a combined multi-stage process (described by Wiesenberger *et al.).* First, the constituents of high molecular weight are separated by a two-stage membrane separation method. The remaining fluid is subjected to a vacuum distillation which removes most of the ethanol.

The main problem with all these procedures arises from the difficulty of retaining in the treated fluid the flavor to which the consumer has become accustomed in the traditional beverage. Alcohol is, itself, a flavor component and it will be impossible to exactly duplicate the original flavor when the alcohol is removed, but other aromatic and flavorful substances are also lost when any of the known methods for alcohol removal are applied. Generally, the problems become greater as more ethanol is removed.

Malt liquors, generally understood as being higher alcohol versions of beer, appeal to a certain segment of the beer-drinking public. No doubt most malt liquors are prepared from worts having higher than normal concentrations of fermentables, using somewhat modified fermentation procedures. They could also be prepared by removing some of the water from a normally fermented beer. According to Dougherty (1977), high gravity brewing has been practiced successfully for many years. This is a method by which a wort is produced and fermented at substantially higher original gravity than usual. It is said that high gravity brewing is advantageous in terms of reduced requirements for brewhouse and cellar capacity, yeast nutrition and management, and finished beer character. Disadvantages are lowered efficiency of wort separation and different fermentation characteristics. The method obviously gives products of higher than normal alcohol content, and some of them may be suitable for sale as malt liquors merely by modifying the final standardization (dilution) step.

The preparation of a flavored liqueur product from a malt-based precursor (or wort) by freeze concentration has been described by Patino *et al.* (1989). Preparation of the wort is by essentially conventional brewing techniques. The fermented wort is filtered and decolorised and most or all of the flavor removed, and as much water removed as is necessary to achieve the desired alcohol content, for example 26% alcohol by volume. Flavorants such as sugar and fruit juices, and appropriate colorants are added to achieve the final liqueur characteristics.

VARIANT PROCESSES

In this section, some old and some new modifications of the brewing process will be described as a means of suggesting directions for further investigations. There is an obvious need for methods which reduce the large amounts of liquid which are present at any given time, so that floor space and equipment costs can be brought down. An obvious way to proceed would be to speed up the steps of fermentation and ruh storage—the same quantity of fluid would be bandied but it would be in the plant for a shorter time. Another way is to ferment and store worts of substantially greater concentration. There are many practical difficulties in each of these approaches. It would certainly seem to be possible to speed up wort cooking by using continuous heat treatment at higher than normal temperatures.

One approach that has received considerable support is to make the brewing process continuous, and, particularly, to shorten the fermentation and rest periods. According to Hough (1985), patented methods of continuous fermentation have existed since about 1905. In 1957, the Morton Coutts and Labatt systems were patented. These plants consisted essentially of three stirred tanks in series. Yeast is introduced into the first tank along with a continuous stream of wort. The wort is fermented and overflows into the next vessel, and this process continues until the end of the line. With fully mixed worts, where the yeast is inoculated once, an equilibrium becomes established in each vessel of the series. The specific gravity and yeast count are determined by the rate of flow of the wort, the temperature, and the wort strength. If yeast is constantly recycled into the first vessel, this will influence the fermentation so that a higher relative flow rate of wort may be employed. In the system described by Hough, the total dwell time of the wort in the series of vessels was 24 to 40 hr. It seems that most of these so-called cascade systems have now been superseded because they proved to be too expensive as compared with modern batch plants.

Tower fermentation is another method which was developed to make some parts of the brewing process continuous. In these procedures, wort is passed through a bed of yeast held within a vertically aligned cylindrical fermentation vessel. The wort is pitched with a strongly sedimenting yeast, but the aggregations of yeasts are deflocculated at the base of the vessel by the high concentration of wort sugars. Some mixing of the contents of the tower occurs, but there is considerable upward plug flow. Wort flow is so adjusted that, when the fermenting wort reaches the top of the vessel, it has been fermented to the required extent. As fermentation progresses, the yeast again acquires its flocculent properties and tends to sediment against the upward flow of wort. A decanting device at the top of the vessel provides an inclined surface to additionally encourage separation of the yeast. Thus, beer substantially free of yeast flows to pest-fermentation equipment. A dwell-time of about eight hours was normally needed to get a result approximating batch fermentation. Highly anaerobic conditions in the tower favor high alcohol yields and minimize the risk of infection while the flow pattern tends to purge the fermenter of nonviable cells and any other nonflocculent organisms. Royston (1966) described the APV tower fermenter which can run continuously for six months and produce a completely acceptable product twenty times faster than batch fermentation methods.

Another tows fermentation system, the Lefrancois plant, has been successfully used to the production of food yeast, and Cauwe (1968) described an adaptation suitable for continuous brewing. Cost of such an installation would be about a third of that required for a conventional plant, yields are greater, (i.e., losses are smaller), and the beer is ready for racking ten hours after brewing. In the Lafrancois tower, the wort is maintained in the form of a perpetually circulating foam, the foam being created by blowing carbon dioxide into the base of the fermenter. The defects with tower fermenters which were observed in practice included difficulties in matching the flavor of batch beers, infection problems with lactic acid bacteria, and a long start-up period of 2 to 3 weeks before a suitable equilibrium state was reached

Another example is the Pablo continuous lautering system (Harsanyi 1968). This method continuously separates the mash into wort and spent grains in a series of centrifugations. The wort extractor consists of a round, horizontally aligned tank that houses a conically shaped sieve drum. Mash is introduced into the narrow end of the drum, and the extracted grains are discharged from the wide end. Wort passes through the perforated walls of the drum and is collected in other vessels. Grain remaining in the drum is further extracted *in situ* by spraying with dilute wort under pressure.

RECENT IMPROVEMENTS

In recent years, there have been a number of techniques proposed for achieving more rapid or more efficient production of beer. Many of these have been concerned with accelerating the primary fermentation step. It is has been known for centuries that raising the wort's temperature during fermentation will increase the rate of alcohol production and shorten the fermentation period as long as the temperature is not so high it damages the yeast. Vigorous agitation, above the agitation normally occurring as a result of carbon dioxide evolution, will also accelerate the fermentation rate. Use of these expedients seems, however, to change the flavor of the beer; they lead to the development of undesirable, so-called "winey" off-flavors, apparently due to the production of increased amounts of volatile compounds such as higher alcohols and esters. They also lead to excessive yeast growth, which is undesirable.

A patented method of continuous fermentation involves the use of yeast immobilised in calcium alginate gel particles which are packed in a reactor through which wort is passed. The inventors claim a significant increase in output per unit volume, for a small-scale plant.

The flavor problems which plague most continuous brewing schemes are apparently due to the reduced time they allow for yeast to modify undesirable aromatic compounds. An example of the unwanted odorous compounds is diacetyl. Although this substance has a buttery flavor which is, in fact, much appreciated in many foods, it is unacceptable in beer. In conventional fermentation processes, the time the yeast is in contact with the wort is sufficient for the cells to absorb diacetyl and to convert diacetyl, precursors to diacetyl which is then absorbed. Other compounds such as hydrogen sulfide and acetaldehyde—which are the principal contributors to the "green" aroma of beer after primary fermentation—are much reduced during maturation. It has been suggested that the addition of diacetyl reductase and its cofactor (nicotinamide adenine dinucleotide) to continuously fermented wort would improve flavor, but the cost would be raised as well, and other problems might result.

Processes involving the use of reactors packed with immobilised yeast present certain difficulties; for example, the wort must be very free of particulates in order to prevent clogging. Also, a considerable amount of fresh wort must be constantly available, necessitating the use of chilled holding vessels to reduce the risk of bacterial contamination and suitable heat exchangers for warming the wort prior to fermentation.

In a patented invention of Hsu (1988), continuous brewing is achieved and some of the disadvantages found in earlier methods are said to be avoided by encapsulating the yeast cells in a semi-permeable matrix material. According to the invention, as applied to beer-making, the batch fermentation process takes place in the same kinds of vessels conventionally employed, such as open or closed tanks. Wort of the usual type, without need for extensive filtration to remove suspended matter, is added to the tank and pitched with yeast in the form of small particles containing yeast cells immobilized in a semi-permeable matrix material. The tank is fitted with a screen or membrane allowing the encapsulated yeast to be restricted to one section of the vessel. Yeast concentrations will general be at least as much as the concentrations employed in conventional brewing. Neither exogenous agitation nor the use of elevated temperatures is required in order to obtain rapid fermentation, so that the production of undesired alcohols and esters or of excess foam is avoided.

To prepare the encapsulated yeast-containing particles described in the Hsu patent, yeast cells are mixed with (for example) a sodium alginate solution which is then gelled by adding a solution containing calcium ions. Conditions of mixing are adjusted so as to result in small particles of the encapsulated yeast.

In the process of Lommi *et al.* (1990), secondary fermentation is reduced from the normal several days or weeks required for the production of lager beer to no more than three hours. The innovations include heat treatment for conversion of diacetyl precursors to diacetyl and then to flavorless compounds in an enzymic reaction, and fermentation with yeast immobilized on granular (diethylaminoethyl)-cellulose. The latter material is said to have been used for many years in the commercial production of high-fructose corn syrup. The immobilised yeast preparation is inclosed in continuous fermentation vessels which have been run for as long as seven months without regeneration. The inventors estimate that capital investment costs and space requirements for the immobilised yeast systems would be about one-eighth that required for a conventional brewery which would have to use lagering tanks, extra space, and miscellaneous equipment instead of the continuous reactors. The product of this test plant is apparently being mixed with the output of a conventional plant and distributed to customers (in Finland) without complaint.

Computer control of the fermentation process, in which temperature, agitation, wort addition, yeast addition, product withdrawal, and as many other factors as possible are controlled by programmed devices, would seem to be an obvious way of improving uniformity, decreasing human errors, and speeding up the process. Whitford (1989) patented a system for automatic control of fermentation in the preparation of alcoholic beverages. Though this invention was strongly oriented toward the making of wine, some of its principles could no doubt be applied to beer fermentation. In one embodiment of the process, the equipment comprises: (1) a yeast propagating tank; (2) a continuous fermenting tank; (3) a first pump having an input pipe connected to a source of sugar solution and an output pipe connected to the continuous fermenting tank; (4) a second pump having an input pipe connected to an outlet of the continuous fermenting tank; (5) a Baume-sensor and a yeast concentration sensor in communication with the contents of the continuous fermenting tank; and (6) a computer connecting the sensors with the pumps so that the rates of input of sugar solution and discharge of product vary in accordance with yeast activity in the continuous fermenting tank so as to retain the Baume and yeast count substantially constant.

DISTILLED PRODUCTS

Ethanol for whiskey, vodka, brandy, and other beverages of high alcoholic content is obtained by distilling worts made by fermenting grain mashes, grape juice, and other natural sources of carbohydrates. Industrial alcohol is generally distilled from cheaper sources of carbohydrate, such as low grade sugar concentrates (e.g., blackatrap molasses), or is made synthetically. The flavor of the finished distilled beverages is not as closely tied to wort composition as is that of beer, since the distillation step eliminates most of the minor flavoring ingredients which develop in the mash.

Table 20.6, which is based on USDA figures, compares the amount of grain sorghum, barley and malt, and corn and corn products utilised in beer with that used in distilled spirits. The figures for distilled spirits are mostly for beverage alcohol but also include some industrial alcohol and may include some fuel alcohol. Brewery consumption of barley and malt far exceeds the usage of these products for distilled spirits, but more corn and corn products are presently being used in distilled spirits. There has been a pronounced increase in the use of grain sorghum for distilled spirits during the last ten years. Of course, other grains, such as rice, much used in beer, and rye, used to some extent in whiskey, are not included in this report.

To prepare mashes for distilled beverage fermentations, corn, rye, or other grain is ground, mixed with water, and cooked under pressure to thoroughly gelatinise the starch and sterilize the mash. After partial cooling, barley malt or another enzyme source is added to hydrolyse the starch to fermentable sugars (principally maltose). The mash is then pumped to fermenters, the temperature is adjusted, and yeast is added. If sour mash whiskey is to be made, some of the residue from previous batches of fermented mash is also added, so as to inoculate the material with microorganisms other than brewers' yeast.

Table 20.6. USAGE OF GRAIN IN ALCOHOL AND DISTILLED SPIRITS

	2003		*2004*	
	Beer	*Distilled spirits*	*Beer*	*Distilled spirits*
	in millions of bushels			
Corn and corn products	47.0	23.2	31.3	77.1
Barley and malt	144.2	3.4	140.5	2.2
Grain sorghum	—	4.1	—	14.6

Under the conditions usually employed, the fermentable sugars are completely converted to alcohol (and other substances) in 48 to 72 hours. Alcohol is then distilled from the mash without further separation of the components. Stills of the continuous column design can be used. Obviously, the fermenting process is simpler and less critical than the method used for fermenting beer wort.

Alcohol for whiskey is distilled at slightly under 160 proof, or 80% ethanol by volume. About 2.5 gallons of absolute alcohol or 5 gallons of 100 proof alcohol can be obtained from a bushel of corn, and slightly less from a bushel of rye. The alcohol is adjusted to the desired proof with plain or distilled water and placed in charred barrels for aging. Flavor of the whiskey depends upon the grain used, fermentation conditions (including inoculum), method of distillation, proof of the distillate, and method and conditions of aging.

21 PROCESSING OF HOT-SERVE CEREALS

There are two processing steps which are common to the manufacture of nearly all uncooked breakfast cereals. One of these is the reduction of particle size and the other is the elimination from the raw material of some of the fibrous substances found in the whole grain. The effect of these operations is to reduce cooking time and to improve the texture and perhaps the digestibility of the cooked food. There is usually no attempt to alter materially the natural flavor of the grain by hydrolysing its starches or caramelising its sugars, although it is true the heat treatment often applied to oatmeal changes its flavor somewhat.

Many consumers find the cooking time required for preparing meals using ingredients containing unaltered grain products to be excessive. To increase convenience, and therefore consumer acceptance, it is highly desirable to decrease the time required for kitchen preparation. Ideally, it should be possible to pour boiling water on the cereal, stir the mixture an few times, and then consume it. This ideal has been achieved with some modifications of oatmeal and wheat farina, although, it is true that the texture of the finished product is not quite the same as that obtained by cooking the unmodified granules.

Some hot-serve cereals are made from mixed grains which have been precooked and then dried, or from a combination of grains with other ingredients such as nonfat dry milk. Cereals for infant feeding may be precooked mixtures of ingredients which are dried in thin flake form. These flakes can be quickly rehydrated by adding the proper amount of hot water and stirring briefly. The consistency or texture of such materials is generally not appreciated by most adults, since the cereals as served tend to be somewhat pasty and sticky.

WHEAT CEREALS

The uncooked wheat cereal having the largest consumption is farina, a typical example being Cream of Wheat. This product is nothing more than the wheat middlings which are described in greater detail in the chapter on Milling. Middlings are chunks of endosperm for all practical purposes free of bran and germ. When reduced in size, middlings become flour. In the manufacture of farina for breakfast cereal, it is necessary to use hard wheat as a raw material since soft wheat yields a product which becomes excessively pasty upon cooking. About 30% of the wheat coming into a mill can be obtained as farina by good milling techniques. It is seldom, if ever, that wheat is milled specifically for the purpose of obtaining farina.

Particle size is thought to be a critical factor influencing consumer acceptance. All the farina should pass through a U. S. Standard No. 20 woven wire cloth sieve; not more than 10.0% should pass through a No. 45 sieve; and not more than 30.0% should pass through a No. 100 sieve. Vitamin and mineral enrichment is usually applied to farina. Vitamins are normally added in the dry state which seems to be satisfactory in practice but does give some opportunity for separation in the package.

Disodium phosphate has been used (at about the 0.25% level) to increase the rate at which farina cooks. Other steps are required to get an "instant" farina which is ready to eat after about one minute of cooking time. One method of decreasing cooking time is to apply proteolytic enzymes (such as bromelin) or fungal enzymes so that microscopic pathways for water penetration are formed in the granule.

Farina flavored with dried malt syrup or with cocoa is marketed. Generally, these products are simple mixtures of the dry flavoring ingredients with middlings.

Whole wheat meal, cracked wheat, flaked wheat, flaked wheat, and farina with bran and germ are sold as hot cereals to a rather limited extent. The shelf-life of these materials is limited by the tendency of germ oils to become rancid unless the product is specially processed.

An instant cook-in-the-bowl cereal made from wheat was described by Spring (1971). Wheat, preferably hard red winter wheat, is milled to a particle size such that at least 90% of it passes through a No. 12 Tyler mesh screen and less than 10% through a 42 mesh screen. The milled fraction is tempered to a moisture content of 15 to 16% and a temperature of 185 to 220°F, and then flaked to 0.007 to 0.008 inch thick by passing the particles between a set of flaking rolls having a slight pressure differential. The flaked grain is then dried to a moisture content of 8 to 9%. The cereal rehydrates readily when mixed with boiling water in a serving bowl.

CORN CEREALS

Corn grits is the maize analogue of farina. For all practical purposes, it is just the endosperm of corn ground into medium coarse granules. Large amounts of grits are consumed in the southern states. They are served with sugar and milk or cream as a breakfast cereal ("mush"). They can also be served as a potato or rice substitute at the noon and evening meals, often being topped with butter or gravy ("grits"). Grits are generally cooked with water, only salt being added. The boiled grits can be allowed to cool and the congealed mass sliced into fairly thick strips and fried (with or without preliminary flouring) to give a culinary delight which is served with syrup or gravy topping.

Corn grits is one of the products obtained in dry milling of corn kernels, a process which is described in considerable detail in a preceding chapter.

OAT CEREALS

The typical commercial oat products used as breakfast cereals or breakfast cereal ingredients can be categorized as (Webster 1986):

1. Rolled oats, produced by flaking whole groats. These are the thickest of standard oat-flake products. Flake thickness varies from 0.020 to 0.030 inch, depending on the intended use. Thicker flakes require longer cooking times and maintain flake integrity during extended holding times.
2. Steel-cut groats are produced by the sectioning of groats into several pieces by a kind of cutting action (as contrasted to crushing); they are used in the preparation of flakes and flour and as a specialty ingredient.
3. Quick oats are flakes produced from steel-cut groats. In this process, oat groats are typically cut into three or four pieces before the final steaming and flaking processes. Quick oats, which are usually 0.0 14 to 0.018 inch thick, require less cooking time than whole-oat flakes.
4. Baby oats are also produced from steel-cut groats, but the flakes are thinner and have a smaller particle size than quick oats. These smaller, thinner flakes cook more rapidly than quick oats and have a smoother texture.
5. Instant oat flakes are produced from "instantised" steel-cut groats. Before cutting, the groats are subjected to a special proprietary process that allows them to acquire a satisfactory eating consistency after a relatively short cooking time. These flakes are typically 0.0 11 to 0.0 13 inch thick.
6. Oat flour is produced by grinding flakes or groats into flour for use as an ingredient in a wide variety of food products.
7. Oat bran is a bran-rich fraction produced by sieving coarsely ground oat flour. In 1990, a committee of the American Association of Cereal

Chemists adopted the following definition of oat bran: "Oat bran is the food which is produced by grinding clean oat groats or rolled oats and separating the resulting oat flour by sieving, bolting, and/or such other suitable means into fractions such that the oat bran fraction is not more than 50% of the starting material, and has a total β-glucan content of at least 5.5% (dry weight basis) and a total dietary fiber content of at least 16% (dry weight basis), and such that at least one-third of the total dietary fiber is soluble fiber."

Oat processing for food involves at least the steps of cleaning, hull removal, steaming, and flaking. Cleaning requires that weed seeds, dirt, and other unwanted materials be removed; this is accomplished through separation of the rubbish by screening, air flotation, and classification by particle shape. Then, the oats are graded by size and reduced in moisture content to permit efficient removal of the hulls. Hulls are then abraded or knocked off the seed by specialized equipment. Each of these steps will be discussed below.

As oats are received at the country elevator, they are weighed and then given a preliminary cleaning by receiving separators. These will be either the vibrating screen type or the rotating reel type. Typically, on the slanted, vibrating screen type, the grain will first pass over a coarse-screen deck that has openings 1 inch by one-half inch. Large piece of impurities are removed at this point. Oats fall through the openings onto a fine screen having triangular perforations 3.5 mm on a side. The desirable kernels pass along the top of this screen while small particles of any description pass through. The oats are carried by the vibration into an aspiration section to remove light weight (low density) impurities from the rest of the grain. The scalper-reel receiving separators require that the oats be fed along the length of a horizontal rotating screen or reel that is fitted with three-quarter inch wire mesh and rotates at about 20 rpm. Large and/or long objects are carried through the inside of the reel to the scrap exit and eventually to a rescalping reel fitted with wire mesh of about 16 mm openings where any oat kernels which have been carried along on the top of large pieces of debris can be recovered. From the original reel, the grain has passed through the 0.75 inch wire mesh and been carried to an aspirating channel where light impurities are blown off and then carried to a dust settling chamber where they are removed by a mechanical conveyor.

The cleaning described in the preceding paragraph is merely a preliminary step intended to give a material which can be handled and stored in the elevator without contaminating other grain with which it comes in contact and without damaging the conveying and weighing equipment. It also makes the subsequent specialised- cleaning operations more efficient. Additional specialised cleaning operations must be applied before the oats are milled. These steps are performed by a screen machine with built-on scalperator, one or more disc separators, width graders, gravity table, and aspirators. In addition to several scrap streams, the oats will be divided into (for example) three streams: stub oats, medium oats, and large oats. A detailed description of the principles of operation of these cleaning machines can he found in the article of Deane and Commers.

Most oats for human consumption are marketed as rolled oats. Some demand also exists for ground oats and steel-cut groats. The initial step in the manufacture of rolled oats is the roasting process. Thoroughly cleaned grains are heated to 212°F for one hour. This roasting procedure reduces the grains moisture content to about 6% and probably at least partially dextrinizes the starch. In addition, the hulls become fragile instead of tough and are more easily removed during subsequent processing.

After cooling, the toasted grains are separated according to size. The hulls are then removed by passing the kernels between two large circular milling stones mounted horizontally with the grinding surfaces separated by a short distance. The upper, or rotating, member of this pair of stones has a very slightly convex milling surface, while the lower stone, which is stationary, has a flat surface. Oats enter at the center of the upper stone and are carried to the periphery by centrifugal force. The distance between the stones is everywhere more than the width of a dehulled kernel, but less than the length of the kernels. As the grains travel outwardly, hulls are removed by the tearing and abrading action of the stones. The mixture of hulls, whole kernels, and brokengrains exiting the mill is screened and subjected to other procedures in order to separate these components. The grain with its hull removed is called a "groat." Hulling can also be performed by impact milling, using such devices as the Entoleter.

The next step is flaking. The groats are steamed before flaking to inactivate enzymes and increase the moisture content. Flaking rollers are about 14 inches in diameter and 28 inches wide; one roller in each pair is fixed and the other is movable so the gap between each pair of rollers can be adjusted. There is a scraper knife on each roll to remove the flakes. The cylinders are often made of chilled iron or centrifugal alloy-iron castings.

Whole groats may be flaked, or they may be first cut into pieces by rotary granulators. The smaller the piece size and the thinner the flake, the quicker the cereal can be cooked. For example, so-called "quick" oats, which are flakes made from a particle about one-fourth to one-third the size of a whole groat, will cook in about five minutes, while flaked whole groats ("regular oats") require ten to fifteen minutes boiling before they are soft enough to satisfy most consumer's requirements. The smaller particles do not stand up as well under prolonged heating, however. Thus, regular oats

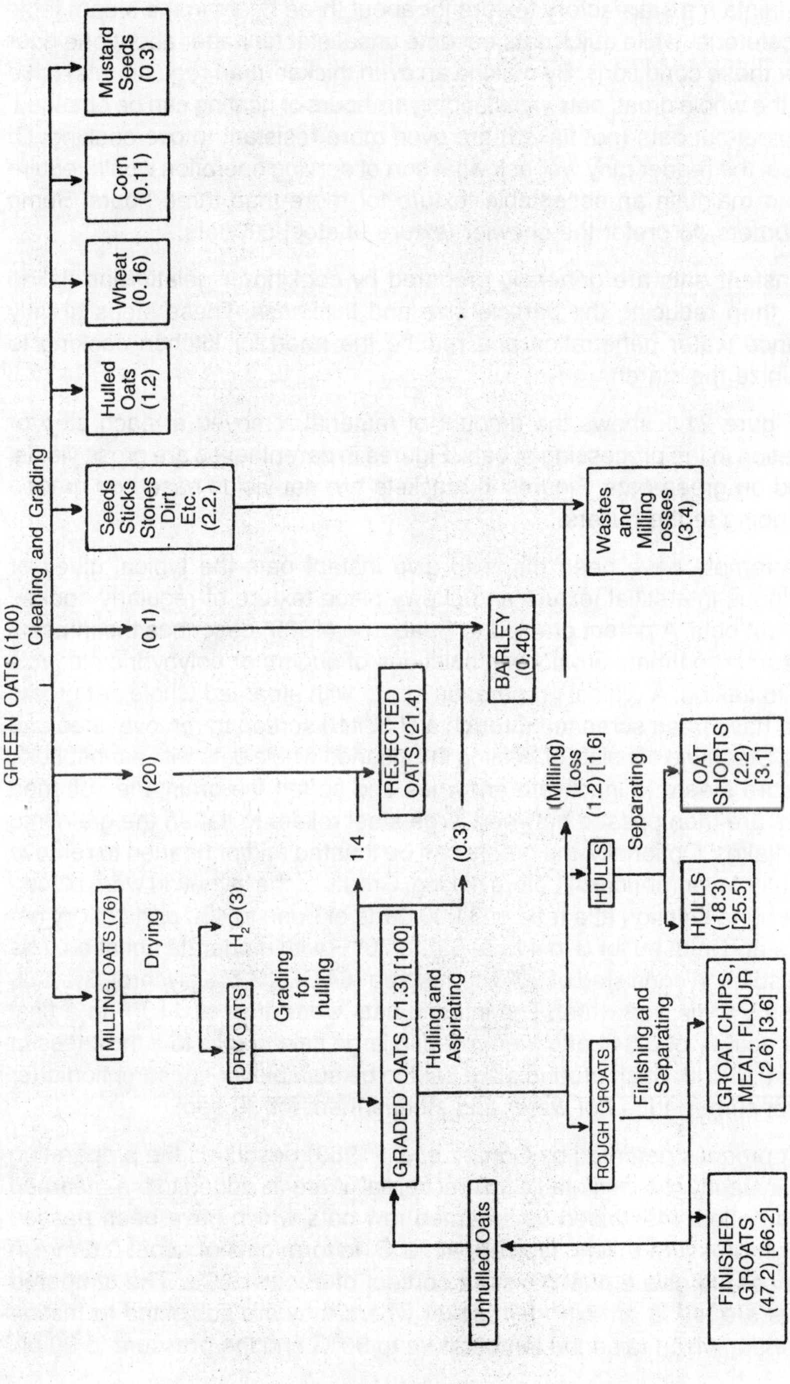

FIG. 21.1: FLOW DIAGRAM OF THE MILLING OF OATS

will maintain a satisfactory texture for about three hours in the steam table of a cafeteria, while quick oats become unsatisfactory after about one hour under these conditions. By making an even thicker (than regular oats) flake from the whole groat, oats withstanding six hours of heating can be obtained, and steel-cut oats (not flaked) are even more resistant to overcooking. Of course, the reader may well ask what sort of serving operation would require oats to maintain an acceptable texture for more than three hours. Some consumers do prefer the chewier texture of steel-cut oats..

Instant oats are generally prepared by cooking or gelatinising flaked oats, then reducing the particle size and thickness. These steps greatly enhance water penetration and reduce the need for kitchen cooking to gelatinize the starch.

Figure 21.1 shows the amount of material removed at each step or operation in the processing of oats. Figures in parentheses are gross yields, based on green oats. Figures in brackets are net yields based on graded oats going to the hullers.

Attempts have been made to give instant oats the typical gluey or gelatinous interstitial texture and chewy piece texture of regularly cooked steel-cut oats. A patent granted to Seaborne (1989) describes the infusion of steamed oatmeal groats with solutions of sugars or polyhydric alcohols prior to flaking. A typical preparation starts with steamed whole oat groats which have been screened through a U.S. #10 screen to remove fines and rocks. Steaming consists of heating the cleaned whole oats with atmospheric pressure steam to inactivate enzymes and soften the grain; the softened groats are then passed between large steel rollers to flatten the grain into large flakes. Optionally, the groats can be toasted and/or pearled to remove the outer layer (pericarp) before flaking. Groats of the invention were placed into a brine solution at a ratio of 3,000 parts of brine to 400 parts of dry oat groats and infused for 3 to 4 hr at 65° to 70° F with moderate agitation. The brine solution consisted of 30% corn syrup (64 DE), 7.5% glycerol, 3% salt, and 59.5% distilled water. The infused oats were dried at 110°F to a final water activity of 0.544 and then rolled in large flaking rolls to a thickness of about 0.025 in. Such products are said to be suitable for consumption after the consumer adds hot water and steeps them for 30 sec.

A process patented by Conroy *et al.* (1989) describes the preparation of an instantly reconstitutable hot oat cereal. Water is added to pre-steamed flaked oatlets (described as steamed raw oats which have been passed through pressure rollers, typically at 80°C, to form oats of about 0.6 mm in thickness) to give a final moisture content of about 18.5%. The tempered oatlets are fed to an extruder cooker where they are subjected to friction and shear which raise the temperature to 90°C and the pressure to 90 psi at the die orifice. At the die face the exudate is cut into pellets weighing about 0.1 g, which are conveyed to flaking rolls where flakes are formed. The flakes are dried to a moisture content of about 7%, then blended with 25% by weight of the pre-steamed (but not extruded) oatlets to form an instantly reconstitutable cereal product.

Pan-toasted oats are subjected to additional heat treatment in gas-heated open "pans" to give a slightly more caramelized or toasted flavor.

OTHER GRAINS AS HOT CEREALS

Whole milled rice is occasionally cooked as a breakfast cereal. Full details on whole milled rice are given in the chapter on Rice Processing. There is also an analogue of wheat farina called Cream of Rice, which consists of milled rice or broken rice which has been ground into particles about the size of those used in Cream of Wheat. The smaller particle size leads to much quicker cooking, compared to whole grain rice, so that the product is essentially instant, that is, it does not require additional heating after the addition of boiling water. A short period of standing after the addition of water is necessary, of course, to allow complete hydration of the granules. Most consumers would doubtless prefer the texture of product given a short cook.

In the Orient, one encounters the product called congee, which is whole rice or broken rice made into a fairly thin gruel. It is usually eaten for breakfast with condiments such as raw eggs, chopped Onions, or dried fish. Cooking with water, and Presumably some salt, is the means of Preparing this food.

There is a retail pack of coarse rye meal, called Cream of Rye, in a container very similar in appearance to the traditional cylindrical oatmeal box, which has a very small share of the hot cereal market and is found in very few outlets. There is also a Roman Meal cookable breakfast cereal consisting of a mixture of grains in small granule form.

PRE-COOKED HOT CEREALS

As described above, and also in the chapter on cereals for special dietary needs, for many years methods have been available for making "instantly" rehydratable cooked cereals. These methods consist essentially of cooking the cereal, often with additives of a nutritional or flavoring nature, then drying the mixture, as on a drum dryer, and grinding the product to give small flakes. Since the flakes are very thin and usually somewhat porous, they allow hot water to penetrate quickly throughout the particle. Since the starch has been completely gelatinised, further cooking is not necessary.

A method for manufacturing a high grain content hot cereal has been patented by Karwowski *et al.* (1989). It is described as a precooked cereal which, after cooking, is dried, formed into flakes, and, optionally, agglomerated. The cereal is colored, flavored, and treated through the use of an enzyme-reacted grain. Basically, the treatment process involves mixing gram and water, adding one or more starch-converting enzymes, and heating at 60° to 80°C until 70 to 80% of the starch has been converted to monosaccharides. A minor amount of this reacted slurry is added to a mixture of raw grains and water, and another heating step performed, after which the cooked grains are dried and converted into flakes. The flakes can be used as the end product or they can be agglomerated with milk solids, corn syrup solids, or other sticky substances. Grains which can be used are wheat, oats, corn, rye, rice, barley, and mixtures of these. The product is intended to be packaged in single-serving size containers for convenience. The consumer opens the package, adds a liquid such as milk or water, and then he the mixture in a microwave oven.

PROCESSING READY-TO-EAT BREAKFAST CEREALS

FLAKES

General considerations— Flaking is a relatively simple process, consisting in its most elemental form of cooking fragments of cereal grains (or in some cases whole grains) with Water, flattening the soft particles between large steel rollers, and toasting the resultant flake at high temperatures. Apparently, the first commercial production of such a food occurred around the turn of the century when J. H. Kellogg and W. H. Kellogg made whole wheat flakes in a barn behind the Battle Creek Sanitorium. Since that time, many complications have been introduced into the process in attempts to improve the flavor of the product and the efficiency of operations, and to gain the uniformity of flake size and appearance which is so desirable to the manufacturer and perhaps even to the consumer.

Flakes owe their popularity with consumers to their crisp but friable texture, to their sweet but rather bland flavor, and to the ease with which they can he readied for consumption.

In the basic processing steps, the raw material undergoes the following changes: (1) the starch is gelatinised and probably slightly hydrolysed; (2) the particle undergoes a browning reaction due probably to interaction of protein and sugars; (3) enzymatic processes are stopped, rendering the final product more stable; (4) dextrinisation and caramelisation of the sugars occur as a result of the high temperatures in the roasting oven; and (5) the flake becomes crisper as a result of reduction of its moisture content to a very low level.

Early methods for making flaked cereals, e.g., wheat or corn flakes, were based on the use of a fairly large chunk of the grain, which retained its integrity throughout the entire process. Conventional corn flakes are still made this way. The technique has some disadvantages, such as the restrictions it places on the size, shape, and composition of the particle. One of the early patents describing a method of circumventing these restrictions was that of Clausi *et al.* In essence, this invention required the extrusion of a dough piece by a pelleting mill, and the subsequent puffing or flaking of the piece. In the words of the patent, the process involved "gelatinising hydrated, ungelatinised cereal dough pieces having a major proportion of at least one highly nutritious cereal flour [and at a moisture content of about 22% to about 36%] at temperatures from about 215° to about 265°F at steam pressures of from about 1 to about 23 psig, cooling the gelatinsed cereal dough pieces to a temperature whereat they are less plastic and their stiffness is increased, by cooling them to temperatures from above about 150° to about 205°F, pelletising the cereal dough pieces, partially drying the gelatinised dough pieces to from about 5% to about 21% moisture, mechanically modifying the shape of the dough piece [as by flaking], and drying the.. .[flakes] to a moisture content of from about 1% to about 3.5% moisture under conditions such that the temperature of the cereal dough pieces does not exceed about 250°F." The patent indicates that pelletising was to be done by a conventional, commercial pelletising machine, which is a much simpler device than the cooking extruders to be discussed later in this chapter.

Table 21.1. FORMULAS FOR PELLETISED AND FLAKED) CEREALS

Formula A		Formula B	
Ingredient	*Per cent by weight*	*Ingrodiont*	*Per cent by weight*
Oat flour	60–70	Soy flour	80.4
Rice flour	7–12	Sucrose	8
Soy flour	5–10	Casein	5
Sucrose	5–15	Malt syrup	4
Lecithin	0.05–0.15	Salt	2.5
Salt	2–4	Vanilla flavor	0.1
Milk casein	1.5–10.0		

The Clausi et al. patent disclosed several formulas which could be used for compounded doughs suitable for processing by the invention. Two of these are shown in Table 21.1.

In the subsequent paragraphs of this section, a fairly straightforward corn flake operation will be described first, followed by a discussion of a wheat flake process which is considerably more complex. Bran flakes, 40% bran flakes, and rice flakes are also marketed. They are manufactured by methods having much similarity to the corn flake process.

Corn flakes— Hybrid yellow corn is most often used as the raw material for corn flakes, although white corn provides an equally satisfactory ingredient. The corn is broken (milled) so as to yield a No. 4 to No. 5 grit free of germ and bran. These large pieces represent about half of a corn kernel and they retain their identity throughout the process, each particle eventually emerging as a corn flake. The hulls resulting from the milling operation are used in animal feeds, and the germs are pressed in expellers to yield the corn oil of commerce and a meal or cake which can serve as a protein enrichment in animal feeds.

Into a cylindrical pressure cooker or retort are placed about 1,700 lb of grits and 36 gal of a flavoring syrup made from sugar, nondiastatic malt, salt, and water. Occasionally, niacin will be added at this point. During cooking, the charge accumulates additional water from the steam which is introduced into the retort, and its moisture content rises to about 33%,

The contents of the slowly rotating retort are cooked at 15 to 23 (typically 18) pounds steam pressure for 1 to 2 hr. Different lots of corn can vary appreciably in their cooking time requirements. The end point can be judged by examining a small sample which is blown out through a gate valve. A uniform transparency in the kernels indicates an adequate cook. At the expiration of the cooking time, pressure in the vessel is reduced to atmospheric level, the retort is opened, and its contents are dumped onto a moving belt.

After the lumps from the cooker are broken down to individual particles by a revolving reel, they are distributed to a set of driers. The latter devices are essentially large tubes or tanks extending vertically for several stories. Wet kernels enter the top and are dried by a countercurrent of hot (150°F) air as they travel to the bottom. Another type of drying equipment consists of horizontal rotating cylinders having numerous steam- heated pipes passing longitudinally through them. Louver driers may also be used.

As they exit the driers, the corn particles contain 19 to 23% moisture, but the water is unevenly distributed, so the material is transferred to tempering bins for several hours (as many as 24) so that the moisture can equilibrate. After tempering, the hard dark brown grits are ready for flaking.

The flaking rolls are steel cylinders weighing over a ton. They revolve at a speed of about 180 to 200 rpm, and are cooled by internal circulation of water. Hydraulic controls maintain a pressure of over 40 tons at the nip of the rollers. According to Fast *et al.* (1990) the most popular sizes of rolls

Fig. 21.2. A Set of Flaking Rolls

are 20 inches in diameter x 30 inches wide and 26x40, with other standards being 32x40, 24x40, and 20x24.5 for ready-to-eat cereals. The cooked dried grits are pressed into thin flakes as they pass between the rolls. The flake is rather flexible at this time, and lacks the desired crispness and toasted flavor of the finished corn flake. Figure 21.2 shows a pair of flaking rolls, such as are used to make corn flakes.

From the rolls, flakes pass directly to a rotating toasting oven which is usually gas-fired. The moist flakes tumble through the perforated drums and pass within a few inches of gas flames. Treatment may be, for example, 50 sec at 575°F or 2 to 3 mm at 550°F. In addition to being thoroughly dehydrated by this process, the flakes are toasted and blistered. They contain less than 3% moisture when they emerge from the oven.

From the ovens, flakes are carried by belts to expansion bins where they are permitted to cool to room temperature. During transfer, the corn flakes are cooled by circulating air and they are usually sprayed with a solution of thiamin and perhaps other B-vitamins.

Corn flakes can also be made by cooking the corn in an extruder, cooling the cooked mass to perhaps 25°C (to eliminate post-extrusion expansion) then passing it through a die to form strands which are cut into short lengths (e.g., 5 mm), A finer grind of corn may be used in this method, as compared to the raw material required in the traditional method described previously, since the size of the flake is not dependent on the dimensions of the corn grit. The cooked pellets are then flaked and toasted in equipment very similar to that used for "old-fashioned" corn flakes. Flaking is done by pairs of large steel cylinders operating at a speed differential that shapes the strands into thin flakes. Adjustments of the rollers can be used to control the thickness, texture, and surface characteristics of the finished flake. Final drying and toasting can be conducted in any convenient type of hot air unit which does not subject the flake to excessive attrition. Belt dryers or fluid bed units are possible choices. In any case, the moisture content of the flake must be reduced from about 20% to about 3 or 4%. Applying the hottest air to the entry point causes blistering of the flake, which is generally considered desirable. It is said that extruded flakes can be completely processed in 30 minutes, or even less, as compared to an 8 hour cycle time for conventional processing. Midden (1989) says there is an 11% savings in costs when corn flakes are made by the extrusion method.

A method similar to that described above was described in a patent granted to Short and Wilkinson (1989). Briefly, this involves extruding pelleted half-products made principally of corn or some other cereal flour, drying these to a moisture content of 9.5 to 17.0%, conditioning the dried half-products to a moisture content of between 17 and 23%, treating the conditioned half-products with a moisture-absorbing compound to reduce the stickiness of their outer surfaces, flaking the half-products by the usual method, reducing the moisture content of the flakes to about 15 to 18%, and toasting the flakes to a final moisture content of 2 to 5%. The method of these inventors for producing cereal flakes from pellets of half products is shown in Figure 21.3.

Wheat flakes— Plump kernels of soft wheat ate frequently used as the raw material for wheat flakes. After cleaning and sorting according to size, the kernels are tempered in steel bins of small diameter by adding moisture and holding at about 80°F for about 24 hr. The wheat may be transferred one or more times during this period if such a procedure is necessary in order to keep the temperature within reasonable limits. After tempering, the wheat is steamed at atmospheric pressure until it reaches 203°F and 21% moisture.

The steamed wheat is bumped between smooth steel rollers set considerably farther apart than are flaking rollers. This treatment flattens the grain slightly, and ruptures the bran coat in several places making the kernel more permeable to the moisture which will be added during the cooking step. Next, the flattened kernels are transferred to pressure cookers,

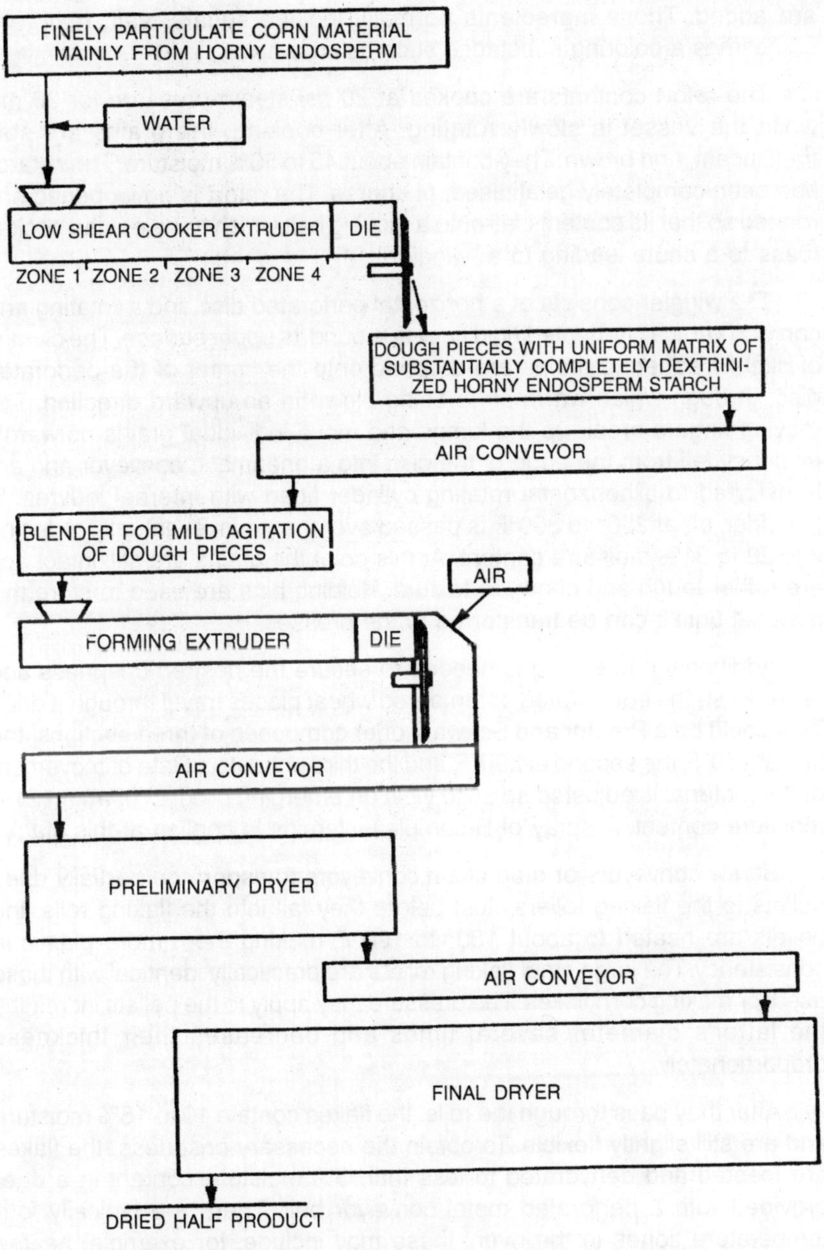

FIG. 21.3: METHOD FOR PREPARING CEREAL FLAKES FROM PELLETED HALF PRODUCTS

which are similar to those used for corn flakes, and the other ingredients are added. These ingredients normally include sugars, salt, malt, and sometimes a coloring substance such as caramel.

The retort contents are cooked at 20 psi steam pressure for 90 min while the vessel is slowly rotating. After cooking, the grains are soft, translucent, and brown. They contain about 45 to 50% moisture. Their starch has been completely gelatinised, of course. The retort is now opened and rotated so that its contents fall onto a moving belt which transfers the cooked mass to a chute leading to a "wiggler."

The wiggler consists of a horizontal perforated disc and a rotating arm carrying vertically-oriented rigid fingers around its upper surface. The clumps of slightly adhering grains are dropped onto the center of the perforated disc, through which warm air is being blown in an upward direction. The moving fingers break up the lumps and move individual grains outwardly until they fall from the edge of the disc into a pneumatic conveyor and are transferred to a horizontal rotating cylinder fitted with internal iouvres. In this drier, air at 250° to 300°F is passed over the grain, eventually reducing it to 28 to 31% moisture content. At this point the grains are still intact and are rather tough and chewy in texture. Holding bins are used to store this material until it can be transferred to the presses.

Additional processing is needed to secure the desired crispness and flavor. First, the equilibrated or tempered wheat pieces travel through a drier. This could be a Proctor and Schwarz drier composed of three sections, the first at 280°F, the second at 290°F, and the third unheated. Rate of movement of the material is adjusted so as to yield an emerging product of about 21% moisture content. A spray of B-complex vitamins is applied at this stage.

Screw conveyors or drag chain conveyors transport the partially dried pellets to the flaking rollers. Just before they fall into the flaking rolls, the pellets are heated to about 180° to 190°F, making them more plastic in consistency. The large steel flaking rollers are practically identical with those used for making corn flakes. The pressure they apply to the pellets increases the latter's diameter several times and decreases their thickness proportionately.

After they pass through the rolls, the flakes contain 10 to 15% moisture and are still slightly flexible. To obtain the necessary crispness, the flakes are toasted and dehydrated to less than 3% moisture content in a drier provided with a perforated metal conveyor belt. There are typically four temperature zones in the oven; these may include, for example, heated sections at 310°, 300°, and 280°F, and an unheated section to partially cool the flakes. The decreasing temperature pattern is said to promote the development of desirable curling and blistering.

A process patented by Benson and Merboth (1967) describes the production of breakfast cereal flakes from a continuous sheet of dough, with the improvement of gaining greater control over size and shape of the finished product. The thickness of the dough is reduced by running the conveyor belt faster than the extruded sheet, and tempering is accomplished by cooling the outer surface of the dough sheet with currents of air.

Like most breakfast cereals, wheat flakes are susceptible to the development of rancidity after extended storage. Addition of the common antioxidants BHA and BHT increases shelf life somewhat. For extruded wheat flakes, they are less satisfactory when added to the pre-mix because the high temperatures of processing tend to destroy or vaporise the antioxidants. Megremis (1990) reveals that mixed tocopherols will survive the conditions of extrusion and substantially extend the storage life of wheat flakes made by this method.

Bran flakes— Bran flakes constituted a rather minor part of the breakfast cereal market until the recent fiber craze, when they began to assume a much more important role. Old-fashioned bran flakes were manufactured by combining a dried portion containing wheat and sufficient amounts of bran to yield flakes containing about four grams of fiber per ounce of cereal. Use of larger amounts of bran, with the aim of providing consumers with a product having greater fiber content, leads to grave difficulties in flaking and soft (not crisp) products. Most cereals of very high bran content are extruded so as to yield, typically, the shreds sold as "All Bran."

To make bran flakes, the dry wheat and bran are combined with a flavoring syrup containing sugar, corn syrup, malt, and salt, then cooked until the starch is completely gelatinised. The cooked particles are partially dried, tempered, flaked by previously described methods, and finally, toasted to give finished flakes having a thickness of 0.005 to 0.040 inch.

Bolles *et al.* (1989) described a method said to give bran flakes containing up to eight grams of fiber per ounce of cereal. Their process involves mixing a grain, such as wheat or rice, with a fiber source, such as wheat bran or oat bran, in a ratio of about 6 to 4, then reacting the mixture with an a-amylase. The enzymes suggested in the patent are bacterial and fungal in origin. It is important that there be limited or partial digestion of the starch, so the amount of enzyme and the reaction conditions are critical. Generally, the combination of bran cracked wheat, and enzyme are mixed thoroughly and heated to a temperature within the range of of 115° to 130°F. Processing times ranging between 2 and 4 minutes are suggested. The digested mixture/is then cooked in a pressurised vessel under conditions which inactivate the enzyme, say, at about 300°F for 35 minutes. The moisture content of the material coming out of the cooking vessel should be about 3%. This is lowered to about 19% by any convenient method, and the agglomerates are tempered and cooled for about 30 to 60 minutes. Subsequently, the lumps are flaked by passing them between rollers in the manner which has already been described for wheat flakes. A flake thickness in the range of 0.005 to 0.040 inch is said to be satisfactory. The flakes are toasted in improve flavor.

Additional comment on extruded bran shreds may be appropriate at this point, although they are not "flakes" by any normal definition. It is characteristic of these products that they contain more fiber than the usual bran flake, as indicated by the trade-names of "40% Bran Flakes" for the former and "All Bran" buds for the latter. In batch production of the shreds, the first step might involve mixing 100 lb wheat bran, 5 lb wheat flour, 7.5 lb of another kind of flour, water, and flavorings. This mixture is pressure cooked at about 260°F for a half hour, then extruded under low shear conditions to form nuggets or buds which are dried and perhaps sprayed with a vitamin solution. Cereals produced by this method generally stay crisp in milk for about 2 to 3 minutes before they start to disintegrate.

A continuous process for mixing, heat processing, and forming a bran cereal composition in a combination cooker-extruder has been described by Calandro *et al.* (1989). Dry ingredients (including at least one cereal bran component) are mixed with a syrup containing at least one sugar component in the blending zone of a twin screw extruder. The wetted bran mixture is then cooked in another zone before it is passed through a headspace zone adjacent to the extrusion die. Extrusion takes place through narrow orifices, and the strands of cereal spontaneously break into pieces which fall onto a moving belt. Note that the strands are not cut into predetermined lengths.

The cooked and fragmented strands are then dried and toasted in an oven. The cereal pieces are described as having a visibly roughened surface and an unplasticised appearance with discrete bran particles. Pressure drop across the die, pressures within the extruder barrel, and temperatures within the extruder are kept low so as to prevent plasticization of the extrudate, since it is desired to avoid producing smooth, continuous, spaghetti-like strands or overexpansion. Pressure within the extruder should be less than 400 psig and the temperature should be 270°F or less. Pressure drop across the die should preferably be 140 to 275 psig.

As it exits the die, the cooked bran will contain about 26% moisture, sugar solids of about 18%, and about 56% bran. There may be a few per cent of minor texturising and flavoring ingredients. This moist material is dried to a water content of 6% or less. It is said the dried and toasted strands, with their uncut ends, remain crisp in milk for at least four minutes. Flavoring and texturising ingredients mentioned in the patent include fruit juices, malt, and flavors such as maple. A formula is 55.5% raw wheat bran, 1.4% malt, 23% sucrose syrup (67% solids), 16.2% water, 1.1% salt, 1.3% fig juice concentrate, 1.3% prune juice concentrate, and 0.2% vitamin premix.

Flakes from other grains— Because of the comparatively high level of fat in oats, flakes made from this grain in the conventional way have a unacceptably short storage life. Lilly and Reinhart (1967) describe a process said to give oat products of satisfactory stability. Oat groats are pressure-cooked until the starch is gelatinised, and then kneaded while being held at a temperature of 150° to 212°F until a plastic dough is formed. The dough is shaped into flakes about 0.011 inch in thickness and these are flash dried to 2 to 10% moisture content by contact with air having a temperature in the range of 400° to 800°F.

Although the author does not know of any commercial breakfast cereal flakes made entirely, or mostly, from barley, it has been suggested that this grain would be suitable for the purpose. According to one authority, "When extruded, barley will yield a harder, more crispy flake than than corn or wheat... . The stronger texture contributed by barley helps minimise breakage to the cereal flakes during transport or consumer handling" Anon. (1989A).

There does not appear to have ever been a rye flake which gained wide commercial distribution, but the patent of Gulstad (1971) describes a method for making such a product. In one example, clean dry rye kernels having a moisture content of about 8.3% were fed into a continuous puffing gun at a feed rate of about 10 lb/min. The following gun conditions were used: Steam pressure 100 psig, steam temperature 385°F, barrel angle of 3 degrees below the horizontal, barrel rotation of 45 rpm, puffing orifice diameter of 0.5 inch, barrel diameter 10 inches, and barrel length 12 ft. The puffed rye was milled into flour on a pin mill. A dough was formed by mixing 388 parts of the rye flour with 54.5 parts sucrose, 11.3 parts salt, and 169 parts water, so as to give a mixture having a moisture content of about 32.5%, The resulting dough was processed in a piston type extruder at a pressure of about 2200 psig, and cut into pellets about 0.25 inch in diameter. After the pellets were surface dried to about 23% moisture, they were passed between a pair of flaking rolls spaced about 0.020 inch apart, then dried in a belt oven to a moisture content of about 1%.

No reference can be found to flakes made from grain sorghum, although these seeds would be likely to respond much like the other grains when subjected to the same type of process. Of course, sorghum grains are much smaller than other cereal kernels, and conditions would have to be adjusted to take this difference into account.

SHREDS

Shredded wheat biscuits— The most popular representative of this class is the pillow-shaped shredded wheat biscuit manufactured by Nabisco. It differs from most other ready-to-eat breakfast cereals in that it is made from whole grain without the addition of any flavor and without removal of the germ or bran. Cooking is typically done at atmospheric pressure in boiling water. After one hour or more of cooking, moisture content of the wheat kernels will have reached 50 to 60% and the grain will be very soft. Some preliminary drying in louvred ovens may follow, but the whole wheat is not brought much below 45 to 50% moisture content. The cooked and slightly dried wheat is transferred to stainless steel bins and tempered for many hours before it goes to the shredding rolls.

The shredding rolls are from 6 to 8 inches in diameter and as wide as the finished biscuit is to be, thus much smaller than flaking rolls. One of the pair of rolls has a series of 20 shallow corrugations or ridges running around its periphery. In cross section, these corrugations may be rectangular, triangular, or a combination of these shapes. The other roll of the pair is smooth-surfaced. Moist, softened wheat is drawn between these rollers as they rotate, and it issues as continuous strands of dough. By cutting grooves perpendicular to the circumferential corrugations, shred layers having a net-like effect can be obtained. Hall and Carpenter (1956) described the

Fig. 21.4. Separating Shredded Wheat into Individual Biscuits.

preparation of a biscuit having a lattice-like network of shreds. Their product may also be puffed, giving an additional variation in texture and appearance.

Biscuits are built up by layering strands on a moving belt which passes under sets of rolls positioned in tandem. Ten to 18 rolls may be used for circular biscuits, while 22 rolls is a common number for rectangular biscuits. In the latter case, layered strands are separated into biscuits by passing them below blunt "knives" which press a thin line of the dough into a solid mass at regular intervals. Figure 21.4 shows the layered strands being separated into biscuits.

Circular biscuits, which are probably not being made anymore in the U.S., were formed quite differently. One end of the sheet formed from layered strands of whole wheat dough is caught up by a smooth roll which rotates just above the belt. This roller turns the layer of strands back upon itself, arid the forward motion of the belt combined with the reverse and upward motion of the cylinder surface, causes the layer to roll up into a circular biscuit. As the biscuit reaches a predetermined diameter, a knife chops down on the belt, severing the strands so that the formed biscuit can be released. Automatic controls vary the speed of the belt as the diameter of the biscuit increases. The completed disc falls into a cup from which it is transferred to a bolt leading to the ovens.

Since the biscuits are formed from dough of relatively high moisture content, they are quite tender and fragile, and must be handled very carefully to prevent distortion. In practice, this means that the transfer steps must proceed more slowly than is necessary with flakes or puffed products.

The wet biscuits are placed on a metal belt moving through a high temperature gas-fired oven. After 10 to 15 minutes, the outside of the product is dry and toasted but the interior is still wet. Then, the biscuits are transferred to another hot air oven (or to a different section of the same oven) where they are dried at 250°F for 30 to 60 minutes through-time, depending on the size of the biscuit and the rate of air flow. Finished moisture content should be about 11%. The combination of heat treatments causes the biscuit to assume the familiar oval cross section (pillow shape) as a result of differential shrinkage of the layers.

A triple shredding mill is used for producing bite-size breakfast cereals. Dough made from wheat, corn, or rice is fed to long, water-cooled shredding rolls. These rolls deposit a shredded dough sheet onto a constant speed conveyor to form a wide, three-layer ribbon. The rolls on the first and third shredding mills extrude dough sheets with a laced pattern, due to the use of combinations of smooth and grooved rolls. The middle set of rolls revolves at higher speed than the other two pairs. As a result, the dough sheet in the middle folds as it falls onto the relatively slow moving conveyor belt which has been covered by the first dough sheet. Sugar is sprinkled over the middle dough sheet, and the top sheet is then added. The combined structure passes between scoring rolls, and the baked cereal is finally broken along scored lines to form individual bite-size pieces.

It can be seen that the process described in the immediately preceding paragraph can be varied to give many different kinds of products; for example, biscuits containing layers of different kinds of grain.

The flavor of shredded wheat differs significantly from that of whole wheat flakes because the latter includes added condiments and is subjected to much more heat in both the cooking and toasting steps. The more rigorous heat treatment applied to flakes results in considerably more caramelisation and other browning reactions in the finished product.

Since shredded wheat is made from the whole kernel, it contains all of the relatively unstable oils from the germ. As a result, rancid odors tend to accumulate in the container if shredded wheat is stored in sealed packages. It is for this reason that the product is normally sold in "breather" boxes without outer or inner linings. When so packaged, the odors of incipient rancidity diffuse from the container, and the product has satisfactory storage stability. Of course, such packages also allow moisture absorption to occur in atmospheres of high relative humidity, with a consequent loss of crispness, but it appears that consumers of this product are not as demanding, in terms of their texture requirements, as are consumers of, say, corn flakes or crisped rice.

A method of making a breakfast type cereal by forming corrugated flakes of non-uniform thickness on a pair of rolls, one of which is grooved. The flakes are said to have thin connecting membranes that dissolve in milk to leave the remainder in the form of shreds. The non-dissolving shreds essentially duplicate in eating qualities a shredded biscuit-type cereal product (Reesman 1974).

Composite biscuits— There are many patents describing the operations of the shredding devices used in the production of shredded wheat and the like. Some significant U.S. patents are 2,008,024, 2,013,003, and 2,693,419, and Canadian patent 674,046. The production of shredded cereal products having a fruit paste filling is described in U.S. patents 2,693,419 and 4,004,035. In the former patent, the shreds are prepared normally by passing cooked wheat between two rollers, at least one of which has circumferentially arranged grooves. After about half the shred layers have been placed on the conveyor belt, a measured amount of fruit paste is deposited on the shreds, then additional layers of wheat shreds are place a on top of the fruit. In a specific example, raisins are deposited over the surface of seven shred layers in a pattern such that the raisins will be centered within the finished biscuits. The composite bed or mat is cut into biscuits using blunt edged knives after seven more layers of shreds have been deposited over the raisins. Other fruits in the form of a ground paste may replace the raisins. Patent 4,004,035 describes the production of a shredded biscuit having a lapped zig-zag configuration of shreds, in which the layers are disposed at an angle relative to the sides and ends of the biscuits. This is supposed to make the biscuit more rugged than one produced from parallel-deposited shreds. By adding a second lapping device to this patented equipment, a flavorful filling can be deposited between the shred layers. An additional advantage of the lapping technique is that more than one layer can be obtained from each shredding mill. That is, one pair of rollers can, through the zig-zag laminating effect, double or triple the number of layers it deposits on the belt. Of course, the length of the layer deposited by the mill is reduced by the the lapping operation so it is difficult to see how the total production rate can be increased.

A recent patent (Leibfred 1989) describes a process for making fruit-filled shredded wheat biscuits having a plurality of textures. Wheat is cooked and tempered in the previously described manner to give the grains a moisture content of 39 to 43%, and is then transferred to a hopper feeding a screw conveyor, thence to a series of shredding rollers via flow tubes or hoppers. The shredding mills comprise a pair of rolls that rotate in opposite directions. One of the rolls has circumferential grooves and cross-hatching grooves which are transverse to them, so as to produce a net-like sheet. Spacing between the rolls is adjusted to avoid the production of webbing, i.e., a continuous film of dough between the netting is not desired. After a certain number of layers has been deposited on an underlying conveyor belt by an equal number of roller pairs, sugar is deposited on the mat, then a rope of flavored paste is extruded on to the shreds. More layers of shreds are laid down on the paste, so as to cover the extrudate completely. The net-like sheets (shred layers) immediately adjacent to the filling should have a relatively high number of cross-hatchings so as to provide a region of dense texture. This enhances the chewiness of the filling. The first and last cereal dough layers to be deposited should also have enough cross-hatching to provide regions of dense texture. For a shredding roller of five inch diameter, about 45 cross-hatchings, equally spaced about the roll, should be adequate. Rolls five inches in rolls will typically have: (1) about 18 to 22 circumferential grooves per inch of width, each groove having a depth of about 0.021 inches and a width of about 0.029 inches, and (2) up to about 120 equally spaced crosshatching grooves having a width of up to 0.040 inches and a depth of 0.002 to 0.008 inches less than the depth of the circumferential grooves.

The sugar deposited in the preceding process should be a humectant sugar such as fructose or corn syrup. It can be applied by any of the commonly known pieces of equipment. Paste is applied through two or more outlet orifices fed by a pump. A strawberry paste might include glycerin, strawberries, high fructose corn syrup, sugar, modified food starch, strawberry juice, natural flavor, pectin, malic acid, sodium alginate, and sodium benzoate. The filling should be formulated to be microbiologically stable, i.e., with a water activity less than about 0.7. Pastes having a higher water activity may be used if they contain appropriate preservatives. Suitable fruit pastes typically have a water content of about 12%. Enough paste is deposited to give at least 15% by weight of filling in the biscuit. The combined deposit of shreds and paste is separated into biscuits by previously described cutting devices.

The cut biscuits are dried, baked, and toasted in conventional equipment. Zones of 200° to 600°F can be used, with a baking time of about 5 to 10 minutes total. Finished products should have average moisture contents within the range of 7 to 8%, and a water activity less than 0.6.

A method for continuously extruding a network of strands utilising two moving sets of orifices and simultaneously extruding a filling could probably be used for making composite types of breakfast cereals (Mercer *et al.* 1986).

GRANULES

The breaking up of a loaf or biscuit is one way of forming cereal granules. The other method is to agglomerate smaller pieces until particles in the desired size range are formed. The first option has been used for several decades in the production of Grape-Nuts, and involves the baking of a dense loaf of simple composition which is then dried and ground.

A stiff dough of about 1,600 pounds weight is prepared from wheat, malted barley flour, salt, dry yeast, and water. This dough is dumped into troughs and stored at 80°F and 80% relative humidity for 4.5 to 5 hr. During this fermentation period, much hydrolysis of the starch to sugars occurs as one result of the action of malt enzymes. Some leavening, or expansion of the dough, takes place because of yeast fermentation. At the end of the fermentation, the dough is formed into loaves and transferred to ovens without the intervention of any proofing time. Baking takes place at 400 degrees F for two hours. The doughs are depanned and then fragmented by shredding knives or saws. The pieces are transferred to secondary ovens after passing through a sizing step which removes fines. The latter are used as ingredients in subsequent doughs. After two hours or more of drying and toasting at about 250°F, the pieces are broken up into small granules which are graded by sieves before packaging. The modern ingredient includes added vitamins and minerals, probably added by spraying on to granules,

Fig. 21.5. Loaves which will be grounded into Cereal Granules.

although some of the more stable compounds may be included in the dough mix. Figure 21.5 shows the baked loaves which are broken up to form cereal granules such as Grape-Nuts.

PUFFED CEREALS

General considerations— All puffed cereal manufacturing process are based on the rapid generation of steam within a plasticised mass which then expands. Puffing may be conducted at atmospheric pressure, as in the preparation of popcorn, or it may involve sudden pressure changes in which a product heated above the boiling point of water in some sort of retort is rapidly transferred to an area of lower (e.g., atmospheric) pressure. In both cases, puffing results from the quick conversion of liquid water to vapor in the interstices of of the cereal particle or dough. The cereal is fixed in its expanded state by the dehydration which results from diffusion of water vapor out of it and also by the cooling. Gun puffing may result in an increase of apparent volume (bulk density decrease) of 8-fold to 16-fold for wheat and 6-fold to 8-fold for rice. Oven puffing leads to a smaller increase in volume for corn, about 3-fold to 4-fold.

Puffed products must be maintained at about 3% moisture or less in order to have satisfactory crispness. Even at 5% moisture a definite toughness becomes evident. These levels are most critical and hardest to maintain in foods which have been gun-puffed.

Oven-puffed rice— This product is prepared from whole kernels of domestic short-grain milled rice. Frequently the rice is parboiled and pearled before being introduced into the puffing plant. Typically, a batch of 1,400 lb of rice is weighed into cookers such as are used in the preparation of corn or wheat flakes. About 535 gal of sugar syrup with salt are added and the mixture is cooked for 5 hr under 15 lb steam pressure. Sometimes non-diastatic malt syrup and enriching ingredients are added before cooking.

The lumps of cooked rice coming from the retorts are broken up and dried to approximately 25 to 30% moisture content in rotating louvred driers. Then, the moisture is allowed to distribute uniformly in the grain by storing the partially dried product in stainless steel bins for about 15 hours. Lumps form during the tempering process and must be broken up before the rice is sent to the flaking rolls.

After the individual kernels are separated and again dried so that a moisture content of 18 to 20% is reached, they are passed under a radiant heater which brings the external layers of the rice to a temperature of about 180°F. This plasticises the outer layers of the kernel so that they do not split when the grain is run through the flaking rolls.

Rollers used in the preparation of oven-puffed rice are set relatively far apart so that the tremendous compression effect necessary in corn flakes manufacture is not achieved. In fact, the rolls contact only the widest part of the kernel. The "bumped" grains are again tempered, this time for about 24 hr. To secure the puffed effect, the cooled and tempered rice is passed for about 30 to 45 sec through toasting ovens held at 450° to 575°F.

A cereal called "Special K," manufactured by the Kellogg Co., is basically a rice kernel which is cooked, then coated while in a moistened condition with wheat gluten, wheat germ meal, dried skim milk, debittered brewers' yeast, and other nutritional additives. Finally, the material is oven-puffed. A more complete description of the method of manufacture has been given by Thompson and Raymer (1958).

Gun-puffed products— The manufacture of a composite cereal by the gun-puffing process will be described since it includes several concepts not previously treated in this chapter. In the preparation of Cheerios, corn cones, oat flour, and a flavor premix consisting of sugar, coloring substances, flavoring compounds, etc., are combined in a screw conveyor having interrupted flights. The homogeneous mixture is dumped through a rotary valve into a continuous steam-jacketed cooker. Water is added by a metering device so that the product going to the extruder is at 38 to 40% moisture content.

In the extruder, auger-induced pressure forces strands of cooked dough from orifices in a circular die plate. A knife rotates over the surface of the die, cutting the strands into short pellets which may or may not have a central hole depending upon the design of the die orifices. These pellets are transferred to a tumbling cooker which reduces the surface moisture and prevents them from sticking together. The product is then deposited in a layer about three inches deep on the metal belt of a Procter and Schwartz oven. Solid pellets of 15 to 16% moisture content can be bumped between steel rollers to cause the disc shape to have serrated edges. Puffing takes place in so-called guns.

The puffing guns are pressure vessels typically with internal diameters of about six inches and a length of about 30 inches. They are provided with a steam inlet, a bleed-off valve, and a means for heating the gun—usually a gas flame directed onto parts of the outer surface. A charge of pellets at 11 to 12% moisture content is dropped into the open end of the gun through a gravity chute leading from storage bins on the floor above. The end of the gun is sealed by a trip-valve as soon as the charge is inserted. If the gun is heated by gas flames, it will be slowly rotated during the pressurising process. The temperature builds up as part of the water content of the pellets is converted to vapor and the steam pressure increases. In about 5 to 7 mm the temperature will reach 500° to 800°F, and the pressure at the end point may be in the range of 100 to 200 psi.

When pressure reaches the predetermined level, the end of the gun is suddenly opened by a trigger mechanism and the contents explode into a cage or bin provided with a floor opening leading to a conveyor belt. The ejected material still too moist to be a finished product and must be further dried, usually in a rotating heated cylinder. Finally, the cereal is cooled, inspected for visual defects, and sent to the packaging line.

Many variations on the preceding method are possible. Cocoa can be added to the dough to make a chocolate-flavored confection. Products may be made of any color for which there is a suitable edible dye, though the high content of voids in the product lightens the color greatly. Shapes may be varied over a wide range. Raw materials may be almost any combination of cereals, although each cereal has different expansion potentialities, mostly related to starch characteristics.

Whole kernels of wheat and rice can be gun-puffed. Usually hard wheat or durum is used as raw material for puffed wheat, in order to gain maximum expansion and crispness, and the kernels may be pearled before puffing to reduce the mount of bran present on the finished product Bran becomes loosened by the puffing process, and it may form an unsightly deposit at the bottom of the retail package.

Puffing by extrusion— Many fancy shapes of puffed breakfast cereals, as well as many kinds of snacks, are being made by extruding superheated and pressurised doughs through a restrictive, shaped orifice into a space at atmospheric pressure. The sudden expansion of water vapor as the excess pressure on the pellets is reduced increases the volume of the cereal several times. Apparent specific volumes can reach or exceed those attained by gun-puffing, and extrusion seems to have several advantages over gun-puffing, not the least of which is the extruder's adaptability to continuous production.

In a typical process, a cereal premix containing on the order of 60 to 75% expandable starch base is moistened with water or steam. The resultant mash is compacted by a screw revolving inside a barrel which may be heated by steam. The thread of the screw has a progressively closer pitch as it approaches the discharge end. Pressurising and steam heating bring the dough to a temperature of around 300° to 350°F and a pressure of 350 to 500 psi at the die head. Under these conditions the dough is quite plastic and easily adapts to complex orifice configurations.

The die head will ordinarily contain several or many orifices, and pieces of correct length will be sliced from the emerging strands by rotating blades which rest on the exterior die surface. Adjustment of the speed of rotation of the knife assembly (relative to the rate of extrusion) controls the piece size. Dough pieces expand very rapidly as they leave the die orifice but the expansion may continue for a few seconds after they emerge since the dough is hot and still flexible, and steam continues to evolve. Even so, the final moisture content will be too high for satisfactory stability, and the pieces must be further dried on vibrating screens in hot-air ovens. Fines and agglomerates are removed at the same time, and the products cooled and packaged.

The following raw materials can be expanded satisfactorily by appropriate types of extrusion equipment:

(1) Rice flour—excellent expander, white and bland tasting products; accepts colors and flavors well.

(2) Corn meal or flour—expands well; texture good; retains corn flavor.

(3) Oat flour—high moisture content required if satisfactory expansion is to be obtained; high temperature also needed.

(4) Wheat flour—high moisture and high temperature required for satisfactory results.

(5) Potato flour—high moisture and high temperature needed.

(6) Tapioca flour—needs high temperature and moderate moisture content; bland taste.

(7) Defatted soy flour—requires high temperature and moderate to high moisture.

(8) Full fat soybeans—should have 3 to 5 minutes preconditioning with steam prior to extrusion; extrude at 250°F.

(9) Plain and add-modified corn and wheat starches-need medium to high temperatures; use either steam or water as moisturiser.

As the fat content of the cereal mixture increases, the expansion tends to decrease, but the pieces become more uniform and their surface becomes smoother and brighter, while the cell size becomes smaller and more uniform. Monoglycerides seem to increase these effects. Sugars modify the flavor and texture, and may help to control shape and size of tough doughs.

Alternative puffing methods— Puffing processes depending on contact of dough pieces with very hot embossed cylinders are in current use. Roll temperatures of 350° to 800°F are said to be within the practical range, and it is likely that most producers employ temperatures in the upper half of this range. Rolls may be heated by radiant (infrared) energy or by the circulation of high temperature fluid media inside the cylinder. In one process (Huber 1955), the dough has a moisture content of 8 to 18% going into the rolls and 6 to 7% after puffing. Doughs may be preheated to temperatures below the boiling point, this technique allowing lower roll temperatures to he used.

SUGARCOATED PRODUCTS

Items which are approximately spherical or disc-shaped, such as puffed wheat and puffed rice, can be coated by a technique very similar to the pan-coating process used in confectionery manufacture. The usual apparatus somewhat resembles a cement mixer in having an open bowl rotating about an axis inclined slightly from the horizontal. The very dry cereal particles are placed in the bowl and, as it rotates, a molten (250°F) sugar syrup is slowly dripped on the bowl's contents. A small amount of coconut oil may be added to decrease foaming of the sugar syrup and to promote separation of the coated particles. The tumbling action of the particles results in each of them remaining separate and becoming uniformly coated with a thin glaze of sugar which hardens upon cooling. From 25 to 60% of the weight of the finished product is glaze. A stream of hot air is usually directed into the coating reel to assist in removal of moisture. Some authorities have suggested a syrup formula of 86% sucrose, 13% corn syrup, and 1% salt. Sometimes 0.01 to 0.05% sodium acetate may be added to prevent crystallisation of the coating.

Other methods of coating breakfast cereal pieces with sweet syrups include stirring the granules or flakes with the syrup in a mixing bowl or spraying the viscous material on a bed or falling stream of the cereal. In all cases, the moisture content of the syrup is kept as low as possible to avoid causing changes in the structure and texture of the cereal. In practice, this generally means applying a molten sugar mixture with less than five per cent of water content, and, preferably, about 1% moisture content. Formation of agglomerates of flakes stuck together with the syrup is a recurring problem, and various methods have been suggested to overcome it. An obvious expedient is to keep the pieces widely separated until the coating hardens and loses much of its stickiness, but this creates difficulties in processing. Other methods include applying a non-sticky powder as the coated flakes are cooling.

Hygroscopic coatings lead to sticky surfaces which cause agglomeration of pieces into clumps of several pieces. King (1990) patented a process which leads to the absorption into the interior of the puffed piece of most of the added sugar. It is particularly useful with honey coatings. According to the invention, a grain cereal is enrobod with honey, then heated in an oven at a temperature which will cause the particle to swell and give off moisture. The honey seeps into the pores of the swollen grain. This removes most of the sweetener from the surface, reducing the stickiness and the clumping problem.

Of course, there is nothing to prevent coating of cereal pieces with artificial sweeteners such as saccharin or aspartame. These substances are not inherently sticky, however, so a problem arises in getting them to adhere to the substrate. In an invention patented in 1976 by Baggerly, aspartame was mixed with water containing containing a relatively high concentration of dextrins, and the solution applied to the cereal pieces by atomisation. Other patents achieve the same purpose, but yield a frosty coating as the result of using maltodextrins as the adhering agent. Also, the use of gums and of water soluble vegetable and protein isolates as adhesives has been described.

Crystallisation in the coating may be deliberately caused in order to give a frosted, or somewhat snowlike appearance to the cereal pieces and to reduce sticking. Crystallised sugar is not sticky, has reduced hygroscopicity, and has an opaque white or frosted appearance. Noncrystalline or glassy sugar is hygroscopic, sticky, and has a transparent glossy appearance. In one patented method for producing frosted pieces, the breakfast cereal is coated with seed crystals of dextrose and sucrose; an aqueous solution of dextrose and sucrose is then uniformly applied to the surface; finally, the moisture content of the cereal is reduced by drying at a temperature below that which can cause browning. Another invention describes mixing coarse crystalline sugar granules with cereal pieces which have been sprayed with an edible binding agent; subsequently, the coated pieces are dried.

A recent patent (Verrico 1989) for applying a snow-like coating to shredded wheat biscuits describes an array of atomising units which spray a sweetener mixture onto a single layer of biscuits conveyed on a wire mesh bolt; the coated material is then quickly dried with air currents (not heated). The sweetener mixture may contain, for example, powdered sugar, water, gelatin, and glycerin—note that this is not a solution.

Publications quoted by Walker (1989) give the following formula for a glaze to be applied to puffed wheat : sucrose 54.5%, water 27.2%, invert syrup 7.8%, honey 1.6%, and dextrins 8.9%. This mixture is to be cooked to 325°F and coated on a equal portion of the puffed cereal. Cereal with a non- sticky, non-glassy coating is said to result when 10 parts of cereal are mixed with 12 parts of crystalline sucrose and 4 parts of a spray containing 7.5% gelatin.

White and Parke (1989) recommended the use of fructose in cereal coating because of the intense sweetness of the hexose and an interaction of the sugar with starch. They say that, when crystalline fructose and an instant starch product are dusted onto a liquid sweetener primer that has been applied to a cereal, shelf life and bowl life are extended.

A one-step process for applying sugar and an edible oil to cereal base was disclosed by Lyall and Johnston (1976). A quantity of edible fat is added to an aqueous sugar solution to make up a syrup emulsion having a moisture content of 9 to 34%. After emulsification at 115° to 155°F, the mixture is heated to about 180°F and used to enrobe cereal particles. The coating is then dried, giving crisp, nonhygroscopic cereal with a softer, less frangible texture than conventional candy coated cereals. Two examples of coating formulas used in this process are shown in Table 21.2.

TABLE 21.2. SWEET COATINGS FOR READY-TO—EAT CEREALS

Formula A		*Formula B*	
Ingredient	*Weight*	*Ingredient*	*Weight*
Water	16 oz	Water	32 oz
Icing sugar	64 oz	Dark brown sugar	48 oz
Soybean oil	7 oz	Coconut oil	15 oz
Distilled monoglycerides	1 oz	Distilled monoglycerides	2 oz
Honey	12 oz	Honey	12 oz
Artificial color	0.5 gm		

Cereals can also be sweetened by enzymatically converting part of their normal starch or cellulose content into sugars. Several patented processes based on this concept have been disclosed over the last few years. One of the more recent ones (Neidleman and Maselli 1989), reveals a process for sweetening with fructose without adding that sugar as a separate ingredient. The inventors enzymatically convert a portion of the cellulose fraction in a fibrous cereal with cellulase (to produce glucose) and glucose isomerase (to convert the glucose to fructose). The starch fraction is the ultimate source of the sweetening hexose in the patent of Maselli *et at.* (1989). The cereal grain, or grain fraction such as bran, is treated with glycoamylase and glucose isomerase, which enzymes are subsequently inactivated by the heat treatment normally applied to processed cereals.

OVENS

Several times in the preceding discussion, it has been mentioned there is a need for drying and/or toasting as one of the final steps in the manufacture of breakfast cereals, Many kinds of ovens have been used for this operation. Some of them were simple adaptations of ovens that had been designed for baking or other food processes. Fast (1990) divided cereal toasting ovens into three major types: rotary toasting ovens, conveyorised or flat band forced-convection ovens, and high velocity fluidised-bed dryers or ovens. A rotary toasting oven will consist of an insulated outer shell, an inner revolving cylinder, gas burners, a waste hopper with screw conveyor, and a drive mechanism. In these ovens, wheat and oat cereals are generally toasted at between 350° and 450°F, rice and corn flakes at 450° to 600°F. Usually, the feed end of the oven is held at a higher temperature than the exit end. Band ovens are similar in many respects to the band ovens used to bake cookies or crackers in large volume factories. They can be either direct- fired or use burners located outside the main oven chamber. Corn or rice strands which are to be puffed will first be dried in this typo of equipment, typically dropping in moisture content from 30% to 11% in 30 to 40 sec. The product is then fluidised and heated to 550° to 600°F to puff it.

Air impingement ovens are based on the jet-tube effect, in which high velocity streams of hot air are directed into the bed of product. When conditions are properly adjusted, the cereal pieces will be suspended in the turbulent currents of gas maintained at, say, 600°F.. These ovens are satisfactory for raw or intermediate particles such as pellets, flakes, and fancy shapes but are normally not adaptable to larger pieces such as shredded wheat biscuits. Sequential zones with different temperatures can be used to achieve special effects. Typically, for puffing intermediate products, the first zone(s) will be maintained at 400° to 500°F and puffing will occur. Temperature in the next zone will be lowered to about 300° to 400°F to prevent burning while the product continues to toast.

22
SPECIAL DIETARY FOODS AND INGREDIENTS

INTRODUCTION

Specially designed foods are needed to meet the nutritional regimens of infants, elderly people, invalids, pregnant and nursing women, athletes, and diabetics, to cause weight loss or weight gain, to permit adequate nutritional intake for people having allergies to certain food components, and to serve as vehicles for added fiber, etc. Doubtless, there are additional reasons which will occur to the reader. To supply these needs, many different combinations of natural foods and synthetic additives have been developed. Some of these combinations include cereal products, either as one of the sources of important nutrients or as a bland, innocuous, and familiar bulking ingredient or carrier for the active component.

There is constant research activity directed toward the development of dietary supplements from cereal grains. Since cereals are not, however, particularly good sources of protein, vitamins (the germs may be used as sources of, or raw materials for, fat soluble vitamins), or minerals, justification for employment of cereals as dietary supplements will most likely be based on their content of "complex carbohydrates" or "dietary fiber." Considerable success has been achieved in developing high fiber foods from bran and other components of millfeed, a by-product of flour milling more commonly used in animal rations.

SPECIAL DIETARY FOODS

HOT CEREALS FOR SMALL CHILDREN

Junior and infant cereals in rehydratable flake form have been a market factor for many years. They are similar in most respects, but infant cereals are expected to reconstitute into a rather smooth, homogeneous paste, while junior cereals are expected to have more texture contrast, with some soft granules or lumps being present. Occasionally, there will be some difference in the enrichment profile, as well.

The infant cereals are derived from single grains or blends of mixed grains combined with flavoring, enriching, and texturising ingredients. Some of the varieties which have been offered are oatmeal, barley cereal, corn cereal, rice cereal, mixed cereal, and high protein cereal. Rice cereal, since it is made from a grain that is considered to be hypoallergenic, has been a particular favorite in the U.S. Consumer acceptance of precooked infant cereals is affected by several convenience factors. For example, the cereal must reconstitute readily with milk or water to give an easy-to-feed paste (Kelly 1985). These rehydratable cereals compete directly with fully prepared cereals in glass jars. They are sometimes used for geriatric feeding and for hospital patients requiring bland or soft diets.

Ingredients other than cereals may be added to improve the convenience of the product and to provide a food that has better nutritional balance. Some of the materials found in commercial products include malt, milk solids, vegetable oil, wheat germ, sugar, cottonseed flour, tri- or dicalcium phosphate, dried yeast, iron supplements, and B vitamins. According to Abeling (1959), the following factors are given primary consideration when developing formulas: (1) allergenicity of the various ingredients, (2) compatibility of the mixed materials to give desired flavor and appearance in end product, (3) availability of raw materials, (4) nutritional aspects of the formula, (5) shelf life of the formula, and (6) ease of manufacture. Amylolytic enzymes may be used to hyrdolyse part of the cereal starch to give a product which does not form lumps when the consumer mixes it with liquid.

The processing method described by Abeling can be summarised as follows. Approximately 150 gallons of water are drawn into a mixing tank. With the agitator in motion, preweighed amounts of grain and flour are sifted into the tank along with premixed minor ingredients so as to make a slurry of 300 lbs of dry material. At this point, the batch may be pumped to a pressure kettle where it is completely cooked (for example, 10 to 20 minutes) or it may remain in the original kettle where a similar or longer cooking process takes place.

After cooking is completed, the batch is pumped to an atmospheric drum drier. This piece of equipment is composed of a pair of rotating hollow steel drums which are horizontally disposed and internally heated. The cereal slurry is pumped between the two drums and dries in a thin sheet on the drum surface. Product is removed from the rolls by knife blades and conveyed to a flaking machine. Here the sheets are broken into small flakes which vary in size, depending on the cereal variety and the manufacturer's specifications. The length of time required to process a batch varies according to the drying capacity, but will ordinarily fall in the range of 20 to 40 minutes. Thickness of the sheet of cereal influences the reconstitution properties of the finished cereal, its density and thus the weight which can be put in a package of given dimensions, and the texture of the prepared food. The flaked cereal is either conveyed directly from the flaking equipment to the packaging line or placed in storage drums for later packaging.

Each of the varieties poses its own special processing and packaging problems. Rice cereal is the most difficult of the infant foods to manufacture, according to Kelly (1985). Rice cereal does not flake well when drum dried, and its bulk density tends to vary. The cereal is not very hygroscopic, however, having an equilibrium moisture content of about 13% when stored at 75% relative humidity. Caking is usually not a problem. The product is usually packaged in a container that does not provide very good protection against the transmission of moisture vapor. Most precooked infant cereals sold in the U.S. are packaged in a bending-grade chip-cylinder board prepared from virgin pulp. The carton may be overwrapped with a glue-mounted pre-printed paper. Other manufacturers package these cereals in preprinted cartons overwrapped with a dear film of cellophane, polyethylene, etc. Cereals containing fruit, and spray-dried rice, milk, and sugar products are hygroscopic and require protection from excessive uptake of moisture vapor.

A cereal and fruit combination in liquid or paste form, particularly suitable for infants, was patented by Reinl and Schmidt (1989). Their invention requires use of an enzymatically hydrolysed cereal in liquid form as an ingredient. The formula contains comminuted fruit (e.g., apples or oranges) and a fatty material such as cream in addition to the treated oatmeal or other cereal. The hydrolysis step is said to allow use of larger percentages of cereal and thus give a product which will appease the appetite of the consumer for a longer period of time.

QUALITY CONTROL

The following specifications for rice flour (based on Kelly 1985) to be used as an ingredient in infant cereal could be adapted for some of the other cereal flours.

Definition: The flour obtained by grinding and bolting clean, sound rice of short- or medium-grain varieties.

Purity: The ingredient must be free of pesticide residues, foreign material, and rodent and insect contamination.

Materials: Only medium- or short-grain varieties of rice shall be used. The rice shall be clean, sound, and scoured, and shall be free from smut, weed seeds, or other foreign matter.

Workmanship: The rice shall be properly ground and bolted, and otherwise processed in accordance with good commercial practice and under strict sanitary conditions.

Containers: The finished flour shall be packed in sound, multi-walled paper bags which meet consolidated freight classifications, are adequately sealed by sewing or taping, and are free from dirt, foreign matter, or adulterating substances.

Net Weight: Net weight of the contents of each bag shall be 100 lb avoirdupois at the time of receipt.

Labeling: Each container shall be clearly and properly labelled with the name of the manufacturer, the net weight, and the name "Rice Flour."

Shipping: The product shall be shipped in first-class transportation equipment that has been thoroughly cleaned to prevent any possible contamination of the product or its containers by material carried over from previous shipments or other deleterious substances.

Compliance: Deliveries shall comply in every respect with the Federal Food, Drug, and Cosmetic Act, and with state and local laws which are applicable to such materials.

Samples: Upon the buyer's request, seller shall furnish representative samples for inspection and testing. These samples shall be drawn from actual lots that will be delivered, and shall be of a size designated by the buyer, or in the absence of a specific designation to the contrary, five pounds.

Testing: Acceptance will be subject to a sampling of the material actually delivered and to testing of these samples according to laboratory instructions in this specification. Chemical and physical tests normally applied include amylograph paste viscosity, color, odor, flavor, and granulation. Microbiological tests include counts of thermophilic spores, fiat sour spores, and thermophilic anaerobes.

Methods: Methods of analysis shall be those described in the methods of the Association of Official Agricultural Chemists or other procedure as specified by the buyer.

Sampling: Representative samples will be obtained from six bags selected at random from the delivered lot and combined into one gallon containers. If resampling is required, representative samples from an additional 12 bags may be tested individually or in any composite form.

Quality assurance evaluation of the finished goods should include microbiological tests for total thermophilic spores, flat sour spores, and thermophilic spores, and organoleptic tests for flavor, consistency, and color. The consistency of infant foods can be evaluated by the Bostwick Consistometer which measures the distance the material will flow in a given time. This does not indicate the shortness or stringiness of the paste, which is evaluated by spooning the product.

JUNIOR CEREALS

As mentioned above, junior cereals tend to have more texture contrast than infant cereals. There is considerable overlap between the two groups, and, in fact, there is no clear definition for either item. Coarser texture has been achieved by adding rolled oats to an edible polysaccharide gum or to a pregelatinised starch. Another suggestion has been to combine pregelatinised base flakes with quick cooking cereal flakes. Also, the addition of dehydrated fruit granules or lumps has been recommended.

A patent granted to Cloud *et al.* (1976) describes the manufacture of a precooked, dehydrated, grain product that is rapidly reconstitutable with liquid (water, milk, or formula) to form a coarse-textured cereal suitable for feeding to young children. The formula and process will be included here as examples of the state of the art.

The patent is distinguished from prior art in providing for reducing sugars in an amount of from about 12 to 30% of the grain slurry and by subjecting the slurry to sterilisation conditions of greater temperature and line pressure, so that the resulting drum-dried product possesses the desired coarse texture.

The exemplary formula for an oatmeal cereal consists of 100 lb oat flour, 5 lb malted barley flour, 1.6 lb calcium sulfate, 1.5 lb vanilla sugar, and 0.31 lb of vitamin and mineral enrichment. After these ingredients are blended, they are slurried with 60 gallons of water. The slurry is heated for about 20 min at 140°F, and then transferred through a tangential heater maintained at 240°F and 50 psig. The resulting gelatinised and sterilised slurry is fed to a conventional double drum dryer, with the drums heated at an internal steam Pressure of about 50 psig. These drums rotate at about four revolutions per minute, and the dried sheets are removed by doctor blades and comminuted to the desired size of 0.25 to 1.0 inches.

A suggested formula for mixed cereal is 40 lb oat flour, 40 lb corn flour, 10 lb soy flour, 5 lb malted barley flour, 3 lb soy oil, 2.2 lb calcium sulfate, 0.35 lb vitamin mix (containing niacinamide, riboflavin, pyridoxine hydrochloride, and thiamin mononitrate), and 0.085 lb electrolytic iron. A variation of this formula was prepared by mixing 75 parts of the preceding dried cereal with 20 parts of rice flakes and 5 parts of soy flakes.

An alternate formula for oatmeal cereal consists of 270 lb oat flour, 18 lb soy flour, 18 lb malt flour, and 2 lb of calcium carbonate. These blended .—ere mixed with 176 gallons of water, then heated for 17 min at 145°F in a cook tank. The hot slurry was passed through a tangential heater maintained at 250°F and 50 psig before being fed to a double drum dryer operating at 4 rpm and an internal steam pressure of 65 psig. The resultant sheet was ground under conditions such that the flakes were retained on sieves having openings of about 7/16 inch.

The preferred moisture content of the finished product is 2 to 5%, and the thickness of the flakes will be within the range of 4 to 7 mils. The coarse texture of the reconstituted product results from the high pressure in-line heating. Sterilisation line back-pressures in excess of 30 psig are required.

Variations which can be made in the above products include the addition of fruit purees (bananas, prunes, strawberries, apples, etc.) and imitation flavors.

BEVERAGES

Health food enthusiasts and persons who avoid caffeine-containing beverages for religious reasons often want a coffee substitute which serves some of the same purposes as the real thing. There have also been many attempts to provide a substitute which is substantially cheaper than coffee. Some of these ersatz beverages have been based on roasted chicory, which is a root vegetable, but many others have used cereal components as the chief ingredients and so are suitable topics for this book. The most popular of these cereal-based coffee imitations in the U.S. has been Postum, now manufactured by General Foods. This is a dark brown powder bearing a superficial resemblance to some forms of dehydrated coffee and yielding, when mixed with the proper amount of hot water, a beverage which resembles coffee in that it is hot and brown. This product has an interesting history.

Postum Cereal, a cereal beverage which had to be prepared by a steeping or extraction process like that applied to ground coffee, was the first product made by the founder of Post Cereals and it originally appeared on the market January 1, 1895. The following description of its manufacture in a Battle Creek, Michigan plant was obtained from General Foods in the 1960s.

Wheat bran is mixed with molasses, then dried and roasted to a uniform color. Whole wheat kernels are roasted separately. Each bran roaster holds 225 lbs of the bran mixture, which is roasted for 45 minutes at 350°F. The cooking vessels for whole wheat kernels roast 11 bushels of the grain for two hours at 425°F.

The roasted bran and molasses mixture is cooled and screened in large shelf-type coolers installed at the rear of the cookers. Roasted wheat is cooled in metal trays and then conveyed to grinders.

Blending scales automatically blend the ground roasted wheat and the roasted bran and molasses mixture in the correct ratio to produce Postum Cereal, which is then packaged.

Instant Postum is a form of the beverage which can be prepared for consumption by mixing a measured quantity of a powder directly with hot water in the cup, thus being the counterpart of instant coffee. It is, or was, made by extracting the previously described Postum Cereal with water and then drying the extract. According to publications obtained from the manufacturer, fifteen thousand pounds of Postum Cereal constitutes a percolator batch. Ten thousand gallons of hot water is percolated through the Postum Cereal and the resulting solution is drawn off through outlets on the front of the percolators.

The cereal infusion goes first to storage tanks and then, after a brief holding period, is clarified by running it through Sharples Centrifugal Clarifiers and Ful-Flo filters. After the clarifying operations, the liquor is pumped to the evaporator system where the water is removed until the material assumes the consistency of molasses. The concentrated syrup is pumped to a series of vacuum drum driers where it is converted to a thin, low moisture film at relatively low temperature. This film is removed in sheets and flakes of mixed sizes and conveyed to bins which are held at a constant low humidity.

From the bins, the dehydrated material passes to grinding rolls where the Instant Postum is ground into the glistening granules characteristic of this product. The finished material is packed by vacuum- fillers in glass jars in rooms that have humidity and temperature controlling means.

There seem to be many more coffee-substitutes available in Europe than in the U.S. Most of these contain cereal products as essential ingredients. An old favorite is Ovaltine. Though in its current form it is primarily a milk flavoring material and nutrient supplement, it was originally a hot-water additive based largely on barley malt syrup, and was promoted for its alleged health-giving properties rather than as a replacement for coffee. Some details regarding its manufacture are included in the malting chapter.

CEREAL-DERIVED SUPPLEMENTS

The cereal-derived dietary supplements of greatest current interest are those described as dietary fiber concentrates. These materials have been obtained not only by special processing of cereal grains but also from by-products of various other processing methods.

Fiber supplementation has been one of the great food "gimmicks" of recent years. Addition of "roughage" to the diet is a rather old concept; for example, the idea that undigestible plant materials had some beneficial effect on "regularity" was one of the justifications for using graham flour as a replacement for white flour. The current fad originated with the publications of a Dr. Denis Burkett, who reported that heart disease, diveticulosis, and cancer of the colon seldom occurred in rural Africans but were fairly common in Africans who had moved to urban areas. He hypothesised that the differences in cancer rates might be the result of a change from a native high-fiber diet containing mostly unrefined foods to an urban diet lower in fiber. Subsequent studies presented a mixed picture, some results appearing to support Burkett's hypothesis while others cast doubt upon it.

DETERMINING FIBER CONTENT OF FOODS

At the heart of this problem is the definition of "fiber." This term has been used to describe a number of different types of substances; but it is generally thought to refer only to certain compounds found in plants, i.e., animal foods do not contain fiber as it is understood in this context. Fiber has not been clearly defined from a structural standpoint and it may be impossible to define it to everyone's satisfaction. From the physiological standpoint, fiber is considered to be the endogenous components of plant materials in the diet which are resistant to digestion by enzymes secreted by the stomach or small intestine. Many of these plant constituents are carbohydrates composed of repeating monosaccharide units; others, such as lignin, have much more complex structures. Some of the substances which are considered to be part of the fiber fraction of foods include cellulose, hemi-cellulose, pectic substances, gums, mucilages, and lignin. Both water insoluble and water soluble materials are found in this category. The water insoluble substances (e.g., cellulose) absorb large amounts of water as they pass through the digestive tract, thus increasing fecal weight, reducing intestinal transit time, slowing starch hydrolysis, and delaying glucose absorption. The water soluble fraction (e.g., pectin) forms gels and delays gastric emptying, decreases glucose absorption, and lowers serum cholesterol levels.

The analytical methods which have been prescribed for determining fiber content are empirical, complex, and time-consuming. There is crude fiber, which is basically the organic substances that survive a harsh acid digestion process during the analysis; then there is dietary fiber which will generally include all the crude fiber plus many gum-like substances soluble or dispersible under very mild conditions and not under any normal set of circumstances capable of forming "fibers." It can be said, as a helpful generalisation, that substances of the dietary fiber type are not digested or are very poorly digested in the human intestinal tract and therefore do not contribute calories to the diet but do bind water and increase bulk of the feces.

The food constituents referred to as crude fiber are the residue of plant materials remaining after solvent extraction followed by digestion with dilute acid and alkali. From the data so obtained is deducted the total of mineral constituents determined by ashing. It is obvious the conditions applied in the test causes changes in the natural constituents not strictly comparable to anything that happens in the human body and so "crude fiber" determinations are of limited value in physiological studies. The acid detergent method was developed to improve the meaningfulness of fiber determinations. In this procedure, a sample is boiled in a solution of cetyl trimethylammonium bromide (the detergent) and in sulfuric acid. The residue is filtered, dried, and weighed. Larger percentages of cellulose and lignin are recovered, as compared to the crude fiber results. Lignin can be determined by further hydrolyzing the residue, using 72% sulfuric acid, and weighing the washed and dried remainder. Later, the neutral detergent fiber method was developed, primarily to permit the determination of cell wall constituents.

Since analysts encountered interference and inaccuracies from other factors when samples of high starch content were analysed by the preceding methods, a procedure was published which involved the inclusion of an a-amylase hydrolysis step. This modification of the neutral detergent fiber analysis has been approved by the American Association of Cereal Chemists as a standard method. By omitting the acid and alkali hydrolysis steps, the fiber is subjected to a much milder treatment, with the result that nearly all of the cellulose, hemicellulose, and lignin can be obtained. The results of this method are being reported as "dietary fiber" in literature and labeling. However, the neutral detergent method, as modified, still omits components that some nutrition scientists consider to be part of the total dietary fiber; for example, the water soluble gums and pectin which are supposed to have a beneficial role in human nutrition. Perhaps the most complete and meaningful analysis involves applying separate and specific tests for each of the fiber constituents and then summing up the individual measurements. Of course, this is a very time-consuming process and subject to considerable experimental error under the best of conditions. A more practical approach was needed, and this was apparently achieved with the publication of a gravimetric method employing enzyme hydrolysis. In this latest version of dietary fiber determination, samples are gelatinised, treated with a-amylase, digested with protease and amyloglucosidase, then mixed with 78% ethanol to precipitate the soluble dietary fiber. The residue is filtered, washed with ethanol and acetone, dried, and weighed. Values for protein and ash in the residue are subtracted, and the difference reported as total dietary fiber. Soluble fiber is determined by adding additional ethanol (95%) to the filtrate and determining the dry weight of the precipitate.

Crude fiber determinations generally amount to about two-thirds of the cellulose (an insoluble fiber) and do not include any of the soluble fiber. Results of the acid detergent method generally report 90% of the cellulose, the lignin, and a small part of the hemicellulose (insoluble substances), and no soluble fiber. The neutral detergent analysis accounts for virtually all the cellulose, lignin, and hemicellulose, part of the insoluble pectins, and none of the soluble fibers. When total dietary fiber is reported, it should include cellulose, lignin, hemicellulose, and polysaccharides not susceptible to enzymic digestion. The total dietary fiber amount will also include ß-glucan, a "soluble fiber" found in appreciable amounts only in oats and barley, and pentosans, a type of insoluble fiber found in oat hulls and the surface layers of other grains.

According to Cummings and Englyst (1987), the crude fiber analytical procedures which have been developed over the past ten years follow two different broad principles: firstly, the enzymatic-gravimetric methods, which attempt to define a fraction of the diet that resist digestion in the human small intestine; secondly, techniques based on carbohydrate chemistry which aim to measure specific constituents of foods and which define fiber as non-starch polysaccharides (non a-glucan polysaccharides, or NSP). In the cited article are reported results of a collaborative study which gave the following values for several cereal products (an NSP method result first, a proposed AOAC method second; in grams of dietary fiber per 100 grams dry matter): white flour 3.2 and 3.8, added bran flour 7.7 and 12.1, wholemeal digestive biscuits 1.3 and 4.7, cornflakes 1.2 and 4.3, bran 36.4 and 53.2, instant porridge 6.6 and 10.7, soy flour 8.4 and 19.4, whole meal bread 9.5 and 13.3, low fiber brown bread 5.6 and 7.8, pea hull bread 6.9 and 9.0, rye bread 3.5 and 5.6, white bread 3.3 and 4.4, and high fiber brown bread 6.5 and 9.7.

The value of dietary fiber in preventing cardiovascular disorders is said to be related to the ability of pectins, gums, etc., to bind bile acids and thereby increase their excretion, thus preventing their absorption and re-use by the body. The reduced supply of bile acids causes more cholesterol to be used as a raw material for making these compounds, so there is a reduction in the amount of cholesterol circulating in the blood. As everone knows (?), a reduction in cholesterol leads to less atherosclerosis, arteriosclerosus, etc. Adverse results of high fiber diets are more immediate and obvious and include unpleasant sensations of abdominal fullness, flatulence, and diarrhea. As one authority states,".. .but these symptoms subside with time."

The uncertainties have not prevented such organisation National Cancer Institute from stating that a high fiber diet is beneficial and urging Americans to consume 25 to 35 grams of fiber per day to reduce their risk of getting cancer. A government report also said, "The average American diet is low in fiber. Eating foods high in fiber tends to reduce the symptoms of chronic constipation, diverticulosis, and some forms of irritable bowel. There is also concern that low fiber [diets] might increase the risk of developing cancer of the colon, but whether this is true or not is not yet known."

It has become apparent that persons consuming a high fiber diet tend to mobilise less of some of the mineral substances in food. For example, fiber binds calcium in the intestines. Zinc deficiencies, hitherto a great rarity in the U.S., have been observed in some food faddists who consumed large quantities of bran.

ENHANCING FIBER CONSUMPTION

The consumer has a choice of several bakery products which will contribute some extra fiber to the diet. The total dietary fiber levels in these products, while somewhat better than in standard white bread, are not particularly impressive. The typical levels are 1.4% crude fiber and 5.2% dietary fiber in whole wheat bread, 2.6% crude fiber and 8.3% dietary fiber in bran bread, 1.4% crude fiber and 45% dietary fiber in multi-grain bread, 3.5% crude fiber and 9.8% dietary fiber for Canadian fiber bread, and 5.0% crude fiber and 12.0% dietary fiber for U.S. reduced calorie bread (Stewart 1987).

In the cookie and cracker categories, some fiber-enhanced products have been available for many years, although they have not been promoted on this basis. Examples are graham crackers and so called digestive biscuits. Cookies and crackers are good candidates for fiber additions because their structure is generally less sensitive to increases in the percentages of inert ingredients in formulas—they do not have the delicate, highly expanded structure of bread and rolls, which is so responsive to minor changes in composition. Particularly suitable as fiber carriers are the shortbread type cookies which undergo very little expansion on baking and are expected to have a solid but tender structure; the large amount of shortening used in these items is also beneficial since it helps overcome the dry and often powdery mouthfeel that all too often accompanies a high fiber content. The author has had good results with a chocolate-flavored shortbread with a 50% fiber content—it is necessary to sweeten this product with artificial sweeteners.

All of the milling by-products of wheat, corn, barley, sorghum, etc., as well as the by-products of wet milling corn and wheat have been investigated as possible fiber supplements for cereal and other foods. In addition, brewers' dried grains with solubles and the distillers' counterpart, which are by-products of the beer brewing and ethanol production (from grain) industries, respectively, have got some attention, although their flavor would seem to be a considerable negative feature. The paper of San Buenaventura *et al.* (1987) listed the total dietary fiber content of wheat, corn, barley, and brown sorghum and of the distillers' dried grains with solubles from these grains.

These were (percentages, dry weight basis; grain first, distillers' by-product second): wheat 10.5 and 34.6, corn 12.1 and 32.0, barley 21.7 and 84.7, and brown sorghum 10.1 and 67.8.

Corn bran, and probably barley bran and sorghum bran, are possible choices for supplementing the fiber content of foods. They have relatively mild flavors, relatively high dietary fiber contents, and are available in large amounts at low prices.

By subjecting bran of any cereal to various known extraction procedures, it would appear to be possible to get a product that analysed close to 100% of the dry matter as dietary fiber. The relatively low yield and the cost of the extraction processes would very likely make the product noncompetitive, from a price standpoint, with (for example) the purified cellulose powder obtained from woodpulp, which is at present an item of commerce. It is also not certain that bran subjected to these purification procedures, which would doubtless significantly alter many of the components remaining in the proposed ingredient, would be acceptable as a food ingredient without lengthy safety testing.

23
Food Additives

Food additives are substances or a mixture of substances, which are added to food but are not commonly regarded as food. These substances can be added at any stage of the manufacturing process viz, processing, storage or packing, and affect the keeping quality, texture, appearance, odor, acidity or alkalinity and the consistency of the food. Colorants, antioxidants, preservatives, emulsifiers and stabilisers as well as numerous miscellaneous additives such as sweeteners, solvents and improving agents fall into the category of food additives. The term does not include contaminants. Food additives can be classified as intentional and unintentional additives.

Intentional additives are substances deliberately added to perform specific functions, while unintentional (non-intentional or incidental) additives are substances, which have no intended function in the finished food but become part of the food product during some phase of production or subsequent handling. Both kinds of additives in excessive amounts can be detrimental to health.

In recent times there has been an increase in public awareness of the potential health effects of the thousands of food additives, which are utilised by the food industry, but unfortunately sufficient information to make informed judgements on their safety is often lacking. The quantities of food additives which may be added to foods are only prescribed for certain categories of additives and in the case of colorants, emulsifiers, stabilisers, solvents and most miscellaneous additives there are mostly no prohibitions to the amounts of these substances which may be used in foods, although their use has been restricted to certain categories of food.

FUNCTIONS AND USES OF FOOD ADDITIVES

Food additives perform several function such as drying, emulsifying, enhancing flavor, enriching, firming, flavoring, foam producing, glazing, leavening, lining food containers, maturing (flour), anticaking, antidrying, antifoaming, antihardening, antispattering, antisticking, bleaching, buffering, chillproofing, clarifying, color retaining, coloring, conditioning (dough), creaming, curing, dispersing, dissolving, sweetening, thickening, preserving, stabilizing and supplementing nutrients.

MAJOR USES OF FOOD ADDITIVES

- Enhancement of the attractiveness of foods by means of coloring and flavoring agents, emulsifiers, stabilisers, thickeners, clarifiers and bleaching agents.
- Maintenance of nutritional quality by the use of antioxidants.
- Facilitating food processing by means of acids, alkalis, buffers sequestrants and various other chemicals.
- Enhancement of keeping quality of stability by the use of antioxidants, antimicrobial agents, inert gases, meat curers, etc.

There are more than thousands of different chemical compounds used as intentional food additives and can be classified into several groups. Some of the important groups are discussed below:

ANTIOXIDANTS

Antioxidants are added to oils and fats and fat containing foods to prevent oxidation and thus prolong their shelf life, wholesomeness and palatability.

Without antioxidants, fatty foods cannot be stored for a long time without becoming rancid. Normally this is best achieved when mixtures of antioxidants are used for this purpose. Natural antioxidants include some vitamins (particularly vitamin E and ubiquinols) and some phenolic compounds occuring in foods, especially spices. An antioxidant should not have any harmful physiological effect and should not impart an objectionable flavor, odor or colour to the food in which it is present. It should be effective in low concentration and be fat-soluble. Some antioxidants used in foods are butylated hydroxy anisole (BHA) butylated hydroxy toluene (BHT) tertiary butyl-hydroquinone (TBHQ) propyl gallate (PG), tocopherols, more expensive naturally occurring vitamin E. sulphur dioxide and ascorbic acid. Ascorbic acid prevents browning caused by enzymatic oxidation of phenolic compounds. Acids such as citric acid and phosphoric increase the effectiveness of ascorbic acid. The natural antioxidants, such as the increase the effectiveness of ascorbic acid. The natural antioxidants, such as the tocopherols (vitamin E) and ubiquinols have a cyclic nucleus and hydrocarbon tail and the antioxidant properties are produced by the cyclic nucleus of these molecules by interrupting the free radical chain reaction involved in lipid oxidation.

PRESERVATIVES

Preservatives are substances which are capable of inhibiting, retarding, or arresting the growth of microorganisms. It may be a chemical or a natural substance (sugar, salt or acid). Food preservation is an old process which has been followed since ancient times and food has been preserved by drying, smoking or by the addition of salt or sugar. Today food preservation has become a huge industry and besides the ancient methods, canning, bottling and refrigeration are extensively used to preserve foods. The use of synthetic, organic and inorganic preservatives has become fashionable in the food industry. The most commonly used inorganic preservatives are sulphur dioxide, nitrates and nitrites. Sulphur dioxide is used in gaseous form, in solution as sulphurous acid or as sulphites of sodium, potassium or calcium. It prevents the browning of foods and also inhibits the growth of moulds, and it is used extensively in the preservation of fruit juices and dried fruits. Sulphur dioxide is known to destroy vitamin B but it helps to preserve vitamin C. Sodium and potassium nitrate and nitrite are used mainly in the curing of meats. The most extensively used organic preservatives are benzoic acids, 4-hydrobenzoates, salicylic acid, parachlorobenzoic acid, acetic acid, propionic acid, sorbic acid and sodium diacetate. Many of these products are used in the preservation of breads and flour confectionary Benzoic acid and benzoates are used for the preservation of some jams, fruit juices, desserts, tinned fruits, salad creams, yoghurt, sauces and margarines. It is also an effective agent against the growth of yeasts and moulds. Sorbic acid is a mould and yeast inhibitor in cheese and baked products, fruit juices, wines and pickles. Chlorine compounds used as germicidal wash for fruits and vegetables are also used as preservatives. The term preservative includes fumigants (e.g., ethylene oxide and ethyl formate) used to control microorganisms on spices, nuts and dried fruits.

SOLVENTS

Solvents are used to dissolve raw materials and concentrates and they are also used to incorporate flavors, oils, colors, antioxidants and vitamins into foods. Many of the compounds used are considered to be health risks, since some are suspected of having carcinogenic properties; and the use of some of these compounds has been banned in some countries.

COLORANTS

These are used in a large number of food items to make them more attractive, appetising and acceptable to the consumer. They may be natural e.g., extract of annatto, caramel, carotene and saffron, or synthetic. Synthetic dyes, besides providing a larger range of colors than natural substances, are generally superior to the latter in coloring power, uniformity and stability of color and are cheaper. Since many adverse reactions due to synthetic colorants have been reported many of these have been banned in some countries and natural colorants are being used more frequently. Natural food colors are becoming most popular and the main classes are the carotenoids, beetroot extract, anthocyanins, riboflavins, chlorophylls and naturally colored foods such as paprika, turmeric and saffron along with extract of these materials. Overall it can be said that avoidance of food colorants can only be of advantage to the consumer.

SWEETENERS

Non carbohydrate sweeteners have been used as substitutes for cane sugar in the preparation of diabetic foods and they are also used in foods that are stored at low temperatures such as ice cream. Substances have been synthesised which are 10 to 3000 times as sweet as sucrose and mainly used in the manufacture of low - calorie soft drinks. They are also added to low calorie liquid foods, canned fruit, frozen desserts, salad dressings, gelatin desserts, and some baked products. These non-sugar sweeteners besides helping to control weight have made it possible for diabetics to enjoy foods they would otherwise not be able to eat it. The first synthetic sweetening agent was saccharin, which is 300 times sweeter than sucrose and has a bitter and unpleasant after-taste. Cyclamates are 15 to 30 times as sweet as sucrose. Aspartame, the methyl ester of aspartyl phenylalanine is about 180 times as sweet as sucrose and does not have any unpleasant after-taste. Glycyrrhizic acid, thaumatin, sucralose alitame are also used as sweeteners. However, use of some of them has been restricted or prohibited because of their adverse effect on health.

FLAVOURING AGENTS AND FLAVOUR ENHANCERS

Flavouring agents and flavour enhancers are those substances, naturally occurring or synthetic, which are responsible for characteristic flavours of almost all the foods in our diet. This is the largest group of food additives and includes about more than two thousand different substances. Spices, herbs, plant extracts (root, leaves, stem, flower) and essential oils are widely used flavouring agents of natural origin. Since the preparation of extracts and essential oils is very costly, synthetic ones are replacing natural flavouring substances.

Esters, aldehydes, ketones, alcohols and esthers having characteristic fruity odors can be easily synthesised and readily replace aromatic substances. Some examples of these are amyl acetate (banana) methyl anthranilate (grapes) and ethyl butyrate (pine apple). Generally, mixing a number of different synthetic substances can reproduce natural flavours. Flavour enhancers do not possess any flavour themselves but they intensify the flavours of other substances through a synergistic effect. The best known, most widely used and somewhat controversial flavour enhancer is monosodium glutamate (MSG); the sodium salt of the naturally occurring glutamic acid an amino acid extracted from seaweeds and soybean. Ribonucleoties extracted from yeast possess ten times the flavour enhancing property of MSG.

EMULSIFIERS AND STABILISERS

Emulsifiers are used to disperse tiny globules of one liquid in another so that they will stay mixed. Their use has made it possible to market oil-containing foods, such as peanut butter and margarines, that will not separate and so are instantly usable. Emulsifiers are used extensively in the baking industry to help increase volume and to effect the firmness. Stabilisers and thickeners are use to bind together solids and liquids so that they will not separate. They are used in ice-cream, cake and pudding mixes, cheese spreads, salad dressings, soups and many others, too numerous to mention. Most commercial stabilisers and thickeners are pure plant extracts and the use of plant gums for this purpose is quite extensive. Gums are extracted from seaweed, trees, and seeds while cellulose derivatives are obtained from wood pulp and cotton. The seaweed extracts include agar, algin, carrageenan, and furcellaran; The tree gums include arabic, ghatti, karaya, larch and tracaganth. Extracts of seeds which include guar, and extracts from the carob bean, and the commonly used cellulose derivatives are methyl cellulose, carboxy methyl cellulose hydroxypropyl methylcellulose. The most commonly used natural emulsifier is lecithin, which is obtained from soybeans, and other vegetable oils. But synthetic, mono, di and trigylycerides are also extensively used. Synthetic stabilisers and emulsifiers are used extensively in the baking and dairy industry; the permitted substances include stearyl tartrate, glycerol esters, acetic and tartaric acid esters of mono and di gylycerides. Some of these compounds are suspected to be carcinogens and the approval for the use of some of the compounds (polyoxyethylene compounds) has been withdrawn in some countries.

Since much work has not been carried out in our country on the toxicological evaluation of food additives, we therefore, depend on the work done in advanced countries as well as by the FAO, WHO and other International organizations. There are situations where food additives are best avoided.

THUS ADDITIVES SHOULD NOT BE USED:

- In baby and invalid food
- To mask the spoilage or bad quality of food and thus deceive the consumer.
- To cover up the defects in handling and processing.
- To make food attractive and appealing to consumers at the expense of its nutritional quality and safety.
- To obtain a desired effect instead of adopting improved process techniques.

Where the addition may modify the nutrients in a food or in any other manner adversely affect the health of the consumer.

Although the above list of food additives is not complete, the above details are worthy to a certain extent. In most countries there is legislation, which enforces the proper labeling of food items sold to the general public, and most nutritional organisations support the right of the public to know what is in the food they buy. Caution is necessary even in using some of the permitted food additives. Since most of the food additives are health hazardous, it is always better to avoid the additives in the food preparations or in the processing stages wherever / whenever possible. Otherwise it is better to go for the natural food additives as an alternative.

24
Use of Antimicrobials in Food Preservation

INTRODUCTION

Food preservation is a continuous fight against microorganisms spoiling the food or making it unsafe. The main purpose of food processing is food preservation, which involves maintaining high quality properties of the food for as long as possible. Preservatives or antimicrobial agents play an important role in todays supply of safe and stable foods. Increasing demand for convenience foods and reasonably long-shelf life of processed foods make the use of antimicrobial food preservatives imperative. Some of the commonly used preservatives- such as sulphites, nitrates, and salts — have been used for centuries in processed meats and wine. These preservatives also minimise damage to some essential amino acids and loss of some vitamins. Anti-microbials prevent the growth of moulds, yeast and bacteria whereas antioxidants keep foods from becoming rancid, brown, or developing black spots. Preservatives are used to prevent deterioration. The choice of an antimicrobial agent has to be based on the knowledge of antimicrobial spectrum of the preservative, the chemical and physical properties of both food and preservative, the conditions of storage and handling, the assurance of a high initial quality of the food to be preserved.

The use of chemicals in foods is a well-known method of food reservation. Additives are used in foods to perform one of the following functions:

- To ensure safety and wholesomeness.
- To improve keeping quality.
- To increase availability from season to season.
- To improve or maintain nutritional value.
- To enhance consumer acceptability.

- To facilitate preparation of the food.
- To make food more readily available.

Chemical preservatives are defined by the Food and Drug Administration as "any chemical that, when added to food, tends to prevent or retard deterioration, but does not include common salt, sugars, vinegars, spices or oils extracted from spices, substances added to food by direct exposure thereof to wood smoke or chemicals applied for their respective insecticidal or herbicidal properties. Food is susceptible to chemical and biological deterioration. Chemical deterioration includes browning, lipid oxidation and staling. Antibrowning agents, antioxidants, or antistaling agents are used to prevent chemical deterioration of the food. The biological deterioration of foods can be prevented using antimicrobials. By preventing or retarding chemical and biological deterioration, the shelf life of foods can be extended by as much as 200%.

The selection of a specific antimicrobial for a specific food depends on: physical and chemical properties of the antimicrobial agents, composition of the food, type of preservation system other than chemicals used in the food, characteristics and number of microorganisms, cost and toxicity of the antimicrobial. The physical and chemical properties considered in selecting an antimicrobial are water solubility, hydrophile - lipophile balance, boiling point, ability to ionize, and potential inactivation with the food constituents. The activity of antimicrobials is reduced as a result of reaction with lipids, proteins or carbohydrates. Further, chemical reaction between antimicrobials and food constituents may result in the formation of off flavors and off colors. Therefore, the antimicrobial used in a food should be carefully selected after considering the necessary factors.

CHEMICALS WITH ANTIMICROBIAL PROPERTIES

2.1 ORGANIC ACIDS

Acids are added to foods as acidulants or antimicrobials. The most common classical preservative agents are the weak organic acids, for example acetic, lactic, benzoic and sorbic acid. The demand for organic acids is steadily increasing because of larger production volumes of acid foods. Citric acid and malic acid are the general-purpose acidulants, with fumaric acid being used in most foods where acidity is desired. These molecules inhibit the outgrowth of both bacterial and fungal cells and are also reported to inhibit the germination and outgrowth of bacterial spores. Weak acid preservatives exist in a pH- dependent equilibrium between the undissociated and dissociated state. Preservatives have optimal inhibitory activity at low pH because this flavours the uncharged, undissociated state of the molecule, which is freely permeable across the plasma membrane and is thus able to enter the cell. The preservative molecule diffuses into the cell until equilibrium is reached in accordance with the pH gradient across the membrane resulting in the accumulation of anions and protons inside the cell. Therefore, inhibition of growth by weak acid preservatives has been proposed to be due to a number of actions including, membrane disruption, inhibition of essential metabolic reactions, stress on intracellular pH homeostasis and the accumulation of toxic anions. In yeasts, it has also been proposed that the actual inhibitory action of weak acid preservatives could be due to the induction of an energetically expensive stress response that attempts to restore homeostasis and results in the reduction of available energy pools for growth and other essential metabolic functions The saturated acids with C10 to C12 chain lengths have optimal antimicrobial activity. Gram-negative bacteria are affected by short (< C6), rather than long fatty acids and their derivatives. Organic acids are more effective antimicrobials than are inorganic acids. Salts of benzoic, propionic and sorbic acids are often used as antimicrobials. Acids such as acetic, citric, propionic, malic, fumaric, and tartaric, are mainly used as acidulants but they also inhibit moulds. Organic acids can also act as chelating agents and thereby inhibit lipid oxidation, control pectin gel formation, inhibit browning, and aid in sucrose inversion (Doores, 1993).

2.1.1 Benzoic acid

One of the oldest chemical used in cosmetics, food, and drug industries is benzoic acid. The sodium salt of benzoic acid was the first chemical preservative approved by the U.S. Food and Drug Administration. Benzoic acid is also naturally present in cranberries, prunes, cinnamon, apples, strawberries, and yogurt (Christiansen and Tanner, 1972). The antimicrobial properties of benzoic acid have been assumed to be expressed by the undissociated acid only. However, benzoic acid also shows certain growth inhibitory capacity in the dissociated state . At pH 3, 93.5 % of the acid exists in the undissociated form; at pH 4, only 59.3% of the acid exists in the undissociated form (Dziezak, 1986). Benzoic acid and sodium benzoate are generally recognized as safe (GRAS) ingredients and are most suitable for foods with a pH <4.5 (Chipley, 1993). Some of the foods preserved with benzoic acid and sodium benzoate include fruit juice, cider, carbonated or noncarbonated drink, bakery products, salad dressings, margarine, tomato ketchup, fruit salads, jams, and jellies. Benzoic acid and sodium benzoate are also used as a fungicide to preserve post harvest diseases of fruits and vegetables. A benzoic acid-based polymer coating was developed to prevent spoilage of apples (Chipley, 1 993). Benzoate acts essentially as a mould and yeast inhibitor in acidic foods. It exhibits optimum activity in the pH range 2.5-4.0, making it well suited for use in acid foods, such as fruit juices, carbonated beverages, pickles. Since the sodium salt of benzoic acid is more soluble in water than the acid form, the former is generally used. The poor activity of benzoate at pH>4.0 limits its use against bacteria. Benzoic acid prevents the outgrowth of vegetative cell from spore after shredding of the spore wall. Often benzoic acid is used in combination with sorbic acid and levels of use usually range from 0.05 to 0.1% by weight.

2.1.2 Citric acid

Citric acid is quantitatively the most widely used organic acid additive in foods and is utilised in many different products. Citric acid has a pleasant acid taste, is very soluble in water, and finds many applications in food, pharmaceutical and cosmetic industries. Citric acid occurs naturally in almost all living things and is the predominant acid in citrus fruits and in many vegetables. Originally this acid was extracted from citrus. It is used as a standard to evaluate the effects of other acidulants in foods. Citric acid can chelate metal ions, allowing antioxidants to function more effectively in retarding lipid oxidation (Dziezak, 1990). Citric acid is particularly inhibitory to flat sour organisms from tomato juice. Other foods preserved with citric acid include ice cream, sherbet, beverage, salad dressing, fruit preserves, jams, and jellies. Citric acid is a precursor of diacetyl and therefore indirectly improves the flavors of cultured dairy products (Doores, 1 993). The production of citric acid is based on fermentation of aspergillus niger. Citric acid is a weak organic acid and is thus not completely dissociated at the pH range of 5-7 of many food commodities. As a metal chelator, citric acid is widely used as an antioxidant agent, and is widely recognized to act as an antioxidant synergist to both ascorbic acid and tocopherols. Due to its ability to chelate metals and decrease pH, citric acid is also used as a browning inhibitor. Citric acid may also affect the growth and survival of microorganisms in foods due to its acidic properties.

2.1.3 Sorbic acid

Sorbic acid is a straight-chain, trans-trans unsaturated fatty acid and it has low solubility (0.15 g/100 mL) in water at room temperature. The sodium and potassium salts of sorbic acid are more soluble in water. Sorbates are stable in the dry form and unstable in aqueous solutions because they decompose through oxidation. The rate of oxidation is increased at low pH, by increased temperature, and by light exposure. Sorbic acid is a naturally occurring compound and is used in wide variety of foods including cheese, baked products, fruit juices, wine, and pickles as the calcium, sodium, or potassium salt. Sorbic acid and sorbates are effective against yeasts and moulds. Sorbates inhibit yeast growth in a variety of foods including wine, fruit juice, dried food, cottage cheese, meat, and fish products, carbonated beverages, and a variety of other foods.

The maximum permissible concentration of sorbates in foods is 0.2 %. Sorbates are generally used in sweetened wines or wines that contain residual sugars to prevent refermentation. At the levels generally used, sorbates do not affect food flavour. However, when used at high levels, it may be detected by some people as an unpleasant flavour. The method of application may involve direct incorporation, surface coatings or incorporation in a wrapping material. Sorbic acid is most effective at pH < 6.0. The activity of sorbic acid increases as pH decreases. Sorbates are primarily effective against yeasts and moulds. Bacteria inhibited by sorbate include S. aureus, Salmonella, coliforms, psychrotrophic spoilage bacteria, and Vibrio parahaemolyticus. Similar to benzoates, sorbates inhibit the amino acid uptake of cells and outgrowth of vegetative cells from spores. Sorbates enhances the heat activation and destruction of spores (Sofas and Busta, 1993). Sorbates at a concentration of 0.4 % inhibits synthesis of protein, RNA, and DNA in Pseudomonas fluorescens (Ecklund, 1 989). Sorbates are mainly used in dairy products, bakery products, vegetables, fruits, beverages, and meat and fish products. Sorbate is less toxic and four times as effective as benzoate or propionate.

2.1.4 Propionic acid

Propionic acid and its sodium and calcium salts exert antimicrobial activity against moulds and a few bacteria. Level of use generally range up to 0.3 % by weight. Propionic acid has a slightly pungent and disagreeable odor. The salts of propionic acid exhibit a cheese like flavor. The propionates have an effective upper pH limit of 5.5. Propionic acid is normally present in cheese and as a metabolite in the ruminant gastrointestinal tract. Propionic acid formed in Swiss Cheeses as a result of the growth and metabolism of propionic bacteria helps prevent mould growth. Propionic acid is used as a mould inhibitor in cheese foods and spreads, and as a mould and rope inhibitor in bread. The sodium salt of propionic acid is used in chemically leavened products because calcium interferes with the leavening action.

2.1.5 Glacial acetic acid

Glacial acetic acid is a GRAS additive and is used as an acidifier and flavoring agent in sliced and canned fruits and vegetables, mayonnaise, salad dressings and sausages. Vinegar containing 5 % acetic acid is more widely used in foods such as salad dressings, mustard, ketchup, and marinades for meat, poultry and fish, and bakery products (Dziezak, 1990). Acetic acid is also effective in sanitization of meat carcasses and decreasing salmonella typhimurium and campylobacter jejuni in poultry scald water (Doores, 1993). Acetic acid is a better inhibitor of bacteria than of yeast and moulds. However, it is effective against bread moulds Aspergillus and Rhizopus (Ecklund, 1989). Acetates of sodium, potassium and calcium are used in bread and other baked goods to prevent ropiness and the growth of moulds, but they do not interfere with yeasts. The antimicrobial activity of acetic acid increases as the pH decreases.

2.1.6 Adipic acid

Adipic acid is the least acidic of the commonly used acidulants. Adipic acid functions as a buffering agent at pH 2.5—3.0, neutralising agent, gelling aid and sequesterant. Adipic acid is used in evaporated milk, instant puddings, gelatin desserts, cheese analogues, powdered concentrates for fruit - flavoured beverages, cake mixes, baking powders and flavoring extracts. The shelf life of dry mixes and baking powders is extended because of the extremely low moisture absorption capacity of adipic acid,

2.1.7 Fumaric acid

Fumaric acid is a dicarboxylic acid, and is the least expensive among the food grade acids in terms of cost and the quantities used in foods. Fumaric acid provides a strong acid taste blends with certain flavoring compounds to intensify the aftertaste of select flavors. Fumaric acid is naturally present in rice, sugar cane, wine, plant leaves, mushrooms, and gelatin. The calcium, magnesium, potassium, and sodium salts of fumaric acid are approved for use in nonstandardised foods. Fumaric acid is used similarly in the food industry as an acidulant, accounting for about 20 % of the total acidulant in the US and is especially suitable for using in dry beverages mixes, where its low hygroscopicity serves to extend the shelf life of other ingredients. This acid accelerates the fixation of color in cured meat and poultry products and can replace tartaric acid in the beverage and baking industries. This acid is used not only as an acidulant but also for candy coatings, emulsifying agents and fat and dough conditioners. Similar to adipic acid, fumaric acid is used in dry mixes because of its strong resistance to moisture absorption. One advantage of fumaric acid is the smaller quantity of acid required to achieve a taste similar to citric, malic or tartaric acids. Fumaric acid is used in fruit juice drinks, gelatin desserts, rye bread, and refrigerated biscuit doughs. Fumaric acid is used as an acidulant and clarifying agent in wine

2.1.8 Malic acid

Malic acid is a naturally occurring acidulant, present in most fruits and vegetables. The traditional method for producing malic acid was by extraction from apple juice (0.4-0.7% malic acid). Malic acid finds its application as an alternative to citric acid in fruit products and lemonades. Malic acid is a GRAS ingredient used in many foods, including nonalcoholic beverages, hard candies, canned tomatoes, and fruit pie fillings. It provides a smooth, tart taste that lingers in the mouth without imparting a burst of flavor. Due to its stronger apparent acidity, malic acid can be used in smaller amount than citric acid

2.2 SULPHUR DIOXIDE AND SULPHITES

Sulphur dioxide has long been used in food as a general food preservative. Currently, the forms employed include sulphur dioxide gas, and the sodium or potassium salts of sulphide, biSulphite or metabisulphite. With the exception of potassium Sulphite, these salts are permitted for use in foods and beverages in the United States. It has been shown that sulphur dioxide is most effective as an antimicrobial agent in acid media, and this effect is believed to result from undissociated sulphurous acid, which is the dominant form below pH 3.0. Of the known inhibitors of nonenzymic browning in food, sulphur dioxide is probably the most effective. Sulphur dioxide also inhibits certain enzyme catalysed reactions, notably enzymic browning. The use of sulphite or metabisulphite sprays or dips with or without added citric acid provides effective control of enzymic browning in prepeeled and presliced potatoes, carrots, and apples. The red color of fresh meat also can be effectively maintained by the presence of sulphur dioxide. In many countries, sulphites are permitted in liquid and egg products, fish fillet, fish paste, and sausage

Bacteria are more sensitive to SO_2 than yeasts and moulds. SO_2 is bacteriostatic (prevention of multiplication of microorganisms) at small concentrations and bactericidal (killing of all micro-organisms) at large concentrations. Yeasts are intermediate to acetic acid and lactic acid bacteria and moulds in their sensitivity to SO_2. Some strains of Saccharomyces produce SO_2 during juice fermentation. Proteins in the cell wall and plasma membrane of microorganisms are the primary targets interacting with sulphite. Sulphite ions react with a range of coenzymes essential for enzymes activity or with prosthetic groups conjugated with biologically active proteins. SO_2 can be used to control undesirable bacteria and wild yeast in fermentations without affecting the SO_2 tolerant cultured yeasts. According to Chichester and Tanner (1968), the undissociated acid is 1,000 times more active than HSO_3 for Escherichia coli, 100 to 500 times for Saccharomyces cerevisiae, and 100 times for Aspergillius niger. The amount of SO_2 added to foods is self-limiting because at levels from 200 to 500 ppm the product may develop an unpleasant off-flavour. The use of SO_2 is not permitted in foods that contain significant quantities of thiamine, because this vitamin is destroyed by SO_2.

SO_2 is also widely used in dried fruits, where levels may be up to 2,000 ppm. SO_2 is the only legal fungicide for grapes. Gassing the fruit storage area with a high concentration of SO_2 completely inhibits mould growth accompanied by severe fruit discoloration. The use of small gassing concentrations three times a week gives better results than gassing once a week with high concentrations. Other applications are in dried vegetables and dried potato products. Because SO_2 is volatile and easily lost to the atmosphere, the residual levels may be much lower than the amounts originally applied. In 1986, the FDA revoked the GRAS status of SO_2 for use on raw fruits and vegetables and established a residual concentration in selected dehydrated foods. The alternatives to SO_2 include polyphenol oxidase inhibitors, ascorbic acid/citric acid based formulations, and complexing agents such as EDTA. So far, no alternative with the multifunctional characteristics of 502 has been reported.

The use of sulphites to preserve meat was known even in the early nineteenth century. Sulphite is added to foods and beverages for one or more of the following reasons: inhibition of enzyme activity, as an antioxidant, inhibition of nonenzymatic browning, inhibition of microbial growth, bleaching of a foodstuff, and as a general aid in food processing. The bound forms of sulphur have little antimicrobial activity. Carbonyl compounds present in foods bind the sulphites, thus reducing the antimicrobial activity. This chemical is used to preserve food items such as baked foods, beer, wine, tea, condiments, vinegar, dairy product, processed seafood products, grain products, gravies, sauces, jam, jellies, nut products, plant protein isolates, dried fruit, fruit juices, fruits, vegetables, filled crackers, soup mixes, sugar, sweet sauces etc. In some countries the use of sulphites is banned on fruits and vegetables intended to be eaten raw, such as in salad bars and also in thiamine rich food such as enriched flour. The major applications of sulphites in the wine making industry include sanitisation of the equipment, inhibiting the growth of microorganisms from freshly squeezed juice, clarifying the wine during fermentation and preventing microbial growth after fermentation

Sulphite treatment improves the color and odor of meats, and retards or prevents growth of surface bacteria. Sulphite treatment, combined with vacuum packaging and a good oxygen barrier film, extends the shelf life of sausage. Browning in fruits and vegetables can be controlled with the use of sulphites. Sulphites are also used to control microbial growth and maintain oxidative stability of carbonated beverages, dehydrated fruits, fruit juices, syrups, concentrates, purees, and fresh shrimp. Fruits and vegetables are sprayed with or dipped in a sulphite solution. Prior to canning sulphite containing foods, sulphites must be removed to prevent generation of hydrogen sulphide and the black precipitates

2.3 NITRITES AND NITRATES

Nitrites are a favourite preservative of meat processors even though its excess use is restricted in many countries. This chemical stabilises the red colour of the meat and gives an appearance of fresh meat. Nitrites are used as a preservative for meat and meat products. Nitrate and nitrite have been used for centuries in curing and preserving meats and fish, and in the manufacture of certain cheeses. For commercial purposes, salt mixtures were found to be more effective in curing processes if they contained saltpetre (potassium nitrate). During preparation, nitrate is reduced to nitrite which is the major active ingredient in these salt mixtures. Nitrate is reduced to nitrite by bacteria under anaerobic conditions, using the molybdopterin-containing nitrate reductase. When added to foods such as cured meats, nitrite has at least three functions Firstly, it contributes to the flavour; this may be due to the inhibition of development of rancid off-flavours. Secondly, it reacts with myoglobin to give mono nitrosylhaemochrome, which gives the characteristic pink colour of cured meat. Thirdly, it inhibits the growth of food spoilage bacteria, and most importantly, Clostridium botulin urn. C. botulinum thrives under anaerobic conditions, and produces a neurotoxin which is one of the most lethal natural products known. Nitrite, together with cooking and addition of salt, is a protection against food poisoning by this microorganism. Nitrate and nitrite occur in the diet from numerous different sources. Vegetables are a major source of nitrates, for example about 1000 mg/kg for leaf vegetables such as lettuce, and 200 mg/kg in root vegetables such as potatoes.

Until the early 1940s, nitrite was added to meats primarily to impart the characteristic flavor and color. The antimicrobial properties of nitrites were demonstrated by the mid 1950s. Nitrous acid derived from nitrite in the acid environment of meat is responsible for microbial inhibition. Nitrite is more effective as an antimicrobial agent at pH< 7.0. Nitrite was believed to prevent outgrowth of spores surviving after heat treatment in canned meat. Until the 1960s, it was believed that the antimicrobial effect of nitrite was caused by the influence of nitrite on water activity of the food. Although nitrite was recognised as an effective antimicrobial agent, the use of nitrite as preservative in cured meats was not popular.

Curing was originally developed to aid in the preservation of food by the addition of sodium chloride. Sodium nitrite, a natural impurity of sodium chloride, was observed to be responsible for the development of pink to red pigment in cured meat. The additives used in curing may include ascorbates, nitrates, nitrites, phosphates, glucono-delta-lactone, and sugars. Sodium nitrite and nitrate stabilize the red meat color and inhibit certain spoilage and food poisoning microorganisms. One of the disadvantages of using nitrite is poor stability to heat and storage. However, many bacteria are capable of utilizing nitrate as an electron acceptor, resulting in the reduction of nitrate to nitrite. In an acid environment, nitrite ionises to yield nitrous oxide. The nitrous oxide further decomposes to nitric oxide. Nitric oxide reacts with myoglobin under reducing conditions to produce the red pigment nitrosomyoglobin.

The most important microorganism inhibited by nitrites is Clostridium botulinum. Nitrite is also effective against C. sporogenes and C. perfringens, the bacteria used in laboratory studies to assess potential antibotulinal effects of nitrites. The antibotulinal effect consists of inhibition of vegetative cell growth and prevention of germination and growth of spores viable after heat processing (Jay, 1992). Low concentrations of nitrite inhibit outgrowth of spores after germination whereas high concentrations inhibit the germination itself. The antimicrobial activity of nitrite depends on the pH, salt content, temperature of incubation, and number of spores.

Because of the antibotulinal effect of nitrite, it is often necessary to add nitrite to cured meats. For the development of flavor and appearance, smaller concentrations (100 ppm) of nitrite are required. However, the antibotulinal effects require larger concentrations (12Opprn) for bacon, comminuted cured ham, and canned, shelf stable luncheon meat. Toxin production in meats can be greatly reduced by using a combination of nitrites, sucrose, and an inoculum of lactic acid bacteria. Only the required quantities of nitrite should be added to the food. The presence of excess concentrations of nitrite results in a green discoloration or nitrite burn in cured meats.

Nitrite is also effective against S. aureus at large concentrations, with the effectiveness increasing as pH decreases. However, nitrite is generally ineffective against Enterobacteriaceae, including Salmonella and lactic acid bacteria. The antibacterial effects of nitrite may be the result of the reaction of nitric oxide with other porphyrin containing compounds such as catalase, peroxidases, and cytochromes. Use of nitrites in meats is controversial in terms of health risks because of the formation of carcinogenic nitrosamines. The reaction between nitrite and secondary, tertiary, or quaternary amines results in the formation of nitrosamines (Jay, 1992). The nitrosamines are powerful carcinogens, and they may be mutagenic and teratogenic as well. It appears that very small amounts of nitrosamines can be formed in certain cured meat products.

The current residual nitrite content of cured meat products is about 10 ppm. In 1975 average residual nitrite content in cured meats was reported as 52.5 ppm.

3. ANTIMICROBIALS NATURALLY PRESENT OR FORMED IN FOOD

In addition to the more traditional and emerging systems that are employed to achieve desired safe shelf life, there is consumer pressure for mild, and more natural means for the preservation of foods. This has concentrated attention on the wide range of effective naturally occurring antimicrobial systems that are employed by animals, plants, and microorganisms with the aim of exploiting some of them in food stuffs (Davidson and Brannen, 1993; Dillon and Board, 1994). Animal derived systems include enzymes such as lysozyme, lactoperoxidase, and other proteins such as lactoferrin, ovotransferrin, serum transferrins etc. and plant derived systems include phytoalexins, lower molecular weight components from herbs and spices, phenolics such as oleuropein from olives, essential oils. Microorganisms derived ones include acids, hydrogen peroxide diacetyl and other low molecular substances and bacteriocins such as nisin and pediocin and many others discovered in the last few years. Few importants ones are described here. It is anticipated that the future potential for application of such systems is substantial.

3.1 LACTOPEROXIDASE SYSTEM (LPS)

The lactoperoxidase system, found in milk, has profound antimicrobial effects against both bacteria and fungi. The system requires hydrogen peroxide and thiocyanate for optimal activity and is thus primarily active against microorganisms producing H_2O_2. Lactoperoxidase is a glycoprotein containing one heme group and 9.9-10.2 % carbohydrate (Wilkins and Board, 1989). The enzyme lactoperoxidase is present in milk in amounts varying between 10 and 30 pg/ ml. For the LPS to function efficiently, 0.5- 1 .0 mg/ ml of the enzyme lactoperoxidase is necessary (Conner, 1993). The enzyme lactoperoxidase forms the LPS in combination with an oxidisable substrate and hydrogen peroxide. The naturally occurring LPS is primarily active against H_2O_2 producing bacteria such as lactococci and lactobacilli.. A wide range of both gram-negative bacteria and gram-positive bacteria are inhibited by the lactoperoxidase system. Gram- negative bacteria includes coliforms, pseudomonas, salmonellae, and shigellae. Gram-positive bacteria, including streptococci and lactobacilli, are only temporarily inhibited. The gram-negative bacteria are more susceptible than the gram-positive. The LPS can be used for preservation of milk, infant formula, and liquid whole eggs. The shelf life of pasteurised milk can be extended by 20 days with use of LPS. When used in milk, the LPS is effective at temperatures below 15°C. A combination of the LPS and mild heat treatment may be an effective preservation method, particularly for minimally processed or heat sensitive foods.

3.2 LYSOZYME

Lysozyme is a lytic enzyme naturally present in plant tissues, milk, and eggs. It is present in a concentration of 0.1 and 0.13 pg/ml in human and bovine milk, respectively. The bactericidal and lytic action of lysozyme depends on the enzyme concentration, ionic strength, and nature of the electrolytes present. Anions such as SCN - and HCO_3 promote bacterial lysis. Lysozyme destroys the cellular integrity via hydrolysis of the ß (1-4) linkages between N-acetylemuramic acid and N-acetylglucosamine of the peptidoglycan layer of the bacteria cell walls (Conner, 1993). Loss of the cell wall allows water uptake leading to cell lysis. Therefore, lysozyme is effective against gram-positive bacteria (Wilkins and Board, 1989). Gram-negative bacteria are more resistant to lysozyme because of the smaller content of peptidoglycan. However, gram-negative bacteria that are sensitive to lysozyme include Salmonella, Pseudomonas, Aeromonas, enteropathogenic E. coli, and some Vibria spp. Few of the gram-positive bacteria, including staphylococci, containing teiechoic acids in the cell wall are resistant to lysozyme (Wilkins and Board, 1989).

Although lysozyme may potentially be used in food systems for its preservative properties, it is used to a limited extent in the food industry. Lysozyme in combination with EDTA (ethylenediaminetetraacetic acid) or TRIS (tris [hydroxymethyl] aminomethane) can be used as a preservative in foods prepared from fresh vegetables (Conner, 1993). EDTA and TRIS act by binding divalent cations Ca^{2+} and Mg^{2+} responsible for maintaining the structural integrity of the outer membrane of gram-negative bacteria (Wilkins and Board, 1989). Lysozyme is approved as a food additive in Europe, Asia, and the United States. In Europe, lysozyme is added in certain hard cheeses to prevent gassing and blowing due to Clostridium. The Japanese use lysozyme to preserve oysters, shrimp as well as other seafood, noodles, potato salad, and custard (Conner, 1993). Lysozyme is the only antimicrobial enzyme that has achieved significant commercial application. It is most effective against thermophilic spore formers. It can be used freely in ripened cheeses, and is in fact the only enzyme permitted as a food preservative.

3.3 LACTOFERRIN

Lactoferrin is a glycoprotein present in milk that acts as an antimicrobial agent by binding the iron needed for growth of the microorganisms. Bovine milk contains very little lactoferrin. Lactoferrin has two iron-binding sites. For each ferric ion bound by lactoferrin, one bicarbonate anion is bound and three protons are released (Conner, 1993). The bacteriostatic (prevention of multiplication of micro-organisms) effects of lactoferrin are expressed against bacteria with high iron requirements such as coliforms. Organisms with low iron requirements such as lactic acid bacteria and streptococci remain unaffected (Wilkins and Board, 1989). Some of the bacteria inhibited by lactoferrin include Listeria monocyto genes, Bacillus subtilis, Bacillus stearothermophilus, Staphylococcus aureus, and E. coil (Wilkins and Board, 1989; Conner, 1993). Lactoferrin is well suited to be used as a dual- purpose additive for its antimicrobial as well as its antioxidant properties in iron supplemented foods e.g. in commercial infant formulas (Satue-Gracia et al., 2000).

4. BACTERIOCINS

Bacteria are a source of antimicrobial peptides, which have been examined for applications in microbial food safety. The bacteriocins were first characterised in gram-negative bacteria. The antimicrobial proteins or peptides produced by bacteria are termed as bacteriocins. Bacteriocins are small proteins by many bacterial genera, including lactic acid bacteria (LAB). Most of the bacteriocins produced by LAB inhibit the growth of other lactic acid bacteria, but some are bactericidal to a number of food pathogens and food-spoilage bacteria. Today, more than 30 different bacteriocins produced by some 17 species of lactic acid bacteria have been identified. Bacteriocins have been shown to be safe, and have potential as effective natural food preservatives. Bacteriocins have applications in hurdle technology, which utilises synergies of combined treatments to more effectively preserve food. The chemical composition and the physical conditions of food can have a significant influence on the activity of the bacteriocins. Nisin, for example, is 228 times more soluble at pH 2 than at pH 8 (Liu and Hansen, 1990). Bacteriocins have been directly added to foods such as cheese to prevent against Clostridium and Listeria.

Bacteriocins may be defined as protein containing macromolecules with a capacity to exert bactericidal action on susceptible bacteria. E. coil produce colicins and lactococci produce nisin and diplococcin. The bacteriocins inhibit some gram-positive bacteria, spore forming bacteria, and food borne pathogens, including Listens monocyto genes. Nisin is approved for use in over 50 countries and has been in use as a food preservative for over 50 years. Nisin inhibits the outgrowth of C. botulinum spores in cheese spreads and it is approved as a food additive in the United States for this purpose. Nisin has many applications in foods and is approved for use in various foods throughout the world.

Nisin is produced by fermentation of a modified milk medium by certain strains of lactic acid bacterium, Lactococcus lactis. The potential application for nisin in food preservation were observed when nisin producing starter cultures prevented clostridial gas formation in cheese. The nisin molecule is acidic in nature and exhibits the greatest stability under acidic condition. Some of the desirable properties of nisin include nontoxicity and heat storage stability; it is a naturally produced additive, is destroyed by digestive enzymes, has a narrow range of antimicrobial acidity, and does not present formation of off flavors or off colors (Jay, 1992).

Nisin possesses antimicrobial properties against certain gram- positive bacteria, including Staphylococcus, Streptococcus, Micrococcus, and lactobacillus. Gram-negative bacteria, yeast and moulds are not affected by nisin. Spores of Bacillus stearothermophilus are more sensitive than spores of B. cereus, B. polymyxa, or B. megaterium. Spores of C. botulinum types A, B, and E are sensitive to nisin. The sensitivity of the spores decreases in the order of type E, B, and A. Lower pH, higher temperature and a longer period of heat shock may be used to increase the effectiveness of nisin in preventing the outgrowth of C. botulinum spores. Nisin is an antibacterial polypeptide produced by some strains of Lactococcus lactis. Nisin like substances are widely produced by lactic acid bacteria. Nisin has been called an antibiotic, but this term is avoided because nisin is not used for therapeutic purposes in humans or animals. Nisin producing organisms occur naturally in milk. Nisin can be used as a processing aid against gram-positive organisms. Because its effectiveness decreases as the bacterial load increases, it is unlikely to be used to cover up unhygienic practices. The use of nisin as a food preservative has been approved in many countries. It has been used effectively in preservation of processed cheese. Nisin also has been used in conjunction with other preservative measures to enhance product safety or quality. Conventional heat treatment of low acid canned food requires a F_o treatment of 6 to 8 mm to inactivate spores of C. botulinum and spoilage organisms. The addition of nisin to low acid foods helps reduce the F_o to 3 mm. The reduced time and temperature results in better quality food (Jay, 1992). In canned foods such as vegetables, soups, and puddings, nisin has been applied in conjunction with heating to successfully counteract heat-resistant spores of flat-sour thermophilic bacteria. Normal heating and nisin may be combined for milk production in countries where pasteurisation, refrigeration and transportation facilities are not adequate and where it is difficult to assure the supply of good quality milk to the public. When nisin is used with acetic, lactic, or citric acid, the effectiveness of blanching and pasteurization may be better than with nisin or the organic acids alone. The use of nisin in combination with nitrate in milk products has been reported frequently. Although the combined operation may allow for less nitrite to exert the identical degree of inhibition of clostridia compared to nitrite alone, the meat system seems to influence the effectiveness of nisin strongly. Inhibition of L. monocyto genes in raw meat, for instance, may continue for two weeks at 5°C, but both the inhibitory effect and the nisin related activity rapidly diminish at room temperature. Comparable findings hold for clostridia suppression in bacon and sausages. Conceivably, binding of nisin in meat particles and high salt concentration may reduce the amount of nisin in solution where it may be active.

5. ANTIBIOTIC

Antibiotics are antimicrobial agents produced naturally by a variety of microorganisms. Antibiotic includes natamycin, tetracycline, subtilin, and tylosin. A related antibacterial substance is natamycin, identical to primaricin. Natamycin is effective in controlling the growth of fungi but has no effect on bacteria or viruses. In fermentation industries, natamycin can be used to control mould or yeast growth. It has a low solubility and therefore can be used as a surface treatment on foods. Natamycin is used in the production of many varieties of cheese. Natamycin is effective against yeasts and moulds but not bacteria. The concentration of natamycin required to inhibit certain strains of moulds is 50-100 times less than the inhibitory concentration of sorbic acid. Compared to nystatin about five times less natamycin is required to control fungi on strawberries and raspberries. Natamycin binds to membrane sterols and induces distortion of selective membrane permeability. The lack of membrane sterols in bacteria explains the ineffectiveness of natamycin. The surface treatment of refrigerated meats with 7 to 10 ppm of chlortetracycline (CTC) results in a shelf life extension of 3 to 5 days. CTC combined with sorbates can prevent spoilage of fish up to 14 days. Heat sensibility and lack of storage stability are the disadvantages to tetracycline. Subtilin produced by some strains of B. subtilis is similar to nisin in its action against gram-positive bacteria and prevention of outgrowth of germinating spores. One ppm of tylosin added to cream style corn containing flat sour spores, followed by thermal process, resulted in the extension of shelf life at 54°C up to 30 days.

6. OTHER PRESERVATIVES

6.1 HYDROGEN PEROXIDE

Hydrogen peroxide is a strong oxidising agent and is also useful as a bleaching agent. It is used for the bleaching of crude soya lecithin. The antimicrobial action of hydrogen peroxide is used for the preservation of cheese milk. Hydrogen peroxide decomposes slowly into water and oxygen; this process is accelerated by increased temperature and the presence of catalysts such as catalase, lacto-peroxidase and heavy metals. Its antimicrobial action increases with temperature. When hydrogen peroxide is used for cheese making, the milk is treated with 0.02 percent hydrogen peroxide followed by catalase to remove the hydrogen peroxide. Hydrogen peroxide can be used for sterilizing food processing equipment and for sterilizing packaging material used in aseptic food packaging systems.

Hydrogen peroxide on its own is also known to be bactericidal depending on the concentrations applied and on environmental factors such as pH and temperature. Temperature is also an extremely important parameter in determining the sporicidal efficacy of hydrogen peroxide. H_2O_2 was found to be weakly sporicidal at room temperatures but very potent at higher temperatures (Toledo, 1975). In the USA, the regulatory authorities allow the direct addition of hydrogen peroxide to food products such as raw milk for the preparation of certain cheese variants; whey intended for use in modified whey preparation; corn starch and dried eggs; and finally, for the decontamination of packaging materials (Toledo, 1975). Several other procedures where H_2O_2 is used as a preservative have been reported, such as fruit and vegetable disinfection (Falik et a!., 1994) and raisin decontamination.

6.2 SALT

Salt has been used for centuries to prevent spoilage of foods. Fish, meats, and vegetables have been preserved with salt. Today, salt is used mainly in combination with other processing methods. The antimicrobial activity of salt is related to its activity to reduce the water activity (aw). Addition of salt disturbs the osmotic balance of the food environment, leading to loss of water from the microbial and food cell. A high concentration of salt exerts a drying effect on both food and microorganisms. Loss of water from microbial cells results in cell inactivation (Jay, 1992). The amount of salt needed to prevent microbial growth depends on the type and growth stage of the microorganisms, type and properties of food, and storage temperature. Xerophilic moulds, osmophilic yeasts and halophilic bacteria can grow at low aw and require salt for their growth. Most food borne pathogenic bacteria do not grow at aw below 0.92 or at salt concentration greater than 10 %. As acidity of food increases, amount of salt needed decreases. Salt adds flavor and inhibits pathogenic bacteria in meat products. A small increase in salt concentration played a major role in delaying the formation of toxin from C. botulinum in meat products. Vacuum packaged meats and sausages containing less than 4 % salt showed little protection from C. botulinum even in the presence of 50 or 100ppm nitrite.

An appropriate concentration of salt in vegetable fermentation extracts nutrients from the plant tissue and allows the correct progression and growth of lactic acid bacteria. Lower concentration of salt in fermented foods results in poor quality and even unsafe products. Salt exhibits synergistic antimicrobial effects with benzoate, sorbate, phosphate, antioxidants, spices, liquid smoke, and isoascorbate. Salt has the following characteristics: it produces an osmotic effect, it limits oxygen solubility, it changes pH, sodium and chloride ions are toxic, and salt contributes to loss of magnesium ions. The use of salt is self-limiting because of its effect on taste.

6.3 SUGAR

Sugar exerts antimicrobial action in a manner similar to salt and is used in many food preservations. The only difference between use of salt and sugar is the high concentration of sugar (six times) needed for the same effect as salt (Jay, 1992). Sugar aids in preservation of products in which it is used. The high osmotic pressure of sugar creates conditions that are unfavorable for the growth and reproduction of most species of bacteria, yeasts, and moulds . The preservative action of moderate strength of sugars can be improved if invertase is used to increase the concentration of glucose relative to sucrose. Foods, in which sugars aid preservation includes syrups, and confectionary products, honey, jams, jellies, mamalandes, and fruits such as dates, sultanas and currants.

7. CONCLUSION

Antimicrobials may be naturally present or added to foods. Their effectiveness depends not only upon the concentration and type of organisms but on the intrinsic properties of the food system. The naturally present antimicrobials and organic acids exhibit good inhibitory properties. However, some of the chemicals used as preservatives are controversial in terms of health risks involved and the benefits of extending the shelf life of the food. Attempts are being made to replace the controversial chemicals with new antimicrobials or combinations of safe chemicals. Naturally occurring antimicrobials are abundant in the environment. Food preservatives of natural origin are generally considered as potential, safe sources of antimicrobials, but their effective use in practice has been established in only a few cases. For the use of naturally occurring antimicrobials to increase, however, research, commercial development, and economic production must occur on an adequate scale; sensory changes in foods must be avoided; food safety must be assured; multifactor preservative systems including natural antimicrobials must be developed. Moreover, the application of new preservation methods needs the approval of governmental authorities. Toxicological data for antimicrobials are often lacking and are as expensive to assemble as data for chemical compounds.

25
Role of Antioxidants in Food Preservation

Taste, flavour and odours are important factors by which the consumer judges a food product. Unfortunately, atmospheric oxidation, common enemy of all edible animal and vegetable fats and oils, causes deterioration in the quality of these oxidative changes, produce rancidity, bitterness and loss of potency in various foods. Lipids in foods are most prone to auto-oxidation resulting in the development of off flavours, production of toxic substances etc., food can even become unfit for human consumption.

Two of the biggest concerns at least those most addressable today are oxidation, especially oxidative rancidity, and microbial growth, especially food-borne pathogens. Protecting against oxidative deterioration requires a straightforward approach: eliminate, minimise or control food contact with oxygen. Microbial concerns are more complex — if the conditions are right (primarily, the presence of nutrients, moisture and oxygen, for aerobic microbes), the harmful bacteria grow quite quickly. On the other hand, if the product is handled correctly, the microbial population can be kept to a minimum until the food is thermally processed, or cooked and consumed.

Oxidation is the major cause of deterioration of food and feed products which contain fats and oils, because it is one of the main causes of rancidity in these products. The factors to consider, when discussing deterioration of fats and oils and methods of prevention, include biochemical processes (enzyme caused deterioration), chemical processes (oxygen caused deterioration or auto-oxidation), nature and condition of substrates, required storage time, light, temperature, etc. Many attempts such as improved methods of food preservation, processing, freezing, refrigeration and packaging under vacuum or inert gas to exclude oxygen have been tried but they are expensive and not completely satisfactory.

Consequently there is a need for substances, which can be directly introduced into the food product to retard the destructive process, which results in rancidity. Antioxidants often are used in products that contain higher levels of fats ; such as meat products and edible oils. But they can be useful in any product containing even a low percentage of unsaturated fats. They are applied to some cereals, for example; if the fat becomes rancid, even if it's a minor percentage of the formulation, it will still spoil that product's flavour.

Antioxidant can be defined as "Substance which when added to food retards or prevents oxidative deterioration of foods and does not include sugars, cereals, oils, flours, herbs and spices is termed as an antioxidant". (Prevention of food adulteration act and rules, Govt. of India, 1955)

D.S. Sastry et al., (1983) defined antioxidants as "Antioxidants as name indicates, are substances that are capable of delaying, retarding or preventing the development of rancidity or similar deterioration in food due to oxidation".

Many products undergo irreversible chemical changes when exposed to oxygen and light. The process of oxidation deteriorates color and flavor of the products containing susceptible fats, and can eventually create odors that render the product inedible. Fortunately, food processors have been able to control this problem through the application of ingredients known as antioxidants or oxidation inhibitors. These products slow down oxidation by disrupting the chemical chain reaction between oxygen and fat. It might be said that they will "sacrifice themselves" to the oxygen. When the antioxidant is depleted, the oxygen reacts with the fat in the food product.

AUTO OXIDATION

The classic route of auto oxidation includes initiation (production of lipid free radicals), propagation and termination (production of non radical products). Antioxidants can interfere with the oxidation process by reacting with free radicals, chelating catalytic metals and also by acting as oxygen scavengers.

INITIATION	$RH \rightarrow R^* + H^*$	(1)
PROPAGATION	$R^* + O_2 \rightarrow ROO^*$	(2)
	$ROO^* + RH \rightarrow R^* + ROOH$	(3)
TERMINATION	$R^* + R^* \rightarrow R - R$ (Non Radical)	(4)
	$R^* + ROO^* \rightarrow ROOR$	(5)
	$ROO^* + ROO^* \rightarrow ROOR + O_2$	(6)

Reaction (1) is thermodynamically difficult (activation energy of about 35 kcal/mol), production of the first few radicals is necessary to begin the propagation reaction Inarwar, 1985.

The reaction of a lipid with molecular oxygen in its excited single state or by metal catalysis or by exposure to light can form lipid peroxy radicals. Lipid radicals are highly reactive and can readily undergo propagation reactions either by abstraction of a hydrogen atom from the alpha position adjacent to a double bond or by reaction with molecular oxygen in its ground state (reaction-2).

The wide array of solid antioxidants and liquid antioxidant blends available in the market makes it essential to consider the following factors before utilising a particular antioxidant in a food material;

(a) The type of oil or fat to be stabilised.

(b) The need for "carry-through" from the oil to the cooked food product.

(c) The ease of antioxidant solubility and disposition into the fat phase of the product.

(d) The presence of metal ions and possible resulting discolouration.

(e) The relative severity of processing (i.e., baking versus frying) and the legality of a specific antioxidant for a specific application.

MECHANISM

Four processing mechanisms for inhibiting lipid oxidation

- Hydrogen donation by the antioxidant
- Electron donation by the antioxidant
- Addition of lipid to aromatic ring of the antioxidant
- Formation of a complex between the lipid and the aromatic ring of the antioxidant

AH antioxidant interferes with lipid oxidation by rapid donation of a hydrogen atom to lipid radicals (reaction 1 and 2). The latter reaction is complete with chain propagation reactions.

$$ROO^* + AH \rightarrow ROOH + A^* \quad (1)$$

$$RO^* + AH \rightarrow ROH + A^* \quad (2)$$

$$ROO^* + A^* \rightarrow ROOOA \quad (3)$$

$$RO^* + A^* \rightarrow ROA \quad (4)$$

The above reactions are exothermic in nature. The resulting phenoxy radical itself must not initiate a new radical or be subjected to rapid oxidation by a chain reaction. In this respect, phenolic antioxidants are excellent hydrogen or electron donors and in addition, their radical intermediates are relatively stable due to resonance delocalisation and lack of suitable site for attack by molecular oxygen.

REQUIREMENTS FOR AN IDEAL FOOD ANTIOXIDANT

1. Lack of toxicity

At the necessary concentration used in food products, the antioxidants should be non toxic and should give rise to non toxic break down products.

2. Effectiveness in low concentrations

The antioxidant should be sufficiently active at low concentrations in the range of 0.01 to 0.02% (based on content) as this is the "permissible range" for the use of such compounds (Prevention of food adulteration act and rules).

3. Ease of application

An antioxidant must be in chemical contact with the material to be protected is in a dispersed phase or when it is a solid non- fatty product, this chemical contact is not easy to achieve. A number of techniques have been developed for the purpose of incorporation of an antioxidant in to food products or fats or oils.

MOST COMMON USES OF ANTIOXIDANTS

Name of the antioxidant	*Most commonly used in*
BHA and BHT	Animal fats, vegetable oils, milk powder, margarine, bakery products, spices, cereals, essential oils, packaging materials, chewing gum base.
Gallates	Animal fats, vegetable oils, whole milk powder, margarine, bakery products, candy, chewing gum base
Tocopherols	Animal fats, hydrogenated whole oil, bakery products.
Ascorbyl	Animal fat, vegetable oils and fats, buttermilk powder, vitamin A concentrates.
Ascorbic acid	Fruit juices, citrus oil, wine, beer, frozen fruits, fish meat and meat products, butter, milk powder
Citric acid	Processed fruits and vegetables, beverages canned foods, vegetable oils, milk powder, frozen sea foods.
Phosphoric acid	Vegetable oils, animal fats.
Disodium EDTA	Canned and cooked crab meat, shell fish, beverages, processed fruits and vegetables, Potato products.

The basic requirement of an antioxidant for this purpose is good solubility in solvents and oils and fats of vegetable or animal origin.

4. Stability at high temperature

The antioxidant should not get lost to the atmosphere at high temperature of frying (in deep frying operations, for instance, using the stabilised oils) or of baking. Such antioxidants which withstand this heat are known to have good carry through properties. The antioxidants should not contribute undesirable odour, flavour, taste or colour or in any way alter these properties of main food products. Finally the antioxidant should be available at reasonable prices with continuity of supply. This factor has paramount importance in Indian conditions as we still depend upon imported materials. Fats, oils, bakery and confectionary products require food antioxidants but the increase in cost due to antioxidant should in no case be such so as to deter the user from using it.

NATURAL ANTIOXIDANTS

Oxidation is a "weak point" of almost all fats and vegetable oils, even those containing natural antioxidants. Beside these synthetic antioxidants are not accepted by consumers and have enzyme-inducing effect in liver and other organs such as lungs and gastro-intestinal tract, mucosa. Apart from traditional antioxidants, a variety of natural antioxidants have been studied and proposed for use in foods. These compounds include cinnamon, clove, cassia, natural flavourings such as extracts of rosemary and sage, compounds found in wood smoke, rice bran oil and water soluble and fat insoluble polyphenolic catechins present in tea.

Natural Antioxidants in Selected Plant Sources

Source material	*Example*	*Antioxidant*
Vegetable Oils	Soybean oil	Tocopherols
Tropical Oils	Palm oil	Tocotrienols
Plant Oils	Palm oil	Carotenoids
Herbs and Spices	Rosemary and Sage	Complex phenolics
Cereals	Wheat and buckwheat	Flavenoids
Legumes	Soybean	Isoflavones
Oil Seeds	Canola and Mustard	Phenolic acids & Phenylpropanoids
Teas	Green Tea	Catechins & Polyphenols
Fruit skin and seeds	Grape seed and skin	Polyphenols & Tannins

The extract produced by extraction, purification and fractionation of rosemary and sage serve as an effective agent to control the oxidation in food. Rosemary extract is available in different forms such as water-soluble rosemary extracts and oil soluble products. Water-soluble rosemary extracts are mostly used in sauces, marinades and salad dressings, white oil soluble rosemary extracts are suitable for lipid based food products. These extracts have lower volatility better stability than BHA and BHT at higher temperature and do not have any adverse effect on human health. These have excellent antioxidant properties at concentrations of 0.02%.

CONCLUSION

Today's popularity of new products changes the picture ever so slightly in terms of preservation not always to an advantage. Consider, for example, the blaze of new no-fat and low-fat products hitting the market. In spite of a reduction in fat, they may still need protection for whatever amount of fat remains in the product. Even no-fat products may still legally contain very small amounts of fat. There is a need for the introduction of these food grade antioxidants for stabilisation of oils used for preparation of popular snacks, and related food items especially in the small sector of food makers in India. A number of such food items are based on deep frying operations. Reports indicate that unrefined groundnut oil was used for the preparation of such foods and the same was subjected to continuous heating for long periods of time, thus oxidising it and also rendering it carcinogenic. In these respects the food grade antioxidants can play a significant role towards reducing the health hazards and increasing the mileage of available oils, fats and foodstuffs made from them. The extra expenditure which is about 0.04% is significant compared to the value of the products and considering the benefits derived. It is a big task for the food technologists to find ways and means of spreading the information and helping the consumers, dealers, and manufactures to know the whys and hows of antioxidant usage for the welfare of the society. Extension of this knowledge to all sectors of society is important, both for the immediate conservation of oils and foodstuff and long term effects on the health of people.

26
PRESERVATION OF FRUITS AND VEGETABLES

Microorganisms on the surfaces of freshly harvested fruits and vegetables include not only those of the normal surface flora but also those from soil and water and perhaps plant pathogens. Genera of bacteria usually present include Pseudomonas, Alkaligenes. Bacillus, Chromobacterium, Enterobacter, Flavobacterium, Lactobacillus, Leuconostoc, Micrococcus, Sarcina, Serratia, Staphylococcus, Streptoccous, and others, plus perhaps genera containing plant pathogens, such as Erwinia and Xanthomonas. Any number or kinds of moulds also may be there and sometimes a few yeasts. If the surfaces are moist or the outer surface has been damaged, growth of some microorganisms may take place between harvesting and processing or consumption of the vegetables. Adequate control of temperature and humidity will reduce such growth.

Microorganisms can be removed partly by washing with a non-ionic detergent solutions, chlorinated water or borax solution, use of heat, use of low temperatures, chilling, freezing, drying or use of preservatives and by irradiation.

PROCESSING, PRESERVATION AND STORAGE

A. DRYING

Preservation of foods by drying is perhaps the oldest method known. Large quantities of fruits are dried in the sun in different parts of the world such as Spain. Asia, Greece, and other Mediterranean countries, Arabia and Afghanistan. The modern method of dehydration i.e., drying fruits and vegetables under controlled atmosphere is however assuming importance.

The main objective of drying is removal of free water (lowering of water activity below 0.7) from fruits and vegetables to the extent, where microorganisms do not surrive and reproduce (Desrosier, 1970; Somogyi and Luh 1975). Simultaneously the total solids, viz., sugars, organic acids etc., are concentrated, exerting osmotic pressure to inhibit the microorganisms. Thus reduction in water content, and packaging, controls the biological, and chemical forces respectively which act upon fruits and vegetables, facilitating preservation of these perishables (Desrosier, 1970). There are many methods by which drying is accomplished such as sundrying, drum drying, vacuum drying and freeze drying etc.

Sun drying: In sun-drying, the sound fruits are loaded on trays, transferred to the sun drying yard and allowed to dry, until the fruits are about two thirds dry. Then the trays are stacked in the shade to allow the later stages of drying, which, proceeds slowly. Apricots, peaches, pears and grapes are some fruits that are sundried (Salunkhe et al, 1976). Among vegetables, cucumbers, potatoes, chillies, ladies finger etc. can also be sun-dried.

Lower capital investment is required to apply this simple method. Since sun-drying depends on uncontrollable factors, production of uniform, and high quality product is not expected. Some over drying, contamination by dust as well as dirt, and insect infestation of the finished product are usually tolerated. The most obvious disadvantages of this technique is its complete dependence upon the sun light. Generally sun drying will not allow the fruit products to dry below 15—20% moisture level. The resulting product will have a limited shelf life.

Incorporating some improvement in the sundrying technique, a hot box process, which improved the product by reducing contamination by dust, insect infestation and animal or human interference was developed in Syria. It reduced the drying time to half the usual time, and the finished product had more appealing appearance and better flavour than that dried in the conventional way. Szulmayer has also described an indirect solar drying process, in which the product is exposed to heated air, rather than to direct sun. Use of hot air reduces relative humidity of the air, thereby leading to drying at a reasonable rate. Solar drying with chimni effect has been claimed to improve the quality of the finished products.

Cabinet Drying: Food products dried in a cabinet dryer are placed on trays and moved into a drying compartment where the product is exposed to the drying air (Fig. 26.1).

Drum Drying: One of the novel products developed from mangoes is fruited cereals namely, mango cereal flakes, which is prepared from mango pulp by drum drying. Mango pulp is blended with a small quantity of edible starch, and the blend adjusted for acidity and pH and then fed on to the heated revolving stainless steel double drum roller drier. Other products like tomato flakes; strained baby foods, guava etc. also can be dried by the

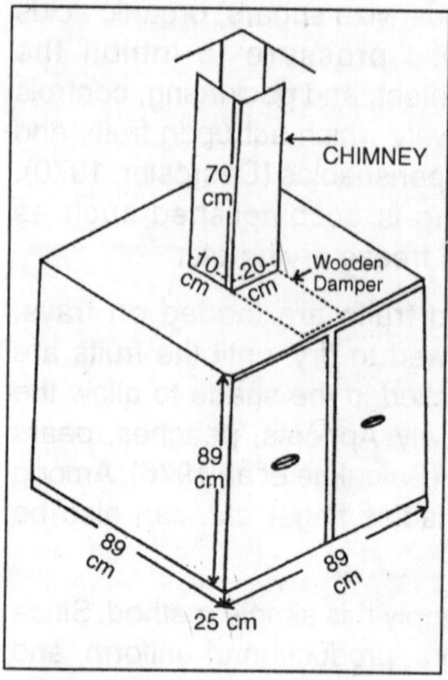

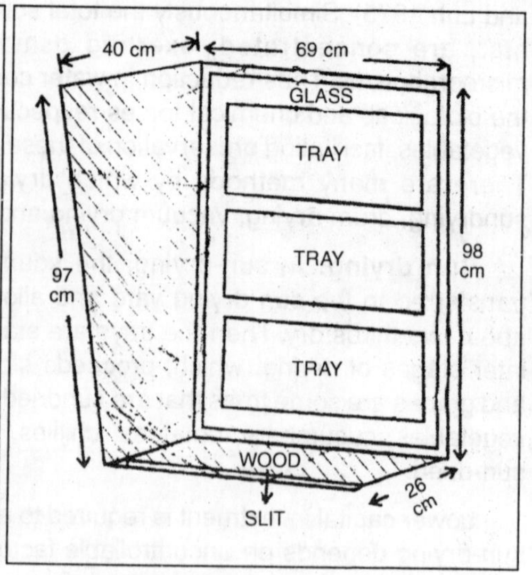

FIG. 26.1: SOLAR DRYER SOLAR DRYER (PLAIN/AMBER GLASS)

above technique.

Vacuum puffing and dehydration: The puffing unit consists essentially of a shallow receptacle with an airtight lid, connected through a quick opening valve to a vacuum reservoir maintained at 62 cm Hg vacuum. The lid of the receptacle can be closed and opened instantly by a pneumatic cylinder, which open by the suction from the reservoir. The entire operation of transferring trays to the receptacle, closing the lid, applying and releasing the vacuum and opening the lid, can be completed with in a short period of 15 seconds. The puffed porous pieces can then he dried in a tunnel (or drier) at about 66°C with an air velocity of 30() metres per mm. The Product has excellent consumer acceptance (Pawar et *al.*, 1988).

Foam-Mat Drying: The foam-mat drying process consists essentially is incorporating small amount suitable foaming agents such as glyceryl mono-stearate. egg albumin, groundnut protein isolate, guar guava and carboxymethyl cellulose into the fluid food materials so that they can be whipped to a low density foam and spread on trays. Drying is done at relatively low temperatures, in an ordinary forced air circulation drier. The dried product can be reconstituted readily. The method is considerably cheaper than puff drying, drying, drum drying etc.

The foaming agent dissolved or dispersed in a small quantity of water, added to the fruit juice concentrate or pulp, mixed in Waring blendor and then foamed in a Hobart mixer fitted with a wire mesh. The foamed material extended into strips, 3-4 in diameter and the strips spread on stainless steel trays. The trays were arranged in a cabinet drier maintained at 65°C to 70°C in such a manner that the strips were parallel to the flow of air. The material dried in 30 to 60 minutes depending upon its nature. The dried strips were Scraped from the trays and filled into air-tight containers as they were hygroscopic. The optimum amount of the foaming agent to be used is 0.3 to 1.5 per cent. The strip could be dried crisp in 30 to 45 minutes to a moisture content of 1.5 to 2.0 per cent. The foam mat drying technique could be successfully employed in the case a variety of fruit pulps, concentrates and similar products by standardizing the conditions in each case.

B. EVAPORATING COOLING — COOL CHAMBERS

Evaporative cooling is Nature's very own method. The ancient Egyptians used a primitive form of evaporative cooling, dating back to about 250() BC. and so did the Mughals a few centuries ago. Evaporation of water produces a considerable cooling effect and the faster the evaporation the greater is the cooling. Evaporative cooling occurs when air, that is not already saturated with water vapour, is blown across any Wet surface. Thus evaporative coolers consist of a wet porous bed through which air is drawn and is cooled and humidified by evaporation of water. Theoretically, the lowest temperature, that can be reached by the evaporation of water is the wet tube temperature (Hall, 1975). Evaporative cooling is widely used for comfort cooling of living and working spaces in hot, dry climates and it has a considerable potential for pre-cooling and even storage of fruits. The principles of evaporative cooling can be gainfully utilised for storage of fresh produce, particularly in rural India, as it can be constructed even in a remote village (Fig.26.2).

Freeze drying: In this method, the material such as fruit juice concentrate, is first poured on trays in the lower chamber of a freeze drier and the frozen material dried in the upper chamber under high vacuum. The material is directly dried by sublimation of ice without passing through the intermediate liquid stage. The dried product is highly hygroscopic and it reconstitutes easily. Mango pulp, orange juice concentrate passion fruit juice and guava pulp have been prepared to give freeze-dried powders of excellent quality in regard to taste, flavour and reconstitution property, etc.

C. ACCELERATED FREEZE DRYING (A.F.D.):

This method which is an adaptation of the freeze drying technique has been developed to a commercial process by the Aberdeen workers for drying fish, meat, etc., to meet Defence Services demands. On account of low temperature employed for drying and the technique of drying the pieces of the product without unduly disturbing their shape and taste the dried material has good reconstitution properties and possesses exact taste and flavour,

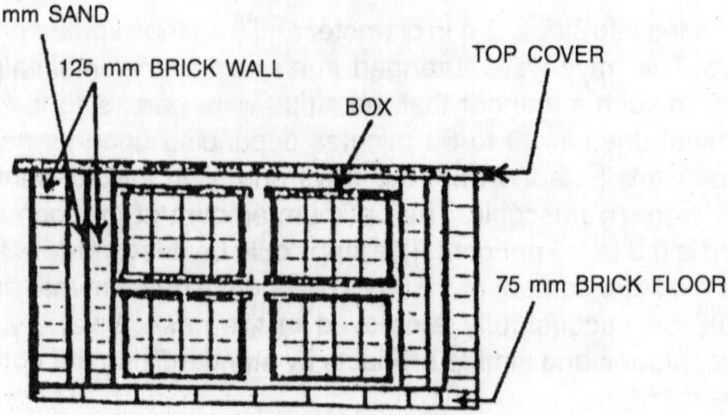

SECTION A—A

PLAN

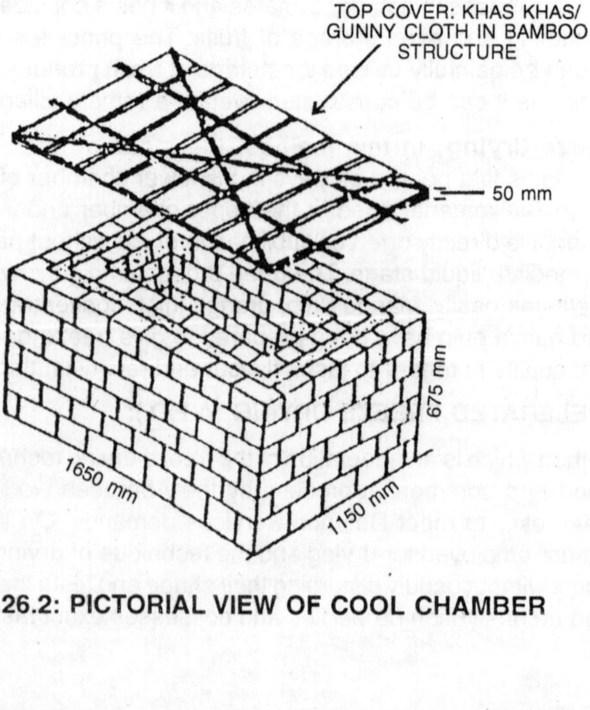

FIG. 26.2: PICTORIAL VIEW OF COOL CHAMBER

and as such, has been well accepted by consumer. Dried products are highly useful in the preparation of emergency food products and rations for use by the Defence Services under difficult and adverse conditions of climate and terrain such as at high altitudes, mountain areas etc. In this method, the pieces of material to be dried are kept in between two perforated or wire mesh trays, inside a cabinet freeze drier. As the material dries, the pieces are gradually reduced in bulk by reducing the clearance between the two trays hydraulically, with the result the dried material retains its normal shape and regains it when rehydrated. This is a highly important consideration in the drying of meat, fish and semi solid pieces of food. The equipment needed for large-scale freeze drying of foods is highly costly. In view of the several advantages, however, the government of India has set up a tonne capacity unit for meeting the needs of the Defence services stationed at high altitudes and on difficult terrains.

D. DEHYDRO-FREEZING:

In this method, the product is first dried partially and then frozen, and is thus slightly different from the usually freeze drying technique.

Dryers commonly used for liquid and solid foods is given below

COMMON DRYER TYPES USED FOR LIQUID AND SOLID FOODS

Dryer type	*Usual food type*
Air convention dryers	
Kiln	pieces
cabinet, tray or pan	pieces, purees, liquids
tunnel	pieces
continuous conveyor belt	purees, liquids
belt through	pieces
air lift	small pieces, granules
fluidised bed	small pieces, granules
spray	liquid, purees
Drum or roller dryers	
atmospheric	purees, liquids
vacuum	purees, liquids
Vacuum dryers	
vacuum shelf	pieces, purees, liquids
vacuum belt	purees, liquids
freeze dryers	pieces, liquids

Sun and solar drying of fruits and vegetables is a cheap method of preservation because it uses the natural resource/source of heat sunlight. This method can be used on a commercial scale as at the village level provided that the climate is hot, relatively dry and free of rainfall during and immediately after the normal harvesting period. The fresh crop should be of good quality and as ripe (mature) as it would need to he if it was going to be used fresh. Poor quality procured cannot be used for natural drying.

Dried fruit and vegetables have certain advantages over those preserved by other methods. They are lighter in wight than their corresponding fresh produce and, at the same time, they do not require refrigerated storage. However, if they are kept at high temperature and have a high moisture content they will turn brown after relatively short periods of storage.

E. CANNING

For canning, fruits and vegetables should be absolutely fresh. 'An hour from the field to the can' is the accepted ideal. The fruit should be ripe but firm, and evenly matured. It should be free from all unsightly blemishes, insect damage, and malformation. Over-ripe fruit is generally infected with micro-organisms, and would yield a pack of poor quality. Under-ripe fruit will generally shrivel and toughen on canning. The vegetables should be tender, except that tomatoes should be firm, fully ripe, and of deep red colour. They should be reasonably free from soil, dirt etc. The main processes of canning are described below (Girdharilal (et al., 1986).

Sorting and Grading: After preliminary sorting, the fruits awl vegetables are graded. This is necessary to obtain a pack of uniform quality as regards size, colour, etc. and is clone by hand or with the help of grading machines. There are several mechanical graders, like the screen graders, roller graders, rope or cable graders etc. Fruits like berries, plums, cherries and olives are graded whole, while peaches, apricots, pears, mangoes, etc., are generally graded after cutting them into halves or slices.

Washing The graded fruits and vegetables are washed with water in different ways, such as soaking or agitating in water, washing with cold or hot water sprays etc. A thorough wash is most essential for good results. Vegetables may preferably be soaked in a dilute solution of potassium permanganate to disinfect them. Agitation of the washing water is effected generally by means of compressed air or a force pump or a propeller type equipment. Spray washing is, however, the most efficient method.

Peeling, coring and pitting: The washed fruits and vegetables are prepared for canning by peeling, coring, blanching etc. Fruits and vegetables are peeled in a variety of ways: (i) by hand or with knife (ii) by machine, (iii) by heat treatment and (iv) by lye solution. Cores and pits in fruits are removed by hand or by means of machine.

Hand peeling: Many of the fruits and vegetables are peeled and cut by hand with the help of special knives. The peeling knife with a curved blade and a special guard to regulate the depth of peeling is of special interest as it can be employed universally for many of the fruits and vegetables.

Peeling, coring, and pitting by machine: Recently mechanical peeling, coring and cubing machines for pears, apples and other fruits and vegetables have been introduced. There are also automatic machines for peaches and cherries. Mechanical peelers are used for root vegetables like carrots, turnips, potatoes etc.

Peeling by heat: Some fruits and vegetables, particularly certain varieties of peaches and potatoes, are scalded in steam or boiling water to soften and loosen the skin which is subsequently removed easily by hand. The latest development of this method consists in exposing the fruit or vegetable to a high temperature of 105°C for 10 to 60 seconds whereby the skin bursts and retracts facilitating its easy removal by means of pressure sprays. For work on large scale, a furnace fitted with variable speed conveyor and temperature control device is employed. To get good results, the fruit or vegetable should be of uniform size and maturity. It is claimed that in this method, there is little loss of flavour, and the product is of uniform colour free from any blemish. The heat peeled fruit absorbs sugar more readily than fruit peeled by other methods.

Lye peeling: Fruits and vegetables like peaches, apricots, quinces, sweet orange, carrots and sweet potatoes are generally peeled by dipping them in boiling caustic soda or lye solution of 1 to 2 per cent strength, for short periods ranging from 30 seconds to 2 minutes (depending on the nature and maturity of the fruit or vegetable). The strength of the boiling lye is adjusted from time to time. The hot lye loosens the skin from the flesh underneath. The peel is then removed easily by hand. Any trace of alkali is removed by washing the fruit or vegetable thoroughly in running cold water or preferably by dipping it for a few seconds in a very week solution of hydrochloric or citric acid. This method is quick and reduces wastage as well as cost of peeling.

The lye-dipping equipment varies from a simple open iron pan. In the lye solution, with iron baskets or cages for holding the fruits or vegetables, to fully automatic machines. The use of aluminium in the lye dipping equipment should be avoided as it reacts with sodium hydroxide Recently, stainless steel equipment has been introduced for lye-peeling of fruits such as rough segments, peaches etc.

Blanching: Treatment of fruits and vegetables with boiling water or steam for short periods followed by cooling prior to canning, is called blanching. This loosens the skin, which process is particular importance in the case of beetroot and tomatoes. It facilitates close filling in the can and drives out the air from the tissues, Further, helps to clean the fruit or vegetable and to eliminate micro-organisms. It also inactivate the enzymes, thus preventing the possibility of discolouration. By removing undesirable acid elements and astringent taste of the peel, it also improves the flavour.

In a small cannery the fruit or vegetable to be blanched is placed in a wire perforated basket, which is first dipped in hot water for a short period, ranging from 2 to 5 minutes, and then dipped in cold water, Hard water should not be used for blanching, as it toughens the tissues and destroys the natural texture, In large canneries, blanching is done on belt conveyors passing through boiling water or steam, or in a rotary horizontal cylinders.

Can Filling: The cans are washed with water or subjected to a steam jet to remove any adhering dust or foreign matter. In large canneries, the cans are washed with jets of compressed air or water. In India where the canning industry has not developed so much as to warrant the use of costly machines, using an empty can in open tanks containing hot water is the usual practice. In some factories, however, simple devices have been made to sterilise the cans in steam, before use. Plain cans are used generally, although in the case of coloured fruits like red plums, black grapes, strawberries, it is desirable to employ fruit-lacquered cans. Automatic can filling machines are in use in large canneries in many countries, but choice grade fruits are generally filled by hand to prevent bruising and also ensuring properly grade pack. In India, filling by hand using rubber gloves is common practice.

Syruping or brining: The cans are filled without sugar syrup for fruits and with hot brine for vegetables. The object of adding syrup or brine is to improve the taste of the canned product to fill up the inter space between the fruits or vegetables in the can. The syrup or brine should be added to the can at a temperature of 79°C to 82°C , leaving suitable head space in the can so that when filled can is closed on the double seaming machine, the space left ranges from 0.32 cm to 0.47 cm.

In some of the large canneries in other countries, syruping or brining is done on automatic machines. These machines are available in various designs and capacities. A simple syruper consists of a 227 litres capacity tank of stainless steel or aluminum metal fitted with a closed steam pipe inside and provide with a delivery valve for filling the cans. The cans travel on a continuous belt in an inclined position below the syrup pipe and get filled, the overflowing excess syrup is pumped back into the syrup tank by a centrifugal pump.

Lidding or clinching: Formerly, the cans after being filled, and covered loosely with the lid and passed through the exhaust boxes for large-scale practice. This had certain disadvantages such as spilling of the contents, toppling of the lids, etc. Lidding has now been modernised, the 'clinching' process in which the lid is partially seamed to the can by a single first roller action of a double seamer. The lid remains loose to permit the escape of dissolved as well as free air from the contents and also the vapour formed during the exhaust process, Counting and coding devices are also generally incorporated in clinching machine.

Exhausting: Before sealing the cans finally, it is necessary to remove all air from the contents. The process by which this is achieved is known as 'exhausting'. By removing air from the containers, risks of contamination of the tin plate and pinholing during storage, as also of discolouration of the product, are reduced, because oxidation is prevented. The temperature of syrup or brine in the can should be 79°C to 82°C. Removal of air also helps in better retention of nutrients especially of vitamin C. Since some of the fruits and vegetables have a tendency to expand or shrivel during heating, the exhaust process will help in avoiding over-filling or underfilling of the can. For instance corn and peas expand when boiled in brine and straw berries shrivel when heated in sugar syrup. The other advantages of the exhaust process are prevention of bulging of the can when stored in hot climates; reduction of chemical reaction; and prevention of excessive pressure during sterilisation. Fruits and vegetables sometimes react slowly with the metal of the can producing hydrogen gas which builds up pressure. If there is no vacuum inside the can to start with, bulging will lake place and before the marketability of the canned product would suffer. Vacuum in the can, after exhaust, depends on several factors, such as the time and temperature of exhaust the headspace in the can, etc. The higher the temperature of exhaust, the more the volume of water vapour formed, and consequently the greater the vacuum inside the can. It is, however, preferable to exhaust the cans at a temperature for a longer time to secure uniform heating. The headspace left after filling the can affects the vacuum; the smaller the headspace the greater the vacuum. A can sealed at a lower altitude will show a lower vacuum at a higher altitude and vice versa. Cans with a low vacuum generally become 'springers' at high altitudes.

Containers are exhausted either by heat treatment or by mechanical. The heat exhaust method is generally used in the case of cans.

Sealing: After exhausting, the cans are sealed by special electrical machines known as double seamers. These are of various designs and capacities. These are hand-operated as well as semi-automatic and fully automatic seams.

In sealing lids on metal cans, a double seam is created by interlocking the curl of the lid and flange of the can. Glass containers are sealed tinder vacuum created mechanically or by steam-flow. The containers are sealed with a close-fitting cover of tin plate or a thread or long cap.

Processing: The term "processing" as used in canning technology, means heating or cooling of canned foods to inactivate bacteria.

Heat-processing: The heat treatment to which foods are subjected after hermatic (air tight) sealing in containers is called the heat process . The temperature and time of processing vary with the nature of the product and the size of the container. Acid products with pH values below 4.5 are readily preserved at the temperature of boiling water. The containers holding these products are processed in atmospheric steam or hot- water cookers.

Non-acid products require higher temperatures for sterilisation and are processed in steam-tight pressure cookers — "retarts" or in "continuous pressure cookers" — usually controlled by automatic devices. In general, the length of the process depends on the processing temperature; the higher the temperature the shorter time required. The characteristics of products cause differences in processing requirements. A viscous liquid will require longer processing time than a less heavy liquid. The size of the can is an important factor in determining the correct combination of time and temperature in processing. Obviously, heat will penetrate to the centre of a small can more quickly then to the centre of a large one. Since it is vital for convey type of product, precise information about the rate of heat penetration is required.

Recently the flame steriliser has been developed for certain products in which the cans are exposed to direct flames while rotating. It is a high-temperature short-time process in which the sealed containers are heated by means of direct contact with flames while rotating rapidly.

Cooling: After the "process" containers are cooled quickly to prevent over-cooking. This may be done with water in the cooker under air pressure or by conveying the containers from the cooker to a rotary cooler with a cold-water spray. Cooling water may be kept sterile with 1 to 2 ppm chlorine.

Labeling and casing: After cooking cooling and drying the containers are ready for labeling. Labeling machines apply glue and labels in one high-speed operation. The labeled cans or jars are conveyed to devices which pack them into shipping cartons. The typical vegetable caning operations are given in Fig. 26.3.

F. DEHYDRATION AND CONCENTRATION :

Dehydration is probably the oldest method of preserving fruits and vegetables. Removal of water from foods is primarily accomplished by application of heat, but new methods employing other sources of energy are being used (Van Arsdel et al., 19; Charman, 1971). Foods are dehydrated to protect against spoilage by microorganisms and to reduce the cost of packaging, handling, storing and transporting. There are several methods of drying used industrially. Forced air drying, drum- drying, spray-drying, vacuum drying, and freeze-drying. Continuous belt conveyor drying have increasingly replaced tray and tunnel dryers in recent years.

Mechanism of dehydration: As water evaporates from the wet fruit or vegetable surface, the diameter of superficial water-filled pores and capillaries diminishes and solid structural elements pull closer together under the influence of surface tension. The effect spreads into deeper layers of tissue and eventually all the way to the centre. Value shrinkage is substantially equal to the volume of water evaporated, and the drying rate per unit of surface remains constant.

A wide variety of dried fruits and vegetables is now on the retail market, and many more are dried for re-manufacturing purposes. For example most of the dehydrated garlic and onions are used as seasoning for such products as canned tomatoes, tomato ketchup, tomato sauce and soups. Dehydration is also being used to convert waste materials into animal feed. Solids from tomato-processing plant, for example can be dried and incorporated into animal feed.

G. PROCESSED PRODUCTS:

Global marketing view of fruit and vegetables is given below:

FRUIT AND VEGETABLES — GLOBAL MARKETING VIEW

PREPARATION OF FRUIT JAM

Jam is prepared by boiling the fruit pulp with sufficient quantity of sugar to a reasonably thick consistency, firm enough to hold fruit tissues in position. It should contain not less than 68.5% soluble solids as determined by a refractometer, when cold and uncorrected for insoluble solids. Jam may be made from a single fruit or from a combination of two or more fruits. The preparation of jam requires several operations.

Selection of fruit: Ripe fruit having good colour, flavour and aroma should he selected. If the fruit is firm and tough allow it to stand for a day or two to develop sweetness arid flavour. Unripe or immature fruits should not be used for this purpose. Wash the fruits thoroughly in fresh water. Remove stems and leaves, if any. Trim the bruised and blemished portions.

Preparation of fruit: Peel the fruits. Remove any stone or core of the fruits. Cut the fruit into small pieces. If the fruit is tough and hard, boil it with small quantity of water to soften it.

Addition of Sugar: To the sour fruits, add an equal quantity of sugar by weight. Add only 3/4 sugar by weight to the sweeter varieties. To ensure a minimum of *68.5%* of Total Soluble Solids (TSS) in the jam. generally 24.9 kg sugar is required for every 20.4 kg fruit taken.

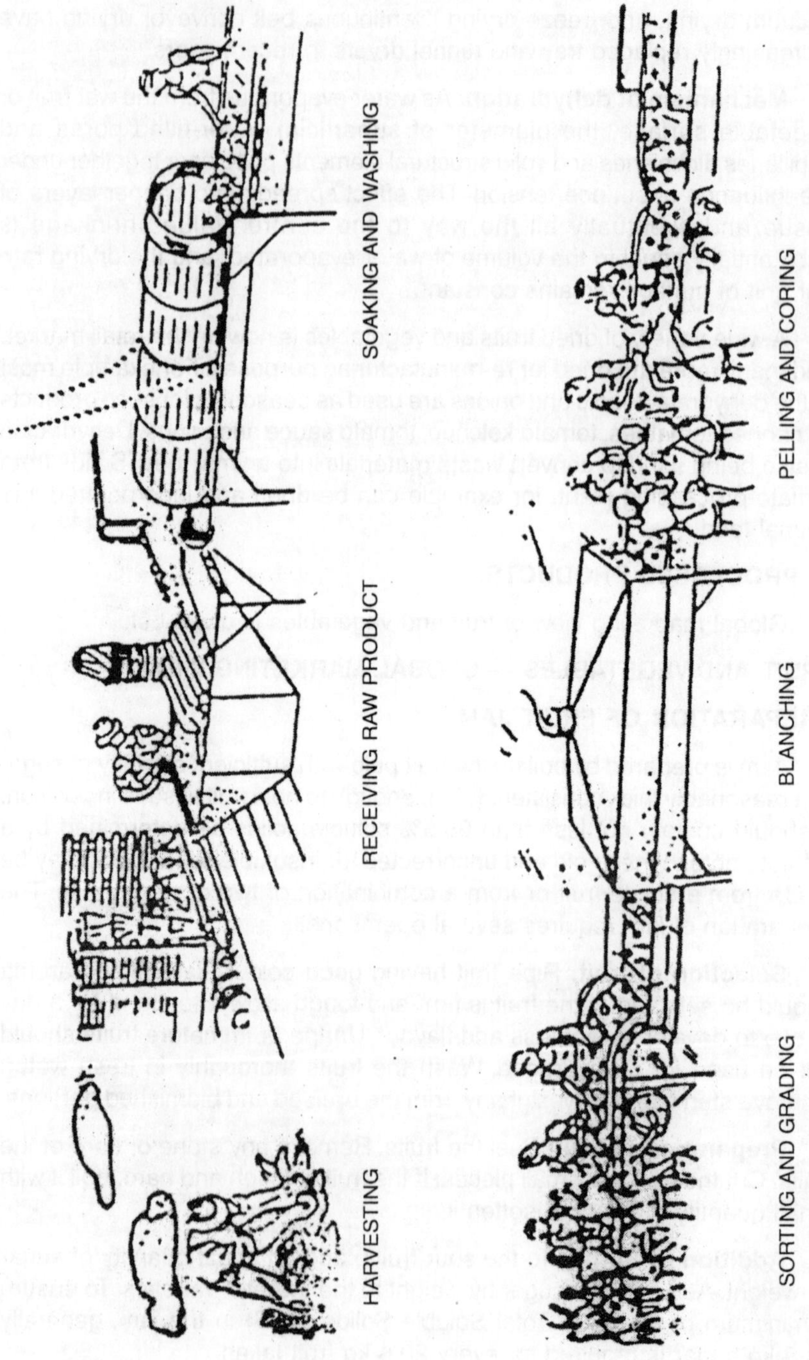
HARVESTING
RECEIVING RAW PRODUCT
SOAKING AND WASHING
SORTING AND GRADING
BLANCHING
PELLING AND CORING

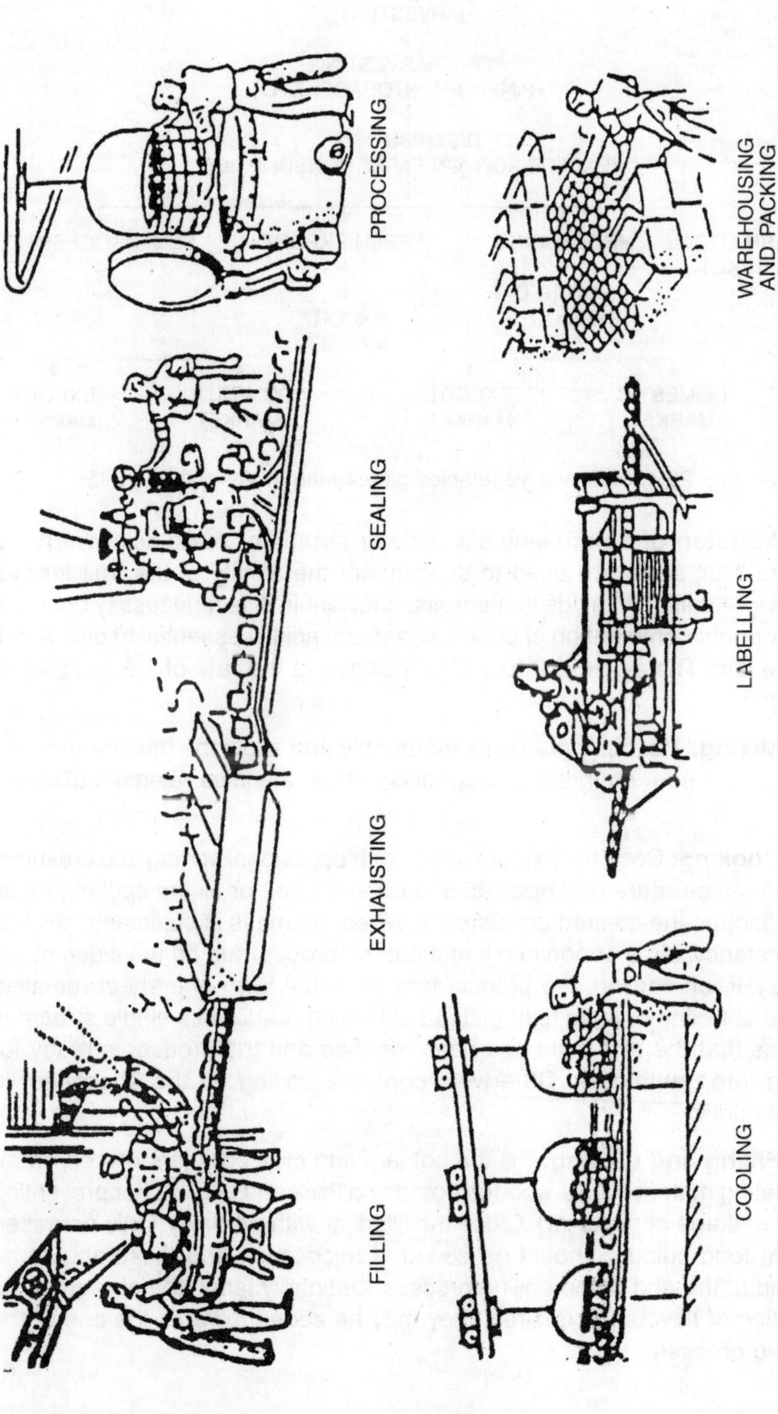

FIG. 26.3: TYPICAL CANNING OPERATIONS

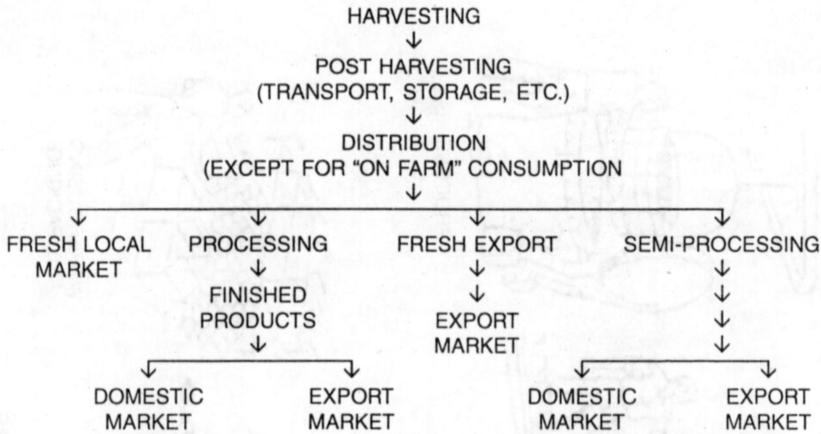

Fig. 26.4: Fruit and Vegetables-global margin Vas (mirue-1995)

Addition of acid: Generally citric or tartaric or malic acid which are natural fruit acids are used to supplement the acidity of the fruit for jam making. Addition of acids to the fruits, deficient in it, is a necessity because appropriate combination of pectin, sugar and acid is essential to give a 'set' to the jam. The acids (0.2 to 0.4%) is added at the rate of 1.5 to 2g/kg of the fruit.

Mixing: Mix the ingredients thoroughly and allow the mixture to stand for 1/2 to 1 hour so that the sugar dissolves in the juice released from the fruit.

Cooking: Cook the mixture slowly with occasional stirring and crushing, till the temperature reaches 105.5°C (at sea level) or till the cooking mass approaches the desired consistency. When the mass is sufficiently thick in consistency, dip a spoon into it and put the product run off the sides of the spoon. If, on cooling, the product falls off in the form of a sheet (detailed under sheeting or ladle test) instead of flowing readily in a single stream, it means that the end point has been reached and the product is ready for filling into containers. Otherwise continue boiling till the sheet test is satisfactory.

Filling and closing: Fill the hot jam into clean dry jars placed on an insulating material like a wooden board or a thick pad of cloth (for preventing the breakage of glass jar). Close the filled jar without delay. Only permitted edible food colours should be added. If necessary, and these should he added at the end of the boiling process. Ordinarily jams do not require the addition of flavours. If desired, they may he added towards the end of the boiling process.

Cooling and storage: Allow it to cool and store in a cool dry place.

PRECAUTIONS

(a) Pectin present in the fruit gives it a good set.

(b) High concentration of sugar facilitates preservation.

(c) Over ripe fruit should not be used as it produces pasty product.

(d) In cases where the fruit is deficient in pectin, pectin from other fruits or commercial liquid or solid pectin may be added.

(e) If the sugar is excess, jam becomes sticky and gummy. Therefore, add pectin or acid or both to counteract the effect of excess sugar.

(f) If Sugar is less, add sugar.

(g) Under exceptional conditions, where more sugar is not added, it would be advisable to add small quantity of sodium bicarbonate to reduce the acidity and thus prevent pre- coagulation.

(h) Finished product should contain:

67.5% total soluble solids by refractometer

0.52% acidity (citric acid)

64% inversion degree

Determination by Sheeting or Ladle Test: This is known as 'cold plate' test, the 'sheet' or the 'flake' test.

Cold plate test: A drop of the boiling juice from the pan is placed on a plate containing water and allowed to cool. If the jelly is about to set the mixture on the plate will rinkle when pushed with a finger. The main drawback in this method is that while the drop on the plate is cooling the jelly mixture continues to boil in the pan with the result that there is risk of over—cooking the product or of missing the correct setting point.

Sheet or flake test: This test is more reliable than the plate test. In this case, a small portion of the jelly is taken with a large spoon or wooden ladle, cooled slightly and then allowed to drop off. If the jelly drops like a syrup, it requires further concentration, but if it falls in the form of flake or sheet, the end point has been reached. After some experience this test can be adopted as a routine measure in the boiling of jelly.

Determination by weighing: Where there is some difficulty in handling the thermometer or in understanding the sheet or flake test, the weighing method is useful. In this method, the boiling pan is weighed before, and again after, transferring the fruit extract and sugar into it. The weight of the finished jelly should be about 1½ times the weight of sugar used. The end point of boiling is determined by weighing the pan with the boiling jelly.

Jelly: In jelly making, pectin is the most essential constituent. Pectin is present in the cell walls of fruits. Its quantity, however varies with the kind of fruit and even with the variety of the same fruit. Some fruits are rich in pectin as well as acid and are thus suitable for jel making.

Selection of fruits: The fruits should be sufficiently ripe, but not over ripe and they should have good flavour. Slightly under ripe fruit yields more pectin than fully ripe fruit. On ripening the pectin present in the fruit, decomposes to pectin acid, which does not form a jelly. After picking, the fruits should be used, without undue delay, for jelly making.

Preparation of fruits: Fruits are washed thoroughly with water to remove any adhering dirt. If the fruit has been sprayed with lead or arsenical sprays, it should be washed in a warm solution of one per cent hydrochloric acid and then washed in water. Fruits are cut (in the case of oranges and lemons, it is necessary to remove the outer yellow portion of the peel to remove the bit-terness) into thin slices so that the acid and pectin in them can be extracted easily.

Extraction of pectin: Only minimum amount of water should be added to the fruits for extraction of pectic. In the case of grapes, water is not added and fruit being heated in its own juice.

Test for pectin: The alcohol precipitation test for pectin which is very simple, quick, is highly useful. Finding the viscosity of the pectin solution by using a jel meter is another method.

Effect of different metals: For boiling fruit juice, copper and iron kettles should not be used. Aluminium equipment is satisfactory. The best equipment made from stainless steel or enamel material or glass.

Straining and clarification: The pectin can be clarified by passing it through cheese cloth and allowed to settle overnight and the supernatent liquid drained off.

Pectin requirement: Usually 0.5 to 1.0 per cent pectin of suitable quality in the extract is sufficient to produce a good jelly.

ESSENTIAL CONSTITUENTS OF A GOOD JELLY

Pectin	1.0 per cent
Sugar	60–65 per cent
Acid	1.0 per cent
Water	33–38 per cent

The rate of formation of jel is influenced by the following factors.

- Concentration of pectin in the solution
- Constitution of pectin

- Hydrogen ion concentration (pH of the pectin solution)
- Concentration of sugar in solution
- Temperature of the mixture

Foaming: Foaming of the jelly tin during boiling can be controlled by adding to the pan a small quantity of edible oil. Generally one tea spoon of the oil is sufficient for a batch containing 45.3 kg of sugar.

CLOUDY OR FOGGY JELLIES

(i) **Cloudy jelly:** This type of jelly is formed if the juice or extract not clarified.

(ii) **Use of immature fruits:** Green, immature fruits contain starch which is insoluble in the juice, and the jelly made from them has, the cloudy appearance.

(iii) **Over-cooking:** Over-cooked jellies are gummy and sticky, on account of their excessive viscosity, they do not become clear after they are poured into containers.

(iv) **Over-cooling:** When the jelly is cooled too much, it becomes viscous and sometimes lumpy. Such a jelly is almost cloudy.

(v) **Faulty pouring into containers:** The jelly should not be poured in containers from a great height because air gets incorporated into the mess and the bubbles formed do not clear easily, especially when the jelly is well made and sets within a spout period. The spout of the pouring vessel should not be more than about 2. 5 cm from the top of the container.

(vi) **Non-removal of scum:** The jelly becomes cloudy also when scum is not removed before pouring.

(vii) **Premature gelation:** If there is excess of pectin in the juice, it cause premature gelation with the result that air may get trapped and make the jelly opaque. This can be avoided by using low pectin.

Formation of Crystals: The formation of sugar crystals in a jelly is caused by adding excess sugar. It is also an indication of over—concentration of the jelly.

In making a jelly from fruits deficient in acid, the mixture should be boiled for a few minutes after adding the sugar so that the sugar is dissolved adequately and it does not crystallise later.

Crystals of cream of tartar sometimes separate out in grape. Although they are harmless, they spoil the appearance of the jelly. The cream of tartar should be eliminated from the grap juice by allowing settling of the juice, and the treated juice only used for making the Jelly.

Syneresis or 'Weeping': The phenomenon of spontaneous exudation of fluid from a gel is syneresis or 'weeping' of jelly. It is caused by several factors such as (1) excess of acid, (2) too low concentration of sugar or soluble solids, (3) insufficient pectin.

FRUIT JUICES AND FRUIT SYRUPS

The consumption of unfermented fruit juices and fruit syrups which have been preserved in sealed bottles or cans is very great in many countries, particularly in U.S.A. and Germany. Their preparation and preservation are many- sided operations, varying according to the nature of the fruit and the type of product required. World trade (imports) in fruit juices and concentrates reached $ 4.36 billion in I 993 a drop from the 1992 figure of $ 5.17 billion but an increase over the $3.97 billion of 1989. The fluctuations over 1989—1994 period reflect not only changes in qualities imported but also movements in price levels and foreign exchange rates. The volume of juices traded internationally increased by over 10 per cent from 1992 to 1993 (Oleson, 1996). Briefly, fruit juice may be considered under the following headings:

Selection of Fruit for juice: As a rule, fruits for juice production should be fully ripe and of good colour and flavour, but not over-ripe ; rotten, mouldy or diseased fruit should on no account be used. In some cases, eg. apples, juice-making is an outlet for fruit which, although sound, is not of marketable quality. i.e. it may be small. With apples also, the colour of the fruit is of little consequence., but the blending of different commercial varieties to obtain a juice of the right degree of sweetness may be desirable. Selection and blending demand considerable skill and judgement.

Extraction of the Juice: It is not proposed here to enter into the mechanical details of extraction; as these must be adapted to the structure of the fruit. In general, the aim is first to disrupt the cells of the juice-bearing tissues so as to release the juice, and secondly to press the juice out. In the case of apples, soft fruits, berries. etc., the whole fruit is milled or grated and then pressed in hydraulic or screw presses. Citrus fruits the rinds con-tam bitter substances which must not be allowed to contaminate the juice proper and the same applies to pomegranate rinds, which are very astringent. For citrus fruits extraction is carried out by revolving burrs or reamers on which the transversely — halved fruits are pressed; for pomegranates and pineapples special presses, cutters and mills have been designed to make the best use of all edible portions. In the case of ripe, soft fruits, berries. etc., in the raw state, the juice contains soluble pectin and small quantities of other colloids which may make it slimy and difficult to press out from the tissues after milling ; moreover, with many fruits, even if the juice can be expressed, die soluble pectic substances quickly form first gels and, finally, flocculent precipitates which carry down all suspended particles and insoluble colouring matters and completely change the character and even the flavour of the juice. To prevent this and to render filtration easy the milled material is treated with an enzyme (pectinol in USA, Filtragol in Europe) produced from the growth of moulds on bran, which converts the pectins partly into soluble reducing sugars and partly into insoluble pectic acid. The enzyme works best at pH 3.0 to 3.5 and, under ideal conditions, it should completely remove the pectin in twenty-four hours.

Juice treated with enzyme should be heated to 170°C for half an hour to inactivate the enzyme and prevent further sedimentation. No doubt flash: heating at a higher temperature would have the same effect.

Deaeration: Deaeration of juices as early as possible in the preserving process, particularly in the case of citrus juices and tomato juice which develop off- flavours and lose vitamin C very rapidly through the action of oxidising enzymes or even by chemical oxidation. They recommend precautions against incorporating air in the juice during extraction, and they carry out the actual deaeration either by spraying the juice into a chamber under vacuum or by allowing it to enter the vacuum chamber as a thin film travelling over baffles. A vacuum of 27.5 inches removes 95 per cent of the dissolved air and is effective in preventing oxidation.

Straining; Filtering; Clarification: Formerly it was fashionable to produce bright and sparkling fruit juices, but clarification to this extent may considerably reduce the flavour of the juice and rob it of much of its character. Moreover, with juices, which owe their colour to insoluble coloured bodies (eg. tomato, apricot) over-filtration will cause decolorisation The modern tendency is to produce juices containing a proportion of suspended matter consisting of fragments of tissue, e.g. orange and lemon juice-sacs, but not of precipitated pectic substance. For this purpose the juice is merely coarsely screened or strained and sold in that condition— usually in cans or opaque glass.

For the production of clear juice several types of filters are available according to the degree of clarity desired. The simplest is the bag filter of flannel or cloth which removes all the larger fragments, while, for greater clarity and output, there are paper—pulp filters to produce a perfectly clear, bright product. High-speed centrifugal separators are used in the production of clear fruit syrups and, for some purposes, recourse is had to the addition of "finings" of casein, gelatin and tannin, or even Bentonite clay.

A certain degree of clarification can be effected by heating, which causes some coagulation of colloidal substances. Heating also stabilises the juice by destroying the pectic enzymes, although some deposition of pectic substances may be expected even with heated juices after prolonged storage. In the case of apple juice which contains starch, starch - splitting as well as proteolytic and pectin - splitting enzymes are used in clarification.

STERILISATION AND PRESERVATION

Pasteurising: The fresh-fruit flavour on which much of the value of fruit juices depends is readily impaired by cooking, the degree of impairment being a function of time and temperature. Hence, pasteurisation is either carried out for a very short time at a high temperature (flash — pasteurisation) or for a longer time at a lower temperature. The times and temperatures recommended depend, in both cases to some extent, on the pH of the juices. Tressler *et* al. (1939) describe several types of flash pasteurisers. These usually consist of tubes, often ribbon-shaped, through which the juice passes and which are heated either by steam or hot water. When the juice has reached the required temperature for sterilisation and enzyme destruction it is cooled quickly to the temperature for filling into cans or bottles, by passage through a cooling coil. Temperature control can be effected by varying the temperature outside the tubes, by altering the rate of flow of juice and, to a lesser extent, by altering its initial temperature. Rapid sterilisation and cooling of liquids, even when packed in cans, is possible if the cans are either rolled or rapidly rotated in the cooker and cooler. Tressler *et at.* (1939) state that the temperatures required to destroy pectic enzymes in citrus fruits are four minutes at 185°F., one minute it 190°F, or a fraction of a minute at 195°F. Fillige temperatures for cans of pasteurised juice are of the order of 170° to 180°. ocanalil a 180°F. Bottles can also be filled at 180°F. but should be warmed before hand and cooled more slowly than cans ; if juice is pasteurised in bottles it should be heated and cooled more slowly than in cans. Some manufacturers, having deaerated the juice, take precautions to exclude air during pasteurisation and cooking, eg. by the use of inert gases, vacuum sealing, etc. This is said to preset-ye the full bouquet of the original juice.

Filtration: The Seitz—Boehi process of removing micro-organisms by filtration has been in use for apple juice on a commercial scale in Germany very successfully for several years. About 0.1 per cent of Filtragol is added to the freshly expressed juice and, after twenty four hours, the sediment is removed in a centrifuge and the juice roughly filtered through clarifying discs. The filtrate is then impregnated with carbon-di-oxide at 120 lb pressure per sq. in. to prevent the growth of yeasts or bacteria and stored in large enamel-lined steel cylinders, holding upto 10,000 gallons, until required for bottling.

Bottling is carried out in a sterile manner with full bacteriological precautions. The carbon dioxide is removed and the liquor rendered brilliant by passing through Seitz clarifying discs and goes through the Seitz sterilising filter which holds Lick all micro—organisms. Bottles, caps, filling machines; in fact, all surfaces with which the juice comes in contact after leaving the filter are sterilised, usually with 2 per cent sulphurous acid, and scrupulous cleanliness of air —filtration, etc., are practised. The juice is usually bottled in the still' condition, but sealing under carbon dioxide at 20 lb. per sq. in. may be used as an extra precaution against fermentation.

The Addition of Preservatives: About 600 parts per million of sulphur dioxide in citrus juices stored in bulk for subsequent bottling or syrup-making (the syrups are made by stirring the requisite amount of dry sugar in the cold, filtered juices until dissolved). For syrups containing 35 to 50 per cent of sugar 200 to 300 parts per million of sulphur dioxide are usually added as potassium meta-bisulphite, calcium bisulphite or sulphurous acid.

Benzoates have become unpopular as preservatives for fruit juices because it is believed that they permit colour deterioration, especially in citrus juices. Tressler and Jeslyn (1971), however, stress the necessary for using sodium benzoate of high purity and state that the deterioration is due rather to oxidation than to any action of the benzoate. If the juice is thoroughly deaerated and stored in the absence of oxygen, 0.05 to 0.1 per cent of benzoate will preserve it effectively and impart less undesirable flavour than sulphur dioxide. It is suggested that combinations of sulphurous acid and benzoate would be satisfactory, the sulphurous acid to retard oxidative changes and the benzoate to suppress spoilage organisms. Like sulphurous acid, sodium benzoate is most effective at high acidity; in fact, it is of no use with non-acid products.

Cold Storage: Like the fruits, fruit juices can be also preserved satisfactorily either raw at 0°F or at higher temperatures, between 14°F to 20°F., if previously heat-treated. Exclusion of air during cold storage helps to preserve the quality of the juice.

OTHER METHODS OF PRESERVATION

(a) Oligodynamic Processes: These depend on the alleged destruction of micro-organisms by minute traces of certain metals, e.g. silver. In the *Matzka process* the juice is allowed to flow in the annular space between two metal tubes insulated from one another. One tube is of silver and the other aluminium or stainless steel. The system is heated by hot water, and it is claimed that a small electric current flowing in the liquid between the two metals carries silver ions which sterilise it. In the opinion of some of the research workers who have investigated the process, the sterilisation is like a flash pasteurisation, although it is true that small traces of silver are present in the juice. The amount of silver can be varied tinder suitable conditions. Its concentration of 0.25 to 1 part per million is said to be sufficient for sterilisation.

In the Schoop process (Swiss) it is claimed that a simple antioxidation treatment effectively suppresses the action of yeast and eliminates the need for high-pressure storage in steel tanks.

Carbonation: Apart from the effect of high-pressure carbonation in suppressing fermentation, carbonation also renders many juices more refreshing and palatable. For bottling or canning purposes 2 to 3 volumes of carbon dioxide are usually added; in terms of pressures, Cruess and Irish (1940) recommend 30 to 40 lb. at 50°F.

For fruit juices low-pressure — low-temperature carbonators are preferred, the juice being cooled to about 32° F before being charged with carbon dioxide in glass-lined, steel tanks. This method is said to give a product of uniform gas pressure and simplifies bottling operations. If the juice only contain 2 or 3 volumes of gas pasteurisation can be carried out at ordinary temperature in sealed cans or bottles.

High-pressure carbonators which charge at higher temperatures can also be used for fruit juices, but must be constructed of non-corrodible materials. There are bottling difficulties with the process however, owing to foaming.

Ready to serve beverages (RTS): Ahmed (1996) formulated ready to serve (RTS) beverages based on banana juice which can be stored at room temperature for a period of 9 months. Saxena *et al.* (1996) reported that the carbonation of RTS blends resulted in sparkling drinks of excellent sensory quality. The blends containing grape-mango (3:1) and grape-pineapple (1:1) received the highest sensory quality scores.

THE CONCENTRATION OF FRUIT JUICES

Concentration by Freezing: When water containing a dissolved substance is progressively cooled pure ice is formed at first and the concentration of the dissolved substance in the liquid phase increases. By removing the ice at a suitable stage we can thus obtain a highly concentrated liquid.

This method was first applied to fruit juices by Gore (1914) who produced a concentrate with a richer flavour than that obtained by any other process because there was no loss of volatile flavours and aromas and the chemical changes which normally take place during heat concentration, did not occur. The fruit juice was simply placed in a freezing room in ordinary ice-cans, surrounded by cold brine, and frozen to a semi-solid cake. This was crushed and placed in the basket of a sugar centrifuge moving at a moderate speed. The liquid passed through the basket was collected; the ice remained behind and, after being washed free from syrup by a fine spray of water, was discarded. This operation was repeated once or twice until a syrup containing about 50 per cent of dissolved solids was obtained. Much of the success of the method depends on having the ice crystals large enough to be held up by the basket of the centrifuge and to permit the free passage of the liquid phase. Too rapid freezing, resulting in very small ice crystals, is unsatisfactory.

Concentration in Vacuum Evaporators: The chief disadvantage of concentration in *vacuo,* even at low temperatures in the neighbourhood of 100°F, is that volatile flavours and aromas are more or less completely lost and, although the vitamin C may be largely retained, the product is usually flat and lacks character. Many attempts have been made to trap the flavours and reintroduce them to the juice after concentration, but it is impossible that such devices should be completely successful. Evaporators for fruit juices range from simple glass-lined vacuum pans to multiple-effect tabular evaporators and evaporators of the climbing and falling film type with tubes of stainless steel. All parts exposed to the action of the juice must be of non-corrodible metal.

CANDIED FRUITS

Glazed fruit: For this purpose a very highly super-satuated syrup containing about 80 per cent or more of sugar is used. The fruit is placed in it while boiling and allowed to cool until local graining can be intruded by stirring at the side of the pan. It is then ladled out and arranged on a suitable wire support to harden and dry. It should not be sticky.

Sauces: Sauces are generally of two kinds i.e. thin and thick. Thin sauces mainly consist of a vinegar extract of various flavouring materials like spices and herbs. Their quality depends mostly on the punjancy of the material used.

Thin sauces: As mentioned above thin sauces mainly consist of a vinegar extract of various flavouring materials like spices and herbs.

Some sauces are matured by storing them in wooden barrels. This develops their flavour and aroma. Freshly prepared products of this kind often taste raw and harsh. For sauces of high quality, the spices, herbs, fruits and vegetables are macerated in cold vinegar. Sometimes, extracts are prepared by boiling them in vinegar. The sauce is filtered through a fine corrosive mesh sieve of non-corrodible metal according to the quality required. The skins, seeds and stalks of spices should not be allowed to pass through the sieve as they spoil the appearance of the sauce. The usual commercial practice is to prepare vinegar extracts of each kind of spice and fruit separately either by maceration or by boiling and then to blend them suitably before putting them into barrels for subsequent maturing.

Soya sauce: Soya sauce is made from soyabeans. The sauce has usually a predominant saltish taste and has a dark brown colour. It is made by cooking soyabeans and wheat, and then allowing the mass to undergo mould fermentation for 3—4 days. The mass is then mixed with strong brine (15—20 per cent) to form a mass which is placed in wooden barrels to bring about bacteriological and chemical changes. In due course, a thick brown liquid is formed. It is then boiled and filtered. To the filtered liquor molasses are added to taste, before bottling.

The other examples for thin sauces are mushroom ketchup, walnut ketchup and worcestershire sauce.

Thick sauces: A sauce which does not flow freely and which has a high viscosity is called a thick sauce. It should contain atleast 3 per cent acetic acid so that it has good keeping quality. The acidity should not, however, exceed 3—4 per cent, otherwise, the sauce would taste sharp. The sugar content may vary from 15 to 30 per cent, according to the kind of sauce made. Usually malt vinegar is used which in addition to producing acidity, improves the flavour. The sweetness is derived partly from fruits like date, raisin, sultanas, apple and tomatoes and partly from the sugar. The colour of the sauce varies with the raw material used. Sometimes a little caramel is used.

Raw materials are generally cut into pieces or slices of the desired size and cooked till they are soft. Slow cooking at temperatures below the boiling point, yields better results than brisk treatment at comparatively higher temperatures. Onion and garlic are added at the start to mellow their strong flavours. Spices are coarsely powdered before they are added. Sometimes vinegar extract of spices is used instead. Thickening agents are added to prevent or retardd sedimentation of the solid practices in suspension. In India, apple pulp is often used for this purpose. Sometimes, the fruit, which is used for making sauce, is boiled, pulped and used as a filler.

The starches of maize, potato, arrow root (cassava starch). sago and rye also are used as thickening agents. The use of Indian gum, locust kernel gum, tragacauth, karaya gum, gelatin, irish moss, pectin and other similar substances is also advised. These are not, however, as good as the starches.

Preparation of Tomato Ketchup: Tomato ketchup is made by concentrating tomato juice or pulp without seeds and pieces of skin. Spices, salt, sugar, vinegar, onion, garlic etc., are added to the extent that ketchup contains not less than 12% tomato solids and 28% total solids.

Raw Material: Select sound ripe tomatoes having deep red colour. Remove all green and yellow portions. Green fruits makes the ketchup inferior in colour and flavour.

Preparation of Pulp and extraction of juice: Collect the prepared fruit in an aluminium or stainless steel vessel and crush thoroughly with a wooden laddle. Cook the crushed mass for 5 minutes and mash it well while cooking. When it is sufficiently soft, strain through fine mosquito net cloth or 1 mm mesh stainless steel sieve. Discard the seeds and skins.

RECIPE

Tomato juice/Pulp (Sp. gr. 1.022 – 1.027)	3.0 kg
Onion (chopped)	37.5 g
Garlic (chopped)	2.5 g
Clover (whole) headless	1.0 g
Cardamom (coarsely powdered) in equal	
Black Pepper (coarsely powdered) quantities	1.2 g
Zira (coarsely powdered)	
Mace (Javatri) not ground	0.25 g
Cinnamon (broken)	1.75 g
Red chilli powder	1.25 g
Salt	31.2 g
Sugar	100.0 g
Vinegar (6% acetic acid)	150.0 ml

***Note:** Sugar can be increased upto about 150 g to get a Ketchup with a slightly sweeter taste.

To the pulp add about 1/3 of the sugar given in the recipe. Place the spices (onion, garlic, cloves, cardamom, black pepper, zira, mace, cinnamon, red chilli powder) in a muslin bag and immerse it into the pulp. Heat the pulp till it thickens and is reduced to 1/3 of its original volume. Remove the muslin bag and squeeze it well to extract the aroma and flavour of the spices. Add vinegar, salt and the remaining sugar. Heat the mass for a few minutes so that the volume of the finished product is about 1/3 of its original pulp.

To a small quantity of finished product, add the preservative 'sodium benzoate' @ 295 mg/kg of the finished product and mix thoroughly. Transfer the dissolved preservative to the rest of the product and mix thoroughly. Pour the finished product into medium size sterilised bottles, seal them air tight with a cransed seal and pasturise in boiling water for 30 minutes. Cool the bottles in air and store in a cool dry place.

Note:

1. Chilli powder, spices, onion, ginger, garlic should be tied loosely in a muslin cloth bag.
2. Acetic acid and colour may be added towards the end of boiling.

3. 1/3 of the sugar may be added in the beginning to preserve the red colour of the pulp.
4. Instead (if clove, cinnamon and cardamom, es-sence of these spices may be added more conveniently.
5. Garlic may or may not be added, depending upon consumer's acceptance.
6. Acid Magenta II colour is avoided. Choose dot red colours or orange colours such as Erythrosine, carmoisine, sunset yellow etc.

Pickling: The preservation of fruits and vegetables in common salt or in vinegar is called pickling. Spices and edible oils may be added to the product. Raw mango, lime, turnip, cabbage, cauliflower, etc. are preserved in the form of pickles, which have become popular in several countries. Pickling is done *(i)* by curing and fermentation with dry salting or fermentation in brine, or salting without fermentation and *(ii)* by finishing, and packing (Giridharilal *et al.,* 1986). In dry salting, for every 100 kg prepared vegetables, 3 kg salt is used in alternate layers in the keg or barrel. After 3/4th filling, the mass is covered with wooden board under some weight. Brine is formed in about 24 hours. Fermentation is usually completed in 8 to 10 days at 27— 32°C, but it may take 2—4 weeks in cold weather. Vegetables such as cucumber, which do not contain sufficient juice to form brine with dry salt are fermented in brine.

Lactic acid fermentation: The addition of salt permits the naturally present lactic acid bacteria naturally present to grow, thereby rapidly producing sufficient acid to supplement the action of salt (Desrosier, 1970). In this process, the fermentable carbohydrate reserve is converted into acid, whose level in cucumber ranges from 0.8 to 1.5% expressed as lactic acid. In the commercial production of fermented salted cucumbers, the salt concentration is maintained at 8—10% during the first week, and thereafter until 16% salt concentration is obtained in solution. The fermentation is completed within 4 to 6 weeks, as evidenced by the change in the tissue characteristics. The salt stock is freshened twice in warm water (43 — 45°C) for 10 to 14 h. The freshened salt stock is packed in consumer units with weak vinegar (2.5% acidity) to prepare sour pickle. Sweet, spiced vinegar is used for sweet pickle. Spices are added to the acidified brine.

Sauerkraut is another lactic acid fermented product made from cabbage. The shredded cabbage is mixed with salt and on an average 1.5 to 2.0% lactic acid is produced, as fermentation may be complete in a little over a week. About one half as much acid is produced, as there is sugar present in the cabbage. In India, oil pickles are highly popular. Cauliflower, lime, mango, turnip, bamboo, jack fruit, kair, karonda etc. are used to make oil pickles. Raw material (whole and cut into desired pieces) is washed, then mixed spices such as chilli powder, turmeric powder, cumin, cardamon, cinnamon, clove, black pepper, fenugreek, nigella, ginger, onion and mustard seed etc. Mustard or gingelly oil is generally used.

The main problem in pickles is the spoilage by either yeasts or moulds, since both can grow in the presence of acid. Thus, an anaerobic environment can control these microorganisms, which can be provided by putting extra layer of oil over the fruits and vegetables in oil pickle and brine or vinegar layer in pickles packed with brine or vinegar. Under properly controlled conditions, the salted fermented cucumber may be held for several years, as the salt protects the fruit pickles against microbial spoilage (Kanekar et *al.,* 1989).

Fruit juice concentrate: This is the fruit juice which has been concentrated by the removal of water either by heat or by freezing.

Sherbats: This is cooling drink of sweetened diluted fruit juice.

Fruit juices are valuable from the nutritional point of view they are rich in minerals, vitamins and other nutritive factors. Besides fruit juices are delicious and have a universal appeal. In developed countries fruit juices commonly form part of the breakfast and are produced in very large quantities. (In the USA. the annual production of juices is more than 50 crore kilolitres). Fruit juices do not form the normal diet in our country and the fruit juice industry is in its infancy in India. Preparation of the juice is limited mostly to home scale production. The fruits generally used for making juice are orange, grape, apple, pomegranate, melon, mango. etc. Of late, the manufacture of squashes on a commercial scale has made some progress.

Fruit juices are best in taste, aroma and colour, when freshly expressed. The most important problem therefore, in the fruit juice industry is to use such methods as would help retain these properties to the maximum extent. The steps involved in the processing of juice are selection of fruit, extraction of juice, deaeration, straining and preservation.

Freshly picked, sound and suitable varieties of fruits are selected and thoroughly washed. The juice is extracted by crushing and pressing the fruits: while extracting the fruit juice, fruit components other than sacs or cells in which juice is present are to be avoided as far as possible. Further, the juice should not be unduly exposed to air. The juice (particularly pure orange juice, which is susceptible to the action of air) is immediately deaerated by subjecting it to a high vacuum. After deaeration, the vacuum is released with nitrogen gas, the juice is transferred into containers which are hermitically sealed and frozen. Fruit juices in sealed containers keep well for about 2 years in the frozen condition. In the alternative, the fruit juice is spray dried.

When clear juice is required, the juice is strained and complete removal of all suspension is effected by fitration and clarification. Clarification needs the removal of colloidal suspensions of the fruit juice. This can be brought about by freezing, heating, use of enzymes or fining agents. The finning agents produce a voluminous floculant precipitate which gradually settles, carrying down with it colloidal suspensions. The clarified juice, as in the case of whole fruit juice, is preserved by freezing, pasteurisation or the addition of chemical preservatives, such as sodium benzoate or bisulphite.

Fruit Juice: The fresh Juices extracted from the various fruits contain mainly sugars and small quantities of vitamins and minerals. The acid taste is due to the presence of organic acids. Fruit juices of various sorts have been prepared for the food-specialty trade for many years, but recent years have seen great advances both in the numbers of these refreshing beverages and their attractiveness and quality. Lime juice from the tropical islands has long been sold by dealers in high-grade food specialities, while grape juice, both red and white, followed there after. A great impetus has taken place in the production and marketing of citrus-fruit juices including those from oranges, lemons, and grape fruit. Some of these are also called fruit cocktails, especially if mixed with other ingredients.

The popularity of these types of product is doubtless due largely in their detectable flavours, and perhaps, in part also, to the emphasis which has been given to vitamins in the past decade, as many fruits contain vitamin C. To secure good quality the fruits used are picked at a definite carefully regulated time as each fruit has a particular period when the acid and sugar content are at an optimum. Oranges for example, should be mature when picked, other wise, the juice is bitter, while grapes may be used for juice when slightly under ripe. The fruit used for juices must be absolutely sound and clean. Rot, mouldiness, fermentation or dirt in crushed fruit spell failure in so far as a high quality beverage is concerned. Each fruit present an individual problem in regard to harvesting. crushing, pressing, clarifying and preserving. In crushing,, for instance, the metal of the crusher should be of such a nature that it is not attacked by the fruit acid, thus imparting colour and changing flavour. Certain fruits darken or lose their attractive appearance on exposure to air even for short periods of time. All fruit juices are subjected to spoilage by microorganisms unless properly handled and stored.

Use of Fining Agents: This method aims at producing a voluminous flocculent precipitate which settles gradually. Carrying down with it divided particles and colloid suspension that are responsible for cloudiness in clarified juices. A number of substances like gelatin, mixture of tannin and gelatin, milk, white of eggs, casein etc. have been used by wine makers and brewers for clarification. The mixture of tannin and gelatin is most widely employed for clarifying fruit juices.

Finings are of three kinds:

(i) Enzymes which destroy the colloids present in the juice.

(ii) Finings which are purely physical in their action. eg: Infusorial earths.

(iii) Chemical finings which act on the gummy and colloidal substances present in the juice to form insoluble coagulates that settle down easily. eg. gelatin, albumen and casein.

I. **Enzymes:** Various kinds of enzymes such as proteolytic, pectin-decomposing, hydrolytic, starch-liquifying enzymes etc. are some times used to remove pectin, proteins, and starch from fruit juices.

2. **Finings having purely physical mechanical action:** Generally infusorial earths such as spanish clay, kaolin, bentonite etc which are known as 'titter— cells' are employed for the clarification of fruit juices. Usually 0.5 to 0.6 per cent of the earth is mixed with the juice and the mixture then passed through the filter press.

3. **Chemical Finings:** The bulk of suspended matter especially in the case of apple juice, consists of proteins arid pectin like substances gelatin, casein and albumen are normally used to clarify the fruit juices.

Clarification by Freezing: Colloidal suspensions when subjected to freezing, are readily precipitated on thawing. Apple juice particularly responds very well to this treatment. The bulk of fruit juice is subjected to refrigeration for several months to complete the precipitation the clear juice is then bottled.

Clarification by heating: It is a well known fact that colloidal material in fruit juices usually coagulates, when the juice is heated, and settles down readily. To get good results, the juice is heated to about 82°C for a minute or less and then cooled down rapidly, the great advantage of this method is that it also removes from the juice those substances which would other wise be precipitated during pasteurisation of the juice. Clarification of pomegranate juice is a typical example of this process.

Cider: Freshly pressed apple juice or sweet cider is a beverage held in high esteem in many parts of this country, particularly in the Northern and Atlantic states where the apple has been the most characteristic nature fruit for generations. With the recent creation of markets for bottled cider which may be held for a considerable period before use, refinements in the clarification of the juice have been developed. One of the methods advocated for this purpose has been the combined utilisation of gelatin and tannin for the precipitation of suspended colloidal material, followed by filteration. Enzyme preparations, capable of attacking pectins and starches which are likely to cause a hauze in the juice, have also been found useful in this respects.

Grape Juice: Grape juice has been a popular beverage for many years. In the usual procedure the grapes are first carefully washed or subjected to a water spray, then crushed and steamed mechanically. Ordinary filteration will not readily remove completely the turbidity of grape juice, but this may be accomplished by adding organic materials such as casein, or through the use of enzyme concentrates derived from moulds. Either of these treatments, followed by filtration, will produce a relatively clear produce. The clarified juice is again heat treated at a temperature of I70°F or more for 30 minutes and filled into the final container which should be sterile.

Orange Juice: Fresh orange juice is one of the most popular fruit beverages, and much efforts have been given to producing high grade commercial products of this nature. To have satisfactory flavour, it is necessary that the total acidity of the orange juice should be at least one per cent. Freezing has also been used as a means of preserving citrus juices. Juice sealed in vacuum and stored in air tight containers at 0^0F is said to keep well.

Grape fruit Juice: The Juice of grape fruit has been canned successfully for a number of years and has obtained considerable popularity. The canning of grape fruit juice consists of extracting and straining the juice adding the sweetening, processing and cooling.

Lemon Juice: The canned juice of lemons is also a common product at present. This fruit is also subject to flavour and colour changes which require the removal of air as far as possible. Lemon juice may also be dried to a powder form using spray—drying equipment.

Tomato Juice: Another relatively recent product which has acquired high popularity not merely for its acceptable taste but also because of its vitamin value.

SQUASHES: The term squash refers to a fruit juice added in the concentrated sugar syrup and preserved.

Essentials of squash:

I. Fruit— Usually, citrus juicy fruits such as lemon, orange, plums, pineapple, grapes, mango, kokum are used.
2. Sugar— It acts as preservative and gives sweet taste.
3. Acid— It acts as preservative and gives sour taste.
4. Chemical Preservatives— Potassium Metabisulphite/Sodium Benzoates.

Steps in squash making:

1. Selection of fruit— Select fresh, juicy, fully riped, firm wholesome and fresh fruit.

2. To soften the fruits, keep them in fresh lukewarm water for ten minutes.
3. Extract the juice and strain it.
4. Calculate the amount of sugar, water and preservative (325 mg of potassium metabisulphate for 450 ml of prepared squash) to be added. (Eg. Lemon juice 30.0%; water 15.0% and Sugar 55.0%) mango juice 45.0%; water 10.0% and sugar 45.0%)
5. Prepare syrup with sugar, citric acid and water and cool it.
6. Add strained fruit juice in the cooled prepared syrup.
7. Add preservative dissolved in small quantity of cooled squash.
8. Add permitted colour and essence in adequate amounts.
9. Pour in dry sterilised bottle through a funnel leaving 2.5 cm headspace.
10. Close the bottle and seal it.

Squashes are prepared by the addition of sugar, organic acids and preservatives to freshly expressed fruit juices. Squashes are usually diluted with water before consumption.

Lime and Lemon squash: Take fresh, fully ripe, sound fruits and wash them thoroughly in fresh water, cut them into halves with a stainless steel knife . Express the juice from the limes in a lime juice squeezer or in small basket press; for lemon use cone type extractor (Mix Master) strain the juice through mosquito net cloth to remove seeds and coarse pulp. Add suitable quantity of edible yellow colour (Permissible brand) to bring out, desired shade in the finished product (Juice 1.0 kg, sugar 1.8 kg and water 1.2 kg).

Orange Squash: Select fresh, fully ripe, sound fruits, and wash them in ample quantity of fresh water. Remove the peal of the loose skinned orange, separate the segments and extract the juice in a screw press. Strain the juice through a coarse muslin, or mosquito net cloth. Cut the tight skinned oranges into halves and express the juice in a cone type extractor (Mix master). Mix thoroughly the ingredients (Juice, 1 kg; sugar 1:7 kg; water 1.3 kg citric acid 30—35 g and orange essence 1½ tsp) till the sugar and citric acid are dissolved. Slightly warm if necessary and strain the mixture through coarse muslin cloth. Add potassium metabisulphite at the rate of 619 ug/kg of finished product. Dissolve this powder in the small quantity of water and mix it thoroughly in the product. Bottle the squash and store, when required, for 1 cup add 3 cups of water.

Cashew apple squash: Extract the juice and clarify using gelatin solution, add 6 g of lime juice, 12 g of citric acid and 670 g of sugar for every kg of clarified cashew apple juice. Mix well till the sugar is dissolved. Add potassium metabisulphite at the rate of 610 ug or sodium benzoate at the rate of 700 ug per kg of the finished product respectively. Fill the squash into clean bottles, cork tightly and store in cool place . As and when required, for every cup of the squash, add 3 cups of chilled water, mix and use as a fresh drink.

Jack fruit squash: Cut the ripe fruit into eight or sixteen pieces first across and then length wise. Remove the gummy core by means of a sharp knife from the bulbs. Smear a little cooking oil on the hand to prevent stickiness. Separate the bulbs from the rind and the surrounding carpels. Trim off the top and bottom of the bulbs remove the seeds and their thin covering. Cut the bulbs into halves, quarters or slices and soften by heating them slowly in about half their weight of water and stirring with a wooden ladle and mash into a fine pulp and mix with sugar syrup. (pulp 1 kg: sugar 1.7 kg, water 1.3 kg and citric acid 40 g). Jack fruit squash is a palatable beverage with pleasant taste and aroma. Before use, dilute it with 3 volumes of water.

Sapota Squash: Pass the fruit segment through a meat mincer and obtain a uniform pulp. Wrap the pulp in thick cloth and press out the juice with gloved hands or a small basket press. Mix the ingredients, (Pulp 1 kg, sugar 1.2 kg, water 1.0 kg and citric acid 40 g) and heat the mixture thoroughly into a uniform syrup mass. Strain it through coarse muslin cloth.

Fruit Juice cordials: Fruit juice cordials differ from the fruit juice squashes in that the suspended fruit pulp has been removed. They are usually dilute with water be lore consumption.

Lime Juice cordial (CFTRI 1990): Extract the juice from limes as is squash and store in glass containers. Winchester bottles or carboys after adding potassium metabisulpite at the rate of 1.5 g/kg of the juice. Allow the juice for about a month to settle. Decant the clear juice without disturbing the sediment and strain it through fine muslin cloth. Mix the ingredients (juice I kg, sugar 1.25 kg arid water 1 kg) thoroughly with slight warming. If necessary, strain the product through fine muslin cloth. Add potassium metabisulphite (preservative) at the rate of 150 mg/kg of the finished product, bottle and store.

CARBONATED BEVERAGES: The production and use of carbonated beverages have increased greatly in recent years. The business has extended from a relatively small, highly seasonal hot—weather industry to one of large proportions. There are over 5.000 establishments in the United States producing carbonated products with an an annual value of over 200 million dolars. Some of these products are carbonated natural-fruit beverage such as grape juice and cider. The great bulk, however, is composed of beverages, of which ginger ale is perhaps the outstanding example, containing as a base a flavoured syrup which may also be fortified with some fruit acid. Although the food value of these products is riot high, they serve a useful function especially in warm weather; and many are pleasant substitute for hot beverage at the table eve ii in the cooler months.

The following federable definition for ginger ale indicates the general composition of this type of carbonated beverage.

Ginger ale is the carbonated beverage prepared from ginger ale, flavour, harmless organic acid, potable water, and a syrup of one or more of the following sugar, invert sugar, dextrose with or without the addition of caramel colour.

Ginger-ale flavour is defined as follows : Ginger-ale flavour, ginger-ale concentrate is the beverage flavour in which ginger is the essential constituent, with or without aromatic and pungent ingredient, citrus oils, fruit juices, and caramel colour.

Ginger ale is one of the most popular beverages and is produced in two common forms, the so-called "golden ginger ale" and "pale dry" ginger ale. The former usually has a sugar concentration between 8.5 and 9.5 while the sugar content of the latter is slightly lower, ranging from 8 to 9 per cent. The "pale dry" is generally more acidic than the "golden".

Other carbonated products some times have flavours made from flavouring oils and occasionally from synthetic organic derivatives. Sassafras flavour, for instance, is prepared from oil of sassafras and methylsalicylate, oil of winter-green.

Most carbonated beverages of the ginger-ale type are not heat-treated and therefore would seem to present the possibilities of spoilage of microorganisms. Fortunately, however, carbondioxide itself when present tinder pressure tends to inhibit the growth of many type of microbes which would otherwise cause spoilage.

The water used requires special consideration from a chemical standpoint also, as the lower the total solids content, the better the product. It is undesirable to employ water having over 15 grains of total solids per gallon, and the presence of calcium sulphate (hard water) should be avoided. Distilled water is suitable for use but is not commonly necessary. It is sometimes necessary to have the water supply chemically treated to make it satisfactory for beverage purposes, because the ability of water to take up carbon dioxide gas properly is of great importance. The necessity of having an odourless and tasteless water supply is equally essential and the final treated water must be clear as crystal.

Another main ingredient of carbonated beverages is the syrup. Although present in relatively small quality in comparison with water, it is the syrup which supplies the flavour and whatever food value the product presents. There are a great variety of syrups, all of which contain sugar and some flavouring material, which may be from natural fruit or more often synthetic flavours.

Fruit acids such as citric acid are commonly used as an important constituent of syrups and tend to accentuate the other flavouring ingredients used. The sugar used in these syrups is largely sucrose, although it is now legally possible to use corn sugar without declaration on the lable. The sugar content of concentrated syrup is usually high enough to restrain growth and to prevent spoilage, even though stored some time before use, but microbes gain entrance if they are not killed by the sugar. Therefore it is essential that the strictest sanitary precaution be taken in making syrups and keeping them chemically and biologically clean during storage. The third ingredient is the carbon dioxide gas. This is usually purchased is cylinder containing the carbon dioxide under high pressure, which facilitates later operations as the pressure is necessary. In order to increase the solubility of carbon dioxide in water, the water in beverage plants is usually cooled close to the freezing point before bottling operations are started. This chilled water is sometimes carbonated previous to the actual filling operations.

The three chief ingredients, syrup, water, and carbon dioxide are ultimately combined in the bottle in definite proportions and in such a manner that the carbon dioxide in the product has a pressure of 3 or 4 atmospheres. The filling operations are carried out in highly automatic machines, to cap the bottle after they are filled. The bottles are usually conveyed through a testing tank filled with water which checks the capping operations, as leaks may be detected by bubbles of carbon dioxide rising to surface.

The bottles used for this industry are generally returnable and thus may be used several times. Therefore another important operation in a beverage plant is the thorough cleaning of all bottles used for the product. Often this equipment is the most expensive apparatus in the plant.

Yeasts and related organisms are the principal causes of spoilage in carbonated beverages, as the acidity and sugar content are favourable to their development, although other microorganisms — bacteria or moulds some times cause trouble. Most bacteria are inhibited by the acidity of beverages of this sort, while moulds are unable to grow when high concentrations of carbon dioxide make up the dissolved gas, and exclude oxygen from the air. Yeasts may cause changes in flavour and produce turbidity and sediment owing to their growth. When such cloudiness occurs and even the actual breakdown of the beverages may take place in an infected product, but careful attention to sanitary procedure throughout the whole chain of operations involved minimises such infection and spoilage. Storage of such bottled products should be at low temperatures and in the absence of sunlight. Carbonated beverages containing certain types of flavouring oils are likely to deteriorate in flavour if exposed to direct sunlight.

TOMATO JUICE: Plant ripened and fully red tomatoes should be used. All green, blemished and over ripe fruits should be rejected as they adversely affect the quality of the product. Juice from over ripe tomatoes is usually thin and not quite pleasant in its taste and aroma. The yield, colour and flavour of the juice depend on the degree of ripeness of the tomatoes, the variety and the place where grown.

1. The juice Should be of deep red colour. As the red colour is contained in the fibres and not in the serum of the juice, the fibrous portion as much as possible should be incorporated in the juice in finely divided condition.
2. The juice should posses the characteristic taste arid flavour of tomato.
3. The acidity of the juice as citric acid should be about 0.4%.
4. For uniformity in quality, either the tomatoes used should be from one stock and place or the juice should be suitably blended.

Washing and Trimming: For thorough cleaning, tomatoes should be washed in plenty of running water. For commercial production, rotary washes or through washers fitted with moving conveyor belt and soft rollen brushes are used.

Crushing: After trimming tomatoes are cut into 4 to 6 pieces for boiling to soften the tissues.

Pulping: Tomatoes can be pulped by the hot process or by the cold process.

Hot Pulping: The crushed tomatoes are boiled in their own juice in steam jacketed stainless steel pans or in aluminium pans for 3 to 5 minutes to facilitate pulping.

Advantages

1. The tendency of the juice to separate into liquid and pulp can be overcome if the pectin naturally present in the seed and in the skin can be incorporated into the juice. During the preliminary boiling, this pectin is released and it thickness the pulp.
2. Boiling sterilises the juice partly, thereby checking to some extent the growth of micro organisms which cause fermentation etc., in the juice essential. It also inactivates the oxidatives enzymes which are responsible for the destruction of vitamin C.
3. A light cooking release the red colour pigment in the skin.
4. Yield of juice is higher.

Cold Pulping: The tomatoes are crushed in the cold and as such passed through a pulper.

Defects

1. As compared to the hot process, the extraction of juice is somewhat difficult and the yield is less.
2. Air gets incorporated into the juice in the process of extraction and this oxidises vitamin C in the juice.
3. Colour of this extraction is low.
4. Microbial spoilage is more.
5. Total solid content is 5.66% at 20°C

Common Salt and Sugar: 4 to 6 kg common salt is added/1000 kg of juice sometimes sugar is also added to improve taste.

Packing: Juice can be packed in glass bottle or- cans. The juice is homogenised, heated to about 180°- 190°F poured into hot sterilised cans, without leaving any head space. The cans are double seamed, sterilised at 212°F for 30 minutes and cooled in running water.

TOMATO COCKTAIL: Tomato cocktail is gaining popularity in many five star hotels and restaurants. It is prepared just before serving and sometimes is also served from stock. Although the recipes vary, the main constituent is tomato juice with common salt, vinegar, worcestrenshine sauce, lemon juice, Tabasco sauce are added in different proportions to suit the palate. Simmer the tomato juice, with the spices loosely tied in a cloth bag for about 20 minutes in a covered vessel. Then add the lime juice, vinegar and common salt. Other fermented juice products are fermented cider (fermented apple juice) apple wine, apple brandy, beer, whisky and scotch.

27
BEVERAGES

ALCOHOLIC BEVERAGES

Alcoholic beverages have been known since antiquity. These are judged in terms of flavour and stimulant effect and hardly at all as sources of calories. However, the calorific value of alcohol in 7 kcal/g and excess of alcohol consumed could add to the total calorie intake of a person. In the case of the distilled liquors (whisky, brandy, gin and rum), the calorific value is only due to alcohol and consumption of 100 ml of these beverages would yield about 230 kcal of energy. Beer and wine contain some nutrients present in the original malted barley and the fruit juice used in their preparation and naturally their energy value would be higher than that of distilled liquors ; 350 ml of beer gives about 150 kcal and 100 ml of wine about 80 kcal.

Alcohol is absorbed without prior digestion but the body has limited capacity to oxidise it. That is the reason why alcoholic beverages are to be sipped instead of gulping them. As a drug the effects of alcohol vary from mild stimulation, when small amounts are consumed to loss of coordination and even death when large amounts are consumed.

There are three main classes of alcoholic beverages such as wines, malted beverages (beer) and distilled liquors. Different starting materials and different methods are used in their manufacture. But there is one common characteristic in all of them, namely, they are made by the process of fermentation. The essential step in all the fermentation processes is the conversion of glucose into alcohol by yeast. The enzymes present in yeast catalyze the breakdown of glucose.

$$C_6H_{12}O_6 \xrightarrow{\text{Yeast enzymes}} 2C_2H_5OH + 2CO_2$$

WINES: Wine is the oldest of the alcoholic beverages made by the fermentation of grape juice. Wine, strictly speaking, is a product of vine, but often includes all fermented liquors obtained from different fruit juices (fruit wines). Wines differ greatly in their character, because grapes grown in different regions differ in their composition, particularly with respect to their volatile components which contribute to flavour and bouquet arid in the method used for wine making (Amerine, 1972 Amerine *et al.* 1972 ; Cruess, 1947).

There are different varieties of wines and in many cases they are named by reference to their place of origin, eg. champagne is produced in the district of Champagne in France. Most of the wines produced in the world tire natural and still (without excess of carbon dioxide). Sparkling wines, such as champagne, contain excess of carbon dioxide due to the secondary fermentation that occurs after bottling. The carbon dioxide generated is stored within the liquid tinder its own pressure and gives the wine a sparkle. Some wines like port and sherry are fortified wines and differ from natural wines in that some alcohol (grape brandy) is added to them before the completion of fermentation. Vermouth is also a fortified wine prepared by the addition of spice mixtures or their extracts at various stages during fermentation.

Wines also differ in their colour. The colour of wine may be white or red. However, the colour does not depend on the colour of the grapes from which it is made in fact, white wines may easily be made from black grapes by using only the juice. In making red wines both juice and skin are used; the pigment giving colour to the grapes lies just tinder the skin and is extracted from it during fermentation. Wines may be either *dry* or *sweet* depending upon the extent to which the fermentation has taken place. If fermentation has taken place until all the sugar is used up, the resulting wine will be dry ; whereas if it is stopped while some sugar remains, it will be sweet. Yeast cannot tolerate an alcohol content greater than 16 per cent. Most of the natural wines contain 8-10 per cent alcohol. Fortified wines contain about 20 per cent alcohol, which is sufficiently high to kill the micro organism that attack natural wines. Wines containing less than 14 per cent alcohol are table wines while those which contain more are dessert wines.

In the manufacture of wine, grapes are picked at the proper time when the sugar and acid contents are in the right proportion. The composition of the grapes varies according to the climatic conditions prevailing during their cultivation and thus the quality of wine varies from one year to another. Therefore, there is a practice of 'vintage dating' the wine with the year of the crop from which it is made. Immediately after picking, in the case of red wines, the grapes are crushed and the juice together with the skin, pulp arid seeds are transferred to the fermentors. After fermentation is completed, the fermented juice is pressed out. In the case of white wines, pressing takes place before fermentation.

'Wild' yeast and other microorganisms are present on the skin of the grapes and these pass into the juicy pulp (known as must) when the fruit is crushed. These are destroyed by adding sulphur dioxide (or potassium metabisulphite) in lie required quantity. If the sugar content is low sucrose is added to the desired strength arid the pH is adjusted to 3.2—3.4 by the addition of tartaric acid. Next, the must is inoculated with a pure culture of actively growing yeast *(Saccharomyces ellipsoideus).* The temperature and duration of fermentation depend upon whether dry or sweet wine is required. Fermentation usually lasts 4 to 10 days. Table wines have a comparatively low content of alcohol and little or no sugar, while dessert wines are forfeited sweet wines.

When fermentation is complete, the clear wine is symphoned from the yeast sediment into barrels (raking) and the wine allowed to age. During this period secondary fermentation takes place and the wine also looses its raw and harsh flavour and mellows down. During this period of maturation clarification takes place in the natural way. It can also be achieved by fining and filtration. Next, the wine is bottled and allowed to mature the time of this maturation extends to a number of years depending upon the quality desired.

Wines are also made from juices of other fruits and berriers. Cider is fermented apple juice. The method of fermentation with fruit juices other than of grapes is almost similar to that of preparation of grape wine. French dry sherry is made from grapes which have a high sugar content. The other wines are perry wine made from pears and mead (honey wine) made from diluted honey (Frazier and Westhoff, 1995).

Beer: Beer, next to wine, is the oldest alcoholic beverage to have been made. There are evidences to shown that fermented beverage from barley existed in Indus Valey civilisation about 5000 years ago in China. Egypt and other cultures even earlier. The first brewery in India was started in 1860, and in 1981 there were 29 breweries and the beer production was about 1.7 million hectolitres, which is very insignificant compared with a world production of 960 million hectolitres in the same year. The chief beer producing countries in the world are the US.A. FDR. USSR, UK and Japan.

The term beer is normally applied to a beverage made by the fermentation of barley malt. However, terms like ale, stout, lager and porter are also used for beer, the difference between them being the method of production. The materials used in the manufacture of beer are barley, malt cereal adjunct, hops, water and yeast. The principal operations involved in the production of beer are malting, mashing and fermentation. The starting material for the production of beer is barley malt.

Starchy materials that are cheaper than malt are used as 'adjuncts' to replace some malt. The most commonly used cereal adjunct is maize in the form of grits or flakes. Other adjuncts suitable for brewing are broken rice, wheat, raw barley, tapioca, starch and sorghum. Such adjuncts should not impede the fermentation process or have an undesirable effect on the quality of the product. The entire starch of the adjunct is to be converted into sugar. Thus, the percentage of adjunct that can be added is restricted by the amount of enzymes in the malt. The introduction of microbial enzymes has increased the flexibility of varying adjunct proportion, as these enzymes supplement malt enzymes. They also reduce the cost of raw material and maintain the quality of beer. Liquid syrup adjuncts can also be used, but they are yet to enter the brewing field in India.

Suitability of water for brewing is of great importance in beer making. Water should be hard, if soft, salts are added to the required hardness. If the water is too hard, it may have to be boiled to remove most of the temporary hardness.

The yeast used depends upon the type of beer to be manufactured. For the production of ale, "top fermentation", systems are used with the yeast Sacharomyces cerevisiae, In top fermentation, the yeast is carried to the top of the fermentating vatt by rapidly evolving bubbles of carbon dioxide. For the production of larger, the "bottom fermentation" system is employed with Sacharomyces carlsbergensis. During fermentation, the yeast settles at the bottom of the vats.

In the manufacture of beer, the malt is mashed *i.e.,* the ground malt is steeped in hot water in vessels called mash tun. Two mashing methods are generally employed : infusion mashing, followed in India, and decoction mashing. In infusion mashing, hot water at 65.6°C is mixed with ground malt to the consistency of porridge. Cereal adjuncts (gelatinised) are added to the malt grit. Sugar syrups, if desired are also added at this stage. The period of infusion is about 2 hours and the temperature is maintained at 65.5°C. During this period, malt amylases degrade starch in aqueous solution to produce sugars approximately in the following ratios : 7-10 per cent monosaccharides. 48-55 per cent disaccharides, 12-15 per cent trisacharides and 20-30 per cent dextrin. By regulating the mashing conditions, the proportion of various carbohydrates can be varied to suit the requirement of the beer to be brewed. When steeping is complete, the extract known as 'wort' is filtered off through barley husks which settle on the perforated false bottom of the mash tun.

The wort is then boiled with hops. This boiling destroys the malt enzymes and sterilises the wort. The essential oil and bitter substances of hops are extracted and the proteins are coagulated. The coagulation of protein assists in clarifying the beer. The liquor is filtered through spent hops which retain the precipitated materials. The liquor, when cold, is seeded with yeast and allowed to ferment for a few days during which time sugar are converted into alcohol. When the fermentation is complete, the beer is allowed to stand for 1 or 2 days when yeast settles down.

After fermentation, the beer is run off to storage tanks for maturing when secondary fermentation takes palce the flavour and bouquet of beer develop. The maturing process varies from only a few days for mild beer to several months for strong beer. Next, the beer is pasteurised or sterile filtered and bottled or canned, with the introduction of carbon dioxide under pressure.

Variation in the quality of beer, such as the strength of alcohol, colour and extractives, depends upon the quality of malt, malt adjuncts used mashing method, amount of hops added and the condition of fermentation. *Beer, ale, porter* and *stout* are beverages produced by top fermentation while lager beer is a product of bottom fermentation. *Ab* is made like lager but is usually stronger in hop character and contains a higher alcohol content. *Porter* is a heavier and darker drink made with longer dried, roasted, or caramelised malt with less hops. *Stout* is like porter except that it has heavier malt flavour much darker than any other malt drink. It has a stronger hop taste than porter. The alcohol content of various beers varies from 2.5 to 7 g per cent. *Beers* produced in India contain 4-5 per cent alcohol and have a calorific value of about 30 kcal per 100 ml.

Sake is Japanese beer, which is made entirely from rice. Whole grain rice is soaked until it is quite soft and then steamed. The steamed rice is partially dried by spreading on straw mats. It is then inoculated with a yeast-like mould and after 10-14 days, the completely fermented material is filtered. This fluid is placed in barrels to settle. After a few days, the clear liquid is withdrawn and pasteurised giving *Saki.* It contains about 14 to 17 per cent or more alcohol by volume.

Sonti is a rice beer or wine of India, The mould *Rhizopus sonti* and yeasts are active in the fermentation.

Pulque is a latin–American beer like beverage containing about 6 per cent alcohol that results from a naturally yeast fermentation of the juice of the agave, or century plant.

Ginger beer is a mildly alcholoic, acid beverage made by the fermentation of a sugar solution flavoured with ginger.

Pilsener is a large type beer, light in colour, containing little remaining fermented carbohydrate.

Bock beer is a very dark beer with a high alcohol content.

Coconut sap or juice is obtained by tapping or cutting the stalk of the young flower bunches of coconut. The main constituent of the fresh juice is sucrose (12.3–17.4 per cent); the juice is rich in ascorbic acid (16— 30 mg/ l00 ml). The juice in the fresh state is sweet toddy or neera and is used as a beverage. Sweet toddy, if carefully collected in sterile vessels, remains unfermented for a considerable time. However, as collected, fermentation gets in the fermented product toddy is used as beverage and contains about 4.0 per cent alcohol. Arrack is the product obtained by the distillation of fermented toddy and contains about 35 per cent alcohol. Coconut sap when strained and evaporated gives jaggery.

Distilled Spirits: Distilled spirits are made by distilling fermented liquors. Whisky is made by the fermentation and distillation of fermented cereal grains, brandy from wine and rum from fermented molasses.

Gin is a distilled spirit flavoured with juniper *(Juniperus Communis)* berries or some other aromatics. Distilled liquors usually have 40 per cent alcohol and thus have excellent keeping qualities. Usually, distilled liquors, other than gin, are allowed to mature before consumption, e.g., whisky is matured in wooden barrels for 5 — 15 years to become smooth and mellow.

An essential stage in making spirits is distillation. The liquid obtained by fermentation from different materials contains dilute alcohol and is concentrated by distillation. Originally, distillation was carried out in a pot still. To obtain a concentrated alcoholic liquor, the distillation in a pot still has to be repeated a number of times. To overcome this disadvantage, continuous distillation still have been developed. In spite of this development, pot still distillation is still used for making the finest *whiskys, brandies* and other renowned *spirits.* Pot still allows many of the volatile components which contribute characteristic and subtle flavours to the drink to pass over with the alcohol during distillation. The best of brandies, cognac, is made by distilling twice in a pot still.

Whisky is made using different cereals. Scotch malt whisky, the original whisky, is made from malted barley and scotch grain whisky from barley malt and other tin- malted cereal grains. US whiskys are generally made from rye (straight lye whisky) and maize (straight maize whisky). Canadian whisky is made from maize, wheat, rye or barley. Irish whisky is made from malted barley alone or with a mixture of unmalted barley, wheat, rye and oats.

In the manufacturing process, the grain is converted into beer except for the omission of hops and is distilled to obtain a distillate containing 80 per cent alcohol by volume. It is then diluted with water and stored in charred barrels. After the desired period of aging, the whisky is adjusted to the required alcohol strength and bottled. The characteristic flavour of scotch whisky is said to be due to the fumes from the peat used for firing malt kilns and the characteristics of the water used.

Brandy can be made from any fruit. Generally, brandy refers only to the distillate from grape wine. Grape wine obtained from selected grapes is completely fermented using pure cultures of yeast and distilled. The brandy obtained is stored in oak casks and is allowed to age in a damp storage building for as long as 20 years.

Rum is an alcoholic beverage distilled directly from fermented sugarcane products, such as sugarcane juice, syrup of molasses. The rum obtained by distillation is stored in either charred, plain or reused barrels or vats. Rum readily improves in characters and flavour with aging. After aging, the strength of alcohols is adjusted to 40 per cent and bottled.

Gin is produced by diluting neutral spirit with distilled water so that the alcohol content is 60 per cent. This is distilled in a pot with juniper berries and other aromatics. During distillation, the alcohol water vapour extracts the flavouring principles. The distillate is then reduced to the required alcohol strength by the addition of water and bottled. No aging is required for gin; in fact, it may be harmful as the essential oils in gin may decompose with time.

Vodka is a distilled liquor without any identifying characteristics except that of dilute alcohol. It is free from all traces of colour and flavour. Vodka is made by diluting neutral spirit obtained from wheat or other cereal crams or potato.

For the preparation of gin arid vodka, and for fortification off any other beverage with alcohol, a colourless and tasteless spirit is required and this can be obtained by distillation in a continuous still. Dilute alcohol from any source when distilled in a continuous still can give 95 per cent alcohol. Such alcohol is very pure and has only the odour and flavour characteristic of alcohol. Such alcohol is known as neutral spirit (silent spirit).

Liquors are products obtained by steeping herbs, fruits, flowers or plants in netural or- distilled spirits and distilling the resulting produce. To the distillate, sugar is added to the extent of 2.5 per cent. As a rule, liquors are sweet, and caramel colour or other colouring may be added. Liquors like Benedictine. Drambuie, Creme-de-menthe are obtained this way. The recipes of most liqueurs are closely guarded secrets.

Traditional eastern alcoholic beverages: Toddy is the sap from palm and other trees which has undergone alcoholic fermentation. The method of tapping the sap differs depending upon the tree species. In the coconut palm, the lower portion of the unopened spadex is bound by a strong cord, and the uncovered portion is pounded with a maliet; the sap that oozes out from the prepared tip is collected in pots tied to it.

Chang is a traditional alcoholic beverage from the North-Western part of India. Cooked rice and other cereals are used as the substrate, called grim, and the inoculum, called phab, is prepared from herbs. The inoculated material is fermented under defined conditions. The extract obtained after fermentation is called chang. Rice beer, shonti annum and other similar beverages are prepared from rice, wheat and huskless barley in different parts of the country, and are called by different names.

Kaomak and **takju** are traditional alcoholic beverages from Thailand. *Kaomak* is prepared from boiled glutinuous rice with species. *Takju* is prepared from barley, corn and wheat.

Feni is a traditional distilled alcoholic beverage of India prepared from the cashew apple in Goa. The juice is fermented, and distillation is carried out in two stages. The distillate of coconut toddy is called coconut feni.

Country liquor is prepared from such raw materials as jaggery, potato, fruits like orange and mango, etc., Spices like cardamom, aniseeds, coriander and ginger, and flower like rose and jasmine, are also used for distinctive perfuming. *Modhuka* is another alcoholic beverage prepared from mahua flowers.

The main types of alcoholic drink and their calorie values are given below.

Type	*Alcohol content*	*Calorie value (cal/100) ml)*
Beers		
Bitter	3	30
Mild	3	25
Cidey		
Dry	4	35
Sweet	4	40
Wines		
White	9	70
Red	9	65
Fortified	16	135
Spirits		
Whisky	31	220
Liqueurs		
Benedictine	39	270

The salient features of traditional methods are:

(a) Use of microorganisms to modify the substrate and release fermentable sugars.

(b) Use of starter cultures prepared under specific conditions, sometimes using natural plant materials.

(c) Absence of rigid temperature control.

(d) Fermentation normally by mixed flora.

(e) Absence of any stringent precautions during fermentation or processing to avoid cross-infection. In contrast, modern conventional fermentations include highly controls and demanding conditions of fermentation and processing.

Traditional alcoholic beverage may be relevant to developing countries on grounds of cost, technology, and availability of infrastructure and raw materials.

28
Sugars and Sweeteners

Sugar is produced by the process of photosynthesis in the leaves of green land plants. The process involves sunlight, combination of carbon dioxide and water in cells which contain chlorophyll and the oxygen is given off. Although sugars are widely distributed in plants, yet, sugar cane and sugar beet store sugar more abundantly than most plants. These two are the major sources of supply of sugar all ever the world.

The commercial value of sugar cane derives from the preponderance of sucrose as a constituent of juice of the mature plant. Other important sugars present in substantial amounts are glucose and fructose.

CANE SUGAR PROCESSING

Weighing. This is important for making the payment to the cane growers and also to find out the yield potential of the canes. The juice contained in the canes determines the sugar recovery. Weighing is done on huge weigh bridges installed at the entry points.

Cutting. The milling process is separated into two steps: (i) Cutting of the canes, and (ii) Grinding of the canes. The cutting is done by revolving cane knives that cut the cane into small chips, but extract no juice.

Crushing and Shredding. Shredders tear the canes into shreds but extract no juice, but the crushers break and crush the structure of the cane, extracting a large portion of the juice. Crushers, in general, consist of two (occasionally three) deeply grooved rollers which crush or break the cane, expressing from 40 to 70 per cent of the juice.

Extraction of Juice. In the milling process, cane parts with 70 to 80 per cent of its weight as juice while passing through the crusher and shredder. No amount of pressure can reduce the final product to anything other than an approximately equal mixture of woody fibre and juice. It is a universal practice to add water or thin juices thus, diluting the contained juice and increasing the extraction as this juice is expressed. This use of water is termed saturation, imbibition, or maceration. The sugar cane residue, called bagasse, contains about 25 per cent juice. It is used to make woodlike structures, paper, and plywood sheets. It also has rich fuel value. Bagasse is also used to run the boilers.

PURIFICATION

(a) Filteration. The raw juice is subjected to course screening during the preliminary treatment. The removal of fibre improves the clarifying capacity and gives better juice clarity.

(b) Defacation Process. Clarification by heat and lime, known as the simple defacation process, is the oldest and probably the most effective means of purifying the juice. In general, sufficient lime is added to neutralise the organic acids present in the juice, after which the temperature is raised to about 95°C or above.

(c) Sedimentation. This lime milk and heat treatment form a precipitate of complex composition; part heavier and part lighter than the juice. The complex may contain insoluble lime, salts, coagulated albumin, and varying proportions of the fats, waxes and the gums. The flocculent precipitate carries with it most of the finely suspended material of the juice that may have escaped mechanical screening.

EVAPORATION

The juice from the clarification system contains natural water, expressed from the cane, together with part of the imbibition water. An average composition may contain 85 per cent water and 15 per cent solids. The major portion of water is now removed to yield a syrup of 60 per cent sollds or more. Therefore, evaporation is a system of removing moisture through the application of heat. An elementary simple evaporator is made up of the closed spaces, separated from one another by thin metal walls in the form of tubes, coils, or plates called the heating surface. Steam enters one of these spaces at a given temperature and pressure, where it condenses, giving up its latent heat. In the other space, a solution at a lower pressure and temperature absorbs this released heat by the evaporation of water.

To evaporate about ½ litre of water, it is necessary to supply the equivalent of its latent heat at the pressure at which evaporation takes place, assuming that solution is at boiling point.

In the multieffect evaporation, the evaporators can be fixed in tandem, the vapour from one becoming steam for the next. It is necessary only to lower the pressure as successive units are added; thus establishing an adequate difference of temperature to enable the operators to function properly.

CRYSTALLISATION

The function of the vacuum pan is to produce and develop satisfactory sugar crystals from the syrup or molasses fed to it. A calandria pan is a specially designed single effect evaporator with large diameter, short tubes and a large pan to facilitate the circulation of heavy viscous massecuite elaborated in batches. Syrup and molasses in certain proportions develop sugar crystals, beginning with the heating-surface covered just sufficiently to obtain circulation and finishing with a full load, called a strike, whose volume is about three times than at the start. When volume of the strike reaches full capacity of the pan, the final concentration is effected by shutting off feed and allowing the evaporation to proceed until the necessary degree Brix is attained.

Thus, in the operation of vacuum pans crystals of the following sizes are produced:

C-Sugar grain footings	0.243 mm
C-Sugar and magma	0.350 mm
Primary footings	0.506 mm
Secondary footings	0.730 mm
Commercial sugar	1.050 mm

Purity of Massecuite. The crystal content of a final low-purity massecuite should be as high as the viscosity of the mother liquor. Low grade massecuites, after having been boiled to maximum workable consistency, are usually discharged to the crystallisers at a temperature of 65 to 70°C The mother liquor of the massecuite cannot be exhausted of crystallisable sucrose at this temperature. Crystallisation should be allowed to continue at the minimum temperature until a saturation temperature suitable for centrifugal processing is attained. The rate of cooling, of course, will depend upon the characteristics of massecuites, the nature of impurities and design of crystalliser. Some important crystallisers are:

1. Air-cooled crystallisers
2. Water-cooled crystallisers
3. Water-jacketed crystallisers
4. Stationery cooling coils
5. Crystalliser with revolving heat exchange elements.

Separation of Crystals and Molasses. The massecuites as delivered from the vacuum pans or from the crystallisers go first to a mixer generally a troughlike container with revolving arms to prevent the crystals from setting. The crystals in the massecuities are separated from the surrounding molasses or syrup by centrifugal force. In the machine, the molasses is expelled into the curb and the crystals are retained. The spinning, called 'purging', continues until the sugar crystals are practically free of molasses. After that, the crystals may be further purged of molasses by spraying the wall of sugar with a measured quantity of water.

Methods of washing the purged sugars have seen tremendous growth and development. Steam washing and hot mingling are some of the notable improvements.

Refining. This involves affination, clarification, decolourisation with absorbents, crystallisation and finishing. Most sugars discharged from the centrifugal machines contain about one per cent of water and are conveyed to distributing bins above the granulators by scroll or belt conveyors. The white sugar then goes through the granulators for drying. The dried sugar goes to a set of screens that classify it according to the size of the crystals. Bulk storage of refined sugar is practised now. The amount of granulated sugar available as expressed in per cent of melt is a figure of interest to refiners. Actually, the yield depends upon the true purity of the raw sugar i.e., per cent of sucrose in the dry solids.

BEET SUGAR

Juice Extraction from Beets. The extraction of juice is affected by treatment of thinly cut beets with hot water, since sugar and non-sugar portions pass through the beet into water by diffusion called the diffusion method.

Different operations involved are:

1. Delivery of beets to the plant
2. Separation of course impurities, such as stones, straws and extraneous materials from the beets.
3. Washing the beets to clean from adhering dirt and microbial load.
4. Transport of washed beets to the beet slicer and weighing them for accounting purpose.

After the sliced beets are placed in water, sugar and other solubles gradually pass from the slice into the water. Inside the slice, the concentration of sugar decreases, while in the surrounding the concentration increases. The movement of soluble solids continues until the concentration inside the beets and in water extract equalises. The spotaneous movement of dissolved substance in the direction of lower concentration is called diffusion. Diffusion is caused by the random movement of the molecules of the dissolved substances moving at first in various directions, the molecules gradually arrange themselves in a pattern of uniform distribution. Diffusion proceeds rather slowly, since heat increases the speed of moving molecules, it accelerates diffusion as well.

It should be stressed that successful extraction of sugar by the diffusion method is continued by heating the beets to the protein coagulation temperature of atleast 60°C. Sugar does not diffuse from fresh beet cells, because the vacuoles containing the juice are surrounded by a layer of protoplasm (Protein) that prevents the passage of sugar molecules and other dissolved substances. On the other hand, sugar diffuses from frozen beets even without preheating, because frozen protoplasm coagulates.

Finally, beet juice is further extracted by pressing the grated beets wrapped in muslin cloth. Hydraulic presses are found best for the pressing purpose. Calcium hydroxide is added to the juice extracted, and carbon dioxide is introduced until virtually all the lime is precipitated in the form of calcium carbonate. The treatment effects both chemical and mechanical purification of the juice. Filteration follows, and the juice is treated again with carbon dioxide to complete the removal of lime. After a second filteration, the juice is treated with sulphur dioxide, filtered a third time and then returned to the evaporators.

The evaporators consist of a number of large boiling vessels which are heated by exhaust steam. Each cell of the evaporator has a higher vacuum than the one preceding, so that the juice boils at progressively lower temperatures. Here, the juice is concentrated to a liquid containing 60 to 70 per cent solids.

After another filteration, the juice is boiled in vacuum pans until crystals forms. In the vacuum pan, the sugar boiler can regulate the Size and uniformly of the crystals in the final sugar. The material discharged from the vacuum pans consists of crystals of sugar suspended in syrup. The syrup is removed by centrifuging and the refined, granulated sugar is washed, dried, screened for size, and packed.

MAIZE SWEETENERS

Commercial maize sweeteners are of four general types:

(a) **Maize Syrups.** Clear, colourless, non-crystallisation viscous liquids consisting of mixture of dextrose, maltose and higher saccharides.

(b) **Maize Syrup Solids.** The solid substance obtained by dehydrating liquid maize syrup.

(c) **Crude Maize Sugar.** A solidified maize sugar "Liquor" consisting essentially of dextrose.

(d) **Dextrose.** A pure crystalline solid.

These products are all starch hydrolyzates and may be classified on the basis of the dextrose equivalent (DE) of the product. It is a measure of the reducing—sugar content of a product calculated as dextrose and expressed as a percentage of the total dry solids.

Maize is one of the major sources of starch which is stored as a source of carbohydrate and energy. Purified starch may be white, dry, granular, insoluble in alcohol and dispersbile in hot water which can also result in the formation of gel. It is an important ingredient in many food products. The maize which is classified as: (i) Common maize, (ii) Waxy maize and (iii) high amylose maize, only the waxy and high amylose types are used for starch production. Starch is the main component used in the production of maize syrups and sugars. Such hydrolyzates can be produced from starch derived from other plant sources by chemical or enzymatic hydrolysis. The process of hydrolysis involves three methods, namely:

(i) Acid conversion

(ii) Acid-enzyme conversion

(iii) Enzyme-enzyme conversion.

Acid-conversion Method. In this method, the only hydrolysing agent is acid which acts as a catalyst. The starch is mixed with water to produce a suspension. About 0.1 per cent of hydrochloric acid is added and temperature is raised to 140 to 160°C with live steam for 10 to 15 minutes. On cooking, the starch is gelatinized to higher polysaccharides. Along the way, other sugars are produced as well. At the desired end point, the heating is stopped and the process of hydrolysis ceases by the addition of neutralising agent like soda ash. The pH should be from 4.5 to 5.5. The suspended materials are filtered out. The filtered syrup is clarified and readied for other uses.

The commercial maize syrups are sold on the Baume basis, which is a measure of specific gravity. Maize syrup solids are the solid substances obtained by dehydrating liquid maize syrup to a low moisture content.

Acid enzyme conversion method. The acid enzyme conversion involves two steps of hydrolysis. After the initial acid hydrolysis, the starch splitting enzyme is introduced. Such enzymes called amylases are of three types:

(a) a-amylase

(b) β-amylase, and

(c) gluco-amylase.

Enzyme-enzyme inversion method. The enzyme activity results in the production of dextrose and maltose in approximately equivalent quantities. However, the dual enzyme system of the syrup production involves a hydrolysis step, where the starchy stuff is subject to et-amylase, followed by fungal-amylase. The dual enzyme system is not common, being more cost intensive.

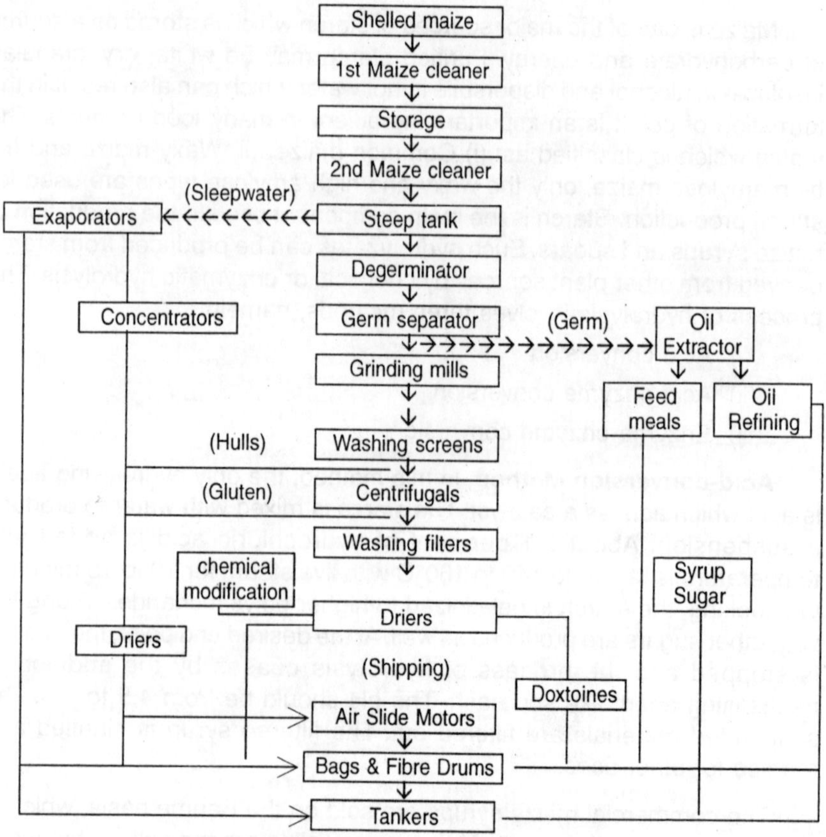

FIG. 28.1. FLOW DIAGRAME OF THE RECOVERY OF STARCH AND SYRUP FROM MAIZE

Dextrose is obtained by the complete hydrolysis of starch, by either of the methods discussed above. The first step envisages enzyme preparation, which is to gelatinize the starch with acid or amylase. The starch concentrate usually is from 30 to 40 per cent. Then gluco-amylase is added undercontrolled conditions of temperature and pH. The time required for the reaction is from 48 to 72 hours at 55 to 60°C. When the hydrolysis is complete, the solution is filtered and concentrated under vacuum to 70 to 75 per cent solids. It is then cooked, pumped to crystallisation pans and seed crystals are added. After the completion of crystallisation process, the crystals are centrifuged from mother liquor, washed and dried. The enc products is dextrose monohydrate.

29
Milk and Milk Products

Milk as an article of food, dates back to the earliest recorded times. However, most of the exact knowledge is the progress of the past 100 years or so. Scientific achievements notwithstanding, our future endeavours would show our accumulated knowledge of the subject to be still very incomplete.

The importance of milk in the human dietary cannot be overstressed. Milk may be defined as the normal secretion of the mammary glands of most mammals. The nature designed milk as a food for the newly borns and the youngs. The perfect composition of milk not only recommends itself for the growing organism, but is also suited to satisfy the energy and vitamin requirements of the adult system. It is a heterogeneous product in which fat, Proteins, sugar, vitamins and mineral salts are held in emulsion, colloidal suspension or solution in the major constituent, i.e., water.

TABLE 29.1. THE CHIEF CONSTITUENTS OF AN AVERAGE SAMPLE OF MILK

Constituent	*Percentage*
Water	87.25
Dry matter	12.75
Fat	3.80
Protein	3.50
Sugar	4.80
Ash	0.65

Palatability of milk foods. The first prerequisite of a food is that it must be palatable. It must be relished and enjoyed when consumed. Milk and milk products are liked by most people. There are a great deal of variations which can be managed to make milk products acceptable by those who do not care for it in its natural state.

Digestibility. Though it is essential that most, if not all, major constituents be present in a food, yet it is more crucial that most of these constituents be readily available for the utilization by human body. The percentage of various food constituents of milk which are digested is very high. It is possible for certain individuals to utilise as much as 98 per cent of proteins and 99 per cent of carbohydrates and fat.

Cleanliness. If a food is inherently clean, it is bound to increase the appeals of the average consumer. The milk and milk products—being clean, wholesome and nutritious—attract the attention of masses and create a desire for such foods. Milk for direct consumption can be prepared under very sanitary conditions maintaining the highest quality.

Economy of milk as food. Certain foods are consumed for meeting the needs of a given number of nutrients: for example, bread is an excellent source of carbohydrates, meats of proteins, leafy vegetables and saag of dietary fibre etc. But these foods do not furnish any considerable quantity of other constituents. In contrast, milk contains constituents of all classes needed by the body.

MILK PRODUCTS

BUTTER

Butter is an important dairy product in India, although relatively little of it is directly utilised for consumption.

Makhan, an indigenous butter, is obtained invariably by churning "dahi" (yoghurt). Almost all of the butter produced is used for the preparation of ghee (clarified butter fat). Creamy butter is also produced for the exclusive use of European residents and a few westernised Indians in cities. The upward trend in the use of creamy butter has been observed lately.

Preparations. The preparation of dahi for the production of butter from raw milk is usually either by self-souring milk or by the addition of a culture or starter. Most commercial makhan is obtained from the unprocessed milk. Sometimes a mixture of boiled and raw milk is used. Most commonly, milk used for makhan is kept simmering for a long time. With inoculation of culture at an appropriate temperature 20°C ± 50°C), the milk is coverted into curd (dahi) before churning it into butter, the fermentation period ranging from 12 to 48 hours.

The isolation of butter from the curdled whole milk is usually carried out with the help of indigenous beaters, made up of wood and run manually. However, electric beaters made up of stainless steel components are now available at the household and commercial scales. The Churning is affected by the beating action of the blades at high speed. During chuming there is no proper control of temperature. However, there is a practice to add water at intervals to control the temperature and/or viscosity of the curd. After the butter grains have formed, these are allowed to settle for 5 to 10 minutes.

The butter milk is then separated and the butter fat makhan is obtained. It has very good initial quality and shelf-life.

The yield of butter depends upon the fat and moisture content of the milk base. It also depends upon the fat recovery method (churning). The moisture content of butter may vary from 20 to 25 per cent, and the fat content is as high as 85 per cent of the original fat available in milk. The cow milk butter is characterised by yellow colour, whereas butter from the buffalo milk is white. The butter from cow milk suffers in body and creamy in texture.

However, the product from mixed heterogeneous milk blends tends to be intermediate in appearance and quality. The flavours of the good quality product should be pleasant and slightly acidic. It should be free from objectionable taint or rancidity.

GHEE

Ghee. It can be defined as the clarified butter fat prepared mainly from makhan. The product is referred to as from cow or buffalo or mixed milks, though small and significant amount of ghee is also prepared from other milk sources such as goat, sheep and camel. The use of ghee is significant in the Indian dietary and the Hindu religious functions. Desi ghee is also believed to be having immense medicinal values.

Ghee is mainly produced for use as food. Only up to 2 per cent of it goes into the ceremonial purposes. People of the Indian continent have developed as special liking for the flavour and aroma of desi ghee. For the table use, it is mostly served as melted product when it is mixed with rice, vegetables, curries to enhance the flavour. The use is also very common to smear the chapatis to improve their texture and flavour. It is also used as a shallow and deep fat trying media.

The high cost of production, availability of cheaper vegetable ghee (shortcomings) as well as refined oils, and the health awareness to reduce the desi ghee consumption owing to its being rich in saturated fatty acids—have resulted in the negative trends seen in the recent past of its use. Nevertheless, it remains very crucial and significant factor in the Indian dietary pattern.

Melting point. It varies from 28° to 44°C while the solidifying point ranges between 15° and 28° C. Since desi ghee is a mixture of glycerides, it does not melt sharply at any fixed temperature.

Specific gravity. it varies from 0.93 to 0.94.

Polenske value. This should not be more than 2. based on the water insoluble fatty acids present in the ghee.

Saponification value. It is less than 2.00.

Iodine value. It is a decree of unsaturation and in ghee it should be between 24 and 36 unit.

TABLE 29.2. CONSTITUENTS OF GHEE

Constituents	*Ghee from*	
	Cow milk	*Bufallo milk*
Fat (%)	99.0-99.5	99.00-99.5
Moisture (%)	< 0.5	<0.5
Carotene pig/g	3.2-7.4	—
Vitamin IU /g	19-34	17-38
Tocopherol mg/g	26-48	18-37
FFA%	2.8	2.8
Casein	trace	trace

Preparation. Desi ghee as it is commonly called in northern India, can be prepared either from the butter (makhan) or cream; the former constituting about 95 per cent of the raw material.

When cream is to be used as a raw material, the non-fatty solids should be washed off to obtain better ghee. The process of conversion, essentially, consists of separating the fat from the water phase. This is rendered comparatively easy by the circumstance that the continuous phase of the butter emulsion consists of electrically neutral particles of fat. By keeping butter at a temperature slightly higher than the one at which it melts, the fat and water layers separate; the curd particles, generally; forming an intermediate complex.

The butter is heated in a pan, heated with careful stirring, low until the mass melts. Between 90° and 100°C the contents start boiling, when the moisture is evaporated and ghee is ready heating is discontinued. The clear ghee is decanted off leaving the sedimentation residues to be used as by-products.

There have been many improvements over the indigenous and traditional methods of ghee making with some aimed at bulk and large-scale production. Although ghee is expected to have a good shelf life, yet it develop undesirable flavour and texture over time. Therefore, proper marketing is essential.

LASSI OR CHHACHH

Lassi or *Chhachh* is known as the buttermilk in the western world. It is a by-product of the butter manufacture process. Following the churning process, the fat is separated from the whey.

This by-product of butter process is largely consumed by the people. It is drank as such, particularly during the summers, to quench the thirst after the addition of sugar or salt depending on the sources and sweetness of the taste. A fried and mildy seasoned recipe called khoru is popular. Basically, Lassi, contains about 90 to 91 per cent; water, 0.1 to 1.0 per cent; fat 3.0 to 3.5 per cent; protein, 0.5 to 1.0 per cent; acid, 0.05 to 0.10 per cent; ash, 0.05 to 0.10 per cent; calcium: and 0.05 to 0.10 per cent phosphorus. It has Lassi to butter ratio of about 50:1.

The *lassi* can be used for the preparation of casein milk protein on commercial scale. Casein can find use in infant foods, ghees, paints and insecticide sprays. It is also an important analytical agent used in the laboratories.

UNFERMENTED MILK PRODUCTS

By reducing the moisture content of raw milk, the volume can be reduced, whereas, making use of the concentrated product containing all major components of food value intact. Some of the products like condensed milk, dry milk, and desiccated products like khoa, rabbari and kheer are prepared. All these products can be classified as the unfermented milk products.

Condensed milk. The concentration of milk to obtain the condensed form is achieved by either one of the two processes namely; Evaporation, or Concentration.

The difference between the two processes is inherent in this fact whether the moisture removal has been secured by evaporation at normal pressures or under vacuum. The milk boils at approximately the same temperature as does the water, i.e.. 100°C, at ordinary pressure. However, if milk is boiled at 100°C, it has deleterious effect on the quality of final product, because some volatile constituents responsible for flavour and body may be lost and the 'cooked' flavour be added. Therefore, concentration under partial vacuum is preferred. Many improvements regarding the making of vacuum pans have been made normally. The milk intended for condensing is placed in a tank, where it is heated to about 60°C. The heating is done by letting in the hot steam; then a partial vacuum is created. The milk enters the side pan through a pipe from the tank. Because a partial vacuum has been created in the pan, the milk is sucked into it, then the live steam is turned in through a coil. The heat evaporates the moisture. However, the condensed milk is not removed from the pan till the desired concentration is achieved. Some of the parameters of determining the concentration are: fat percentage, total milk solids, total solids, and sugar if added during the condensing process.

After the condensing is complete, the condensed milk is analysed for the quality and legal standards. A condensed milk is used in the home in cooking for any purpose for which ordinary milk is used. A large number of recipes have been prepared for home cooking based on condensed milk. It is also used in large quantities by bakers as well as candy and ice cream manufacturers.

Khoa. This is one of the most important unfermented milk products. It is prepared by partially desiccating the whole milk in open pans by the direct application of heat. The keeping quality of the milk constituents is enhanced by the desiccation into semi-solid form by tending to reduce the bacterial growth and by reducing the water activity (AW) of the products.

Average composition of khoa ranges as—moisture 19 to 20 per cent, fat 25 to 45 per cent, protein 19 to 25 per cent, lactose 25 to 30 per cent, ash 3 to 5 per cent,—depending upon the source of milk and the extent of concentration.

A 100 kg batch of milk (mixed) can yield about 20 kg of khoa which is mostly used in the preparation of sweets (mithai). It can hold well for about 4 to 5 days of its own.

Preparation. Main reaction in the preparation of khoa is the heat denaturation and coagulation of the milk proteins. Most of the albumin and globulin are rapidly denatured. The protective properties of other colloids are destroyed early in the boiling process, which is accelerated by the incorporation of air during the constant stirring.

In its preparation, milk is boiled in a suitable open pan like a karahi over a brisk fire and it is stirred continuously with circular motion by the flattened end of a khunti. A constant evaporation of water takes place, resulting in progressive thickness; heating is continued till the viscous product reaches a paste consistency and begins to dry up. The finished product is turned into small balls or flat cubes of a uniform size and weight.

Milk solids, mostly conserved in the form of khoa, are mainly used as a base for many preparations like Barfi and Gulab Jamun. In South India, whole milk is desiccated with sugar aided during the later stages of concentration to yield a product called thirallupal.

Other important desiccated and non-fermented milk products include kheer. This is also a partially desiccated product, but with higher moisture and cooked with rice; it is also sweetened to suit the taste. Kheer is served fresh and sometimes garnished with coconut, almonds slices and resins to increase its attractiveness and appeal.

Rabbri. While preparing rabbri, milk is not stirred and the solids are separated from the milk. When the amount is reduced to about one-fifth of the original volume, it is removed from the heat, sugar is then added and product allowed to cool. It is essentially a clotted cream, skimmed off from slowly evaporating milk and is a delicious preparation.

Mallai. It is obtained by simmering large quantities of milk until a thick layer of milk fat and coagulated protein form a thick layer on the surface. The product is smooth and white in colour and has a characteristic flavour and texture.

Paneer. Indian cheese also called paneer is another useful delicacy prepared from unfermented milk. In social gatherings, the paneer preparation is believed to be a substitute of non-vegetarian dish.

It is prepared from the whole milk which is clotted with rennet, and the resulting curd is filled into muslin bags or wicker baskets. A suitable weight can be rested at the top to facilitate whey extraction. Lumps of casein with entrained in ilk fats, arc formed as soon as the acid or rennet is added to the milk. The semisolid mass is then cut into small cubes and used in the preparation of several recipes.

Cottage cheese. Skimmed milk can be easily used in the preparation of soft cheese known as the cottage cheese, and products are very common and popular in the Western societies. In its preparation, milk is coagulated and separated from whey. The coagulation can be brought about by the lactic acid bacteria added in the form of starter with the help of bacterial action emanating from rennet addition. The end-product is creamed for fat enrichment and salted to taste.

Ice Creams. Ice cream is a product which may contain a variety of ingredients in addition to milk, cream, and sugar in frozen state. However, it is impossible to state definitely the composition of commercial ice creams, as it depends upon a number of ingredients used.

In commercial ice cream an emulsifier and stabiliser is used to prevent formation of water crystals as well as to give a fluffy texture to the product. Flavouring extracts like chocolates, fruits, nuts, candies and baked goods are added to enhance their flavour and acceptability.

There are two general types of freezers used in the ice cream manufacture. The batch type freezers are common. However, continuous types freezers are more useful where large quantities of better quality ice creams are produced. Sometimes, the ice cream mixes are subjected to instantaneous quick freezing (IQF) to avoid any separation of the ingredients during the freezing process.

30 Meat and Meat Products

Man has satisfied his hunger with animal food from the earliest of times. The term meat refers to muscle of warm-blooded terrestrial animals; the chief ones being cattle, sheep and pigs. Meat also includes the glands and organs of these animals. Meat products include many of the by-products from animal slaughter such as animal gut used for sausage the fat from the meat used in the manufacture of lard, gelatin, and others.

The annual consumption of meat of any country depends upon its economic status; affluent countries consuming more than others. The per capita consumption of meat in India is of the order of 1.5 kg per annum. The world demand for meat is growing up steadily, because of the preference based on palatability.

COMPOSITION OF MEAT

Meat contains 15 to 20 per cent proteins of outstanding nutritive value. The lean meal contains 20 to 22 per cent proteins. Of the total nitrogen content of meat, approximately 95 per cent is protein and 5 per cent is smaller peptides and amino acids. The amino acid make-up of meat proteins is very good for the maintenance and growth of human tissues.

The fat content of meat varies from 5 to 40 per cent with the type, breed, feed and age of animal. When the animal is well fed, fat deposits subcutaneously as a protective layer around the organs. Then it accumulates around and between muscles. Finally, fat penetrates between the muscle fibre bundles and this is known as "marbling". Marbling is desirable with some meats, because the amount of fat and, consequently, the water holding capacity of the meat greatly influences juiciness.

Meat fats are rich in saturated fatty acids and it is likely that it produces certain forms of atherosclerosis. The cholesterol content of meat is about 75 mg per 100g. The lean portion of meat contains greater proportions of phospholipids (0.5 to 1.0 per cent), and these are located in the membranes of the cell. The fatty acids in the lean portion of meat have a higher proportion of unsaturated fatty acids than tissue fats.

Carbohydrates are found only in very small quantities in meat. Two carbohydrates found in meat are glycogen and glucose. Meat is an excellent source of some of the vitamins of the B complex and a good source of iron and phosphorus. Meat also contains sodium and potassium. The vitamins and minerals are found in the lean portion of the meat. Meat contains the protein hydrolysing enzymes, cathepsins, and these are responsible for the increased tenderness of meat during ageing. The colour of meat is due primarily to myoglobin. Variations in colour of meat depend upon the chemical state of myoglobin is stable. Haemoglobin also contributes to the colour of meat to some extent.

CLASSIFICATION OF MEAT

Mutton

Sheep carcasses, based largely on the age of the animal, are classified under three main classes:

Lamb. The flesh of young ovine animals of both sexes whose age is twelve months or under. Lamb carcasses, as a group, are distinguished from mutton carcasses by their smaller and lighter bones, lighter coloured flesh and softer and whiter external and internal fats. The usual test for lamb carcass is the "break joint" of foreleg. When the foot is broken off sharply from the leg above the regular joint, the break shows four distinct ridges that appear smooth, moist and red with blood.

Yearling Mutton. Carcasses of young sheep, usually from 12 to about 20 months older, are termed yearling mutton. Such carcasses are distinguished from lamb carcasses by harder and whiter bones, darker and somewhat coarser flesh and thicker external and internal fat. The break joint of the foreleg usually breaks in ridges similar in shape to a lamb joint, but the surface is rough, porous, dry and lacks redness.

Mature Mutton. This is the flesh of both males (castrated as well as uncastrated) and females of the ovine species that are 20 months in age at the time of slaughter. The colour of the mature mutton ranges from light to dark red. The break joint fails to break due to the hardening and ossification of bones. Mutton has a strong characteristic flavour different from the delicate flavour of lamb. With proper preparation, however, either lamb or mutton will be acceptable to the most people.

Pork

Pork is the meat of swine. Good quality pork is obtained from animals between the ages of 3 to 22 months before the amount of fat becomes excessive. Pork is not differentiated according to the age and the size of pigs. Generally, pork has more fat than other meats. Because of this, pork is a tender meat. The colour of young lean pork is highly pink and changes to rose as the animals matures. Bacon is the cut from the belly portion of hog carcass and has a high percentage of fat.

Organs Meats

These include liver, kidney, heart, sweetbread (thymus and pancreas), brain, lung, tripe (first and second stomach of the ruminants), head and tail of the animal. From the point of view of economy, variety and nutritive value, these organ meats are less expensive and more nutritive.

Sausages

These are made of ground or minced meat. Mostly cured meat and, to a lesser extent, uncured meat are used for this purpose. There are hundreds of varieties of sausages marketed under different classes depending upon whether the ground meat is fresh or cured, and whether the sausage is cooked or uncooked, smoked or unsmoked, and dried or not during manufacture. The cooked and smoked sausages are known as table readymeats.

COOKING OF MEATS

Cooking can make meat more or less tender than the original raw cut. When meat is cooked, three types of changes contribute to the increased tenderness. They are: the melting of fat, dissolution of collagen in hot liquids to become soft gelatin, and tissue softening and muscle fibre separation. There are also toughening influences of heating. Overheating can cause muscle fibres to contract and meat to shrink and become tougher; evaporation of moisture occurs and dried out tissues become tougher.

There are two methods of cooking meat: dry heat and moist heat methods. Selection of the method to use for a meat cut depends upon whether it is a tender or less tender cut. Less tender cuts become more tender when prepared by moist heat methods, because this provides a means for the conversion of collagen to gelatin. Moist heat methods of cooking include braising, stewing (cooking in simmering water) arid pressure cooking. Tender cuts do not require the conversion of connective tissue. Then, they are cooked by dry heat methods, which include roasting, broiling, pan broiling and frying.

For any method of cooking, an appropriate cooking temperature must be chosen. Generally, lower cooking temperature for a longer period of time is better than a higher temperature for a short period of time for any degree of doneness. This results in decreased drip loss, less shrinkage, increased juiciness and more uniform colour throughout the cut.

Testing for doneness is an important aspect in meat cookery. This is tested by the use of a meat thermometer. The recommended temperatures in the centre of the cut for rare, medium, and well done stages for lamb are 77°C, 79°C and 82°C, respectively; and for boar 60°C, 71°C and 77°C. Fresh pork is to be heated to well done stage 70°C, to destroy Trichinella spiralis. Moist heat methods will produce well done meats in every instance. It is not necessary to use a thermometer when employing moist heat cookery methods.

Dry Heat Methods

Tender cuts of lamb and pork may be cooked by these methods. Use of dry heat permits selection of the desired final interior temperature of meat. Some of these are:

Roasting. It is one of the simplest and most commonly used method of cooking meats. The meat is placed uncovered on a rack in a shallow pan to keep it out of drippings. A meat thermometer is inserted into the thickest part of the meat, taking care that it does not touch bones or fat. The roasting pan is placed in the centre of the oven and an oven temperature of 163°C is maintained till the desired internal temperature is indicated on the meat thermometer. This ensures adequate browning of meat for good flavour and appearance. For small roasts, an oven temperature of 177°C is used. Roasts continue to cook at the centre even after they have been removed from the oven. This is because heat is transmitted into the interior from the outer surface.

Broiling. This consists of cooking meat by direct radiant heat such as the open fire of a gas flame, live coals, or electric oven. In open fire or coal broiling, heat comes from below; whereas in oven broiling, the heat comes from above. Broiling is applied to tender cuts that are at least 2.5 cm thick. Thinner cuts will he too dry, if broiled.

To broil, meat is placed on a rack; and the rack is adjusted in such a way that the top of the meat is some 5 to 10 cm from the source of heat. Shorter distances are used for thinner cuts of meat .A tray should be placed beneath the meat rack to collect the melted fat. Broiling is carried out at a temperature of 176°C until the top side is brown.

Pan Broiling. In pan broiling, heat is transferred to meat primarily by conduction from the pan or griddle. Meat is placed in a cold griddle and heated so that the meat cooks slowly. Any fat that accumulates in the pan is removed in order that the meat will continue to pan broil rather than pan fry. Pan broiling is the preferred method of cooking for thin cuts of meats, because the equipment required for cooking is simpler. A low temperature is sufficient to brown the meat. Pan-broiled meat should be turned occasionally to ensure uniform heat penetration.

Frying. This is a useful method for cooking tender cuts of meat which are thin (about 1 to 1.5 cm thick). There are two methods of frying: pan frying and deep-fat frying. In pan frying, a small amount of fat is added to the frying pan so that the melted fat is about 0.5 cm deep. In deep-fat frying, the melted fat will be deep enough to cover the meat.

In pan frying, as with pan broiling, it may be necessary to turn meat occasionally to develop an even colour on the meat; but the turnings should be kept to a minimum. The temperature is to be controlled such that the meat does not develop a broiled flavour and dryness. With high temperatures, fat decomposes to acrolein which impairs the flavour of meat. With thin cuts and a properly controlled temperature, the interior of the meat will be well done before the exterior becomes too brown.

In deep-fat frying also, the control of temperature is very important. Too high a temperature not only causes the fat to smoke but also the meat to be undergone in the middle, when the outside has a pleasing colour. If the temperature is too low, it will lengthen the frying time and result in a greasier product.

Moist Heat Methods

Moist heat methods are used for less tender cuts of meat. There are:

Braising. In this method of cooking, the meat is first carefully browned on all sides by broiling, pan broiling or frying. Then a small amount of water is usually added to the browned meat and the pan is covered with a tight fitting lid and cooking is continued with a low heat until the meat becomes tender.

It is not necessary to add water in braising, because steam from the water in the meat itself can provide the moisture needed for changes that take place in meat during braising. Water, when added, should be kept to a minimum. The cooking liquid from the braised meat is very flavourful and can be used for making gravy or sauce.

Stewing. Large pieces of tough cuts are cooked in water until tender. Meats that are to be stewed may be browned, if desired, or simmered in water with no preliminary browning at all. The meat is placed in a kettle or vessel with sufficient water to cover the meat. The vessel is then covered and heated so that the water simmers.

Pressure Cooking. Braising as well as simmering of meat takes a long time for cooking. In pressure cooking, a relatively short cooking time is required, as cooking is done in steam at a temperature higher than that of boiling water. Pressure cooking brings about the same changes in meat as in other methods of cooking with moist heat. However, pressure-cooked meats are less juicy and cooking losses are great.

Cooking Frozen Meat

Frozen meats may be cooked by the usual cooking methods, either in the frozen condition or after thawing. Frozen meats take about one-and-a-half times more time to cook than the unfrozen cuts of the same size and shape. Frozen meat may be thawed in a refrigerator or room temperature or in running water. Refrigerator thawing is recommended, as it results in uniform thawing as well as the best appearance of the meat. there are no differences in the tenderness, juiciness and flavour associated with the cooking of frozen or thawed cuts of meats.

Curing of Meat

The prime object of ageing or ripening as well as use of tenderisers is to increase the tenderness of meat. The curing of meat has additional objectives. Curing brings about the modification of meat that effects preservation, flavour, colour and tenderness due to added curing agents.

Originally, curing was practised as a means of preservation prior to pre-refrigeration days. In less developed countries, curing is still an important method of preservation. When modem methods of preservation are available, the prime purpose of curing is to produce the unique flavoured meat products; and a special purpose is to preserve the red colour of meat. Thus, cured meat remains red on cooking, while in the uncured condition they become brown.

The ingredients used for curing are: common salt, sodium nitrate or nitrite, sugar, and spices. Salt retards microbial growth and gives flavour to the meat. Nitrite fixes the red colour of myoglobin. Nitrite also has a beneficial effect on the flavour of cured meats as well as an inhibitory effect on Clostridium botulinum.. Sugar helps stabilise colour, counteract saltiness and also adds flavour, while spices are added mainly for flavour.

During curing process, the curing mixture may be rubbed dry on the surface of a cut of meat or the meat may be immersed in a solution of the curing agent (pickling). These processes of curing are slow when the meat cut is large. The curing ingredients may be much more rapidly and uniformly distributed throughout the meat by pumping the solution via an artery is intact or the cure may be injected with multiple needles into the cut of meat.

During curing by salt, the high osmotic pressure of the external fluid initially draws water and soluble proteins out of the meat. Later, salt diffuses into the meat and binds to the proteins, causing some expelled protein to diffuse back in. This causes a swelling of the meat. The salt-protein complex that forms bind water well.

Smoking

The cured meat may be dried and smoked. Smoking was also used originally as a method of preservation, but today smoking is used mostly for its flavour contribution and coagulation of proteins. Ham is frequently processed by smoking. The sawdust from hardwoods is used as a fuel for smoking. Slow smoking is preferable, since the extended period enables more drying to occur on the surface. Drying is responsible for much of the preservative action of smoking. The smoke contains compounds having antiseptic properties, which destroy the microorganisms present in meat. Smoking also prevents the development of rancidity in meat.

31
Sea Foods

Fish is found abundantly in all natural waters. It is a valuable source of food and has been used by man from antiquity. With mounting population pressures, most nations are expanding their fish catching power. In addition to fishing in vast oceans, fish cultivation on a large-scale is gaining major significance in may lands. Tapping the wealth of the oceans and inland waters as well as its efficient utilisation have become urgent for the survival of the human race. About 10 per cent of world's fish catch is from inland fisheries.

TYPES OF FISH

It is estimated that there are about 25,000 species of fish living today, varying in size from very small fish to very large sharks. They are second to insects in the largeness of population and outnumber all other vertebrates (backbone animals), mammals, birds, reptiles and amphibians put together.

About 250 different species of fish are used for edible purposes. Edible fishe are classified into two major categories based on their anatomical differences. Fish having vertebrae with fin-appendages, which help balance and steer the body in its movements through water, are termed as finfish. The skin of these fish is covered with protective scales and is abundantly coated with mucous. Fish without a skeleton, but covered with some type of hard shell, are known as shellfish.

The shellfish are of two types: the molluscs and crustaceans. The former have soft unsegmented body, while the latter have segmented bodies. The molluscs are either partially or wholly enclosed in a hard shell that is largely of mineral composition. These include oysters, clams, scallops and mussels. The crustaceans are covered with crustlike shells and they include lobsters, crabs, shrimps and crayfish. Edible shellfish are mainly salt water fishes.

The kinds of finfish available for food are more than those of shellfish and the types differ in different locations. They are found both in salt water and fresh water. The flavour and quality depends partly on the water in which they are grown. Saltwater fish have a more distinctive flavour than fresh water fish. The common sea or marine fish available in the country are all types of shark, salmon, mackerel, Bombay duck, ribbon fish, pomfret, sole, tuna, etc. Fish from fresh water include sardine, mullet, catfish, perch, pearlespot, etc.

Fish are also classified, based on their fat content, as lean (less than 2 per cent), medium (2 to 5 per cent) and fat (more than 5 per cent). Bombay duck, halibut, cod, porch and sole are examples of lean fish. Fat fish include salmon, sardine, mackerel, tuna, etc. In fish with more than 5 per cent fat, the flesh is usually more highly pigmented than that of the low-fat varieties which are generally white fleshed.

COMPOSITION AND NUTRITIVE VALUE

The composition of fish varies considerably, amongst other factors, due to variation in fat content, which varies from 0.1 per cent to about 25 per cent. Many factors like the season, sex and stage of maturity determine the fat content of fish. In all cases, the liver and viscera (the pyloric caecum and mesenteria) constitute the location of fat depot. However, fats are also encountered in muscle tissue, skin, mutt and roe (mass of egg fish).

The principal component of most fish are glycerides of fatty acids which make up 95 per cent of the oil. Fish oils differ remarkably from vegetable oils in containing a great variety of fatty acids, specially highly unsaturated fatty acids having four to six unsaturated linkages.

Fish is an excellent source of protein. The protein content of fin fish is, on an average, about 20 per cent. The muscles of some lean fish, as compared to the best meat, contain exceptionally higher levels of proteins. Asa whole, the protein content of shellfish is lower than that of fin fish.

Fish contains some glycogen, shellfish containing a higher proportion some shell fish have 3 to 5 per cent glycogen. The sweet taste of various shell fish is due to glucose formed from the glycogen by enzymic action. Fish is a good source of minerals. It contains more minerals than other types of meats. Fish meat is a good source of copper, sulpher and phosphorus.

Fish oils are the richest known sources of vitamins A and D. However, there are extreme differences in the vitamin reserves of different species. Fish flesh is a fair source of thiamine, being somewhat poorer in this vitamin than most meats.

Fish proteins are also easily digested. The amino acid pattern of fish protein closely approximates that found in any other class of animal protein. Generally, fish meat has lysine and histidine at a high level and, occasionally, methionine and tryptophan on the low side of mammalian meat. Because of their high nutritive value, fish protein concentrates (FPC) have been developed from inexpensive and surplus fish to combat malnutrition of people around the world.

PRESERVATION AND PROCESSING

As fish is a highly perishable commodity, various methods have been devised to preserve it. Before preservation fish is washed with clean water to remove slime, blood stains, etc. Larger fish are gutted (i.e., all the internal organs or viscera are removed) and the body cavity is washed. The various methods adopted for preservation are: drying, salting, smoking, freezing, and canning.

Sun-drying is the most ancient method. Drying removes moisture from the tissues and helps to arrest bacterial and enzymatic putrefaction. In India, over 35 per cent of the total catch of sea fish is cured in the sun. This method is not hygienic; there is an appreciable percentage of loss due to putrefaction and spillage, and the dried fish develops a peculiar odour.

Salting (pickling) is also widely used in India. The dry-salting or wet-salting method is used. In the former method, fish is first rubbed with salt powder and then packed in tubes with dry salt powder sprinkled in between layers of fish. After a period of about 10 to 20 hours, the fish is removed, washed in brine and dried in the sun for 2 to 3 days. In wet-salting, cleaned fish is packed in large vats containing concentrated salt solutions and stirred daily till properly pickled. With large-sized fish, longitudinal slits are made in the flesh to allow penetration of salt. After pickling for 7 to 10 days, the salty water that oozes out from the fish is allowed to drain off. Wet-salted fish is sold without drying. In does not keep for long and, therefore, has to be used within 3 to 4 months. It some countries fish soaked in salt solution are taken out and smoked. Smoked fish is not popular in India.

The above method semployed for curing fish are rather crude and primitive; hence, the products are unattractive. Case hardening, rancidity development, colour changes, mold growth and attack by insects and mites are some of the common defects of fish cured by sun-drying and salting.

Chemicals such as acids, sodium benzoate and ethylene oxide as well as the antibiotic aureomycin can prolong the life of fish. However, many countries do not permit the use of these preservatives. Irradiation of fish by Y-radiations prolongs their storage life by 20 to 25 days. But the current methods of importance, for preserving quality fish, are freezing and canning.

Freezing. This method of preservation can greatly extend the storage period and is effective in keeping the fish in a condition similar to that of fresh fish, if the fish is gutted and frozen down to—29°C within two hours of its catch. In some cases, clean whole fish is frozen. Fin fish are usually frozen as fillets (lengthwise cuts), steaks (crosscut section) or sticks (lengthwise or crosswise cuts from fillers or steaks). Large fish are frozen by the sharp freeze, a comparatively slow freeze. Small fish, fillets and steaks are quick frozen. This type of freezing gives a better produce. The storage life of quality frozen fish, with a low fat content, can be as long as two years.

Some undesirable changes can also take place, if proper care is not taken during freezing. Slow freezing can result in protein denaturation. As the water in the fish freezes, the salt concentration of the muscle tissue increases which causes denaturation of the protein, making it tough and rubbery. Another effect of freezing is desiccation or drying, caused by the freezing equipment. Frozen fish undergo oxidative changes, and fatty fish become rancid more quickly than the lean ones. Desiccation and oxidation can be prevented by protecting fish properly with suitable wrappers before freezing.

Preservation of fish by freezing is not yet widespread in India. Cold storage facilities are available in areas where fisheries are highly developed.

Canning. While high-fat fish do not store as well as low-fat fish in the frozen state, oily fish are the most suitable for canning. Salmon, tuna, sardine, herring, lobster, shrimp, etc., are canned. In the case of salmon, tuna, sardine and mackerel additional fish or vegetable oil is commonly added to the fish prior to can closure; shrimps are canned in brine. Canning retains the natural flavour of the fish. Large quantities of certain types of fish are canned in this country mostly for export purposes.

Shell fish become dark or discoloured during canned storage. This is due to the release of hydrogen sulphide from the sulphur components of the fish, which reacts with the iron in the can to give black iron sulphide. This can be avoided by using an enamel, specially enamel containing zinc, since the zinc sulphide formed is white in colour.

FISH PRODUCTS

A number of products are prepared from fish. These include fish meal used as animal feed, fish flour used for protein enrichment of human food, fish oils used for feeding and industrial purposes, fish glue, isinglass—a high grade fish collagen used for the clarification of wines, beer, vinegar, etc.

Fish Meal. It is prepared from the parts of fish not used for human food, and sometimes from the whole fish of less flavoured species, by grinding the material usually with the removal of some oil, followed by dehydration. Fish meal, on an average, is composed of proteins 55 to 70 per cent; fat 2 to 5 per cent minerals 10 to 12 per cent; and moisture 6 to 12 per cent. Fish meal is used as animal and poultry feeds. Low grade fish meal is used as manure in plantations of tea, coffee and tobacco. Considerable quantities of fish meal are produced in India.

Fish Flour. It is possible to extract oils and fatty substances from ground fish tissues by solvent extraction to such an extent that no fishy odour or flavour remains. The fat extracted tissue, after stripping off solvent, dehydration and milling, gives a bland highly nutritious powder rich in high quality protein and minerals. This product, when produced underproper bacteriological and sanitary control, is good for use as human food and is known as fish flour or fish protein concentrate (FPC).

Fish flour, properly manufactured and packaged, can retain bland and nutritive properties almost indefinitely. The flour can be incorporated at 3 to 10 per cent levels into a variety of dishes without any adverse effect upon their acceptability. Fish flour contains 85 to 90 per cent of high quality proteins. It is estimated that food shortages and high quality protein needs in several areas of the world can be alleviated by fish flour at a very low cost.

Fish Oils. These are of two kinds: liver oil and fish body oil. Liver oil is the principal natural source of vitamin A and, to a lesser extent of vitamin D. Fish such as cod, halibut, tuna, and shark are good sources of fish liver oils. The oil and vitamin A contents vary in different fish. Body oil is obtained from fish such as sardine, herring and salmon.

Liver oil is obtained by different methods. The most common method is by cooking good quality minced fish liver at 85° to 95°C. This results in the disintegration of liver cells and freeing of oil. The oil floating on the steam condensate can be skimmed off or separated by centrifugation.

Fish body oils are produced along with fish meal. Fish is first ground to a pulp and steamed. The oil and water get separated from the protein. The cooked flesh is then pressed. The "press cake" is worked up for fish meal. The press liquor or "stick water" is concentrated and oil recovered.

32
Poultry, Eggs and Egg Products

The term 'Poultry' refers to the domestic fowls reared for their flesh, eggs, or feathers and includes chicken, ducks, geese, turkeys and pigeons? Of these, chickens and turkeys are most commonly used for their me.

CLASSIFICATION

Chickens are classified into different types, depending on the fowl's ability to produce a product of commercial value; egg type, meat type, dual- purpose type, and miscellaneous type. Meat types are generally large in size with plenty of flesh but they are not good layers. The meat is tender. The dual-purpose types also yield meat of excel lent quality alongwith a good number of eggs. The classification, according to Indian standards is as follows:

Broiler or Fryer. Chicken of 8 to 10 weeks of age of either sex, tender-meated with soft, pliable, smooth textured skin and flexible breastbone cartilage.

Rooster. A young chicken, usually 3 to 5 months of age, of either sex, tendermeated with soft, pliable, smooth textured skin and breastbone cartilage that may be somewhat less flexible than that of die broiler or fryer.

Stag. A male chicken, usually under 10 months of age, with coarse skin somewhat toughened and darkened flesh, and a considerable hardening of the breastbone cartilage.

Stewing Chicken or Fowl. A mature chicken, usually more than 10 months of age, with meat less tender than that of a roaster and non-flexible breastbone tip.

Cock. A mature male chicken, usually over 10 months of age with coarse skin, toughened as well as darkened meat and hardened breastbone tip.

Other forms of poultry are classified in a similar way.

POULTRY PROCESSING

Plants for dressing poultry will vary with size upto the largest that can process 10,000 birds per hour. These modern plants are efficient continuous line facilities, in which the birds are moved from operation to operation via monorail. Live birds are chalked, electrically stunned, bled, scalded to facilitate feather removal, plucked off feathers, eviscerated, government inspected, washed and chilled, dried, packaged, and frozen (if production calls for freezing). The operations can be partially mechanised and are highly efficient in large plants since the birds purchased are remarkably uniform with respect to size, shape, weight, and other characteristics. To ensure high quality uniform birds, large processors, generally contract with the growers far in advance and set up rigid specifications on the kind of bird they want.

Slaughter and Bleeding. Birds, generally, are not fed for 12 hours before slaughter to ensure that their corps are empty, which makes for cleaner operations. Bleeding time depends upon efficiency of the cut, type of bird, and whether the bird was electrically stunned or not before cutting. Bleeding may take anywhere from 1 to 3 minutes depending upon these factors. But bleeding must be quite complete in order to produce the desirable white yellow skin colour in the final dressed bird.

Scalding. After bleeding, the birds are conveyed through a scalding tank. Scalding loosens the feathers and makes for easier plucking and pinfeather removal. The higher the temperature, the shorter the time required; but careful time as well as temperature control is very important, because at higher temperatures there is a greater danger of removal of portions of skin in the defeathering machines. Scalding may be done at 60°C in about 45 seconds, or more safely with less chance of skin removal at 52°C in about 2 minutes. Optimum conditions must be established for the kind of bird being dressed.

Defeathering. This is commonly done mechanically by a device that has a multiplicity of rotating rubber fingers. This removes all but a few remaining pinfeathers, which are then removed by dipping the bird in melted wax. Chilling to harden the wax, and then peeling.

Evisceration. This is generally done in a separate cool room. Evisceration includes inspection of the viscera by a veterinarian or someone under his supervision. The lungs and other organs that are difficult to dislodge may be removed by suction tubes. Birds passing inspection are thoroughly washed.

Chilling. The washed birds are rapidly chilled from about 32°C to 1.7°C to prevent bacterial spoilage and to preserve quality. Chilling is done with ice- slush, amid the birds absorb a small amount of moisture from the slush which makes them more succulent after packaging. But the maximum allowable water pickup is fixed by law. After chilling, birds are drained of excess moisture and sized as well as graded for quality.

Packaging. The graded poultry may be packaged as fresh poultry in boxes surrounded by crushed ice. If so, birds must be kept below 4.4°C and moved to retail channels rapidly, because shelf-life may be only a few days. Shelf-life will depend upon the bacterial load. Should this be about 10,000 organisms per square centimeter of surface, which is not uncommon, odour and slime will develop even at 4.4°C in about 6 days.

To prolong storage life, much poultry is individually wrapped in low-moisture and low-oxygen transmission films or bags and is frozen. When this is done, the bags are made to fit snugly; and the birds are vacuum packed in the bags to remove all air, since the fat of chicken is highly susceptible to oxidation.

NUTRITIVE VALUE

The composition of the edible parts of chicken depends upon the cut and the method of cooking. Roasted white meat, without the skin, will contain about 64 per cent water, 32 per cent protein, and 3.5 per cent fat. Roasted dark meat, without the skin, contains about 65 per cent water, 28 per cent protein, and 6 per cent fat. The skin is higher in fat. Chicken flesh contains more protein and less fat than red meat. The protein is of excellent quality and contains all of the essential amino acids needed by man. The fat is more unsaturated than the fat of red meat and this can provide nutritional advantages. Like other animal tissue, poultry flesh is a good source of vitamin B and minerals. Because of this high protein to fat ratio, it is a favoured food for weight watchers, elder people who must restrict their intake of fat, and patients with vascular sclerotic tendencies. Of course, poultry is also an all around excellent food from babyhood to old age.

EGGS AND EGG PRODUCTS

The eggs of many species of birds have been in use as an item of food from prehistoric times. An average Indian's diet is seriously deficient in important proteins of animal origin. It is now widely recognised that the easiest and most practical method of removing this inadequacy from our diet is to supplement it with eggs. There is a misconception among people that egg is non-vegetarian. But practically all the eggs sold in the market are infertile (lifeless) and, therefore, they may be termed vegetarian eggs. Vegetarians who have no objection to take milk, should have no objection to take eggs. However, there is still a need to popularise the consumption of eggs. The demand for eggs in the country is increasing rapidly and currently it is of the order of 15,000 mill ion per annum.

NUTRITIVE VALUE

Eggs have an excellent nutritive value. They contain 12 to 14 per cent proteins, which are well-balanced with respect to all the essential amino acids. The egg prow ins are easily digested and their quality is comparable to that of meat. The lipids of egg constitute 10 to 12 per cent and they are composed of a high percentage of unsaturated fatty acids. Much of the calorie (about 80 Kcal per egg) contribution is due to the fat contained in yolk. Minerals are present to the extent of 1 per cent in egg. They include iron, phosphorus, calcium and sulphur. The yolk is a particularly important source of iron (1.42 mg per egg); practically the whole of iron is present in a form in which it can be easily utilised.

Eggs are an excellent source of vitamin A which, again, is present in the yolk. The yolk is also a good source of vitamin D, which is not commonly found in other foods. The egg-yolk is second only to fish oil in this respect. The quantity of vitamin D depends upon the amount of direct sunshine the layers get. Egg is also a good source of vitamin B. The yolk of the egg also contains about 250 mg of cholesterol, a fact which makes it necessary for some people on special diets to restrict their intake of eggs. Thus, with its rich protein, lipid, mineral, and vitamin contents as well as good storage qualities, egg is more useful as food than even milk.

EGG QUALITY

Egg is an excellent food for man and, as such, its quality is of very great importance. If proper care is not taken, the egg quality deteriorates rapidly and its food value is adversely affected. A number of factors constitute egg quality including both external and internal factors. External factors include the size and the shape of the egg as well as condition of the shell. Internal factors determining the quality are the size of the air cell and condition of the albumen, yolk and the germ spot.

The size of an egg is indicated by the weight of the newly laid egg. Hens lay eggs of different sizes, varying from 49 to 70g. The size of the egg depends upon the hen's inheritance, body size, age, diet, stage of laying, season of laying, and health of the bird. The indigenous Indian hens, however, usually lay eggs weighing less than 45 g. The size does not reflect the quality and, similarly, the grade of the eggs does not give an indication of its size. A point of favour of small eggs is that they contain a relatively higher proportion of yolk than large eggs.

The factors affecting the conditions of the shell are its strength, porosity, soundness, texture, colour, and cleanliness. The strength of the shell depends upon its thickness which, in turn, depends upon the nutrition of the bird and other factors. A porous shell is graded lower than a shell with fine pores. The texture of the egg shell varies. This does not materially affect the quality of the inner contents. However, there should not be ridges or grooves spread over a large area of the shell. As already stated, the colour of the shell varies but has nothing to do with the quality of the edible portion of the egg. Finally, eggs must be clean. Any dirt on the egg shell means the presence of a large number of contaminating microorganisms. Eggs may be dry cleaned or wiped with a piece of moist cloth, if they are slightly soiled, or washed with warm water of a temperature of about 10°C higher than that of the egg.

The quality of the internal contents of the egg is determined by the size of the air cell, the denseness of the egg white as well as the size, distinctness, colour and mobility of the yolk. As the quality of the egg deteriorates, the size of the air cell increases and the white becomes thinner. The yolk should be centred in the egg and its position tends to drift off-centre when the egg becomes stale. Since yolk colour depends largely on the colour of the chicken feed, the colour is not an indication of the egg quality; though eggs with darker yolks are preferred. The yolk should be free from abnormalities, which include blood spots embryonic development, mold growth, discolouration and other signs of spoilage.

EVALUATION OF EGG QUALITY

The quality of egg in the shell is evaluated, most commonly, by a process known as candling. The egg is held up to a light source in a dark room and is viewed in silhouette, while being rotated. Candling will reveal a crack in the shell, the size of the air cell, the firmness of albumen, the position as well as mobility of yolk, and the possible presence of foreign substances. Sometimes the quality of egg is determined by dropping the egg in water. If the egg sinks, it is considered good; while it is considered to be of poor quality if it floats. However this is not an effective method for determining the egg quality. It only gives a rough idea and shows that the egg floating in water has lost in weight due to dehydration.

Where it is feasible, the quality of an egg can be graded by breaking the egg Out of the shell. The appearance of the shelled egg is an excellent indication of its freshness. Fresh egg have a high yolk rather than a flat yolk, i.e., the yolk index, a figure derived by dividing the height of the yolk by its diameter, is high in fresh eggs. Also, the height of the thick albumen (albumen index) indicates the quality of egg; fresh eggs have a larger amount of thick white relative to runny thin white. This causes a stale egg to spread out over a larger area than a fresh egg.

EGG GRADING

Eggs, whose quality has been determined, are graded for marketing purposes. They are graded according to size and quality, which are independent of each other. In India, eggs are graded according to weight into four grades, whose weight specification is as indicated in table. In the US, based on minimum weight, eggs are graded into six classes: as jumbo, extra-large, large, medium, small and pee wee. Grading according to size helps the buyer obtain a particular quality of the food material for a given price.

Clean eggs with unbroken shell are graded on quality depending upon the depth of air-cell, centering of egg yolk and freedom from defects, as Grade A and B in India. These are further subdivided based on size. In the US, eggs are classified into three groups as AA, A and B.

TABLE. 32.1 WEIGHT SPECIFICATION OF HEN EGGS

Grade	*Weight of individual egg (g)*
Extra-large	above 60
Large	53-59
Medium	45-52
Small	Below 45

EGG PROCESSING

Egg Freezing. Eggs, in addition to storage in the shell, may be preserved by freezing or by the drying of their contents. An egg cannot be frozen in the shell, since the egg shell would crack with the expansion of liquids when frozen. Therefore, the whole of the liquid content of the egg is frozen or it is separated into yolk and white, and then frozen.

One of the important problems in freezing is the control of micro organisms. To reduce contamination, the shells are usually washed just before the eggs are broken from the shell, and then freezing is done as quickly as possible. Because of the prevalence of Salmonella which are pathogenic, it is better to pasteurise the white, yolk, or whole egg. Egg-white is very sensitive to heat, being easily coagulated very near the pasteurisation temperature. By heating for 2 minutes at 58°C albumen becomes turbid and viscous and loses the foaming properties. Whole egg or yolk, in contrast, can be pasteurised at 60° to 61.5°C for 3.5 to 4.0 minutes, without significant changes in physical and functional properties. The pasteurised whole or separated eggs are placed in cans or suitable containers and frozen in a sharp freezer room with circulating air — 29°C. Freezing may take from about 48 to 72 hours.

While the frozen egg white retains its qualities fairly well, yolk and whole egg cannot be frozen satisfactorily. On freezing, the yolk or whole egg becomes viscous and gummy, a condition known as 'gelation' resulting in altered functional properties. Yolk gelation is due to the formation of ice crystals on the lowering of the storage temperature to below 6°C (the freezing point of yolk is about 1.0°C). Freezing also reduces the distance between reactants, such as lipoproteins, which enhance their aggregation. This is prevented by the addition of sugar, salt or maize syrup to the egg yolk and whole egg before freezing. Sugared yolk is used satisfactorily in dessert products, confectionery and other products that tolerate sugar, while salted yolk is used in the manufacture of mayonnaise. By enzyme treatment with pepsin, it is claimed that egg yolk maintains functional properties during frozen storage.

Dried Eggs. Drying is another method of egg preservation and there is a demand for egg powder for the preparation of commercial egg products. The white, yolk or whole egg, after pasteurisation, may be dried by any of the several methods of drying. The most common method employed for drying egg is spray drying. The liquid egg is forced through an atomizer as a fine spray into a drying chamber through which hot air is blown. The powdered egg is cooled, collected and packaged.

Egg white contains traces of glucose. When the dehydrated white or whole egg is stored at temperatures much above freezing, the glucose combines with egg proteins resulting in browning. To prevent this, glucose is to be removed with glucose oxidase or by fermentation with yeast prior to drying.

The functional properties of an egg are not adversely affected by drying. The heat coagulation properties remain practically the same. Dried eggs keep best when the moisture content is low, and if they are kept in tightly sealed containers. Dried egg white is quite stable during storage. However, objectionable changes in colour, flavour, odour and solubility occur when either dried yolks or whole eggs are held at temperatures higher than 5°C. A lower temperature retards the undesirable changes, until at 18°C when very little change occurs. Dried eggs may be reconstituted before use by mixing with an appropriate quantity of water. The nutritive value of frozen eggs and dried eggs will practically be the same as that of shell eggs, if properly stored.

EGG SUBSTITUTES

Because of the high cholesterol contents of egg yolk several commercial egg substitutes have been introduced for a cholesterol-free diet. The basic principle of these substitutes is to eliminate the egg yolk and to retain the natural egg white. Various ingredients are added to the egg white to simulate the whole fresh egg. Egg substitutes are available in fresh, refrigerated or frozen forms. The nutritional and caloric values of the substitute depend upon the ingredients. Though they are used in various products where the whole fresh egg is an ingredient, the result is not frequently identical to the product made using fresh egg. However, for some preparations like scrambled egg and French omelette so they are found quite satisfactory.

OTHER PRODUCTS

The egg is important as a food and food ingredient. It is one of the most nutritious foods we consume, and can be prepared in many different ways by itself such as scrambled eggs. It is also a major ingredient in dishes such as souffles, and is an essential part of many baked goods, candies, and other foods. The egg functions in many different ways to give food products, in which it is used, certain desirable characteristics. It leavens, binds, thickens emulsifies, tenderises, retains moisture, adds flavour as well as colour, and improves nutritive value.

Eggs are consumed as shell eggs and as further processed egg products. Egg production has changed through the years; from small farm flocks of less than 100 to larger flocks producing eggs under more closely con trolled conditions. Now flocks of 100,000 birds are common.

The egg and component parts of the egg are very unique materials. The composition of the basic parts and the mixture of these parts ; egg white, egg yolk, and whole egg. Whole egg is actually a mixture of the white and yolk in natural proportions. There are 60 parts by weight of liquid white to 40 parts by weight of liquid yolk. The commercial yolk shown is not actually pure yolk but has about 10 per cent egg white, which stays with the yolk during breaking and separating. Pure yolk with the adhering white removed would have 51 per cent solids, of which 16 per cent is protein and 31 per cent lipids.

Egg white is made up of mostly proteins which have rather unusual properties. Egg yolk is a very complex mixture of essential lipids and proteins. It is further complicated by the inclusion of whites. Half of the water in egg is distributed as free water and the rest is bound to three distinct fractions; the water soluble protein, the high-density lipoprotein, and the low-density lipoprotein. Most of the lipids are in the low-density lipoprotein fraction which, in unaltered egg yolk liquid, is in a finely dispersed state. It has been postulated that the triglycerides make up the inner core of the highly emulsified shell and then protein molecules are wrapped around the shell. The high-density lipoproteins are contained in granules which can be removed by centrifuging. All of the lipids of unaltered egg yolk are associated with lipoproteins.

LEAVENING POWER

This is sometimes called the aerating, foaming, or whipping property of eggs. It means the ability to incorporate air by itself or in a mixture with other ingredients and to hold the aerated structure long enough so that it can be set by heat, drying, or other means. Foams created by egg white are some what different from these created by whole egg and yolk.

BINDING AND THICKENING

Proteins of egg coagulate during heating and, thus, give to eggs the ability to bind pieces of food together or to thicken foods such as custard and puddings. Coagulation is sometimes referred to as denaturation or gelation. Eggs go through the denaturation, flocculation, and insolubility stages during heat coagulation.

EMULSIFYING POWER

Egg yolk, whole egg, and egg white are all good emulsifiers. Actually, egg yolk is rated as four times as effective an emulsifier as egg white; and whole egg is intermediate between the two. There are excellent emulsifying properties of egg yolk are attributed to the lecithoproteins. However, it has been observed that the ether-insoluble portion of whole egg is the most important emulsifying substance.

TENDERISING

Eggs contribute to smoothness, moistness, and a desirable texture in baked products. One reason for this is that they are known to retard crystallisation of sugar.

MOISTURE RETENTION

In baked goods, eggs help to retain moisture during baking and also during storage. Eggs bind the ingredients together and offer a barrier through which it is difficult for moisture to escape.

FLAVOUR

Eggs are, of course, good for eating by themselves. They have a distinct flavour which affects baked products. They also help flavour by imparting better mouth feel to these products.

NUTRITION

Eggs have the highest quality proteins of any food and they have most of the essential vitamins. The lipids are easily digested, and there are more unsaturated fats than in any other animal product.

COLOUR

Eggs add colour to the products in which they are used, though this colour can be easily substituted by the use of other colouring materials. There are some products, however, in which the Standards of Identity will not permit other colouring added and where colour of the eggs is essential to indicate richness of the product. An example is egg noodles.

33
Candied Foods

A fruit impregnated with cane sugar and glucose, and subsequently drained and dried, is called as candied fruit. Candied fruits covered or coated with a thin transparent coating of sugar, which imparts it a glossy appearance, are called glaced fruits. When candied fruit is coated with crystals of sugar, either by rolling it in finely powdered sugar or by allowing the sugar crystals from a dense syrup to deposit on it, it becomes what is called crystallised fruit.

CANDY MAKING

The process for making a fruit candy or candied fruit, is practically the same as that employed in the case of preserves, with the only difference that the fruit is impregnaled with a higher percentage of sugar or glucose. A certain amount of invert sugar or glucose is substituted in place of cane sugar. The total sugar content of the impregnated fruit is kept at about 75 per cent to prevent fermentation. The process of impregnation with sugar must not be hurried through, because otherwise, the fruit would shrivel and sweat and become unfit for glaceing and crystallising.

Fruit and sugar are the main raw materials required for candying. The most suitable fruits are those which posses pronounced flavour, e.g., pineapple, peach, peels of orange, lemon, grapefruit, citron, cherry, ginger, etc. Slightly unripe fruits should be taken, because fully ripe and over-ripe fruits develop jam-like consistency in the syruping process. Canned fruits of good quality can also be used.

Cane sugar is employed in conjunction with glucose or with invert sugar. Glucose and invert sugar are commercially available under different names. They are briefly described here.

Confectioner's Glucose. This is also known as maize syrup, crystal syrup or commercial glucose. It is a heavy, slightly sweet, colourless, and semifluid substance.

Dextrose. It is slightly less sweet than cane sugar and is quite stable. It gives very fine granular crystals. When mixed with cane sugar in small proportions, it induces crystal formation in cane sugar also. Thus, it helps in imparting smoothness as well as softness to the candy.

Invert Sugar. When cane sugar is boiled with a small quantity of an organic acid like acetic, citric, or tartaric acid or with cream of tartar, it is hydrolysed into invert sugar, which is a mixture of glucose and laevulose. Usually, 14 g of the acid is added for every 50kg of sugar taken. On hydrolysis, dextrose and laevulose are formed in equal proportions, and the mixture is much sweeter than cane sugar alone. Moreover, invert sugar does not crystallise. It also prevents crystallisation of cane sugar in heavy sugar syrups.

BULK STORAGE OF FRUITS

Fruits like *amla* and *myrobalan*, and citrus peels are kept in a strong solution of common salt to remove their astringency. They are usually stored tightly packed in barrels to which brine containing 15 per cent common salt and sulphurous acid equivalent to 2,000 ppm of sulphur dioxide are added to avoid fermentation and undue softening of the fruit. At the time of use, the stored fruit or peel is taken out from the barrel and washed thoroughly in running cold water to leach out as much of the brine as possible. The fruit or peel is then placed in a cooking pan and boiled for about 15 minutes to remove traces of salt as well as to soften its texture. It is then steeped in fresh cold water for about 12 hours; the water being changed 4 to 5 times. This completes the leaching process and makes the fruit firm in texture.

SYRUP TREATMENT

The fruit or peel (after brining, where necessary) is boiled in cane sugar syrup of about 300 Brix containing 0.1 per cent citric or tartaric acid (about l00g of the acid per 100kg of syrup) for 10 to 15 minutes and, thereafter, left in the syrup for about 24 hours. The Brix of the syrup is then raised to 400 by adding more of cane sugar. The whole mass is boiled for about 5 minutes and left for another 24 hours. This procedure is repeated until the Brix of the syrup reaches 600. After that, the strength of the syrup is progressively increased (50 at a time) by adding more sugar and boiling the mass on every alternate day until the final concentration reaches 75° Brix.

The total amount of sugar required for candying is much more than what is really absorbed by the fruit. It varies with the fruit used. The quantity of sugar requires for preparing 1.0kg of candied orange or lemon peel, petha or ash gourd (Benincase cerifera) and carrot is given in the table 33.1.

The syrup left over from the candying process can be used in various ways, i.e., for sweetening chutneys, sauces and pickles; in vinegar making, for candying another batch of the same kind of fruit after suitable dilution.

DRAINING AND DRYING

After the syruping treatment has been completed satisfactorily, the fruit may be removed from the syrup and drained for about half an hour. The drained fruit is placed on the sorting tables to separate any defective and unwanted pieces. The fruit or peel is then wiped with a wet sponge. Sometimes it is dipped for a moment in boiling water to remove the adhering syrup. This is followed by slow drying in the shade, or in a drier at about 66°C for 8 to 10 hours. Candied citrus peel needs drying for 10 to 12 hours.

TABLE 33.1. SUGAR REQUIREMENTS FOR CANDYING

Fruit	*Total Sugar required per kg of candy*		*Sugar actually absorbed by the fruit*
	(kg)	*(g)*	*(g)*
Orange peel	1	106	400
Lemon peel	1	113	380
Petha (ash gourd)	0.45	340	354
Carrot	0	170	377

GLACEING

Syrup just sufficient for the glaceing process is made by boiling a mixture of cane sugar and water in the proportion of 2:1, in a steam-pan at 113° to 114°C and skimming off the impurities as they come up. Heating is then discontinued and the syrup cooled to 93°C. Granulation of the sugar is achieved by rubbing the syrup with a wooden ladle on the side of the pan. Dried candied fruits are passed through this granulated portion of the syrup one by one by means of a fork, and then placed on trays, which are kept in a warm dry room. To hasten the process, the fruit may be dried in a drier at 49°C for 2 to 3 hours. When it becomes crisp, it is packed in airtight containers.

CRYSTALLISED FRUITS

The process of crystallising candied fruit is quite different from that employed for glaceing, but is almost similar to the crystallising of confectionery. Syrup of 700 Brix is employed. To avoid premature granulation of sugar, a sheet of waxed paper is placed on the surface of the syrup. The candied fruit is placed on a wire mesh tray which, in turn, is placed in a deep vessel. The cooled syrup is then gently poured over the fruit so as to cover it entirely. To prevent the fruit from floating, another wire mesh tray is placed on it, and a sheet of waxed paper is placed on the surface of the syrup. The whole mass is left undisturbed for 12 to 18 hours, at the end of which a thin crust of crystallised sugar will be formed. The tray containing the fruit is then removed carefully from the pan, and the surplus syrup drained off. The drained fruits are spread in single layers on wire mesh trays and allowed to dry at room temperature or in driers at about 49°C.

SPOILAGE

There is a likelihood of spoilage occurring due to fermentation, specially in the initial stages of preparation of preserves and candies when the concentration of sugar in the syrup is low. This can, however, be controlled by boiling the product at proper intervals. If candied and crystallised fruits are stored under humid conditions, they throw off some of their sugar owing to absorption of moisture from the air. Further, they become moldy, if they are packed in wet instead of dry containers. There is also the danger of their being attacked by mold, if they have not been sufficiently dried.

PETHA *(BENINCASE CERIFERA)* PREPARATIONS

Take fully mature petha and cut longitudinally into fairly large pieces. Remove the fluffy portion from inside of the slices, and peel each slice separately. Soak the peeled slices for about 30 minutes in lime water diluted with three times the quantity of water. Prick the pieces with a stainless steel needle or fork with pointed bamboo pricks, and cut the slices into pieces of suitable size. Next, prepare 2 to 3 per cent alum solution and bring it to boil. Boil the pieces in this solution till they become tender. Drain and cool them in running cold water. If it is desired to make the pieces perfectly white, a small quantity of sodium sulphite may be added to the alum solution while cooking the slices in it. Now arrange the prepared slices in alternate layers with sugar (half their weight) in a vessel and allow them to stand for 24 hours. During this interval, pieces will give cut sufficient water in which the sugar will dissolve. Ordinarily, the syrup thus formed will be 500 to 600 Brix. Also add citric or tartaric acid at the rate of 0.62 g of the acid for every kilogram of sugar used. Alternatively, add 25 per cent by weight of invert sugar or maize syrup to raise the syrup strength. Boil the slices and the syrup together for about 10 minutes and set them aside for 24 hours. Subsequently, increase the strength of the syrup by 50 Brix on every alternate day till its Brix reaches 700. Allow the pieces to remain in this syrup for 4 to 6 weeks. The product thus got is known as petha preserve, and is highly popular in north India as a sweet delicacy. For candying, bring the whole mass of petha and syrup to boil ; and while still hot, drain the syrup. Roll the drained pieces in finely powdered sugar and dry them on trays at ordinary room temperature.

34
Fruits and Fruit Products

The commercial canning of fruits has increased rapidly during the present century. The use of fruit varieties specially suited to canning and the careful adherencc to established commercial size and quality grades are the two most important fundamentals in the successful commercial canning of fruits. Upgraded canned fruit is unattractive in appearance; is uneven in colour, texture, and maturity ; and is not a product that will command a high enough price to return a reasonable profit to the canner and the grower.

The fruits must be gathered at the proper stage of maturity for canning; i.e., usually it should not be so ripe or so soft as that for eating fresh, yet it should have attained the flavour characteristics of the ripe fruit. The fruits should be picked carefully and transported to the cannery quickly without bruising.

Boxes must be clean and must not be permitted to become moldy and heavily impregnated with fermented and sourced fruit juice or pulp. Painting the boxes with a special coating to preserve the wood and prevent molding, is common practice.

A clean factory operated with strict observance of the fundamental principles of sanitation is essential mandatory to the production of canned fruits of high quality.

CANNING OF FRUITS

APPLES

Apples generally are not canned to any great extent, since they can be kept in refrigerated or controlled atmosphere storage for practically the whole year from one season to another. Canned apples, which are usually available in the larger sizes of cans, are generally used in pies. The canning of apples is considered a by-product industry in most apple-growing countries end as a means of utilising the best quality of culls. The fruit for canning purposes should be of fair size and reasonably free from blemishes. Apples unfit for canning may often be used for cider or vinegar. The two principal forms are quarters or saegments in water and canned apple sauce. Apples for canning should be firm and hold their shape in the can. They should be of good flavour, colour and texture. Acid varieties of white flesh are preferred.

Ripeness of the apples has a pronounced effect on the flavour, colour and character of the finished product. Therefore, maturity is a factor which must be considered in packing apple slices. Excessively green apples tend to produce an excessively firm, green end product, which does not have a desirable flavour. Overripe apples, on the other hand, produce a soft or mushy pack having a bland flavour.

Storage

For temporary or short-term storage between harvest and canning, it is preferable to use stacked bins so as to permit good air circulation rather than bulk storage. When bulk storage is necessary, small piles are preferable and some provision for air circulation is desirable. For prolonged storage, storage at 0°C or controlled atmosphere cold storage should be used for best results.

Washing

Many canners presoak the apples before washing by fluming them in water from the receiving areas to the washers. Mechanical washers equipped with either paddles or high pressure jets are used for washing apples before peeling. In areas where lead arsenic sprays are used, it is advisable to add 1.0 to 1.5 per cent hydrochloric acid to the water in order to remove the residual spray material from the apples. The apples should then be given a fresh rinse to remove the acid.

Grading

The purpose of grading for size is to improve the efficiency of the peeling operation as well as to increase yields by removing small apples and grading the remaining fruits into two or more size groups for delivery to separate peeling lines. The smallest apples may be diverted to juice, the other graded sizes can be handled on peelers set more efficiently for the fruits of one particular diameter size range. In this manner, peeling loss is reduced and skips can be largely eliminated, there by reducing trimming labour. Decayed apples should be removed and discarded by inspectors prior to grading.

Peeling and Coring

The fruit should be washed and sorted before it goes to the preparation tables. It is peeled by mechanical peelers, operated by power, the apples are placed on the peeling knives of the machine by hand. The peeled and cored fruit is trimmed by women, who work at another belt to which the fruit is delivered by conveyor, those who do the trimming also out the fruit into quarters or smaller segments. Ordinarily, the fruit is put immediately in dilute brine to prevent oxidation and browning. The peels and cores, which normally represent 30 to 40 per cent of the weight of the fresh fruit, are usually sent to the vinegar factory to be crushed and pressed for vineger, although some factories have found it profitable to dehydrate the peels and cores for the use for jelly and pectin manufacturers.

Blanching

Before the apples are canned they are usually blanched in one of several ways. A simple process of blanching consists in passing the quartered or sectioned apples through a steam box to soften them, to destroy the oxidase, and to expel the air from the fruit, thereby reducing pinholing of the tin plate. In some canneries, the fruit is immersed in boiling 3 per cent brine for 3 or 4 minutes to accomplish the results mentioned above. It is possible to remove the air by placing the fruit in dilute brine or water and subjecting it to a high vacuum. The air is effectively removed and water enters the fruit tissues to replace the expelled air, thereby increasing the weight of the fruit considerably. Another method in fairly common use consists in heating the fruit several hours in water at 50°C, or lower temperature. And it is found that this treatment removes oxygen from the tissues.

Canning

Following the blanching operation, the hot fruit is packed at once into cans as a solid pack, or a small amount of boiling hot water is added. In most cases, however, the can is practically filled in solid-pack style, and very little liquid is necessary. Type L or similar corrosion-resistant cans should be used.

Filling

The apple slices are filled by semi-automatic or automatic fillers, of which several types are available. It is important to fill the cans hot, adding sufficient hot water or syrup to fill the spaces between the slices. A filling temperature of between 70°C and 80°C is desirable since it is very difficult to bring the centre temperature after closing to the desired processing temperature, specially if the fill is a heavy pack.

Exhausting

More trouble has been experienced by corrosion and pinholing of the tin plate by apples than by other canned fruits. It has been proved by some reputed investigators that corrosion is caused by the malic acid of apples in the presence of air or oxygen and that corrosion can be limited or reduced to a negligible extent if the air is thoroughly expelled from the fruits by blanching and from the can and contents by thorough exhausting.

Sterilising

Apples are easily sterilised on account of their high acidity, but because the fruit is packed tightly in the cans, heat penetration is not very rapid. Nevertheless, sterilisation of 8 to 10 minutes at 100°C in a continuously agitating steriliser has been considered sufficient, if the cans have been filled and sealed above 70°C.

Cooling

Immediately after sterilising, the cans should be water cooled until the average temperature of the contents 35°C to 40°C. Casing canned apple slices at high temperatures may result in softening, loss of normal colour, or darkening or pink discolouration of the product (stack bum).

MANGOES

India is the home of mangoes. A large number of varieties are found in almost all parts of the country. According to statistics collected by the Fruit Development Adviser, Government of India, out of the total fruit acreage, mangoes alone cover about 70 per cent. Uttar pradesh, Tamil Nadu, Karnataka, Bihar and West Bengal lead in mango growing.

Among the numerous varieties, Safaida and Dusehri of U.P.; Alphonso of Ratnagiri, Badami of Mysore, Benishan of East Coast; and Raspuri , Neelam and Mulgoa of Tamil Nadu and Karnataka are the most important varieties for canning. The Bangalora or Totapari mango, which is an assured as well as heavy annual bearer and also yields an excellent pulp or juice, is sometimes canned to give a fairly good canned product. Juicy and fibrous varieties are not quite suitable for canning. Hence, they are mostly used for making juice, squash, nectar, chutney and pickles.

Firm ripe mangoes, that are just developing colour, are picked and ripened in straw. As they ripen, canning ripe fruits are selected daily from the lot. They are washed in water and peeled with hand, and the fruit is cut into 6 to 8 longitudinal slices. For canning as halves, the cheeks or the two broad sides are taken. The slices are placed in 2 per cent common salt solution to prevent their enzymic browning. Plain cans are used. As some of the table varieties have a pH slightly higher than the critical pH of 4.2, it is necessary to add 0.3 to 0.5 per cent citric acid to the syrup for safe processing of the cans in the open cookers. Now-a-days, the practice is to sterilise the cans first in open cookers and then in closed retorts at 0.07 to 0.14 kg/sq. cm as an additional safety measure. The trimmings of the slices and the pulp adhering to the stone can be utilised profitably for the preparation of mango squashes and mango jam.

Mango, being the most important and unique commercial fruit of India and known as the king of fruits, calls for the development of a large-scale canning and preservation of the fruit. Considerable amount of scientific and developmental work has been done in the Central Food Technological Research Institute, Mysore, on various aspects concerning the mango including the storage and long distance transport. Mango products are lickly to find increasing markets in many countries of the world. Canned mango would, in many respects, compare well with the well-known canned peach of commerce.

ORANGES

Oranges are canned to a limited extent only. Satsuma, Mandarin, and Unshu of Japan are the important canning varieties. Being practically seedless unlike the Indian mandarin oranges, such as the loose-jacket mandarin oranges of Nagpur, Coorg, Assam and a few other regions, they are preferred for canning. The segments are easier to handle without much breakage, which would otherwise occur while attempting to remove the seeds. Sathgudi and Malta oranges, which are tight-skinned like the Valencia orange (Citrus aurantium or C. reticulata) , have been found to yield comparatively good canned products. There is a considerable export potential for canned mandarin orange segments. A great deal of care as well as sophisticated techniques for peeling, exhausting, processing and cooling the cans is needed to get a really good canned product.

The peel of the loose jacket oranges can be removed easily with hand. In case of tight skinned oranges prior dipping of fruits in boiling water, as in the case of grapefruits, is necessary to loosen the skin. The segments are separated and the adhering fibres removed. They are then dipped in boiling lye solution of 1 to 2 per cent strength for 20 to 30 seconds, rinsed in warm water, dipped in dilute hydrochloric acid of 0.5 to 1.0 per cent strength to remove traces of alkali, and finally rinsed well in cold water. Any adhering membrane and also seeds are removed by hand. The segments are then carefully filled into plain cans containing some water, to prevent undue breakage of the segments during filling. The filled cans are then drained. A small amount of orange flavour may be added to the syrup. The cans are closed preferably on a vacuum double seamer. Alternatively, the filled cans are exhausted for 15 to 20 minutes at 82°C in a rocking type pasteuriser in an open tank of water. After processing, the cans are cooled in a rocking type cooler. Precautions are necessary to prevent undue breakage of segments and to minimise the loss of delicate flavour of the orange. Orange segments can also be canned as salad alongwith other fruits like mango, pineapple, jackfruit, banana, etc. Canning of sliced oranges, instead of segments, has been found to give a novel product. This approaches the new concept of using the 'whole fruit' as in the case of fruit drinks. Broken segments can be profitably utilised for orange jam, juice, squash, etc.

At present, the internal market for canned oranges is rather limited. There is, however, good scope for developing an export market for the product.

PAPAYA

Papaya slices or cubes can be used for canning. About 0.5 per cent citric acid should be added to the syrup to counteract the high pH of the fruit. Papaya could be canned along with other fruits like pineapple, mango, banana, etc. to get a product similar to the one commercially packed in Australia. Papaya, being a quick-growing fruit, can form the basis for a thriving canning industry. It also yields valuable by-products, such as the enzyme papain and jelly-forming pectin.

PINEAPPLE

The pineapple is a native American product, having been found first in Central and South America, and from these countries the plants have been taken to all tropical sections of the world. It is badly misnamed, as the plant is neither a pine nor an apple. The fruit is produced by the fusion of many flowers produced on a stall. The fruit is highly esteemed, but is very perishable after it has once ripened. Pineapples were canned in Maryland in a small way early in the history of the canning industry.

In India, pineapple are grown mostly in Assam and West Bengal, along the western coast, and in the Godawari district in Andhra Pradesh. Recently, pineapples of an excellent quality with regard to texture, taste and flavour, and canning quality have been grown on an increasing scale in the coorg area of Karanataka state. They have been found to yield a canned product of premium quality. Giant Kew and Queen are the two important varieties. In India, kew is, however, preferred for canning, and the area under it is steadily increasing to meet the mounting demand for canned pineapple within industry.

Harvesting

The fruit is allowed to reach full maturity, not only for maximum flavour and quality, but also texture so that the optimum canning cutout and yields may be attained. Workmen walk along the rows and pick the pineapples from the plants by bending the pineapple sharply. They then cutoff the crown with a sharp knife and place the pineapple on a belt of an extended boom that carries it to a large bin on a special truck. The truck also moves the harvesting machine. When the bin is full, the harvesting machine lifts itself off the truck by four hydraulic lift legs, and the truck drives the bin to the cannery or to the barge for transportation to the cannery. Another truck drives under the harvestor, and the picking continues.

Most of the crop is picked in June, July, August and September, although in the other eight months of the year there is usually enough fruit to permit canning operations for several days of the week on a partial-capacity basis.

The Ginaca Machine

The fruit bins from the fields are lifted mechanically from the trucks and conveyed to a central dumping station. The bins, each holding about 8 tons of fruit, are dumped and pineapples are graded mechanically for size ; each size goes to a Ginaca machine adjusted to its diameter. This machine is entirely automatic in operation. It cuts a cylinder from the centre portion of each fruit, removes the shell, cuts off the shell portions at each end of the cylinder, and removes the core. An eradicator scraps the edible flesh frorn the shell, as completely as possible, for use in the crushed pineapple products or for juice.

In India, however, power driven slicing machines and hand punches, corers and eye removers, are generally employed. As the fruit contains highly active proteolytic enzymes, injurious to the skin, the worker should wear rubber gloves. The fruit, which is at the canning-ripe stage, is sliced on a power-driven slicing machine and the slices are fed to the workers, who remove the outer peel with a curved knife fixed to the edge of the workable. It is, however, preferable to slice the unpeeled whole fruit and then punch out the rings from the slices. From the peeled slices, a circular ring is punched out using stainless steel punches of different diameter ranging from 5.6 to 8.8 cm, the core is then removed with a corer and any remaining eyes and hard portions in the outer periphery of the ring are trimmod off carefully without breaking it. The rings thus prepared are graded visually for size by stringing them on to a stick, dipped in water to remove the adhering broken bits, etc., and then filled into cans.

Trimming

The cylinders from the Ginaca machine are conveyed by belt to the trimmers who inspect each cylinder carefully and trim away any small portions such as the bits of adhering shells at the ends being unsuitable for canning.

Slicing

The trimmed cylinders are carried by chain conveyors through a spray washer to the slicing machine. This machine slices them transversely into rings 1.25 cm thick for No. A 2½ cans.

Grading and Packing

From the slicer, the pieces of pineapple pass on to endless belt conveyors from which they are removed by operators who pack them into cans. The grading for different grades is done while passing over the belt Certain of the packers pick out the pineapple which is to go into the fancy grade; other pick out seconds and broken slices which are packed separately. After band filling into the cans, the pineapple goes either to an exhaust chamber or to the vacuumising chamber, or goes directly to the syruper.

Prevacuumising

The filled cans enter a vacuumising chamber, where they are subjected to vacuum for 5 to 10 seconds. This operation removes air from the tissues of the fruits and changes their appearance from a chalky white to semitransluscency; and gives the product a more uniform colour after canning.

Syruping

The cans are syrupped in a conventional syruper like that used for canned peaches. The syrup is made up, in part from juice expressed from the shells and other by-products. The juice is neutralised with lime, heated to throw out calcium citrate filtered, treated in ion-exchange columns and partially concentrated in vacuum before it is mixed with cane sugar syrup and added to the cans of pineapple. Citric acid is made from calcium citrate.

Double Seaming

The cans are sealed under vacuum by the usual double-seaming operations. The prevacuumising operation and sealing in vacuum make it unnecessary to heat the cans of fruit in an exhaust box.

Processing

The cans of pineapple are processed in continuous pressure cookers at a temperature somewhat above boiling until temperature in the centre of the cans reaches 90°C. The length of process will vary according to the size of can and other conditions. The cans are cooled in water and are trayed and stored in the cooling room until required for labelling and casing.

Cooling

The cans should be cooled in cold water after processing when using rotating cooker, the cans pass from the cooker to a rotating cooker.

Crushed Pineapple

The previously mentioned shredded material is pumped into steam-jacketed kettles and heated to 90°C. Some of the juice is drained away to give a product optimum consistency. If it is to be sweetened, sufficiently heavy syrup is added to give the desired sugar content. The hot mix is packed into cans automatically, sealed, given a short process to ensure keeping quality, and cooled.

By-Products

Shells, trimmings, and other by-product materials are shredded and pressed in a continuous press to recover as much juice as possible. The juice is refined as previously mentioned and is used in canning of the pineapple after mixing with cane sugar syrup. The press cake is dried in rotary drum driers, and the dried product is sold as pineapple bran for feeding to live-stock. Ctiric acid is recovered from the juice, as previously described.

PEACHES

A larger quantity of peaches is canned than that of any other single fruit, although pineapple is now a close rival. Its delicate flavour which persists after canning, its firm texture which persists sterilisation without disintegration, its attractive appearance, and its moderate price have combined to give the peaches its present popularity in western countries. There are two types of peaches: the clingstone and the freestone. Among the former, the Tuscan, which is an early ripening variety. Elberta, Lovell and J.H. Hale are freestone peaches suitable for canning; while Muir is good for drying only. Other varieties are Sherbati, Shani-Punjab, Red Haven and Atom.

Peaches for canning should be of large uniform size, of symmetrical shape, of yellow colour, of close tender fibre, not coarse or ragged, and of good cooking quality, i.e., they should retain their form, size, flavour, colour and aroma during sterilisation in the can. The pit should be small in order to given thick halves that do not flatten during heating.

Grading

Peaches received at the cannery usually include a wide range of sizes and maturities. It is the normal custom to grade the peaches according to size and maturity by means of a mechanical grader. This pre-grading and sizing is accomplished before the fruit has reached canning maturity so as to eliminate or minimise the bruising of the fruit.

Cutting and Pitting

Earlier cutting and halving was done mannually, but now it can be done by machines. All selling peaches are now pitted by machine. Freestone peaches are also pitted by machines unless peaches with split-pits are numerous.

Cutting and Pitting by Hand

A fruit-cutting knife is used to cut the cling peach around the suture from the surface to the pit. A spoon-shaped knife is then inserted from the stem end of the peach, and with this instrument the flesh is cut from the pit.

Freestone varieties are halved and the pit is then easily removed with the cutting knife.

Cutting and Pitting by Machine

The peach is first cut around the suture by machine, then the two halves in the tight grasp of two cups are rotated in opposite directions to free them from the whole pits. Fruit halves and pits are then separated by screen. The pit cavity has a slightly roughened surface that resembles that of the freestone peach.

Peeling and Washing of Clingstone of Peaches

The pitted halves are conveyed (cup down) on a screen conveyor through a spray-type lye peeler in which the lye solution wets only the outer (or skin) surface and not the pit cavity. In this way, the attractive naturally rough surface of the pit cavity is retained and loss of flesh by lye action in the cavity is avoided.

The concentration of the peeling solution is normally between 1 and 2.5 per cent, and the length of application is 30 to 60 seconds. Green fruit requires a stronger solution than the ripe fruit. The concentration of the lye is maintained by adding concentrated lye solution or the dry flake caustic (Flake, NaOH); such addition is necessary because dilution and neutralisation of the lye reduce its strength rapidly.

If the solution is too strong, too much of the flesh is removed entailing excessive loss in weight and decrease in diameter of the fruit. If it is too weak, the fruit is imperfectly peeled and much hand trimming may

Lye-peeled fruit is thoroughly sprayed with cold water to effect complete removal of the peel and the lye residue.

Slicing

Fruit that is not canned as halves is usually discharged from the canning belt to the slicing machine.

Cans

Cans made of 50-25 differential plain electrolytic plate bodies and enamelled electrolytic 25-25 plate ends are recommended for syrup or water pack peaches. For sliced peaches, plain electrolytic bodies and enamelled electrolytic cans are recommended when no colour has been added, but for highly coloured varieties or when colour has been added, inside enamelled electrolytic plate can must be used.

Filling

The peach halves are filled almost exclusively by in-line and rotary type fillers. They should be filled as rapidly as possible after peeling and grading to avoid discolouration from exposure to the air. The cans should be filled with peaches as full as practicable without impairment of quality.

Slices should go over an inspection belt for removal of defective pieces. The slices then are discharged to handpack fillers. Both a rotary and a straight line filler have been used for filling slices.

Syruping

The standards of identity for canned peached specify the densities of the cutout syrup that correspond to label names such as 'heavy syrup' or 'light syrup'.

Syruping of canned peaches is accomplished by rotary and straight line syrupers or by re-vacuumising syrupers. The PVS machine pre-vacuumises the can containing the peaches and allows the syrup to flow into the can while dissipating the vacuum. Its main advantages are a substantial saving of the syrup by providing a constant fill of syrup and, when used in conjunction with a vacuum closing machine or a Steam-Vac closure, exhausting is not required.

If either hot 88°C or deacrated syrup is filled through a valve that will fill to a definite controlled head space, the peel and the lye residue otherwise will darken the surface rapidly.

Peeling and Washing, Freestone Peaches

Steaming

This is considered the most satisfactory method of peeling fully ripened freestone peaches, but does not work for green fruits. The most satisfactory means of steaming consists of placing the halves (pil cavity down) on a suitable belt or in pans, which pass through a scalder. There after having been cooled with water sprays, the skin is lifted from the peaches without picking up the halves. The peaches may then be filled directly from the belt or pans. The time of steaming required is from 1/2 to 2 minutes, depending on the size and maturity of fruit being handled. Longer steaming period tends to reduce oxidative browning that occurs following peeling. Steaming may be accomplished in tomato scalders if available.

Scalding in Water

Peaches may be scalded in very hot water and peeled by hand although this method is not considered as satisfactory as steaming. It does however, result in less mechanical damage than is the case with lye peeling, but requires somewhat more hand labour for peeling.

Combination Steam and Lye

There is a steam and lye combination peeling system. It consists essentially of a long conveyor on which the halved and pitted peaches are placed cup down and then conveyed through a steam scalding section, a lye cascade with a short reaction time, and finally a high pressure spray washing chamber.

Sorting

The peeled fruit passes from the lye peeler on to a slowly moving belt, from which the sorters remove blemished, partly peeled, broken and other unfit pieces. The prime fruit travels to the size-grading machine.

Grading

Usually 5 or 6 size grades are made; the smallest often going to the low- grade line and the largest to the slicers. Cans may be closed satisfactorily without subsequent exhausting by using a Steam-Vac closure.

Exhausting

If thermal exhausting is employed, the cans are given a steam exhaust for approximately 6 minutes at 87°C to 90°C following the syruping operation. Some canners maintain that a longer exhaust (8 minutes) results in better colour, particularly if some oxidative browning has occurred prior to exhausting.

Closing

Following the exhaust period and provided the minimum average closing temperature cannot be maintained above 70°C, it is advisable to use steam-flow closure. In both Steam-Vac and machine vacuum closure, it is essential that the cans have a gross headspace of 8 mm.

If the pre-vaccumising syruper is used for canned peaches, it cannot be used alone to ensure vacuum in cans ; but must be used in conjunction with a Steam-Vac or mechanical vacuum closure, as the syrup is filled relatively cold.

Processing

Cans of peaches should be closed immediately after exhausting and processed at once so that the heat of the exhaust is not lost before processing begins.

Solid pack fruit is normally filled as slices or quarters with as little free liquid as possible. The process required to obtain the desired texture is somewhat longer than that required to obtain commercial sterility. The product is normally filled at a temperature of 93°C and sterility may be obtained by air cooling. However, processes up to 30 minutes at 100°C in rotating cookers or up to 40 minutes at 104°C in still retorts are employed to obtain the desired texture.

Cooling

Immediately after processing, the cans should be water cooled until the average temperature of the contents reaches 35°C — 40°C. If the cans are not cooled sufficiently, the cooking process will continue in the can with the result that the peaches become soft and acquire a dark or pink colour.

Storage

Formerly, the cans were placed on the warehouse floor in stacks approximately 4 to 6 metres high. The warehouse should be cool, dry and well ventilated, and the cans must be protected against the accumulation of moisture to prevent rusting.

PEARS

While there are very many varieties of peas, the Bartlett is unquestionably the one best suited for canning. Its size, regularity in shape, fine texture, bright colour, and excellent flavour are combined better features than those of any other variety. In India, pears are grown in abundance in the Kullu and Kashmir valleys and to some extent, in the hilly areas of south India.

The pear is a fruit which should be picked when firm, i.e.. just before softening. Maturation should be completed in the lug box, in cold storage while this takes place. In purchasing they must have a diameter of atleast 5.5 cm. Pears of Kullu should be picked at a pressure of about 0.91 to 0.98 kg/sq cm. These are subsequently ripened at 23°C to 26°C, when they develop a light yellow colour, and the white pulp becomes fairly soft and develops the characteristic pleasant taste and aroma.

Grading

Pears are graded for size mechanically prior to peeling, and the pieces are again graded for size by hand before being filled into the cans. Small size pears are not accepted at canneries.

Peeling and Coring

Peeling of Bartlett pears is carried out mechanically. These machines also core the pears as well as peel them. The peeling and coring of Indian pears generally is carried out by hand. On account of the tough skin of this variety of pear, it is difficult to peel it with a mechanical peeler. The fruit is peeled with a knife from stem-end to bottom-end, is cut longitudinally into two halves, and then the core is removed with a double edged coring knife. The core, stem as well as bottom ends, and all the bruised and discoloured spots are carefully removed. Pears start to turn brown very soon after they are peeled, if exposed to the air. For this reason, they should be kept under water until they are canned ; and if they cannot be handled promptly, they should be kept under a weak salt solution (about 10 g to 1 litre). Brine checks the action of oxidase — the enzyme responsible for browning. The waste during peeling, coring and stemming is usually 30 to 35 per cent. The cores and peels can be used in the preparation of vinegar, brandy or denatured alcohol ; although in most factories the waste material is discarded by grinding and washing down the sewer with ample water.

Grading and Filling

The grading is again done while doing the peeling and the filling into cans. The peelers divide the halves into 3 or 4 different sizes to the best of their ability as judged by the eye. Any pieces that are off-colour or otherwise defective should be placed in layers in order to fill the spaces and get full weight.

Syruping

The syrups used for the different grades are 40°, 30°, 20° and 10° Balling and water, respectively. Owing to the pear's low acidity, the 40° syrup is sufficient for the best grade; syrups higher in sugar than 40° Balling imparting too sweet a taste.

Exhausting

Cans of pear should be exhausted preferably in a steam exhaust box until the temperature at the centre of the cans is 70° to 75°C. This will generally require 8 to 12 minutes.

Closing

Following the exhaust period and provided the above minimum average closing temperatures are attained, an adequate vacuum can be attained with atmospheric closure. However, if the minimum average closing temperature cannot be maintained above 70°C, it is advisable to use steam-flow closure.

If the pre-vacuumising syruper is used for canned pears, it can not be used alone to ensure vacuum closure. When either closure is used, it is essential that the cans have a headspace of 8 mm.

Process

Pears are processed in boiling water temperature (100°C) and the time for sterilisation will vary from 15 to 25 minutes. Pears in heavy syrup require a longer process than those in light syrup. Sometimes a longer time is required to soften the pieces properly than is necessary in the case of sterilisation.

Occasionally, heating times in excess of those required to give commercial sterility are necessary to give pears the proper texture. Excessive heating time should be avoided, as this may cause pink discolouration of the product.

Cooling

It is important that the cans be immediately and thoroughly cooled after processing to an average can-centre temperature between 35°C and 40°C. If the cooling is not complete, the edges of the pieces may become too soft and a general dull appearance may result. Processing for too long a time or stacking away hot may cause the pears to turn pink.

PREPARATION OF FRUIT JUICES, SQUASHES AND CORDIALS

In India, cold drinks are in demand practically throughout the year. Among these, fruit juices have an important place. Being rich in essential minerals, vitamins and other nutritive factors, they are quite popular. Besides, they are delicious and have universal appeal unlike other beverages.

The nutritive value of real fruit beverages is far greater than that of synthetic product which are, at present, being bottled and sold in large quantities throughout the country. The annual production of carbonated beverages like lemonade, orange, strawberry, lime juice, etc., as well as various kinds of sherbet and other artificially flavoured beverages runs into several million bottles. If real fruit juices could be substituted for these synthetic preparations, it would be a boon to the consumer as well as to the fruit grower. There is, therefore, great scope in the country for the production of fruit juices and other fruit-based beverages.

With the rapid progress in fruit farming that has taken place during the last two decades, fresh fruit juices are being increasingly sold, by vendors in some of the larger towns. The demand for fresh fruit juices is on the increase, but these cannot be had easily, when the fruits are out of season. Fruit juices have, therefore, to be preserved in a form in which they can be made available to the public during the off-season.

Preparation of fruit beverages on a commercial scale was practically unknown in the country till about 1930. New products such as squashes and cordials are, however, now being packed to the extent of more than three million bottles annually. If aerated water factories begin to use pure fruit juices instead of synthetic colours and flavours, that alone will create a steady demand for utilisation of several thousand tones of fruit every year.

In India, the pure fruit juice industry is still in its infancy. Preparation of these juices is limited to small-scale productions only, because the equipment required for production of the best quality fruit juices is rather sophisticated and costly. Quite recently, however, a few units have come into existence to pack fairly large quantities of pure fruit juices from citrus fruits, pineapples, grape, apple, etc. Fruits such as apple, grape, pomegranate, mulberry, jamun (Eugenia jambolana), phalsa (Grewia asiatica), mango, pineapple, etc., are generally utilised for the preparation of juices. The scope for large-scale production of fruit juices is, however, limited at present, as these are not yet included to any considerable extent in the normal diet of the people. However, tomato juice, which is in fair demand already, has considerable scope for large-scale production.

SHERBET

It consists of sugar syrups flavoured with artificial essence of fruits or herbs, and has been produced in India from times immemorial and are, therefore, well known practically throughout the country.

Of late, large-scale manufacture of squashes, orange lemon and lime juice cordial, has made considerable progress in different parts of the country. Proper education and publicity of the dietetic value of fruit beverages is necessary to stimulate a general demand for them.

Fruit juices, specially orange, apple and grape juices, are concentrated using modern equipment so that there is practically very little loss in their nutritional properties and flavour characteristics. Sometimes, the recovered flavour is added back to the concentrate to get full fruit taste and flavour on dilution for serving. These concentrates are used as basis for soft drinks, pharmaceutical preparations, baby foods, tonic foods, etc. The frozen orange juice concentrate (four to one) is an excellent example in this case.

Conventional equipments such as climbing and falling film evaporators and more recently, the centrifugal evaporators etc., are being employed. Fruit juices and concentrates are further converted into free-flowing fruit juice powders by adopting methods such as, puff-drying, foam mat drying, freeze drying, etc. Sometimes, sealed-in flavours are blended with the powders so as to get natural fruit juices on reconstitution for serving as beverages.

EQUIPMENT FOR FRUIT JUICES

Until recently, the equipment used for the extraction of fruit juices was similar to that used in the manufacture of wine, vinegar, etc. There has, however, been a rapid advance in the fruit juice industry in the U.S.A., U.K., and several other countries. Consequently, one can now get equipment ranging from the simple household juice extractor or press, to the fully automatic juice lines capable of handling several thousand bottles daily. Particularly, the development of the citrus juice industry, has been the most important factor in revolutionising the entire fruit juice industry. It is essential that suitable equipment is employed for the successful operation of this industry.

Washing Equipment

For washing apples, citrus fruit, tomatoes, berries, etc., different kinds of equipment are available. Tender fruits like berries, tomatoes, etc., are usually washed with fine overhead sprays of water, whereas the fruits travel on a continuous woven wire belt. A rotating rod-cylinder with a helical screw inside to push the fruit along and fitted with jets of water forced by a centrifugal pump, has been found highly useful for washing loose jacket mandarin oranges. On a small-scale, cement or galvanised iron tanks for holding water are quite useful. A battery of these will be adequate even for a factory of moderate size.

Sorting Equipment

In large factories, a continuous broad belt made of woven metal is generally employed for sorting the fruits. In smaller factories, however, batch sorting will suffice.

Extraction Equipment

There are two types of extractions. In one case, the fruits are crushed and pressed continuously in one operation, whereas in the other, the fruits are crushed or cut into small pieces or comminuted in a mill, and these are subsequently pressed in a suitable press.

In case of the citrus fruits, the juice is enclosed in small natural sacs. Besides, there are other adhering tissues also in the fruit. The peel consists of an inner white spongy portion called the albedo, and an outer yellow coloured portion called the flavado. The oil glands are embedded in the flavado and are easily ruptured even with a gentle pressure. Substances which are responsible for the bitterness of the juice are located chiefly in: (i) the fruit tissues in which the juice sacs are embedded, (ii) the inner portion of the flavedo, (iii) the albedo, and (iv) the seeds. The presence of these (containing bitter substances) makes it rather difficult to extract the juice free from bitterness. An ideal equipment would be the one in which the juice is extracted from the juice sacs only without its coming into contact with the other tissues of the fruit. No perfect mechanical device has so far been developed for this. With the existing equipment, the bitter substances are also extracted to varying extents and get incorporated with the juice. Extraction of juice from peeled segments as such, or from segments dipped in dye solution for removing most of the adhereing tissues, helps to minimise the incorporation of bitter substances into the juice.

Halving and Turning Machines

Malta orange or Sathgudi or musambi oranges, grapefruit, lemon and gal gal are cut by a special machine, in which the fruit is placed in a conical cup in a wheel which brings the fruits against a stationery or revolving knife.

The fruit is cut into two halves, which drop into a receptacle placed below. The burrs (or roses) are generally made of stainless steel, monel metal, aluminium, nickel, or non-odorous hard wood. They are conical in shape and are ribbed. They are driven by a motor. The cut half of the fruit is held against the revolving burr and the reamed juice is collected in a vessel kept below. There are generally, two buns, one each on either side of the shaft. Several single burrs can also be fitted in series. By regulating the speed of the burr and the pressure on the fruit held against it, any excessive tearing of the tissues can be avoided.

Continuous Screw Expeller Press

These presses are similar in principle to the familiar household meat mincer. The segments of the fruit are fed through a hopper at one end of a feeding screw, revolving inside a conical jacket, which is perforated in sections or throughout. The juice flows out through the perforations and the pomace comes out at the end of the conical jacket. The flow of pomace and, hence, the pressing pressure of the screw can be adjusted, to some extent, by means of a movable disc at the conical end of the perforated jacket Small power driven screw type extractors (1/2 to 1 HP) have now been introduced in several factories in the country. Very large units are not, however, in general use at present. The juice extracted is generally thick, cloudy, and contains a considerable amount of mascerated pulp. The juice should be passed through sieves to remove the pulp to the desired extent Screw-type juice extractors are useful in the case of tomatoes, grapes, etc. In the case of pineapple, however, the pieces of fruit are first crushed in a screw-type crusher and then from the crushed material, the juice is separated effectively in a centrifuge (hydroextractor) which is, by and large, a suspended basket centrifuge widely employed in the sugar and chemical industries.

Plunger-Type Press

The halved citrus fruit is held on an inverted cup, in which it is pressed by an automatic adjustment against a metallic cone fitting into the cup. The clearance between the cup and cone is slightly greater than the usual thickness of the peel of the fruit, so that very little of the peel oil or emulsion is pressed out. This type of press is being used only in one or two factories in the country.

Roller-Type Press

Roller presses, made of hard granite or wood, are specially designed to extract juice from sour limes (Citrus medica) which are popularly known as kagzinimboo or limboo. The whole lime is fed through the rollers. These presses are in extensive use in West Indies and Jamaica. They have been introduced in some of the Indian factories also.

Double Operation

Fruits like apples, grapes, berries, etc., are first crushed in a grater or crusher or comminuting mill, and the juice them extracted from the crushed material by means of a hydraulic press. In large-scale production, as in the case of apple juice, the crushing device forms an integral part of the press itself.

Basket Press

In the industry, two types of presses are used for pressing the juice from the crushed fruit. They are: (i) the basket press, and (ii) the rack and cloth press. Basket presses, which are of various designs and capacities, are operated manually by hydraulic pressure. The manually operated press consists of a strong cylindrical basket made of wooden slates, which rest on a wooden or metallic base. There is a strong screw at the top of the frame. The crushed fruit is folded in a piece of strong cloth and placed inside the basket. By turning the screw by hand or with a hydraulic pump, the juice is pressed out. It flows out through the slates in the basket into the bottom tray, from which it is channelled into a collecting vessel. The basket press has been found useful in the case of apple, grape, pomegranate, phalsa, etc.

Rack and Cloth Press

In this type of press, the crushed fruit is spread as a layer in a coarse woven cloth of cotton or nylon and folded into a squat suited to the size of the platform of the press. Several such layers are arranged alternately between racks built of wooden slates. The built up layers are subjected to hydraulic pressure by means of a pump. The juice is pressed out gradually due to increasing pressure in the pile. The released juice is collected at the base of the pile. Various types of these presses, which are in use in several countries, are claimed to give higher yields of clear juice than the basket type presses. Rack and cloth presses are in use in a few factories in India specialising in the production of apple juice.

Fruit juices, extracted or pressed by any of the methods described, contain suspended matter like coarse fruit tissues, pieces of skin, seeds, and finely divided fruit pulp. These are separated from the juice in various ways, depending upon the nature of the product required, e.g., cloudy, sparkling, clear, etc. Three important methods in common use are (i) straining or screening, (ii) settling or sedimentation, and (iii) filtration.

STRAINING OR SCREENING EQUIPMENT

Several types of equipment, varying in design and capacity, are in use for straining juices. A pulper made of stainless steel with power-driven wooden, metallic or brush paddles which revolve inside has been highly useful in the case of citrus, tomato and mango juices. The fruit, which is fed through a hopper, is crushed and pressed by the paddles against the sieve. The juice flows out through the sieve into the jacket and is collected at the outlet below, while the coarse residue passes out at the lower end of the sieve.

For sedimentation and settling of the juices, only a few wooden barrels or stainless steel tanks are required.

FILTRATION EQUIPMENT

Finely suspended particles in the juice are removed with a special equipment known as filter press. Filter presses are of various designs and capacities. The filtering media may be finely woven cloth, canvas, fibre, asbestos pads, cotton or wood pulp discs, porous porcelain wares, etc. The frame and filter press, which is similar to that used in sugar factories but made of wood, has been highly effective for the clarification of lime juice required for the preparation of lime juice cordial. Seitz filters of various designs and sizes are widely employed for filtering wines, spirits, sugar, syrups, cordials, apple, and other fruit juices etc.

A simple filtering device, however, is a large conical bag of heavy drill cloth or feel, similar to the ordinary jelly bag. The juice is heated with filter aid and placed inside the bag. Filtration is rather slow, but the output can be increased by having a battery of such filter bags.

DEAERATOR AND FLASH PASTEURISER

Freshly extracted and screened juices contain appreciable quantity of oxygen which should be removed before packing. The special equipment used for the purpose is called a deaerator. The deaerated juice is subsequently heated in a flash-pasteurisation equipment. Commercial deaerators and Cash pasteurisers vary greatly in design, construction and capacity.

FRUIT BEVERAGES

Fruit juices are preserved in different forms such as pure juices, squashes, cordials, fermented juices, etc. These are broadly defined as follows:

Unfermented Juice or Pure Fruit Juice. This is the natural juice pressed out of the fruit, and remains practically unaltered in its composition during preparation and preservation.

Fruit Juice Beverage. This is a fruit juice which is considerably altered in composition before consumption. It may be diluted before it is served as a drink.

Fermented Fruit Beverage. This is a fruit juice which has undergone alcoholic fermentation by yeast. The product contains varying amounts of alcohol. Grape wine, apple ciders, berry wines etc., are typical examples of this kind of beverage.

Fruit Juice Squash. This consists essentially of strained of juice containing moderate quantities of fruit pulp to which cane sugar is added for sweetening, e.g., orange squash, lemon squash, pineapple squash, mango squash.

Fruit juice Cordial. This is a sparkling, clear sweetened fruit juice from which all the pulp and other suspended materials have been completely eliminated, e.g., sherbets of sandal, orange, almond, rose, khuskhus, sarasaparilla, kewra, etc.

Fruit Juice Concentrate. This is a fruit juice which has been concentrated by the removal of water either by heat or by freezing. Carbonated beverages and other products are made from this.

Fruit Juice Powder. This is a fruit juice which has been converted into a free-flowing, highly hygroscopic powder, to which natural fruit flavour in powder form is incorporated to compensate for any loss of flavour in concentration, dehydration, etc. Freeze-dried fruit juice powders form the last word among sophisticated fruit juice products. They are reconstituted readily to yield full-strength, full-fruit, frult juice drinks.

Preparation and Preservation

Fruit juices have their best taste, aroma and colour when they are freshly extracted or expressed. All subsequent efforts to preserve them adversely affect their quality to varying degrees, depending upon the method of preservation employed. The most important problem, therefore, is to adopt only such methods that would help retain their quality to the maximum extent possible.

The most important steps in processing fruit juices are: (i) selection and preparation of fruit, (ii) extraction of juice, (iii) deaeration, (iv) straining, filtration and clarification, and (v) preservation. The quality of the juice will depend on the manner in which these several processes are carried out.

Selection and Preparation of Fruit

All fruits are not suitable for making fruit-juice, either because of difficulties in the extraction of juice, or because the juice got is of poor quality. Even some of the juicy fruits are not quite suited, as they do not yield juice of good beverage quality. The variety of fruit, its maturity, and the locality in which it is grown, have a marked effect on its flavour as well as keeping quality. The best juice is, therefore, extracted from freshly picked, sound, and suitable varieties when they are at an optimum state of maturity.

The fruits should be washed thoroughly with water, and in some cases scrubbed also, to remove any adhering dust and other extraneous matter. Residues of sprays of arsenic and lead should be removed with dilute hydrochloric acid. All mouldy and decayed parts should be removed, as in the case of fruits prepared for canning.

Juice Extraction

The method of juice extraction will differ with the structure and composition of the fruit. Generally, juice from fresh fruits is extracted by crushing and pressing them. In the case of fruits, in which the juice is in sacs or in cells during the extraction of the juice, the other tissues of the fruit in which these sacs or cells are embedded and also broken or crushed, resulting in the corporation of some undesirable constituents in the juice. The admixture of these extraneous constituents with the juice should be avoided as far as possible by adopting a suitable method of extraction. Further, during extraction the juice should not be unduly exposed to air, as oxygen of the air will not only adversely affect the colour, taste and aroma but also reduce the vitamin content of the juice.

Deaeration

In spite of all improvements made so far in the extraction equipment, fruit juices do retain some air. This is due to the difficulty of extracting the juice without some aeration, and also owing to the presence of air in the inter-cell surface of the fruit particles ; while some is found dissolved in the juice. In the case of citrus juices, particularly orange juice which is highly susceptible to the adverse action of the residual air, immediately after extraction the juice is subjected to a high vacuum, whereby most of the air as well as other gases are removed. This process is known as deaeration.

Straining, Filtration and Clarification

Fruit juices, after extraction, always contain varying amounts of suspended matter which consists of broken fruit tissue, seed, and skin ; and also various gums, pectic substances and proteins in colloidal suspension. Usually, coarse particles of pulp, seeds and pieces of skin are removed by means of screens in the case of almost juices.

Coarse particles of suspensions in the juice are removed either by straining through sieves of non-corrodible metal, or by sedimentation. For sedimentation, the juice is stored in carboys or barrels, adding a chemical preservative to ensure that the juice does not undergo fermentation during storage. The coarse particles settle down gradually over a period of a few days. The supernatant juice, which contains mostly fine suspended particles and colloidal suspensions, is syphoned off for subsequent treatment. The type of equipment used for straining the juice depends upon the kind of juice. It is fitted with screens having holes of varying dimensions. The juice is passed through the sieves soon after extraction. Coarse particles of tissues, skins and seeds are separated by vibratory action, and the juice still retaining the desired amount of fine pulp and juice sacs is collected in a vessel. When perfectly clear juices are required, complete removal of all suspensions is effected either by filtration or by clarification. For this, enzymes and fining agents are employed.

Filtration is necessary for removing completely all the fine and colloidal suspensions. In this process which is physical in nature, the juice, which has been strained and from which the coarse particles have already been removed, is forced through a filtering medium. The filtering medium usually consists of woven fibre cloth, asbestos pads, cotton pulp, porous porcelain or wood pulp. The colloidal suspension tends to clog the filters in the press. In order to minimise this, filter aids such as diatomaceous or infusorial earth, also known as kieselguhr, kaolin, Spanish clay, etc., are added to the juice, so that the filtering medium is coated with these without blocking the fine pores and thereby facilitating filtration. The use of these filter aids, however, tends to impart to the juice a slight amount of earthy taste, which may be unacceptable to some persons.

Use of Fining Agents

This method aims at producing a voluminous flocculent precipitate which settles gradually, carrying down with it finely divided particles and colloidal suspensions that are responsible for cloudiness or haze in clarified juices.

Finings are of three kinds: (i) enzymes which destroy the colloids present in the juice, (ii) finings which are purely physical in their action, e.g., infusorial earths, and (iii) chemical findings which act on the gummy and colloidal substances present in the juice to form insoluble coagulates that settle down easily, e.g.. gelatin, albumen and casein.

ENZYMES

Various kinds of enzymes such as proteolytic, pectin decomposing, hydrolytic, starch-liquefying enzymes, etc., are sometimes used to remove pectin, proteins and starch from juices. In the trade, these enzyme preparations are sold under different brand names such as Pectinol, Filtragol, Ido, Pectasine, etc. Each class of enzymes has a different type of action on the colloids present in the juice. The process of clarification differs according to the particular enzyme used.

Chemical Finings

The bulk of suspended matter, specially in the case of apple juice, consists of proteins and pectin-like substances. The colloidal substances carry on them electrical charge, generally negative, and are precipitated when this charge is neutralised by the addition of positively charged colloids. Gelatin and casein act partly in this manner, and partly by forming insoluble precipitates with the constituents of the juice. For instance, casein combines with the acids, and gelatin with the tannins of the juice. On allowing the treated juice to settle, the precipitates formed carry down with them other suspended particles also.

Clarification by Freezing

Colloidal suspensions, when subjected to freezing, are readily precipitated on thawing. Apple juice, particularly, responds very well to this treatment. Freshly extracted grape juice, besides containing the usual suspension of pulp, skin, etc., also carries varying quantities of cream of tartar or potassium hydrogen tartar. When the juice is bottled in the usual way, the cream of tartar goes on precipitating gradually in the form of fine crystals. The presence of these crystals in the juice is rather objectionable In order to stop this slow precipitation, the bulk of the juice is subjected to refrigeration for several months to complete the precipitation. The clear juice is then bottled. Grape wines also behave like grape juice and are, therefore treated similarly.

Clarification by Heating

It is a well known fact that colloidal material in fruit juices usually coagulates, when the juice is heated, and settles down readily. To get good results, the juice is heated to about 82°C for a minute or less, and then cooled down rapidly. The heating is effected in flash-heaters to avoid oxidation by air and to minimize the loss of flavouring materials. After flash heating and cooling, the juice is mixed with the filter aid and passed through the filter press. One great advantage of this method is that it also removes from the juice those substances which would otherwise be precipitated during pasteurisation of the juice. Clarification of pomegranate juice is a typical example of this process.

PRESERVATION OF FRUIT JUICES

Freshly extracted juices are highly attractive in appearance and possess good taste and aroma, but deteriorate rapidly, if kept for some time. This is on account of several causes which are stated below:

1. Fermentation may be caused by mold, yeast and bacteria.
2. Enzymes present in the juice may affect the colour and flavour adversely. For example, apple juice turns brown due to the activity of oxidative enzymes present in it.
3. Chemicals present in the juice may react with one another and spoil the taste and aroma of the juice.

4. Air coming in contact with the juice, may react with the glucosidal material in the juice and render the juice bitter. Thus, the juices from navel orange and sweet lime often turn bitter, when they are exposed to air even for a short time.
5. Metals from the equipment may get into the juice and spoil its taste and aroma.

To retain the natural taste and aroma of the juice, it is necessary to preserve it soon after extraction without allowing into stand for any length of time. Various methods of preservation are employed, and each has its own merits. The methods generally used are: (i) pasteurisation (ii) addition of chemicals, (iii) addition of sugar, (iv) freezing, (v) drying, and (vi) filtration. Other methods such as preservation by pressure by gases, by electric current, etc., are generally not employed on any large-scale.

PASTEURISATION

Preservation of fruit juices by heat is the most popular method. The method consists essentially in heating the juice to 100°C, or slightly below, for a sufficient time to kill microorganisms, which cause spoilage, and the process of heating is called pasteurisation. The juice is hermetically sealed in containers, which remain sealed against the entry of microorganisms from outside. Pasteurisation temperatures do not kill all the microorganisms present in the juice. Some spores and spore-bearing bacteria like B. subtilis and B. mesentericus can survive the process and multiply later on. These survivals are, however, generally too weak to cause any spoilage of the juice. Further, these organisms are highly sensitive to acids and cannot grow in acid fruit and acid vegetable juices.

Fruit juices are pasteurised at such temperatures and for such periods as would render them sterile, without impairing their flavour. Usually, the juices are pasteurised at about 85° for 25 to 30 minutes, according to the nature of the juice and the size of the container. Acid fruit juices require lower temperature and less time for pasteurisation than the less acid ones. To obtain satisfactory results, it is essential to keep all equipment perfectly clean and to carry out the work under hygienic conditions.

Juices can be pasteurised in two ways: (i) by heating the juice at a low temperature for a long period, and (ii) by heating the juice at a high temperature for a short time only (HTST method).

BOTTLE METHOD OR 'HOLDING' PASTEURISATION

This method is commonly used for the preservation of fruit juices on a home-scale. The extracted juice is strained, filtered and/or clarified, as the case may be, and filled into bottles leaving proper head space for the expansion of the juice during heating. The bottles are then sealed, air tight and pasteurised.

PASTEURISATION BY OVER-FLOW METHOD

In this method, the juice is heated to a temperature of about 2.5°C higher than the pasteurisation temperature, and filled into hot sterilised bottles up to the brim, taking care to see that during filling and sealing, the temperature of the juice does not fall below the pasteurisation temperature. The bottles should be hot at the time of the filling to safeguard against fall of temperature of the juice.

PREPARATION OF FRUIT BEVERAGES

FRUIT BEVERAGES

Fruits most commonly used for preparing beverages are: sweet oranges, mandarin (sangtra) loose jacket orange, sour lime (kagzi nimboo or limboo), lemon, grapefruit, grapes, apple, mango, pomegranate, phalsa (Grevia asiatica) jamun (Eugenia jambolana), mulberry, passion-fruit, pineapple, etc. Tomato juice also has become quite popular. Among the squashes, sweetened orange juice known as orange squash, lemon squash and pineapple squash are the most popular ones.

SQUASHES AND CORDIALS

Fruit juices are most commonly packed as squashes or cordials in this country, although canned pure fruit juices like orange and pineapple juices and, quite recently, mango juice are gaining importance. Methods of preparing some of the more important squashes and cordials are dealt with briefly in the following sections.

ORANGE SQUASH

Extraction of Juice

Orange squash is prepared from tight-skinned oranges such as malta, sathgudi or chinese and musambi oranges as well as from loose-skinned oranges like Nagpur and Coorg oranges. Tight-skinned oranges are cut into halves either with a knife by hand or by means of a halving machine having a circular knife. The halves are pressed by hand against a revolving burr or rose fitted to rosing machine. The reamed juice is collected in a vessel. It contains plenty of coarse tissues, seeds, etc. To remove these, it is filtered through a net cloth or passed through a sieving machine known as pulper, in which the juice gets brushed through a stationary perforated cylinder by revolving paddles of stainless steel, wood or fibre brush. The sieved juice is utilised for making squash.

Dipping of the segments in hot lye solution for 1/2 to 1 minute removes most of parchment-like material enclosing the juice sacs in the segments, and the juice obtained from the treated acid-dipped and washed segments is practically free from substances that subsequently cause bitterness in the juice. This juice has been found to be highly satisfactory for canning as pure orange juice as well as for making orange squash. The segments are passed through a screw-type juice extractor.

Preparation of Squash

Sugar, citric acid, flavouring materials, colour and preservatives are added to the juice in correct proportions. Sugar, citric acid and water are mixed and heated. Any dirt is skimmed off. The syrup is cooled slightly and filtered through cloth. The clean syrup is blended with the juice. To improve flavour, peal emulsion of 2 to 4 oranges for every l00 oranges taken or an appropriate quantity of an essential oil and orange essence is added to the squash.

After mixing all the ingredients, a calculated amount of a chemical preservative, namely potassium metabisulphite, approximately about 30gm for every 500 ml of squash dissolved previously in a small quantity of the juice or water, is added to the squash. While using stored and sulphur dioxide preserved orange juice for making the squash, allowances should be made for the acid as well as sulphur dioxide added to the juice for preserving it. The amount of sulphur dioxide in the final product should not exceed 350 ppm., which is the upper limit permitted by law. The bottles are cleaned and washed in a bottle- washing machine, fitted with revolving brushes or in a washing machine fitted with jets of hot lye, hot water and steam, to clean and dry the bottles. The sterile bottles are rinsed with hot water before filling them with the squash, leaving about 1.2 to 2.5cm of head space. The bottles are then closed with crown corks or pilfer-proof closures, which have been dipped in one per cent potassium metabisulphite solution to sterilise them. The bottles are washed, dried and labelled.

TABLE 34.1. ORANGE SQUASH RECIPES

Ingredients	*45°Brix.* 1.5% acidity (kg)*	*45°Brix,** 1.5% acidity (kg)*	*65°Brix* 2.0% acidity (kg)*	*65°Brix** 2.0% acidity (kg)*
Orange Juice 100Brix 0.8% acidity	100.0	100.0	100.0	100.0
Sugar	165.0	120.0	240.0	180.0
Citric acid	5.0	2.5	6.5	5.0
Essence of orange water	2.5	2.0	3.0	2.5
Orange colour Preservative (Potassium metabisulphite)	0.10	0.07	0.10	0.07

GRAPEFRUIT SQUASH

The methods of preparation of juice for grapefruit squash is the same as that employed in the case of orange squash.

TABLE 34.2. GRAPEFRUIT SQUASH RECIPE

Ingredients	*45°Brix.* 1.5% acidity (kg)*	*45°Brix,** 1.5% acidity (kg)*	*65°Brix* 2.0% acidity (kg)*	*65°Brix** 2.0% acidity (kg)*
Grapefruit (juice 10°Brix, 1.25% acidity).	100.0	100.0	100.0	100.0
Sugar	165.0	120.0	240.0	62.0
Citric acid	5.0	2.5	6.5	40.0
Water	125.0	73.0	46.0	11.0
Essence of grapefruit	2.5	2.0	2.5	2.5
Potassium metabisulphite	0.10	0.07	0.10	0.07

* 2.5% Fruit Juice Ingredient
** 33% Fruit Juice Ingredient

LEMON SQUASH

European lemon, Eureka lemon, and gal gal (Citrus limonia) are generally used for the preparation of lemon squash. Lemon squash requires addition of flavour to improve its taste. The method of preparing the juice and squash is practically the same as that employed in the case of tight-skinned orange for manufacture of orange squash. The juice is extracted by reaming.

TABLE 34.3. LEMON SQUASH RECIPES

Ingredients	*45°Brix.* 1.5% acidity (kg)*	*45°Brix,** 1.6% acidity (kg)*	*65°Brix* 2.0% acidity (kg)*	*65°Brix** 1.6% acidity (kg)*
Juice Lemon (100Brix, 5% acidity)	100.0	100.0	100.0	100.0
Sugar	165.0	125.0	245.0	180.0
Citric acid	2.5	—	3.0	—
Water	125.0	70.0	55.0	15.0
Essence of lemon	2.5	2.0	2.5	2.5
Preservative (potassium metabisulphite)	0.1	0.1	0.1	0.1

* 2.5% Fruit Juice Ingredient
** 33% Fruit Juice Ingredient

LIME SQUASH

Kagzi nimboo is widely used for making lime squash. These limes are available in large quantities in Gujarat, Maharashtra, Andhra Pradesh Karnataka, Tamil Nadu, etc. The fruit is cut into halves with a knife and the juice pressed out from the halves be means of small wooden squeezers or by means of stone roller type presses. The juice is sometimes pressed from the cut fruit by means of a wooden basket press. Seeds are removed by sieving through cloth.

TABLE 34.4. LIME SQUASH RECIPE

Ingredients	*45°Brix.* 1.5% acidity (kg)*	*45°Brix,** 2.0% acidity (kg)*	*65°Brix* 1.5% acidity (kg)*	*65°Brix** 2.0% acidity (kg)*
Lime juice (10° Brix, 6.0% acidity)	100.0	100.0	100.0	100.0
Sugar	165.0	120.0	250.0	180.0
Water	130.0	75.0	50.0	15.0
Preservative (potassium metabisulphite)	0.1	0.1	0.1	0.1

* 2.5% Fruit Juice Ingredient

** 33% Fruit Juice Ingredient

LIME JUICE CORDIAL

Lime juice is stored in large carboys or upright wooden barrels lined with microcrystalline wax. Fifty-six gm of potassium metabisulphite is added to every 45kg of the juice to preserve it during storage The juice settles gradually, and the ediment forms a compact layer at the bottom, leaving a clear juice at the top. This process takes 2 to 3 months. The clear juice is syphoned off. This method is rather slow and time-consuming. Clarification of the juice can also be achieved quickly by adding gelatin and tannin in proper proportion, based on preliminary laboratory trials. Sugar, water, colour if necessary and preservative are added to the clear juice, and the mixture is then filtered by means of a filter press. Filter aids are added in this process to facilitate filteration, the clear cordial is bottled as usual.

Sugar is added in the form of syrup. The quantity of preservative added to the juice for storage is taken into account while adding the required quantity of it to the cordial. Only a small quantity of colour should be added.

JAMAN SQUASH OR SYRUP

Jaman fruit is crushed and heated in its own juice gently for 5 to 10 minutes at about 60°C to extract the rich purple colour. The heated material is pressed in cloth in a basket press and the clear purple coloured juice is used for making the squash, which is highly attractive in appearance and possesses a pleasant taste and flavour with a slight astringency.

TABLE 34.5. LIME JUICE CORDIAL RECIPE

Ingredients	*35°Brix.* 1.5% acidity (kg)*	*35°Brix,** 2.0% acidity (kg)*	*50°Brix* 1.5% acidity (kg)*	*50°Brix** 2.0% acidity (kg)*
Clarified lime juice, 10°Brix, 6% acidity	100.0	100.0	100.0	100.0
Sugar	128.0	90.0	190.0	140.0
Water	170.0	100.0	110.0	130.0
Colour	q.s.	q.s.	q.s.	q.s.
Preservative (potassium metabisulphite)	0.1	0.1	0.1	0.1

* 2.5% Fruit Juice Ingredient
** 33% Fruit Juice Ingredient

TABLE 34.6. JAMAN SQUASH RECIPE

Ingredients	*45° Brix* 1.5% acidity (kg)*
Jaman juice, 14°Brix, 0.75% acidity	100.0
Sugar	70.0
Citric acid	2.0
Water	240.0
Preservative (sodium benzoate)	0.1

* 50% Fruit Juice Ingredients

Mango Squash

Juicy varieties of mangoes are preferred for making mango squash. Fully ripe fruit is taken and washed well. The stem portion is cut off and four vertical slits are given to each fruit to facilitate pulping. The fruits are then passed through a pulping machine to separate the skins and the stones. The fine smooth pulp is used for making squash.

Sugar is added in the form of syrup. The squash may be strained through cloth before bottling.

PEACH SQUASH

White juicy peaches are good for making squash. The pulp is heated with half its weight of water for about 15 minutes at 82°C, and the juice is pressed from the softened pulp in a basket Press. The thick pulpy juice issued for making peach squash. Potassium metabisulphite is added as preservative.

PHALSA SQUASH

The method of preparing phalsa squash is similar to that described for making jaman squash. As the juice itself is sufficiently acidic, extra citric acid is not added to the squash.

PINEAPPLE SQUASH

Pineapple squash, and pineapple crush, which is similar to the squash but with a higher sugar content, have become highly popular in this country in recent years. There is a growing demand for the product practically all over the country. The fruit is sliced and the outer skin peeled off with a curved knife. The peeled slices are cored and then cut into small pieces, which are passed through a screw- type crusher and extractor. Broken fruit slices, which are less than quarters, can be used for the preparation of juice for squash. From the crushed material juice is pressed in a basket press, or in a centrifugal extractor. The clear juice is used in the preparation of squash.

PLUM SQUASH

Juicy plums like the alucha plum are preferred for the preparation of plum squash. To extract the colour from the skin, the plums are heated at 82°C for about 30 minutes, in their weight of water. The heated fruit is passed through a pulper to extract juice. The juice is made into squash of 45 to 550 Brix. Sodium benzoate is added as preservative.

SYRUPS

Syrups of rose, sandal, almond, sarsaparilla, kewra, Strawberry, pineapple, raspberry, orange, mulberry, etc., are highly popular as summer drinks in different parts of the country. They are generally prepared from extracts of natural material, or by using artificial colours and syrups of 70 to 75°Brix. To prevent crystallisation, sugar is inverted by heating it in water, to which a small quantity of citric acid is added.

Many of these synthetic syrups can be gradually replaced with real fruit syrups which are more nutritive.

TABLE 34.7. FRUIT SYRUPS

Ingredients	*Orange*	*Lemon*	*Pineapple*	*Raspberry*	*Strawberry*
Syrup of 70° Brix (litres)	1.0	1.0	1.0	1.0	1.0
Citric acid gm	82.0	122.0	82.0	40.0	22.0
Colour (q.s.)	Orange Yellow	Yellow	Yellow	Red	Strawberry
Essence gm	Soluble essence sweet orange	Lemon essence cloudy	Soluble essence, Pineapple sweet	Essence of Rasberry	Essence of Strawberry

35
Vegetables and Vegetable Products

Vegetables such as peas, beans, carrot, beetroot, tomato, asparagus, etc., are canned in large quantities in different parts of the world. In India, there is a good market for canned peas, green as well as processed ones. Carrot, cabbage, potato, cauliflower, tomato, etc. are canned in the brine in their natural form or in curried style using spices, fat etc., as the covering liquid.

COMPARISON OF FRUITS AND VEGETABLES

In general, we may consider canned vegetables as staple foods and the higher grades of canned fruits as dessert products. Vegetables differ from fruits in chemical composition, and for this reason the process of canning vegetables differ from those used for fruits. Most vegetables contain more starch than sugar, as contrasted to the fruits, which are high in sugar and low in starch.

The acidity of vegetables is generally much lower than that of fruits. Vegetables are grown in or near the ground in contrast to fruits, which are borne on trees, at a considerable distance from the soil. Vegetables, therefore, usually contain more of the resistant soil organisms than fruits and usually require more cooking than fruits to develop their most desirable flavour and texture.

Consequently, generally require a more severe processing than do the fruits in order to render them sterile and to cook them sufficiently for table use. Vegetables often contain disagreeable flavours or compounds, which should be removed before canning, or some must be wilted by heating before canning. For these reasons, they are usually blanched before being filled into the cans. But this process is not necessary with most fruits.

Vegetables are grown as annual field crops. Thus, it is possible for the canner to contract for each year's supply of peas or tomatoes in current year and to a large degree he can plan to control the quantum of his seasonal pack.

In general, vegetable for canning purposes should be uniform in colour and quality, tender, and in prime condition. Because of the rapid deterioration of vegetables after gathering, they should be transported from the field to the cannery in as short a time as possible.

OKRA

Okra is a staple garden crop. The pods resemble pepper in appearance and contain a nucilaginous substance that thickens soups. A fertile sandy loam soil is most favourable for growth of okra A monthly average maximum temperature of 36°C with a minimum average above l7°C provides optimum conditions for growth and high-quality pods.

Conspicuous cleanliness must be maintained at all times to pack okra of good quality. Cutting knives, pans, tanks, etc., must be kept free from conditions which tend to take iron into solution (iron darkens okra). They should be made from non-corrosive metal. Water, high in iron, also contributes to the discolouration. Fermenting and decaying juices produce acidity which, in turn, dissolves traces of iron. Cutters should be blown with steam every two hours. If this is not done, a black discolouraton of the cut surface of the okra is likely to occur.

The okra should be handled quickly from the fields to the soaking tanks. Do not allow it to lie around in the fields or at the cannery. Tough pods of okra should be picked out and discarded.

There are two methods of preparing okra. It is either canned fresh or soaked in brine for a period of time.

Fresh Okra. If packed fresh, it is blanched in boiling water for 2 minutes, followed by a spray of cold water to cool it It is then passed through a cutter to cut into pieces of the proper length, placed immediately in cans, and covered with boiling hot 2 per cent brine.

Soaked Okra. If the okra is to be soaked, the stem is removed and the okra is thoroughly washed. It is then placed in brine made by dissolving salt @ 1.6 kg/100 litres of water. The soaking period is about 18 hours. It varies somewhat according to the size of the okra. The okra is removed from the soaking tanks, blanched in boiling water for 2 to 3 minutes, sprayed with cold water, and then immediately put through the cutter, unless it is to be canned whole.

FILLING AND EXHAUSTING

Fill the cans full, cover with 2 per cent boiling hot brine, exhaust for at least 4 minutes in steam for all cans smaller than No. 10 size. The No. 10 cans should be exhausted for 8 to 10 minutes.

The standard of identity permits citric acid treatment of okra to control an iron induced discolouration. 400 to 1000 ppm citric acid provided by combination salt tablets containing 4-10 per cent citric acid is commonly, employed.

The processed cans are cooled rapidly in water, dried, labelled, and packed into cardboard cases.

MUSHROOMS

Edible mushrooms, which are not poisonous, are canned in the U.K. and the U.S.A. canned mushroom is a delicacy in India also. As some of the mushrooms are poisonous, great care is necessary in selecting them for canning, as such or in the form of soup. Mushroom cultivation has gained popularity recently in some parts of India. There is scope for canning as well as dehydration of mushrooms in the country. Much progress in the technical knowledge base and mechanisation of the canning operations has come about in the recent decade. Researches conducted coupled with the practical experiences have confirmed the merit of new or modified handling, cold storage, vacuumising, blanching and sterilisation practices in terms of improving processed yields and quality of canned mushrooms.

Fresh mushrooms are white, without dark marks of either cap or stem. The veil is closed and the gills are not visible. The upper surface of the caps should be strongly convex and stems should be plump, rather than elongated.

Mushrooms are grown on spawn compost, usually in mushroom houses where the temperature and humidity can be kept within desirable ranges. They are harvested daily, cooled immediately, and processed the same day. If the mushrooms are to be kept for more than a few hours before processing, they should be refrigerated in plastic bags to delay veil opening as well as to reduce weight loss.

SORTING OF WASHING

Mushrooms are sorted first for quality. The best mushrooms will go to the button line and those with slight discolouration or open veils to the pieces and stems line. The mushrooms are next soaked and washed in rod reel or soak tank washers. The button pack mushrooms are size-graded; the larger ones being used for slicing.

BLANCHING

Mushrooms should be steam or water blanched at 100°C for 5 to 7 minutes in a rotary screw-type conveyor made of stainless steel. Some plants blanch the mushrooms in slightly acidified water to improve the colour of the canned product. Different blanching times should be used for the various sizes ; thus, preventing over-blanching and shrinkage. The blanching process removes the gases from the mushroom tissue, inactivates the polyphenol oxidase enzymes, improves the texture for slicing, and reduces the bacterial counts. A blancher I m in diameter and 4 m long can blanch 1.5 tons of mushrooms per hour. A short spray of cold water should follow the blanching process to cool the mushrooms to 36°C or lower.

SIZE-GRADING

The blanched and cooled mushrooms are separated into various sizes in a rotary size-grader. The mushrooms are inspected and destemmed or sliced after blanching and size-grading. Most defects will show up then and weak veils will have opened.

FILLING

Mushrooms may be filled into cans by hand or mechanically. Hot brine or hot water and a salt tablet are added. The brine or water may contain the juice lost from the mushrooms during steam-blanching, the juice improves the flavour, but darkens the mushrooms slightly. Ascorbic acid is an optional ingredient.

CANNING

If the brine is boiling hot when added, exhausting is unnecessary; otherwise, cans should be exhausted to reach a centre temperature of 75°C and closed. They may be processed in retorts, continuous cookers, or by the newer Steri flamme Process.

PEAS

Canned fresh green peas stand out predominantly among canned vegetables. In India, Bonneville, Kinnauri, Lincoln, and VL-3 varieties have become popular for canning. Work is continuing to develop the right varieties for canning.

Peas for canning should be uniformly ripe and should retain their green colour, even after processing. They should possess good texture and flavour. Large sized peas are generally preferred for canning, although the petite pois, the little smooth peas, have stood out as a class by themselves in several countries.

The time of harvesting is determined largely by the appearance of the pods, which should be swollen and well filled with young succulent peas that change in colour from dark to light green. But in recent years, instruments such as the Tenderometer and Maturemeter have been introduced to measure the tenderness of the peas and to predict the most suitable time for harvesting the pods from the vines in the field and even to forecast the harvesting period.

VINING

The vining or shelling is done immediately after harvesting. A delay in vining results in deterioration in quality and may even cause loss of sugar, sweating and fermentation. Peas are shelled by means of a pea-podding machine which consists of a perforated revolving cylinder with paddles or beaters inside on a central shaft. The cylinder revolves slowly, while the beater revolves rapidly. The peas are hulled by impact with the beaters and fall through the openings in the cylinder.

CLEANING

The peas from the vines are first put through a special dry cleaner. A blast of air removes light material and a series of screens remove heavy large pieces such as pods and sticks and also the fine material. Then peas go to a special washing machine. They first pass over a series of ripples which collect stones and other heavy material. The second section floats off any chaff, empty skins, etc. The third part is a revolving screen with strong sprays of water which give a final thorough rinse.

GRADING

Grading is usually done by passing the peas through a slowly revolving screen cylinder or through a series of parallel screens; in either case the screens have holes of varying diameters. An important requirement for satisfactory size- grading is that the grader be fed at a uniform rate. Frequently, two or more sizes are combined into a single grade.

Peas are passed over picking tables for inspection, either after grading and before blanching, or else after blanching. The general practice is to inspect them for foreign material and discoloured peas after grading. A few packers make this inspection after the peas are blanched.

BLANCHING

After size-grading or inspection, the peas are pumped to the blanching section. The hot water used in blanching removes most of the dried coating of vine juice. Blanching removes the slight raw taste and odour of shelled peas as well as the air entrapped in the pea tissues. It also softens the peas so that a more uniform fill of the cans is obtained.

The blanchers consist of an outer steel drum which contains heated water; in this drum is a revolving perforated galvanised steel drum, inside of which an welded to the walls is a spiral (several inches deep) made of steel metal. The peas are fed into one end of the revolving drum, and the spiral carries them through the hot water in the outer drum. The water is heated by steam supplied by perforated pipes. Water is fed continuously into the discharge end of the blancher, so that the peas encounter water of increasing freshness as they pass through the machine. In some blanchers, a rotary screen is installed beyond the outlet spout, so that the peas may be spray washed as they emerge after blanching. A blanch of 3 minutes at 85° to 95°C is common for peas of average maturity and size. Water used for blanching should be soft, because the calcium in hard water will harden the peas. Steam-blanching for only 30 seconds prepares peas adequately for canning. More valuable nutrients are lost in water—than in steam-blanching. However, steam-blanching does not have as great cleansing and plumping action as water-blanching. But it is advocated to reduce the amount of soluble constituents that are removed. It is difficult to ensure that each pea gets the same heat treatment while handling a large volume of peas in steam- blanching.

GRADING AND MATURITY

Older peas are distinctly heavier than the younger ones, so that a separation by gravity is possible. Salt solutions of varying specific gravities are used to separate the older and heavier peas from the younger ones. There are several machines in the market for making this separation. Since much of the air in the peas is removed during blanching, a somewhat better gravity separation is possible after blanching. The successful separation or peas by gravity requires considerable guidance and the assistance of a trained food scientist is advisable.

BRINE

The brine should be added to the peas at or near the boiling temperature, and sufficient brine should be used to fill the cans as full as possible without interfering with the sealing operation. Hard water should not be used.

There is such a wide variation with regard to the amount of sugar and salt used in the brine that it is difficult to give an average figure. Probably, this would be around 8kg of salt and 12kg of sugar per five hundred litres of water. As high as 12 kg of salt and 20 kg of sugar per five hundred litres of water are used by some packers. Many packers use more sugar with sweet peas. Salt tablets or salt- sugar tablets and water may be added instead of brine.

FILL OF CANS

There is Standard Fill of Container for canned peas. To meet this standard without, overfilling the cans, it requires considerable experience and continual care. Most peas shrink slightly on canning. Nearly mature peas may increase the size on cooking, so the "fill-in" volume must be cut down accordingly.

EXHAUSTING

Shelf size of can need not be exhausted, if the brine is boiling hot when added. When peas are quality graded after blanching and filled in No. 10

cans, exhausting is necessary to obtain a desirable closing temperature. There is also need to exhaust when No. 10 cans are used and are processed at 120°C.

COOLING

Cooling should be rapid following sterilisation to avoid excessive softening and the formation of a cloudy brine through gelatinisation of starch.

CABBAGE

Early season cabbage, with tender, yellowish leaves, is used for canning. The head is either cut into 4 to 8 places or shredded into pieces about 2.5 cms thick. The pieces are generally blanched for 5 to 6 minutes in boiling citric or tartaric acid solution of 1.0 per cent strength; and, subsequently, cooled in 2.0 per cent to prevent discolouration. Plain cans and 2.0 per cent brine are used for canning. Pink discolouration in the canned product is a problem which requires more work to determine its cause and prevention. Canning varieties are Pride of India, Golden Acre, Pusa Drum Head.

PUMPKIN

Pumpkin, for canning purposes, should be deep yellow or orange in colour; should have a firm, dry, thick meal, and during the ripening period should possess no green colour in the rind. Most canners prefer a fine, rather than a coarse ; grained meal. The flesh should be golden yellow and of good texture.

WASHING AND PREPARATION FOR CANNING

Pumpkins, as delivered to the cannery, have more or less adhering soil, which be soaked before it is readily removed. The soak water should be kept lukewarm. After thorough soaking, adhering clay soil and silt are easily removed by hand scrubbing with common scrub brush. This should be followed by passing the pumpkins under a spray to thoroughly rinse them, as any soil adhering to them at the time they are cut results in a gritty pack.

After thorough cleansing, the stems are removed and the pumpkins are cut into pieces by large knives or hatchets or by special roller disks. The pieces are washed in a revolving circular screen washer to remove seeds and fibre ; or the seeds and fibre are removed by a revolving blunt and broad cone, against which the halved pumpkins is held by hand.

The pieces are steamed in retorts at 115°C for 20 minutes or until well-softened, or they may be steamed at atmospheric pressure in a continuous steam cooker designed for the purpose.

PULPING

The pulp is separated from the skin and tough fibre in a tomato pulper. It is then passed through a finisher, evaporated in open kettles to a heavy density, filled hot, and sealed. Enamel-lined cans should be use to prevent darkening of the product.

CANNING

The cans are sealed hot. The process is usually conducted at 120°C for 75 to 90 minutes.

A good can of pumpkin should be smooth, evenly screened, free from fibre and uniformly coloured. When opened, the can should be filled to within 25cm of the top.

BEANS

Green lima beans are canned after having been shelled from the pods. The bush variety is grown for canning purposes and is handled in much the same manner as peas. Veriety are SVM-1, Premier, Cortender, Laxmi, UP Bauni-I, Pusa Parbati.

VINING

Lima beans, are harvested in somewhat the same manner as peas when they have reached the stage of maturity most desirable for canning. The vines are passed through a viner which threshes out the beans from the pods and separales the vines and pods from the beans. The beans should be canned promptly after vining, as delay results in rapid deterioration in colour, flavour, and quality.

GRADING

The beans are cleaned and graded for size diameter. The various sizes are known as Tiny, Fancy, Medium, Standard, and Mammoth. The smallest sizes are the tenderest and sweetest, and are the most desirable for canning purposes.

Before canning, the over mature beans may be soaked in water until plump and canned as "soaked beans".

BLANCHING

The green beans are blanched in water at 85°C to 95°C or in boiling water, as described for peas, and dilute brine added to fill. The cans require no exhaust, if filled hot.

FILLING

The beans may be filled by hand. Any of the different types of hand filling machines is satisfactory. The filled cans are passed to the briner where a boiling hot 1½ per cent (1.5 kg of salt to 100 litres of water) salt brine is added to completely fill the can. Tumble fillers are now generally used.

EXHAUST

It is not necessary to exhaust the smaller size cans, when the brine is added boiling hot. With No. 10 cans, special care should be taken to make sure the brine is added boiling hot. If the temperature at which the cans are sealed is too low, buckling of No. 10 cans may occur during processing. To prevent this, many packers pass the No. 10 cans through an exhaust box with the steam turned on full.

COOLING

The cans should be water cooled 35°C to 40°C immediately after processing.

POTATOES

Potatoes are canned whole or as slices. For the most suited variety, specific gravity test is sometimes used. Potatoes having specific gravity of about 1.075 are better suiled for canning. Potatoes for canning, should be carefully inspected for injuries and other defects. If too many potatoes show defects or damage, the additional labour cost of inspection and trimming may make the cost of canning prohibitive.

When potatoes are to be stored several days before canning, they should be held in a cool place away from directly sure light to avoid losses through rot and to prevent greening. This green discolouration is not readily removed by normal peeling and may contribute a bitter taste to the canned product. Potatoes should be stored in a well-ventilated area to minimise losses through bacteriological and undesirable physiological changes.

If the sugar content of the potatoes is high as a result of low-temperature storage or other causes, the canned product may be somewhat discoloured. Freshly harvested potatoes yield a better quality canned product, are easier to peel, and require less labour for inspection and trimming than the stored potatoes.

WASHING

Prior to peeling, the surface dirt must be removed from the potatoes. Reel- type washers with strong sprays of water are usually used. Spiral flights may be employed to control the time for which potatoes are retained in the washer. Where stones are a problem, they may be removed by discharging potatoes from the washer into a through with rapidly flowing water moving over two sets of wooden riffles properly spaced at the bottom of the trough. The potatoes are carried along by the stream of water, and then washed again on a conveyor with a spray of water.

PREHEATING

Sometimes potatoes are preheated in water, prior to peeling, in order to reduce the heat load on the peeler; thereby increasing its capacity. This operation is said to be effective in preventing enzymatic discolouration, which may occur when potatoes arc taken directly from cool storage and subjected to high- temperature peeling.

PEELING

Steam, lye, and abrasion peeling as well as their combinations are used in the canning of potatoes. Both batch and continuous high-pressure steam peeling equipments are used. Batch steam peelers consist of a cylindrical drum equipped with a mechanism for rotating the drum slowly. Potatoes are filled into the drum with 250 to 500 kg capacity, lid locked, and steam at about 50kg pressure per sq. cm is let into the chamber.

The drum is slowly revolved to promote even heating as well as assist in removing peel loosened by the action of the high-temperature steam. After a short interval, the drum is stopped and the pressure released. The potatoes are discharged by inverting the peeler and allowing them to fall into water, which transports them to the washer.

Reel or drum-typo lye peeler and draper belt in tank types are also in general use. The concentration of lye in the solution may vary from 5 to 15 per cent. The temperature of the solution is usually maintained near the boiling point. The time for satisfactory peeling depends on the size of potatoes and the temperature and strength of the lye solution. The concentration of the lye in the peeler should be maintained at a roasonably uniform level.

It is essential that the peeled product be discharged immediately into a washer equipped with high-pressure water sprays, so that the peel can be removed before it has a chance to harden. Reel-type washers are generally used with water sprays operating at 40 to 50kg pressure per sq cm. Sprays should be regulated so that the skins are removed by the water as well as by the tumbling action of potatoes without roughening the surface of the potatoes.

Abrasion peelers are sometimes used by small processors where the operation size does not justify more expensive lye or steam peelers. Peeling losses are much greater with this type of peeling than with either steam or lye peeling.

Anew method of dry caustic peeling has been introduced. The potatoes are exposed to hot dilute caustic, drained, held, and subjected to infrared radiation while tumbling in a barrel. After peeling on rollers having rubber fingers, the last vestiges of peel are removed by a water wash. This commercially used process can markedly reduce water pollution in the effluents of potato-processing plants.

INSPECTION AND TRIMMING

While some trimmings to remove shallow unpeeled eyes, small pieces of skin, and other defects may be advantageous, it is often cheaper to sort these out from the cleanly peeled potatoes and send them through the lye peeler again.

SIZE-GRADING

A more uniformly sized product is obtained, if potatoes are sized after peeling. Perforated belts and screens, rubber spools and diverging belt graders are used for sizing potatoes.

Smaller sizes of potatoes (2.50 to 1.25 cms) are normally canned whole, since they command a premium price ; while the larger sizes may be sliced. Cutting and slicing equipment should be maintained in good condition to minimise the amount of chips and fines. The small pieces are removed from the product by screening.

FILLING

Whole and cut potatoes are filled into the cans by automatic as well as rotary hand-pack fillers. Cans made with electrolytic plate bodies and inside enamelled electrolytic plate ends are generally used.

Either boiling water or brine containing 1.5 to 3.0 per cent salt should be added to the container. Where boiling water is used, a salt tablet of proper size is added to each container prior to sealing.

Addition of calcium in the form of calcium chloride, calcium sulphate, calcium citrate, or monocalcium phosphate is permitted. The total calcium content must not exceed 0.051 per cent of the net weight of the finished product calcium chloride is usually used because of its ready solubility.

SEALING AND PROCESSING

The filled can should be sealed at 70°C, if ordinary closure is to be used. Steam flow or vacuum closure may also be used to obtain desirable can vacuum.

COOLING

The heat-processed cans are water-cooled promptly to 38°C. Casing and stacking of the packed cans at temperature in excess of this temperature may result in quality deterioration known as stacking-burning. If the temperature is much lower than 38°C, the cans may not dry properly resulting in the external rusting of containers.

CARROTS

Carrots are canned in diced, sliced, halved, quartered, and whole. Varieties for canning should have smooth contour free of deep folds or wrinkles, tender texture, and flesh of attractive orange colour. The carrot should not have a white or light-yellow core, but the flesh should be well coloured throughout.

Carrots store well in the cold storage, if humidity of the air is maintained at a high enough level to minimise evaporation of moisture. If the carrots lose moisture excessively, they become limp and rubbery. Best quality is attained by canning soon after harvesting.

WASHING

Generally speaking, carrots are easy to wash. Usually, the ordinary efficient spray wash is all that is required. If there is much dirt adhering to the carrots, they should be soaked in water before passing under the spray. Or carrots can be thoroughly washed in rotating drums with heavy sprays of water to remove adhering soil that would otherwise collect as mud in the tank of the lye peeling machine or interfere in abrasion peeling.

GRADING

The carrots are size-graded ; common sizes being 2.50 cm or less in diameter, 2.5 to 3.00cm, and above 3.0cm. Some of the smaller sizes are canned whole. The larger ones are sliced or cut in strips. They may also be cut lengthwise into quarters or halves.

BLANCHING

Carrots should be blanched for a short time before they are peeled. Time of the blanch depends upon the size and the general condition of the carrots. From 2 to 4 minutes in water at 88°C to 100°C is usually sufficient.

PEELING

The washed carrots are peeled in one of three ways, viz., by abrasion peeler, by hot lye solution, or by high-temperature steam-peeling. If the carrots are to be adrasion-peeled, a short blanch at 85°C to 90°C to well loosen the skin and thus facilitate peeling. In lye peeling, a solution containing 5 to 10 per cent NaOH is used, preferably in a spray-type lye peeler.

In steam peeling, the carrots are conveyed continuously in a closed chamber, heated briefly at about 150°C and then ejected continuously from the heating chamber. Since the skin and the flesh immediately beneath the skin are at a very high temperature, steam forms with explosive effect beneath the skin, forcing it off the vegetable with a minimum loss of flesh. Following either lye peeling or steam peeling, the disintegrated skins are washed away under heavy sprays of water in a rotating drum washer. The peeled carrots are trimmed by hand from a slowly moving belt to remove the roots, green flesh and defective areas.

SLICING OR DICING

The larger carrots are sliced, diced or cut into rings by a vegetable cutting machine. Diced or cut carrots should be screened under sprays of water to remove fines. The diced carrot pieces should be 0.5 to 10 cm in diameter. The smallest carrot pieces should be canned whole. The carrots are usually blanched in live steam or in water at 88°C for 2 to 4 minutes. Whole carrots are packed into cans by hand, and the cut carrots are filled by machine.

CANNING

Salt tablets are added by dispenser to the cans, which are then filled with very hot water, or the cans are filled with hot brine at 6 to 8 salometre (1.5 to 2 per cent salt).

In order to maintain firmness, addition of 0.035 per cent calcium is recommended. Brine containing 800 ppm monocalcium disodium salt of ethylene diaminetetra-acetic acid (EDTA) helps in retaining better colour and texture.

Exhausting. It is betters to exhaust even the small sized can. However, it is necessary to exhaust the large sized cans.

36

Processing of Foods Using High Hydrostatic Pressure

Exposure of foods to high hydrostatic pressures causes inactivation of microorganisms, denaturation, association and gel formation of biopolymers resulting in modifi-cation of foods such as appearance, texture, susceptibility to enzymes etc. The treatment can help hygienisation and shelf life extension of foods. The effect of high pressure in decreasing the freezing point of water favours development of high quality frozen foods, conditions for their better thawing as well as storage in non-frozen state under subzero conditions. Unlike thermal treatment, high pressure treatment is less energy intensive and does not generate newer compounds in foods. Advantages of the technique in processing of various foods are briefly discussed.

INTRODUCTION

High hydrostatic pressure (HHP) treatment is one of the conventional techniques practised in ceramics technology for development of electronic components having specific properties. Investigations on the application of high pressure for food processing started one century ago. Hite in 1899 demonstrated that HHP could coagulate egg albumen. In 1924, the potential of HHP in commercial fruit and vegetable processing was recognised. Serious attempts to use this technology for food processing on a commercial scale was initiated in Japan by the Japanese Ministry of Agriculture, Forestries and Fisheries in collaboration with several food industries in 1989. This has resulted in development of several HHP processed foods. The European Commission has also initiated a programme on HHP with particular interest in development of machinery for processing. This article deal with potential application of high hydrostatic pressure in food product development, wit particular reference to seafoods

UNITS OF PRESSURE

The unit of pressure generally used in food processing is Pascal (Pa) which is equivalent to 10 dynes/cm^6 or 6.893x10^3 psi. The interrelationships between Pa and other units as follows: 10^5 Pa or 0.l MPa = 1 Bar 0.987 atmosphere = 1 kg/cm^2 = 10^6 dynes/cm^2. In addition, 1 KBar is also equivalent to 100 MPa. The usual unit referred in food processing by high pressure is MPa. Generally, foods are treated to pressure of the order of 400 to 600 MPa.

BASIC PRINCIPLES

Two basic principles determine the effect of high pressure on foods. Pascal's isostatic principle, indicates that pressure applied to a sample including biological products is transmitted in a uniform and quasi-instantaneous manner. The pressurisation process is independent of sample volume, product size and geometry, in contrast to thermal processing. Processing by high hydrostatic pressure is usually carried out in a low-compressibility liquid such as water. The second principle is that of Le Chatelier, which states that phenomena of phase transition, chemical changes etc., which are accompanied by decrease in volume are favoured by pressure and vice-versa. Pressure influences most biochemical reactions occurring in foods since they often involve a change in volume. Pressure may also inhibit the availability of energy by affecting energy-producing enzymatic reactions. The effect of hydrostatic pressure in a food product is dependent upon the amount of pressure applied, duration of compression, depressurisation rate, temperature of treatment, product pH, water activity, salt concentration etc. There are also other salient features which are unique

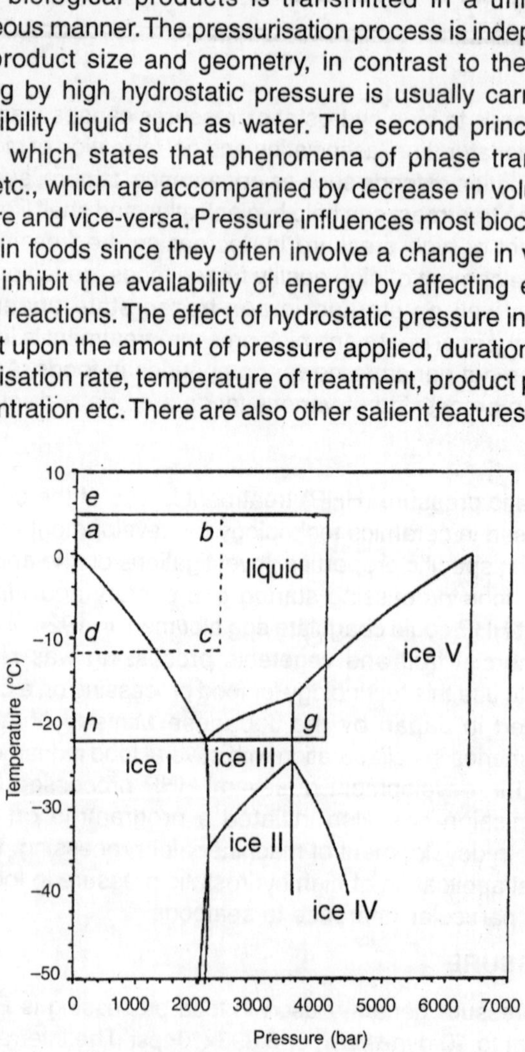

Fig. 36.1: Effect of high Pressure on liquid solid phase transition of water

for HHP processing of foods. As compared with thermal processing, HHP treatment consumes less energy (e.g. energy required pressurisation at 400 MPa is equivalent to heating the same material to 30°C).

EFFECT OF HHP ON WATER

Since water is the main component of foods, the influence of pressure on it has been examined in detail. Unlike gases, HHP causes minimum decrease in volume of water i.e., a maximum of 15% in volume of water is decreased at a pressure of 600 MPa. Foods that contain much water and little gas have a compressibility similar to that of water. Pressure treatment can also cause a decrease in pH of the foods containing significant amount of water; a treatment at 400 MPa causing a reduction of pH up to 0.7. The behaviour of water under high pressure at subzero temperatures has been studied in detail by Bridgman as early as 1912. The freezing point of water is lowered depending upon the pressure, as shown by the solid liquid phase diagram of water (Fig. 36.1). Further, the physical nature of ice that is formed under pressure is also different as compared to conventional ice.

Freezing point of water decreases with increasing pressure; the freezing point is —5°C at 70 MPa, -10°C at 125 MPa, -20°C at 200 MPa and —22°C at 207 MPa. Release of pressure helps in rapid and uniform nucleation and growth of smaller ice crystals in the food, causing minimum damage (see 'abcd' in Fig. 36.1). To enable complete freezing of the sample, additional cooling is needed because of the large heat of fusion of ice formation. This technique also helps in increased freezing rates as compared to a conventional freezing process at ambient pressure.

In an analogus way, pressurassisted thawing involves pressurising a frozen sample up to the liquid area of the phase diagram, thus increasing the thawing rate, if the appropriate heat of fusion is provided (path 'dcba', in Fig. 36.1). The use of high pressure on water offers the possibility to obtain other ice polymorphs instead of normal ice, i.e., ice I (e.g. ice II, III, IV, V etc.), all of which have a smaller volume as compared to the liquid state as observed by Bridgman. Other ice polymorphs can be obtained by direct pressurization at sub-zero temperature (e.g. path "hg" Fig. 36.1) or alternatively by pressurizing a liquid sample above 200 MPa and subsequently cooling the sample (e.g. path "efg", Fig. 36.1). Depressurisation of the sample will result in the formation of ice I. The phase transitions of water occurring during the pressure treatment under different conditions may also influence the functional properties of other food constituents.

EFFECT ON OTHER MAJOR FEED COMPONENTS

Proteins are composed of covalently linked amino acids which are further stabilised by non-covalent interactions such as hydrogen bonds, ionic bonds, hydrophobic attractions etc. The functional properties of proteins, such as oil emulsification and foaming capacities, solubility, textural attributes etc., in foods are due to their characteristic three-dimensional structures. Any processing operation which destroys the native structure of the proteins also changes their functional properties, whereas thermal processing causes covalent bond breakage in the proteins resulting in formation of newer compounds, HHP affects only non- covalent interactions in the proteins and therefore, does not give rise to newer compounds. Nevertheless, the effect of HHP in the range of 400 to 600 MPa on non-covalent bonds may lead to unfolding of the polypeptide chain leading to denaturation, gel formation, precipitation, association, aggregation, polymerisation and coagulation of proteins. Such changes lead to modifications of functional properties and also their susceptibility to proteolytic digestion by enzymes such as trypsin, pepsin etc. Starch components undergo gelatinisation and modification of its susceptibility to enzymatic hydrolysis. Isolated lipids, particularly unsaturated ones, are more prone to auto- oxidation, and are further influenced by the presence of metal ions, oxygen etc. Enzymes are generally stable to pressure treatment. Although some enzymes such as fish myosin may be activated, activity of methyl esterase, peroxidase, polyphenol oxidase or lipoxygenase remains unchanged. Therefore, food products may have to be subjected to an initial blanching before HHP treatment to inactivate the enzymes.

EFFECT ON MICROORGANISMS

The resistance of microorganisms to pressure is extremely variable. The extent of inactivation depends on several par meters, such as the type of microorganism, the pressure level, the process temperature and time and the composition of the dispersion medium. Vegetative cells in the early growth phase are more sensitive than cells in the stationary phase. Gram-positive bacteria are more resistant than gram-negative bacteria. Vegetative cells and also spores of yeasts and moulds are inactivated at 200 to 300 MPa, whereas, bacterial spores are very resistant and can even survive pressures above 1000 MPa. Some viruses are also very resistant to pressure. DNA replication and transcription and protein synthesis are inhibited at much lower pressure levels in Escherichia cali. The effect of HHP is essentially due to change in permeability of cell membrane and associated leakage of intercellular material. Further, membrane-bound AT Pase is denatured and displaced. The lowering of pH due to HHP also leads to loss of viability of microorganisms. Studies in our laboratory have shown that Salmonella typhimurium and Listeria monocytogens could be inactivated by a factor of 7 and 2 log cycles, respectively, by exposure to 200 MPa pressure for 10 min. A combination of gamma irradiation (2-4 kGy) and 400

MPa could reduce bacterial spore load more effectively than the individual treatment per se.

A large volume of studies has been made on the effect of HHP on microorganisms in foods. A Japanese study on pressure-pasteurisation using various microorganisms has shown that the decimal reduction time of 2-11 mm at 300 MPa and 20°C Pressure processing of pork homogenate at neutral pH and 400 MPa caused 6 log cycle inactivation of several microorganisms including E. coli, Campylo bacter jejuni, Salmonella typhimurium, Yersinia enterocolitica, Sacharomyces cerevisae. Bacillus cereus spores were not inactivated. Listeria monocytogenes were inactivated in milk when exposed to 340 MPa at 23°C.

HHP treated foods differ significantly from their thermally treated counterparts, whereas, heat treatment makes large changes in colour, density, flavour and elasticity. Such changes are minimal in pressure treated foods. On the other hand, significant improvements in transparency, smoothness, adhesiveness and gloss of the product could be achieved by pressure processing. While both thermal and pressure treatments cause denaturation and coagulation of proteins, gelatinisation of starch, chemical changes such as Maillard reaction and loss of vitamins are minimal during pressure treatment. While both heat and pressure inactivate vegetative cells of microorganisms as well as insects and their larvae, pressure processing does not inactivate spores of microorganisms. The advantages and disadvantages of HHP processing are given in Table 36.1.

GENERAL APPLICATIONS

RAPID FREEZING AND THAWING OPERATIONS

Conventional freezing techniques are known to have detrimental effects. The optimum freezing rate for food products or living cells is highly system-dependent. Slow freezing (>30 mm) generally results in larger ice-crystal formation, which may cause extensive mechanical damage, accelerated enzyme and microbiological activities as well as potentially increased oxidation rates, resulting from the increasing substrate concentration and the insolubility of oxygen in ice. Ultra-rapid freezing (e.g. cryogenic freezing) may cause lethal intracellular ice crystallization or mechanical cracking. Pressure-assisted freezing occurs as an impact of the pressure-induced freezing point depression which enables water still in the liquid phase at high pressures. The behaviour of water under pressure offers potential applications in food processing, such as pressure-assisted freezing (pressure-shift freezing) and pressure-assisted thawing (pressure-shift thawing), non-frozen storage under pressure at sub-zero temperature and formation of different ice polymorphs. Pressure-assisted freezing and pressure-assisted thawing have been examined on a variety of foods. For example, pressure-assisted thawing of tuna and carp meat resulted in a better quality of the products. Pressure-assisted freezing and thawing are particularly beneficial for preventing quality loss during freezing and thawing of fishery products since such frozen products form the major components of international seafood trade.

Table. 36.1 Advantages and Disadvantages of High Pressure Food Processing

Advantages	*Disadvantages*
Operation at low or ambient temperature. Hence, minimum change in food quality occurs. No newer compounds are formed due to degradation of food constituents. Unlike heating, no covalent bond breakage and formation of newer compounds occur. Minimum changes in flavour and vitamins.	Food enzymes generally require very high pressure for inactivation. At usual range of pressures used, an increase or decrease in enzyme activity may result, affecting the food quality. A blanching process needs to be included to inactivate the enzymes.
Pressure coagulated food proteins, e.g. egg. Soy, beef, pork and fish meat are glossy transparent, dense, smooth and soft as compared to heated ones. The unique properties of pressure-procesed protein-rich foods can help development of novel foods.	Residual enzyme activity and dissolved oxygen results in enzymatic and oxidative degradation of food components.
Less use of food additives	Most pressure-processed foods need low temperature storage and distribution to retain their sensory properties.
Less energy requirement	Spores of microorganisms are resistant
Uniformity of application	
The treatment is instantaneous	
Does not damage packaging because the treatment is isostatic (uniform throughout the food)	
Irreversible effects on biological material at >100 MPa. Therefore, 100-1000 MPa used.	
Better hygienic quality. Environmentally-friendly process.	

STORAGE OF FOODS UNDER SUB-ZERO TEMPERATURE UNDER NON-FROZEN STATE

The use of moderate hydrostatic pressure in combination with sub-zero temperatures, has been proposed as means of storing food products without the formation of ice, avoiding damage due to freezing and microbial spoilage. Further, significant energy could be saved using pressure-assisted rather than frozen storage. Product deterioration due to freezing and thawing effects is also avoided.

APPLICATION TO FOODS AGRICULTURAL PRODUCE

Fruit juices were the early successful candidates for pressure-processing, since the pressure-resistant bacterial spores could be inhibited by low pH. Pressure treatment of non-pasteurised citrus juice resulted in a product having flavour close to fresh juice with no loss of vitamin C and a shelf life up to 17 months. HHP processed strawberries jam retained 95% of initial ascorbic acid content and was preferred by a taste panel to heat-processed jam. Pressure-treated jams are currently available in Japanese markets. Strawberries and tomatoes maintained their fresh taste and colour on storage for a few days or weeks under 50-200 MPa at -5° to —20°C Preliminary studies carried out in Germany have shown that high-pressure treatment and freezing can influence the dehydration and subsequent rehydration of potatoes, green beans and carrots. Potential applications of HHP to various food items are shown in Table 36.2.

ANIMAL PRODUCTS

Boiled eggs have a sulphur flavour, while pressure-treated eggs have no such flavour. Fresh egg white became opaque when treated at 500 MPa and was only partially coagulated, while hard gels were formed at pressure above 600 MPa. Egg yolk formed a gel when subjected to a pressure of 400 MPa for 30 min at 25°C, kept its original colour and was soft and adhesive. The hardest gels obtained by pressure treatment were only one sixth the strength of the heat-induced gels. Pressure- treated rabbit meat maintained their native colour and flavour. They were also glossy, smooth and soft, with greater elasticity than heat-induced gels. Gel hardness tended to increase with the pressure used, while adhesiveness decreased. Cured and non-cured pork increased in hardness when subjected to 4000 kg/cm^2 for 30 mm at 25°C. Such treatment increased the digestibility of non-cured pork by trypsin. Raw pork could be successfully stored, avoiding the drip losses occurring after thawing. The microbial counts in ground beef were reduced by low temperature storage under pressure of 200 MPa at -20°C Chicken could be preserved at -8° or —15°C under 170 MPa for 50 days, without significant change in texture. However, enzyme activity under these conditions may be a problem. Thus, unlike frozen storage, enzymatic degradation of ATP occurred at appreciable levels during pressure-chill storage. Therefore, the technique has to be evaluated depending upon the type of foods. Table 36.2 summarises the different food processing applications.

Subjecting fish meat such as those from cod, mackerel etc. to high hydrostatic pressure at refrigerated temperatures can result in changes in their colour, visual appearance and physicochemical properties of components. This is due to destruction of the arrangement of myofibrils, although no degradation through destruction of covalent bonds in the

Table 36.2. Effect of Pressure on Some Individual Food Items

Food Item	*Pressure (MPa)*	*Quality*
Juices (strawberry, grapefruit and mandarin)	400-500	Superior quality. Low temperature storage required; HP prevents bitterness development in grape juice and moulds and yeasts in mandarin. Available in Japanese markets.
Jams (strawberries, kiwifruit, apples)	400-500	Natural colour and taste. Available in Japanese markets
Pears	500 for 15 mm	retained organoleptic qualifies
Soybean, rice, potato	500	Texture turned pliable
Sweet potato	500	Sweetness increased
Guava *puree*	400	Superior quality
Carrot	High pressure freezing at 200-400 MPa	Better texture and histological structure
Beef	200-350	Pinker meat
Sausages	300	Changes in functionality. Increase in lightness
Tea	700 MPa, 50°C, 30 min heating	Sterilised tea. Less change in flavour.
Beef	400 (10 mm)	No change in flavour. When surface is slightly baked, the product tasted like steaks
Ham	400-500	HP helps to reduce salt content
Fish paste	400-500	HP helps to reduce salt content
Oyster	300-400 (10 min)	No change in flavour
Shrimp	400 (10 mm)	Meat coagulation as boiled shrimp. No change in colour.
Surimi from different fish species	300-500	Gelation of protein without heat treatment

myofibrillar proteins occurs. Marine lipids are characterised by a high level of poly-unsaturated fatty acids (PUFAs) such as eicosapentaenoic acid and docosahexaenoic acid. PUFAs are sensitive to oxidation, which in turn, affects the quality of the product, including colour, texture and nutritional value. Pressurization of cod at 405 MPa also helps in inhibition of phospholipid degradation resulting in lower amounts of free fatty acids. High pressure has been shown to enhance lipid autooxidation in fish meat.

EXTENSION OF REFRIGERATED SHELF LIFE

The sensitivity of microorganisms to HHP can be advantageously used for preser-vation of fishery products. However, at mode-rate pressure ranges, namely 400 to 800 MPa, sterilisation of the product cannot be achieved. For example, subjecting squid mantle flesh and tuna meat to 450 MPa at 25°C for 15 mm could lower the initial counts from 5.2×10^3 and 1.9×10^3 to about 300 organisms per g, respectively. Such non-sterile products, however, should be stored under refrigerated conditions to control the proliferation of surviving microorganisms and also to ensure safety from any contaminated spores of Ciostridium botulinum which can germinate at temperatures above 3.5°C and produce toxin. Nevertheless, because of the lower number of surviving microorganisms, the treated products can have longer shelf life than that of untreated control samples under refrigerated conditions. Carp could be preserved at —8°C or —15°C under 170 MPa for 50 days, without significant change in texture. Combination of other processing techniques such as modified atmosphere storage, salting, heat pasteurisation, gamma irradiation etc., along with HHP can further enhance chilled storage life of these products because of the synergestic effect of these processing techniques on viability of surviving microorganisms.

DEVELOPMENT OF SEAFOODS HAVING NOVEL TEXTURE

The possibilities for modification of proteins through pressure-induced changes in non- covalent interactions of polypeptide moieties offer potentials for development of fish products having novel textural attributes. Although, at present, most of these applications of high pressure have been carried out only at laboratory scale, these could be scaled up on a commercial scale. For example, the reddish fresh mackerel meat could be changed to opaque, as if it has been grilled or boiled. Similarly, the transparent nature of cod meat also can be converted into opaque by HHP at 608 MPa for 15 min.

Surimi is a washed fish meat, which forms a gel with excellent texture when heated. Surimi, when mixed with small amounts of salt and subjected to heating can form gel. The gelation property has been used commercially to develop high value items such as lobster tails, shrimp etc. from meat of several low-cost fish. Using ingredients such as egg white and suitable moulds, it is possible to prepare fish and shellfish analogues. Instead of heat, HHP can be used to induce gelation of surimi. Pressure-induced surimi gels from marine species were smoother and more elastic than those produced by heat and were considered to be organoleptically superior. Excellent gels could be produced from pollack, sardine, skipjack and tuna meat at 400 MPa and from squid at 600 MPa. High pressure is very effective in producing highly appealing kamaboko, a Japanese product made from surimi. It has been however, generally observed that instead of surimi, if other fish are used for HHP treatment, they should be of low fat content, since HHP can enhance oxidation of lipids present in the meat.

EQUIPMENT

Initial equipment used for food processing were those used for ceramic processing for electronic components, which were modified with additional sensors. The machines presently available are batch type having limited volume. It may be mentioned that in HHP processing, a 50 litre equipment is comparable to 200 litre heating vessel and a time of 15 mm for HHP is equivalent to one hr in heating and cooling operations. Conventionally, food items packaged in pouches made from conventionally plastic materials is charged into a high pressure vessel filled with normal tap water. The vessel is closed and the pressure therein is increased to the necessary value and then decompressed to ambient pressure again. The treated package is dried which is ready for distribution. The former is used for packaged foods and the latter for liquid items. Some of the companies manufacturing equipment for high pressure food processing include ABB Autoclave Systems Inc, Columbus, Ohio, USA and Mark Freeman, Stansted Fluid Power Ltd., Essex, CM 24, 8HT, UK. The 'Quintus' research high pressure food system developed by ABB Autoclave Systems Inc., S-721 66, Sweden consists of pre-stressed, wire-bound isostatic pressure containment system, intensifier — based electrohydraulic pumping system, water circulation system and control module. The equipment can withstand 900 MPa (130,500 psi) and a temperature of 80°C. A semi-continuous system of 1-4 tonne per hr treatment is also available.

PACKAGING AND STORAGE

Plastic films are generally acceptable for HHP, which are not generally suitable for high temperature processing. However, metal cans and glass containers are not suitable for HHP. Packaging materials for high pressure processed foods should preferably be oxygen impermeable to avoid the adverse interactions between food components such as unsaturated lipids with oxygen under the treatment conditions. There is a need for development of such packaging materials which prevent oxygen permeability and light exposure for keeping fresh colour and flavour of HHP processed foods.

ADVANTAGES TO THE FOOD INDUSTRY

The main benefits of HHP in food processing, as discussed above, include inactivation of microorganisms, structural modifications of biopolymers and depression of freezing point of water. These could be advantageously used in several segments of food industry including seafood industry. In the case of meat industry, the treatment helps to retain functional properties of pre-rigor meat and improve its quality, avoids chilling immediately after slaughtering thus saving energy, improves meat tenderisation and cohesive properties between meat particles and ingredients in restructured products. In the dairy industry, the benefits of HHP include hygienisation of milk and milk products, stabilisation of fermented and dairy products, improved rennet and acid coagulation of milk and preparation of dairy gels and emulsions with novel texture. Poultry industry can use HHP to develop superior soft gels from egg without loss in flavour and nutritional value. The major potential benefits of HHP in protein foods processing could be sanitation of products such as raw milk, cheese, curd, processed meat and seafood products by removing pathogenic microorganisms such as Salmonella, Listeria etc. Since several seafood items are eaten raw in several parts of the world, sanitation of such products definitely has advantage in reducing the risk of food- borne diseases, apart from developing novel products. Other benefits include prolongation of refrigerated shelf life of perishable items such as spreads, emulsified sauces etc. Some other potential applications include improvement of tenderness of pre-rigor beef muscle, selective removal of ß-lactoglobulin from whey concontrates and acceleration of bovine milk curdling by rennet.

PRESSURE PROCESSED COMMERCIAL FOODS

In the year 1990, Meijiya Food Co., Japan, first introduced three kinds of jams (strawberries, kiwifruit and apples) made by HHP treatment without application of heat. High pressure has subsequently been applied to the processing of orange juice to prevent the development of a bitter taste. At present, the company is producing several food sauces and desserts using HHP processing. Several HHP processed fruit juices and jams, pickles, soybean paste, rice, seaweeds are available in the Japanese markets. Some commercial fish items such as fish sausages subjected to HHP are currently available in Japan and more such products are likely to appear in Japanese supermarkets.

37
Technology for Pellet based Snacks

PELLETS

Pellet, a semi-finished product, is the core of snack industry since its characteristics - shape, texture and partly the taste determine the characteristics of the edible snack after frying. The inventor of pellets used the same expansion principle of 'popcorns', creating a starchy matrix with a vitreous structure, which 'bursts' when submitted to powerful thermic treatment.

Raw material with high quantity of starch are necessary to obtain a vitreous structure, which becomes amorphous once it is gelatinised and dried.

In the past, pellets were manufactured in manual way, by means of dough vapour cooking, cut and finally sun-dried. Nowadays, highly sophisticated technologies are utilised to mix powder ingredients, to extrude and cook the dough, to shape the pellet. Die forming, stamping and piercing, are traditional systems of shaping the pellet, while the most recent technologies allow to obtain 3D and pillow shapes by bringing and cutting two sheets of dough together.

A pellet-based snack offers **significant advantages** in comparison with natural potato crisps, in terms of **Profitability** thanks to:

- higher selling price, due to the uniqueness of the snack;
- reduced investments for processing lines and manufacturing facilities;
- easy transportation and handling of pellets, which have long term stability of their characteristics and do not need strict storing conditions (that is why pellets can be delivered everywhere World-wide);
- absence of extra-costs for decontamination of water wastes or potato scraps;

- simple know-how required for frying, flavouring and packing, which reduces the number of workers and the required skills to run the manufacturing operation.

2. OIL

Frying Oil has a strong impact on the shelf life of the snack. The frying temperature for pellets depends on its characteristics but typically, it ranges between 185-200°C. In case of natural potato crisps, it ranges between 160-180°C. Because of the high processing temperature, it is necessary to use oils with peculiar characteristics- like oils with low acidity level. As a matter of fact, triglycerides are made of polyunsaturated fatty acids and are not very stable at high temperatures, since they are sensitive to oxidation, they cause rancidity of the oil absorbed by the pellet.

As a general indication, a good oil for frying pellets should maintain the following acidity values:

- Free Fatty Acids (FFA) < 0.4 - 0.5 %
- Peroxide Index Value (PIV) < 8.0 - 9.0

Higher levels could cause higher oil deterioration and shorter shelf life of the finished snack packed into bags.

MAIN TYPES OF OIL

- **Sunflower Oil:** It is known to cause gumming in fryers due to the formation of high molecular weight polymers. As a consequence, it leads to an increase in oil viscosity. It needs regular cleaning to avoid oil deterioration. Its stability is not sufficient for frying temperatures higher than 180°C.
- **Fractionated Palm Oil (Palmolein):** Chemically and physically, it appears to be particularly stable and clean for frying as well as relatively cheap. Since it contains relatively low fat percentage and natural anti-oxidants, further chemical additions are not required. It is considered the most suitable for frying pellets.
- **Maize or Corn Oil:** It is not widely used for commercial frying and its problems are commonly related to gumming in the fryer and its relatively short life, unless they are partially hydrogenated.
- **Cottonseed Oil:** It causes less problems regarding gumming than sunflower, but nevertheless it still presents some difficulties. Hydrogenation increases its stability and the shelf life of fried products.
- **Pure Soya and Rapeseed Oil:** These are generally regarded as unsuitable for frying without hydrogenation.

Where the oil may have a questionable stability at high temperature, essential to achieve an adequate shelf life are:

- suitable fryer design;
- handling of the fryer to ensure a short oil turnover time;
- good cleaning practices to reduce to the minimum the formation of products with high molecular weight.

3. FLAVOUR

Taste and texture being the two basic organoleptic characteristics while eating a snack, it is easy to understand how important 'flavour' is for the success of a snack.

Flavours are natural or synthetic extract blends, added with salt and maltodextrins, which allow an effective distribution of seasoning powder on the pellet while going through the drum.

Since tastes are related to the local gastronomic tradition, each country has its own preferred flavours, which may differ, even significantly, from those preferred in a neighbour country.

The most important flavour manufacturers can develop tailor-made flavours by adopting ingredients and percentage of salt. Normally, flavour manufacturers give exclusivity for tailor-made products, which is fundamental to keep uniqueness of the snack in the domestic market.

When a new flavour is selected to be launched, it is wise to make atleast limited market tests to evaluate in advance its acceptability by target consumers.

4. PACKAGING FILM

Pillow bags are the most popular packaging format for snacks World-wide.

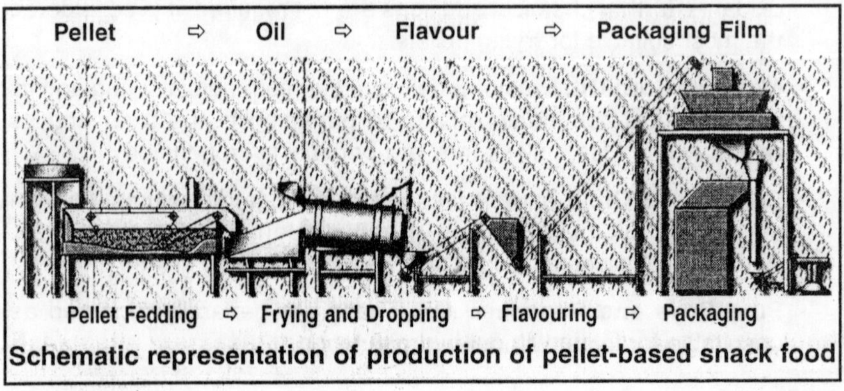

Schematic representation of production of pellet-based snack food

Snacks are normally regarded as 'impulse' products. According to a recent survey, an attractive bag can weigh upto 50% when deciding to buy a bag of snacks for the first time.

A Bag should offer the following characteristics:

- capability to attract consumers' attention in terms of brand name, dimension, lay-out and colours;
- high barrier to humidity to keep the product fragrant and crispy for the longest possible time, as well as high barrier to oxygen and UV (ultra violent) rays, which are required to limit oil degradation that causes rancidity. In other words, to grant the longest shelf life;
- the best protection of product integrity.

Generally speaking, the film is obtained by coupling different layers. Commonly used film is based on by-oriented polypropylene, and can also have a metalised internal surface as a protection from gases and light.

The degree of protection offered by a film is the result of a combination of choices-number and thickness of layers, eventual presence of metalisation, windows and colours.

However, given the design of the fryer, type of oil and process handling, the shelf life of a product mainly depends on the packaging film.

When the environment is characterised by critical conditions (high temperatures and humidity), nitrogen can be blown inside the bag before sealing. To this purpose, a special device on the packaging machine and facilities for manufacturing nitrogen must be available.

A product packed in bags should have a shelf life of atleast three months, but local rules may require longer period.

TECHNOLOGY

1. Pellet Feeding grants the feeding of a constant and uniform quantity of pellet. Normally, frying is done in an oil bath, but could also be achieved through 'expansion' in a hot air oven. A good Dosing Unit should grant:

- feeding of constant and uniform quantity according to process capacity;
- reproducible processing parameters;
- gentle' handling of the pellet in order to avoid breakage;
- reliability.

Pellet feeding can be performed by means of several technologies-

- **Vibrating doser:** it is the most economical system, but does not allow to have precise feeding and information concerning production capacity and quantity processed;

- **Volumetric doser:** it is a reliable way in terms of constant dosing, but similar to vibrating doser, it does not give indications concerning the quantity processed;
- **Weighing doser:** it is the most reliable system, and it allows knowing how much quantity of pellet is processed every hour. As a consequence, it is the most expensive one.

2. FRYING AND DROPPING

Normally, the heat is transferred through edible oil, but there are other means to obtain expansion—

- frying
- hot air
- microwave
- infrared rays.

(the last two having no known industrial application for expanding pellet).

Frying: This phase represents the heart of the whole frying process, as the immersion of pellet into the oil bath causes its expansion, the final step is the snack.

The key principle is that the quick heating of the pellet (frying temperature ranges between 185- 200°C) causes the softening of the gel and the very quick transformation of its residual water in vapour so that the consequent pressure produces the expansion of the pellet.

A good fryer for pellets should grant—

- uniform treatment of all pieces immersed into the oil;
- constant processing time into the oil bath for all pellets;
- steady and uniform distribution of heat in all the different points of the oil bath;
- the smallest possibility of oil deterioration.

Some elements can positively influence the performance of the fryer, and the reaching of the above goals:

Oil recycling system: Forced oil turbulence in the bath grants uniform distribution of heat. A quicker circulation results in a smaller possibility of oil deterioration because of the reduced time of contact with the heating surface. Furthermore, oil turbulence has a positive impact on the expansion of 3D and grid shapes, as oil can easily enter the inside part of the pillow, making the pellets to expand uniformly.

Conveyor system: Forwards the expanding pellet into the oil bath and keeps processing time 'constant'. One solution is a submerging belt, which forwards the pellet as soon as it starts expanding and floating on the oil bath surface. An alternative can be a belt with paddles, which encloses the pellets into cells, where they expand while they are forwarded. The latter solution grants very uniform processing time of the pellet, but can cause small percentage of breakage due to the impact of the product with the paddles of the belt.

Oil turnover: It should not be longer than three hours, and it is influenced by the ratio between the dimensions of oil bath and production capacity, as well as from the percentage of oil absorption depending on pellet characteristics.

Vapour exhausting and **oil filtering** are recommended in order to eliminate dirt and scrapes as natural consequences of the frying and dropping process.

The fryer has to be run always at the maximum capacity, compatible with the pellet to be expanded so that the oil turnover is carried out in the quickest way. To this purpose, the packaging system must be suitable for processing such capacity.

Hot Air: A good hot air oven should grant—

- uniform treatment of all pieces passing through it;
- constant and uniform permanence time;
- gentle handling of expanding pellets;
- steady and uniform distribution of the heat in all points of the expanding section of tho oven.

Most popular hot-air ovens are based on cyclone technology, drum technology and vibrating conveyors with orientable air injection system technology.

Dropping: A good dropping system should grant—

- The most effective dropping in the shortest possible time. Indeed, many kinds of oil are not liquid at room temperature so that the cooling of the fried snack may reduce its ability to lose the excess of oil;
- Gentle handling of fried products.

3. FLAVOURING

Fried snacks are flavoured according to consumer tastes and the type of pellet to be used.

From the technical point of view, it is necessary that flavouring be made immediately after the frying process so that the absorption of the oil in the surface is complete.

A good flavouring system should grant—

- a uniform distribution of snack seasoning, avoiding the formation of lumps;
- reduced quantity of flavour waste;
- gentle handling of snacks.

Dispersion of the seasoning is generally made by means of a flavouring drum, where pellets are put into and are continuously overturned due the rotation of the drum. The flavour is sprayed on the pellet in order to avoid the formation of lumps. A system used recently is the electrostatic drum, by means of which flavour powder and the fried pellet get fed with the oppostite electrostatic values in order to cause reciprocal attraction.

In the case of **hot-air** expansion, it is necessary to spray first the oil and then the flavour on the pellets; as a consequence, the total oil content is normally kept under 10%.

Before passing to the packaging phase, the flavoured snack must rest for a few minutes so as to become less oily and to minimise its tendency to oil the internal surface of the bag.

Sometimes, there are pauses of the bag-maker. Hence it is necessary to add a by-pass phase between flavouring and packaging in which the snacks are temporarily accumulated.

PACKAGING

Finally, the snack is conveyed to the packaging system, where it is packed with the bag size designed according to market demand.

Packaging process is split into two phases:

- weighing of the pellet
- forming and filling of the bag by means of a bag-maker

WEIGHING OF THE PELLET

A good weighing system should grant—

- a high speed weighing in terms of number of bags weighed per minute;
- high precision, even with small bag sizes;
- reliability;
- gentle handling of snack.

Normally, the best performances are reached with multi-head weighing machines, which grant high precision with different bag sizes, and an error margin of about 'zero'. It is important to minimise the error margin, as flavoured snack has the major incidence on the cost of the bag and wastes can increase direct variable manufacturing costs.

FORMING AND FILLING OF THE BAG BY MEANS OF A BAG-MAKER

A good bag-maker should grant—

- speed according to weighing process in terms of number of bags per minute;
- gentle handling of snacks and film;
- reliability.

Generally speaking, bag-maker speed is measured in number of beats per minute so that its production capacity depends on the weight of the bag. The bags being equal, production capacity of a bag-maker depends on the flowing speed of snacks.

The bag-maker production capacity is suggested to be slightly higher than that of the fryer.

38
CONFECTIONERY, COCOA, COFFEE AND TEA

CANDY PRODUCTS AND CONFECTIONERY

Chocolate Peanut Bars

Sugar	3 lb	Water	1 pt
Corn Syrup	3 lb		

Cook to 240° F. Then add 8 pounds of washed peanuts and cook for 10 minutes. Remove from fire, and roll out on a slab. Cut into small pieces and dip in chocolate.

Coffee Caramels

Sugar	4 lb	Cream	½ gal
Corn Syrup	3 lb	Good Java Coffee	½ gal

Cook the above to 238° F. Then add 1 quart sweet cream and cook to about 242° F. Remove from fire, pour on greased slab.

Butterscotch Squares

Sugar	10 lb	water	3 pt
Corn Syrup	4 lb		

Cook to 285° F. Add 4 ounces of butter, ½ teaspoonful of salt. Stir and cook to 295° F. When cooled down flavor with oil of lemon. Pour on greased slabs.

Everton Toffee

Sugar	4 lb	Cream of Tartar	½ tsp
Water	3 cups	Butter	2 oz

Put the water, sugar, and cream of tartar into a pan and stir until they boil, but no longer. Add the butter after the other comes off the fire, but do not stir it in.

Licorice Drops

Sugar	12½ lb	Oil of Wintergreen	30 min
Water	3 pt	Oil of Anise	20 min
Cream of Tartar	1 dr	Powdered Charcoal	1dr
Powdered Extract of Licorice	1 oz		

Cook the sugar, water, and cream of tartar to 340° F. Pour out on an oiled slab. Add the other ingredients, and fold and knead until well mixed. Then stamp into drops.

Fruit Jelly Candies

Fruit Juice	2 qt	Corn Syrup or Invert Syrup	3 lb
Sugar	3 lb	Commercial Pectin Syrup	1 qt

Mix fruit juice and pectin syrup. Add the sugar and corn, or invert, syrup. Boil to 222-223° F. Remove from fire. Pour into starch molds or oiled pans, about ½ inch deep. Allow to harden 24 hours. Remove from molds and dust with powdered sugar or dip in chocolate.

Fruit Caramels

Sugar	2 lb	Ground Dried Fruit	1 lb
Chopped Walnuts	½ Pt	Butter	2 oz
Corn Syrup	1¼ lb	Whipping Cream	2 qt

Cook sugar, corn syrup, and one-half of cream to 238°F. Then add one-half of the remaining cream and cook to 242° F. Add remaining cream, dried fruit, butter, and chopped nuts and cook to 248° F. Pour into an oiled pan or on a slab to cool and harden.

Fruit Marshmallows

Powdered Edible Gelatin	4 oz	Dried Apricots, Figs, Prunes, Pears, Chopped or Whole Raisins	3 lb
Hot Water	1 pt		
Corn Syrup	2½ lb		
Powdered Sugar	2½ lb		

Dissolve the gelatin in hot water. Cook corn syrup to 250° F. Beat into it the dissolved gelatin and powdered sugar until the mixture is light. Flavor with vanilla. Then add the dried fruit. Beat a short time and pour on oiled paper or a slab to harden. Three-quarters of a pint of fruit syrup may be used instead of dried fruit.

Molasses Wafers

Sugar	5 lb	New Orleans Molasses	1 Pt
Corn Syrup	1 lb	Butter	¼ lb
Water	1½ pt		

Stir and cook to 290° F. Roll out on a greased slab.

Maraschino Cherries

Place firm ripe Royal Ann Cherries in a paraffin-lined barrel, a crock, or a bottle, depending upon amount. Do not remove the stems. Cover the cherries with the solution made as follows:

Water	1 gal	Citric Acid	½ oz
Bisulfite of Soda	1 gal	Salt	6 oz

Dissolve the above ingredients. Let stand until cherries are bleached, which may take 2 weeks or longer. Then discard the solution. Stem and pit the fruit. Boil the fruit in five or six changes of water until free from sulfur taste and tender. Prepare a 40% sugar solution, and for each 10 gallons of cherries dissolve ¼ ounce of certified red color, Ponceaux 3R. Also add teaspoonful citric acid. Now cover cherries with this colored sugar solution, and cook for 10 minutes. After 24 hours, cook cherries and syrup again, after adding 10 pounds of sugar. Repeat this again on third day. -Then allow to remain in crock for 2 weeks. Now add ¼ ounce of bitter almond oil dissolved in a little alcohol, for flavor. Instead of the red, a green food color may be used, and instead of wild cherry, mint flavor may be added.

Wild Cherry Drops

Sugar (Crystal A)	4 lb	Extract of Bitter Almonds	3 dr
Water	1 pt	Powdered Orris	3 dr
Cream of Tartar	24 gr	Red Color	Sufficient

Cook the sugar, water, and cream of tartar to 335° F. Pour out on an oiled slab. Let it cool a little. Add the extract, the orris and the color. When cool enough, work thoroughly and stamp into drops.

Aniseed Drops

Sugar (Crystal A)	5 lb	Oil of Anise	40 mm
Water	22 oz	Red Color	Sufficient
Cream of Tartar	40 gr		

Put the sugar in a suitable container. Add the water and the cream of tartar. Cook to 335° F. Pour out on an oiled slab. As it cools, add the oil of anise and the color. Fold over until cool enough to handle. Then work thoroughly and stamp into drops.

Nut Glazes

Sugar	10 lb	Water	3 pt
Corn Syrup	2½ lb		

Cook sugar and water to 290° F. Shut off heat and drop in nuts to be sugar coated or glazed. Remove with fork.

Revivifying Dry Popcorn

Popcorn which pops poorly because of having become too dry may be restored to good popping condition by the following method:

Put 40 pounds of corn into a 10-gallon can. Add 1 to 3 pounds of water, according to the dryness of the corn, as indicated by the way it pops. If its popping yield is less than one-third the normal yield of the variety, add 3 pounds of water; if it is two-thirds normal, add only 1 pound. For intermediate degrees of popping add intermediate quantities of water. For different varieties of popcorn the normal popping yield varies from 15 to about 30 volumes.

Put on the cover, using a rubber gasket, and clamp it down tightly. Shake thoroughly. Let it stand 2 days or longer before popping.

The poor popping quality of some lots of corn is due to other causes than lack of moisture. In such cases the popping cannot be improved by adding water.

The above method of restoring poppability is applicable only to small quantities of corn. When it becomes necessary to increase the moisture content of a large quantity of popcorn, it should be done by storing the corn in a cool, damp place, as, for example, in a shed outside during winter, or in a basement room during summer.

Popcorn Fruit Crisp

Sugar	3 lb	Butter	3 tbsp
Corn Syrup	1½ lb	Chopped Dried Fruit	3/4 lb
Water	1 pt	Salt	Sufficient to flavor
Popped Popcorn	4½ qt		

Cook sugar, corn syrup and water to 285°F. Add the butter, salt and fruit, and stir. Now stir in the popcorn. More or less popcorn may be added to suit.

Salted Peanuts

Heat coconut oil in a kettle on a gas flame to about 300°F. Put shelled Spanish peanuts into a basket. Immerse this basket in the hot oil, and roast until brown. Now pour peanuts over a fine sieve, and when the oil has drained off add the salt.

Unwrapped Licorice Caramels

Cane Sugar	60 lb	Sweetened Whole Condensed Milk (8%)	3 gal
Corn Syrup (430 Be)	50 lb	Table Salt	6 oz
Cream (40%)	4 gal	Fat (140° F m.p.) (Hydrogenated Peanut or Cottonseed Stearine)	2 lb
Fresh Unsweetened Whole Condensed Milk (10%)	5 gal	Licorice Syrup	8 lb

Put all ingredients except licorice in kettle. Cook to a soft ball. Add licorice syrup and black color. Cook batch to hard ball in cold water. Pour on slab and let stand overnight. Cut to size desired. No wrapper is required for this excellent "stand-up" caramel. Put in waxed paper cups.

Licorice Taffy

Cane Sugar	15 lb	Cocoa Butter	1 lb
Licorice Syrup	8 lb	Corn Syrup (430 Be)	13 lb

Place in kettle. Cook to soft ball in cold water and add licorice syrup. Cook to hard ball, add black color, and spread out on marble to desired thickness. Let cool and cut to suit. Wrapper should be about 20-pound white waxed.

This is a splendid number for wax-wrapped five- and ten- cent bars. May also be used to increase variety and give novelty to chocolate and bonbon centers. Makes an excellent center for pan goods.

Licorice Jelly Gum Drops

Gum Arabic	50 lb	Corn Syrup (430 Be)	5 lb
Cane Sugar	80 lb	Water	4 gal
Licorice Syrup	12 lb		

Soak gum in hot water, using 1 pound of gum to 1 quart of water. Let stand in hot room overnight. Skim off and strain through very fine sieve. Cook sugar, corn syrup, and water to 250° F. Add licorice syrup and black color and continue to cook to 255° F. Add gum and cast in starch. Put in hot room for 48 hours. Take out and let stand until cool. When cool, remove from starch and place in crystal pans. Use crystal cold, cook to 232° F. Leave in crystal overnight.

The smaller sizes of licorice jelly gum drops make excellent centers for pan work. For this work they are, of course, not crystallised. Put them in the pan after removing them from starch and handle them the same as you would jelly beans or cordial drops. Do not color the syrup but finish white.

Chocolate or bonbon-coated, this luscious jelly gum drop makes an excellent addition to the conventional cordial box or summer package.

Hard Licorice Drops (Pastilles)

Gum Arabic	60 lb	Licorice Syrup	12 lb
Cane Sugar	36 lb	Corn Syrup	6 lb
Glycerin	3 oz		

Melt gum in the proportion of 1 pound to 1 quart of hot water, and let set overnight in hot room. Bring to a boil next day and strain through a very fine sieve. Cook sugar and corn syrup to 280°F. Add gum, licorice syrup, and black color, and put in hot room overnight. Next morning, skim off and cast in starch.

Place in hot room again and allow to set for three days. Temperature of hot room should be maintained between 130 and 140°F. After removing from the hot room, let stand for about 24 hours to cool. Clean off starch and return to hot room until product is hot, rub in refined petrolatum (white vaseline) until the desired shine is obtained.

Wrapped Licorice Caramels

Corn Syrup (43° Be)	10 lb	Cream (40%)	4 gal
Cane Sugar	30 lb	Licorice Syrup	6 lb
Cocoa Butter	3 lb		

Put all ingredients except black color and licorice syrup in kettle. Cook to a soft ball. Add licorice syrup and black color. Cook to a hard ball in cold water. Pour on slab and allow to stand overnight. Cut and wrap.

Licorice Marshmallow Caramels

Cane sugar	60 lb	Sweetened Whole Condensed Milk (8%)	3 gal
Corn Syrup (430 Be)	50 lb	Table Salt	6 oz
Cream (40%)	4 gal	Licorice Syrup	8 lb
Fresh Unsweetened Whole Condensed Milk (10%)	5 gal		

Put all ingredients except color and licorice in kettle. Cook to a soft ball. Add licorice syrup and black color. Cook batch to a hard ball in cold water. Turn out 1/8 inch thick. On this lay a sheet of sheet marshmallow. Put top piece of licorice caramel on when batch is cool enough to handle.

Cut and pack in waxed paper cups, straight-packed or in assortments, alternating rows with plain licorice caramels.

Licorice Caramel-Nougat Center for Chocolates or Bonbons

Corn Syrup (43° Be)	10 lb	Cream (40%)	4 gal
Cane Sugar	30 lb	Licorice Syrup	4 lb
Cocoa Butter	3 lb		

Mix equal quantities of this licorice caramel and a vanilla nougat. Do not add any additional color. The resulting batch will be lighter than licorice caramel but of good color.

The licorice-caramel-nougat mixture makes a particularly fine eating piece of candy and is confidently recommended to those who seek something distinctive in the way of chocolate or bonbon centers.

Licorice Turkish Paste

Cane Sugar	75 lb	Cream of Tartar	6 oz
Corn Syrup (430 Be)	15 lb	Licorice Syrup	20 lb
Cooking Starch	9 lb	Water	4 gal

Put sugar, corn syrup, and water in kettle and bring to boil. Add cooking starch which has previously been soaked in 1 gallon of cold water. After batch has boiled 10 minutes, add cream of tartar which was previously melted in 6 ounces of water. Next, add licorice syrup and continue boiling until batch is finished. Cook until it drops easily from a knife.

This constitutes a licorice confection of mild character and velvety texture.

Licorice Strings, Opera Drops or A. B. Gum-Work

Cane Sugar	50 lb	Special Thick-Boiling Starch	20 lb
Corn Syrup (430 Be)	135 lb	Licorice Syrup	12 lb
Cream of Tartar	2½ oz	Water	8 gal
Tartaric Acid	1½ oz		

Put sugar and corn syrup in kettle with water. Bring to a boil. Add starch, which has been previously dissolved in 3 gallons of cold water, and cream of tartar. Cook 1 hour. Add licorice syrup. Cook for another ½ hour, making a total cooking time of 1½ hours. Turn off steam. Add vegetable black color, and finally add acid which has been melted in a little hot water.

Cast in blood-warm starch (98-100° F). Leave in hot room, at 140°F, for 3 days. Take out of hot room and let stand until cold. When cold, sugar up and let stand in hot room or a very dry room for 24 hours.

Cook crystal to 233°F and apply, while hot, to goods. Leave goods in crystal for 10 hours. Drain off crystal and empty crystal pans into boards. Be sure goods are thoroughly dry before packing.

This formula makes a tender and delicious string or drop. It may also be used for A.B. gums, if desired.

Licorice Paste for Bag Work

Powdered XXXX Sugar	10 lb	Well Beaten Whites of Eggs	8 oz
Licorice Syrup	1 lb		

Beat egg whites to a stiff fluff. Add sugar and licorice syrup, and sufficient black vegetable color to get the desired shade. Keep this paste in a covered container and use as needed. It sets up brittle and crunchy, like a biscuit. It is a deliciously flavored paste for making dominoes, clubs and spades, Hallowe'en witches, black cats, and all sorts of holiday bag work and bag work novelties.

Licorice Bonbon Fondant (Natural Color)

Cane Sugar	80 lb	Water	2½ gal
Egg Whites	1 pt	Licorice Syrup	8 lb

Cook sugar and water to 242°F. Pour on ball beater and let cool. Beat egg whites to a stiff fluff, add to batch, and start beater. When thoroughly mixed, add licorice syrup. Use no color. When fondant is finished, put it in a cream tank. Do not use a wet cloth to cover fondant; use a metal or wood cover instead.

This is a mild flavored bonbon coating of natural light brown color. It adds a new piquant note to the character of bonbons and advances but does not dominate the flavor of the center.

Cocoanut Center for Licorice Bonbons

Fresh Grated Cocoanut	55 lb	Cane Sugar	15 lb
Corn Syrup (430 Be)	35 lb	Table Salt	¼ Oz

Put all of the above ingredients in steam kettle and cook to a soft ball. Add 10 pounds of nougat cream and 4 ounces vanilla extract. Pour on marble. Let cool. •Cut or roll to desired size. Fork-dip in licorice bonbon coating.

This is a delicious fresh cocoanut bonbon for the high-class retail trade. A less perishable center can be made using desiccated instead of fresh cocoanut.

Low-Priced Wrapped Licorice Caramels
(Natural Color or Colored)

Corn Syrup (43°Be)	60 lb	Whole Sweetened Condensed Milk	25 lb
Cane Sugar	40 lb	Vanilla Extract	4 oz
Cocoanut Butter (92°F)	8 lb	Licorice Syrup	8 lb
Full Cream Caramel Paste	25 lb		

Put all the ingredients, except licorice syrup and vanilla extract, in kettle. Cook to a soft ball. Add licorice syrup and vanilla extract. Add black color, if desired. Cook to a hard ball in cold water. Pour on slab and allow to stand overnight. Cut and wrap.

This is an inexpensive caramel of excellent stand-up and eating qualities.

Licorice Wrapped Kisses
(Semi-Nougat Type)

Corn Syrup (43°Be)	20 lb	Whole Sweetened Condensed Milk	1¼ lb
Cane Sugar	10 lb	Licorice Syrup	1½ lb
Cocoa Butter	¾ lb	Color	Sufficient

Put all materials together in kettle. Cook to 255°F. Pour on slab and let cool. Pull for five minutes. Spin out and cut to suit.

This is a pleasing departure from the ordinary run of wrapped kiss formula. This licorice kiss is inexpensive to make, will stay soft, and is easy to eat.

Almond Licorice Nougat

Cane Sugar	80 lb	Licorice Syrup	10 lb
Corn Syrup (43°Be)	70 lb	Water	8 gal
Almonds	15 lb	Egg Albumen (Good Beating Quality)	1¼ lb

Soak -egg albumen in water overnight. Then put in nougat kettle and beat 5 minutes. Cook sugar, corn syrup, and water to 240°F. Take 3 quarts of this mixture and beat into egg fluff very slowly. Cook balance of sugar and corn syrup batch to 300°F. Add slowly to batch in nougat kettle until all are thoroughly mixed. Now add licorice syrup, almonds, and sufficient vegetable color to get a good black color.

If a short nougat is desired, the batch should be beaten about hour. If a chewy nougat is preferred, 15 minutes beating will be sufficient.

Turn nougat out into steel or wood trays and cut the following day.

This makes a high-class, cut nougat which is without equal for adding color contrast and flavor variety to pallid vacation numbers, summer packages, and straight nougat assortments:

Genuine Licorice Anthracite

Licorice Syrup	12 lb	Whole 8% Sweetened Condensed Milk	5 gal
Granulated Cane Sugar	50 lb	Salt	½ lb
Corn Syrup (43°Be)	60 lb	Cocoanut Butter (92°F m.p.)	6 lb
Hard Fat (Hydrogenated Peanut or Cottonseed Stearine)	2 lb		

Put all raw materials in kettle, with the exception of licorice syrup, and cook to a crack. Add licorice syrup and black vegetable color to suit. Cook to a hard crack. Pour on marble slab and allow to cool. Cut into irregular chunks resenibling coal.

A rich, delicious piece of the butter-toffee variety. Has the novel appearance of anthracite and a savory background of licorice.

Genuine Licorice Black Birds

Cane Sugar	12 lb	Corn Syrup (43°Be)	30 lb
Refined Dextrose (Corn Products Cerelose or Equivalent)	20 lb	Thin Boiling Starch	9 lb
		Gelatin	3¾ lb
		Licorice Syrup	5 lb

Dissolve cane sugar, dextrose, and corn syrup in 4½ gallons of water. Cook as for a regular high-cooked gum drop. Suspend 9 pounds of thin boiling starch in 2 gallons of water and add gradually to the boiling batch. The cooking is continued until a high-cooked gum drop results.

Dissolve 3¾ pounds of gelatin in 5½ quarts of water and warm up. Mix this in with the remainder of the batch toward the end of the boil. Finally, add licorice syrup and black vegetable color to suit. It is customary to give this piece a high gloss after taking it out of starch.

This is the popular chewy black licorice drop in the appealing all-licorice flavour. Those desiring a still chewier drop will find that they can vary the above formula by adding to the gelatin solution an equal amount of gum arabic dissolved in water.

Sugar Coating for Candy

Cocoa Butter Substitute	35 lb	Powdered Sugar	50 lb
Powdered Skim Milk	15 lb	Salt	2oz
Vanillin	½ oz		

This may be colored and flavored with oil-soluble colors. After melting the cocoa butter substitute, add the other materials gradually in a dough mixer and finally run over finishing rolls at a temperature of 110°F. In using, run on enrober at 104°F.

Chocolate Coating

Cocoa Butter Substitute	28 lb	XXXX Powdered Sugar	52 lb
Cocoa Powder	10 lb	Vanillin	½ oz
Skim Milk Powder	10 lb	Salt	2 oz

Melt fat and mix thoroughly. This coating may be used at a temperature of about 110°F. For summer use, add 2% cottonseed stearine (140°F m.p.).

Vanilla Marshmallows

Water	3 qt	Corn Syrup	15 lb
Gelatin	15 oz	XXXX Sugar	15 lb)

Dissolve gelatin in 3 quarts of hot water and set aside. Heat the corn syrup to 250°F in a kettle. Remove from heat and, while mixing, add 15 pounds of XXXX sugar. Now pour into the batch, through a strainer, the 3 quarts of gelatin. Work the whole lot together and flavor with vanilla. Transfer the batch to the marshmallow beater, and beat until very stiff. Then pour it on a slab previously powdered with XXXX sugar. Let stand 4 to 5 hours. Then cut into marshmallow size. Press knife down and cut.

Agar Jelly Gum Drops

Agar-Agar	10 oz	Water	5 gal
Sugar	18 lb	Corn Starch	1 lb
Corn Syrup	8 lb		

Soak 10 ounces of agar in 4 gallons of water, overnight. In the morning cook up the agar for several minutes, and then strain into the sugar and corn syrup. Now bring the batch to a boil, while stirring. When the batch comes to a boil, add the 1 pound of corn starch made into a paste with 1 gallon of water. Cook the entire batch up to about 230°F or to a stiff string and then cast in starch. Add color and flavor, after removing batch from the heat. For fruit flavors, use 1 or 2 ounces of citric acid.

British Unwrapped Caramels

Condensed Whole Milk (40% Sugar)	50 lb	Corn Syrup	20lb
		Nulomoline	5 lb
Salted Dairy Butter	5 lb	Brown Sugar	10 lb
Hard Coconut Butter (88-90° F m. p.)	10 lb	Rice Flour	5 lb
		Salt	3 lb

Flavor with a combination of:

Vanilla Flavor	Strong
Violet Flavor	Trace
Maple Flavor	Moderately strong

Place the condensed milk, butter, coconut butter, corn syrup, and Nulomoline into a kettle, heat, and mix until the fats are melted. Add the sugar and rice flour, mix, and boil the batch to a firm ball. Now add the salt and flavors, mix well and spread the batch out to cool, then size and cut;

North Carolina Caramels
(For Caramel Twirls)

Condensed Skim Milk (40% Sugar)	35 lb	Fine Granulated Sugar	20 lb
		Soft Winter Wheat Flour	10 lb
Corn Syrup	50 lb	Salt	6 oz
Coconut Oil (760 F m.p.)	5 lb	Basic Fondant	15 lb
Nulomoline	10 lb	Flavor and Color	As desired

Heat the Nulomoline, corn syrup, milk and coconut oil, then add the sugar, which has been mixed with the flour, and stir. Cook the batch to a hard ball. Add the fondant, salt, flavor and color, and mix well. Then spread the batch out to cool.

Roll the batch into thin sheets, placing a layer of nougat (New York Nougat) on the caramel. Then roll it up in much the same manner as jelly rolls. Spin the caramel into strips about 1 inch in diameter and later cut into pieces of the desired size.

Basic Fondant

Fine Granulated Sugar	80 lb	Water	To Dissolve the Sugar
Corn Syrup	20 lb		
Nulomoline	10 lb		

Cook together to 244°F.

Smyrna Caramels

Corn Syrup	10 lb	Salt	4 oz
Nulomoline	10 lb	Ground Figs	30 lb
Coconut Oil (76° F m.p.)	5 lb	Red Color	
Sugar	15 lb	Roman Punch Flavor	
Condensed Whole Milk (40% Sugar)	20 lb		

Heat the corn syrup, Nulomoline, coconut oil and condensed milk together. Add the sugar. Continue to stir and bring the batch to a boil. Now add the ground figs and cook to a firm ball. Then add the salt, flavor and color. Spread the batch out to cool. Cut into squares and wrap in cellophane or coat in chocolate or pack in parchment paper cups.

Swiss Caramels (Unwrapped)

Sugar	45 lb	Egg Whites (Fresh or Frozen) or 2 lb of Albumen Dissolved in 4 lb of Water	10 lb
Nulomoline	5 lb		
Corn Syrup	40 lb		
Cream (20% Butter Fat)	100 lb	Salt	2 oz
		Coffee Flavor	

Mix the egg whites or albumen solution with the cream. Meanwhile, place the sugar, Nulomoline and corn syrup in a kettle. Add enough of the cream to dissolve the sugar and bring the batch to the boiling point. Gradually add the balance of the cream and egg mixture and boil the batch to a medium firm ball. Add the salt, flavor, and color if wanted, and spread the batch out to cool. Different flavors and nut meats can be added to this batch to produce a variety of caramels.

Butterscotch (Squares and Slabs)

Refined Sugar	10 lb	Lecithin	½ oz
Brown Sugar	10 lb	Special Caramel Paste	10 lb
Corn Syrup	10 lb	Frappe No. 1	2 lb
Nulomoline	5 lb	Salt	3 oz
Water	6 lb	Vanilla Flavor	Strong
Salted Dairy Butter	3 lb	Bergamot Oil	Trace
Coconut Oil (76° F m.p.)	2 lb	Nutmeg Oil	Trace

Melt the butter and coconut oil, add the lecithin and stir until it is melted, then add the sugars, corn syrup, Nulomoline and water and boil together to 280° F. Gradually add the caramel paste. Mix well and continue to cook the batch to the first crack. Turn off the heat. Add the frappe, salt and flavors and spread the batch out between iron bars so that it will be approximately ½ inch thick. Mark with a cutting frame, Then cut-into bars. This makes a good five-cent item for wrapping in waxed paper or cellophane.

Special Caramel Paste

Corn Syrup	35 lb	Coconut Oil (76°F m.p.)	10 lb
Condensed Whole Milk		Granlated Sugar	20 lb
(40% Sugar)	45 lb	Salt	½ lb

Heat the corn syrup, coconut oil and condensed milk. Add the sugar and salt and heat until the sugar is dissolved. Then cook to a soft paste and spread out to cool.

Frappe No. 1

Nulomoline	50 lb	Albumen	3 lb
Corn Syrup	50 lb	Cold Water	2 lb

Boil the corn syrup to approximately 245°F. Shut off the steam. Add the Nulomoline cold and stir until it is melted. Place the batch in a marshmallow beater. Start the beater. Then gradually add the albumen, dissolved in the water, and beat until light.

French Chewing Candy (Mixture No. 1)

Corn Syrup	25 lb	Albumen—Dissolved in	3 lb
Nulomoline	25 lb	Water	6 lb

Boil the corn syrup to 245°F. Add the Nulomoline and stir until it is melted. Place the batch into a beater. Start the beater. Then gradually add the aqueous albumen solution and beat until light.

French Chewing Candy (Mixture No. 2)

Sugar	30 lb	Cream (20% Butter Fat)	10 lb
Nulomoline	5 lb	Coconut Oil (76°F m.p.)	2 lb
Corn Syrup	25 lb		

Boil altogether to 290° F. Pour this into 20 pounds of Mixture No. 1, adding 6 ounces of gelatin that has been previously soaked in 6 ounces of hot water, and beat until quite light. Now add 10 pounds of roasted cashew nuts, 2 pounds of unsweetened chocolate and vanilla flavor. When the hatch is almost cold, spin it into round sticks about 1½ inches in diameter. Then cut these sticks or rolls into pieces approximately 6 inches long and wrap in cellophane or heavy waxed paper. This may also be cut into blocks or bars.

Japanese Strips (Coconut Pieces)

Corn Syrup	20 lb	Coconut Oil (760 F m.p.)	3 lb
Water	8 lb	Desiccated Coconut	25 lb
Brown Sugar	5 lb	Salt	2 oz
Nulomoline	5 lb	Red Color	
Condensed Whole Milk		Oil of Cinnamon (Ceylon)	
(40% Sugar)	10 lb	Currants	7 lb

Heat the corn syrup, water, Nulomoline, sugar, condensed milk and coconut oil to the boiling point. Add the coconut, continue to mix and cook to a medium firm paste, then add the color, salt, and flavor, mix well, then add the currants. Mix and spread out to cool on an oiled slab dusted with XXXX sugar. Then roll the batch down and, when cold, size, cut and roll in sugar.

Mandarin Slices (Coconut Cut Pieces)

Sugar	15 lb	Desiccated Coconut	25 lb
Water	10 lb	Kumquat Pieces	10 lb
Nulomoline	10 lb	Preserved Ginger	4 lb
Corn Syrup	25 lb	Yellow Color	

Heat the sugar, water, Nulomoline and corn syrup to the boiling point. Then add the coconut and stir and cook to a medium firm paste. Add the kumquat pieces, ginger and color, and mix well. If the fruit contains an excess amount of water, cook the batch to a firm paste.

Spread the batch out on an oiled slab dusted with XXXX sugar and, before the batch is quite cold, form into rolls about 1 inch in diameter. When cold, moisten the rolls with simple syrup or thin icing and roll at once in sesame seeds. The rolls may later be cut into slices and placed in paper cups.

Mont Royale (Fudge Coconut Kisses) [Mixture No. 1]

Desiccated Coconut		Nulomoline	5 lb
(Fancy Shred)	50 lb	Hot Water	5 lb

Mix the Nulomoline with tho hot water, then mix it through the coconut and allow to set for ½ hour before using.

Mont Royale (Fudge Coconut Kisses) [Mixture No. 2]

Condensed Whole Milk		Winter Wheat Flour	5 lb
(40% Sugar)	35 lb	Basic Fondant—made	
Corn Syrup	25 lb	from:	100 lb
Nulomoline	15 lb	80 lbs Sugar	
Brown Sugar	15 lb	20 lbs Corn Syrup	
Coconut Oil (76°F m.p)	9 lb	10 lbs Nulomoline	
Salt	8 oz	Water to Dissolve the Sugar	

Cook to 244° F.

Heat the condensed milk, corn syrup, Nulomoline and coconut oil together. Add the sugar and flour and continue to stir and cook the batch to a firm ball. Then add the salt, fondant and vanilla flavor and mix well. Now add the coconut (Mixture No. 1). Mix well and spoon the batch out into roughly formed kisses, or it may be formed into bars or egg shapes and coated in chocolate.

Sicilano Coconut Cuts (Licorice Flavor)

Sugar	12 lb	Desiccated Coconut	25 lb
Nulomoline	8 lb	Gelatin (Soaked in 8 oz of Water)	8 oz
Corn Syrup	20 lb		
Water	8 lb	Salt	1 oz
Coconut Oil (76°F m.p.)	2 lb	Black Color	
Licorice Paste (Properly Dissolved)	3 lb	Anise Flavor (Optional)	
		Almonds	4 lb

Heat the sugar, Nulomoline, corn syrup and water to the boiling point. Add the properly dissolved licorice paste, then the coconut and stir and cook the batch to a medium firm paste. Now add the soaked gelatin, salt, coconut oil, color, flavor and almonds and mix well. Spread the batch out on an oiled slab dusted with XXXX sugar that has been colored black. Roll the batch down to the desired thickness using colored XXXX sugar, and when cold cut into pieces.

Massachusetts Molasses Mint Cream Centers (Short-Cast Cream Centers)

Mixture No. I

Basic Fondant—made from:	100 lb	Nulomoline	10 lb
		Water	To Dissolve the Sugar
Sugar	80 lb		
Corn Syrup	20 lb		

Cook together to 242° F.

Mixture No. 2

Dark Grandma's Molasses	25 lb	Frappe No. 1	15 lb
		Convertit	2 oz
Sugar	20 lb	Mint Flavor	Sufficient
Water	5 lb		

Place the fondant (Mixture No. 1) into a cream-melting kettle and heat the batch to approximately 120°F. Meanwhile, boil the molasses, sugar and water to 234°F. Then, pour this at once on top of the fondant and mix thoroughly. Now add the frappe and convertit, mix well, then work in the flavor. The casting temperature is approximately 140 to 145°F.

Frappe No. 1

Nulomoline	50 lb	Albumen	1 lb
Corn Syrup	50 lb	Cold Water	2 lb

Boil the corn syrup to approximately 245° F. Shut off the steam, add the Nulomoline and stir until melted. Place the batch in a marshmallow beater. Start the beater, then gradually add the albumen, in aqueous solution, and beat until light.

Pennsylvania Pudding
(Cast Whipped Creams—Chocolate Flavor)
Mixture No. 1

Sugar	80 lb	Nulomoline	10 lb
Corn Syrup	20 lb	Water	20 lb

Boil together to 242° F. Then cool to 110° F and beat into fondant in the usual manner.

Mixture No. 2

Corn Syrup	50 lb	Soaked in Cold Water	3 lb
Nulomoline	50 lb	Albumen	1½ lb
Good Grade Gelatin	1½ lb	Soaked in Cold Water	3 lb

Boil the corn syrup to 245° F. Add the Nulomoline and stir until it is melted. Place the batch in a marshmallow beater, add the gelatin solution. Start the beater, then gradually add the albumen solution and beat until quite light.

Melt 100 pounds of fondant (Mixture No. 1) to 150° F. Add 5 pounds of unsweetened chocolate, 2 ounces of salt and vanilla or rum flavor, and mix well. Then add 30 pounds of frappe (Mixture No. 2) and mix well. Cast the batch into starch at 140 to 145° F. This is suitable for small or large pieces.

Virginia Variety Creams (Crystallised Creams)

First prepare a fondant as follows

Sugar	80 lb	Water	To Dissolve
Corn Syrup	15 lb		the Sugar
Nulomoline	5 lb		

Boil all together to 246° F and cream as usual. Prepare a bob as follows:

Sugar	80 lb	Water	To Dissolve
Corn Syrup	10 lb		the Sugar
Nulomoline	5 lb		

Boil together to 245° F.

Place 100 pounds of the fondant in a clean cream-melting kettle. Turn the steam on partly and heat the fondant to approximately 125°F. Then add color and flavor and mix well. Now gradually add the boiled bob and mix thoroughly.

Have the hopper of the depositor heated to approximately 125°F.

Cast into fancy shaped starch impressions and later crystallise the creams using a syrup of 34° Bé at a temperature of 75°F.

Italian Cream Fudge (Mixture No. 1)

Sugar	80 lb	Cream (26% Butter Fat)	20 lb
Nulomoline	20 lb		

Place the sugar, Nulomoline and 15 pounds of the cream into a kettle, stir the batch constantly until it boils, then wash down all grains of sugar that adhere to the interior of the kettle. Now add the remaining cream and boil the batch to 240° F. Pour the batch onto a cream cooler and do not disturb until it has cooled to approximately 110° F. Then beat into fondant in the usual manner.

Italian Cream Fudge (Mixture No. 2)

Sugar	50 lb	Hard Coconut Butter	
Corn Syrup	20 lb	(86°F m.p.)	14 lb
Condensed Whole Milk		Salt	10 oz
(40% Sugar)	40 lb	Frappe No. 1	10 lb
		Vanilla Flavor	

Place the condensed milk, corn syrup and coconut butter into a kettle and heat until the fat is melted. Then add the sugar and stir. Cook to 240°F. Turn off the heat. Add the salt, flavor, nuts as desired, and frappe. Add 100 pounds of Mixture No. 1, and mix thoroughly. Then spread the batch out on oiled paper to set.

Frappe No. 1

Nulomoline	50 lb	Albumen	1 lb
Corn Syrup	50 lb	Dissolved in Cold Water	2 lb

Boil the corn syrup to approximately 245°F. Shut off the steam. Add the Nulomoline, cold, and stir until it is melted. Place the batch in a marshmallow beater. Start the beater. Then gradually add the albumen solution and beat until light.

Georgia Gum Drops (Starch Jelly Gums)

Sugar	40 lb	Corn Starch (No. 50—60)	10½ lb
Nulomoline	10 lb	Cold Water	100 lb
Corn Syrup	50 lb	Cream of Tartar	2 oz

Place the water, sugar, starch and 30 pounds of the corn syrup in a kettle equipped with a good stirring device. Turn the steam on partly, and allow the batch gradually to reach the boiling point. Add the cream of tartar. Turn the steam on full and boil the batch as rapidly as possible, using 80 to 100 pounds steam pressure. Cook the batch to a string. Turn off the heat. Add the balance of the corn syrup and the Nulomoline, then color and flavor. Mix thoroughly and cast the batch into starch. The temperature of the starch into which the jellies are cast may range from 65 to 175°F.

If a continuous starch drier is available, heat the starch to 160 to 175°F. Then cast the batch into the starch and leave the jellies in a room at normal temperature for at least 10 hours. They may then be removed from the starch, moistened with steam vapor and sanded with fine granulated sugar.

In the absence of a continuous starch drier the jellies may be placed in a drying room, heated to 140°F, and allowed to dry for 24 to 48 hours.

Moscow Jellies (Cut Agar-agar Jellies) [Mixture No. 1]

Sugar	30 lb	Japanese Gelatin (Agar-Agar No.1)	1 lb
Nulomoline	20 lb		
Water	40 lb		

Moscow Jellies (Cut Agar-agar Jellies) [Mixture No. 1]

XXXX Sugar (Berry Sugar)	225 lb	Green Coloring	
		Peppermint and Cara way Oils	Combination

Mixture No. 1: Soak the agar-agar in the water for several hours, preferably overnight. Then boil the agar-agar and water for several minutes, stirring occasionally. Strain the agar solution through a No. 30 sieve. Add the sugar and Nulomoline and boil to 222° F. Allow the batch to cool to 140°F.

When the batch has cooled to 140° F, add the color, flavors and XXXX sugar and mix well, pouring the batch into trays which have first been lined with ordinary wrapping paper.

When the jelly has set, sprinkle the surface with XXXX sugar, remove the paper from the jelly sheets, sprinkle them well with XXXX sugar and cut into pieces of the desired size. Then sand well and let them dry before packing.

Swan Marmalade (Cast)
Apricot Starch Jellies

Dry Apricots (Soaked in Water until Soft)	20 lb	Starch (No. 50—60)	10 lb
		Cream of Tartar	1 oz
Sugar	50 lb	water	90 lb
Nulomoline	10 lb	Red Coloring	
Corn Syrup	40 lb		

Rub the apricots through a No. 20 sieve to remove the skins. Then place the apricot pulp in a kettle. Add the sugar, Nulomoline, corn syrup, starch, water and cream of tartar, and boil all together to a good string. Add the red coloring. Mix well and cast the batch into warm dry starch.

Place the jellies in a dry room at 130°F for 24 hours and, when cold, remove from the starch, run them through a sanding machine and sand them in granulated sugar which has been colored yellow.

New Jersey Jelly
(Agar Jelly for Cutting or Casting)

Sugar	50 lb	Japanese Gelatin No. 1	
Corn Syrup	25 lb	(Agar-Agar)	13/4 lb
Nulomoline	25 lb	Water	75 lb
Flavor and Color	As desired		

Soak the gelatin in the water for at least 2 hours, preferably overnight. Place the soaked gelatin in a kettle arid boil for several minutes, stirring occasionally, then strain through a No. 30 sieve. Add the sugar and Nulomoline to the strained gelatin and boil the batch to 224° F. Turn off the heat. Add the corn syrup. Mix well, and, when the batch has cooled to approximately 125° F, add flavor and color. The batch may now be poured into trays that have been lined with wrapping paper or it may be cast into warm dry starch,

If the jelly is poured into trays, allow it to remain undisturbed until set, then turn the jelly sheet upside-down. Moisten the paper with water. Peel off the paper and roll the jellies in XXXX sugar. Then cut and roll again in XXXX sugar and let the pieces dry before they are packed into containers.

If aerated jelly is desired, as soon as the batch has boiled to 224° F, place it at once in a marshmallow beater. Start the beater. Then gradually add pound of albumen, dissolved in 1 pound of water, and beat the batch until white.

Acid or flavors containing acid should be added when the batch has cooled to 125° F or less.

Turkish Paste (Starch Jellies–Cast into Starch)

Sugar	55 lb	Water	100 lb
Nulomoline	45 lb	Cream of Tartar	2 oz
Thin Boiling Starch No. 50–60	12 lb	Color and Flavor	As desired

Place the sugar, Nulomoline, water, starch and cream of tartar into a kettle and cook and stir the batch occasionally until it reaches the boiling point. Continue to stir and boil the batch to a good string. Turn off the heat. Add color and flavor and cast the batch into dry starch.

Place the jellies in a drying room overnight. Then remove the jellies from the drying room and clean well. Run them through a sanding machine. When the jellies are quite dry, they are ready to be packed.

Delaware Desserts (Plain Marshmallow)

First Grade Gelatin	212 lb	Corn Syrup	40 lb
Water	32 lb	Nulomoline	10 lb
Fine Granulated Sugar	60 lb		

Mix the gelatin with 17 pounds of cold water. Place the remaining 15 pounds of water in a kettle and add the sugar. Heat and stir until the sugar is dissolved. Do not boil. Then add the soaked gelatin and stir until it is dissolved. Now add the corn syrup and Nulomoline and beat the batch until 1 gallon measure filled with the marshmallow weighs approximately 4 pounds. Add the flavor. Mix well and place the batch into the hopper of the depositor, which should be heated to approximately 100° F.

Cast the marshmallow into starch, containing not more than 8% moisture and heated to 90 to 95°F. Place the trays containing the marshmallow in a room at normal temperature for 10 to 20 hours.

After a slight crust has formed on the marshmallows, remove them from the starch. If they are to be packed plain, dust them with a combination of 9 pounds of dry powdered sugar to 1 pound of dry starch. Let them remain covered with the starch- sugar mixture for several hours before packing.

These marshmallows can also be placed in a revolving pan and coated with colored and flavored jelly (made by formula for New Jersey Jolly). After the marshmallows are well coated with the jelly, add desiccated coconut or colored sugar and turn them alit to set.

Maryland Marshmallow (Toasted Coconut Cut Marshmallow)

Granulated Sugar	25 lb	Water	18 lb
Nulomoline	15 lb	Good Grade Gelatin	2½ lb
Corn Syrup	60 lb		

Soak the gelatin for at least 15 minutes in 10 pounds of cold water. Meanwhile, heat the sugar with the remaining 8 pounds of water until it is dissolved. Do not permit the batch to boil. Turn off the heat, add the Nulomoline and soaked gelatin and stir until the gelatin is completely dissolved. Then add the corn syrup. Place the batch in a beater and beat until quite light. Add flavor and color as desired. Spread in paper-lined or greased trays, and immediately sprinkle the surface with toasted coconut. When the marshmallow has set, cut it into squares or bars and roll in toasted coconut. Permit the bars to dry for several hours before packing.

Danske Nuga (Fluffy Short Nougat) [Part No. 1]

Albumen	12 oz	Tapioca Flour	12 oz
Dissolved in Water	2 lb	Grandma's Molasses	4 lb

Place the albumen solution, tapioca flour and Grandma's Molasses in an upright beating bowl and beat until rather stiff.

Danske Nuga (Fluffy Short Nougat) [Part No. 2]

Sugar	35 lb	Nulomoline	5 lb
Corn Syrup	15 lb	water	8 lb

Boil all together to 245°F. Add 2 gallons of this syrup to Part No. 1, heating at second speed. Boil the remainder of the syrup batch to 250°F. Gradually add this to the beaten batch, and continue the beating until quite light. Add 2 ounces of powdered sugar to start the grain when making the first batch.

When grain becomes visible add 5 pounds of powdered skimmed milk, 3 pounds of hard coconut butter (88°F m.p.), 2 ounces of salt, vanilla flavor and broken walnut pieces.

Spread the batch out on an oiled and dusted wood or metal slab and, when it has set, cut into bars of the desired size, and coat with chocolate or icing.

Montelemar Nougat (Mixture No. 1)

Honey	10 lb	Albumen	3½ lb
Corn Syrup	10 lb	Dissolved in Water	7 lb
Nulomoline	10 lb		

Heat the Nulomoline, honey and corn syrup until they are melted. Place this mixture in a beater. Gradually add the dissolved albumen, and beat until quite light.

Montelemar Nougat (Mixture No. 2)

Corn Syrup	40 lb	Orange Flower Flavor	
Sugar	60 lb	Vanilla Flavor	
Nulomoline	10 lb	Pistachio Nuts	10 lb
Water	15 lb	Blanched Almonds	15 lb
Coconut Oil (76°F m.p.)	2 lb	Lightly Roasted Almonds	10 lb
Salt	4 oz		

Boil the corn syrup, sugar, Nulomoline and water to 280°F. Pour this mixture gradually into Mixture No. 1, beating well. Add the flavors, salt, nuts and coconut oil and mix well. Then spread the batch on an oiled slab and, while warm, cut into bars.

New York Nougat (Mixture No. 1)

Albumen	2 lb	Dissolved in Water	4½ lb

Beat until light, then place in a cold kettle.

New York Nougat (Mixture No. 2)

Sugar	75 lb	Water	16 lb
Corn Syrup	50 lb		

Cook all together to 243°F. Draw off about 25 pounds of the syrup, and pour it slowly into the beaten albumen, stirring constantly.

Cook the remainder of the batch (Mixture No. 2) to 270°F. Add this to the beaten batch and beat until grain is visible, then add Mixture No. 3.

New York Nougat (Mixture No. 3)

Nulomoline	10 lb	Corn Syrup	10 lb

Boil together to 265° F. Pour this into the beaten batch. Add 3 pounds of coconut butter, 4 ounçes of salt, flavor, nuts or diced fruits, and mix well. Spread the batch out on an oiled slab to set.

This makes an ideal layer to be used between caramels or coconut work. It may also be wrapped plain or coated in chocolate.

English Toffee Nougats (Chewing)

Corn Syrup	38 lb	Brown Sugar	15 lb
Nulomoline	10 lb	Fine Granulated Sugar	20 lb
Dairy Butter (Salted)	5 lb	Salt	5 oz
Coconut Butter (86°F m.p.)	10 lb	Flavor with a combination of Clove-Oil, Almond Oil and Vanilla	
Condensed Whole Milk (40% Sugar)	40 lb		

Place the following Ingredients in a caramel cooking kettle: Nulomoline, corn syrup, butter, coconut butter and condensed milk. Give the steam valve a few turns and allow the batch to mix until the fats are melted and mixed with the other ingredients. Then add the brown and white sugar, turn the steam on full and cook the batch as rapidly as possible to a firm ball.

This toffee can be cooked quite successfully, using as much as 110 pounds of steam pressure. After the batch has been cooked to the desired consistency, turn off the heat. Add the salt and flavor and mix thoroughly. Spread the batch out at once to cool. Then gradually fold it together so as to secure an even temperature throughout the batch. It is then ready to pass through drop rolls.

After the toffee nuggets are cold, place them in a revolving pan. Spray them well with melted hard coconut butter. Then add powdered sugar that has been flavored with mint oil. Allow the candies to revolve until they are well coated, spread them out to set. Then pack.

Rum-Butter Toffee (Wrapped)

Condensed Whole Milk (40% Sugar)	40 lb	Fine Granulated Sugar	30 lb
Corn Syrup	30 lb	Hard Coconut Butter—No. 90	15 lb
Nulomoline	10 lb	Salt	5 oz
Grandma's Molasses	5 lb	Rum and Butter Flavor	

Place the condensed milk, corn syrup, Nulomoline, molasses and hard coconut butter in a caramel cooking kettle equipped with double action mixers. Turn the heat on partly and mix the batch until the fat is completely melted. Then add the granulated sugar. Mix well. Turn the steam on full and boil the batch as rapidly as possible to a medium firm ball. Turn off the heat. Add the salt and the rum-butter flavor, and mix thoroughly.

Spread the batch out to cool. Then cut into pieces of the desired size and wrap.

Barcelona Brittle (Chocolate Flavored)

Sugar	15 lb	Coconut Oil (76° Fm.p.)	7 lb
Water	4 lb	Unsweetened Chocolate	2 lb
Nulomoline	3 lb	Lecithin	2 oz
Corn Syrup	2 lb	Salt	2 oz
Salted Dairy Butter	3 lb	Ground Roasted Almonds	5 lb
Condensed Whole Milk (40% Sugar)	4 lb	Ground Roasted Filberts	5 lb

Place the coconut oil and chocolate into a kettle and heat until melted. Add the lecithin and mix until it is dissolved. Then add the sugar, Nulomoline, corn syrup, water, butter and condensed milk and cook the batch to 300°F. Now add the ground roasted nuts. Mix thoroughly and turn the batch out on an oiled slab. Then roll as thinly as possible and cut into squares.

It is also possible to grind this brittle roughly and work it into ice cream or use it as a topping for sundaes. It can also be worked into chewing nougat to replace fruits, nuts, etc.

Glasgow Crackle

Sugar	15 lb	Water	2 lb
Nulomoline	3 lb	Ground Roasted Peanuts	Maximum amount
Salted Dairy Butter	2 lb		
Coconut Oil (76°F m.p.)	8 lb	Salt	2 oz
Lecithin	1½ oz	Rum Butter Flavor	

Melt the dairy butter and coconut oil. Add the lecithin and stir until it is melted. Then add the sugar, Nulomoline and water and boil all together to 310°F. Now add the maximum amount of ground roasted peanuts, the salt and flavor, and mix well.

Spread the batch out on an oiled slab. Roll into a thin sheet and cut with a roller knife.

This piece may be coated in chocolate or wrapped in cellophane or waxed paper, and used either for packages or bars. It is also possible to grind this candy roughly and work it into ice cream or use it as a topping for sundaes. It may also be worked into chewing nougat to replace fruits, nuts, etc.

CHEWING GUM

Chewing Gum Bases

a Bubble Gum Base		Washed Gutta Katian	400 lb
Washed Pontianak		Washed Gutta Soh	75 lb
Gum	425 lb	Candelilla Wax	10 lb

The mixed gums and wax are heated until the total batch contains only 8 to 9% moisture.

b Stick Gum Base		Gutta Katian	400 lb
Pontianak Gum	425 lb	Gutta Soh	75 lb
		Candelilla Wax	60 lb

Ball Gum

Base *b* (above)	22 lb	Wax	1½ lb
Corn Syrup	48 lb	Caramel Paste	2½ lb
Sugar	117 lb	Flavor	22/3 oz
Chicle	3 lb		

Penny Stick Gum

Base *a* (above)	40 lb	Sugar	140 lb
Corn Syrup	40 lb	Flavor	30 oz

Bubble Gum

Base a (above)	35 lb	Sugar	115 lb
Pontianak Gum	5 lb	Flavor	28 oz
Corn Syrup	45 lb		

ICE-CREAM POWDER

Ice-cream powder is the perfect smoothener for ice cream and other frozen preparations. It consists of:

Powdered Sugar	48 lb	Gum Karaya	50 lb
White Gum Acacia	2 lb		

It is a pure vegetable compound which has the following advantages:

1. It can be used to advantage in the manufacture of the best grade of sherbets and ice cream, as well as cheaper grades.

2. Although it contains no gelatin, it can be used to replace gelatin entirely.
3. It will cause milk and cream to beat up to more than double their original volume.
4. It will make ice cream stand up, preventing it from melting quickly and giving it a firm substance. It prevents ice cream from becoming snowy or rough and from shrinking in volume while being stored or shipped.
5. It renders all water ices smoother and richer.
6. It is an incomparable thickener.

Directions for Use

Straight Cream	2 oz to 10-gal freezer
¼ Milk and 3/4 Cream	4 oz to 10-gal freezer
2/3 Milk and 1/3 Cream	8 oz to 10-gal freezer
Straight Milk	12 oz to 10-gal freezer

The specified quantity of ice cream powder should be thoroughly incorporated with the amount of sugar which is used with the batch of 10 gallons of ice cream. Into this mixture sufficient straight milk, or cream and milk combined, should be stirred to make a smooth paste. To this paste, the balance of the milk and cream should he slowly added. Stir and mix constantly until the whole is dissolved. When dissolved, freeze the batch in the usual way.

Ice-Cream Preparation (Freeze-It)

Albumen	10 oz	or:	
XXXX Sugar	80 oz	Dried Milk	50 oz
Whole Dried Milk	10 oz	XXXX Sugar	50 oz
Indian Gum	5 oz	Cream of Tartar	42/5 oz
Vanillin	1½ oz	Sodium Carbonate	2 oz
Vanillin	0.06 oz		

Package 4½ ounces = 127.5 grams

Stir contents of the package into ½ pint (1 cup) cold milk. Stir until dissolved. Whip ½ pint (1 cup) chilled whipping cream. Add the dissolved Freeze-It to the whipped cream and mix. Freeze.

Chocolate Ice Cream

Milk	32 oz	Eggs	4 oz
Sugar	16 oz	Cream	32 oz
Flour	2 oz	Vanillin	¼ oz
Salt	1/8 oz	Unsweetened Chocolate	4 oz

Heat milk and add flour, salt, and sugar. Stir thoroughly in double boiler for 20 minutes after batch is brought to a boil. After the mass thickens, add the beaten eggs and cook for 5 minutes longer with constant stirring. Cool, add cream which has been whipped into a still paste, and then add the flavoring. Add the melted chocolate which was previously mixed with a little sugar and warm milk to form a paste. Put in a refrigerator or pack in ice and salt until frozen.

Ice Cream Without Gelatin

Butter Fat	12 lb	Milk Serum Solids	113/4 lb
Granulated Sugar	12 lb	Vanilla Flavor	To suit
Cerelose (Corn Sugar)	4 lb		

WATER ICES AND SHERBETS

The figures are given on the basis of 100 pounds of mix, which is about 10½ gallons.

Water Ice

Cane Sugar	25 lb	Water, Fruit, Fruit Acid,	
Corn Sugar	7 lb	Flavor and Color	672/5 lb
Gum Tragacanth or Gala-		Agar (3.2 oz or 90.6 g)	1/5 lb
gum C (6.4 oz or 181.2 g)	2/5 lb		

Overrun 20 to 25% Total yield 13 gallons

Sherbet Using Milk

Cane Sugar	25 lb	90.6 g)	1/5 lb
Corn Sugar	7 lb	Whole Milk	50 lb
Agar (3.2 oz or 96.6 g)	1/5 lb	Water, Fruit, Fruit	
Gum Tragacanth or		Acid, Flavor and	
Galagum C (3.2 oz or		Color	173/5 lb

Overrun 25 to 30% Total yield 13.5 gallons

Sherbet Using Ice-Cream Mix

Cane Sugar	25 lb	Ice-Cream Mix, without	
Corn Sugar	7 lb	Sugar or Gelatin	10 lb
Agar (3.2 oz or 90.6 g)	1/5 lb	Water, Fruit, Fruit Acid,	
Gum Tragacanth or Gala-		Flavor and color	$57^3/_5$ lb
gum C (3.2 oz or 90.6 g)	1/5 lb		

Overrun 25 to 30% Total yield 13.5 gallons

Orange Water Ice (For 10 Gal Batch)

Granulated Sugar	21 lb	Orange Juice (Or Its	
Corn Sugar	7 lb	Equivalent in Orange	
Galagum C	3 oz	Flavor)	1 gal
Citric Acid	To suit		

Make up to 10 gallons with water. Takes no overrun.

Orange Sherbet (10 Gal Mix)

Cane Sugar	22½ lb	Orange Concentrate	4 oz
Cerelose (Corn Sugar)	7½ lb	Citric Acid	To suit
Milk	4 gal	Color	To suit
Gelatin	11 oz		

Make up to 10 gallons with water.

Cocoa Junket

Cocoa	2 oz	Junket Tablets	2
Boiling Water	4 oz	Cold Water	1 oz
Sugar	4 oz	Vanilla Extract	¼ oz
Milk	32 oz		

Cook mixture of cocoa and water in double boiler for 5 minutes. Add sugar, stir until dissolved, and then add milk which has been preheated to 100°F. Add vanilla extract and heat to 120°F. Stir in junket tablets which are dissolved first in a little water. Pour into containers immediately, let stand until set.

COCOA AND CHOCOLATE PRODUCTS

Cacao (cocoa) is derived from the seeds of Theobroma Cacao. The cacao, often called cocoa, tree is indigenous to Brazil, Venezuela, Ecuador, and Mexico, thriving only in a tropical climate in localities that have well-watered, well-drained soils, and plenty of rainfall. It is a medium-sized tree, 20 to 30 feet high. The fruit is a pod, having a hard, thick shell, and is from 8 to 10 inches long and from 3 to 4 inches thick. There are forty or more beans in each pod.

DIFFERENT KINDS OF COCOA BEANS

Porto Cabello or Caracas

These beans are large, but not very uniform in size. They are covered with a reddish, sometimes silver-gray dust. The husks are thicker than on ordinary beans and are of dark red color inside. Ninety-nine hundredths of 1 % is theobromine. The small Caracas bean has less fat and is therefore cheaper.

Trinidads

These beans are nearly flat. The husk is dark gray, and the kernels are almost black. Ninety-two hundredths of 1 % is theobromine. This is a good bean for the price.

Guayaquils (Ecuador)

These are large, flat, irregular-shaped beans. The husk and kernel are brown. They have a fine strong flavor.

Cubans

These are egg-shaped, flat beans. The husk is mauve, and the kernel is dark brown.

Paras (Brazil)

These beans are irregular in size, and long and flat on one side. The husk is gray or reddish, and the kernel is light brown. They are rich in fat, and good for a filler.

Grenadas

These are similar to Paras.

Javas

These are oval, slightly flattened beans. The husk is thin and easily peeled. The kernel is light brown, of bitter, but agreeable, taste. One and twenty-two hundredths per cent is theobromine. They have a fine flavor, but are high in price.

Bahias

These beans are flat, triangular in shape and rough. The yellow-looking bean is the best, the grayish-red one, inferior. The kernel is mauve in color arid produces a dark liquor. This is a very popular bean in the United States.

TEST FOR RIPENESS OF A CACAO BEAN

Cut the bean with a knife. If it slices and no shell falls off, the bean is unripe.

THE (COCOA) CACAO BEAN AND ITS PRODUCTS

Cocoa has been cultivated since ancient times, but this plant and its products were unknown to Europe until the beginning of the sixteenth century, when Cortez and his soldiers became acquainted with it upon their landing in Mexico. From then on the use of cocoa spread very rapidly throughout the civilized world.

Cocoa is grown almost entirely south of the equator, the largest crops coming from the west (Gold Coast) of Africa. The next largest crop comes from Ecuador. The cocoa from each country has a distinctive character and flavor of its own. The coco as coming from Venezuela are the finest. The cheapest are from San Domingo.

Cocoa beans are the seeds of a tree that grows in most tropical countries. The seeds grow in pods very much like the seeds of the pumpkin and squash, and hang from both the branches and trunks of the trees. When ripe they are picked from the tree and gathered into large piles. They are then cut open and the seeds and pulp scraped out.

The seeds with their surrounding pulpy mass are placed into large vats or pits and allowed to ferment. The time of fermentation varies according to the kind of cocoa. The sweeter variety requires a shorter fermentation while the coarser or more ordinary type requires a longer fermentation.

During the fermentation starch is converted by the diastase present into soluble sugars, which are further fermented into alcohol, and finally converted to acetic acid. The pulpy mass is decomposed and flows away as a vinegar-smelling fluid. During the fermentation, care must be taken that sufficient air is circulated through the beans, otherwise, butyl alcohols are formed which give the cocoa a bad odor. To prevent this the beans are turned over (every day. Fermentation changes the color of the bean from a light to a dark, rich, red-brown, liberates the alkaloid theobromine, and lessens its bitter and astringent taste.

When the fermentation is completed the beans are separated from any remaining pulp, dried, and sometimes polished. The drying must be done very carefully, as improperly dried beans are apt to become moldy. The best cocoa is obtained by drying in the sun, although methods using steam- or water-heated pipes are also in use.

Upon importation into the -United States, the beans are inspected and are rejected if they contain more than 5% of either wormy or moldy beans.

The raw cocoa beans are cleaned by passing them over a shaking-table covered with a metal screen which has holes smaller in size than the beans. Sand, dust, and other foreign materials are screened out. At the end of the shaking-table, the beans drop into a chute located at the bottom of an air duct. The cleaned beans are carried up by air suction, and deposited into a conveyor. Stones, metals, and other heavy materials drop to the bottom of the chute, which is counterpoised by a weighted lever. When sufficient heavy material has gathered, the bottom opens and the foreign material drops to a receiving pan.

The clean raw cocoa beans are run into a roaster of approximately 600 pounds capacity, of the revoking drum type, which is heated by coal fire using forced draft, or by gas or super heated steam. A roast usually requires 45 minutes, depending on the type of cocoa beans, and the kind of roast desired. The final flavor of the cocoa powder and chocolate depends a great deal on the proper roasting of the cocoa beans.

The cocoa beans attain a temperature from 240 to 300°F at the end of the roast, are quickly discharged into a cooling truck with a perforated metal bottom, and are quickly cooled by cold air suction.

The cooled beans are carried to a cracker and fanner device, which cracks up the beans and blows the shells aside. The cocoa germs and fines are separated from the broken nibs by sieving them through a rotating cylinder covered with screening of Increasing mesh. The clean nibs are carried to hoppers which iced a battery of triple stone mills, and are ground into a heavy, viscous fluid known as chocolate liquor, which is the starting point in the manufacture of cocoa powder and chocolate.

In the manufacture of cocoa powder the chocolate liquor is transferred to hydraulic presses, and pressed from 8 minutes to 13/4 hours, depending on the amount of fat that is to be left in the cocoa powder. The cocoa press cake is cooled, and broken up by a cracking device, passed over a magnetic belt to remove stray iron, and then put through a micro-pulveriser. The ground press cake is cooled on a conveyer, and is refined by being passed through silk bolting cloth used as a sieve; or a current of air is played on the particles of cocoa in such manner as to separate the fine cocoa from the coarse. The coarse cocoa, or cocoa tailings, are returned to the grinders and reground over and over again, until the particles are fine enough to pass through the sieve, or can be separated by air flotation.

There are many kinds of cocoas, but they can be divided into two main classifications: (a) natural process cocoa and (b) Dutch process cocoa.

Natural process cocoas are cocoas to which no alkalies or dutching agents have been added during manufacture.

Dutch process cocoas are cocoas to which an alkali has been added. In preparing Dutched cocoas, the clean nibs are boiled in a solution of alkali, such as potassium, sodium or ammonium bicarbonate, or carbonate. The water is evaporated and the Dutched nibs dried in a roaster. The nibs are milled, the liquor pressed, and the cocoa refined in the same manner as natural process cocoas.

Dutched cocoas are darker in color, less acid, and less bitter than natural cocoas. They are more economical to use, and, for certain purposes, cannot be replaced by natural cocoas.

The various types of cocoas can be described as follows:

1. Semi-cocoas, cocoa nuggets, cocoa crumbles, cocoa chips, etc., are prepared by crumbling press cake, or by mixing chocolate liquor with a quantity of cocoa to reduce the fat. In the latter case, the product is molded into thin cakes, and then broken into small chips. Because of the high fat content, 32 to 45%, and chocolate flavor, they are used extensively for fine quality ice cream, and for fancy icings.
2. High-quality cocoas usually contain from 25 to 32% cocoa butter. They are made from select quality cocoa beans and are carefully

blended. These cocoas are either Dutched, natural, or semi-Dutched. They are used for fancy ice cream, for drinking, for icing, as a filler between layers of cakes, and for syrups.

3. Breakfast cocoas contain not less than 22% cocoa butter. The natural process and semi-Dutched breakfast cocoas are used for drinking, syrups, and general household use. The Dutched type breakfast cocoas are used for chocolate biscuits and crackers, for devil's food cakes, and for home made candy, such as chocolate fudge.
4. Semi-dry cocoas usually contain 15 to 18% fat. The natural and semi-Dutched cocoas are used for malted milk mixtures, cocoa milk drinks, chocolate flavored desserts, chocolate pies and chocolate-flavored syrups. The percentage of fat they contain is just right for use in the products mentioned.
5. Dry cocoas contain 10 to 12% fat, and are used for miscellaneous purposes. The natural process cocoa is used for milk drinks, cocoa skim milk mixtures, sweet cocoas, icings, etc. The Dutch process cocoa is used for cocoa extracts, for baking, and devil's food mixtures. These cocoas are the most common type found on the market, and are used where low cost is of importance.
6. Extra dry cocoas contain 8 to 9% cocoa fat. They are used for thin syrups and other mixtures where any excess fat is not desired.
7. Very dry cocoas contain 6½ to 7¾% fat, and this fat content is about the limit for cocoas made by pressing the fat from the chocolate liquor. They are used for making substitute or imitation chocolate coatings by incorporating sugar and another fat, such as cocoanut oil. They are desired for their low fat content, because of the difficulty of blending cocoa butter and cocoanut oil. This cocoa is used as a dusting powder in confectionery.
8. Solvent-extracted cocoas, or defatted cocoas, contain from ½ to 3% fat. They are usually manufactured from cheap low-fat cocoa cake, by extracting the remaining fat by means of a solvent. Solvent-extracted cocoas have almost no chocolate flavor. Some have a faint odor and taste of the solvent used for their extraction. They are usually high in moisture content, which is, at Times, as high as 10%. Solvent-extracted cocoas are used as dusting powders in confectionery, and for imitation chocolate.
9. By-product cocoa and cocoa cake usually contain 5½ to 11% cocoa fat. This product is obtained by passing cocoa fines and dust through the Anderson expeller, which removes a portion of

the fat. The by-product cake has a limited use as a fertiliser ingredient, as raw material for theobromine extraction, and for cattle feed for which it has not been very successfully used.

10. Prepared cocoas are cocoa mixtures, such as cocoa and sugar, cocoa skim milk and sugar, and cocoa malt skim milk and sugar. They are used for instant chocolate and milk drinks in ice cream parlors, and are also put up in envelopes of the proper weight sufficient for one cup.

MANUFACTURE OF CHOCOLATE

Chocolate, because of its very fine flavor, its concentrated food value, pleasing appearance, good keeping qualities, and convenience in handling, is a food of exceptional value to all.

The definition of chocolate, technically speaking, is the solid or plastic mass obtained by grinding cocoa nibs free from shell or husk and germs, and is the product commonly known as chocolate liquor. By common usage, however, the word chocolate is usually applied to Sweet chocolate, milk chocolate, and chocolate covered centers.

Although chocolates may be similar in composition as to percentages of chocolate liquor, sugar, added cocoa butter, and milk solids, there is a great deal of difference in their flavor and texture.

Of the many varieties of cocoa beans, approximately thirty are used in the larger chocolate factories. The cocoa beans vary in color, chocolate character, pungency, acidity, mildness, bitterness, and creaminess. The delicate flavors of the cocoa beans are developed by careful roasting, cleaning, and milling. The flavor of the resulting chocolate depends on the skill used in blending, milling, and conching the various varieties of cocoa nibs with the proper amount of sugar and cocoa butter, with or without milk solids, and flavors.

The possibility of developing blends of chocolate is tin- limited. Most formulas are limited to blends of one to six varieties The number of combinations that can be made with thirty varieties of cocoa beans, blended with varying percentages of sugar, cocoa butter, milk solids, and flavors, and milled to various degrees of fineness, and adjusted to various vis cosities and colors, is astounding.

There are many varieties of chocolates on the market, but they can be classified into the following general types: bitter, bittersweet, dark sweet, medium dark sweet, light sweet, milk chocolate, ice-cream coating, skim milk, buttermilk, malted milk, imitation, and lecithin coatings.

It is difficult to state exactly what type of chocolate coating is best suited for a particular center. It depends on a number of factors among which are sweetness, texture, and blending properties of both the center and coating. As a rule, chocolate liquors and bittersweets are used for every sweet center. Dark sweets and medium dark sweet coatings are used for moderately sweet centers. Milk chocolates are used for caramels, nougatines, marshmallows, etc. Light sweets are used for not-too- sweet centers and for candy bars.

The chocolate liquor of commerce is also known as chocolate, bitter chocolate, chocolate liquor, chocolate paste, bitter chocolate coating, and unsweetened chocolate. It is the product obtained by grinding cocoa nibs free from shell or husk and germs, usually through triple stone mills, Bausman disc, or similar devices.

The above product comes in two types, natural process and Dutch process. The Dutch process type, or alkalised type, is prepared in the same manner as described for cocoas except that none of the fat is expressed. The natural chocolate liquor has a pH 5.1 to 6.0. The Dutched chocolate liquor has a pH 6.0 to 7.8, depending on the original pH of the nibs, and the amount and kind of alkali used. If more than 1½ % alkali is used the liquor has a tendency to develop a saponified taste.

Chocolate liquors are molded into ten-pound cakes for commercial use, and in one-quarter- to one-pound cakes for household use. Chocolate liquor is used for coating very sweet centers, such as hand roll centers and butter creams. It is also used as an ingredient for ice cream, candy, culinary products, and chocolate syrup. The Dutched type of chocolate liquor is used for flavoring tobacco, and for general uses where a milder and darker product is desired. Chocolate liquor is often used in place of cocoa powder when a creamier and richer product is desired. The high fat content, 50 to 56%, however, makes its use difficult without such aids as homogenisers or emulsifiers.

Chocolate liquor is considered pure if it contains not less than 50% cocoa fat, and, on the moisture and fat-free basis, not more than 8% total ash, not more than 0.4% ash insoluble in hydrochloric acid, and not more than 7% crude fiber. The standards for Dutched liquor are the same as for natural process liquor, after allowance is made for the kind and amount of alkaline substance added. The amount of alkaline substance permitted is not more than 3 pounds of potassium carbonate, or its neutralising equivalent in other alkaline substances to each 100 pounds of cocoa nibs,

Sweet chocolate, sweet chocolate coating, is chocolate mixed with sugar and/or dextrose with or without the addition of cocoa butter, spices, or other flavoring ingredients. This definition applies to all sweet coatings regardless of the amount of sugar and chocolate liquor they contain. The phrase, other flavoring ingredients, is somewhat vague, and has led to some misunderstanding. The definitions for food products are so framed as to exclude anything not mentioned by name, but the strict interpretation of flavor would include any and all flavoring ingredients such as small amounts of malt, malted milk, skim milk, dairy butter, essential oil, etc.

Although dextrose, corn sugar, is permitted in chocolate, either alone or mixed with sucrose (cane sugar or beet sugar), it has been used only to a very limited extent, and has not been studied sufficiently to have its virtues discussed.

Bittersweet coatings contain from 80 to 95% chocolate liquor and 5 to 20% sugar. Since the cocoa butter content is very high, 40 to 50%, and the viscosity low, the addition of extra cocoa butter is not required. These coatings are prepared by adding sugar to chocolate liquor with or without flavor and refining. Bittersweet chocolates are dark in color and are used as couvertures for cordials, peppermint creams, fudge, whipped cream, Italian creams, hand rolls, butter creams, and marshmallow centers.

Mild bittersweet coatings contain from 50 to 75% chocolate liquor, from 25 to 38% sugar, and from 38 to 42.% cocoa butter. As the sugar content increases and the chocolate liquor content decreases, it becomes necessary to add additional cocoa butter to obtain the proper viscosity. Mild bittersweet coatings are used for practically the same type of centers as bittersweet coatings, and are used to some extent for covering marshmallow crackers.

Dark sweet chocolates contain from 25 to 45% chocolate liquor, from 40 to 50% sugar, and vary in total cocoa butter content from 34 to 42%, depending on the desired viscosity of the finished coating. Dark sweet chocolates are used for enrobing such centers as nougats, cordials, peppermints, fudge, and nut-flavored cream fondants.

Medium dark sweet coatings are the most popular used, to a great extent, for molding chocolate bars and a variety of solid chocolate items, which are neither too sweet nor bitter for the average consumer's taste. They contain from 20 to 40% chocolate liquor, from 45 to 55% sugar, and from 32 to 42% total cocoa butter. The commercial product is sold in molded ten- pound cakes, and is used for enrobing such centers as caramels, nougats, fruit-flavored cream fondants, jelly centers, cocoanut cream fondants, vanilla cream fondants, nut clusters, raisin clusters, dates, figs, marshmallows, nut-flavored cream fondants, cocoanut, sponge, chip and marshmallow cracker.

Light sweet coatings are of two types, the expensive type and the cheaper type. The expensive types are prepared from blends of light-colored and mild but chocolate-like cocoa nibs such as Java, Ceylon, Maracaibo, etc., and a moderate amount of sugar, usually 45%. These coatings are very expensive, and are used for enrobing moderately sweet centers of the better sort. They are finely milled, conched, delicately flavored, and are representative of the chocolate expert's skill in the art of fine chocolate making.

The cheap type of light sweet chocolate coatings owe their light color to the small amount of chocolate liquor and the large amount of sugar used in their manufacture. They usually cons tam from 5 to 15% chocolate liquor, from 55 to 68% sugar, and a total cocoa butter content of 31 to 39%, depending on the fineness of grinding and their ultimate use. - These coatings are used for special purposes, and for enrobing nut rolls, nuts, nut clusters, nut chews, raisin clusters, and for candy rolls containing peanuts, marshmallows, caramels, fudge, and other ingredients. The light sweet coating, although lacking in chocolate flavor and excessively sweet, nevertheless, blends in nicely with the types of centers mentioned.

Milk chocolate, sweet milk chocolate, is the product obtained by grinding chocolate with sucrose and/or dextrose, with the solids of whole milk, or the constituents of milk solids in the proportion normal for whole milk, and with or without cocoa butter, and/or flavoring material. It contains not less than 12% milk solids. Milk chocolates usually contain 7 to 17% chocolate liquor, 35 to 55% sugar, and a total fat content of 28 to 39%. There are many types of milk chocolate, varying in their degrees of milkiness, chocolate character, color, fineness, and viscosity. Milk chocolates are prepared from fresh whole milk which is first evaporated, and from milk powders, both spray and roller process types, and from skim milk powder to which has been added an amount of milk fat either in the form of dairy butter, or butter fat, necessary to convert the skim milk solids to whole milk solids.

In converting skim milk solids to whole milk solids by the addition of dairy butter, it is necessary to bear in mind the fact that dairy butter contains 80 to 84% milk fat, and approximately 16% water. The difficulties of removing the water and of blending the dairy butter with the skim milk solids, and the fact that 100 pounds of dairy butter yields approximately 80 pounds of milk fat, make this method of milk chocolate preparation undesirable, and often more expensive than the method using whole milk solids.

Milk chocolates owe their popularity to their delicate milk flavor, and their lack of a harsh or bitter taste. They are particularly liked by women and children. The manufacture of milk chocolate with a very fine milky flavor is a difficult art, and is a secret closely guarded by chocolate manufacturers. Milk chocolates are sold over the counter of the ice-cream parlors and candy stores as broken milk chocolate, and in the form of bars which vary from a fraction of an ounce to a pound. Milk chocolate coatings are molded in ten-pound cakes and are used for enrobing such centers as nougats, vanilla cream fondants, nut rolls, nuts, nut clusters, and nut-chews.

Ice cream coatings are chocolate coatings of high cocoa butter content containing from 50 to 60% fat. Their high fat content is necessary to obtain a very thin running chocolate, which will quickly drain off the solid ice cream center when dipped. Ice cream coatings may be of the dark sweet, medium dark sweet, light sweet, and milk chocolate types. Allowance should be made for the high fat content. As their name implies, they are used exclusively for dipping ice cream in the manufacture of ice cream pops and Eskimo Pies. Since ice cream coatings are frozen instantly on the - ice cream, and the ice cream is kept at temperatures below freezing, the user of ice cream coatings is not concerned with exact enrobing temperatures, nor with fat or sugar bloom. His chief problem is to combat the thickening-up of the chocolate due to moisture absorption from the melting ice cream. This difficulty is often remedied by the incorporation of 3/10 of 1% lecithin in cocoa butter.

Skim milk, buttermilk and milk chocolate coatings are sweet chocolate coatings containing not-less than 12% of, respectively, skim milk solids, buttermilk solids, or malted milk and milk solids. These coatings are not defined in F.I.D. 191, or later additions to the Federal Pure Food Laws. Buttermilk coatings, and skim milk coatings, have become popular in the last few years. They are a cross between milk chocolate coatings and light sweet coatings. Skim milk and buttermilk cut down the excessive sweetness of a light sweet coating without sacrificing the light color. These coatings are used for enrobing the same types of centers as light sweet coatings, and in some cases, milk chocolate coatings. These coatings, in the absence of a published definition for them, should be labeled and sold for exactly what they are, namely, skim milk, buttermilk, or malted milk chocolate coatings.

Modified chocolate coatings are sweet chocolate coatings of various types, such as dark sweets, light sweets, and ice cream coatings, to which has been added a small amount of skim milk, buttermilk, whole milk, or malt sugar. The amount added is usually 3 to 5%. These ingredients are added as flavoring ingredients, and to cut down the excessive sweetness of light sweet coating, and also to cut the bitterness or sharpness of a dark sweet coating. The above ingredients are used to some extent in ice cream coatings for the reasons mentioned, and for obtaining a softer eating chocolate of less brittleness than the ordinary chocolate coating, when it is frozen on the ice cream.

Imitation chocolate coatings are mixtures of cocoa, sugar, and a substitute fat such as cocoanut oil, cocoanut stearines, illipe oil, etc., with or without flavoring ingredients. They are used mostly for enrobing cheap centers, and for medicated products where a higher melting-point chocolate is desired than is obtained with cocoa butter. Cocoanut oil coatings are used to some extent for ice cream. Imitation coatings are what their names imply, imitation chocolate coatings often lacking the true flavor and taste of pure chocolate.

Lecithin chocolate coatings are chocolate coatings of all types to which has been added a small amount of lecithin, usually not exceeding 4/10 of 1% lecithin in cocoa butter. Lecithin modifies the physical properties of chocolate to some textent. Coatings can be made with 3 to 8 pounds less of added cocoa butter per 100 pounds of chocolate, making them less fatty. Lecithin coatings resist thickening-up due to moisture, allow greater flexibility in enrobing temperature, and cover centers more uniformly. Lecithin stabilises chocolate coatings so that the viscosity is only slightly changed on aging, heating, or mechanical manipulation.

Cocoa butter, is the only fat common to chocolate, and is the edible fat obtained from sound cocoa beans either before or after roasting. It is a yellowish-white solid having a faint, agreeable odor, and a bland chocolate-like taste, and is usually brittle at temperatures below 25°C (77°F). It is slightly soluble in alcohol, but is soluble in ether, chloroform, petroleum benzin, benzene, and in many other solvents. It has a specific gravity of approximately 0.8580 at 100°C (212°F), and 0.9100 at 40°C (104°F), when compared with an equal volume of water at 25°C (77°F). Cocoa butter melts between 30 and 35°C (86 and 95°F), has a refractive index of approximately 1.4578 at 40°C (104°F), a saponification value of 188 to 195, an iodine value of 33 to 38, and a free fatty acid content of 0.70 to 1.4% calculated as oleic acid.

Cocoa butter is obtained by pressing chocolate liquor in the manufacture of cocoa powder, by passing cocoa fines through the expeller, and by solvent extractions from low-fat cocoa press cake and cocoa fines. Cocoa butter is used mostly for the manufacture of chocolate and confectionery, and to some extent for the manufacture of suppositories, creams, lotions, ointments, and soaps. It is also used for the treatment of burns, sunburn, and for massaging:

Chocolate, when properly molded, possesses a gloss which, if not protected, soon becomes dull in appearance. Both heat and moisture rapidly destroy the luster of chocolate, and cause a mottled gray surface commonly known as bloom.

Chocolate must be carefully' melted, carefully tempered, and carefully cooled when manufactured, otherwise bloom may develop in a short time. The handling of chocolate is a fine art and requires very careful attention to details. If chocolate is cooled too rapidly, the outer surface will solidify, trapping the latent heat within, which will gradually find its way to the surface and cause fat bloom. The proper temperature for storing chocolate is 55 to 65°F, and the proper relative humidity 60 to 65%.

USES OF COCOA

	Semi-Cocoas, Cocoa Nuggets, Cocoa Crumblers, Cocoa Chips, 32–45% Fat		High Quality Cocoas 25–32% Fat		Breakfast Cocoas Not less than 22% Fat		Semi Dry Cocoas 15–18% Fat		Dry Cocoas 10–12% Fat		Extra Dry Cocoas, 8–9% Fat	Very Dry Cocoas, 6½–7¾% Fat	Defatted or Solvent extracted Cocoas, ½–3% Fat	By-product Cocoa and Cocoa Cake, 5½–11% Fat	Prepared Cocoas Sweet Cocoas
	Natural	Dutched	Natural	Dutched	Natural	Dutched	Natural	Dutched	Natural	Dutched					
Baking					•	•	•	•	•	•					
Beverages			•	•	•	•	•	•	•	•					
Cake fillers			•	•											
Cattle feed														•	
chocolate biscuits						•		•		•					
chocolate crackers						•		•		•					
choc. flavored desserts					•	•	•	•	•	•					
Chocolate pies					•	•	•	•	•	•					
cocoa, malt, sugar mixt							•	•	•	•					
Cocoa milks							•	•	•	•	•	•			
confectionery, fudge			•	•	•	•	•	•	•	•					
Devil's food cake						•		•		•					
Dusting powder												•	•	•	
Fertilisers														•	
Household use			•	•					•	•					
icecream	•	•	•	•											
icings	•	•	•	•											
imitation choc. coatings									•		•	•			
Medicinal powders or tablets					•	•	•	•	•						
Sweet cocoas					•	•	•	•	•	•					•
Syrups			•	•	•	•	•	•	•	•	•				
Theobromine													•	•	
Thin syrups									•		•	•			
Tobacco			•	•	•	•	•	•	•	•					

USES OF CHOCOLATE

	Chocolate Liquor	Bitter sweet	Dark Sweet	Medium Dark Sweet	Light Sweet	Milk Chocolate	Ice Cream Coating	skim Milk, Buttermilk	Imitation Coating	Coca Butter
Butter creams	•	•	•							
Candy bars				•	•	•		•		
Caramels				•	•			•		
chocolate bars				•	•	•				
Chocolate ice cream	•									
Chocolate pops							•		•	
Chocolate syrup	•									
Cocoanut creams				•					•	
Cordials		•	•							
Culinary products	•									
Frappe		•							•	
Fruit-flavored creams				•					•	
Fudge	•	•	•		•			•		
Hand rolls	•	•								
Ice cream bars							•		•	
Italian creams		•								
Jelly centers					•				•	
Lotions		•	•	•	•			•		•
Marshmallows, marshmallow crackers		•	•	•	•	•		•	•	
Nougats			•	•	•			•		
Nuts, nut clusters, nut rolls			•	•	•			•		
Nut-flavored creams			•	•					•	
Ointments										•
Peppermint creams	•	•	•							
Raisins, dates, figs				•		•		•		
Sponge centers				•					•	
Suppositories										•
Tobacco	•									
Vanilla-creams				•		•		•	•	

If chocolate is taken out of a cold room and placed in a warm or damp room, a film of moisture forms on the surface. The fine sugar particles dissolve and form a thin layer of syrup. On evaporation of the moisture, the sugar crystallises in minute form, giving the chocolate a rough, grayish appearance, sometimes mottled by red-brown spots due to the solution of the coloring matter of the chocolate in the moisture. This phenomenon is known as sugar bloom.

If chocolate is stored in a warm place or exposed to heat, the cocoa butter softens or melts, and expands, forcing its way through the spaces between the sugar and cocoa particles to the surface. On cooling, the cocoa butter crystallises, forming a grayish-white film which is greasy to the touch. This type of bloom is known as fat bloom, and is a source of trouble during the summer months. Although the flavor is usually not impaired, the grayish appearance of the chocolate is considered by the public to be a sign of staleness, and this results in great economic loss to the manufacturer. Chocolate picks up foreign odors readily, and should be stored in a. clean room with free circulation of air.

APPROXIMATE COMPOSITION OF CHOCOLATE COATINGS

	Chocolate Liquor	*Sugar*	*Total Fat*	*Whole Milk Solids*	*Skim Milk or Butter-milk Solids*
Bitter	100	0	50-56	0	0
Bittersweet	80-95	5-20	40-50	0	0
Mild bittersweet	50-75	25-38	38-42	0	0
Dark sweet	25-45	40-50	34-42	0	0
Medium dark sweet	20-40	45-55	32-42	0	0
High grade lt. sweet	15-25	40-50	34-39	0	0
Low grade lt. sweet	5-15	55-68	31-39	0	0
Sweet milk	7-17	35-55	28-39	12+	0
Ice cream bar	9-29	29-39	50-60	12+	0-6
Skim milk, butter-milk, malted milk	7-17	35-55	30-40	0	12+

Small quantities of flavoring materials such as vanillin, coumarin, coffee cinnamon, peppermint, orange, lemon, anise, and synthetic cocoa bean flavor may also be used.

Cocoa shells are a by-product of the cocoa and chocolate industries. They are used chiefly as a fertiliser ingredient, and for the extraction of their fat and theobromine content.

COFFEE

Coffee is the fruit of Coffea arabica, indigenous to tropical Africa, especially Abyssinia, from where its growth undoubtedly spread across the continent to Liberia, where it grows wild and is now extensively cultivated. The Liberian coffee plant is a distinct species, which seems to be less subject to disease and which has been successfully introduced into the East Indies. The cultivation soon spread to the Western world, Cuba, Mexico, Central and South America. At the present time Brazil produces about three-quarters of the whole world market.

In its wild state, the coffee tree attains a height of from 20 to 30 feet and looks somewhat like a cherry tree. In cultivation, it is trimmed down to the height of about 6 feet. The coffee tree develops best in rich soil and in a tropical climate where the rainfall exceeds 75 inches per year.

The fruit is an oval, deep purple, two-seeded drupe. The parchment-like endocarp incloses two plano-convex seeds, which are placed together by their flat sides and constitute the raw coffee of commerce. There are two general varieties:

I Brazil coffees

II Mild coffees

The Brazil coffees include the Santos and Rio coffees. The mild coffees include the Java, Mocha, Bogota, Guatemala, Porto Rican, Mexican, Maracaibo and a few others.

Santos coffee is shipped from the port of Santos. It is mild and sweet. Santos coffee is usually blended with Bogota to obtain a good flavor and color.

Rio coffee is shipped from the port of Rio de Janeiro. It is rather pungent.

The roasting of coffee results in a notable reduction of some of the constituents, especially the caffein, fat and sugar. When roasting is properly conducted, the total loss in weight amounts to from 12 to 18%, of which about 8% is moisture.

Coffee is sometimes glazed with sugar before roasting. According to Hilger and Juckenack, glazed coffee must be heated to a much higher temperature. This results in about double the loss of caffein and fat. French roasted coffees belong to this class.

TEA

The tea plant is an evergreen shrub, which grows to a height of from 12 to 15 feet in the wild state, but under cultivation is kept about 4 feet high. Tea will grow in a variety of climates, but a sub-tropical climate, especially in sections where the rainfall is about 50 inches annually seems to be the best. There are three different kinds of tea, depending on the method of curing.

I Green or un fermented tea

II Black or fermented tea

III Oolong or semi—fermented tea

All of these teas can be produced from leaves picked from the same bush.

GREEN TEAS

A Japan Green Teas

1 Basket-fired green tea (long leaves)

2 Pan-fired green tea (short leaves)

B China Green Teas

1 Gunpowders (small round rolled leaves)

2 Imperials (large round rolled leaves)

3 Young hysons (long rolled leaves)

There is no difference in the drinking qualities of these subdivisions, only in appearance. China green teas are generally known as Souchong.

OOLONG TEAS

Oolong teas are produced on the Island of Formosa. They are fired when the leaves are only half fermented.

BLACK TEAS

A. Black teas produced in China are called English breakfast tea or Congou tea.

B. Black teas produced in India, Ceylon, Java, and Sumatra are classified according to the size of the leaf. The three young shoots at the tip are known as Orange Pekoe and Pekoe, which contain the least fiber, most juice, and produce the finest grade of tea. The leaves immediately below the Pekoe are named Souchong, a tea of popular price. Pekoe and Souchong are sometimes mixed and sold as Pekoe Souchong.

The difference between green and black tea is due to the fact that the green tea is dried shortly after gathering, and then rolled and carefully fired, whereas black tea is made up into heaps, which are exposed to the air for some time before firing and allowed to undergo fermentation, resulting in the conversion of its original olive green color to a black color.

39
PLANT ECONOMICS OF ALCOHOLIC BEVERAGES AND VINEGAR FROM COCONUT WATER

Rated Plant Capacity = 3000 LIT./Day

LAND & BUILDING (Land Area 2 Acre) = Rs. 43,50,000.00

PLANT & MACHINERY

1. Coconut breaking unit
2. Coconut Water Collection tank
3. Candle filter with complete accessories
4. Plate heat exchanger
5. Fermenters for Alcohol
6. Fermenters for Vinegar
7. Starter Tank
8. Distillation column
9. Rectification Column
10. Condenser
11. Automatic Weighing filling and bottle sealing machine
12. Automatic labelling machine
13. Stainless steel storage tank
14. Steam Bottle Steriliser
15. Carton sealing machine
16. Water treatment unit
17. Laboratory equipment
18. Pipes,Pumps,Valves fittings, structures, conveyers, and miscellaneous. equipments
19. Instrumentations & process control equipments
20. Electrical fittings, cables, switch gears and other.
21. Boiler

FIXED CAPITAL

1. LAND & BUILDING	Rs.	43,50,000.00
2. PLANT & MACHINERY	Rs.	88,90,000.00
3. OTHER FIXED ASSETS	Rs.	23,80,000.00
TOTAL	Rs.	1,56,20,000.00

RAW MATERIALS

1. Coconut Green
2. Yeast,Chemicals nutrients
3. Glass bottle
4. Glass bottle for Vinegar
5. Crown Caps, P.P.
6. Labels
7. Corrugated Cardboard boxes
8. Miscellaneous, consumables

TOTAL WORKING CAPITAL/MONTH

1. RAW MATERIAL	Rs.	21,75,750.00
2. SALARY & WAGES	Rs.	3,32,750.00
3. UTILITIES & OVERHEADS	Rs.	5,40,000.00
TOTAL	Rs.	30,48,500.00

TOTAL CAPITAL INVESTMENT

TOTAL FIXED CAPITAL	Rs.	1,56,20,000.00
TOTAL WORKING CAPITAL FOR 1 MONTH	Rs.	30,48,500.00
TOTAL	Rs.	1,86,68,500.00

TURN OVER/ANNUM

1. By sale of Coconut Feni (Alcohol beverages)750 ml size bottle (without excise duty)
2. By sale of Coconut Vinegar 500 ml size, (without excise duty)

TOTAL	Rs.	6,36,00,000.00

PROFIT SALES RATIO = Profit / Sales x 100 = 34%

RATE OF RETURN = Operating profit / T.C.I x 100 = 115%

BREAK EVEN POINT (B.E.P) = 32%

40
PLANT ECONOMICS OF AQUACULTURE PRAWN FARMING

Rated Plant Capacity = 4 TON/Day

LAND & BUILDING (Land Area 120 Hectares) = Rs. 4,60,00,000.00

PLANT & MACHINERY

1. Water Pump
2. Fishing nets Nylon yarn
3. Oxygen rating devices, insect killing and filtration equipments.
4. Temperature control equipments.
5. Small Canoes.
6. Cold Storage equipments
7. Conveyor belt
8. Washing tank(s)
9. Miscellaneous equipments(Test Kits)
10. Pollution control equipments

FIXED CAPITAL

1. LAND & BUILDING	Rs.	4,60,00,000.00
2. PLANT & MACHINERY	Rs.	35,30,000.00
3. OTHER FIXED ASSETS	Rs.	18,50,000.00
TOTAL	Rs.	5,13,80,000.00

RAW MATERIALS

1. Prawn fish seedlings
2. Fish meal
3. Medicine, insecticides, other chemicals, water treatments chemicals.

TOTAL WORKING CAPITAL/ANNUM

1. RAW MATERIAL	Rs.	1,63,00,000.00
2. SALARY & WAGES	Rs.	14,25,952.00
3. UTILITIES & OVERHEADS	Rs.	19,29,000.00
TOTAL	Rs.	1,96,54,952.00

TOTAL CAPITAL INVESTMENT

TOTAL FIXED CAPITAL	Rs.	5,13,80,000.00
TOTAL WORKING CAPITAL FOR 3 MONTHS	Rs.	49,13,738.00
TOTAL	Rs.	5,62,93,738.00

TURN OVER/ANNUM

By sale of 1200 Tons of Prawn	Rs.	8,40,00,000.00

PROFIT SALES RATIO = Profit / Sales x 100 = 60%

RATE OF RETURN = Operating profit / T.C.I x 100 = 90%

BREAK EVEN POINT (B.E.P) = 23%

41

PLANT ECONOMICS OF BAKERY UNIT, BUNS, CAKE, TOFFEE

Rated Plant Capacity	= 1243.70 KGS/Day
LAND & BUILDING (Land Area 500 Sq.mt.)	= Rs. 12,00,000.00

PLANT & MACHINERY

1. Auto Sifter
2. Dough Kneader
3. Dough Grinder
4. State Convet
5. Dough Rounder
6. Dough Moulder
7. Diesel Rotary Rock oven
8. Cooling rack
9. Trolley
10. Automatic Slice
11. Dies and Mold
12. Electrically Heating Kettle
13. Cooling Chamber
14. Packing, and sealing Machine
15. Miscellaneous Machine

FIXED CAPITAL

1. LAND & BUILDING		Rs.	12,00,000.00
2. PLANT & MACHINERY		Rs.	9,43,500.00
3. OTHER FIXED ASSETS		Rs.	3,20,000.00
	TOTAL	Rs.	24,63,500.00

RAW MATERIALS

1. Flour
2. Shortening
3. Salt
4. Sugar
5. Egg
6. Milk Solid
7. Yeast
8. Butter
9. Glucose solid

TOTAL WORKING CAPITAL/MONTH

1. RAW MATERIAL		Rs.	4,28,933.00
2. SALARY & WAGES		Rs.	54,240.00
3. UTILITIES & OVERHEADS		Rs.	46,000.00
	TOTAL	Rs.	5,29,173.00

TOTAL CAPITAL INVESTMENT

TOTAL FIXED CAPITAL		Rs.	24,63,500.00
TOTAL WORKING CAPITAL FOR 3 MONTHS		Rs.	15,87,519.00
	TOTAL	Rs.	40,51,019.00

TURN OVER/ANNUM

1. Pastry Products: 120000 Kgs.
2. Paste 30000 Kgs.
3. Bread/Bun 99540 kgs
4. Toffee 123570 Kgs

TOTAL	Rs.	1,07,50,200.00

PROFIT SALES RATIO = Profit / Sales x 100 = 33%

RATE OF RETURN = Operating profit / T.C.I x 100 = 88%

BREAK EVEN POINT (B.E.P) = 27%

42
PLANT ECONOMICS OF BREAD PLANT

Rated Plant Capacity	= 10000 Loaves/Day
LAND & BUILDING (Land Area 668 sq.mt)	= Rs. 19,81,700.00

FIXED CAPITAL

1. LAND & BUILDING		Rs.	19,81,700.00
2. PLANT & MACHINERY		Rs.	15,50,000.00
3. OTHER FIXED ASSETS		Rs.	5,35,000.00
	TOTAL	Rs.	40,66,700.00

RAW MATERIALS

1. Wheat Flour
2. Salt
3. Sugar
4. Milk Powder
5. Edible oil
6. Shortening
7. Yeast
8. Wrappers & Other Misc.

TOTAL WORKING CAPITAL/MONTH

1. RAW MATERIAL		Rs.	24,58,125.00
2. SALARY & WAGES		Rs.	1,35,010.00
3. UTILITIES & OVERHEADS		Rs.	2,97,350.00
	TOTAL	Rs.	28,90,485.00

TOTAL CAPITAL INVESTMENT

TOTAL FIXED CAPITAL		Rs.	40,66,700.00
TOTAL WORKING CAPITAL FOR 1 MONTHS		Rs.	28,90,485.00
	TOTAL	Rs.	69,57,185.00

TURN OVER/ANNUM

1. Receipt from sales of 10,000 × 300 loaves of 800 gms.
2. By sale of 10000 × 300 loaves of 400 gm.

TOTAL	Rs.	4,20,00,000.00

PROFIT SALES RATIO = Profit / Sales x 100 = 14%

RATE OF RETURN = Operating profit / T.C.I x 100 = 85%

BREAK EVEN POINT (B.E.P) = 37%

43
PLANT ECONOMICS OF BEER INDUSTRY (EXPORT ORIENTED)

Rated Plant Capacity = 22000 LIT/Day

LAND & BUILDING (Land Area 5 Acres) = Rs. 1,00,34,300.00

PLANT & MACHINERY

1. Malt Handling Section
2. Brew House Section
3. Wort Treatment Section
4. Yeast Propagation, Storage and Pitching Section
5. Fermentation and Lagering Section
6. Filtration and Carbonation Section
7. Bright Beer Section
8. C.I.P. System
9. Bottling Hall Equipments Complete
10. Refrigeration Section
11. Steam and fuel oil Section
12. Water treatment Section
13. Compressed Air Section
14. Carbon dioxide Section
15. Electrical Section
16. Miscellaneous Items
17. Sales tax, packing charge, forwarding charge, transportation, loading and unloading charges etc.

FIXED CAPITAL

1. LAND & BUILDING	Rs.	1,00,34,300.00
2. PLANT & MACHINERY	Rs.	11,30,33,513.00
3. OTHER FIXED ASSETS	Rs.	4,48,25,000.00
TOTAL	Rs.	16,78,92,813.00

RAW MATERIALS

1. Barley Malt
2. Brewers Yeast good quality
3. Hops
4. Glass Bottles
5. Other Miscellaneous (a) Urea, (b) Ammonium Nitrate, (C) Enzyme

TOTAL WORKING CAPITAL/MONTH

1. RAW MATERIAL	Rs.	40,26,665.00
2. SALARY & WAGES	Rs.	5,59,375.00
3. UTILITIES & OVERHEADS	Rs.	15,25,000.00
TOTAL	Rs.	61,11,040.00

TOTAL CAPITAL INVESTMENT

TOTAL FIXED CAPITAL	Rs.	16,78,92,813.00
TOTAL WORKING CAPITAL FOR 3 MONTHS	Rs.	1,83,33,120.00
TOTAL	Rs.	18,62,25,933.00

TURN OVER/ANNUM

By Sale of 8000000 Bottles of Beer	Rs.	18,40,00,000.00

PROFIT SALES RATIO = Profit / Sales x 100 = 22%

RATE OF RETURN = Operating profit / T.C.I x 100 = 22%

BREAK EVEN POINT (B.E.P) = 66%

44
PLANT ECONOMICS OF CONFECTIONERY INDUSTRY

Rated Plant Capacity = 4.00 Ton./Day

LAND & BUILDING (Land 500 Sq.mt.) = Rs. 15,00,000.00

PLANT & MACHINERY

1. Toffee cut & wrap machine.
2. Cooker (S.S)
3. Boiler
4. Candy forming machine
5. Candy wrapping Machine
6. Pouch making machine.
7. Tabletting Machine
8. Powder mixer.
9. Granulator
10. Grinding machine.
11. Genset

FIXED CAPITAL

1.	LAND & BUILDING	Rs.	15,00,000.00
2.	PLANT & MACHINERY	Rs.	20,35,000.00
3.	OTHER FIXED ASSETS	Rs.	4,85,000.00
	TOTAL	Rs.	40,20,000.00

RAW MATERIALS

1. Sugar
2. Glucose (liquid)

3. Butter
4. Colour
5. Flavours
6. Ingredients for ayurvedic products (salt,spices,sugar & others)
7. Packaging materials, printed film, cartons, sticker, etc.

TOTAL WORKING CAPITAL/MONTH

1. RAW MATERIAL	Rs.	20,04,570.00
2. SALARY & WAGES	Rs.	93,060.00
3. UTILITIES & OVERHEADS	Rs.	2,05,250.00
TOTAL	Rs.	23,02,880.00

TOTAL CAPITAL INVESTMENT

TOTAL FIXED CAPITAL	Rs.	40,20,000.00
TOTAL WORKING CAPITAL FOR 3 MONTHS	Rs.	69,08,640.00
TOTAL	Rs.	1,09,28,640.00

TURN OVER/ANNUM

1. By selling 300 tons of toffee
2. By selling 600 tons of hard candy,
3. By sale of 300 MT products

TOTAL	Rs.	3,48,00,000.00

PROFIT SALES RATIO = Profit / Sales x 100 = 15%

RATE OF RETURN = Operating profit / T.C.I x 100 = 48%

BREAK EVEN POINT (B.E.P) = 40%

45
PLANT ECONOMICS OF CORN FLAKES

Rated Plant Capacity = 1 TON/Day

LAND & BUILDING (Land Area 2000 Sq. Mt.) = Rs. 58,00,000.00

PLANT & MACHINERY

1. Silo
2. Air classifiers
3. Separator
4. Storage bin
5. Weight balance
6. Rotary steam cooker
7. Agitator or lump breaker
8. Pan cooler or steamer
9. Germ Separator
10. Heavy flaking machine
11. Rotary oven
12. Conveyor
13. Inspection conveyor
14. Packing Machine
15. Screening and cooling Equipment
16. Mixer for flavouring syrup
17. Boiler
18. Sifter

FIXED CAPITAL

1. LAND & BUILDING	Rs.	58,00,000.00
2. PLANT & MACHINERY	Rs.	9,30,000.00
3. OTHER FIXED ASSETS	Rs.	4,36,500.00
TOTAL	Rs.	71,66,500.00

RAW MATERIALS

1. Corn Grain
2. Sugar
3. Salt
4. Polythene bags of different sizes

TOTAL WORKING CAPITAL/MONTH

1. RAW MATERIAL	Rs.	3,92,050.00
2. SALARY & WAGES	Rs.	1,52,790.00
3. UTILITIES & OVERHEADS	Rs.	68,350.00
TOTAL	Rs.	6,13,190.00

TOTAL CAPITAL INVESTMENT

TOTAL FIXED CAPITAL	Rs.	71,66,500.00
TOTAL WORKING CAPITAL FOR 1 MONTHS	Rs.	6,13,190.00
TOTAL	Rs.	77,79,690.00

TURN OVER/ANNUM

By sales of 300 ton of corn flakes.	Rs.	1,35,00,000.00

PROFIT SALES RATIO = Profit / Sales x 100 = 33%

RATE OF RETURN = Operating profit / T.C.I x 100 = 58%

BREAK EVEN POINT (B.E.P) = 38%

46
PLANT ECONOMICS OF CHEWING GUM

Rated Plant Capacity = 400 KG/Day

LAND & BUILDING (Land Area 500 sq.mts.) = Rs. 7,00,000.00

PLANT & MACHINERY

1. Dry solid Blender
2. High Intensity Mixer
3. Intermediate Intensity Mixer
4. Rapid Efficient Mixer
5. Dough Mixing Kettle
6. Cooling bath
7. Crimple Machine
8. Packing machine
9. Storage tanks

FIXED CAPITAL

1. LAND & BUILDING	Rs.	7,00,000.00
2. PLANT & MACHINERY	Rs.	8,90,000.00
3. OTHER FIXED ASSETS	Rs.	2,08,500.00
TOTAL	Rs.	17,98,500.00

RAW MATERIALS

1. Synthetic gum
2. Ester gum
3. Polyvinyl Acetate
4. Cocoa butter

5. Glycerol Monosterate
6. Calcium Carbonate
7. TiO2
8. Flavour
9. Corn Syrup
10. Packaging Material

TOTAL WORKING CAPITAL/MONTH

1. RAW MATERIAL	Rs.	2,01,950.00
2. SALARY & WAGES	Rs.	58,622.00
3. UTILITIES & OVERHEADS	Rs.	89,000.00
TOTAL	Rs.	3,49,572.00

TOTAL CAPITAL INVESTMENT

TOTAL FIXED CAPITAL	Rs.	17,98,500.00
TOTAL WORKING CAPITAL FOR 3 MONTHS	Rs.	10,48,716.00
TOTAL	Rs.	28,47,216.00

TURN OVER/ANNUM

By sale of 1,20,000 kg. of chewing gum per annum Rs. 68,40,000.00

PROFIT SALES RATIO = Profit / Sales x 100 = 27%

RATE OF RETURN = Operating profit / T.C.I x 100 = 65%

BREAK EVEN POINT (B.E.P) = 44%

47
PLANT ECONOMICS OF CATTLE FEED

Rated Plant Capacity = 30 TON/Day

LAND & BUILDING (Land Area 1500 sq. mt.) = Rs. 30,10,000.00

PLANT & MACHINERY

1. Pulveriser
2. Ribbon blender
3. Storage Silo
4. Belt Conveyer
5. Automatic bag filling, sealing and packaging Machine.
6. Weighing Machine bridge type with complete accessories.
7. Magnetic separator.
8. Pelleting Machine & Miscellaneous others.

FIXED CAPITAL

1.	LAND & BUILDING	Rs.	30,10,000.00
2.	PLANT & MACHINERY	Rs.	19,40,000.00
3.	OTHER FIXED ASSETS	Rs.	2,35,000.00
	TOTAL	Rs.	51,85,000.00

RAW MATERIALS

1. Ground nut cake
2. Wheat bran/Rice bran
3. Maize
4. Wheat/rice grit
5. Maize-gluten meal

6. Molasses
7. Mineral Mixture
8. Salt
9. Vitamin mixture

TOTAL WORKING CAPITAL/MONTH

1. RAW MATERIAL	Rs.	15,83,000.00
2. SALARY & WAGES	Rs.	1,31,875.00
3. UTILITIES & OVERHEADS	Rs.	4,12,000.00
TOTAL	Rs.	21,26,875.00

TOTAL CAPITAL INVESTMENT

TOTAL FIXED CAPITAL	Rs.	51,85,000.00
TOTAL WORKING CAPITAL FOR 3 MONTHS	Rs.	63,80,625.00
TOTAL	Rs.	1,15,65,625.00

TURN OVER/ANNUM

By Sale of 9000 Mts. of Cattle Feed	Rs.	3,82,50,000.00

PROFIT SALES RATIO = Profit / Sales x 100 = 25%

RATE OF RETURN = Operating profit / T.C.I x 100 = 82%

BREAK EVEN POINT (B.E.P) = 38%

48
PLANT ECONOMICS OF COCONUT PRODUCTS & BYE PRODUCTS PROCESSING UNIT

Rated Plant Capacity = 92.55 MT/Day

LAND & BUILDING (Land Area 8 Acre) = Rs. 4,52,40,000.00

PLANT & MACHINERY

1. Coconut Husk Removing Machine (Automatic)
2. Coconut Breaking Machine Continuous Hydraulic Press type
3. Coconut Kernel Shreddler
4. Coconut Grating Machine fine Type
5. Continuous Conveyer Belt Dryer with S.S. Belt &Counter Current Airflow Size (20 x 5 x 7 ft.)
6. Automatic Sieving Machine
7. Automatic Desiccated Powder Packing Machine
8. Lab. Testing Equipments
9. Coconut Milk, M. Beverage/M. Powder Section : shelled coconut kernel soaking tank s.s.
10. Water Heating Tank (SS)
11. Long Strainer (SS) with Bottom Size milk collecting trays
12. Coconut Milk Storage Tank (SS Made)
13. Coconut Milk Pasteuriser (PHE)
14. Milk Chiller
15. Milk Beverage Making Tank (SS made) with Stirrer
16. Automatic Weighing, filling, sealing, bottling machine
17. Cream Separator Centrifuge (SS lining)
18. Refrigeration Machine

19. Cream Pasteuriser
20. Cream filling in moulds by weighing filling machine
21. Coconut Cream Slabs Wrapping Machine
22. Conveyer Belts (SS Made) with Roller
23. Vacuum Pan Evaporation
24. Double Drum Drier
25. Micro Pulveriser
26. SS Sieving Machine
27. Coconut Powder Automatic Weighing, Filling and Sealing Machine
28. Activated Chamber
29. Boilers
30. Bolting Machine (Automatic)
31. Coconut Water Processing Stainless Steel Storage Tank
32. Other misc. Machineries/Tools and accessories

FIXED CAPITAL

1. LAND & BUILDING	Rs.	4,52,40,000.00
2. PLANT & MACHINERY	Rs.	3,59,50,000.00
3. OTHER FIXED ASSETS	Rs.	3,38,00,000.00
TOTAL	Rs.	11,49,90,000.00

RAW MATERIALS

1. Coconut
2. Chemicals
3. Packaging Materials
4. Other misc. expenses

TOTAL WORKING CAPITAL/MONTH

1. RAW MATERIAL	Rs.	3,99,00,000.00
2. SALARY & WAGES	Rs.	14,33,000.00
3. UTILITIES & OVERHEADS	Rs.	37,48,000.00
TOTAL	Rs.	4,50,81,000.00

TOTAL CAPITAL INVESTMENT

TOTAL FIXED CAPITAL	Rs.	11,49,90,000.00
TOTAL WORKING CAPITAL FOR 3 MONTHS	Rs.	13,52,43,000.00
TOTAL	Rs.	25,02,33,000.00

TURN OVER/ANNUM

1. By sale of DESICCATED COCONUT POWDER (1500 MT)
2. By sale of COCONUT WATER (9000 MT)
3. By sale of COCONUT OIL (240 MT)
4. By sale of COCONUT MILK LIQUID (900 MT)
5. By sale of COCONUT MILK BEVERAGE (525 MT)
6. By sale of SKIMMED MILK POWDER (1050 MT)
7. By sale of COCONUT CREAM (2100 MT)
8. By sale of COCONUT FLOUR (4950 MT)
9. By sale of PARING OIL (330 MT)
10. By sale of COIR (4920 MT)
11. By sale of COCONUT SHELL POWDER (1500 MT)
12. By sale of ACTIVATED CARBON (750 MT)

TOTAL Rs. 73,37,40,000.00

PROFIT SALES RATIO = Profit / Sales x 100 = 20%

RATE OF RETURN = Operating profit / T.C.I x 100 = 57%

BREAK EVEN POINT (B.E.P) = 31%

49
PLANT ECONOMICS OF COIR PITH

Rated Plant Capacity = 50 MT/Day

LAND & BUILDING (Land Area 10 acre) = Rs. 63,24,000.00

PLANT & MACHINERY

1. Bale-Opener
2. Beating Machine (Having mallet type hammering action) fitted with motor
3. Water Wetting Tanks
4. Pollution Treatment Plant (Water effluent Treatment Plant)
5. Belt Conveyor System for conveying of Husk to the Processing Site
6. Lab Equipments
7. Miscellaneous tools jigs, tools, fixture etc.

FIXED CAPITAL

1.	LAND & BUILDING	Rs.	63,24,000.00
2.	PLANT & MACHINERY	Rs.	18,50,000.00
3.	OTHER FIXED ASSETS	Rs.	7,90,000.00
	TOTAL	Rs.	89,64,000.00

RAW MATERIALS

1. Coconut Husks
2. Transport Charges for transporting Husks
3. Packaging Material Gunny Bags

TOTAL WORKING CAPITAL/MONTH

1. RAW MATERIAL	Rs.	54,62,500.00
2. SALARY & WAGES	Rs.	2,67,000.00
3. UTILITIES & OVERHEADS	Rs.	1,75,000.00
TOTAL	Rs.	59,04,500.00

TOTAL CAPITAL INVESTMENT

TOTAL FIXED CAPITAL	Rs.	89,64,000.00
TOTAL WORKING CAPITAL FOR 1 MONTHS	Rs.	59,04,500.00
TOTAL	Rs.	1,48,68,500.00

TURN OVER/ANNUM

1. Coir Pith 15000 mt.
2. Husks Fibres 30,000 mt.

TOTAL	Rs.	9,67,50,000.00

PROFIT SALES RATIO = Profit / Sales x 100 = 24%

RATE OF RETURN = Operating profit / T.C.I x 100 = 157%

BREAK EVEN POINT (B.E.P) = 17%

50
PLANT ECONOMICS OF DESICCATED COCONUT POWDER FROM COCONUT

Rated Plant Capacity = 200 KGS/Day

LAND & BUILDING (Land Area 1200 Sq.mt.) = Rs. 36,77,500.00

PLANT & MACHINERY

1. Disintegrator(a)breaking kernel
2. Wooden washing vats for kernel washing with water spray nozzles and other accessories
3. Cabinet dryer, fitted with electric
4. Pulveriser
5. Vibrating screen
6. Packing appliances
7. Lab. Testing Equipments
8. Drum (S.S.)
9. Miscellaneous

FIXED CAPITAL

1.	LAND & BUILDING	Rs.	36,77,500.00
2.	PLANT & MACHINERY	Rs.	2,91,000.00
3.	OTHER FIXED ASSETS	Rs.	2,05,000.00
	TOTAL	Rs.	41,73,500.00

RAW MATERIALS

1. Coconuts
2. Packing material for packing

TOTAL WORKING CAPITAL/MONTH

1.	RAW MATERIAL	Rs.	94,000.00
2.	SALARY & WAGES	Rs.	1,01,280.00
3.	UTILITIES & OVERHEADS	Rs.	36,500.00
	TOTAL	Rs.	2,31,780.00

TOTAL CAPITAL INVESTMENT

TOTAL FIXED CAPITAL	Rs.	41,73,500.00
TOTAL WORKING CAPITAL FOR 1 MONTH	Rs.	2,31,780.00
TOTAL	Rs.	44,05,280.00

TURN OVER/ANNUM

1. By sale of 60 MT of 60,000 kgs of DESICCATED COCONUT POWDER
2. By sale of oil (This oil is assume to be 3 kg from 10,000 nuts)
3. By sale of unprocessed coir 21.8 MT
4. By sale of coir dust 5.45 MT
5. By sale of Broken shell 21.8 MT
6. By sale of poonac 100 kg.

TOTAL Rs. 42,95,800.00

PROFIT SALES RATIO = Profit / Sales x 100 = 14%

RATE OF RETURN = Operating profit / T.C.I x 100 = 14%

BREAK EVEN POINT (B.E.P) = 72%

51
PLANT ECONOMICS OF DALL MILL

Rated Plant Capacity	=	Channa Dal 2670 Tons/Annum Moong wash 2670 Tons/Annum Urad wash 2670 Tons/Annum Toor 2670 Tons/Annum Yellow pea split 2670 Tons/Annum Husk 1500 Tons/Annum
LAND & BUILDING (Land Area 2000 sq.mt)	=	Rs. 39,50,000.00

PLANT & MACHINERY

1. Dall mill complete with automatic feed Hopper with accessories
2. Belt conveyer system with drive
3. Tray Driers, Handling
4. Sheller
5. Polisher, Husk separator
6. Cleaning sieves
7. Suction Fan
8. Elevators
9. Self oil drum
10. Maintenance Tools, Jigs, trolleys
11. Moistening Tanks
12. Weighing machine
13. 5 H.P. Motor with starter

FIXED CAPITAL

1. LAND & BUILDING	Rs.	39,50,000.00
2. PLANT & MACHINERY	Rs.	12,06,000.00
3. OTHER FIXED ASSETS	Rs.	2,20,000.00
TOTAL	Rs.	53,76,000.00

RAW MATERIALS

1. Channa
2. Moong
3. Urad
4. Toor
5. Yellow pea

TOTAL WORKING CAPITAL/MONTH

1. RAW MATERIAL	Rs.	77,17,500.00
2. SALARY & WAGES	Rs.	1,15,000.00
3. UTILITIES & OVERHEADS	Rs.	1,55,250.00
TOTAL	Rs.	79,87,750.00

TOTAL CAPITAL INVESTMENT

TOTAL FIXED CAPITAL	Rs.	53,76,000.00
TOTAL WORKING CAPITAL FOR 3 MONTHS	Rs.	2,39,63,250.00
TOTAL	Rs.	2,93,39,250.00

TURN OVER/ANNUM

1. By sale of Channa Dal 2670 Tons
2. Moong wash 2670 Tons
3. Urad wash 2670 Tons
4. Toor 2670 Tons
5. Yellow pea split 2670 Tons

TOTAL Rs. 12,12,30,000.00

PROFIT SALES RATIO = Profit/Sales x 100 = 15%

RATE OF RETURN = Operating profit / T.C.I x 100 = 63%

BREAK EVEN POINT (B.E.P) = 31%

52
PLANT ECONOMICS OF DAIRY PRODUCTS & MILK PACKAGING IN POUCHES

Rated Plant Capacity = 1390 KG/Day

LAND & BUILDING (Land Area 2000 Sq.mts.) = Rs. 17,40,000.00

PLANT & MACHINERY

1. Centrifuge or Cream separator
2. Pasteuriser
3. Refrigeration system
4. Filter ordinary
5. Milk reception tank
6. Water softener unit
7. Steam boiler
8. Miscellaneous equipments as laboratory testing equipments
9. Automatic Pouch filling & sealing machine.
10. Vacuum Pan Evaporator
11. Vertical Storage Tank
12. Neutralization tank
13. Pasteurization vessel
14. Fermenting tank
15. Churner
16. Ghee receiving kettle
17. Pipe fitting, pumps, motor, valve and other miscellaneous machinery
18. Screw Press
19. Oscillating Granulator
20. Tray Dryer

21. Grinding Machine
22. Wash Water Storage tank

FIXED CAPITAL

1. LAND & BUILDING	Rs	17,40,000.00
2. PLANT & MACHINERY	Rs	42,20,000.00
3. OTHER FIXED ASSETS	Rs	9,75,000.00
TOTAL	Rs	69,35,000.00

RAW MATERIALS

1. Milk
2. Chemicals for butter paneer
3. Hydrochloric Acid
4. Cans, Polyethene, packets, Corrugated boxes etc.

TOTAL WORKING CAPITAL/MONTH

1. RAW MATERIAL	Rs	36,73,400.00
2. SALARY & WAGES	Rs	1,00,750.00
3. UTILITIES & OVERHEADS	Rs	1,97,500.00
TOTAL	Rs	39,71,650.00

TOTAL CAPITAL INVESTMENT

TOTAL FIXED CAPITAL	Rs	69,35,000.00
TOTAL WORKING CAPITAL FOR 1 MONTH	Rs	39,71,650.00
TOTAL	Rs	1,09,06,650.00

TURN OVER/ANNUM

1. PANEER 60000 KGS.
2. Butter 150000 Kgs
3. Ghee 186000 Kgs
4. Casein 21000 kgs.
5. Milk 600000 litres in pouches

TOTAL	Rs	6,06,60,000.00

PROFIT SALES RATIO = Profit / Sales x 100 = 17%

RATE OF RETURN = Operating profit / T.C.I x 100 = 96%

BREAK EVEN POINT (B.E.P) = 27%

53

PLANT ECONOMICS OF EGG POWDER

Rated Plant Capacity	= 36 MT/Day
LAND & BUILDING (Land Area 10 Acres)	= Rs. 1,87,50,000.00

FIXED CAPITAL

1. LAND & BUILDING	Rs.	1,87,50,000.00
2. PLANT & MACHINERY	Rs.	7,30,00,000.00
3. OTHER FIXED ASSETS	Rs.	1,86,00,000.00
TOTAL	Rs.	11,03,50,000.00

RAW MATERIALS

1. Eggs
2. Chemicals & Preservatives
3. Packaging materials pouches, tin
4. Miscellaneous

TOTAL WORKING CAPITAL/MONTH

1. RAW MATERIAL	Rs	4,58,50,000.00
2. SALARY & WAGES	Rs.	5,87,075.00
3. UTILITIES & OVERHEADS	Rs.	14,53,000.00
TOTAL	Rs.	4,78,90,075.00

TOTAL CAPITAL INVESTMENT

TOTAL FIXED CAPITAL	Rs.	11,03,50,000.00
TOTAL WORKING CAPITAL FOR 3 MONTHS	Rs.	14,36,70,225.00
TOTAL	Rs.	25,40,20,225.00

TURN OVER/ANNUM

By sale of 10,800 MT Egg Powder	Rs.	75,60,00,000.00

PROFIT SALES RATIO = Profit / Sales x 100 = 17%
RATE OF RETURN = Operating profit / T.C.I x 100 = 52%
BREAK EVEN POINT (B.E.P) = 31%

54
PLANT ECONOMICS OF FOOD DEHYDRATION

Rated Plant Capacity	= 2.50 TON/Day
LAND & BUILDING (Land Area 3000 sq.mt)	= Rs. 50,20,000.00

PLANT & MACHINERY

1. Roller grading machine
2. Screen Grading machine with various types of screen
3. Rotary Fruit and Vegetable washing machine (Drum type)
4. Automatic peeling machine (blade type peeling machine)
5. Vertical stone remover
6. Belt type cutter
7. Cabbage dividing machine
8. Universed slicing and shredding machine
9. Tomato Dividing machine
10. Automatic blanching machine with complete accessories
11. Boiler
12. Preparation table of Aluminium
13. Elevator
14. Conveyor
15. Weighing machine
16. Laboratory testing equipments
17. Cold storage
18. Tunnel dryer
19. Vacuum pouch packaging machine semiautomatic
20. Stainless steel tank for SO2 treatment
21. Miscellaneous machineries tanks, pumps, valves, pipe fittings and others

FIXED CAPITAL

1. LAND & BUILDING	Rs.	50,20,000.00
2. PLANT & MACHINERY	Rs.	42,00,000.00
3. OTHER FIXED ASSETS	Rs.	17,50,000.00
TOTAL	Rs.	1,09,70,000.00

RAW MATERIALS

1. Fruits of different variety : Fruits (apple, Banana, Grape, Mango & Gauva)
2. Vegetable (Cabbage, Carrot, Cauliflower, potato & carrot, spinach, tomato)
3. Miscellaneous Preservatives i.e. Sodium benzoate Potassium metabisulfite
4. Packing material (Polythene bags)

TOTAL WORKING CAPITAL/MONTH

1. RAW MATERIAL	Rs.	23,37,500.00
2. SALARY & WAGES	Rs.	1,09,312.00
3. UTILITIES & OVERHEADS	Rs.	2,78,000.00
TOTAL	Rs.	27,24,812.00

TOTAL CAPITAL INVESTMENT

TOTAL FIXED CAPITAL	Rs.	1,09,70,000.00
TOTAL WORKING CAPITAL FOR 2 MONTHS	Rs.	54,49,624.00
TOTAL	Rs.	1,64,19,624.00

TURN OVER/ANNUM

1. Total Receipt by sales Dehydrated fruits 375 tons
2. By sale of dehydrated vegetables 375 tons

TOTAL	Rs.	4,53,75,000.00

PROFIT SALES RATIO = Profit / Sales x 100 = 21%

RATE OF RETURN = Operating profit / T.C.I x 100 = 59%

BREAK EVEN POINT (B.E.P) = 34%

55
PLANT ECONOMICS OF FRUIT JUICE MAKING & PACKING IN PLASTIC CONTAINERS

Rated Plant Capacity = 12000 LTS/Day

LAND & BUILDING (Land Area 2 acres) = Rs. 42,80,000.00

PLANT & MACHINERY

1. Fruit Storage Tanks
2. Washing/Steaming/lye treatment vessel
3. Automatic pineapple processing machine
4. Comminutor
5. Blancher
6. Shredding M/c.
7. Juice Extractor (Vertical press master).
8. Filter press
9. Juice processing vessels (chemical treatment cum thermal pasteurisation vessel).
10. Intermediate Juice storage tanks
11. Deaeration Unit, with vacuum pump
12. Filling & Packing M/c. (Automatic)
13. Chilling Units
14. Weighing M/c. (Weigh Bridge)
15. Boiler
16. Laboratory Equipments
17. Pipe fittings, Pumps & valves etc.
18. Miscellaneous Expenses
19. Erection & Commissioning charge etc.

FIXED CAPITAL

1.	LAND & BUILDING	Rs.	42,80,000.00
2.	PLANT & MACHINERY	Rs.	56,00,000.00
3.	OTHER FIXED ASSETS	Rs.	14,45,000.00
	TOTAL	Rs.	1,13,25,000.00

RAW MATERIALS

1. Mango Fresh Fruit
2. Apple Fresh Fruit
3. Pineapple
4. Litchi
5. Preservatives (like citric acid, sod, benzoate etc.), sugar, salt barley water essences etc.
6. Plastic Pouches (laminated) labels,

TOTAL WORKING CAPITAL/MONTH

1.	RAW MATERIAL	Rs.	75,71,000.00
2.	SALARY & WAGES	Rs.	2,09,375.00
3.	UTILITIES & OVERHEADS	Rs.	6,18,000.00
	TOTAL	Rs.	83,98,375.00

TOTAL CAPITAL INVESTMENT

TOTAL FIXED CAPITAL	Rs.	1,13,25,000.00
TOTAL WORKING CAPITAL FOR 1 MONTHS	Rs.	83,98,375.00
TOTAL	Rs.	1,97,23,375.00

TURN OVER/ANNUM

1. By sale of 9,00,000 litres of Mango Juice
2. By sale of 9,00,000 litres of Apple juice.
3. By sale of 9,00,000 litres of Pine apple.
4. By sale of 9,00,000 litres of Litchi Juice.

TOTAL Rs. 12,42,00,000.00

PROFIT SALES RATIO = Profit / Sales x 100 = 16%

RATE OF RETURN = Operating profit / T.C.I x 100 = 98%

BREAK EVEN POINT (B.E.P) = 30%

56
PLANT ECONOMICS OF FEED MILL FOR MIXED FEED (POULTRY & CATTLE)

Rated Plant Capacity	= 30 MT/Day
LAND & BUILDING (Land Area 1200 sq.mt.)	= Rs. 32,50,000.00

PLANT & MACHINERY

1. Disintegrator with motor Starter Pulley, V Belt, Stand sieve & cyclone etc.
2. Ribbon blender with motor starter, reduction gear, gear box etc.
3. Sifter with motor starter extra sieve etc.
4. Platform weighing Machine
5. Gunny Bag Sealing Machine
6. Laboratory Testing Equipment
7. Depolluting equipments
8. Miscellaneous

FIXED CAPITAL

1. LAND & BUILDING	Rs.	32,50,000.00
2. PLANT & MACHINERY	Rs.	10,97,000.00
3. OTHER FIXED ASSETS	Rs.	3,15,000.00
TOTAL	Rs.	46,62,000.00

RAW MATERIALS

1. Maize
2. Rice Polish
3. Rice germ

4. Damaged wheat
5. Molasses
6. Ground Nut Cake
7. Alfalfa Meal
8. Fish Meal
9. Sunflower cake
10. Mineral Mix
11. Vitamins Mix
12. Miscellaneous

TOTAL WORKING CAPITAL/MONTH

1. RAW MATERIAL	Rs.	50,45,500.00
2. SALARY & WAGES	Rs.	2,13,584.00
3. UTILITIES & OVERHEADS	Rs.	2,77,480.00
TOTAL	Rs.	55,36,564.00

TOTAL CAPITAL INVESTMENT

TOTAL FIXED CAPITAL	Rs.	46,62,000.00
TOTAL WORKING CAPITAL FOR 2 MONTHS	Rs.	1,10,73,128.00
TOTAL	Rs.	1,57,35,128.00

TURN OVER/ANNUM

By sale of 9000 Tons of Mix Cattle and Poultry Feed	Rs.	8,28,00,000.00

PROFIT SALES RATIO = Profit / Sales x 100 = 17%

RATE OF RETURN = Operating profit / T.C.I x 100 = 89%

BREAK EVEN POINT (B.E.P) = 26%

57
PLANT ECONOMICS OF INSTANT NOODLES WITH TASTE MAKER SPICE

Rated Plant Capacity = 1 MT/Day

LAND & BUILDING (Land Area 1200 Sq.Mt.) = Rs. 42,80,000.00

PLANT & MACHINERY

1. Flour mixer
2. Shaper
3. Boiling machine
4. Cutting machine
5. Frying machine
6. Cooler
7. Boiler
8. Horizontal packaging machine
9. Powder packaging machine
10. Taste Maker Equipments e.g. Grinder SS Vessels, Mixing Machine, Vibratory Screen, Packing M/c. etc.

FIXED CAPITAL

1.	LAND & BUILDING	Rs.	42,80,000.00
2.	PLANT & MACHINERY	Rs.	27,50,000.05
3.	OTHER FIXED ASSETS	Rs.	8,75,000.00
	TOTAL	Rs.	79,05,000.05

RAW MATERIALS

1. Flour
2. Edible additives
3. Salt alkali
4. Stabilizers & Antioxidants
5. Water
6. Spices & Packaging Material

TOTAL WORKING CAPITAL/MONTH

1. RAW MATERIAL	Rs.	3,00,000.00
2. SALARY & WAGES	Rs.	1,39,375.00
3. UTILITIES & OVERHEADS	Rs.	2,46,000.00
TOTAL	Rs.	6,85,375.00

TOTAL CAPITAL INVESTMENT

TOTAL FIXED CAPITAL	Rs.	79,05,000.05
TOTAL WORKING CAPITAL FOR 2 MONTHS	Rs.	13,70,750.00
TOTAL	Rs.	92,75,750.05

TURN OVER/ANNUM

By sale of 300 MT. of Instant Noodles (with Taste Maker)	Rs.	1,44,00,000.00

PROFIT SALES RATIO = Profit / Sales x 100 = 28%

RATE OF RETURN = Operating profit / T.C.I x 100 = 44%

BREAK EVEN POINT (B.E.P) = 50%

58
PLANT ECONOMICS OF INDIAN MADE FOREIGN LIQUOR

Rated Plant Capacity = 1200 GLN/Day

LAND & BUILDING (Land Area 4000 sq.mts.) = Rs. 97,50,000.00

PLANT & MACHINERY

1. Fruit Crushing mill, Roller type
2. Mixing Tank
3. Cleaning tank
4. Seed Tank
5. Scrubber
6. Filter press
7. Fermentor
8. Analyser
9. Rectifying Column
10. Condensers with Accumulater
11. Baby Boiler
12. Product Storage tank
13. Storage tank
14. Cooling Tower
15. Pumps & piping
16. Bottles Washing Machine
17. Bottles filling & sealing machine
18. Miscellaneous

FIXED CAPITAL

1. LAND & BUILDING	Rs.	97,50,000.00
2. PLANT & MACHINERY	Rs.	34,01,000.00
3. OTHER FIXED ASSETS	Rs.	5,44,600.00
TOTAL	Rs.	1,36,95,600.00

RAW MATERIALS

1. Grape & Other fruits
2. Yeast, variable amount required
3. Other Chemicals i.e. Sodium sulphite, minerals acids enzymes etc.

TOTAL WORKING CAPITAL/MONTH

1. RAW MATERIAL	Rs.	53,00,000.00
2. SALARY & WAGES	Rs.	2,13,625.00
3. UTILITIES & OVERHEADS	Rs.	7,77,000.00
TOTAL	Rs.	62,90,625.00

TOTAL CAPITAL INVESTMENT

TOTAL FIXED CAPITAL	Rs.	1,36,95,600.00
TOTAL WORKING CAPITAL FOR 1 MONTH	Rs.	62,90,625.00
TOTAL	Rs.	1,99,86,225.00

TURN OVER/ANNUM

By sale of 3,60,000 gallons of Alcohol in different packings	Rs.	9,36,00,000.00

PROFIT SALES RATIO = Profit / Sales x 100 = 15%

RATE OF RETURN = Operating profit / T.C.I x 100 = 70%

BREAK EVEN POINT (B.E.P) = 39%

59
PLANT ECONOMICS OF MEAT

Rated Plant Capacity	=	1500000 Kg Mutton/ Annum 600000 Kg Chicken Products/ Annum 150000 Kg Edible Offals/ Annum 750000 Kg Edible Offals/ Annum
LAND & BUILDING (Land Area 3000 sq.mt)	=	Rs. 23,50,000.00

PLANT & MACHINERY

1. Cutters & Choppers
2. Disintegrator Capable of producing homogenization of meat & mincer
3. Deep freezers with all accessories
4. Mincer S.S. complete with motor & starter
5. Preparation table (Aluminium Tops)
6. Jacketed kettle (S.S.)
7. Vessels of Aluminium & stainless steel of various sizes
8. Weighing Plate form
9. Exhaust Box
10. Retort with thermometer & Pressure gauge
11. Plastic crates
12. Baby Boiler
13. Tanks for curing, blanching etc.
14. Other Ancillaries

FIXED CAPITAL

1. LAND & BUILDING		Rs.	23,50,000.00
2. PLANT & MACHINERY		Rs.	9,57,000.00
3. OTHER FIXED ASSETS		Rs.	9,40,000.00
	TOTAL	Rs.	42,47,000.00

RAW MATERIALS

1. Sheep
2. Broiler
3. Preservative & salt

TOTAL WORKING CAPITAL/MONTH

1. RAW MATERIAL		Rs.	56,27,000.00
2. SALARY & WAGES		Rs.	33,600.00
3. UTILITIES & OVERHEADS		Rs.	23,500.00
	TOTAL	Rs.	56,84,100.00

TOTAL CAPITAL INVESTMENT

TOTAL FIXED CAPITAL		Rs.	42,47,000.00
TOTAL WORKING CAPITAL FOR 3 MONTHS		Rs.	1,70,52,300.00
	TOTAL	Rs.	2,12,99,300.00

TURN OVER/ANNUM

1. By sale of 5000 × 12 × 25 kg of Mutton Processed & canned products
2. By sale of 2000 × 12 × 25 kg of Chicken processed products
3. By sale of edible offals of 500 × 12 × 25kg
4. By sale of non-edible offals of 2500 × 12 × 25 kg

TOTAL Rs. 8,50,50,000.00

PROFIT SALES RATIO = Profit / Sales x 100 = 16%

RATE OF RETURN = Operating profit / T.C.I x 100 = 65%

BREAK EVEN POINT (B.E.P) = 19%

60
PLANT ECONOMICS OF MACARONI

Rated Plant Capacity = 55517 Nos./Day

LAND & BUILDING (Land Area 2000 Sq. Mt.) = Rs. 44,92,500.00

PLANT & MACHINERY

1. NOODLE MAKING EQUIPMENT
   Whirl Round Kneader
2. Table Feeder
3. Compound Pressing Roll Machine
4. Extending roll
5. Pressing & Cutting Roll Machine
6. STEAMING & MEASURING CUTTER EQPNTS.
   Stainless steel tunnel
7. Stainless net conveyor
8. Measuring Cutter Machine
9. Steam Exhaust Blower
10. FRYING EQUIPMENTS: Frying Machine
11. Exhaust Blower
12. Edible oil pump
13. Heavy oil pump
14. Special Chain with case
15. Case cover conveyor
16. Chain driving unit
17. Heavy oil burner with preheater, Frame-eye
18. Automatic float-switch for heavy tank
19. Automatic elevating equipment
20. COOLING EQUIPMENT: Blower
21. Cooling conveyor with driving unit
22. Steam Boiler

23. Edible & heavy oil tanks
24. Furnace Materials
25. Office and laboratory apparatus
26. Miscellaneous

FIXED CAPITAL

1.	LAND & BUILDING	Rs.	44,92,500.00
2.	PLANT & MACHINERY	Rs.	1,01,80,000.00
3.	OTHER FIXED ASSETS	Rs.	5,25,000.00
	TOTAL	Rs.	1,51,97,500.00

RAW MATERIALS

1. Flour
2. Alkaline Powder
3. Sodium Bicarbonate
4. Poly-phosphoric solution
5. Salt
6. Edible colour
7. Ghee
8. Soup

TOTAL WORKING CAPITAL/ANNUM

1.	RAW MATERIAL	Rs.	3,53,23,680.00
2.	SALARY & WAGES	Rs.	18,88,500.00
3.	UTILITIES & OVERHEADS	Rs.	10,68,200.00
	TOTAL	Rs.	3,82,80,380.00

TOTAL CAPITAL INVESTMENT

TOTAL FIXED CAPITAL	Rs.	1,51,97,500.00
TOTAL WORKING CAPITAL FOR 2 MONTHS	Rs.	63,80,063.33
TOTAL	Rs.	2,15,77,563.33

TURN OVER/ANNUM

By sales of 1,66,55,100 Macaroni Packets	Rs.	6,66,20,400.00

PROFIT SALES RATIO = Profit / Sales x 100 = 34%

RATE OF RETURN = Operating profit / T.C.I x 100 = 106%

BREAK EVEN POINT (B.E.P) = 23%

61

PLANT ECONOMICS OF PROCESSED FOOD (FRUIT JUICE, KETCHUP JELLY CANNING OF FRUITS, PICKLES ETC.)

Rated Plant Capacity = 10000 BOT/Day

LAND & BUILDING (Land Area 2000 sq.mt.) = Rs. 30,00,000.00

PLANT & MACHINERY

1. Hammer Mill
2. Neutralizing vessel, equipped with jacket, agitator etc.
3. Filtration press
4. S.S. Lining mixers equipped with agitator, motor etc.
5. Pressure storage tanks & Sealing
6. Automatic bottling machine
7. Cooling/Conditioning Units
8. Clarification Vessels
9. Centrifuges
10. Evaporators
11. Deaerator
12. Paseurisation units
13. Spray Drier
14. Motor pipes and other accessories
15. Boilers
16. Generator

FIXED CAPITAL

1. LAND & BUILDING	Rs.	30,00,000.00
2. PLANT & MACHINERY	Rs.	36,86,000.00
3. OTHER FIXED ASSETS	Rs.	11,75,000.00
TOTAL	Rs.	78,61,000.00

RAW MATERIALS

1. Fruits
2. Sugar
3. Citric Acid
4. Other additives
5. Glass bottles
6. Vegetables

TOTAL WORKING CAPITAL/MONTH

1. RAW MATERIAL	Rs.	28,18,000.00
2. SALARY & WAGES	Rs.	3,06,250.00
3. UTILITIES & OVERHEADS	Rs.	3,49,000.00
TOTAL	Rs.	34,73,250.00

TOTAL CAPITAL INVESTMENT

TOTAL FIXED CAPITAL	Rs.	78,61,000.00
TOTAL WORKING CAPITAL FOR 1 MONTH	Rs.	34,73,250.00
TOTAL	Rs.	1,13,34,250.00

TURN OVER/ANNUM

Receipt of 30,00,000 bottles of Squash, Pickles, Jams, Juices etc.	Rs.	6,00,00,000.00

PROFIT SALES RATIO = Profit / Sales x 100 = 26%

RATE OF RETURN = Operating profit / T.C.I x 100 = 139%

BREAK EVEN POINT (B.E.P) = 27%

62
PLANT ECONOMICS OF PALM OIL

Rated Plant Capacity = 24 TON (F.F.B.)/Day

LAND & BUILDING (Land Area 5000 Sq.mts.) = Rs. 37,70,000.00

PLANT & MACHINERY

1. Fruit bunch Elevator
2. Sterilizing Plant
3. Stripping plant including stalk in cinerator
4. Extracting Station including dirgester & screw press
5. Clarification plant including settling tank and reheater
6. Oil storage tanks with drum and lorry filling equipment
7. Weight Bridge
8. Kernel plant with equipment for nut/fibre separation
9. Steam Boiler
10. Miscellaneous Tool Equipment and elevator, conveyer instrument Pump etc.
11. Oil filling machine

FIXED CAPITAL

1.	LAND & BUILDING	Rs.	37,70,000.00
2.	PLANT & MACHINERY	Rs.	1,00,00,000.00
3.	OTHER FIXED ASSETS	Rs.	25,00,000.00
	TOTAL	Rs.	1,62,70,000.00

RAW MATERIALS

1. Fresh Fruit bunches of Palm tree
2. Packing material mild steel drum
3. Miscellaneous

TOTAL WORKING CAPITAL/MONTH

1. RAW MATERIAL	Rs.	27,65,000.00
2. SALARY & WAGES	Rs.	1,51,125.00
3. UTILITIES & OVERHEADS	Rs.	9,81,000.00
TOTAL	Rs.	38,97,125.00

TOTAL CAPITAL INVESTMENT

TOTAL FIXED CAPITAL	Rs.	1,62,70,000.00
TOTAL WORKING CAPITAL FOR 3 MONTHS	Rs.	1,16,91,375.00
TOTAL	Rs.	2,79,61,375.00

TURN OVER/ANNUM

1. Receipt by Sale of Palm oil (Pure) 1512 Ton
2. By sale of palm kernel 288 ton

TOTAL Rs. 6,13,44,000.00

PROFIT SALES RATIO = Profit / Sales x 100 = 14%

RATE OF RETURN = Operating profit / T.C.I x 100 = 30%

BREAK EVEN POINT (B.E.P) = 58%

63
PLANT ECONOMICS OF PROTEIN AND PROTEIN BASED PRODUCTS

Rated Plant Capacity =
1. Soya Milk 600 MT./Annum
2. Soya Paneer 400 MT./Annum
3. Soya Bariyan/Chunk (Nugget Nutrela type) 300 MT./Annum
4. Casein Powder (30,000 Kgs.) and Caseine by Products (30,000 Kgs.)/ Annum
5. 36,000 Kgs.(90,000 Packs of 400 Gm) Processed Cheese/Annum
6. 30,000 Kgs.(1,50,000 Packs of 200 Gms.) of processed cheese/Annum
7. 21,000 Kgs. of Cream/Annum
8. Corn Flakes 300 Tons/Annum
9. Egg Noodles 450 Tons/Annum

LAND & BUILDING (Land Area 5500 Sq. Mts.) = Rs. 1,00,00,000.00

PLANT & MACHINERY

1. A. Soya Milk & Paneer:-
   Soya Machinery Wet Grinder
2. Dry Roller Grinder
3. Husk Separator
4. Air Blower Fan
5. Blancher
6. Homogenizer
7. Pasteuriser
8. Tanks
9. Chilling Plant/Ice Plant
10. Packing Machine
11. Circulator
13. Water Softening Plant
17. Double-Jacketed Vat for Milk-heating
18. Blending/Mixing Vessel
21. Centrifuge
23. B. For Soya Bariyan/Chunk(Nuggets Nutrela type):- Mixer(Blender) with Motor & Z Type Blade

24. Extruder Cooker (S.S) with Accessories & cutting system
25. Drying Oven
26. Cooling Water System
27. Automatic Pouch Packing Machine
28. Dump Tank for Milk SS made thickness and 8 MM with Washing Devices
29. Weigh Bridge arrangement
30. Cream Separator
31. Cream Storage Tank
33. Wooden Tank
34. Tray Dryer
35. Drying Ovens
36. Oscillating Granulator
37. Milling Machine
38. Electrical Furnace with Tempt Controlled Chamber
40. C. For Processed Cheese:-
    Cheese Vat (Jacketed) (S.S)
41. Cheese Vat (Jacketed) (S.S)
42. Cream Separator
43. Milk Can (Aluminium alloy)
44. Cheese Cutting Table (S.S)
45. Cheese Knives
46. Cheese Hoops
47. cheese Press, Hydraulic Vertical
48. Cheese Grinder (S.S)
49. Ghee Kettle (S.S) Pre-startification
51. Weighing Balance
52. Deep Freezer Large vertical multidoor
53. S.S. Pump
54. Bulk Cooler
55. Plastic Vats
56. Centrifuge for fat test (both electrically/manually tested
57. Cheese filling & Packaging Machine (Automatic Type)
58. Processed Cheese Kettle (S.S.) (Jacketed Type)
61. Air Classifier with all Accessories
62. Separator
63. Storage bin
64. Weighing Balance
65. Rotary Steam Cooker
66. Agitator or Lump Breaker
67. Pan Cooler or Steamer

68. Germ Separator
69. Heavy Flaking Machine
70. Rotary Oven
71. Conveyor
73. Packing Machine
74. Screening and Cooling Equipment
75. Mixer for Flavouring Syrup
76. Sifter for Egg Noodles
77. Mixer (Stainless Steel) Complete with all Accessories
78. Whirl round Kneader (S.S) Complete with all Accessories
79. Noodles sheeter (S.S) with all accessories
80. Noodle cutter (S.S) with all accessories
81. Pre-drier (Hot Air Blower)
82. Electrically operated and Thermo Statically Controlled Cabinet Drier
83. Packaging Machine Vacuum Pack
84. Trays, bins, check balance etc.
85. Lab Testing Equipments
86. Instrumentation and Process Control Equipments

FIXED CAPITAL

1.	LAND & BUILDING	Rs.	1,00,00,000.00
2.	PLANT & MACHINERY	Rs.	69,34,100.00
3.	OTHER FIXED ASSETS	Rs.	13,10,000.00
	TOTAL	Rs.	1,82,44,100.00

RAW MATERIALS

1. A. For Soya Milk & Paneer Soybean
2. Lactic Acid Rennel coagulator
3. Salt, Acid & Sugar for blending with milk
4. Packaging etc.
5. B. For Soya Bariyan/Chunk Soya Oil Cake
6. Miscellaneous viz packaging
7. C. For Casein Milk
8. Miscellaneous Chemical Hcl
9. D. For Processed Cheese Milk
10. Starter
11. Colour, Salt, Etc.
12. Packaging Material with labels,
13. E. For Corn Flakes:- Corn Grain
14. Sugar

15. Salt
16. Polythene bags of different sizes
17. Flour
18. Disodium Phosphate
19. Onion
20. Garlic
21. Salt
22. Capsicum
23. Packaging Materials

TOTAL WORKING CAPITAL/MONTH

1. RAW MATERIAL		Rs.	27,27,298.00
2. SALARY & WAGES		Rs.	2,83,560.00
3. UTILITIES & OVERHEADS		Rs.	1,64,600.00
	TOTAL	Rs.	31,75,458.00

TOTAL CAPITAL INVESTMENT

TOTAL FIXED CAPITAL		Rs.	1,82,44,100.00
TOTAL WORKING CAPITAL FOR 2 MONTHS		Rs.	63,50,916.00
	TOTAL	Rs.	2,45,95,016.00

TURN OVER/ANNUM

1. Soya Milk 600 MT.
2. Soya Panoer 400 MT.
3. Soya Bariyan/Chunk (Nugget Nutrela type) 300 MT.
4. Casein Powder (30,000 Kgs.) and Caseine by Products (30,000 Kgs.)
5. 36,000 Kgs.(90,000 Packs of 400 Gm) Processed Cheese
6. 30,000 Kgs.(1,50,000 Packs of 200 Gms.) of processed cheese
7. 21,000 Kgs. of Cream
8. Corn Flakes 300 Tons
9. Egg Noodles 450 Tons

TOTAL	Rs.	7,09,60,000.00

PROFIT SALES RATIO = Profit / Sales x 100 = 39%

RATE OF RETURN = Operating profit / T.C.I x 100 = 111%

BREAK EVEN POINT (B.E.P) = 22%

64

PLANT ECONOMICS OF POULTRY & BROILER (HATCHERY) FARMING

Rated Plant Capacity = 367 Nos./Day

LAND & BUILDING (Land Area 500 sq.mts.) = Rs. 14,12,500.00

PLANT & MACHINERY

1. Cages
2. Blowers & Exhaust Fans
3. Electric Heaters
4. Room type incubator with sophisticated controls to maintain optimum conditions for hatchability
5. Eggs storing Racks
6. Food feeder with suitable distribution system
7. Automatic vaccination
8. Watering devices for keeping water clean & cool & warm as reqde. Fully sealed & automatic.
9. Laying cages
10. Belt conveyor for egg collection
11. Three-wheel manure cleaning machine used under cages
12. Diesel engine operated dumpers for disposable of liquid, semi liquid manures, with hydraulic tripper
13. Manure handling drum-type dryer
14. Tube wells
15. Diesel Generating
16. Lighting system
17. Black lamps candler (for detecting low quality eggs)
18. Egg packing table on rails

19. Water and temperature control equipments
20. Depolluting equipments
21. miscellaneous

FIXED CAPITAL

1. LAND & BUILDING	Rs.	14,12,500.00
2. PLANT & MACHINERY	Rs.	16,29,700.00
3. OTHER FIXED ASSETS	Rs.	2,64,000.00
TOTAL	Rs.	33,06,200.00

RAW MATERIALS

1. Alfa meal dehydrated
2. Medicines, feed supplements for nutrition.
3. Packing Materials e.g. Cardboard cartons, Egg. trays etc.

TOTAL WORKING CAPITAL/MONTH

1. RAW MATERIAL	Rs.	1,15,500.00
2. SALARY & WAGES	Rs.	74,375.00
3. UTILITIES & OVERHEADS	Rs.	39,500.00
TOTAL	Rs.	2,29,375.00

TOTAL CAPITAL INVESTMENT

TOTAL FIXED CAPITAL	Rs.	33,06,200.00
TOTAL WORKING CAPITAL FOR 2 MONTHS	Rs.	4,58,750.00
TOTAL	Rs.	37,64,950.00

TURN OVER/ANNUM

1. By sale of Egg 30,00000 Nos.
2. Broilers 1,10,000 Nos.
3. Chicks (one day old) 90,000 Nos
4. Culled chickens, 20,000 Nos.
5. Parent Birds 1000 Nos
6. Recovering by sales of poultry manures 30 MT
7. Feathers

TOTAL Rs. 58,98,200.00

PROFIT SALES RATIO = Profit / Sales x 100 = 37%

RATE OF RETURN = Operating profit / T.C.I x 100 = 57%

BREAK EVEN POINT (B.E.P) = 41%

65
PLANT ECONOMICS OF ROLLER FLOUR MILL

Rated Plant Capacity	= 30 MT/Day
LAND & BUILDING (Land Area 7.5 Acre)	= Rs. 1,99,40,000.00

PLANT & MACHINERY

1. Washer
2. Breale roller
3. Plansifier having Sections
4. Double Deck Purifies
5. Roller mill with locks
6. Bran finisher with all accessories
7. Sieving machine with motor
8. Conveyers
9. Packaging machine
10. Installation & Erection
11. Generator
12. Misc. Equipments & Office furniture

FIXED CAPITAL

1. LAND & BUILDING	Rs.	1,99,40,000.00
2. PLANT & MACHINERY	Rs.	24,05,000.00
3. OTHER FIXED ASSETS	Rs.	1,70,000.00
TOTAL	Rs.	2,25,15,000.00

RAW MATERIALS

1. Wheat
2. Packaging material
3. Other miscellaneous chemicals

TOTAL WORKING CAPITAL/MONTH

1. RAW MATERIAL	Rs.	38,75,000.00
2. SALARY & WAGES	Rs.	1,33,125.00
3. UTILITIES & OVERHEADS	Rs.	44,500.00
TOTAL	Rs.	40,52,625.00

TOTAL CAPITAL INVESTMENT

TOTAL FIXED CAPITAL	Rs.	2,25,15,000.00
TOTAL WORKING CAPITAL FOR 3 MONTHS	Rs.	1,21,57,875.00
TOTAL	Rs.	3,46,72,875.00

TURN OVER/ANNUM

1. By sale of Flour 5000 Ton
2. Suji 500 Ton, Maida 3000 Ton, Bran 150 Ton and other products 350 Ton

TOTAL	Rs.	6,60,00,000.00

PROFIT SALES RATIO = Profit/Sales x 100 = 12%

RATE OF RETURN = Operating profit / T.C.I x 100 = 23%

BREAK EVEN POINT (B.E.P) = 57%

66
PLANT ECONOMICS OF MODERN RICE MILL

Rated Plant Capacity	= Rice 19500 MT/ Annum Broken Rice 1500 MT/ Annum Bran 1500 MT/ Annum Husks 6600 MT/ Annum
LAND & BUILDING (Land Area 4.5 Acres)	= Rs. 2,07,87,500.00

PLANT & MACHINERY

1. Drum Sieve
2. Paddy Cleaner
3. Gravity Selector
4. Horizontal Cyclone
5. Bucket Elevator
6. Ducting, Gravity, Packing, Chuts, Hopper and other.
7. Magnets.
8. Grain Separator
9. Rubber roll Paddy Dehusker
10. Paddy Separator
11. Cone Polisher
12. Sieve Separator Aspiration Channels Cyclone, Air Seal etc.
13. Indented Grader
14. Bucket Elevator
15. Magnet
16. Bran Conveying System
17. Ducting Gravity, Packing Spot etc.
18. Erection Changes
19. Technical Consultancy charges

FIXED CAPITAL

1. LAND & BUILDING	Rs.	2,07,87,500.00
2. PLANT & MACHINERY	Rs.	59,52,000.00
3. OTHER FIXED ASSETS	Rs.	23,00,000.00
TOTAL	Rs.	2,90,39,500.00

RAW MATERIALS

1. Paddy
2. Gunny Bags
3. Jute Twine
4. Miscellaneous. Consumables.

TOTAL WORKING CAPITAL/MONTH

1. RAW MATERIAL	Rs.	1,29,82,000.00
2. SALARY & WAGES	Rs.	5,26,080.00
3. UTILITIES & OVERHEADS	Rs.	13,97,000.00
TOTAL	Rs.	1,49,05,080.00

TOTAL CAPITAL INVESTMENT

TOTAL FIXED CAPITAL	Rs.	2,90,39,500.00
TOTAL WORKING CAPITAL FOR 2 MONTHS	Rs.	2,98,10,160.00
TOTAL	Rs.	5,88,49,660.00

TURN OVER/ANNUM

1. By Sale of Rice 19500 M.T.
2. Broken Rice 1500 M.T.
3. Bran 1500 M.T.
4. Husks 6600 M.T.

TOTAL Rs. 23,03,70,000.00

PROFIT SALES RATIO = Profit / Sales x 100 = 18%

RATE OF RETURN = Operating profit / T.C.I x 100 = 70%

BREAK EVEN POINT (B.E.P) = 32%

67 PLANT ECONOMICS OF SNACK FOOD (CRAX SIZE), (ROLL & BALL TYPE)

Rated Plant Capacity = 2400 Pouches/Day

LAND & BUILDING (Land Area 800 sq.mtr.) = Rs. 18,32,500.00

PLANT & MACHINERY

1. Grinding Machine
2. Dough making machine
3. Humidifier
4. Grain Puff Machine
5. Cutting machine
6. Rotary Oven
7. Rotary Seasoning Machine
8. Seasoning Spray System
9. Automatic Weighing Machine
10. Automatic Packing Machine
11. Conveyor
12. Genset
13. Lab testing equipments, Pumps Compressors, Valves etc.

FIXED CAPITAL

1. LAND & BUILDING		Rs.	18,32,500.00
2. PLANT & MACHINERY		Rs.	14,65,000.00
3. OTHER FIXED ASSETS		Rs.	5,70,000.00
	TOTAL	Rs.	38,67,500.00

RAW MATERIALS

1. Rice
2. Edible Oil
3. Salt, Spices, Masala & Other Flavours
4. Packing Materials

TOTAL WORKING CAPITAL/MONTH

1. RAW MATERIAL		Rs.	4,01,800.00
2. SALARY & WAGES		Rs.	81,875.00
3. UTILITIES & OVERHEADS		Rs.	1,13,900.00
	TOTAL	Rs.	5,97,575.00

TOTAL CAPITAL INVESTMENT

TOTAL FIXED CAPITAL		Rs.	38,67,500.00
TOTAL WORKING CAPITAL FOR 2 MONTHS		Rs.	11,95,150.00
	TOTAL	Rs.	50,62,650.00

TURN OVER/ANNUM

By sale of 7,20,000 Nos. pouches of snacks
(each of 250 gms) Rs. 1,44,00,000.00

PROFIT SALES RATIO = Profit / Sales x 100 = 43%

RATE OF RETURN = Operating profit / T.C.I x 100 = 122%

BREAK EVEN POINT (B.E.P) = 25%

68 PLANT ECONOMICS OF SOYBEAN PRODUCTS

Rated Plant Capacity = Milk 3000000 Litre/Annum
Bariya 3000 Tons/Annum
Oil 3000 Tons/Annum
Cake 4500 Tons/Annum

LAND & BUILDING (Land Area 2000 sq.mts.) = Rs. 67,50,000.00

PLANT & MACHINERY

1. Seeking tank
2. Crusher
3. Extractor (solvent)
4. Distillation column for recovery of solvent
5. Refining Unit
6. Boiling vessel
7. Filtration Unit
8. Mixer
9. Collection Unit for Bariya with complete accessories
10. Boiler
11. Drying Unit for Bariya with complete accessories
12. Miscellaneous expenses
13. Electrification and Installation charge

FIXED CAPITAL

1.	LAND & BUILDING	Rs.	67,50,000.00
2.	PLANT & MACHINERY	Rs.	31,90,000.00
3.	OTHER FIXED ASSETS	Rs.	3,75,000.00
	TOTAL	Rs.	1,03,15,000.00

RAW MATERIALS

1. Soybean
2. Other ingredients like corn flour salt etc.
3. Miscellaneous chemicals

TOTAL WORKING CAPITAL/MONTH

1.	RAW MATERIAL	Rs.	1,13,25,000.00
2.	SALARY & WAGES	Rs.	3,88,500.00
3.	UTILITIES & OVERHEADS	Rs.	4,48,500.00
	TOTAL	Rs.	1,21,62,000.00

TOTAL CAPITAL INVESTMENT

TOTAL FIXED CAPITAL	Rs.	1,03,15,000.00
TOTAL WORKING CAPITAL FOR 3 MONTHS	Rs.	3,64,86,000.00
TOTAL	Rs.	4,68,01,000.00

TURN OVER/ANNUM

1. Milk 3000000 Litre
2. Bariya 3000 Tons
3. Oll 3000 Tons
4. Cake 4500 Tons

TOTAL	Rs.	22,44,00,000.00

PROFIT SALES RATIO = Profit / Sales x 100 = 32%

RATE OF RETURN = Operating profit / T.C.I x 100 = 153%

BREAK EVEN POINT (B.E.P) = 13%

69
PLANT ECONOMICS OF SOYA MILK & SOYA PANEER

Rated Plant Capacity = 3.33 Ton/Day

LAND & BUILDING (Land Area 2000 sq.mt.) = Rs. 45,20,000.00

PLANT & MACHINERY

1. SOYA MACHINERY: Wet Grinder
2. Dry Roller Grinder For Del Making
3. Husk Separator
4. Air blower fan
5. Blancher
6. Homogenizers
7. Pasteuriser
8. 10 M-que Tanks
9. Cholliy Plant/Ice Plant
10. Packing Plant
11. Circulator
12. Lab. equipments & fittings
13. Water softener
14. MANUFACTURERS OF PANEER:-
    Storage tank of Plastic
15. Transfer/transportation cans for milk & Starter
16. Cans to carry milk
17. Double jacketed vat for milk - heating
18. Blending/mixing vessel
19. Coal fired small industrial Boiler complete with all mounting & accessiones.
20. Hydrantically operated press with all accessories and ten moulds.

21. Contrifuge
22. Strainers, Hair sieve knives dry & wet bulb thermometer Thermometers, Lactomet, Pans, para. weight m/c etc.

FIXED CAPITAL

1. LAND & BUILDING		Rs.	45,20,000.00
2. PLANT & MACHINERY		Rs.	21,43,500.00
3. OTHER FIXED ASSETS		Rs.	2,50,000.00
	TOTAL	Rs.	69,13,500.00

RAW MATERIALS

1. Soybean
2. Lactic Acid of grade
3. Salt, Acid and Sugar for blending with milk
4. Coal fuel for boiler
5. Lubricating oil, & packaging etc.

TOTAL WORKING CAPITAL/MONTH

1. RAW MATERIAL		Rs.	11,70,000.00
2. SALARY & WAGES		Rs.	1,05,375.00
3. UTILITIES & OVERHEADS		Rs.	35,300.00
	TOTAL	Rs.	13,10,675.00

TOTAL CAPITAL INVESTMENT

TOTAL FIXED CAPITAL		Rs.	69,13,500.00
TOTAL WORKING CAPITAL FOR 2 MONTHS		Rs.	26,21,350.00
	TOTAL	Rs.	95,34,850.00

TURN OVER/ANNUM

1. By sale of 600 tons of soyamilk
2. By sale of 400 MT of soyapaneer

TOTAL	Rs.	2,08,00,000.00

PROFIT SALES RATIO = Profit / Sales x 100 = 15%

RATE OF RETURN = Operating profit / T.C.I x 100 = 32%

BREAK EVEN POINT (B.E.P) = 47%

70
PLANT ECONOMICS OF SUGAR PLANT

Rated Plant Capacity = 450000 MT./Annum

LAND & BUILDING (Land Area 100 acres) = Rs. 7,20,00,000.00

PLANT & MACHINERY

1. Pully conveyor belt system
2. Cane cutter(consist of cylindrical shaft revolving
3. Roll crushing unit
4. Strainer made by stainless steel
5. Plate type Heat Exchanger
6. Clarification tank
7. Filtration unit
8. Sulphitation tank
9. Sulfur furnace
10. Tripple effect Evaporator
11. Crystalizer
12. Centrifugal Machine
13. Drier
14. Pumps, fittings, lines
15. Vertical type oil fired boiler
16. Miscellaneous equipments
17. D. G. Sets.

FIXED CAPITAL

1.	LAND & BUILDING	Rs.	7,20,00,000.00
2.	PLANT & MACHINERY	Rs.	45,00,00,000.00
3.	OTHER FIXED ASSETS	Rs.	5,65,00,000.00
	TOTAL	Rs.	57,85,00,000.00

RAW MATERIALS

1. Cane
2. Lime
3. Sulfur
4. Gunny bags
5. Coke
6. Caustic Soda
7. Misc. Chemicals as activated carbon Flueculant etc.

TOTAL WORKING CAPITAL/ANNUM

1. RAW MATERIAL	Rs.	35,44,40,000.00
2. SALARY & WAGES	Rs.	95,62,560.00
3. UTILITIES & OVERHEADS	Rs.	3,81,70,000.00
TOTAL	Rs.	40,21,72,560.00

TOTAL CAPITAL INVESTMENT

TOTAL FIXED CAPITAL	Rs.	57,85,00,000.00
TOTAL WORKING CAPITAL FOR 2 MONTHS	Rs.	6,70,28,760.00
TOTAL	Rs.	64,55,28,760.00

TURN OVER/ANNUM

1. By selling sugar 4,50,000 Qts.
2. Molasses 90,000 MT.
3. Bagasse 1,35,000 MT.
4. Pressed Mud 22500 MT.

TOTAL Rs. 78,63,75,000.00

PROFIT SALES RATIO = Profit / Sales x 100 = 30%

RATE OF RETURN = Operating profit / T.C.I x 100 = 29%

BREAK EVEN POINT (B.E.P) = 53%

71
PLANT ECONOMICS OF TEA PROCESSING AND PACKAGING

Rated Plant Capacity	= 40 TONS./Day
LAND & BUILDING (Land Area 30,000 sq.mts.)	= Rs. 5,40,00,000.00

PLANT & MACHINERY

1. Withering Machine (Drum Type)
2. Rolling Machine (Rotarvane roller)
3. Fermenting Machine
4. Boiler
5. Blender (S.S.)with accessories
6. Roaster (S.S.)
7. Automatic Sieving machine with 5 HP motor & accessories,
8. Pulveriser
9. Automatic pouch weighing, filling, sealing packaging machine
10. Mono box packaging machine
11. Master Carton strap packing machine
12. Platform type weighing scale (Electronic systems)
13. Tea Testing apparatus (a) Electronic Weighing Scale, (b) Water Dispenser, (c) other equipments etc.
14. Storage Bin
15. Pollution Control Equipments (Dust Collector) etc.
16. Automatic Printing Machine
17. Winnowing Machine

18. Rotary sifter fitted
19. Tray Drier for firing with accessories

FIXED CAPITAL

1. LAND & BUILDING	Rs.	5,40,00,000.00
2. PLANT & MACHINERY	Rs.	3,02,50,000.00
3. OTHER FIXED ASSETS	Rs.	1,25,00,000.00
TOTAL	Rs.	9,67,50,000.00

RAW MATERIALS

1. Tea leaves
2. Misc Chemicals
3. Packaging material,polyethene film, laminated printed pouches,cardboard boxes,cartons,packaging straps, Adhesive tapes, stickers etc.
4. Miscellaneous items

TOTAL WORKING CAPITAL/MONTH

1. RAW MATERIAL	Rs.	4,20,00,000.00
2. SALARY & WAGES	Rs.	5,53,750.00
3. UTILITIES & OVERHEADS	Rs.	75,02,000.00
TOTAL	Rs.	5,00,55,750.00

TOTAL CAPITAL INVESTMENT

TOTAL FIXED CAPITAL	Rs.	9,67,50,000.00
TOTAL WORKING CAPITAL FOR 3 MONTHS	Rs.	15,01,67,250.00
TOTAL	Rs.	24,69,17,250.00

TURN OVER/ANNUM

By sale of 12000 Ton of Tea in various packaging size (100 gms, 250 gms,500 gms)	Rs.	78,00,00,000.00

PROFIT SALES RATIO = Profit / Sales x 100 = 17%

RATE OF RETURN = Operating profit / T.C.I x 100 = 55%

BREAK EVEN POINT (B.E.P) = 38%

72
PLANT ECONOMICS OF VERMICELLI

Rated Plant Capacity	= 1 TON/Day
LAND & BUILDING (Land Area 400 Sq. Mt.)	= Rs. 8,64,000.00

PLANT & MACHINERY

1. Platform Weighing Balance
2. Motorized Dough Making Machine With All Accessories And Other Parts For Mixing Kneading.
3. Ribbon Type Mixer
4. Motorized Extrusion Press, Attached With Strains to Form Vermicelli
5. Electrically Operated And Thermo-statically Controlled Cabinet Type Drier For Cross Flow
6. Miscellaneous Equipments Such As Trays, Bins, Check Balance Tools Etc.

FIXED CAPITAL

1. LAND & BUILDING	Rs.	8,64,000.00
2. PLANT & MACHINERY	Rs.	4,10,000.00
3. OTHER FIXED ASSETS	Rs.	1,15,000.00
TOTAL	Rs.	13,89,000.00

RAW MATERIALS

1. Wheat Flour
2. Maida
3. Packing Material Like Polythene Bags, Cartoons Etc.

TOTAL WORKING CAPITAL/MONTH

1. RAW MATERIAL	Rs.	2,33,750.00
2. SALARY & WAGES	Rs.	99,000.00
3. UTILITIES & OVERHEADS	Rs.	39,650.00
TOTAL	Rs.	3,72,400.00

TOTAL CAPITAL INVESTMENT

TOTAL FIXED CAPITAL	Rs.	13,89,000.00
TOTAL WORKING CAPITAL FOR 2 MONTHS	Rs.	7,44,800.00
TOTAL	Rs.	21,33,800.00

TURN OVER/ANNUM

Receipt By Sale of 300 Tons of VERMICELLI (Packed)	Rs.	60,00,000.00

PROFIT SALES RATIO = Profit / Sales x 100 = 18%

RATE OF RETURN = Operating profit / T.C.I x 100 = 52%

BREAK EVEN POINT (B.E.P) = 50%

73
PLANT ECONOMICS OF WHEAT PORRIDGE (DALIA)

Rated Plant Capacity = 5 TON/Day

LAND & BUILDING (Land Area 1 Acre.) = Rs. 52,00,000.00

PLANT & MACHINERY

1. Bucket Elevator
2. Automatic Sieving Machine
3. Washing Tank
4. Conveyor Belt
5. Drying Chamber with warm air blowing arrangement.
6. Storage Silo M.S.
7. Pulveriser
8. Conveyor
9. Mixing or Blending Machine.
10. Roasting Machine with automatic temperature controller.
11. Cooling Chamber with conveyor.
12. Automatic Weighing, Filling, Sealing Nitrogen Flush Pouch Packaging Machine.
13. Laboratory Testing Equipment.
14. Pipes, Fitting, Pumps, Valves, and other miscellaneous construction.
15. Tools, Jigs, Fixtures, Instrumentations and Process Control Equipment

FIXED CAPITAL

1. LAND & BUILDING		Rs.	52,00,000.00
2. PLANT & MACHINERY		Rs.	94,20,000.00
3. OTHER FIXED ASSETS		Rs.	28,50,000.00
	TOTAL	Rs.	1,74,70,000.00

RAW MATERIALS

1. Wheat
2. Salt
3. Malt Extract
4. Packaging Material
5. Nitrogen Gas

TOTAL WORKING CAPITAL/MONTH

1. RAW MATERIAL		Rs.	16,45,000.00
2. SALARY & WAGES		Rs.	2,82,125.00
3. UTILITIES & OVERHEADS		Rs.	5,04,000.00
	TOTAL	Rs.	24,31,125.00

TOTAL CAPITAL INVESTMENT

TOTAL FIXED CAPITAL		Rs.	1,74,70,000.00
TOTAL WORKING CAPITAL FOR 1 MONTH		Rs.	24,31,125.00
	TOTAL	Rs.	1,99,01,125.00

TURN OVER/ANNUM

By Sale of Whole Wheat Porridge (Dalia) in 200 Gms.Pack (=1500 Tons) or (75,00,000 Packs) Rs. 4,87,50,000.00

PROFIT SALES RATIO = Profit / Sales x 100 = 29%

RATE OF RETURN = Operating profit / T.C.I x 100 = 72%

BREAK EVEN POINT (B.E.P) = 39%

74
SUPPLIERS OF PLANT AND MACHINERY

FLOUR MILL MACHINERY

1. Rajni Metal Works
   B/h Union Bank Of India,
   39, Chinanibaug Est.
   Ahmedabad, Gujarat-380004
   India
   TEL : +91 (0) 79 25621972

2. Flow Tech Engineering Pvt. Ltd.
   16/5, Mathura Rd.
   Faridabad, Haryana-121001
   India
   TEL : +91 (0) 129 25263017
   FAX : +91 (0) 129 25291556

3. Sadhana Engg. Industries
   Municipal Mkt. Bldg.
   Kokkalai
   Thrissur, Kerala-680021
   India
   TEL : +91 (0) 487 2442390
   FAX : +91 (0) 487 2442390
   E-mail: sadhana@surfy.net

4. Industrial Fasteners
   14, Rambali Ngr.
   Fort, Indore,
   Madhya Pradesh-452006
   India
   TEL : +91 (0) 731 2410710

5. Agromech Engineers
   374, Patel Rd.
   Coimbatore,
   Tamil Nadu-641009, India
   TEL : +91 (0) 422 2235054
   FAX : +91 (0) 422 2235054

6. Anamtham Industries
   96, G N Chetty Rd., T Ngr.,
   Chennai, Tamil Nadu-600017, India
   TEL : +91 (0) 44 28266768

7. Gurucharan Engg. Works
   142, Indl. Est., Nunhai
   Agra, Uttar Pradesh-282006
   India
   TEL : +91 (0) 562 2345452

8. Mukul Enterprises
   Mala Roller Flour Mills Compound
   Delhi Road, Partapur,
   Meerut-250103, U.P., India
   TEL : +91 (0) 121 2512284

9. AT Mohsin & Co.
   P.O. Box 2736, 71/B N S Rd.
   Kolkata, West Bengal-700001,
   India
   TEL : +91 (0) 33 22433777
   FAX : +91 (0) 33 22252319
   E-mail: firozukani@sify.com

10. Raghavendra Innovative Industries
    3-55, Gopal Puram, Hanmakonda,
    Andhra Pradesh-506015, India
    TEL : +91 (0) 8712 2565669

BAKERY MACHINERY

1. Aifso Enterprises
   A-1, Veena Beena Apts.
   Sewree (W) Mumbai,
   Maharashtra-400015, India
   TEL : +91 (0) 22 24130926
   FAX : +91 (0) 22 24137339
   E-mail: aifso@bom3.vsnl.net.in

2. Sun Beam Machines (India) Pvt. Ltd.
Plot No. 141, IDA
Bollaram, Hyderabad,
Andhra Pradesh-502325, India
TEL : +91 (0) 8458 279723
FAX : +91 (0) 8458 279078
E-mail: smipl@satyam.net.in

3. NSW India Ltd.
Plot No. 43, Sect. 34
EHTP, Gurgaon,
Haryana-122001, India
TEL : +91 (0) 124 26371106
FAX : +91 (0) 124 26372859
E-mail: corporate@nswindia.com

4. New Era Machines Pvt. Ltd.
Campa Cola Lane
Dhandari Kalan
G T Rd., Ludhiana,
Punjab-141010, India
TEL : +91 (0) 161 2510777
FAX : +91 (0) 161 2510776
E-mail:
sales@neweramachines.com

5. Reliance Engineering Works
Kothi No. 4065
Sect. 46-D, Chandigarh,
Chandigarh (UT)-160047, India
TEL : +91 (0) 172 2605682
FAX : +91 (0) 172 2652781

6. A1 Baker Enterprises
23, Bhera Enclave
New Delhi, NCT of Delhi-110087
India
TEL : +91 (0) 11 25586150

7. Bismac Manufacturers
35/3, R R Cmplx.
100 Ft. Rd., Peenya
Bangalore, Karnataka-560057
India
TEL : +91 (0) 80 28399616
FAX : +91 (0) 80 28393781
E-mail:
bismac2002in@yahoo.com.in

8. Arihant Engineering Works
124, Guru Nanak Timber Mkt.
Dhar Rd. Indore,
Madhya Pradesh-452002, India
TEL : +91 (0) 731 2380535
FAX : +91 (0) 731 2380537
E-mail:
arihantengineering@epatra.com

9. Techman Enterprises
A-82, Sect. 58, Noida,
Uttar Pradesh-201301, India
TEL : +91 (0) 120 24582680

10. Balilias Engineering Company Pvt. Ltd.
6th Flr., Commerce House,
Room No. 6A, 2
Ganesh Chandra Avenue
Kolkata, West Bengal-700013
India
TEL : +91 (0) 33 22377877
FAX : +91 (0) 33 22482070

PASTA MACHINERY

1. Saraswathi Industries
278, Sivasakthi Cly.
Ganapathy, Coimbatore,
Tamil Nadu-641006, India
TEL : +91 (0) 422 2531536
FAX : +91 (0) 422 2531536

2. Sesha Enterprises
Plot No. 266
2nd Main Rd., Nehru Ngr.
Chennai, Tamil Nadu-600096
India
TEL : +91 (0) 44 24927536

3. Spantek Projects
#7, Amir Terrace,
Al-Ameen Soc., Gultekdi
Pune, Maharashtra-411037
India
TEL : +91 (0) 20 24269393
FAX : +91 (0) 20 24269562
E-mail: spantek@hotmail.com

FRUIT PROCESSING MACHINERY

1. Shriram Temp-X-Changers (I)
   991/2-A, GIDC
   Makarpura, Vadodara,
   Gujarat-390010, India
   TEL : +91 (0) 265 2645129
   FAX : +91 (0) 265 2643504
2. Sifter International
   227, Sect. 24, Faridabad,
   Haryana-121005, India
   TEL : +91 (0) 129 25231154
   FAX : +91 (0) 129 25230039
   E-mail: sifter@tatanova.com
3. SSP Pvt. Ltd.
   13/4, Mathura Rd., Faridabad,
   Haryana-121003, India
   TEL : +91 (0) 129 25275441
   FAX : +91 (0) 129 25277441
   E-mail:
   sspgroup@del2.vsnl.net.in
4. Kaps Engineers
   Samraat Silk Mills Compound
   LBS Marg, Vikhroli (W)
   Mumbai, Maharashtra-400079
   India
   TEL : +91 (0) 22 25781933
   FAX : +91 (0) 22 25785741
   E-mail:
   vmsrehls@bom4.vsnl.net.in
5. Praj Industries Ltd.
   "Praj House", Bavdhan
   Pune, Maharashtra-411021
   India
   TEL : +91 (0) 20 22951511
   FAX : +91 (0) 20 22951718
   E-mail: info@praj.net
6. Food Tech Engineers
   31/A, Ghanshyam Indl. Est.
   Veera Desai Rd., Andheri (W)
   Mumbai, Maharashtra-400053
   India
   TEL : +91 (0) 22 26369106
   FAX : +91 (0) 22 26369106
   E-mail: foodtech@hotmail.com
7. Doris (India) Engineers Pvt. Ltd.
   No. 389, 390, Arcot Rd.
   Kodambakkam, Chennai,
   Tamil Nadu-600024, India
   TEL : +91 (0) 44 24801098
   FAX : +91 (0) 44 24815652
   E-mail:
   machines@dorisindia.com
8. Bajaj Maschinen Pvt. Ltd.
   7/20, 7/27, Site IV
   Sahibabad Indl. Area
   Ghaziabad,
   Uttar Pradesh-201010, India
   TEL : +91 (0) 120 24775119
   FAX : +91 (0) 120 24775137
   E-mail: bajaj@del3.vsnl.net.in
9. Asian Power Cyclopes
   Rochipura, Majra
   Dehradun, Uttaranchal-248171
   India
   TEL : +91 (0) 135 2620488
   FAX : +91 (0) 135 2620961
   E-mail: asian@nde.vsnl.net.in
10. Propac Enterprises
    B2C/23B, Janak Puri
    New Delhi,
    NCT of Delhi-110058, India
    TEL : +91 (0) 11 25610240
    FAX : +91 (0) 11 25550443
    E-mail: propac@del3.vsnl.net.in

FEED MILL MACHINERY

1. Spectoms Engineering Pvt. Ltd.
   Makarpura Stn. Rd.
   Maneja, Vadodara,
   Gujarat-390013, India
   TEL : +91 (0) 265 2638641
   FAX : +91 (0) 265 2644592
   E-mail: spectoms@sify.com
2. Dhopeshwar Engineering Pvt. Ltd.
   A-16, CIE, Balanagar
   Hyderabad,
   Andhra Pradesh-500037, India
   TEL : +91 (0) 40 23771579
   FAX : +91 (0) 40 23772450
   E-mail: dhopesh@hd2.dot.net.in

FISH PROCESSING MACHINERY

1. Wintech Taparia Ltd.
3rd Flr., Shreesh Chmbrs.,.
25/1, Y N Rd., Indore,
Madhya Pradesh-452003, India
TEL : +91 (0) 731 2433950
FAX : +91 (0) 731 2430527
E-mail:
sales@wintechtaparia.com

2. Stadler Corporation
A-3/3, Surjit Singh Compound,
Shivaji Ngr., Off Vakola Bridge
Santacruz (E), Mumbai,
Maharashtra-400055, India
TEL : +91 (0) 22 26105212
FAX : +91 (0) 22 26105093
E-mail: stadler44@hotmail.com

3. Han-Ul Engg. Pvt. Ltd.
203, Aurora Towers, (West Wing)
M G Rd., Pune,
Maharashtra-411001, India
TEL : +91 (0) 20 2631567
FAX : +91 (0) 20 2630707
E-mail:
hanul@giaspn01.vsnl.net.in

4. Rajma Engg. Industries
14/OM, Anand Indl. Est.
Mohanji Sunderji Rd.
Raghunath Ngr.
Thane, Maharashtra-400604
India
TEL : +91 (0) 22 25821892
FAX : +91 (0) 22 2582741r
E-mail: rajma_engg@hotmail.com

TEA PROCESSING MACHINERY

1. Netlon India Divn. Of Parry & Company Ltd.
201/202, Regent Tower
Race Course Circle
Vadodara, Gujarat-390007, India
TEL : +91 (0) 265 2332581
FAX : +91 (0) 265 2339352
E-mail: netlon@tuflex.net

2. Bedi & Bedi Pvt. Ltd.
"Casa Grande", 18/13
Nandidurg Extn.
Jayamahal, Bangalore,
Karnataka-560046, India
TEL : +91 (0) 80 23330445
FAX : +91 (0) 80 23332764
E-mail: bedibedi@vsnl.com

3. Kaps Engineers
Samraat Silk Mills Compound
LBS Marg, Vikhroli (W), Mumbai,
Maharashtra-400079, India
TEL : +91 (0) 22 25781933
FAX : +91 (0) 22 25785741
E-mail:
vmsrehls@bom4.vsnl.net.in

4. Plantation Guide Engineering Industries
Nr. Sree Ram Weigh Bridge, 11/2
Thadagam Rd.
Edayarpalayam (P.O.)
Coimbatore, Tamil Nadu-641025
India
TEL : +91 (0) 422 2404594

5. Aarkay Industries
1st Flr., 97, Park St.
Kolkata, West Bengal-700016
India
TEL : +91 (0) 33 22266431
FAX : +91 (0) 33 22265874
E-mail: aarkay@aarkay.net

6. Aluminium Industries (Assam) Pvt. Ltd.
4th Flr., 23/A, N S Rd.
Kolkata, West Bengal-700001
India
TEL : +91 (0) 33 22201120
FAX : +91 (0) 33 22211193

7. CM Ho & Co.
9th Flr., Suit No. 92
Gulmohar, Middleton St.
Kolkata, West Bengal-700071
India
TEL : +91 (0) 33 22475587
FAX : +91 (0) 33 22478171
E-mail:
cmhoco@giascl01.vsnl.net.in

8. Gem Tea Machinery Pvt. Ltd.
   13, Brabourne Rd., Kolkata,
   West Bengal-700001, India
   TEL : +91 (0) 33 22428789
   FAX : +91 (0) 33 22427131
   E-mail:
   gem.forgings@gems.vsnl.net.in
9. Vikram Engg. & Allied Industries Ltd.
   Tobacco House, 4th Flr.,
   1 & 2, Old Court House Corner
   Kolkata, West Bengal-700001
   India
   TEL : +91 (0) 33 22207629
   FAX : +91 (0) 33 22484881
10. Mittal Collection
    7, Netaji Subhash Marg
    Darya Ganj New Delhi,
    NCT of Delhi-110002, India
    TEL : +91 (0) 11 23271810
    FAX : +91 (0) 11 23271218

RICE MILLS/CEREAL MILLS

1. Kiran Engineering Works
   111, Ajay Bizli Mkt., 2865/66
   Shah Ganj, G B Rd., Delhi,
   NCT of Delhi-110009, India
   TEL : +91 (0) 11 23219310
   FAX : +91 (0) 11 23210002
   E-mail: kewbbb@vsnl.net.in
2. Central Engineering Corporation
   Bhaktinagar Stn. Rd.
   P.O. Box 540 & 104
   Bhaktinagar, Rajkot,
   Gujarat-360002, India
   TEL : +91 (0) 281 2462003
   FAX : +91 (0) 281 2461590
   E-mail:
   centralengg01@hotmail.com
3. Amira India
   P.O. Box No. 8
   12/7, Urban Est.
   Gurgaon, Haryana-122001, India
   TEL : +91 (0) 124 26373010
   FAX : +91 (0) 124 26322997
   E-mail: septu@del3.vsnl.net.in
4. Saboo Stone Flour Mills Pvt. Ltd.
   10/5, New Palasia
   Indore, Madhya Pradesh-452001
   India
   TEL : +91 (0) 731 2432562
   FAX : +91 (0) 731 2433239
   E-mail:
   sabstone@bom4.vsnl.net.in
5. Garima Global Enterprises
   215, Ruby Indl. Est.
   Off New Link Rd., Malad (W)
   Mumbai, Maharashtra-400064
   India
   TEL : +91 (0) 22 28771656
   FAX : +91 (0) 22 28765693
   E-mail: garima@bom3.vsnl.net.in
6. Majestic Auto Components
   D-8/9, Focal Point
   Rajpura, Punjab-140401, India
   TEL : +91 (0) 1762 2424276
7. Navdeep Products
   123-124, Nr. Pital Factory
   Pink City Tower, Jaipur,
   Rajasthan-302016, India
   TEL : +91 (0) 141 22304006
   FAX : +91 (0) 141 22304006
8. Sri Rudran Instruments Co.
   56, Vaikundapuram 2nd St.
   Nungambakkam, Chennai,
   Tamil Nadu-600034, India
   TEL : +91 (0) 44 28172803
   FAX : +91 (0) 44 28175843
   E-mail: srico@satyam.net.in
9. Gurucharan Engg. Works
   142, Indl. Est., Nunhai
   Agra, Uttar Pradesh-282006
   India
   TEL : +91 (0) 562 2345452
10. AT Mohsin & Co.
    P.O. Box 2736,
    71/B, N S Rd.
    Kolkata, West Bengal-700001
    India
    TEL : +91 (0) 33 22433777
    FAX : +91 (0) 33 22252319
    E-mail: firozukani@sify.com

GRAIN PROCESSING MACHINERY

1. Satake Corp.
   11th Flr., Dr. Gopal Das Bhavan
   Barakhamba Rd., New Delhi,
   NCT of Delhi-110001, India
   TEL : +91 (0) 11 23738646
   FAX : +91 (0) 11 23738647
   E-mail: satake@del2.vsnl.net.in
2. Goldin (India) Equipment Pvt. Ltd.
   F-29, BIDC Est., Gorwa
   Vadodara, Gujarat-390016, India
   TEL : +91 (0) 265 2280168
   FAX : +91 (0) 265 2280461
   E-mail: sales@goldinequip.com
3. Indopol Food Processing Machinery Pvt. Ltd.
   Indl. Plot No. 28
   Sect. 27-C, Faridabad,
   Haryana-121003, India
   TEL : +91 (0) 129 25276161
   FAX : +91 (0) 129 25720549
   E-mail: info@indopol.com
4. Arihant Engineering Works
   124, Guru Nanak Timber Mkt.
   Dhar Rd., Indore,
   Madhya Pradesh-452002, India
   TEL : +91 (0) 731 2380535
   FAX : +91 (0) 731 2380537
   E-mail:
   arihantengineering@epatra.com
5. Kaps Engineers
   Samraat Silk Mills Compound
   LBS Marg, Vikhroli (W)
   Mumbai, Maharashtra-400079
   India
   TEL : +91 (0) 22 25781933
   FAX : +91 (0) 22 25785741
   E-mail:
   vmsrehls@bom4.vsnl.net.in
6. Guru Nanak Engineering & Foundry Works
   166, Indl. Focal Point
   Mehta Rd., Amritsar,
   Punjab-143039, India
   TEL : +91 (0) 183 2583542
   FAX : +91 (0) 183 2587944
   E-mail: sharanji@jla.vsnl.net.in
7. Agromech Engineers
   374, Patel Rd., Coimbatore,
   Tamil Nadu-641009, India
   TEL : +91 (0) 422 2235054
   FAX : +91 (0) 422 2235054
8. Sree Balaji Industries
   283, Dr. Ambedkar Rd.
   Velandipalayam
   Coimbatore, Tamil Nadu-641025
   India
   TEL : +91 (0) 422 2430510
   FAX : +91 (0) 422 2301598
9. SK Engg. & Allied Works
   5, Digiha, Stn. Rd., Bahraich,
   Uttar Pradesh-271801, India
   TEL : +91 (0) 5252 232964
   FAX : +91 (0) 5252 232904
   E-mail: skengg16@hotmail.com
10. Capco Engg. Pvt. Ltd.
    2-27-16, Gokul St.
    Srinagar, Kakinada,
    Andhra Pradesh-533005, India
    TEL : +91 (0) 884 28311
    FAX : +91 (0) 884 272100

BREWERY MACHINERY

1. Praj Industries Ltd.
   "Praj House", Bavdhan
   Pune, Maharashtra-411021
   India
   TEL : +91 (0) 20 22951511
   FAX : +91 (0) 20 22951718
   E-mail: info@praj.net
2. Sneha Engg. Equipment Pvt. Ltd.
   D-12, Phase-IV Extn., IDA
   Jeedimetla, Hyderabad,
   Andhra Pradesh-500055, India
   TEL : +91 (0) 40 23096386
   FAX : +91 (0) 40 23091065
   E-mail: chidkuri@hd2.vsnl.net.in
3. Breweries Engineering Pvt. Ltd.
   A-10, Gali No. 4
   Anand Parbat Indl. Area
   New Delhi, NCT of Delhi-110005
   India
   TEL : +91 (0) 11 25723331
   FAX : +91 (0) 11 25784682

4. Breweries Filter System Pvt. Ltd.
Plot No. 219, Udyog Ngr.
Swaran Park, Mundka, Delhi,
NCT of Delhi-110041, India
TEL : +91 (0) 11 25475794
E-mail: brewfil@yahoo.com

5. Metal & Forming Industries
147, Sect. 24, Faridabad,
Haryana-121005, India
TEL : +91 (0) 129 25234667
E-mail: vikas809@hotmail.com

6. Alfa Laval (I) Ltd.
Dapodi, Pune,
Maharashtra-411012, India
TEL : +91 (0) 20 27147721
FAX : +91 (0) 20 27147711
E-mail:
satish.tandon@alfalaval.com

7. Chetan Enterprise
No. 6, Nehru Ngr.
Old Mahabalipuram Rd.
Kottivakkam, Chennai,
Tamil Nadu-600041, India
TEL : +91 (0) 44 24925547
FAX : +91 (0) 44 24925030
E-mail: dhaman_a@hotmail.com

8. Anand Dis-Brew Engg. Works
5, Rajinder Ngr. Indl. Area
Mohan Ngr., Ghaziabad,
Uttar Pradesh-201007, India
TEL : +91 (0) 120 24627318
FAX : +91 (0) 120 24629210
E-mail:
anand_disbrew@yahoo.co.in

9. KBK Plascon Pvt. Ltd.
24/168, P.O.Box 158
Phool Bagh Crossing
Birhana Rd., Kanpur,
Uttar Pradesh-208001, India
TEL : +91 (0) 512 2369353
FAX : +91 (0) 512 2352058
E-mail: kbk@lw1.vsnl.net.in

10. Sutdhar Machinery Manufacturers
Plot No. 1, Rajender Ngr. Indl. Est.
P.O. Mohan Ngr., Ghaziabad,
Uttar Pradesh-201005, India
TEL : +91 (0) 120 24624381

DISTILLING MACHINERY

1. Praj Industries Ltd.
"Praj House", Bavdhan
Pune, Maharashtra-411021
India
TEL : +91 (0) 20 22951511
FAX : +91 (0) 20 22951718
E-mail: info@praj.net

2. Dipesh Engineering Works
3, Sheroo Villa
87, J P Rd., Andheri (W)
Mumbai, Maharashtra-400053
India
TEL : +91 (0) 22 26336729
FAX : +91 (0) 22 26315507
E-mail: kjpatel_71@hotmail.com

3. Dhopeshwar Engineering Pvt. Ltd.
A-16, CIE, Balanagar
Hyderabad,
Andhra Pradesh-500037, India
TEL : +91 (0) 40 23771579
FAX : +91 (0) 40 23772450
E-mail: dhopesh@hd2.dot.net.in

4. Eskeyar Pvt. Ltd.
B-126, 1st Stage
Peenya Indl. Est., Bangalore,
Karnataka-560058, India
TEL : +91 (0) 80 28394596

5. Gem Pharma Machineries
Unit No. A-82
Rd. No. 16, Towards Kisan Ngr.
Wagle Indl. Est.
Thane, Maharashtra-400604
India
TEL : +91 (0) 22 25820257
FAX : +91 (0) 22 25826387
E-mail:
gemmumbai@hotmail.com

6. Kothari Pharma
C-11, M K Brothers Indl. Est.,
Jarimari, Andheri-Kurla Rd.
Andheri (E), Mumbai,
Maharashtra-400072, India
TEL : +91 (0) 22 28510837
FAX : +91 (0) 22 28513584
E-mail:
chandrakant@kothariapharma.com

7. Mamko Machines Fabricators Pvt. Ltd.
   105, Heera Panna Indl. Est.
   Western Express Highway
   Goregaon (E), Mumbai,
   Maharashtra-400063, India
   TEL : +91 (0) 22 28756309
   FAX : +91 (0) 22 28752535
   E-mail:
   vvchavan@bom5.vsnl.net.in
8. Metal Plants
   17, Anupam Indl. Est. No. 2
   Off Pt. M M Malviya Marg
   Mulund (W), Mumbai,
   Maharashtra-400080, India
   TEL : +91 (0) 22 25654607
   FAX : +91 (0) 22 25610628
   E-mail: koppa@bol.net.in
9. Anand Dis-Brew Engg. Works
   5, Rajinder Ngr. Indl. Area
   Mohan Ngr., Ghaziabad,
   Uttar Pradesh-201007, India
   TEL : +91 (0) 120 24627318
   FAX : +91 (0) 120 24629210
   E-mail:
   anand_disbrew@yahoo.co.in
10. Steel Crafts Fabrications
    C-349, Sect. 10, Noida,
    Uttar Pradesh-201301, India
    TEL : +91 (0) 120 24554241
    FAX : +91 (0) 120 24441212
    E-mail: steelcraft@rediffmail.com

SUGAR MACHINERY

1. Cenlub Systems
   184, Sect. 16, Faridabad,
   Haryana-121002, India
   TEL : +91 (0) 129 25277746
   FAX : +91 (0) 129 25277747
   E-mail: cenlub@ndb.vsnl.net.in
2. Techno Crafts
   E-38, SSGT Rd. Indl. Area
   Ghaziabad,
   Uttar Pradesh-201009, India
   TEL : +91 (0) 120 24841082
   FAX : +91 (0) 120 24841081
   E-mail:
   technocrafts@rediffmail.com
3. Stotz Blacksmiths Ltd.
   1304, Regent Chmbrs., 13th Flr.
   Nariman Point, Mumbai,
   Maharashtra-400021, India
   TEL : +91 (0) 22 22311531
   FAX : +91 (0) 22 22048172
   E-mail: metle@bom3.vsnl.net.in
4. Capco Engg. Pvt. Ltd.
   2-27-16, Gokul St., Srinagar
   Kakinada, Andhra Pradesh-533005
   India
   TEL : +91 (0) 884 28311
   FAX : +91 (0) 884 272100
5. Ashoka Technologies
   A-15, Phase-I, Mayapuri Indl. Area
   New Delhi, NCT of Delhi-110064
   India
   TEL : +91 (0) 11 25135308
   FAX : +91 (0) 11 25138250
   E-mail: amtc@ndb.vsnl.net.in
6. Whirler Centrifugals Pvt. Ltd.
   1213, Phase-III, GIDC Est.
   Vatva, Ahmedabad,
   Gujarat-382445, India
   TEL : +91 (0) 79 25890021
   FAX : +91 (0) 79 25830442
   E-mail: whirlcent@whirlcent.com
7. Ambala Machine Tools
   G T Rd. (Sirhind Side)
   Ambay Mill Rd., Mandi Gobindgarh,
   Punjab-147301, India
   TEL : +91 (0) 1765 254057
   FAX : +91 (0) 1765 254057
   E-mail: info@ambalamachines.com
8. Binny Engg. Ltd.
   P. O. Box 8677
   Meenambakkam, Chennai,
   Tamil Nadu-600114, India
   TEL : +91 (0) 44 22341151
   FAX : +91 (0) 44 22345251
   E-mail: bew@vsnl.com
9. Saraswati Industrial Syndicate Ltd.
   A-4, Sect. 24, Noida,
   Uttar Pradesh-201301, India
   TEL : +91 (0) 120 24524071
   FAX : +91 (0) 120 24542072
   E-mail: exports@isgec.com

10. Uttam Industrial Engg. Pvt. Ltd.
    A-8, Meerut Rd., Indl. Area
    Ghaziabad, Uttar Pradesh-201003
    India
    TEL : +91 (0) 120 24713212
    FAX : +91 (0) 120 24723133
    E-mail: ranjan@del2.vsnl.net.in

DAIRY MACHINERY

1. Mellcon Engineers Pvt. Ltd.
   B-297, Phase-I, Okhla Indl. Area
   New Delhi, NCT of Delhi-110020
   India
   TEL : +91 (0) 11 26816530
   FAX : +91 (0) 11 26816573
   E-mail: mellcon@vsnl.net
   www.mellcon.com
2. Ved Engg.
   B-38, Sect. 60, Noida,
   Uttar Pradesh-201301, India
   TEL : +91 (0) 118 24580507
   FAX : +91 (0) 118 24580815
   E-mail: vaidant@del3.vsnl.net.in
3. Dipesh Engineering Works
   3, Sheroo Villa
   87, J P Rd., Andheri (W)
   Mumbai, Maharashtra-400053
   India
   TEL : +91 (0) 22 26336729
   FAX : +91 (0) 22 26315507
   E-mail: kjpatel_71@hotmail.com
4. Chengalva Engineers Ltd.
   405, Shashank Residency,
   St. No. 11, Tarnaka
   Hyderabad,
   Andhra Pradesh-500017, India
   TEL : +91 (0) 40 27017397
   FAX : +91 (0) 40 27018517
   E-mail: chenga@hd1.vsnl.net.in
5. Harikrushna Technopride
   Engineering
   52, Shanakr Indl. Est.
   Nr. Revabhai Est., CTM
   Amraiwadi, Ahmedabad,
   Gujarat-380026, India
   TEL : +91 (0) 79 25861526
   FAX : +91 (0) 79 25860186
   E-mail: hte@satyam.net.in
6. Aashit Engg. Works
   A-14, Nawada Rd.
   Dabua, Faridabad,
   Haryana-121001, India
   TEL : +91 (0) 129 25214804
7. Ambica Engg. Works
   16/A, 1st Main,
   Modi Hospital Rd.,
   W.O.C Road, 2nd Stage.
   Bangalore, Karnataka-560086
   India
   TEL : +91 (0) 80 23495370
   FAX : +91 (0) 80 23496120
   E-mail: ambica_e_w@vsnl.com
8. Aggarwal Dairy Equipment Co.
   Opp. Bus Stand,
   37, Dhayan Singh Comml. Cmplx.
   Ludhiana, Punjab-141001, India
   TEL : +91 (0) 161 2447984
   FAX : +91 (0) 161 2447984
   E-mail: adec@satyam.net.in
9. RPM Engineers (I) Ltd.
   14 (NP), Developed Plots
   TVK Indl. Est., Ekkattuthangal
   Chennai, Tamil Nadu-600097
   India
   TEL : +91 (0) 44 22325596
   FAX : +91 (0) 44 22321639
   E-mail: rpm@md3.vsnl.net.in
10. Pasteur Engg. Company Pvt. Ltd.
    15/8/A, The Mall, Dum Dum
    Kolkata, West Bengal-700080
    India
    TEL : +91 (0) 33 25593015
    FAX : +91 (0) 33 25593015

MEAT PROCESSING MACHINERY

1. Superfreeze India Ltd.
   WZ-92-A, Raja Garden
   Ring Rd., New Delhi,
   NCT of Delhi-110015, India
   TEL : +91 (0) 11 25122667
   FAX : +91 (0) 11 25101061
   E-mail:
   corporate@superfreezeindia.com

2. Wintech Taparia Ltd.
   3rd Flr., Shreesh Chmbrs.,
   25/1, Y N Rd., Indore,
   Madhya Pradesh-452003, India
   TEL : +91 (0) 731 2433950
   FAX : +91 (0) 731 2430527
   E-mail: sales@wintechtaparia.com

3. Chengalva Engineers Ltd.
   405, Shashank Residency,
   St. No. 11, Tarnaka
   Hyderabad,
   Andhra Pradesh-500017, India
   TEL : +91 (0) 40 27017397
   FAX : +91 (0) 40 27018517
   E-mail: chenga@hd1.vsnl.net.in

CONFECTIONERY MACHINERY

1. Dhiman Industries (Regd.)
   Dakhni Gate
   Nakodar, Punjab-144040, India
   TEL : +91 (0) 1821 220018
   FAX : +91 (0) 1821 221118
   E-mail: info@dhimangroup.com

2. NSW India Ltd.
   Plot No. 43, Sect. 34
   EHTP, Gurgaon,
   Haryana-122001, India
   TEL : +91 (0) 124 26371106
   FAX : +91 (0) 124 26372859
   E-mail: corporate@nswindia.com

3. Sun Beam Machines (India) Pvt. Ltd.
   Plot No. 141, IDA, Bollaram
   Hyderabad,
   Andhra Pradesh-502325, India
   TEL : +91 (0) 8458 279723
   FAX : +91 (0) 8458 279078
   E-mail: smipl@satyam.net.in

4. Reliance Engineering Works
   Kothi No. 4065, Sect. 46-D
   Chandigarh,
   Chandigarh (UT)-160047, India
   TEL : +91 (0) 172 2605682
   FAX : +91 (0) 172 2652781

5. Flora Engg. Corp.
   28-A, Phool Bagh
   Rampura, Delhi,
   NCT of Delhi-110035, India
   TEL : +91 (0) 11 25415335

6. Ahimsa Industries Pvt. Ltd.
   212, Sakar V
   B/h Natraj Cinema
   Off Ashram Rd., Ahmedabad,
   Gujarat-380009, India
   TEL : +91 (0) 79 26583897
   FAX : +91 (0) 79 26585103
   E-mail: ahimsa@icenet.net

7. Kaps Engineers
   Samraat Silk Mills Compound
   LBS Marg
   Vikhroli (W)
   Mumbai, Maharashtra-400079
   India
   TEL : +91 (0) 22 25781933
   FAX : +91 (0) 22 25785741
   E-mail: vmsrehls@bom4.vsnl.net.in

8. Dhiman Udyog
   6026, Opp. Residence
   (S. Gurbachan Singh Dhiman)
   Nr. Dakhni Gate
   Nakodar, Punjab-144040
   India
   TEL : +91 (0) 1821 220891
   FAX : +91 (0) 1821 222891

9. GR International
   13, Old Trunk Rd.
   Pallavaram, Chennai,
   Tamil Nadu-600043, India
   TEL : +91 (0) 44 22366419
   FAX : +91 (0) 44 22366964
   E-mail: grint@giasmd01.vsnl.net.in

10. Jay Kay Enterprises India (Regd.)
    H-23-25, Sect. 9, Noida,
    Uttar Pradesh-201301, India
    TEL : +91 (0) 120 24557023
    FAX : +91 (0) 120 24535045
    E-mail:
    jaykayenterprises@hotmail.com

POULTRY PROCESSING MACHINERY

1. Stadler Corporation
   A-3/3, Surjit Singh Compound,
   Shivaji Ngr., Off Vakola Bridge
   Santacruz (E), Mumbai,
   Maharashtra-400055, India
   TEL : +91 (0) 22 26105212
   FAX : +91 (0) 22 26105093
   E-mail: stadler44@hotmail.com

2. Dhopeshwar Engineering Pvt. Ltd.
   A-16, CIE, Balanagar
   Hyderabad,
   Andhra Pradesh-500037, India
   TEL : +91 (0) 40 23771579
   FAX : +91 (0) 40 23772450
   E-mail: dhopesh@hd2.dot.net.in

VEGETABLE PROCESSING MACHINERY

1. Doris (India) Engineers Pvt. Ltd.
   No. 389, 390, Arcot Rd.
   Kodambakkam, Chennai,
   Tamil Nadu-600024, India
   TEL : +91 (0) 44 24801098
   FAX : +91 (0) 44 24815652
   E-mail: machines@dorisindia.com

2. Asian Power Cyclopes
   Rochipura, Majra
   Dehradun, Uttaranchal-248171
   India
   TEL : +91 (0) 135 2620488
   FAX : +91 (0) 135 2620961
   E-mail: asian@nde.vsnl.net.in

3. Spantek Projects
   #7, Amir Terrace, Al-Ameen Soc.
   Gultekdi, Pune,
   Maharashtra-411037, India
   TEL : +91 (0) 20 24269393
   FAX : +91 (0) 20 24269562
   E-mail: spantek@hotmail.com

FOOD PACKAGING MACHINERY

1. EC Packaging Pvt. Ltd.
   14/7, Milestone, Mathura Rd.
   Faridabad, Haryana-121003
   India
   TEL : +91 (0) 129 25277796
   FAX : +91 (0) 129 25255602
   E-mail: ecppl@del3.vsnl.net.in

2. Indian Packaging Machineries
   I-15, Phase-I, DLF Indl. Area
   Faridabad, Haryana-121003
   India
   TEL : +91 (0) 129 25276112
   FAX : +91 (0) 129 25274518
   E-mail: indian@del6.vsnl.net.in

3. Target Engineers Co.
   H-91, Sect. 9, Noida,
   Uttar Pradesh-201301, India
   TEL : +91 (0) 120 24530586
   FAX : +91 (0) 120 24557670
   E-mail: target@mantraonline.com

4. Orbit Equipments Pvt. Ltd.
   1, Venkat Reddy Cmplx.
   Tarbund, Secunderabad,
   Andhra Pradesh-500009, India
   TEL : +91 (0) 40 27817296
   FAX : +91 (0) 40 27813877
   E-mail: orbiteqp@hd2.dot.net.in

5. Canflex Engineering Pvt. Ltd.
   Formerly Cannon Engineering Industries
   C-8/3 Indl. Est., Sanathnagar
   P.O. Box No. 1919, Hyderabad,
   Andhra Pradesh-500018, India
   TEL : +91 (0) 40 23774967
   FAX : +91 (0) 40 23730123
   E-mail: info@cannonindia.com

6. Artek Enterprises Pvt. Ltd.
   45, Deepak Bldg.
   13, Nehru Place, New Delhi,
   NCT of Delhi-110019, India
   TEL : +91 (0) 11 28618378
   FAX : +91 (0) 11 26216934
   E-mail: arteke@vsnl.com

7. New Indo International
   135-A, Begumpur, Malviya Ngr.
   New Delhi, NCT of Delhi-110017
   India
   TEL : +91 (0) 11 26683289
   FAX : +91 (0) 11 26688290
   E-mail: nii@ndf.vsnl.net.in
8. Packmech Engineers
   23/4, Kailash Indl. Est., B/h CMC
   Odhav, Ahmedabad,
   Gujarat-382415, India
   TEL : +91 (0) 79 22876181
   FAX : +91 (0) 79 22876893
   E-mail: powervac@satyam.net.in
9. Oval Engineers
   117B, 9th 'A' Cross
   Ganapathi Ngr.
   Peenya Phase-III
   Bangalore, Karnataka-560058
   India
   TEL : +91 (0) 80 28364087
   FAX : +91 (0) 80 28364087
   E-mail: oval@peenyaindarea.com
10. A-Variety Scales
    13/2, Chhoti Gwaltoli
    Asian Tower
    Indore, Madhya Pradesh-452001
    India
    TEL : +91 (0) 731 2762601
    FAX : +91 (0) 731 2446144
    E-mail: varietyscales@yahoo.com
11. NSL Fabricators
    Plot No. 206/6, Phase-II, IDA
    Cherlapally, Hyderabad,
    Andhra Pradesh-500051, India
    TEL : +91 (0) 40 27261612
    FAX : +91 (0) 40 27261612
    E-mail: nslfab@rediffmail.com
12. Manoj Plastics
    A-99/1, Phase-II, Okhla Indl. Area
    New Delhi, NCT of Delhi-110020
    India
    TEL : +91 (0) 11 26839693
    FAX : +91 (0) 11 26913011
    E-mail: mperiwal@del3.vsnl.net.in
13. Mamata Machinery Pvt. Ltd.
    5/1/1A, Phase-I, GIDC
    Vatva, Ahmedabad,
    Gujarat-382445, India
    TEL : +91 (0) 79 25832023
    FAX : +91 (0) 79 25832026
    E-mail: mmpl@ad1.vsnl.net.in
14. Saiman Engineers Pvt. Ltd.
    D/3, Hari Bhakti Indl. Est.
    Old Ghod Bunder Rd.
    P.O. Mira, Thane,
    Maharashtra-401104, India
    TEL : +91 (0) 22 28458206
    FAX : +91 (0) 22 28458466
    E-mail:
    saimanengg@hotmail.com
15. Nishad Process Equipments Pvt. Ltd.
    5-B/118, D N Ngr.
    Kalapradarshini Lane
    Andheri (W), Mumbai,
    Maharashtra-400053, India
    TEL : +91 (0) 22 26239447
16. Samarpan Fabricators Ltd.
    Plot A-182/A-183
    Lane Z, Rd. 16, Wagle Indl. Est.
    Thane, Maharashtra-400604
    India
    TEL : +91 (0) 22 25820373
    FAX : +91 (0) 22 25820033
    E-mail: samarpan1@vsnl.com
17. Khosla Machines Pvt. Ltd.
    B-17, Phase-II, Indl. Area
    Mohali, Punjab-160051, India
    TEL : +91 (0) 172 2670587
    FAX : +91 (0) 172 2260146
    E-mail:
    khosla@khoslamachines.com
18. Vikaash Packaging
    120, Mugappair Rd.
    Padi, Chennai,
    Tamil Nadu-600050, India
    TEL : +91 (0) 44 26521703
    FAX : +91 (0) 44 26521703
    E-mail: rvs@eth.net

19. GR International
13, Old Trunk Rd.
Pallavaram, Chennai,
Tamil Nadu-600043, India
TEL : +91 (0) 44 22366419
FAX : +91 (0) 44 22366964
E-mail: grint@giasmd01.vsnl.net.in

20. Bajaj Maschinen Pvt. Ltd.
7/20, 7/27, Site IV
Sahibabad Indl. Area, Ghaziabad,
Uttar Pradesh-201010, India
TEL : +91 (0) 120 24775119
FAX : +91 (0) 120 24775137
E-mail: bajaj@del3.vsnl.net.in

FOOD PROCESSING MACHINERY

1. Kaps Engineers
Samraat Silk Mills Compound
LBS Marg, Vikhroli (W)
Mumbai, Maharashtra-400079
India
TEL : +91 (0) 22 25781933
FAX : +91 (0) 22 25785741
E-mail: vmsrehls@bom4.vsnl.net.in

2. Jay Kay Enterprises India (Regd.)
H-23-25, Sect. 9
Noida, Uttar Pradesh-201301
India
TEL : +91 (0) 120 24557023
FAX : +91 (0) 120 24535045
E-mail:
jaykayenterprises@hotmail.com

3. NSW India Ltd.
Plot No. 43, Sect. 34
EHTP, Gurgaon,
Haryana-122001, India
TEL : +91 (0) 124 26371106
FAX : +91 (0) 124 26372859
E-mail: corporate@nswindia.com

4. BR Industries
Flat No. 103, Karnik Towers
Khairatabad, Hyderabad,
Andhra Pradesh-500004, India
TEL : +91 (0) 40 26665408
FAX : +91 (0) 40 26660004
E-mail: bri@rediffmail.com

5. Maxcare Marketing & Technical Services
J-188, Saket
New Delhi, NCT of Delhi-110017
India
TEL : +91 (0) 11 26967273
FAX : +91 (0) 11 26866464
E-mail: maxcare188@hotmail.com

6. Kevin Engineering Pvt. Ltd.
A/1/3706, GIDC, Phase-IV
Vatva, Ahmedabad,
Gujarat-382445, India
TEL : +91 (0) 79 25841503
FAX : +91 (0) 79 25841243
E-mail: info@kevinindia.com

7. Ambica Engg. Works
16/A, 1st Main,
Modi Hospital Rd.,
W.O.C Road, 2nd Stage.
Bangalore, Karnataka-560086
India
TEL : +91 (0) 80 23495370
FAX : +91 (0) 80 23496120
E-mail: ambica_e_w@vsnl.com

8. Arihant Engineering Works
124, Guru Nanak Timber Mkt.
Dhar Rd., Indore,
Madhya Pradesh-452002, India
TEL : +91 (0) 731 2380535
FAX : +91 (0) 731 2380537
E-mail:
arihantengineering@epatra.com

9. Sabko Industries
Sanatorium Rd. Madar
Ajmer, Rajasthan-305024, India
TEL : +91 (0) 145 2429750
FAX : +91 (0) 145 2426684
E-mail: sabko@sabko.com

10. Doris (India) Engineers Pvt. Ltd.
No. 389, 390, Arcot Rd.
Kodambakkam, Chennai,
Tamil Nadu-600024, India
TEL : +91 (0) 44 24801098
FAX : +91 (0) 44 24815652
E-mail: machines@dorisindia.com

LIST OF THE READY AVAILABLE DETAILED PROJECT REPORTS

AUTOMOBILES, MECHANICAL & METALLURGICAL

1. AGRICULTRAL EQUIPMENTS
2. AGRICULTRAL EQUIPMENTS INCLUDING THRESHERS
3. AIR BRAKE HELICAL COIL
4. AIR COOLER
5. AIR FILTERS(FOR SCOOTER CAR & EXCAVATORS ETC.)
6. ALUMINIUM & ALUMINIUM ALLOYS FROM ALUMINIUM SCRAP TO MAKE UTENSILS (INDUCTION FURNACE MELTED)
7. ALUMINIUM ALLOY WHEELS
8. ALUMINIUM ALLOYS FROM ALUMINIUM SCRAP TO MAKE UTENSILS (INDUCTION FURNACE)
9. ALUMINIUM HOT & COLD ROLLING MILL
10. ALUMINIUM BOTTLE MANUFACTURING (COLD EXTRUSION OF ALUMINIUM)
11. ALUMINIUM/COPPER CABLE LUGS
12. ALUMINIUM CANS FOR BEER PACKAGING
13. ALUMINIUM CANS FOR CAPACITORS
14. ALUMINIUM CAPS FOR INJECTION VIALS
15. ALUMINIUM EXTRUSION
16. ALUMINIUM FURNITURE & HARDWARE
17. ALUMINIUM SHEET ROLLING MILL
18. ALUMINIUM UTENSILS
19. ALUMINIUM UTENSILS & SCHOOL BOXES
20. ALUMINIUM WIRE DRAWING AND SUPER ENAMELLING FOR WINDING
21. ANODISED ALUMINIUM UTENSILS
22. ANODIZING OF ALUMINIUM
23. ANTIMONY OXIDE FROM LEAD SCRAP
24. ARC WELDING FILTER GLASS
25. ALUMINIUM FOIL CUTTING & ROLL MAKING
26. AUTO FLAPS FOR TRUCKS & BUSES
27. AUTOMOBILE WORKSHOP (GARAGE & SERVICE CENTRE)
28. AUTO GEARS
29. AUTO HORNS
30. AUTO LEAF SPRING
31. AUTO TUBES
32. AUTO PISTON RING
33. AUTO PISTON
34. BAKERY AND BISCUITS EQUIPMENTS FABRICATION
35. BALL POINT PEN REFILLS
36. BALL ROLLER & TAPER BEARING
37. BAND SAW BLADES
38. BARBED WIRE
39. BICYCLE SPOKES
40. BRAKE LINING ASBESTOES/ RESIN BASED & ASBESTOES FREE
41. BRASS ARTWARE/HOLLOW WARE CASTING (WITH THE HELP OF PHENOLIC RESIN)
42. BRASS CASTING
43. BRASS PIPES FROM BRASS SHEET WITH LONGITUDINALLY WELDING
44. BRASS WARE BY CASTING METHOD (BRASS ARTICLES VIZ. BRASS POOJA LAMPS AND OTHER CASTED)
45. BRIGHT BARS
46. BUFFING AND POLISHING INDUSTRY (JOB WORK)
47. BUTT HINGE (BRASS SHEET)
48. CARBON BRUSH HOLDER & SLIP RING
49. CO_2 WELDING WIRE ELECTRODES (COPPER/ COPPER ALLOY COATED M.S.WIRE)
50. CARBON FILM RESISTORS
51. CARBURETTORS
52. CAST STEEL PANES FOR MELTING FURNACE
53. CHEMICAL ETCHING OF STAINLESS STEEL
54. CHEMICAL RESISTANT IRON & STEEL
55. COLD FORM SECTION MILL
56. COLD ROLLED FORMING OF SECTION AND OTHER SECTIONS
57. COLD ROLLING OF MS STRIP
58. COLD TWISTED DE-FORMED RIBBED STEEL
59. COMPRESSOR (HERMETIC) FOR AIR CONDITIONERS
60. COMPRESSED NATURAL GAS (CNG KIT) FOR AUTOVEHICLE
61. CONTINUOUSLY CAST STEEL WIRE RODS (5 mm)
62. CONTINUOUS CASTING COPPER WIRE RODS
63. CONVEYOR BELTINGS
64. CONVEYOR BELT, TRANSM -ISSION BELT & V BELTS
65. COOKING RANGES
66. COPPER/BRASS SHEETS, CIRCLE & UTENSILS
67. COPPER FOIL
68. COPPER INGOTS, RODS MAKING & WIRE DRAWING
69. COPPER PRODUCTS FROM COPPER SCRAP
70. COPPER SMELTING PLANT
71. COPPER WIRE RODS FROM COPPER SCRAP
72. CORRUGATED BOX MAKING MACHINERY AND OTHER THEIR PARTS
73. CYLINDER LINER FOR AUTOMOBILES
74. DOOR LOCKS/PAD LOCKS
75. DRILL BITS & TOOL BITS
76. DRUM CLOSURES
77. ERW STEEL CONDUIT PIPE
78. EARTH MOVING EQPT.
79. ENGINE VALVES FOR AUTOMOBILES
80. FABRICATION OF HEAT EXCHANGER
81. FABRICATION OF STORAGE TANKS AND M.S. DRUM
82. FERROUS ALLOY NI-HARDY I.V CASTING
83. FERROUS Mn ALLOY CASTING BY ALUMINA THERMIC PROCESS
84. FERRO ALLOYS
85. FERRO SILICON & FERRO MANGANESE FROM DOLOMITE (SMS GRADE)
86. FIRE EXTINGUISHERS
87. FLIP-TONE CANS
88. FORGED CONECTING ROD
89. FORGING UNIT
90. FOUNTAIN PEN NIBS
91. FOUNDRY SAND
92. FUEL INJECTION SYSTEM
93. GALVANIZED M.S.STRIPS
94. GALVANIZING PLANT
95. GALVANIZED IRON WIRE
96. GAS WELDING TORCHES AND NOZZLES
97. GASKET SHEET
98. GATE GRILLS & WINDOW FRAMES
99. GENERATING SET (DIESEL)
100. HARD ANODISED ALUMINIUM
101. HOSPITAL WARES
102. HOSPITAL FURNITURES
103. HOT DIP GALVANIZING
104. HOT FORGED FASTENERS
105. HOT MIX PLANT
106. INJECTION MOULDED PLASTIC COMPOUNDS WITH TOOL ROOM
107. INJECTION MOULDED PLASTIC COMPONENTS AND METAL PIPE SPINNING UNIT
108. INVESTMENT CASTING
109. IRON/STEEL WIRE GAUGE
110. IRON TAWA
111. KNIVES (S.S.KNIVES)
112. KITCHEN SINK (S.S.)
113. L.P.G REGULATORS
114. MACHINE SCREWS & SELF TAPPING SCREWS
115. MARUTI WORKSHOP CUM SERVICE STATION
116. MAGNESIUM INGOTS & BULLETS CASTING

Above all the "Detailed Project Reports" are available at *"ENGINEERS INDIA RESEARCH INSTITUTE"*. 4449, Nai Sarak (D), Main Road Delhi - 110 006 (India) ● Ph : 91-11-23918117, 2391 6431, 2384 0361 ● Fax : 91-11- 2391 6431 ●E-Mail : eirisidi@bol.net.in ● WebSite : www.eiriindia.org

117. MANUFACTURE OF TIN CONTAINERS
118. MANUFACTURE OF STORAGE TANKS, PRESSURE VESSELS, HEAT EXCHANGERS
119. MARK II HAND PUMPS
120. MARUTI WORKSHOP CUM - SERVICE STATION
121. MECHANICAL JACKS
122. METAL CUTTING DIE DESIGN
123. METAL CUTTING OF AND GRINDING WHEELS (ABBRASIVE CUTTING WHEELS)
124. METAL HOOKS & CLIPS
125. METAL SEPARATION (COPPER, TIN, LEAD) FROM SPENT WASH ACID
126. METALLIC RING JOINTS
127. METALLIC GASKET (SPIRAL WOUND)
128. MICROVEE & ABSOLUTE FILTER
129. MICROWAVE OVEN
130. MILD STEEL INGOTS
131. MINI STEEL PLANT
132. MODERN VEHICLE WORKSHOP
133. MOPED
134. M.S.HINGES
135. M.S.INGOT AND HR. STEEL STRUCTURALS
136. M.S.INGOT BY INDUCTION FURNACES
137. M.S.PIPES
138. M.S. WELDING ELECTRODE
139. MUFFLERS & SILENCERS FOR THREE WHEELERS
140. NAIL CUTTER WITH FILER & MANICURE
141. NICHROME WIRE
142. NICKEL LINED SCREENS
143. NON-FERROUS ALLOY ROLLING
144. NON-FERROUS FORGING
145. NON-FERROUS FOUNDRY
146. NON PRESSURE
147. INCANDESCENT LAMP
148. NUMBER COMBINATION LOCKS FOR LUGGAGES
149. NUTS & BOLTS
150. PAPER COATED ALUMINIUM AND COPPER WIRE
151. PETROMAX CONTAINER
152. PHOTO ETCHING OF STAINLESS STEEL PLATES
153. PIPE GALVANIZING PLANT
154. PISTON RING-AUTOMOBILE
155. PLANT PROTECTION EQUIPMENTS
156. PLATINUM LABORATORY APPARATUS
157. PRESSURE COOKER & ALUMINIUM UTENSILS
158. PRESSURE COOKER (ALUMINIUM)
159. PRESSURE DIE CASTING
160. PRINTED ALUMINIUM COLLAPSIBLE TUBES
161. PRINTED TIN CONTAINERS
162. PRINTING PRESS (CYLINDER MACHINE)
163. PUMPS FOR CHEMICAL INDUSTRY (SPECIAL)
164. RAILWAY SLEEPERS (M.S.)
165. RAZOR TWIN BLADE
166. R.C.C SPUN PIPES
167. RECONDITIONING OF M.S. DRUMS/BARRELS
168. RE-ROLLING COPPER AND BRASS SHEET AND RODS
169. RE-ROLLING MILLS
170. RESIN COATED SAND
171. RESIN CORED SOFT SOLDER WIRES
172. ROLLING MILL (BY INDUCTION FURNACE) & MANUFACTURE OF BARS, ANGLES, SQUARES, TUBES AND OTHERS
173. ROLLER BEARING & FORGING
174. ROLLING OF STAINLESS STEEL PATTA
175. RUBBER INSULATED PLIERS (HAND TOOLS)
176. RUBBING COMPOUND FOR AUTOMOBILES
177. SCIENTIFIC LABORATORY EQUIPMENTS
178. SCOOTER ASSEMBLING
179. SECONDARY LEAD EXTRAC-TION BY SCRAP BATTERY PLATES,PIPES & SHEET
180. SEAMLESS M.S. TUBES & PIPES
181. SELF TAPPING STEEL SCREW
182. SEWING NEEDLES
183. S.G. IRON & ALLOY STEEL
184. SHEET METAL PRODUCTS, (FERROUS/NON-FERROUS)
185. SHIP/MARINE CONTAINER
186. SHOCK ABSORBERS
187. SHOE EYELETS
188. SHOT AND GRITS BY AUTOMIZATION PROCESS
189. SHOVELS
190. SILICO MANGANESE ALLOYS
191. SILENCERS (MUFFLERS) EXHAUST & TAIL PIPE FOR ALL TYPES OF VEHICLES
192. SINTERED BEARING
193. SINTERED BUSHES
194. SINTERED METAL PRODUCTS
195. SOFT AND HARD FERRITES
196. SPANNERS
197. SPARK PLUGS
198. STEEL PLANT (ELECTRIC ARC FURNACE BASED- EAF)
199. SPHERIODAL GRAPHITE CAST IRON
200. SPRAY DRYER
201. STAINLESS STEEL HINGES
202. STAINLESS STEEL SHEET ROLLING TO PRODUCE STAINLESS STEEL UTENSILS
203. STAINLESS STEEL UTENSILS
204. STAPLE PINS,PAPER PIN, GEM CLIPS ETC.
205. STEEL CASTINGS
206. STEEL CHAIN
207. STEEL FOUNDRY
208. STEEL FURNITURES AND ELECTRICAL APPLIANCES
209. STEEL PLANT (MINI)
210. STEEL RODS AND COILS FROM SCRAPS
211. STEEL ROLLING MILL
212. STEEL STRIPS (COLD ROLLED) SILICON WITH GRAIN RIENTED FOR ELECTRIC USE
213. STEEL TRANSMISSION LINE TOWERS & ROLLING MILL TO PRODUCE STEEL SECTION
214. STEEL FURNITURES AND ELECTRICAL APPLIANCES
215. STEEL WIRE DRAWING AND GALVANIZING
216. STEEL WOOL
217. SUBMERGED ARC WELDED PIPES
218. SUBMERSIBLE PUMP MANUFACTURING
219. SUPER ENAMELLED COPPER WIRE
220. THREE WHEELERS
221. TIE-ROD ENDS
222. TIN CONTAINERS
223. TOOLROOM AND SHEET METAL PRODUCTS
224. TRACTOR TRAILERS
225. TRANSMISSION POWER FITTING
226. TUBULAR POLES
227. SUPER ENAMELLED COPPER WIRES
228. TUBULAR POLES FOR ELECTRICAL TRANSMISSION (BY FABRICATION PROCESS)
229. TUBULAR POLES OF M.S. & HIGH TENSILE STEEL
230. VACUUM CLEANERS
231. VACUUM FLASK (STAINLESS STEEL)
232. VALVES FOR REFRIGERA TION AND AIR-CONDITION
233. VEHICLE WELDING & PAINTING
234. VENETION BLIND
235. WASHING MACHINES (AUTOMATIC & COMPUTERISED)
236. WATER CONTROLLER (AUTOMATIC)
237. WATCH STRAPS/CHAINS/ BRACELETS/BELT BRASS & STAINLESS STEEL
238. WATER COOLERS
239. WELDED WIRE MESH
240. WELDING ELECTRODES
241. WICK STOVES
242. WIND MILL WINDOW FRAME (FERROUS & NON-FERROUS)
243. WRIST WATCH

359. DI ETHYL OXALATE
360. DI METHYL ORTHOPHTHALATE
361. DI-METHYL PHTHALATE
362. DICLOFENAC GEL
363. DIOCTYL PHTHALATE (DOP)
364. DI PHENYL GLYCERINE
365. DI PHENYL OXIDE
366. DINITRO-CHLORO BENZENE
367. DISTILLED WATER
368. DODECYL BENZENE SULPHONATE
369. DUSTLESS CHALK
370. EDTA & ITS SALTS
371. ELECTROLESS NICKEL PLATING ON PLASTICS
372. ENDOSULFAN
373. EPOXY RESIN BASED COMPOUND
374. ETHYL ACETATE
375. EHTYL ETHER
376. ETHYL ALCOHOL (POTABLE LIQUOR)
377. ETHYL HEXANOL
378. EXTRACTION OF ESSENTIAL OILS BY SUGAR CRITICAL FLUID (CARBON DIOXIDE) METHOD FROM FLOWERS, HERBAL & SPICES
379. FERRIC ALUM
380. FERRO CHROME LIGNO SULPHONATE
381. FERRO MANGANESE
382. FERRO SILICONE
383. FERRO VANADIUM FROM VANADIUM SLUDGE
384. FERROUS SILICATE
385. FERROUS SULPHATE
386. FERTILIZER FROM ANIMAL BLOOD & LEATHER WASTE
387. FLUORESCENT TUBE LIGHT POWDER
388. FOAMED PVC COMPOUNDING & ITS PRODUCTS
389. FORMALDEHYDE
390. FRACTIONAL DISTILLATION OF D.M.O (DEMENTHOLIZED OIL)
391. FRACTIONAL DISTILLATION OF ESSENTIAL OIL & MEDICINAL PLANT EXTRACT
392. FRICTION DUST (LIQUID & POWDER) FROM CNSL
393. FRUIT FLAVOURS
394. FURFURAL FROM RICE HUSK
395. GARLIC ACID
396. GASKET SHELLAC COMPOUND
397. GEAR OIL
398. GIBBERELLIC ACID
399. GLASS PUTTY
400. GLYCERINE
401. GOSSYPOL (POLY PHENOL) FROM COTTON SEED OIL
402. GUAR GUM POWDER
403. HAIR FIXER (HAIR GEL TYPE)
404. H - ACID
405. HENNA PASTE MAKING
406. HEPTAL DEHYDE
407. HIGH CARBON FERRO CHROME
408. HYDRATED CALCIUM SILICATE BRICK
409. HYDRATED LIME FROM SEA SHELL
410. HYDROCHLORIC ACID
411. HYDRO FLUORIC ACID
412. HYDROGEN PEROXIDE (BY AUTO-OXIDATION PROCESS)
413. ICE PACKS (SOLUTIONS TYPE, WHITE GEL TYPE, VIOLET SEMI SOLID POLYMER TYPE)
414. IMPROVING DROP POINT PARAFFIN WAX FROM 45-50^{0}C TO 75-80^{0}C
415. INDUSTRIAL ALCOHOL
416. INTEGERATED COMPLEX OF EASTER & ALLIED PRODUCTS (D.O.P, D.B.P, ETHYL ACETATE WIRE ENAMEL & CABLE JELLY)
417. IMFL (WHISKY) & COUNTRY LIQUOR
418. IRON OXIDE FOR MAKING FERITTE
419. IRON SULPHIDE
420. JUTE BATCHING OIL
421. KESH KALA TEL (HAIR DYE LOTION) (VASMOL 33, BLACK NITE TYPE)
422. L-LYSINE MONOHYDROCHLORIDE
423. LACTIC ACID FROM WHITE SUGAR BY FERMENTATION PROCESS
424. LDPE GRANULES FROM VIRGIN (LDPE RESIN)
425. LEAD EXTRACTION FROM BATTERY SCRAP
426. LEAD OXIDE (A) LEAD MONOXIDE (B) LEAD TETRA OXIDE (C) GREYLEAD OXIDE
427. LIQUID GLUCOSE & ITS BY PRODUCTS
428. LIQUID OXYGEN BOTTLING PLANT
429. LIQUID SHOE POLISH
430. LIQUID FLOOR POLISH
431. LUBE OIL VISCOSITY IMPROVED FOR P.P.G/P.E.G.
432. LUBRICANTS ASHLESS 100% COMBUSTION
433. MAGNESIUM CARBONATE AND MAGNESIUM BICARMONATE
434. MAGNESIUM HYDROXIDE POWDER
435. MAGNESIUM SILICATE
436. MAGNESIUM SULPHATE
437. MALACHITE GREEN
438. MALEIC ANHYDRIDE
439. MANGANESE SULPHATE
440. MANUFACTURING OF CARBON MONO-OXIDE WATER GAS
441. MENTHOL BOLD CRYSTALS FROM FLAKES
442. MENTHOL CRYSTAL & MENTHA OIL
443. MERCURIC OXIDE
444. METAL PRE-TREATMENT CHEMICALS
445. METHANE GAS BY SODIUM ACETATE & SODA LIME
446. METHYL ACETYL RICINOLATE
447. METOL
448. METOL FROM HYDROQUINONE & METHYLAMINE
449. MICANITE
450. MICRO NUTRIENT MIXTURE
451. MINERAL WATER
452. MINERAL WATER AND PET BOTTILNG PLANT
453. MINERAL WATER IN BOTTLES, GLASS AND POUCHES
454. MINI CEMENT PLANT (BY ROTARY KILN PROCESS)
455. MIXED FERTILIZER
456. MOSQUITO & FLIES REPELLENT AGARBATTI (INCENSE STICKS)
457. MONO CHLORO ACETIC ACID
458. MONOCROTOPHOS (TECHNICAL)
459. MOSQUITO COIL
460. MOSQUITO COIL & MAT
461. MOSQUITO MAT
462. MOTHER TINCTURE & BIO CHEMIC MEDICINES
463. NAPHTHALENE & PHENYL (INTEGRATED UNIT)
464. NATURAL MINERAL WATER BY REVERSE OSMOSIS PROCESS
465. NICKEL PLATING BRIGHTNER (PRIMARY OR CARRIER BRIGHTNER & SECONDARY BRIGHTNER)
466. NICKEL SULPHATE
467. NICOTINE FROM TOBACCO WASTE
468. NICOTINE SULPHATE FROM TOBACCO WASTE
469. NITRO BENZENE
470. NITRO CELLULOSE SANDING SEALER/LACQUER
471. NITRO MUSK
472. NITROGEN & OXYGEN GAS PLANT
473. NON-IONIC SURFACTANT (WETTING AGENT)
474. NO-CARB PASTE
475. OCTANOL
476. ORTHO NITRO PHENOL
477. OXALIC ACID FROM MOLASSES
478. OXALIC ACID FROMRICE HUSK
479. OXALIC ACID FROM TREE BARK
470. OXALIC ACID FROM WASTE VEGETABLES
471. OXYGEN GAS PLANT
472. OXYGEN GAS PLANT (AIR SEPERATION METHOD)
473. PARA-AMINO BENZOIC ACID
474. PARA-AMINO PHENOL
475. PARA TOLUENE SULPHONIC ACID
476. PECTIN FROM RAW PAPAYA
477. PERFUME (LEMON & OTHERS)

CRUDE NAPHTHA
570. TRIMETHYL AMMONIUM CHLORIDE
571. TRIPHENYL PHOSPHITE (T.P.P)
572. ULTRAMARINE BLUE (LIQUID)
573. UREA FORMALDEHYDE & MELAMINE FORMALDEHYDE POWDER
574. UNDECYLINIC ACID
575. VINYL ACETATE MONOMER
576. VITAMIN C
577. VITAMIN E
578. WASTE WATER TREATMENT PLANT FOR INDUSTRIAL SECTOR IN INDIA (ONLY MARKER SURVEY)
579. WIRE DRAWING LUBRICANT
580. WIRE ENAMEL
581. XANTHATES
582. YELLOW DEXTRIN
583. ZINC CHLORIDE
584. ZINC OXIDE
585. ZINC PHOSPHATING BY COLD PROCESS
586. ZINC SILICATE
587. ZINC STEARATE
588. ZINC SULPHATE
589. ZINC SULPHATE MONOHYDRATE
590. ACID BLACK
591. AURAMINE'O'
592. AZO DYES STUFF
593. DYE & DYE INTERMEDIATE
594. DYE INTERMEDIATES
595. MALACHITE GREEN
596. METHYLENE BLUE
597. PHTHALOCYANINE BLUE
598. PHTHALOCYANINE BLUE & GREEN
599. REACTIVE DYES
600. SULPHUR BLACK DYE
601. VAT DYES
602. WATER CHILLING PLANT
603. WADDING OIL (100%) FOR WADDING OF COTTON HOSIERY CLOTH IN THE DYEING PROCESS
604. WHITE OIL
605. WAX FLOOR POLISH

ELECTRICAL, ELECTONICS, COMPUTERS AND INFOTECH/IT PROJECTS

606. AIR CONDITIONING
607. ALUMINIUM ALLOY CONDUCTOR
608. ALUMINIUM CABLE
609. ALUMINIUM ELECTROYTIC CAPACITORS
610. AUDIO CASSETTE ASSEMBLING & RECORDING
611. AUDIO CASSETTES DUPLICATING RECORDING
612. AUDIO CASSETTES & AUDIO STUDIO
613. AUDIO CASSETTES PLANE & RECORDED
614. AUDIO MAGNETIC HEADS
615. AUDIO MAGNETIC TAPE
616. AUDIO/VIDEO CASSETTES
617. AUTO BULB/LAMPS
618. AUTOMATIC VOLTAGE STABILIZER
619. BATTERY PLATES
620. BACK OFFICE (Rs. 5000/-)
621. B/W TV & COMPUTER MONITOR PICTURE TUBE
622. BREAD BOARDS
623. CALL CENTRE
624. CAMERA (35 MM)
625. CAPACITORS
626. CARBON ELECTRODE USED FOR BATTERY CELL
627. CARBON POTETIOMETERS
628. CEILING FAN
629. CERAMIC INSULATOR
630. CHILDREN INFOTECH TRAINING INSTITUTE (Rs. 5000/-)
631. CHOKE AND PATTI
632. CHOKE AND STARTER
633. CHOKE USED FOR FLUORESCENT LAMPS
634. COLOUR TELEVISION
635. COLOUR AND BLACK & WHITE TELEVISION
636. COMPACT DISC
637. COMPACT DISC PLAYER (AUDIO/VIDEO)
638. COMPUTER EDUCATION INSTITUTE
639. COMPUTER ASSEMBLY
640. COMPUTER HARDWARE
641. COMPUTER KEYBOARD
642. COMPUTER PERIPHERALS
643. COMPUTER PRINTERS
644. COMPUTER RIBBON
645. COMPUTER RIBBON REINKING OR REFILLING
646. COMPUTER STATIONERY
647. COMPUTER STATIONERY &

IMPORTED HARDWARE PARTS
648. COMPUTER TERMINALS
649. COMPUTERISED WASHING MACHINE (AUTOMATIC)
650. COMPUTER SOFTWARE
651. CONDENSER FOR MOTOR USING MPP FILM
652. CONTENT DEVELOPMENT CENTRE (EOU) (Rs. 5000/-)
653. CONTROL PANEL BOARD
654. COOLING COIL FOR AIR CONDITIONERS
655. COPPER STRIP COIL FROM SCRAP
656. CORDLESS TELEPHONES
657. CYBER CAFE
658. CYBERKIOSK (Rs. 5000/-)
659. DATA PROCESSING CENTRE (Rs. 5000/-)
660. D.C. MICRO MOTORS
661. D.G.SETS
662. DISH ANTENNA AND CABLE T.V. NETWORK EQUIPMENT
663. DISTRIBUTION TRANSFORMERS & REPAIRS
664. DOMESTIC ELECTRICAL APPLIANCES- ROOM COOLER, WASHING MACHINE, WATER HEATER, ELECTRIC ROOM HEATER
665. E-SCHOOL
666. E-COMMERCE/BUSINESS
667. ELECTRIC ENERGY METER
668. ELECTRIC FANS
669. ELECTRIC HORN FOR AUTOMOBILE
670. ELECTRIC LAMP/GLS (INCANDESCENT LAMP)
671. ELECTRIC MIXER
672. ELECTRIC MOTORS UP TO 10 HP. REWINDING OF ALL TYPES OF MOTORS WATER PUMPS
673. ELECTRIC MOTOR WINDING (FOR FAN, MIXIES, ETC.)
674. ELECTRIC STEAM IRON
675. ELECTRICAL APPLIANCES
676. ELECTRICAL FIXTURES
677. ELECTRICAL STAMPING
678. ELECTROLYTIC CAPACITORS
679. ELECTROMAGNETIC RELAY
680. ELECTRONIC BALAST/CHOK
681. ELECTRICAL CHOKE
682. ELECTRONIC DIGITAL WATCHES
683. ELECTRONIC DIGITAL WEIGHING MACHINE
684. ELECTRONIC FIRE ALARM
685. ELECTRONIC GAS STOVE LIGHTERS
686. ELECTRONIC PRESSURE INDICATORS, ELECTRICALS, ELECTRONIC LIQUID LEVEL INDICATORS, ELECTRONIC TEMPERATURE INDICATOR, DIGITAL TACHOMETER
687. ELECTRONIC TELEPHONE INSTRUMENTS
688. ELECTRONIC TOYS
689. ELECTRONIC WATCHES & CLOCKS
690. FAX MACHINES
691. F.H.P MOTORS
692. FLOPPY DISKETTES
693. FLUORESCENT LAMP STARTER
694. FLUORESCENT TUBULAR

LAMPS WITH INTRODUCTION TO MERCURY VAPOUR LAMP
695. FRANCHISEE COMPUTER EDUCATION CENTRE (Rs. 5000)
696. GAS DETECTOR (L.P.G)
697. GENERATOR SET & PUMP SETS
698. GENERATOR (BATTERY OPERATED)
699. GIS SERVICE CENTRE (GEOGRAPHICAL INFORMATION SYSTEMS)
700. HARDWARE FITTING FOR TRANSMISSION LINE OVERHEAD LINE MATERIAL
701. HEADERS FOR TRANSISTOR ICS SEMI CONDUCTOR
702. H.T & L.T INSULATORS
703. H.T & M.V INDUSTRIAL CUBICAL SWITCH BOARD
704. INFORMATION MOVING DISPLAY (L.E.D TYPE)
705. INSURANCE CLAIM PROCESSING CENTRE (EOU) (Rs. 5000/-)
706. INTEGRATED CIRCUITS
707. INTERNET BASED STOCK TRADING (Rs. 5000/-)
708. INTERNET SERVICE PROVIDER (I.S.P.)
709. JELLY FILLED TELEPHONE CABLES
710. LAP TOP COMPUTERS
711. LEAD ACID BATTERIES
712. LEAD ACID BATTERY PLATES AND ASSEMBLING OF BATTERY
713. LEGAL TRANSCRIPTION & SECRETARIAL SERVICES CENTER (EOU)(Rs. 5000/-)
714. LIGHT EMITTING DIODES (L.E.D)
715. LINEAR ICS TRAINER KIT
716. LOUD SPEAKER
717. L.T TRANSFORMER REPAIRING
718. MEDICAL TRANSCRIPTION CENTRE
719. METAL FILM RESISTORS
720. METALLISED POLYPROPYLENE, POLYESTER FILM CAPACITOR
721. MICA BASE ELECTRONIC COMPONENTS
722. MICA PAPER WASTE PAPER FROM MICA WASTE
723. MICRO PROCESSORS TRAINER KITS BASED ON MICRO PROCESSORS
724. MINI COMPUTER (PERSONAL COMPUTER)
725. MINIATURE CIRCUIT BREAKER (M.C.B)
726. MINIATURE WATCH BATTERIES (BUTTON CELL)
727. MIXER/GRINDER (MIXI)
728. MONO CHROME COMPUTER MONITOR
729. MOTOR START ELECTROLYTIC CAPACITOR
730. MULTI LAYER P.C.B
731. MULTIPLE RELAY FOR LOW VOLTAGE
732. NEON INDICATOR
733. NEON SIGN MANUFACTURE
734. OPTICAL FIBRE CABLES
735. ON LINE SHOPPING MALL (Rs. 5000/-)
736. OPTO MECHANICAL & ELECTRICAL EQUIPMENTS
737. PHOTO COLOUR LAB
738. PICTURE TUBE (B/W)
739. PLAIN PAPER COPIER
740. PLASTIC FILM CAPACITORS
741. POLYESTER CAPACITORS
742. PORTABLE GENERATOR SET
743. PORTAL
744. PORTABLE TELEVISION(TV)
745. POWER CAPACITORS
746. POWER INVERTERS
747. POWER PLANT
748. POWER TRANSFORMERS UP TO 600 KVA
749. PRINTED CIRCUIT BOARD
750. PVC WIRES & CABLES
751. RE-CONDITIONING OF PICTURE TUBE
752. RESIN CAST CT & PT (1 KV)
753. SEMI CONDUCTOR DEVICE
754. SEMI CONDUCTORS FOR TRANSISTORS & DIODES
755. SETTING UP OF A VIDEO STUDIO
756. SMOKE DETECTORS
757. SOLAR CELLS
758. SOLAR MODULES
759. SOLAR PHOTO VOLTAIC SYSTEM
760. SOLDER FLUXES
761. SOLAR WATER HEATING PANELS
762. STEEL FURNITURE & ELECTRICAL APPLIANCES
763. STEREO AMPLIFIERS
764. STEREO CASSETTE RECORDERS/PLAYERS
765. STREET LIGHT FITTINGS SURGE SUPPRESSOR
766. TANTALUM CAPACITORS
767. TEFLON COATED ELECTRIC CABLE
768. TELEMEDICINE (DISTANCE HEALTH CARE) (Rs. 5000/-)
769. TELEPHONE CORD/CABLE
770. TELEPHONE (PUSH BUTTON TYPE)
771. TELEPHONE (PUSH BUTTON & CORDLESS)
772. TELEVISION (CTV & B/W)
773. TELEVISION (3-D)
774. TELEVISION DEFLECTION COMPONENTS
775. TELEVISION SIGNAL BOOSTERS
776. TELEVISION TUNERS
777. TRACTION BATTERIES
778. TRAINING INSTITUTE OF MEDICAL TRANSCRIPTION
779. TRANSFORMER FOR B/W TV
780. TRANSFORMER FOR VOLTAGE STABILIZER & E.H.T
781. TRANSMISSION POWER LINE FITTING
782. TRANSMISSION TOWER FITTING
783. TV AUDIO EQUIPMENT CABINETS & THEIR ASSEMBLING UNIT
784. UN-INTERRUPTED POWER SUPPLY (U.P.S)
785. VARIABLE FREQUENCY
786. VARIABLE VOLTAGE A.C. DRIVE
787. VIDEO CASSETTES (COMPLETE MANUFACTURING & ASSEMBLING)
788. VIDEO CASSETTES RECORDER (V.C.R)
789. VIDEO FILM STUDIO
790. VOLTAGE REGULATOR FOR AUTOMOBILES
791. VOLTAGE STABILIZERS
792. VOLTAGE STABLIZER & T.V. GAIN BOOSTER
793. WAX AND CHEMICAL COATED, BRAIDED TINSEL WIRE
794. WEBSITE DESIGN & E-MAIL REGISTERING
795. WELDING ELECTRODES
796. WIND ENERGY POWER PROJECT (10 MW) WIRE WOUND POTENTIOMETERS

FOOD, AGRO FOOD, PROCESSED FOOD, AGRO PLANTATION, CULTIVATION, FARMING, DAIRY/MILK, TOBACCO/PAN MASALA, BREWERY & DISTILLERY, EDIBLE OILS, EOU FOOD PRODUCTS AND ALLIED PRODUCTS

797. ALCOHOLIC BEVERAGES & VENEGAR FROM COCONUT WATER
798. ALCOHOL DRINKS FROM ETHYL ALCOHOL BY MIXING OF VARIOUS FLAVOURS
799. ANTI SCALE COMPOUND FOR ADDING INTO SUGAR JUICE BOILING
800. APPLE JUICE CONCENTRATED & DEHYDRATED FRUIT & VEGETABLES
801. ARTIFICIAL FISH MEAL FOR POULTRY FEED
802. AUTOMATIC BISCUIT PLANT
803. BABY CEREAL FOOD AND MILK POWDER
804. BACTERIA FOR CANE JUICE
805. BAKER'S YEAST
806. BAKERY INDUSTRY
807. BANANA PUREE
808. BEER & WINE
809. BEER PLANT (BREWERY)
810. BIDI
811. BIDI & CIGARETTE
812. BISCUIT PLANT

813. BREAD (AUTOMATIC PLANT)
814. BLACK PEPPER (SPICES)
815. BREAD AND BISCUITS
816. BREEDING FARM
817. BROILER CHICKEN
819. BUTTON MUSHROOM CULTIVATION & PROCESSING
820. CANNING OF RASAGULLAS IN METAL CANS
821. CAFFEIN FROM TEA WASTE
822. CANNING OF FRUITS & VEGETABLES
823. CASEIN AND BY-PRODUCTS
824. CASHEW FRUIT JUICE FROM CASHEW FRUIT APPLE
825. CASHEWNUT KERNEL EXTRACTION FROM CASHEWNUT FRUIT
826. CASHEWNUT SHELL LIQUID & KERNEL PROCESSING
827. CASHEW FENI
828. CATECHEU (BY CHEMICAL PROCESS)
829. CATTLE FEED FROM TAPIOCA
830. CHEWING & BUBBLE GUM
831. CHICKEN/SHEEP MEAT PROCESSING
832. CHOCOLATE (MILK)
833. CIGARETTE AND BEEDIES
834. COCOA BUTTER FROM COCOA MASS
835. COCONUT PRODUCTS & BY PRODUCTS PROCESS COMPLEX
836. COLD/SOFT DRINKS
837. COLLECTION OF MILK AND MILK MAKING POWDER
838. COLLECTION OF MILK AND PACKING IN POLYTHENE POUCH (1/2 KG. 1 KG. & 2 KG.)
839. CONDENSED MILK (SWEETNED)
840. CONFECTIONERY INDUSTRY (TOFFEE & CANDY, SEMI-AUTOMATIC PLANT)
841. COUNTRY LIQUOR FROM MOLASSES
842. CIGARETTE
843. DAIRY FARM AND DAIRY (MILK) PRODUCTS (PASTEURISED MILK, BUTTER, GHEE, PANEER)
844. DAIRY FARM TO PRODUCE MILK & PACKING IN POUCHES (50%) & CAN(50%)
845. DAIRY FOR MILK PROCESSING
846. DAIRY FARM (BUFALO)
847. DAL (PULSE) MILL UNIT
848. DEHYDRATION OF CARROT & GARLIC
849. DEHYDRATION & CANNING OF FRUITS & VEGETABLES
850. DEHYDRATION OF FIGS
851. DEHYDRATION OF FRUITS AND VEGETABLES
852. DEHYDRATED ONIONS AND ONION POWDER
853. DRY ICE BY BREAKING OF AIR
854. DRYING OF RED CHILLIES, HALDI, DHANIA, AND GREEN PEAS
855. EGG POWDER (40,000 EGGS PROCESSING PER DAY)
856. EXPORT OF PROCESSED FOODS AND MARINE PRODUCTS
857. FISH CANNING & POUCHING
859. FISH FARMING (PRAWN & OTHER MARINE PRODUCTS)
860. FISH MEAL
861. FLOUR MILL AND MUSTARD OIL
862. FOOD COLOUR & ORASTED GROUNDNUT GRAM PEAS, ETC IN POUCHES
863. FROG LEGS PROCESSING
864. FROZEN MEATS PROCESSING
865. FOOD FLAVOURS (WHISKY). VODKA, GRAPE, BUTTER SCOTCH)
866. FOOD PRODUCTS COMPLEX (DEHYDRATED ONIONS, GARLIC POWDER & FLAKES, CATTLE FEED, TOMATO POWDER, TOMATO PRODUCTS, CANNED FRUITS & VEGETABLES, TOMATO PURE, GROUN NUT OIL, REFIND OIL, DEHYDRATED GRAPES, BANANA POWDER & WAFFERS)
867. FRUIT JUICE, JAM, JELLIES & ALLIED PRODUCTS
868. FRUIT JUICE, PICKLES PROCESSING AND CANNING
869. FRUIT JUICE MAKING & PACKING IN PLASTIC CONTAINER/POUCHES
870. FRUIT PROCESSING (JAM & JELLIES)
871. FRUIT PULP & JUICE CONCENTRATES
872. FRUIT & VEGETABLE DRYING (FREEZE DRYING METHOD)
873. GOAT & SHEEP FARMING
874. GRAM DALL/PULSE MILL
875. GRAPE DEHYDRATION
876. HARD BOILED CANDY (TOFFEE & CANDY)
877. HERBAL CIGARETTES
878. HONEY PROCESSING & PACKAGING
879. ICE CREAM OF DIFFERENT FLAVOURS
880. ICE CREAM STABILIZER
881. ICE MAKING PLANT
882. INDIAN MADE FOREIGN LIQUOR (I.M.F.L)
883. INSTANT FOOD (IDLI MIX, DOSA MIX, GULAB JAMUN MIX)
884. INSTANT FOOD (INSTANT FOOD & FAST FOOD PARLOUR)
885. INSTANT NOODLES
886. INSTANT TEA
887. INSTANT TEA FROM BLACK TEA
888 INTEGERATED STARCH BAKING POWDER/YEAST INDUSTRY
889. IODIZED SALT
890. IODIZED SALT (ORDINARY MOISTURE-LESS/FREE FLOWING IN PLASTIC BAGS AND CONTAINERS)
891. JAM, JELLIES, FRUIT JUICE & ALLIED PRODUCTS
892. KATHA AND CUTCH
893. KHANDSARI SUGAR
894. KHANDSARI SUGAR & IMFL
895. LACTIC ACID FROM WHITE SUGAR BY FERMENTATION PROCESS
896. LACTOSE & BY PRODUCTS PROCESSING FROM MILK
897. LIQUID GLUCOSE AND ITS BYE PRODUCTS
898. MACRONI AND VERMICILLI
899. MALT EXTRACTION FROM BARLEY
900. MANGO PROCESSING (MANGO PULP, JUICE & SLICES)
901. MAYUR BRAND TYPE CHEWING TOBACCO
902. MINERAL WATER
903. MILK PRESERVATION & MARKETING TO WHOLE SELLERS (INPOUCH PACKING BY UHT TECHNOLOGY)
904. MILK PROCESSING AND PACKAGING OF MILK PRODUCTS
905. MILK PRODUCTS (CASEIN, LACTOSE, GHEE & WHEY POWDER)
906. MILK TOFFEE
907. MINI FLOUR MILL
908. MINI SUGAR PLANT
909. MISRI (PEARL SUGAR CANDIES)
910. MODERN RICE MILL
911. MURABBA
912. MUSTARD OIL EXTRACTION & REFINING
913. MUTTON TALLOW
914. NAMKEEN INDUSTRY (BHUJIA, CHANA CHUR ETC.)
915. NAMKEEN & SWEETS
916. NON-BASMATI RICE FROM PADDY
917. OLEORESIN, ESSENTIAL OIL, DYES & POWDER OF SPICES
918. OLEORESIN EXTRACTION FROM DIPTERO-CARPUT TURMINATUS AND PINUS KHASYANA
919. OLEORESIN EXTRACTION FROM CHILLI
920. PAN MASALA AND POUCH

1059. BUFFALO HORN TIP, HOOF
1060. BANQUET HALL
1061. BUTTON
1062. CALCINED PETROLEUM (C.P) COKE
1063. CANVAS SHOES
1064. CANVAS SHOES, JUNGLE BOOTS
1065. CARBON BRUSH, BRUSH HOLDER & SLIP RING
1066. CEMENT SHEETS WITH COIR FIBRE & OTHER SEGMENTS
1067. CERAMIC TILES (GLAZED) BY DOUBLE FIRING/HEATING
1068. CHILDREN RECREATION CENTRE
1069. COAL BRIQUETTES
1070. COLD STORAGE & ICE
1071. COLD STORAGE FOR FRUITS AND VEGETABLES
1072. COMPRESSOR (HERMETIC) FOR AIR CONDITIONER
1073. COSTUME JEWELLERY/ IMITATION JEWELLERY
1074. DECORATIVE LAMINATED SHEET (SUNMICA)
1075. DIAMOND CUTTING & EXPORTS
1076. DRINKING STRAW FROM PROPYLENE
1077. ENGINEERING COLLEGE
1078. ENTERTAINMENT CLUB
1079. FASHION TECHNOLOGY INSTITUTE
1080. FAST FOOD PARLOUR
1081. FAST FOOD (INSTANT FOOD & FAST FOOD PARLOUR)
1082. FIRE EXTINGUISHERS (SODA ACID TYPE)
1083. FISH NET
1084. FLORICULTURE (CUT FLOWER ROSE) WITH GREEN HOUSE
1085. FLOOR COVERING SHEET
1086. FILM STUDIO (VIDEO)
1087. FLUSH DOOR, CHIP BOARD, WOOD WOOL & OTHER INSULATING BOARDS
1088. GAS DETECTORS OF L.P.G
1089. GEMS MANUFACTURING
1090. GLASS BOTTLE BY SCRAP
1092. GOAT & SHEEP FARMING
1093. GOLD ELECTROPLATING
1094. GOLD JEWELLERY (E.O.U)
1095. GOLD PLATED SILVER JEWELLERY & CUTLERY
1096. GRANITE SLAB AND TILES
1097. GREEN HOUSE
1098. HARD CHROMIUM PLATING
1099. HEALTH CLUB AND BEAUTY PARLOUR CUM HAIR SALOON WITH SONA BATH
1100. HEALTH CLUB CUM BEAUTY PARLOUR TRAININGINSTITUTE
1101. HORN TIP,HOOVE BUTTON
1102. HOSPITAL
1103. HOSPITAL (100 BEDS)
1104. HOSPITAL (200 BEDS)
1105. ICE MAKING PLANT
1106. IMITATION AND COSTUME
1107. JEWELLERY (NECKLACE, EARRINGS EAR TOP ETC.)
1108. INITMATE SCENT CHEMICALS FROM ALL TYPES OF FLAVOUR
1109. INVESTMENT CASTING
1110. JUTE, COIR, GLASS ROPE/ SUTLI
1111. JUTE TWINE
1112. L.P.G BOTTLING PLANT
1113. L.P.G REGULATOR (DOMESTIC PURPOSE)
1114. LAMINATED PARTICLE BOARD & HARD BOARD
1115. LAMINATED SAFETY AND TOUGHENED GLASS
1116. LEASING & HIRE PURCHASE
1117. LICHEN (CHARILA)
1118. MANILA ROPES
1119. MEDICAL COLLEGE
1120. MATCH UNIT FROM WAXED PAPER
1121. MEDIUM DENSITY FIBRE BOARD
1122. MELAMINE CROCKERY
1123. MINERAL WATER
1124. MINI CEMENT PLANT
1125. MIRROR SILVER, GOLDEN, PINK, BLACK & SMOKES
1126. MODERN ADVERTISING AGENCY WITH DTP & FILM STUDIO
1127. MOTEL/SMALL HOTEL
1128. MULTI COLOUR PRINTING
1129. MULTI STOREY COMMERCIAL COMPLEX ALONGWITH RESIDENTIAL AND DELUX FLATS FOR FOREIGN TOURISTS & REVOLVING RESTAURENT AT THE TOP
1130. MULTIPLE LAMINATION INDUSTRY
1131. MUSHROOM GROWING AND PROCESSING (BY DEEP FREEZING METHOD)
1132. NEWS PAPER PRINTING
1133. NICKEL LINED INDUSTRIAL SCREEN
1134. OFFSET COLOUR PRINTING PRESS (SIX COLOUR)
1135. OFFSET PRINTING PRESS
1136. P.C.C ELECTRIC POLES
1137. PHOTOGRAPHIC DEVELOPER & FIXER
1138. PVC EXTRUSION PROFILE (DOOR & WINDOWS)
1139. POP-CORN
1140. PHOTO ETCHING OF S.S.
1141. PRE STRESSED CEMENT CONCRETE PIPES
1142. PILFER PROOF CAPS
1143. PILFER PROOF CAPS AND CROWN CAP
1144. POUCH MAKING & GRAVURE PRINTING (ROTO PRINTING)
1145. POULTRY & FISH FARMING (INTEGERATED UNIT)
1146. PRINTING OF TIN SHEETS
1147. READYMADE GARMENTS
1148. RESTAURANT
1149. ROSE PLANTATION AND ROSE OIL EXTRACTION
1150. ROTOGRAVURE PRINTING
1151. SAFETY BELTS
1152. SAFETY MATCHES
1153. SHOE LACES
1154. SILK COCOON CULTIVATION (GROWING OF SILK COCOON WARM)
1155. SILK SCREEN PRINTING FORMULATIONS FOR PLASTIC, PAPER & CLOTH
1156. SPIKENARD (JATAMANSI)
1157. STENCIL COATING SOLUTION
1158. SUGAR CANDY (MISRI)
1159. SUGAR CANE PLANTATION
1160. SUGAR CANE JUICE PRESERVATION
1161. SURAT ZARI
1162. SYNTHETIC SHOES & SOLES
1163. TEA PACKAGING INDUSTRY
1164. TENNIS BALLS
1165. THREE STAR HOTEL
1166. TRAVELLING AGENCY
1167. TRAYS, TROLLEYS FOR HOSPITAL WITH SCRATCHLESS COATING
1168. WAX EXTRACTS (TANNING POWDER)
1169. WIRE ROPE SLINGS
1170. WOOD WOOL SLAB
1171. WOODEN CANE FURNITURE WITH EXPORT POTENTIAL
1172. WOODEN FURNITURE
1173. WOODEN PANEL INCLUDING KILN SEASONING
1174. WOODEN FURNITURE
1175. WATCH CASE BUFFING
1176. WATCH DIAL
1177. WRIST WATCHES
1178. WATCHES (ELECTRONIC)
1179. ZEDOARY (KACHUR)

EDIBLE OILS, ESSENTIAL OILS LURICATIING OILS, GREASES, VEGETABLE OILS, WAXES, CAMPHOR, PERFUMES & PERFUMERY COMPOUNDS AND REFINED OILS ETC.

1180. AROMATIC PERFUMERY COMPOUND
1181. AEROSOL
1182. AGARBATTI PERFUMERY COMPOUND
1183. BEES WAX MANUFACTURE
1184. CAMPHOR
1185. CARDANOL FROM CASHEW NUT SHELL LIQUID
1186. CASTOR OIL
1187. CASTOR OIL DERIVATIVE OLEORESINS
1188. CHILLI OIL
1189. CITRONELLA OILS
1190. CLOVE OIL
1191. CONCENTRATE OF ROSE JASMINE & LILY ETC.
1192. COLOURED FLAME CANDLE

1193. CANDLES (SEMI-AUTOMATIC)
1194. CORN OIL (MAIZE OIL)
1195. DEHYDRATED CASTOR OIL
1196. EUGENOL FROM CINNAMON LEAF OIL
1197. EXTRACTION OF ESSENTIAL OIL (CARDAMON, JEERA, AJOWAN, GINGER OILS ETC. & PACKAGING OF GROUND SPICES)
1198. EXTRACTION OF JASMINE ESSENCE
1199. EXTRACTION OF ESSENTIAL OILS BY SUPER CRITICAL FLUID METHOD FROM FLOWERS, HERBS & SPICES
1200. EUCALYPTUS OIL
1201. EXTRACTION OF OIL FROM OIL SEED EXPANDEREXTRUSION TECHNOLOGY)
1202. FAT LIQUOR SULPHATED OIL
1203. FLAVOURS FOR FOOD
1204. GARLIC OIL & POWDER
1205. GINGER OIL, SANDALWOOD OIL AND NAGARMOTHA OIL
1206. GINGER OIL
1207. GINGER OIL & GINGER DUST
1208. INTEGERATED WAX COMPLEX
1209. IONONE FROM LEMON GRASS OIL
1210. JASMINE & LILLY FLOWER OIL
1211. LEMON GRASS OIL
1212. LIQUID PARAFFIN
1213. LUBE OIL & GREASE
1214. LUBRICATING OIL
1215. MENTHOL CRYSTALS
1216. MENTHOL OIL & CRYSTAL
1217. MICRO CRYSTALLINE WAX
1218. MUSTARD OIL (EDIBLE OIL)
1219. OIL FROM ARTEMISIA HERBS
1220. PALM OIL CRUSHING UNIT
1221. PAN MASALA
1222. PARAFFIN WAX
1223. PARAFFIN WAX FROM SLACK WAX
1224. REFINED OIL-SUN FLOWER OIL, GROUNDNUT OIL, STAFF FLOWER OIL & COTTON SEED OIL
1225. REFINED VEGETABLE OIL
1226. RECLAMATION OF USED ENGINE OIL
1227. RICE BRAN OIL (R.B.O)
1228. ROSE OIL EXTRACTION
1229. SMOKE LESS CANDLE
1230. SPICE OIL & OLEORESINS
1231. SOLVENT EXTRACTION PLANT (OIL CAKE BASED)
1232. SYNTHETIC ALMOND OIL
1233. SYNTHETIC TALLOW
1234. SYNTHETIC GHEE
1235. VEGETABLE OIL EXTRACTION & REFINING
1236. WADDING OIL (100%) FOR WADDING OF COTTON HOSIERY CLOTH IN DYEING PROCESS
1237. WAX EMULSION FOR TEXTILE
1238. WAX FLOOR POLISH

PAINT, ENAMEL, SOLVENTS, THINNERS, INKS & VARNISH

1239. ACRYLIC EMULSION PAINTS
1240. ALUMINIUM PAINT
1241. AUTOMOBILE PAINTS
1242. BALL POINT PEN REFILL INK
1243. BITUMINIOUS ROAD EMULSION
1244. BITUMEN
1245. BITUMINIOUS FELTS FOR WATER & DAMP PROOFING
1246. BITUMINIOUS ROAD EMULSION RAPID MEDIUM & SLOW SETTING
1247. BUFFING & POLISHING
1248. CEMENT PAINT FOR WHITE & GREY CEMENT

1249. DISPERSANT
1250. DRY DISTEMPER
1251. DRY DISTEMPER & CEMENT PAINT
1252. DUPLICATING INK BLACK FOR GESTNER DUPLICATOR
1255. EMULSION PAINTS (WATER BASED)
1256. HAMMERTONE PAINT
1257. INSULATING VARNISH & WIRE ENAMEL
1258. IRON OXIDE PIGMENTS
1259. INSULATING VARNISH (POLY VINYL BUTYRAL BASED, FFC GRADE)
1260. LIME COLOUR (CEMENT COLOUR)
1261. SYNTHETIC RED OXIDE FOR FLOORINGS
1262. SOLVENT & THINNERS
1263. MARKING INKS (WATER PROOF)
1264. METAL NAPHTHANATE (AS DRIER FOR PAINTS)
1265. N.C.PUTTY
1266. OFFSET PRINTING INK
1267. OIL BOUND DISTEMPER PAINT
1268. PAINT BRUSHES
1269. PAINT REMOVERS
1270. PAINT INDUSTRY
1271. PAINT & VARNISH
1272. PICTURE VARNISH
1273. POWDER COATING PAINT
1274. PRINTING INKS (OFFSET, FLEXO & ROTO GRAVURE)
1275. PRIMER PAINT & ENAMEL PAINT
1276. PUTTY & WATER PROOFING PAINT
1277. PRINTING INKS (FLEXO-GRAPHIC INK)
1278. PUTTY (METAL CASEMENT)
1279. RED OXIDE PRIMER (ANTI CORROSIVE)
1280. REFRECTORY PAINT (GRAPHITE BASED)
1281. SCREEN PRINTING INKS
1282. SILK SCREEN PRINTING INK FORMULATION FOR PLASTIC, PAPER, CLOTH
1283. STAMP & PAD INK
1284. STOVING PAINT
1285. SPIRIT SOLUBLE MALEIC RESIN
1286. TEXTURE PAINT
1287. THINNERS AND ITS ALLIED PRODUCTS
1288. TONER INK
1289. VARNISH THINNER (SOLVENT)
1290. VACUUM METALLIZING LACQUERS
1291. WOOD PRIMER

PHARMACEUTICAL, DRUGS, AYURVEDIC/HERBAL COSMETICS & MEDICINES, HOMOEOPATHIC MEDICINES, DISPOSABLE SYRINGE, DENTAL COLLEGE & FINE CHEMICALS ETC.

1292. AROMATIC PILLS
1293. ASPIRIN
1294. AYURVEDIC PAIN BALM OINTMENTS
1295. AYURVEDIC CHURAN AND TABLETS
1296. AYURVEDIC TABLETS (HAJMOLA TYPE)
1297. AYURVEDIC/HERBAL PHARMACY
1298. AYURVEDIC SHERBATS
1299. AYURVEDIC PRODUCTS
1300. BULK DRUGS (E.O.U)
1301. BLOOD BAGS
1302. CALCIUM GLUCONATE
1303. CAPSULE, TABLET & INJECTION WITH MODERN INSTRUMENTS
1304. CASHEW FENI
1305. CHLOROQUINONE PHOSPHATE (BULK DRUGS)
1306. CLINICAL THERMOMETER
1307. DENTAL CLINIC

Above all the "Detailed Project Reports" are available at *"ENGINEERS INDIA RESEARCH INSTITUTE"*. 4449, Nai Sarak (D), Main Road Delhi - 110 006 (India) ● Ph : 91-11-23918117, 2391 6431, 2384 0361 ● Fax : 91-11- 2391 6431 ●E-Mail : eirisidi@bol.net.in ● WebSite : www.eiriindia.org

1308. DENTAL COLLEGE
1309. DENTAL GRADE EUGENOL
1310. DEXTROSE MONOHYDRATE, LIQUID GLUCOSE
1311. DEHYDRATED ONION & ONION POWDER
1312. DEXTROSE POWDER (ANHYDROUS FROM STARCH)
1314. DEXTROSE SALINE SOLUTION
1315. DISTILLERY (I.M.F.L)
1316. DISPOSABLE NEEDLES FOR SYRINGES
1317. DISPRIN
1318. DISTILLED WATER
1319. EMPTY HARD GELATINE CAPSULES
1320. FILLING & PACKING OF CAPSULES
1321. GLUCOSE - D - POWDER
1322. GLYCERINE
1323. HERBAL COSMETICS
1324. HERBAL SHAMPOO
1325. HERBAL HAIR OILS (AYURVEDIC)
1326. HOMOE & BIO-MEDICINES WITH MOTHER TINCTURE
1327. HOMOEPATHIC MEDICINES
1328. HYPODERMIC NEEDLES
1329. I.V. FLUIDS
1330. IBUPROFEN
1331. INFUSION & TRANSFUSION SETS (I.V. SET)
1332. INJECTABLE FOR PHARMACEUTICALS
1333. INJECTION AMPOULES PACKAGING BOX
1334. INTEGERATED SURGICAL COTTON
1335. ICE MAKING PLANT
1336. ICE & COLD STORAGE
1337. LACTOSE & BY PRODUCTS PROCESSING FROM MILK
1338. LICHEN (JATAMANSI CHARILA)
1339. LIQUID GLUCOSE AND ITS BY-PRODUCTS
1340. L-LYSINE MONOHYDRO CHLORIDE
1341. LIQUID GLUCOSE FROM POTATOES
1342. MEDICAL COLLEGE
1343. NICOTINE FROM TOBACCO WASTE
1344. OINTMENT-AYURVEDIC (YELLOW & WHITE)
1345. PHARMACEUTICAL AND FOOD GRADE GELATINE
1346. PHARMACEUTICAL INDUSTRY (TABLETS, CAPSULES, LIQUID, GEL, OINTMENT POWDER INJECTABLE)
1347. PHARMACEUTICAL UNIT (EOU) WITH FORMULA TIONS, INJECTABLES, ETC. PYRIDINE & DERIVATIVES
1348. SALT (IODIZED SALT)
1349. SALINE & INJECTION WATER
1350. SALINE WATER & DEXTROSE SOLUTION (I.V.FLUID IN PLASTIC BOTTLES)
1351. SORBITOL
1352. STARCH (MAIZE)
1353. SURGICAL ADHESIVE PLASTER
1354. SURGICAL BANDAGES
1355. SURGICAL GLOVES
1357. SURGICAL COTTON
1358. SURGICAL COTTON AND BANDAGE
1359. SYNTHETIC CAMPHOR POWDER
1360. TABLETS & CAPSULES
1361. TISSUE CULTURE
1362. TINCTURE FROM RECTIFIED SPIRIT
1363. TRIMETHOPIME
1364. VETERENARY MEDICINES (ONLY FORMULATIONS)
1365. VITAMIN 'C', SORBITOL' ANHYDROUS DEXTROSE, STARCH

PULP, PAPER, STRAW/GREY BOARD, KRAFT PAPER, PACKAGING, PAPER CARRY BAGE, PAPER FROM AGRO WASTE & STATIONERY ETC.

1366. AMMONIA PAPER
1367. AUTOMATIC BOOK BINDING
1368. ADHESIVE (FEVICOL TYPE)
1369. ALL PIN & GEM CLIPS
1370. CARBON PAPER
1371. CARD BOARD
1372. CARBON LESS PAPER
1373. CELLPHANE PAPER
1374. COMPUTER FORMS & SECURITY PRINTING PRESS
1375. CORRUGATED BOARD & BOX (PRINTED & LAMINATED)
1376. CORRUGATED BOARD AND BOXES FROM FROM CARD BOARDS
1377. CORRUGATED CARTONS FROM PLAIN PAPERS
1378. CORRUGATRED PACKING & MATERIAL (BULB & TUBES PACKING)
1379. DESK TOP PUBLISHING
1380. DEFOAMING AGENT FOR PAPER PLANT
1381. DRINKING STRAW PAPER
1382. D.T.P CUM OFFSET PRESS
1383. EGG TRAYS
1384. EXERCISE NOTE BOOK, REGISTER AND PAD
1385. FLEXOGRAPHIC INK
1386. GREETING CARD BY OFFSET PRESS
1387. HAND MADE PAPER FILTER PAPER
1388. HARD BOARD
1389. INJECTION AMPOULES PACKAGING BOXES
1390. INSULATIING PAPER
1391. KRAFT PAPER
1392. KRAFT PAPER FROM BAGASSE
1393. LAMINATED PACKAGING PAPER WITH PRINTING
1394. LAMINATION & COATING ON PAPER
1395. M.G. PAPER FROM WASTE PAPER
1396. MILL PAPER FROM WASTE PAPER
1397. MILL BOARD FROM RICE & WHEAT STRAWS
1398. MILL BOARD FROM WASTE PAPER
1399. MINI PAPER PLANT FROM SISAL
1400. MINI PAPER PLANT
1401. MULTI WALL PAPER SACKS
1402. NEWS PAPER FOR CHILDREN
1403. NEWS PRINT PAPER FROM RICE STRAW BAGASSE
1404. NEWS PAPER CHILDRENS
1405. NEWS PRINT PAPER
1406. OFFSET AND TREADLE TYPE PRINTING PRESS
1407. MILL BOARD BASED ON RICE STRAW
1408. PAPER AND BOARD FROM STRAW
1409. PAPER & PAPER PRODUCTS
1410. PAPER ENVELOPES
1411. PAPER CARRY BAGS
1412. PAPER BOARD CARTON
1413. PAPER CONES FOR LOUD SPEAKERS
1414. PAPER FROM AKRA
1415. PAPER FROM BAGASSE WITH CORRUGATED BOARD & BOXES
1416. PAPER FROM BAMBOO
1417. PAPER GLASSES FOR BEVERAGES
1418. PAPER FROM RICE HUSK & WHEAT HUSK
1419. PAPER FROM TREE BARK, EUCALYPRUS WOOD
1420. PAPER PRODUCTS
1421. PAPER PLANT (WHITE WRITING & NEWS PAPER FOR PULP & WASTE PAPER)
1422. PAPER PLATES, PAPER GLASS
1423. PAPER CONES & TUBES
1425. PAPER PLANT WITH DTP & PRINTING & PUBLISHING UNIT
1426. PAPER BASED PHENOLIC SHEET
1427. PAPER CUP FOR ICE CREAM
1428. PAPER TUBES SPIRAL WINDING COMPOSIT CONTAINER
1429. PAPER LABLE FOR BEER BOTTLES
1430. PARTICLE BOARD & BLACK BOARD WITH SANDING & LAMINATION OF PARTICLE BOARD
1431. PARTICLE BOARD FROM RICE HUSK
1432. POUCH FILLING & MAKING FOR TOMATO SAUCE
1433. POUCH MAKING &

GRAVURE PRINTING
1434. PROCESSING OF PAPER FOR FEEDING IN COMPUTER
1435. PULP FROM BAMBOO & WOOD
1436. PAPER FILES
1437. PLAYING CARDS
1438. ROSIN SIZING AGENT (FOR PAPER PLANT)
1439. SAND PAPER
1440. SANITRY NAPKINS
1441. SILICON COATED PAPER
1442. STENCIL PAPER
1443. STRAW BOARD AND GREY BOARD
1444. STRAW BOARD & MILL BOARD
1445. STRAW BOARD AND PAPER BOARD
1446. TISSUE PAPER FACIAL
1447. TISSUE MOIST TOILETERY CLEANSING TISSUE AND RELATED PRODUCTS
1448. TISSUE PAPER ROLLS
1449. TETRA PACK FOR MILK PACKAGING, GHEE & OTHER LIQUIDS
1450. TOILET PAPER ROLLS
1451. TOILET PAPER & NAPKINS
1452. WAX COATED PRINTED PAPER
1453. WET FACE FRESHNER TISSUE
1454. WHITE WRITING & PRINTING PAPER
1455. WRITING & PRINTING PAPER (PAPER MILLS)

PLASTIC, B.O.P.P, ACRYLIC, DISPOSABLE PLASTIC PRODUCTS, PET PRODUCTS, P.V.C, H.D.P.E, P.P, L.D.P.E., P.U, A.B.S, THERMOFOARMING, MASTER BATCHES, & POLYMER AND RUBBER PRODUCTS, TYRE, TUBE, ADHESIVE, SHEET, COIR & MANY OTHERS

1456. ABS GRANULES FROM ABS SCRAPS FROM OLD T.V. CABINETS, WHITE GOODS ETC.
1457. ACRYLIC BEADS
1458. ACRYLIC COPOLYMER EMULSION
1459. ACRYLIC LATEX
1460. ACRYLIC SHEET
1461. ACRYLIC SHEET & MOULDED PRODUCTS
1462. ACRYLIC TEETH
1463. AUTO TUBES
1464. AUTO FLAPS FOR TRUCKS & BUSES
1465. AUTO TYRES & TUBES
1466. BABY BOTTLES (PLASTIC) WITH WHITESILICON RUBBER NIPPLES
1467. B.O.P.P. FILM
1468. B.O.P.P. PRESSURE SENSITIVE SELF ADHESIVE TAPE
1469. BABY NIPPLE (SILICON)
1470. BABY NIPPLE (BIG SIZE)
1471. BALLOON PLASTIC ADVERTISING
1472. BLISTER FILM PVC
1473. BLISTER PACKAGING & POUCH PAKAGING
1474. BLOW MOULDING PLASTIC CONTAINER
1475. COATING ON METALIZED POLYESTER FILM/METALISED PAPER/ ALIMINIUM FOIL
1476. COATING ON PLASTIC (ELECTROLYSIS) & GLASS
1477. COIR FOAM (RUBBERISED)
1478. COLOUR COATING ON PLASTICS
1479. COLOUR MASTER BATCHES FOR VARIOUS PLASTICS
1480. CYCLE TYRES AND TUBES
1481. DISPOSABLE PLASTIC CUPS GLASSES, ETC.
1482. DISPOSABLE PLASTIC SYRINGES & NEEDLES
1483. DISPOSABLE PLASTIC SYRINGES
1484. DOUGH MOULDING COMPOUND (D.M.C)
1485. EPOXY RESIN
1486. EXPANDED POLYESTRENE MOULDING (THERMOCOLE)
1487. F.R.P AUTO,SCOOTER ROOFS & CEILINGS
1488. F.R.P PRODUCTS (HELMET, WASHBASIN SHEETS, ROOFING SHEETS)
1489. FIBRE REINFORCED PLASTIC (HIGH PRESSURE MOULDING WITH SMC BMC AND DMC)
1490. FIELD RUBBER CONVERTED TO THE 60% LATEX RUBBER
1491. FLEXIBLE P.U. FOAM
1492. FORMALDEHYDE CROCKERY & OTHER ITEMS
1493. FORMALDEHYDE RESIN (UREA, PHENOL,MELEMINE)
1494. GASKET SHEET
1495. GUM BOTTLE (PVC)
1496. GLASS BEADS
1497. HDPE COATED PAPER SACK
1498. H.D.P.E. BAGS
1499. H.D.P.E. CONTAINERS (BLOW MOULDING)
1500. H.D.P.E. CONTAINER, POLY JARS BY INJECTION MOULDING (FOOD GRADE)
1501. H.D.P.E. JERRY CANS
1502. HDPE MANUFACTURING FROM ETHYLALCOHOL
1503. H.D.P.E PIPE AND FITTINGS
1504. H.D.P.E. PIPES
1505. H.D.P.E PRINTED BAGS
1506. H.D.P.E TWINES AND ROPES
1507. H.D.P.E. & L.D.P.E PIPES AND FITTINGS
1508. H.D.P.E/PP BOX STRAPPING
1509. H.D.P.E/PP WOVEN SACKS USING PLAIN LOOMS
1510. HOLOGRAM STICKERS-3D
1511. H.M BAG PLANT WITH PRINTING UNIT
1512. HAWAI CHAPPALS (RUBBER)
1513. I.V PLASTIC BOTTLE
1514. ICE CREAM CUP (PLASTIC)
1515. INJECTION MOULDED AUTO COMPONENTS
1516. INJECTION & BLOW MOULDED PLASTIC PRODUCTS
1517. INJECTION MOULDED PLASTIC PRODUCTS
1518. INTEGERATED COMPLEX ESTER'S & ALLIED PRODUCTS (D.O.P,D.B.P, & ETHYL ACETATE, BUYTL ACETATE, WIRE ENAMELS, JELLY CABLE COMPOUND)
1519. L.D.P.E. (LOW DENSITY POLY ETHYLENE) GRANULES FROM VIRGIN (L.D.P.E. RESIN)
1520. INTEGERATED SURGICAL RUBBER GOODS INDUSTRY
1521. INJECTION MOULDED PLASTIC BALLS
1522. L.D.P.E FROM ETHYL ALCOHOL
1523. LDPE MOULDED PRODUCTS
1524. LAMINATION OF COEXTRUSION MULTILAYER FILM IN ROLL FORM
1525. LATEX RUBBER
1526. LATEX RUBBER CONDOM
1527. MASTER BATCHES (COLOURED, P.V.C, L.D.P.E, H.D.P.E, ETC.)
1528. MELAMINE FORMALHYDE RESIN
1529. MOULDED LUGGAGE
1530. MULTI-LAYER (3 LAYER BAGS)
1531. MULTI-LAYER (3 LAYER) FILM WITH LAMINATION & PRINTING
1532. OIL SEAL
1533. PET BOTTLE/CONTAINERS
1534. PET BOTTLES FROM PRE FORM
1535. PET BOTTLE & MINERAL WATER
1536. PET PRE-FORM FROM PET RESIN
1537. PET PRE-FORM CUM PET BOTTLES
1538. PET PRE-FORM PET BOTTLES CUM MINERAL WATERS
1539. POLY CARBONATE RESIN
1540. PTFE COMPONENTS
1541. PU/PVC SOLE FOR SPORT SHOE BY IMPORTED M/C.
1542. PVC BATTERY SEPARATOR
1543. P.V.C COMPOUNDS (FRESH)
1544. P.V.C COMPOUNDS (SCRAP)
1545. P.V.C ELECTRICAL INSULATING TAPE
1546. P.V.C. EXTRUSION PROFILES
1547. P.V.C FITTINGS
1548. P.V.C FLEXIBLE FUSIBLE POWDER HEAT FUSIBLE POWDER
1549. P.V.C GRANULES (FOR

INSULATION & SHEETS GRADES)
1550. P.V.C GRANULES FROM PVC SCRAPS (WITH POLLUTION CONTROL)
1551. P.V.C HOSES
1552. P.V.C LEATHER CLOTH
1553. P.V.C FLEXIBLE PIPES
1554. P.V.C PIPES AND FITTINGS
1555. POLYTHENE BAGS (PRINTED)
1556. PVC PLASTICS FILM SHEET SOFT/RIGID
1557. PVC RESIN AND COMPOUND
1558. PVC RULAR
1559. PVC STABLIZERS (SINGLE PACK SYSTEM)
1560. PVC WIRE AND CABLES
1561. PAPER BASED PHENOLIC SHEET FOR ELECTRICAL
1562. PHENOL FORMALDEHYDE RESIN
1563. PHENOLIC RESIN
1564. PLASTIC BEADS FROM PLASTIC SCRAPS
1565. PLASTIC BUTTONS
1566. PLASTIC CANS
1567. PLASTIC COLLAPSIBLE TUBE
1568. PLASTIC CORRUGATED SHEET & BOXES
1569. PLASTIC FILM AND SHEETS WITH PRINTING FLEXO & ROTO/LDPE/HDPE/PP/HM/PVC
1570. PLASTIC FILTER MASTER BATCH & OTHER MASTER BATCHES FOR VARIOUS PLASTICS
1571. PLASTIC JERRY CANS
1572. PLASTIC GRANULES OR POWDER FROM PLASTIC SCRAP
1573. PLASTIC INJECTION MOULDED T.V. CABINETS
1574. PLASTIC ITEMS MANUFAC TURE FROM POWDER MELAMINE
1575. PLASTIC GOODS
1576. PLASTIC PIPES & TARPAULINES
1577. PLASTIC SHEET FROM SCRAP
1578. PLASTIC PLANT (BLOW MOULDING & INJECTION MOULDING)
1579. PLASTIC PRODUCTS (GOLD, SILVER, NICKEL)
1580. PLASTIC TOYS
1581. POLYESTER BEADING
1582. POLYESTER FILM
1583. POLYTHENE BAGS & AUTOMATIC PRINTING
1584. POLYTHENE PRINTED BAGS
1585. POLYURETHANE FOAM AND ITS PRODUCTS
1586. PROPYLENE FILM (PRINTED) & BAG MANUFACTURING
1587. PLASTIC MATS
1588. RAINBOW COLOUR ON PVC FILM & SHEET
1589. RED MUD PVC PIPES AND FITTINGS
1590. RE-RUBBERISED OF SOLID TYPE
1591. RESIN COATED SAND REXINE
1592. REXINE CLOTH & ALLIED PRODUCTS
1593. RUBBER ADHESIVE
1594. RUBBER AUTO PARTS
1595. RUBBER BELTING
1596. RUBBER MOULDING UNIT INCLUDING LINING RUBBER SHEETING
1597. RUBBER RECLAIMING
1598. RUBBER ROLLERS FOR TEXTILE MILLS & PAPER INDUSTRIES
1599. RUBBER & PLASTIC SHEETS, MATS & FLAPS
1600. RUBBER SHEET AND ALLIED HOSPITAL RUBBER GOODS
1601. RUBBERIZED PVC GASKET
1602. RUBBERISED COIR
1603. RUBBER COMPOUND FOR AUTOMOBILES
1604. SAFETY BELTS
1605. SILVER AND GOLD PLATING ON PVC AND NYLON-6
1606. SILICONE RUBBER NIPPLES/ TEATS
1607. SPECTACLE FRAMES (PLASTIC)
1608. SPUNGE RUBBER
1609. SURGICAL EXAMINATION GLOVES
1610. SYNTHETIC PEARL COATING ON POLYSTYRENE BEADS
1611. SYNTHETIC RUBBER ADHESIVE
1612. TEFLON MANUFACTURING
1613. TEFLON TAPE
1614. TEFLON TAPES & CABLES
1615. THERMOCOLE SHEET AND MOULDED PRODUCTS EXPANDED POLYESTERENE EXTRUSION PROFILES
1616. THERMOFORMED PACKAGING (BLISTER PACKAGING & POUCH PACKAGING)
1617. THERMOPLASTIC POLYURETHANE
1618. THERMOFORMED CUPS, PLATES & GLASS WITH HIPS SHEET
1619. THERMOCOLE
1620. THERMOCOLE BASED DISPOSABLE GLASS, CUPS & PLATES
1621. TOOTH BRUSHES
1622. TOY BALLOON, DECORA TIVE & INDUSTRIAL BALLOONS
1623. TREAD RUBBER
1624. TYRE RETREADING (HOT)
1625. TYRE RETREADING BY COLD PROCESS
1626. TYRE TUBES & FLAPS
1627. TYRE & TUBES
1628. UNSATURATED POLYESTER FOR REXINE
1629. V-BELT AND FAN BELT
1630. VINYL ASBESTOS AND PVC WALL PAPER
1631. VITON (FLUORO ELASTOMER)

SOAP, COSMETICS & PERFUMS

1632. ACID SLURRY, SYNTHETIC DETERGENT POWDER
1632. ACID SLURRY
1633. AGARBATTI SYNTHETIC, PERFUMERY COMPOUND
1634. AFTER SHAVE LOTION
1635. ANTISEPTIC CREAM
1636. BETA IONONE
1637. BLEACHING POWDER
1638. BLUE DETERGENT POWDER
1639. CLEANING POWDER (VIMTYPE)
1640. COLD CREAM
1641. COLOURED FLAME & PERFUMED CANDLES (RED, BLUE, GREEN FLAME)
1642. COSMETIC INDUSTRY (MODERN)
1643. COSMETIC INDUSTRY (SHAMPOO, SPRAY PERFUME, TALCUM POWDER
1644. DETERGENT POWDER (ARIEL TYPE)
1645. DETERGENT POWDER (NIRMA TYPE) FULLY AUTOMATIC PLANT
1646. DETERGENT WASHING POWDER
1647. FISH OIL SOAP
1648. GLYCERINE TRANSPARENT SOAP
1649. HAIR REMOVING CREAM
1650. HERBAL COSMETICS
1651. HERBAL SHAMPO & CREAM
1652. HERBAL/AYURVEDIC COSMETICS
1653. INCENSE POWDER, INCENSE STICKS & INCENSE CAKE
1654. OPTICAL WHITENERS
1655. ROSE OIL EXTRACTION
1656. SHAMPOOS (COCONUT OIL BASED COLD PROCESS)
1657. SHAVING CREAM
1658. SINDUR (KUMKUM)
1659. SOAP COATED PAPER
1660. SPRAY DRIED DETERGENT POWDER
1661. STAIN REMOVER
1662. TALCUM POWDER (FACE & TOILET POWDER)
1663. TOILET AND HERBAL SOAP
1664. TOOTH PASTE & POWDER
1665. WASHING DETERGENT POWDER AND WASHING SOAP
1666. WASHING POWDER LIQUID DETERGENTS, LOTION & SHAMPOO

TEXTILE INDUSTRIES, READYMADE GARMENTS, COTTON, DYEING, BLEACHING, CLOTH, HOSIERY, POWER LOOM, HAND LOOM, WOOLLEN, SILK, SOCKS, SURGICAL COTTON & MANY OTHERS

1667. ANGORA RABBIT WOOL
1668. BUCKRAM
1669. CANVAS SHOES, JUNGLE BOOT, BOOT RUBBER KNEES & BOOT COMBAT
1670. CARPET FROM COTTON WASTE
1671. CERAMIC THREAD GUIDE
1672. COTTON BUDS/SWABS
1673. COTTON FROM WASTE YARN
1674. COTTON ROLLS
1675. COTTON SPIDERS FOR LOUD SPEAKERS
1676. DENIM CLOTH
1677. DENIM CLOTH (INTEGERATED UNIT WITH BLEACHING, DYEING AND PRINTING)
1678. DISPERSENT FOR TEXTILE
1679. DYEING & BLEACHING
1680. DYEING OF HANK YARN
1681. EMULSIFIER FOR WOOL BATCHING OIL
1682. EMBROIDERY ON FABRICS
1683. GARMENT DYEING, WASHING & STITCHING (JEANS, JACKETS, SKIRTS & SHIRTS)
1684. GOVES KNITTING
1685. GUNNY BAGS
1687. I IDPE WOVEN SACKS
1688. HDPE TARPAULINS USING PLAIN LOOM WITH LAMINATION
1689. HDPE/PP WOVEN SACKS USING CIRCULAR LOOMS
1690. HOSIERY CLOTH (COTTON) PROCESSING (BLEACHING, DYEING, FINISHING OF CLOTH)
1691. HOSIERY INDUSTRY
1692. HOSIERY MERCERISING
1693. HOSIERY PRODUCTS LIKE VEST, BRIEF, T-SHIRTS & SOCKS
1694. JACQUARD FABRICS
1695. JUTE COIR, GRASS ROPE/ SUTLI MAKING
1696. JUTE FELT
1697. JUTE TWINES
1698. KNITTED FABRICS
1699. LAMINATED JUTE BAGS
1700. LAMINATION OF HDPE WOVEN CLOTH (JUTE,COTTON, PAPER)
1701. NYLON YARN CRIMPING, DOUBLING AND BLEACHING
1702. PIGMENT BINDER FOR TEXTILE PRINTING
1704. POLYESTER RESIN FOR WIRE ENAMEL
1705. POLYESTER RESIN
1706. POLYESTER YARN FROM WASTE POLYESTER ZIP FASTENERS
1707. POWER LOOM
1708. READYMADE GARMENTS & HOSIERY
1709. READYMADE GARMENTS MERCHANDISE
1710. READYMADE GARMENTS & COVERS
1711. READYMADE GARMENTS & EMBROIDERY OF GOWNS, SHIRTS, BLOUSES, T-SHIRTS ETC. (ONLY LADIES)
1712 READYMADE SALWAR SUIT
1713. RECOVERY OF NYLON FROM NYLON WASTE
1714. ROTARY PRINTING AND DYEING ON COTTON, SYNTHETIC TEXTILE
1715. SANITARY NAPKINS
1716. SCREEN PRINTING ON COTTON CLOTH
1717. SEWING THREAD REELS & BALLS MAKING INDUSTRIES
1718. SCREEN PRINTING ON COTTON, POLYESTER & ACRYLIC
1719. SHAWLS (WOOLLEN)
1720. SHOE LACES
1721. SILK FABRICS ON HANDLOOM
1722. SOCKS KNITTING
1723. SPINNING, DOUBLING DYEING MERCERISING & BLEACHING OF COTTON YARN
1724. SPINNING & CARDING OF WOOL INTO YARNS
1725. STARCH BOOK BINDING CLOTH
1726. SURAT JARI
1727. SURGICAL COTTON & BANDAGE
1728. SYNTHETIC TEXTILE INDUSTRY(SUITING, SHIRTING, SAREES) TERRY CLOTH
1729. T-SHIRTS
1730. TOWELS, BED SHEET COVERS
1731. TERRY TOWEL
1732. TERRY FABRICS WEAVING UNIT
1733. TEXTILE AUXILLIARIES & CHEMICALS
1734. TEXTILE BLEACHING, DYEING & FINISHING & PRINTING OF COTTON FABRICS
1735. TEXTILE (HOSIERY)
1736. TEXTILE MILL
1737. TEXTILE DYEING & PRINTING
1738. TEXTILE PRINTING (JOB WORK)
1739. TEXTILE PIGMENT PRINTING BINDER
1740. TOWEL (TERRY)
1741. VELVET CLOTH BY FLOCKING PROCESS
1742. VISCOSE STAPLE FIBRE
1743. WADDING OIL (100%) FOR WADDING OF COTTON HOSIERY CLOTH IN THE DYEING PROCESS
1744. WEAVING OF DASUTI CLOTH WITH PRINTING, DYEING, EMBROIDERY & FINISHING
1745. WASHING OF JEANS & OTHER GARMENTS
1746. WORSTED WOOLLEN YARN CLOTH
1747. ZARI GLITTER SALMA SITARA OF PLASTIC FILM

INFOTECH/IT, HOSPITALITY, HOSPITAL, COLLEGE, SCHOOL, MEDICAL, ENTERTAINMENT CLUB, WARE HOUSING & REAL ESTATE, PROJECTS

1748. AMUSEMENT PARK
1749. AMUSEMENT PARK CUM WATER PARK
1750. BANQUET HALL
1751. CALL CENTER (DOMESTIC)
1752. CALL CENTER (INTERNATIONAL)
1753. CHILDREN RECREATION CENTRE
1754. COLD STORAGE
1755. COMMUNITY HALL
1756. COMPUTER EDUCATION INSTITUTE
1757. COMPUTER SOFTWARE
1758. COLLEGE
1759. CYBER CAFE
1760. DENTAL CLINIC
1701. DENTAL COLLEGE
1762. DIAGONOSTIC CENTRE
1763. E-COMMERCE/BUSINESS
1764. E-SCHOOL (Rs. 5000/-)
1765. ENGINEERING COLLEGE
1766. ENTERTAINMENT CLUB
1767. ENTERTAINMENT CLUB, HOLIDAY RESORT, 4 STAR HOTEL, AMUSEMENT PARK CUM WATER PARK, MUSHROOM & ITS PRODUCTS, FISH FARMING, LAKE FOR BOATING, DEER PARK
1768. FASHION TECHNOLOGY INSTITUTE
1769. FAST FOOD PARLOUR
1770. FIVE STAR HOTEL
1771. FOOD PARLOUR
1772. FRANCHISE TRAINING PROGRAMME FOR IIT & ENGINEERING ENTRANCE EXAMS.
1773. GOLF COURSE
1774. HEALTH CLUB, BEAUTY PARLOUR
1775. HEALTH CLUB AND FITNESS CENTER
1776. HEALTH RESORTS
1777. HOLIDAY RESORTS
1778. HOLIDAY RESORT CUM

ENTERTAINMENT CLUB WITH 4 STAR HOTEL
1779. HOSPITALS
1780. ICE CREAM PARLOUR
1781. INTERNET SERVICE PROVIDER (I.S.P.)
1782. MEDICAL COLLEGE
1783. MEDICAL COLLEGE, HOSPITAL & RESEARCH INSTITUTE
1784. MEDICAL TRANSCRIPTION CENTRE
1785. MENTAL RETARDATION HOSPITAL & CEREBRAL PALSY
1786. MOTEL/SMALL HOTEL
1787. MULTISTOREY COMMERCIAL COMPLEX
1788. MULTISTOREY RESIDENTIAL COMPLEX
1789. NURSERY SCHOOL
1790. NATURE CARE CENTRE
1791. NURSING HOME
1792. ONLINE SHOPPING MALL (RS. 5000/- REPORT)
1793. PORTAL
1794. REHABILITATION CENTRE FOR AGED & NEEDY PERSONS
1795. RESIDENTIAL CUM COMMERCIAL COMPLEX
1796. RESTAURANT
1797. RESTAURANT WITH PUB
1798. SCHOOL (PRIMARY)
1799. SCHOOL (HIGHER SECONDARY)
1800. THREE STAR HOTEL
1801. TOURIST CLUB
1802. TRAINING INSTITUTE FOR MEDICAL TRANSCRIPTION
1803. VIDEO FILM STUDIO
1804. WARE HOUSE
1805. WEBSITE DESIGN & E-MAIL REGISTERING

AGRO BASED INDUSTRIES

1806. COAL BRIQUETTES FROM AGROWASTE
1807. FURFURALFROM RICEHULL
1808. MUSHROOM CULTIVATION & PROCESSING (BUTTON)
1809. MUSHROOM GROWING & PROCESSING WITH AIR CONDITIONING
1810. MUSHROOM CULTIVATION & PROCESSING UNIT DEHYDRATION & PACKAGING OF OYSTER & PADDY STRAW MUSHROOMS
1811. ORGANIC MANURE
1812. PAPAYA CULTIVATION
1813. PAPAYA & TOMATO CULTIVATION
1814. PROCESSING & UTILISATION OF COCONUT
1815. PROCESSING OF SHEEP HAIR TO PRODUCE WOOL

BAKERY, CONFECTIONERY & FOOD PRODUCTS

1816. AGROLACTOR SOYA MILK
1817. APPLE FRUIT JUICE WITH CANNING BOTTLING
1818. AYURVEDIC SHARBAT
1819. BAKERY UNIT (PASTRIES, BREAD, BUNS, CAKE, TOFFEE ETC.)
1820. BAKING POWDER
1821. BANANA & ITS BY PRODUCTS
1822. BANANA POWDER
1823. BANANA WAFERS
1824. BANANA CULTIVATION
1825. BEER INDUSTRY
1826. DEHULLING OF JAUN FOR BEER
1827. BEER & WINE
1828. BEER, ALCOHOL, IMFL
1829. BESEN PLANT
1830. BISCUIT PLANT
1831. BREAD & BISCUIT PLANT
1832. BOTTLING PLANT COUNTRY LIQUOR FROM RECTIFIED SPIRIT
1833. BRANDY
1834. BREAD RUSKS
1835. CANNED FRUITS & VEGETABLES
1836. CANNING & PRESERVATION OF MEAT
1837. CANNING & PRESERVATION OF VEGETABLES
1838. CANNING OF MANGO PULP & MANGO SLICES
1839. CARBONATED BEVERAGS
1840. CASHEW FENI
1841. CASHEW NUT (DRIED & FRIED)
1842. CATTLE BREEDING
1843. CATTLE BREEDING & DAIRY FARM TO PRODUCE MILK
1844. CATTLE FEED FROM TAPIOCA
1845. CHEWING GINGER & AMLOKI
1846. CHEWING GUM
1847. CHILLI SAUCE
1848. CHILLI POWDER
1849. CHOCOLATE
1850. CIDER PLANT
1851. COCOA POWDER
1852. COCOA BUTTER & COCOA POWDER
1853. COCONUT SHELL POWDER
1854. COCONUT WATER
1855. COCONUT SWEET (WATERY)
1856. COCONUT MILK POWDER (DEHYDRATED)
1857. COCONUT PRODUCTS & BY PRODUCTS (INTEGRATED PLANT)
1858. COLD DRINK
1859. CURRY POWDER
1860. DAIRY FOR MILK PROCESSING (GHEE, BUTTER & PANEER)
1861. DAIRY PRODUCTS
1862. DAIRY PRODUCTS MILK PACKAGING IN POUCH (GHEE, BUTTER, ETC.
1863. DAIRY FARM TO PRDUCE MILK WITH PACKAGING (COW)
1864. DAIRY FARM TO PRDUCE MILK WITH PACKAGING (BUFALLOE)
1865. DAIRY FARM & MILK PRODUCTS
1866. DAL MOTH, CHANACHUR & BHUJIYA
1867. DEHYDRATION OF FRUITS & VEGETABLE
1868. DESICCATED COCONUT POWDER FROM COCONUTS
1869. DEHYDRATION & CANNING OF FRUITS & VEGETABLES
1870. DRY FRUIT ROASTING & PACKAGING
1871. DRYING OF RED CHILLIES, HALDI, DHANIYA, PEAS & GROUND NUT
1872. EGG POWDER
1873. FISH CANNING IN TIN & POUCHES
1874. FISH DEHYRATION (DRYING OF FISH)
1875. FISH MEAL
1876. FISH PROCESSING (BEAST FREEZING PROCESSES)
1877. FLAVOURS FOR FOOD INDUSTRIES
1878. FLOUR MILL (ROLLER)
1879. FROZEN MEAT
1880. FOOD DEHYDRATION (FRUITS & VEGETABLES)
1881. FRIED & ROASTED GROUND NUT, GRAMS, PEAR ETC.
1882. FRUIT JUICE MAKING & PACKAGING IN PLASTIC CONTAINER
1883. FRUIT JUICE IN TETRA PACK (DRINKS)
1884. FRUIT JUICE, SQUASHES, SAUCE & KETCHUP, JAM, JELLY, VINEGAR ETC.
1885. GARLIC FLAKES
1886. GARLIC POWDER
1887. GHEE & BUTTER
1888. GINGER (PULVERISED)
1889. GINGER GLAZING & PRESERVATION
1890. GINGER STORAGE
1891. GINGER PROCESSING
1892. GINGER OIL & GINGER DUST
1893. GINGER POWDER (DRY) & OLEORESIN
1894. GRAPE DEHYDRATION
1895. GRAPE CULTIVATION
1896. GRAPE JUICE
1897. HONEY PROCESSING & PACKAGING
1898. ICE CREAM & ICE CANDY
1899. ICE CUBE
1900. INVERT SUGAR
1901. IDLI MIX, DOSA MIX SAMBHAR MIX, VADA MIX, GULAB JAMUN MIX
1902. INSTANT COFFEE & INSTANT TEA

1903. INSTANT NOODLES
1904. INSTANT SOUPS
1905. IODIZED SALT FROM CRUDE SALT
1906. JAM CHUTNEY PICKLES & SQUASHES
1907. KATHA MANUFACTURING
1908. LECITHIN (SOYA BASED)
1909. LEMON & ITS PRODUCTS
1910. MACARONI MANUFACTURING
1911. MACARONI, SPAGHETTI, VERMICELLI & NOODLES
1912. MAIZE & ITS BY PRODUCTS MALTING PLANT
1913. MANGO PAPPAD (AAM PAPPAD)
1914. MANGO POWDER RIPE
1915. MANGO POWDER
1916. MANGO PROCESSING & CANNING (MANGO PULP)
1917. MEAT PROCESSING (CHICKEN MUTTON)
1918. MEAT PROCESSING (BUFFALO)
1919. MENTHOL BOLD FROM MENTHOL FLAKES
1020. MILK POWDER
1921. MILK POWDER & GHEE
1922. MILK POWDER, GHEE & SPICES
1923. MILK PRESERVATION & MARKETING TO WHOLE SELLERS
1924. MILK PRESERVATION & MARKETING TO WHOLE SELLERS (IN POUCHES)
1925. MILK TOFFEE MANUFACTURES
1926. MINERAL WATER
1927. MINERAL WATER IN POUCHES
1928. MINI FLOUR MILL ATTA MAIDA, SUJI & WHEAT BRAN
1929. MITHAI/HALWAI (SWEET & NAMKEEN)
1930. MUTTON PROCESSING
1931. PAN MASALA (MEETHA, SADA, ZARDA) MAKING & PACKING
1932. PAN MASALA AND POUCH MAKING
1933. PANEER (CHEESE)
1934. PAPAD & BARIYAN
1935. PAPAD PLANT
1936. PEPSICOLA IN POLYTUBES
1937. PETHA PACKAGING
1938. PICKLES
1939. PIGGERY/MEAT/CHICKEN PROCESSING
1940. PINE APPLE JUICE CANNING
1941. POTATO & ONION POWDER
1942. POTATO & ONION FLAKES
1943. POTATO CHIPS
1944. POTATO GRANULES
1945. POUCH FILLING FOR SAUNF SUPARI ILAICHI ETC.
1946. PRESERVATION OF RAWS MANGO JUICE
1947. PROCESSED CHEESE & MARINE PDTS.
1948. PULP FROM TARMARIND
1949. READYMATE PROCESSED FOOD
1950. RICE & CORN FLAKES
1951. RICE BASMATI (TRADING)
1952. RICE POLISHING & PACKAGING IN POUCH
1953. ROASTED/SALTED/MASALA/ CASHEW NUTS ALMONDS & PEA NUT
1954. ROLLER FLOUR MILL

INFOTECH/IT PROJECTS

1955. MEDICAL TRANSCRIPTION
1956. E-COMMERCE
1957. CYBERCAFE
1958. INTERNET SERVICE PROVIDER (ISP)
1959. COMPUTER EDUCATION CENTRE
1960. PORTAL (WEBSITE DESIGN)
1961. CALL CENTRE

TERMS AND CONDITIONS

FOR INDIA

1. Please ask for Quotations/ Proforma Invoice for Each ***"Market Survey Cum Detailed Techno Economic Feasibility Report"***. Payable in advance through Draft/M.O./Cash in favour of 'ENGINEERS INDIA RESEARCH INSTITUTE', Delhi. Delivery by Regd. Post within 2 Days. (Postage Free)

2. Ask for a Hi Tech Projects, monthly magazine. Each issue covers approx. 75 project profiles.

FOR OVERSEAS

1. Please ask for Quotations/ Proforma Invoice in US $ for Each ***"Market Survey Cum Detailed Techno Economic Feasibility Report"***. Payable in advance through Draft in favour of 'ENGINEERS INDIA RESEARCH INSTITUTE', Delhi (Payable in India). Delivery by Regd. Air Mail Post within 3 Days. (Postage Free).

2. Ask for a Hi Tech Projects, monthly magazine. Each issue covers approx. 75 project profiles.

ENGINEERS INDIA RESEARCH INSTITUTE

4449, Nai Sarak (D), Main Road, Delhi - 110 006 (India)
Ph:. 91-11- 23918117, 23916431, 23840361, 9312282370
Fax: 91-11- 23916431 E-Mail : eirisidi@bol.net.in
Website:www.eiriindia.org
Also at : 4/27, Roop Nagar, Near Roop Nagar No. 1 School, Delhi - 110 007 (India) Ph:. 91-11-2384 0361